D0706528

After Pentecost

The Scripture and Hermeneutics Series

Craig Bartholomew, Series Editor
Colin Greene, Consultant Editor

Editorial Advisory Board
Fred Hughes
Gordon McConville
Christopher Seitz
Janet Martin Soskice
Anthony Thiselton
Nicholas Wolterstorff

Vol. 1 *Renewing Biblical Interpretation*
Vol. 2 *After Pentecost: Language and Biblical Interpretation*

Forthcoming volume 3, November 2002:

A Royal Priesthood: The Use of the Bible Ethically and Politically

After Pentecost
Language and Biblical Interpretation

Edited by
Craig Bartholomew
Colin Greene
Karl Möller

paternoster
press

GRAND RAPIDS, MICHIGAN 49530

CHELTENHAM
&
GLOUCESTER
College of Higher Education

bible society

First published 2001 jointly
in the UK by Paternoster Press, an imprint of Paternoster Publishing,
P.O. Box 300, Carlisle, Cumbria, CA3 OQS
Website: www.paternoster-publishing.com
and in the United States of America by
Zondervan
5300 Patterson Ave SE, Grand Rapids, Michigan 49530

07 06 05 04 03 02 01 / DC / 7 6 5 4 3 2 1

British Library Cataloguing in Publication Data
A catalogue record for this book is available from the British Library
ISBN 1-84227-066-4

Library of Congress Cataloguing in Publication Data
After Pentecost: Language and Biblical Interpretation / Craig Bartholomew,
series editor, Colin Greene, consultant editor, Karl Möller, editor
p.cm. — (Scripture and Hermeneutics series: v. 2)
Includes bibliographical references
ISBN 0-310-23412-3
1. Bible—Hermeneutics. I. Bartholomew, Craig G., 1961– II. Greene, Colin
III Möller, Karl. IV. Series.
BS476.A35 2001
220.6'01'4—dc21
2001026321

Typeset by WestKey Ltd, Falmouth, Cornwall
Printed in the United States of America
Printed on acid free paper

*For Professor Canon Anthony Thiselton on his retirement,
in recognition of his work in biblical hermeneutics.*

Contents

Contributors

Craig G. Bartholomew is Research Fellow at Cheltenham and Gloucester College of Higher Education. He is the author of *Reading Ecclesiastes: Old Testament Exegesis and Hermeneutical Theory.* He has also edited *In the Fields of the Lord: A Calvin Seerveld Reader* and co-edited *Christ and Consumerism: A Critical Analysis of the Spirit of the Age* and *Renewing Biblical Interpretation.* He is the series editor for the Scripture and Hermeneutics Series.

Colin Greene is Head of Theology and Public Policy at the British and Foreign Bible Society, and Visiting Professor of Systematic Theology at Seattle Pacific University. He is the author of *Christology and Atonement in Historical Context* and *Marking Out the Horizons: Christology in Cultural Perspective.* He has also co-edited *Renewing Biblical Interpretation.*

Kathryn Greene-McCreight is Lecturer in the Department of Religion and Biblical Literature at Smith College, Northampton, Massachusetts. She is the author of *Ad Litteram: How Augustine, Calvin and Barth Read the 'Plain Sense' of Genesis 1–3* and *Feminist Reconstructions of Christian Doctrine.* She has also co-edited *Theological Exegesis: Essays in Honor of Brevard S. Childs.*

Mary B. Hesse, FBA is a historian and philosopher of science, and Emeritus Professor in Philosophy of Science in the University of Cambridge. She has authored numerous books, including *Revolutions and Reconstructions in the Philosophy of Science, The Structure of Scientific Inference* and *Models and Analogies in Science.*

Brian Ingraffia is Associate Professor of English at Biola University, La Mirada, California. He is the author of *Postmodern Theory and Biblical Theology: Vanquishing God's Shadow.*

David Lyle Jeffrey is Distinguished Professor of Literature and Humanities at Baylor University. He is also Professor Emeritus of English Literature at the University of Ottawa, and has been Guest Professor at Peking University (Beijing) since 1996. He is general editor and co-author of *A Dictionary of*

Biblical Tradition in English Literature. Among his other books are *The Early English Lyric and Franciscan Spirituality, By Things Seen: Reference and Recognition in Medieval Thought, Chaucer and Scriptural Tradition, English Spirituality in the Age of Wesley, English Spirituality in the Age of Wyclif,* and *People of the Book: Christian Identity and Literary Culture.* He has also co-edited and co-authored *Rethinking the Future of the University.*

Gregory J. Laughery is associated with the Swiss L'Abri Fellowship. He has published a short commentary on the apocalypse and has translated *The First Christian Historian: The Acts of the Apostles* (forthcoming).

Gordon McConville is Senior Lecturer in Old Testament and Hebrew at Cheltenham and Gloucester College of Higher Education. He books include *Law and Theology in Deuteronomy, Grace in the End* and *Judgment and Promise.* He has also co-authored *Time and Place in Deuteronomy* and co-edited *Reconsidering Israel and Judah: Recent Studies on the Deuteronomistic History.*

Neil B. MacDonald has lectured at the University of St Andrews and the University of Edinburgh and is the author of *Karl Barth and the Strange New World Within the Bible: Barth, Wittgenstein and the Metadilemmas of the Enlightenment.*

Karl Möller is a researcher in the School of Theology and Religious Studies, Cheltenham and Gloucester College of Higher Education. He is the author of *A Prophet in Debate: The Rhetoric of Persuasion in the Book of Amos* (forthcoming). He has also co-edited *Renewing Biblical Interpretation.*

William Olhausen is an Anglican clergyman serving as assistant curate in Reading. He is also researching for a PhD in biblical interpretation at Cheltenham and Gloucester College of Higher Education.

Ian Paul is Associate Minister of St Mary's, Poole, Dorset; Managing Editor of Grove Books; and Theological Adviser to the Board of Ministry in the Anglican Diocese of Salisbury. He is the author of *Through the Eyes of Mark* and *Ministry of the Word.* A revised version of his thesis on Ricœur's hermeneutic of metaphor and the book of Revelation is due to be published in 2002.

Todd Pickett is Associate Professor of English at Biola University in La Mirada, California, where he teaches Victorian literature and courses in literature and theology. His reviews and review essays have appeared in *Christianity and Literature* and *Religion and Literature.*

Dan R. Stiver is Professor of Theology at the Logsdon School of Theology, Hardin-Simmons University, Abilene, Texas. He is the author of *The Philosophy of Religious Language* and *Theology after Ricœur* (forthcoming). From 1994 to 1998 he was editor of the *Review and Expositor.*

Anthony C. Thiselton is Professor of Christian Theology in the University of Nottingham, and is also Canon Theologian both of Leicester Cathedral and of Southwell Minster. His books include *The Two Horizons, New Horizons in Hermeneutics, Interpreting God and the Postmodern Self, The Promise of Hermeneutics* (co-author) and *The First Epistle to the Corinthians: A Commentary on the Greek Text.* He is President of the Society for the Study of Theology and a member of the Church of England Doctrine Commission, of which he is also a former Vice-Chairman.

Kevin J. Vanhoozer is Research Professor of Theology at the Divinity School of Trinity International University in Deerfield, Illinois. He is the author of *Is There a Meaning in this Text? The Bible, the Reader, and the Morality of Literary Knowledge.* He is also co-chair of the Christian Systematic Theology Group of the American Academy of Religion.

Raymond C. Van Leeuwen is Professor of Biblical Studies at Eastern College in St Davids, Pennsylvania. He is the author of *Context and Meaning in Proverbs 25–29* and of a commentary on *The Book of Proverbs* in *The New Interpreter's Bible.*

Nicholas Wolterstorff is Noah Porter Professor of Philosophical Theology at Yale University. He has authored numerous books, including *John Locke and the Ethics of Belief, Divine Discourse: Philosophical Reflections on the Claim that God Speaks, Reason within the Bounds of Religion, Works and Worlds of Art* and *Thomas Reid and the Story of Epistemology.*

Stephen Wright is Director of the College of Preachers and Associate Lecturer at Spurgeon's College, London. He is the author of *The Voice of Jesus: Studies in the Interpretation of Six Gospel Parables.*

Abbreviations

AARDS	American Academy of Religion Dissertation Series
AGJU	Arbeiten zur Geschichte des antiken Judentums und des Urchristentums
AUMSR	Andrews University Monograph Studies in Religion
BBB	Bonner biblische Beiträge
BibInt	*Biblical Interpretation*
BT	*The Bible Translator*
BZAW	Beihefte zur Zeitschrift für die alttestamentliche Wissenschaft
CBQ	*Catholic Biblical Quarterly*
ChrLit	*Christianity and Literature*
ConBOT	Coniectanea biblica: Old Testament Series
CRBS	*Currents in Research: Biblical Studies*
EuroJT	*European Journal of Theology*
EvT	*Evangelische Theologie*
ExAud	*Ex auditu*
ExpTim	*Expository Times*
FF	Foundations and Facets
GBS	Guides to Biblical Scholarship
GNB	Good News Bible
HTR	*Harvard Theological Review*
ICC	International Critical Commentary
Int	*Interpretation*
JBL	*Journal of Biblical Literature*
JBMW	*Journal for Biblical Manhood and Womanhood*
JETS	*Journal of the Evangelical Theological Society*
JR	*Journal of Religion*
JSNTSup	Journal for the Study of the New Testament: Supplement Series
JSOTSup	Journal for the Study of the Old Testament: Supplement Series
KD	*Kerygma und Dogma*
KJV	King James Version

LCL	Loeb Classical Library
LXX	Septuagint
NASB	New American Standard Bible
NIBCOT	New International Biblical Commentary on the Old Testament
NICOT	New International Commentary on the Old Testament
NIDNTT	*New International Dictionary of New Testament Theology*
NIV	New International Version
NJB	New Jerusalem Bible
NRSV	New Revised Standard Version
NTS	*New Testament Studies*
OBS	Oxford Bible Series
OBT	Overtures to Biblical Theology
OTL	Old Testament Library
OTS	Old Testament Studies
QR	*Quarterly Review*
REB	Revised English Bible
RevExp	*Review and Expositor*
RSV	Revised Standard Version
SBLDS	Society of Biblical Literature Dissertation Series
SBT	Studies in Biblical Theology
SBTS	Sources for Biblical and Theological Study
SHANE	Studies in the History of the Ancient Near East
SHS	Scripture and Hermeneutics Series
SJT	*Scottish Journal of Theology*
SNTSMS	Society for New Testament Studies Monograph Series
StABH	Studies in American Biblical Hermeneutics
TS	*Theological Studies*
ThTo	*Theology Today*
TCW	*Tydskrif vir Christelike Wetenskap*
TDNT	*Theological Dictionary of the New Testament*
TEV	Today's English Version
TynBul	*Tyndale Bulletin*
VSH	*Vanderbilt Studies in the Humanities*
VT	*Vetus Testamentum*
VTSup	Supplements to Vetus Testamentum
WBC	Word Biblical Commentary
WdF	Wege der Forschung
WMANT	Wissenschaftliche Monographien zum Alten und Neuen Testament
ZAW	*Zeitschrift für die alttestamentliche Wissenschaft*
ZDMG	*Zeitschrift der deutschen morgenländischen Gesellschaft*

The Artists

Zak Benjamin

Zak Benjamin was born in 1951. He completed a BA Fine Arts degree, taught art and has worked full-time as an artist since 1991. His work is represented in collections internationally. He is married and lives in Vereeniging, South Africa, and has two daughters.

Painter and Printmaker

Born Izak Benjamin de Villiers, the artist grew up in Pretoria, a member of a typical middle-class Afrikaner family. His father was a senior government official. Benjamin was sent to Sunday school, belonged to the Voortrekker movement and signed up as a member of the Nationalist Party Youth Movement. The discrepancies between the Christian values taught at church and the policies of the Nationalist government, and their expression in the status-seeking materialist Afrikaner middle class, made him rebel against his background. In the mid-1980s, Benjamin experienced a profound religious conversion that led to his friendship with sculptor Gert Swart in their mutual struggle to discover what it means to make contemporary art as Christians.

Benjamin's frustration with lingering apartheid in the Dutch Reformed Church and the challenges facing Christians in post-apartheid South Africa provide themes for some of his work. Calvin Seerveld has thus characterized his style: '… bright gaiety and humour combined with an ethereal seriousness. Like the unusual world of *One Hundred Years of Solitude* (Gabriel Marquez), the paintings hold together, as natural, the most outlandish realities. Bold naïveté of forms and colours, stories of mysteries and conflict, trouble and healing – with a difference: friendly, zany, readable, provoking the viewer to look again … a wholesome pleasure in the grit of life.'

http://zakbenjaminartist.homestead.com/index.html

Gert Swart

Gert Swart was born in Durban, South Africa, where he qualified and worked as a public health inspector before studying fine art for two years at the Natal Technikon. He now resides and works as a sculptor in Pietermaritzburg, South Africa. He is married to Istine Rodseth.

For the past ten years Gert Swart has lived and worked in Pietermaritzburg. His most important exhibition of this period was staged at the Tatham Art Gallery in 1997. This exhibition, titled 'Contemplation: a body of work by Gert Swart', expressed the redemption of an individual as a metamorphosis from the curse of death to the hope of resurrection and how this transition affects the individual's relationship to society, nature and God.

One of Swart's most significant commissions of the past decade was a monument erected on the battlefield at Isandlwana in 1999. Although the battle of Isandlwana is known for its stunning defeat of a colonial army by an unconventional army, only monuments to fallen British soldiers had been erected on it in the past. It was a privilege to be involved in redressing this injustice and a challenge to design a monument that honours the fallen Zulu warriors but does not glorify war.

Gert met Zak Benjamin at a Christian Arts Festival some twelve years ago. He and Benjamin were among the founder members of the Christian Worldview Network initiated by Craig Bartholomew. They enjoy a rich friendship that is currently finding expression in the joint design of book covers for this series in collaboration with Craig. This design project is the fruit of Craig's concern for Christian artists and his friendship with Gert and Zak.

http://gertswartsculptor.homestead.com/index.html

Introduction

Craig G. Bartholomew

The group that was to become The Scripture and Hermeneutics Seminar met for the first time in Cheltenham in April 1998. There can't be many consultations that have met with our agenda. Our task was to discuss 'the crisis' in biblical interpretation, and to consider speech-act theory as a possible resource for responding to it! Here at Cheltenham and Gloucester College of Higher Education, the hosting institution, several meetings were arranged prior to the consultation to help those involved get up to speed on speech-act theory, as this is not a standard part of a biblical scholar's education.

A distinguished group gathered for the consultation. It included prominent scholars like Nicholas Wolterstorff, Anthony Thiselton, Francis Watson and Kevin Vanhoozer, all of whom in different ways argue that speech-act theory, the philosophy of language emerging from the work of Austin and Searle,[1] can really help us with the present challenges in biblical interpretation. Also present were Mary Hesse and others who are cautious about the benefits of speech-act theory and who incline towards a strongly metaphorical view of language.[2] Mary Hesse is well known for her work on science and metaphor.

Needless to say, we were not all agreed about speech-act theory and its benefits for biblical interpretation. However, we agreed unanimously that any renewal of biblical interpretation in our day would have to attend closely to philosophy and theology of language and biblical interpretation. This was high on the ten-year agenda that we mapped out at the end of that first, memorable consultation. Indeed, language has been the first major issue the Seminar has addressed. In 1999 we met in Cambridge to revisit and assess in detail the current state of biblical interpretation. The results of that consultation are published in *Renewing Biblical Interpretation*, which sets out the issues that need to be tackled if biblical interpretation is to be renewed. Then, in

---

[1] See esp. Austin, *How to Do Things With Words* and Searle, *Speech Acts*.
[2] See, e.g., Hesse, 'Cognitive Claims', 'Theories' and 'Models, Metaphors and Truth'.

August 2000, the Seminar met at Redeemer University College in Ancaster, Ontario, Canada to explore the interfaces of philosophy and theology of language and biblical interpretation. The present volume results from that consultation.

It is entirely appropriate that we should focus on language early in the Scripture and Hermeneutics process. Dan Stiver rightly says of the twentieth century, 'When future philosophers assess this century's major philosophical emphasis, it surely will be claimed as the century of the linguistic turn.'[3] Inevitably the linguistic turn in philosophy[4] caught up with biblical interpretation, and we continue to feel its effects. In the 1960s we became aware, courtesy of James Barr, that linguistics, which exploded as a discipline in the twentieth century, was vitally important for biblical interpretation – and that word studies could not continue as usual.[5] In the 1970s, the literary turn alerted us to the radical interpretative implications of considering the Bible as literature. Since the 1980s and 1990s, language has been at the heart of postmodernism, which confronts biblical interpretation with a veritable smorgasbord of problems and opportunities. It was with all these challenges in mind that we met in Canada.

After Pentecost: **The Table and the Tree**[6]

The title of this volume, and of the cover image by Gert Swart and Zak Benjamin, alludes, of course, to George Steiner and his distinguished book on language, *After Babel*. Steiner's book is a *tour de force* examining, *inter alia*, the influence of the Babel story on the history of reflection on language. At the end of *Real Presences*, Steiner's book on literature and art, Steiner calls his approach to language and art that of 'the long day's journey of the Saturday'. He contrasts this somewhat[7] with the 'Sunday' approach of Christians, in which

---

[3] *Philosophy*, 1.

[4] See, e.g., Rorty (ed.), *Linguistic Turn*.

[5] See Barr, *Semantics* and *Biblical Words*.

[6] I am grateful to Gert and Istine Swart, Erna Buber-de Villiers and Zak Benjamin for their help with this section.

[7] The 'somewhat' should be emphasized. See *Real Presences*, 231, 232, for the moving way Steiner concludes.

the aesthetic will, presumably, no longer have logic or necessity. The apprehensions and figurations in the play of metaphysical imagining, in the poem and the music, which tell of pain and of hope, of the flesh which is said to taste of ash and of the spirit which is said to have the savour of fire, are always Sabbatarian.[8]

Although Steiner here distinguishes his approach from a Christian one, and although our title might (incorrectly) be read as a polemical contrast with Steiner, this is not the case. In my own chapter in particular, I have drawn deeply on Steiner's work. Indeed, if I had my way, *Real Presences* would be compulsory reading for every biblical studies and theology student. It is, in my opinion, in a class of its own. Rather than being polemical, *After Pentecost* relates to our desire to take absolutely seriously Steiner's proposal that a healthy understanding of language requires a wager on God as transcendent creator whose presence underlies the real presences we experience in and through art and language.

The Scripture and Hermeneutics Seminar is made up of a group of interdisciplinary, Christian scholars. The participants vary somewhat from year to year, depending on the subject being addressed. The one rule for the Seminar is that faith – in our case Christian faith – is not to be excluded from or marginalized in the debates, as has been the case in so much modern scholarship. We want to wager seriously on God as the transcendent creator and redeemer. We aim to work at a rigorously academic and critical level, but in a way that manifests 'faith seeking understanding'. It is this that our title seeks to express, and which the cover image articulates so very well.

The painting positions us as the reader/s of Scripture – one enters the painting, as it were, by assuming the hands of the reader. The picture within the painting alerts us to the elements shaping the context within which we read – there is an intriguing pull in the composition between the book and the picture on the easel, so that the viewer is pulled back to the book as she or he focuses on the painting on the easel. This is a powerful reminder that we are always working with some 'storied' understanding of language in our interpretation of the Bible. Indeed, the somewhat hieroglyphic nature of the script in the Bible, as well as the effort required in reading indicated by the slightly raised right hand, clue us in to the inevitability and the struggle of interpretation. This is not to deny what has been called the perspicuity of Scripture but, like all good metaphors, 'perspicuity' must not be over-read. Perspicuity should be complemented by an understanding of the Bible as a partially closed book that needs interpretation for it to become more open.[9] As Ray van Leeuwen argues in his chapter in this volume, the Bible requires commentary

---

[8] Steiner, *Real Presences*, 232.
[9] I heard this expression from John Stott.

and interpretation. The cover image reminds us that in our interpretation we need an understanding of language that fits with the Bible.

And, as one looks closely at the picture on the easel, it is clear that there is more to the story of language than Babel. In the background of the painting towers a giant anachronistic structure, its electronic 'ear' incongruous with its ancient arches and ladders. Babel – the structure is deliberately reminiscent of Bruegel's 'Tower of Babel' – has become a powerful and dominant symbol in our day for language and postmodernism. Countless book covers portray Bruegel's image. In the postmodern context Babel has become a symbol for contemporary fragmentation, cultural diversity and wild pluralism. Many, but certainly not Steiner, tear the Babel story loose from its context in creation and redemption, so that our story, our metanarrative if you like, becomes Babel alone.

The picture on the easel takes Babel seriously, and it is represented very much like Bruegel's Tower, with one huge exception – the large satellite dish and the other signs of modern communication aerials on the top of the Tower. The dish reminds us of the challenges to language that the modern communications highway presents, and perhaps alerts us to the particular danger of the idolatry of Babel in today's context. However, it also reminds us that the basic danger remains the same: in vain the huge satellite dish listens and listens, but it does not hear a sound from the universe.

The picture contextualizes Babel by denying it the central place it always holds in Bruegel's representations, and by setting it in a broader theological context, namely that of the table (the sacraments) and the tree (of life). The tree of life connects back into creation (Gen. 2:9) and forward into re-creation (Rev. 22), but, standing next to the sacraments, it does so in a deeply Christian way. The table, standing for and inviting us to participate in Christ's redemptive work, reminds us that Christ, the Word, is *the* clue to creation and the answer to Babel.[10] From this perspective, certainly, it would be madness to let Babel have the final word in our reading of Scripture. It is rather a sacramental hermeneutic that will enable us to read so as to hear the living Word and thus partake of the tree of life.

So much is made nowadays of Babel, and relatively little is made of its New Testament counterpoint, Pentecost. By invoking Pentecost we have no desire to deny that 'ours is the long day's journey of the Saturday'.[11] Indeed, elements of this are present in the painting: an artist sits before an *unfinished* picture standing on an easel. The table is vulnerable and relatively powerless against the might of the Tower. The serious human faces evoke the uncertainties and

---

[10]   Steiner's title 'Real Presences' likewise suggests, in a Catholic way, the link between the Eucharist and language.

[11]   Steiner, *Real Presences*, 232.

in-betweenness of life. We have called this book 'After Pentecost' in order to suggest that Babel needs to be contextualized by what comes before Babel – that is, creation – and after Babel – namely redemption, or what Christians might call 'Pentecost'. Certainly if Christians are to engage in faith seeking understanding, they should resist attempts to stop with Babel, and should insist that language and hermeneutics need to be understood 'After Pentecost'.

Taking an 'After Pentecost' perspective seriously in biblical hermeneutics should not be considered a negative agenda. It would resist absolutizing Babel in a Gnostic way,[12] but, as Thiselton and many others note, contemporary hermeneutics is full of promise for biblical interpretation. A theological understanding of language would seek to capitalize on the very best of these insights.[13] This is well captured by the image: the Book is open, and the table and tree are set against Babel, with the paintbrushes corresponding diametrically to the tree, and not to Babel. The work as a whole is suffused with warmth, as if lit by the flames of Pentecost. As Kevin Vanhoozer says:

> We may likewise celebrate the feast of interpretation. The Spirit of Pentecost overcomes the cultural and ideological biases that distort communication and so restores language as a medium of communion … We now enjoy only the first-fruits of understanding, but we look forward to that day when we will understand as we have been understood. *Veni spiritus interpres!* Come interpreter Spirit![14]

Language and Biblical Exegesis

Volumes like this on philosophy and theology of language and biblical interpretation are not common, and the biblical exegete may well wonder just what difference attention to such issues will make in the practice of biblical interpretation. How does celebrating the feast of interpretation help us in the actual tasks of doing exegesis? This is fair comment. Biblical studies has become such a specialized discipline that it is hard enough to become an expert in the area without straying into philosophy and theology of language. Unless it can be shown that philosophy and theology of language really do make a difference to exegesis, biblical scholars might be well advised to ignore such issues.

In my opinion, issues of language are *always* already at work in interpretation, and they cannot be avoided. However, that does not mean that we are

---

[12] See the discussions of Gnosticism and postmodernism in my chapter.

[13] I do not wish to suggest that all the contributors to this volume agree about the relationship between philosophy and theology of language and how they relate to exegesis. The Seminar is, however, committed to taking faith seriously in scholarship and exegesis.

[14] Vanhoozer, 'Spirit', 165.

necessarily conscious of them. Exegetes often work unconsciously with
certain views of language, and there is great benefit to be gained from becoming more conscious of what views of language are at work in exegesis and
interpretation. To illustrate this point, I will discuss one example from the
interpretation of Leviticus. Leviticus may seem an obscure example to choose,
but if we want to know how language affects actual exegesis, then it is actual
exegesis that we will have to explore, with particular examples. Readers with
(understandably) no interest in this sort of detailed exegetical discussion should
move on to the next section.

The example in Leviticus that I will discuss came up in one of our regular
Biblical Studies Seminars here in Cheltenham, through a presentation by one
of our doctoral students.[15] In other words, it is not untypical of the sort of thing
a doctoral student in biblical studies might encounter.

In his major commentary on Leviticus,[16] Jacob Milgrom argues that in the
Old Testament cultic texts, the Hebrew verb אשם (= ʾāšam)[17] is best translated
as 'to feel guilty'.[18] Milgrom asserts that this translation is highly significant:
'The critical importance of this new rendering is that it necessitates an overhaul
of every cultic passage in which the verb ʾāšam occurs without an object.'[19]
Milgrom gives six examples of such passages. One of them is Leviticus 5:17.
The RSV translates this verse as: 'If anyone sins, doing any of the things which
the LORD has commanded not to be done, though he does not know it, yet *he
is guilty* and shall bear his iniquity.'[20] NIV similarly translates *asham* as 'he is
guilty'. NRSV translates it as '*you have incurred guilt* and are subject to punishment'. However, Milgrom translates this verse as 'If, however, a person errs by
violating any of the Lord's prohibitive commandments without knowing it
and *he feels guilt*, he shall bear his responsibility …'[21] The other verses Milgrom

---

[15] I am grateful to Jay Sklar for drawing my attention to this issue and for his help with
some of the details in this discussion. Gordon Wenham and Karl Möller have also provided helpful comment on this section.

[16] Freedman, 'Preface', ix, says of Milgrom's first volume on Leviticus that 'this magisterial undertaking has already established itself as a classic, the standard by which all
future works must be judged, and a standing challenge to scholars in coming generations'. I do not wish to detract from Milgrom's achievement in my analysis of a small
part of his work. I merely wish to demonstrate how issues of language are present in
often surprising ways in scholarship of even this calibre, and that we could all benefit
from taking them more seriously.

[17] For this introduction I will use the simple transliteration of this verb as *asham*.

[18] Milgrom, *Leviticus 1–16*, 343. Kiuchi, *Purification Offering*, by comparison, argues
that we should understand *asham* as 'to realize one's guilt'.

[19] Milgrom, *Leviticus 1–16*, 343.

[20] The rendering of *asham* in English is italicized in the translations referred to.

[21] Ibid., 319.

refers to are Leviticus 5:23a, 5:5; Numbers 5:6b–7; Leviticus 5:2–4 and 4:27–28.

It is a moot point how much hangs on deciding how to translate *asham* at these points. For our purposes, it is important to note that these discussions are the bread and butter issues biblical scholars deal with every day. And what do bear scrutiny are the arguments Milgrom marshals in favour of this translation. I cannot here discuss these in detail, but essentially they go as follows:

Milgrom argues that *asham* is a consequential verb in the Old Testament cultic texts. That is, whereas in some parts of the Old Testament *asham* refers to being culpable, in the priestly material it refers to the consequences of guilt. For the sake of the argument let us concede this point. Milgrom says that there is also a psychological component to the consequential *asham* in Leviticus. Immediately having said this he continues, 'The ancients did not distinguish between emotional and physical suffering; the same language describes pangs of conscience and physical pains …'[22] In support of this he states that in the penitential psalms it is hard to know whether the penitent is suffering emotionally or physically. The reason for this, according to Milgrom, is that unexplainable suffering may be regarded as the result of sin so that the penitent is most concerned to discover the offence that caused the plight.

> Thus it is logical to expect that a language that, as observed, will express the consequential syndrome of sin-punishment by a single word will also have at least one root in its lexicon to express another consequential relationship, that which exists between sin-punishment and guilt feelings. This root, I submit, is ʾšm.[23]

Secondly, Milgrom asserts that while non-legal texts use metaphorical language to describe the feelings of guilt,[24] legal and cultic texts eschew metaphor so that in Leviticus a precise term would be needed to 'pinpoint the existence of guilt'.[25] This is the verb *asham*.

A third prong in Milgrom's argument is that of 'redundancy'. In Leviticus 5:17 *asham* cannot, in his view, be translated as 'incurring guilt' or 'is guilty' because the contiguous 'shall bear his responsibility' would make it tautologous.[26]

What is important for our purposes is that an understanding of how language works is influencing Milgrom's decision to translate *asham* as 'to feel

---

[22] Ibid., 342.

[23] Ibid., 343.

[24] E.g., 'David's heart smote him' (1 Sam. 24:5; 2 Sam. 24:10); 'a stumbling [offence] of the heart' (1 Sam. 25:31); 'my kidneys have whipped me' (Ps. 16:7).

[25] Ibid.

[26] Ibid.

guilty'. That is inevitable, but the question is, how helpful is his view of language? We could ask:

- Is it true that the ancients did not distinguish between emotional and physical suffering?
- Why would we expect Hebrew to have a root that expresses the connection between sin and the feeling of guilt?
- Do legal texts avoid metaphorical language in their need for precision?
- Is metaphorical language imprecise?
- Is Milgrom correct about redundancy in the texts he refers to?
- How would different answers to the above help with the translation of *asham*?

We could, obviously, discuss these issues at length. Suffice it here to note that much of Milgrom's case rests on inadequate views of language. That similar vocabulary might be used for physical and emotional suffering does not mean that the ancients were unable to distinguish conceptually between them. Such an argument buys into the very logico-grammatical parallelism that Barr refuted. Barr long ago exposed the weakness of the Biblical Theology Movement in its suggestion that the vocabulary of the language of a people is closely related to how the people think. As Barr says of the Biblical Theology Movement,

> All this can be summarized by saying that where linguistic evidence has been used in the Greek-Hebrew contrast it has not been adequately protected against, or indeed has positively presupposed, the idea of a logico-grammatical parallelism, a doctrine which can be traced from Aristotle through scholasticism, and which gained some of its plausibility from the predominant position of Latin and the corresponding attempt to force the forms of other languages into the moulds of Latin grammar.[27]

A case could be made that the ancients understood only too well the psychosomatic connections between physical and mental and emotional pain, but it is clear in the Psalms that these different sufferings are not collapsed into one category.

Similarly, I cannot imagine why we should expect there to be a root in Hebrew expressing the consequential link between sin and the experience of guilt. Milgrom's logic is hard to follow at this point, but it does seem to rest on the same logico-grammatical parallelism that Barr critiques.

Thirdly, legal texts do differ in their use of language from, say, poetic texts, where metaphor abounds. Compare, for example, Psalm 42 with Leviticus 6:1–7. But the difference is one of degree and not one of the presence versus

---

[27] Barr, *Semantics*, 43.

the absence of metaphor. There is perhaps also a difference in kind and function of metaphor. In the priestly literature there *are* central metaphors, such as clean/unclean, and holy/unholy, that structure the entire discourse. In the early chapters of Leviticus there are other common metaphors, such as 'without blemish' and 'pleasing odour'. Then there are further important metaphors in later chapters of Leviticus:

- 18:6–23: the use of 'uncover' for sexual intercourse
- 18:25: the land became defiled … the land vomited out its inhabitants
- 18:29: whoever commits any of these abominations shall be 'cut off' from their people
- 18:30: defile yourselves
- 25:1: the land shall observe a Sabbath

An expression like 'cut off' is clearly metaphorical and imprecise in terms of the exact penalty envisaged, as the scholarly discussion of just what is involved indicates.[28] It is a central clause expressing the penalty for very serious crimes. It is clear that 'cut off' means that God will act decisively and probably through premature death, but it is never clear how God will achieve this, or when.[29] The metaphor is very clear and yet open-ended. It may be that legal language avoids being metaphorical in the same way as poetry, but clearly it is metaphorical in its own way. It must also be borne in mind that a text like Leviticus is more than a legal text; it is also educative material. And it can be argued that, in educational material, metaphors play a crucial role.[30]

Milgrom's view of metaphor appears to be the popular one that metaphor is ornamental and has no place in scientific texts. However, it is wrong to think that metaphorical language is necessarily imprecise and that scientific texts eschew metaphor.[31] Considerable work has been done in recent decades on vagueness, ambiguity, metaphor and literal language.[32] Some studies of metaphor have argued that all language is metaphorical, albeit in different ways.[33]

---

[28] See, e.g., Wold, 'The Karet Penalty in P'.

[29] Jay Sklar has helpfully alerted me to the considerable body of literature on the subject of being 'cut off'. It is not possible to interact with that literature here. My limited goal is to demonstrate that identifying 'cut off' as a metaphor is an important part of understanding its function.

[30] Petrie, 'Metaphor'.

[31] See, e.g., Botha, 'Metaphorical Models', and the articles mentioned earlier by Hesse.

[32] See, e.g., Scheffler, *Beyond the Letter*; Lakoff and Johnson, *Metaphors*; *Philosophy*; Ricœur, *Rule*; Soskice, *Metaphor*.

[33] Hesse, 'Cognitive Claims', 1, says that 'I am going to argue here for a radically different theory, which I shall call the *network* theory of meaning, and for a related thesis that "all language is metaphorical" '.

Certainly a more refined view of language is required to handle the data with which Milgrom is dealing. If, for example, Milgrom is right about the consequential use of *asham* in Leviticus, might it not be the case that *asham* is being employed somewhat differently from its normal usage precisely in order to evoke the range of consequences associated with being guilty of sin? Thus, the term could be precise – the state or experience of guilt – and deliberately encompassing in terms of the effects at the same time. Feeling guilty would be one manifestation of the state, but it may be that the text deliberately refers to the experience in its totality without specifying the precise means.[34]

One is also surprised to encounter Milgrom's arguments about redundancy. In the study of the Psalms and the Pentateuch, redundancy has been exposed repeatedly as not truly redundant and thus as inadequate argument.[35] However, it may be that redundancy is far less common in legal texts, in which case this might support Milgrom's case. Nevertheless, the case for redundancy in Leviticus 5:17 would still depend on the precise relationship between 'become guilty' and 'subject to punishment'. Might it not be that this verse stresses the fact that lack of awareness at the time of the deed does not mean that one escapes the responsibilities of guilt?

No doubt, the debate about how to translate *asham* in Leviticus will continue. But I hope it is clear that the debate ought not to continue uninformed by linguistic insight. How we conceive the relationship between language and thought, how we think about metaphor and literal language, what we make of redundancy in texts – these and a myriad of other issues of language inevitably shape our reading of the Bible, right down to the detail of how we translate *asham*.

Content

Meir Sternberg maintains that,

> Since biblical study is not a discipline by any stretch of the term but the intersection of the humanities par excellence, the progress it so badly needs is conditional either on all-round expertise, not given to humans, or on a truly common pursuit of knowledge.[36]

Whether Sternberg is right or not about biblical study being *a* discipline, he is certainly right about the number of disciplines and elements that intersect in

---

[34] This would support the standard translation of *asham* as to be or become guilty.

[35] See, e.g., Sternberg, *Poetics*.

[36] *Poetics*, 21–22.

biblical interpretation. Biblical hermeneutics is a kind of ecological habitat in which all sorts of components interact with each other in a delicate balance, so that it is difficult and necessarily distorting to abstract out of the ecology one single aspect – in our case, language. However, as I hope this volume demonstrates, there are also considerable advantages to be gained from such abstraction, provided one always keeps in mind the holistic context from which one is abstracting.

The study of language is nowadays a huge, complex and growing area, and it is not an easy area to navigate. Fortunately, scholars such as Anthony Thiselton[37] have spent many years working in this field, and there is now a growing corpus of literature on language and biblical interpretation. This volume leans on the fine work that scholars like Thiselton, Wolterstorff and others have done. It seeks to evaluate and develop their work, while also attending to the multitude of issues that language raises for biblical interpretation. Not only do issues of language inevitably connect with other issues in interpretation, but it is also hard to separate out different aspects of language – such as theology and philosophy, translation and literature. Indeed, one deliberate aim of the Seminar is to assert the fecundity of attending to the connections. This does mean, however, that it is difficult to classify the chapters that follow into any clear-cut categories.

In the area of *speech-act theory* and biblical interpretation, Thiselton, Wolterstorff and Vanhoozer have published highly creative work in recent years, although they appropriate speech-act theory in quite distinct ways. In this volume Wolterstorff, Stiver and Vanhoozer, in particular, focus on speech-act theory. Vanhoozer makes a rigorous, creative case for all that speech-act theory has to offer in biblical interpretation. He integrates a theology of covenant with speech-act theory to argue for a covenantal theology of discourse/language that can inform our discourse of the covenant – that is, our reading and interpretation of Scripture. In this way Scripture informs and shapes our view of language, which again shapes our interpretation of Scripture. Vanhoozer's is a thorough and stimulating chapter, ranging across philosophy and theology of language, and leading to a theology of the Bible as Scripture with examples of biblical interpretation. Vanhoozer responds to some of his critics and develops his view of language and biblical hermeneutics further and draws, *inter alia*, on Alston's recently published *Illocutionary Acts and Sentence Meaning*. Stiver focuses on the difficult issue of treating the Gospels as literary and yet also as historical. He argues that speech-act theory, as developed by Austin and Ricœur, can help us to understand how the Gospels can indeed be both literary and historical.

---

[37] See Thiselton *Two Horizons, New Horizons*.

In *Divine Discourse* Wolterstorff uses the notion of double-agency discourse from speech-act theory to argue for a biblical hermeneutic that has as its goal hearing what God has said, and is saying, to us. The goal of interpretation becomes to hear the divine discourse. In his chapter in this volume on 'The Promise of Speech-Act Theory for Biblical Interpretation', Wolterstorff starts out with a masterly assessment of the widespread rejection of authorial-intention hermeneutics (à la Hirsch) and the appropriation of textual-sense interpretation. By means of an analysis of Derrida's critique of the latter, Wolterstorff makes his case for *authorial-discourse interpretation*, which is aimed at what the speaker said – that is, which illocutionary act he or she performed. Wolterstorff argues that this approach holds considerable promise for interpreting Scripture as divine discourse. Such a biblical hermeneutic is dogmatic in its explicit use of theological convictions in interpretation, notably at the 'second hermeneutic' of the double agency, in which one inquires after God's illocution in appropriating this text. Biblical scholars tend to be good at the first hermeneutic but, if we are after divine discourse, then the second is the really important one. Finally, Wolterstorff discusses some objections that have emerged to his authorial-discourse hermeneutic.

Hidden beneath arguments about interpretation are massive philosophical issues. This is clear from the first part of Wolterstorff's paper, and even more so, perhaps, from Mary Hesse's response. Hesse picks up on Wolterstorff's agreement – against Derrida – with Frege's idealism of 'sense'. She argues that, historically, this is related to the view stemming from a reading of the Genesis creation narratives that there is in principle an ideal language, and that this view, with its trust in hard science, has been decisively refuted by Kuhn, Feyerabend and others. Thus, in an exhilarating dialogue, Hesse probes Wolterstorff's position from a postmodern perspective. At our consultation the Hesse-Wolterstorff dialogue was one of the real high points, and readers will be aware that here is a discussion that needs to be pursued.

Thiselton explores the thorny issues of reference and indeterminacy in relation to biblical interpretation. At a popular level, in terms of the way in which texts are read, the biblical studies student may nowadays feel caught between advocates of radical indeterminacy on the one hand, and rigid determinacy on the other. Thiselton takes up the metaphors of 'behind', 'within' and 'in front of' the text, explains their development and assesses their strengths and weaknesses. Always aware of textual particularities – his chapter is peppered with illustrations from his magisterial work on 1 Corinthians – Thiselton nevertheless asserts the inseparability of the 'three metaphors'. He particularly commends the developing interest in *Wirkungsgeschichte* in exegesis, even as he refuses to concede the dichotomy between radical indeterminacy and single determinate meaning. In his response to Thiselton, Olhausen suggests that 'politeness theory' may have much to offer for developing Thiselton's use of speech-act theory, and also probes the theological dimension of Thiselton's hermeneutics.

The above 'philosophical' chapters are also highly theological – especially those of Vanhoozer and Thiselton. Others focus more specifically on the *theology of language* and biblical interpretation. Bartholomew suggests that the challenge of postmodernism in particular necessitates an exploration of theology of language and the implications of this for biblical interpretation. He examines George Steiner's and John Milbank's proposals for a theology of language, and suggests that Steiner's *Real Presences* is a superb example of what theology of language can provide for biblical interpretation. Bartholomew, like Hesse, suggests that continental philosophies of language may be more fertile for biblical interpretation than analytic philosophies like speech-act theory.

Laughery addresses two questions: how does religious language relate to other language and, secondly, in the light of this question, should Scripture be read as any other book? He articulates a realist theology of language that provides a way of differentiating religious language from other forms of language without driving a wedge between them. Laughery resists the dichotomy of either reading the Bible as any other book or reading it distinctly. He argues that a theology of language enables us to nuance this polarization in more helpful ways.

Greene searches for a theology of language that is focused firmly on the cross and resurrection, but which nevertheless fully takes into account the challenge of postmodernism. Greene, in dialogue with Tom Wright, focuses on apocalyptic and the kingdom of God, and argues that a Christology that takes seriously the fracturedness of history illumines language and history such that biblical interpretation could play a key role in religion recovering a public presence.

The *literary turn* in biblical studies in the 1970s continues to affect biblical interpretation in powerful ways. Through a dialogue with Stephen Prickett's *Words and the Word*, Stephen Wright demonstrates how sensitivity to the Bible as literature illuminates texts like the story of Jesus' exorcism in the Capernaum synagogue (Mk 1:21–28) without necessarily undermining its historicity. Ingraffia and Pickett continue Wright's discussion about the Bible as literature. In dialogue with Vanhoozer, Ingraffia argues that we must read the Bible with a trust that we bestow on no other book. As a complement to Ingraffia, Pickett demonstrates how literature can help our reading of Scripture.

Recent decades have alerted us all to the knotty problem of the relationship between *gender and language*, and for biblical scholars this is frequently focused in issues of translation. David Lyle Jeffrey interacts with contemporary trends towards inclusive language and examines the theological and hermeneutical implications of some of the more radical proposals. He encourages us to recover the authority of Jesus. Kathryn Greene-McCreight interacts with

Jeffrey's views in her response, suggesting that the underlying issue is whether or not God has revealed himself.

Ray Van Leeuwen revisits the perennial issue of *Bible translation* and argues for a renewal of translations that are more direct and transparent in relation to the original languages. At least, functional equivalent translations need supplementation by more direct translations. Woven into Van Leeuwen's detailed case is an argument for the canon as the main literary context within which we should read the Bible and which needs to be taken seriously in translations, as well as an apology for commentary, both of the academic written sort and of the oral, teaching and preaching sort.

Hans Frei's legacy continues to be felt in the renewed interest nowadays in theological, and particularly narrative, interpretation of the Bible. Neil Beaton MacDonald examines Frei's account of the move from pre-critical to critical biblical hermeneutics, and he argues that Frei's account of biblical narrative needs to be supplemented by the illocutionary stance of historical truth-telling, and that the critical shift took place at the level of epistemic stance towards belief.

A great concern of the Seminar is that our work on biblical hermeneutics should come home to roost, as it were, in *actual biblical interpretation*. Most of the chapters in this volume manifest this concern, and three in particular weigh in strongly on interpretative issues. Karl Möller draws on rhetorical criticism, speech-act theory and studies of metaphor, to chart a creative way forward in the reading of the oracles of judgement in Amos. Gordon McConville ranges across the history of interpretation of Deuteronomy to show how issues of language have influenced, and should influence, its interpretation. Ian Paul draws on Ricœur's theory of metaphor to interpret Revelation 12.

It will be hard, I think, to emerge from this volume without being aware of just how significant issues of language are for biblical interpretation. If that is true, then a major aim of the Seminar will have been achieved. Half the battle is to persuade biblical exegetes that linguistics and philosophy and theology of language really matter in interpretation. The more difficult issue is to chart the way forward in our understandings of language and interpretation. This volume builds on some of the most creative work of recent decades and identifies work sites that require ongoing attention. For example, if theology of language is taken seriously as a constituent part of a biblical hermeneutic, how do we relate the more analytical speech-act approaches to more continental approaches such as that of Steiner and Hesse? This volume opens up this sort of question, and invites readers concerned with a renewal of biblical interpretation into this exhilarating and challenging discussion.

Bibliography

Austin, J., *How to Do Things With Words* (Cambridge, MA: Harvard University Press, 2nd edn, 1975)

Barr, J., *The Semantics of Biblical Language* (Oxford: OUP, 1961)

—, *Biblical Words for Time* (London: SCM Press, 2nd edn, 1969)

Botha, M.E., 'Metaphorical Models and Scientific Realism', in *Proceedings of the 1986 Biennial Meeting of the Philosophy of Science Association*, I (ed. A. Fine and P. Machamer; Michigan: Philosophy of Science Association, 1986), 374–83

Freedman, D.N., 'Preface', in *Pomegranates and Golden Bells: Studies in Biblical, Jewish, and Near Eastern Ritual, Law, and Literature in Honor of Jacob Milgrom* (ed. D.P. Wright, D.N. Freedman and A. Hurvitz; Winona Lake, IN: Eisenbrauns, 1995), ix–xi

Hesse, M., 'The Cognitive Claim of Metaphor', *The Journal of Speculative Philosophy* II.1 (1988), 1–16

—, 'Theories, Family Resemblances and Analogy', in *Analogical Reasoning* (ed. D.H. Helman; Dordrecht: Kluwer Academic, 1988), 317–40

—, 'Model, Metaphors and Truth', in *Knowledge and Language*, III: *Knowledge and Metaphor* (ed. F.R. Ankersmit and J.J.A. Mooij; Dordrecht: Kluwer Academic, 1992), 49-66

Kiuchi, N., *The Purification Offering in the Priestly Literature: Its Meaning and Function* (JSOTSup 56; Sheffield: JSOT Press, 1987)

Lakoff, G., and M. Johnson, *Metaphors We Live By* (Chicago and London: Chicago University Press, 1980)

—, *Philosophy in the Flesh: The Embodied Mind and Its Challenge to Western Thought* (New York: Basic Books, 1999)

Milgrom, J., *Leviticus 1–16* (Anchor Bible; New York: Doubleday, 1991)

Petrie, H.G., 'Metaphor and Learning', in *Metaphor and Thought* (ed. A. Ortony; Cambridge: CUP, 1979), 438–61

Ricœur, P., *The Rule of Metaphor: Multi-disciplinary Studies of the Creation of Meaning in Language* (London: Routledge, 1978)

Rorty, R. (ed.), *The Linguistic Turn: Recent Essays in Philosophical Methodology* (Chicago: Chicago University Press, 1967)

Scheffler, I., *Beyond the Letter: A Philosophical Inquiry into Ambiguity, Vagueness and Metaphor in Language* (London: Routledge and Kegan Paul, 1979)

Searle, J.R., *Speech Acts: An Essay in the Philosophy of Language* (Cambridge: CUP, 1983)

Soskice, J.M., *Metaphor and Religious Language* (Oxford: Clarendon Press, 1985)

Steiner, G., *After Babel: Aspects of Language and Interpretation* (Oxford and New York: OUP, 3rd edn, 1998)

—, *Real Presences: Is There Anything in What We Say?* (London and Boston: Faber and Faber, 1989)

Sternberg, M., *The Poetics of Biblical Narrative: Ideological Literature and the Drama of Reading* (Bloomington, IN: Indiana University Press, 1987)

Stiver, D.R., *The Philosophy of Religious Language: Sign, Symbol and Story* (Malden, MA and Oxford: Basil Blackwell, 1996)

Thiselton, A.C., *The Two Horizons: New Testament Hermeneutics and Philosophical Description* (Carlisle: Paternoster; Grand Rapids: Eerdmans, 1980)

—, *New Horizons in Hermeneutics: The Theory and Practice of Transforming Biblical Reading* (Grand Rapids: Zondervan, 1992)

Vanhoozer, K.J., 'The Spirit of Understanding: Special Revelation and General Hermeneutics', in *Disciplining Hermeneutics. Interpretation in Christian Perspective* (ed. R. Lundin; Grand Rapids: Eerdmans; Leicester: Apollos, 1997), 131–65

Wold, D.J., 'The Karet Penalty in P: Rationale and Cases', in *SBL Seminar Papers* (1979), 1–45

Wolterstorff, N., *Divine Discourse: Philosophical Reflections on the Claim that God Speaks* (Cambridge: CUP, 1995)

1

From Speech Acts to Scripture Acts

The Covenant of Discourse and the Discourse of the Covenant

Kevin J. Vanhoozer

Introduction: Language in Jerusalem and Athens

A word is dead
When it is said
Some say.

I say it just
Begins to live
That day.
   Emily Dickinson

'Know thyself'. Socrates' demand that philosophers reflect on what it is to be human has been taken up by many in other disciplines as well. It is possible to study the functions of humans considered as biological organisms (physiology) as well as human emotional and mental dysfunctions (psychology); the actions of individuals in the past (history) as well as the behavior of various human groups (sociology). The study of human language is similarly interdisciplinary. It can be studied by linguists, cognitive psychologists, historians, logicians, philosophers – and, yes, theologians. If the third-century theologian Tertullian was correct in defining a 'person' as a being who speaks and acts (which is not so very far from what a philosopher, Peter Strawson, would say about individuals some seventeen hundred years later), then it may well be that we have to treat both topics – language and humanity – *together*.

To study language, then, is to touch on issues involving a whole world and life view. Some approaches to the study of language's origin and purpose, for example, presuppose that human existence and behavior is best explained in terms of Darwinian evolution. In their highly regarded work on linguistic relevance, for instance, Dan Sperber and Deirdre Wilson suggest that human cognition is a biological function whose mechanisms result from a process of natural selection: 'Human beings are efficient information-processing devices'.[1] For Sperber and Wilson, language is essentially a cognitive rather than communicative tool that enables an organism (or device) with memory to process information.[2] On the other hand, George Steiner claims, on the basis of his experience of transcendence in literature, that 'God underwrites language'.[3] Such disparate analyses should give philosophers pause. They also raise the question as to whether Christians should not approach the study of language from an explicitly Christian point of view. Such, however, is the intent of the present article: to reflect on language from out of the convictions of Christian faith.

Craig Bartholomew has recently called for those interested in the theological interpretation of Scripture to clarify just how the relation of philosophy to theology bears on biblical study.[4] Here we probably do not want to follow Tertullian's suggestion, stated in the form of a rhetorical question, that Jerusalem (theology) has nothing to do with Athens (philosophy). We would do better to follow Alvin Plantinga's advice to Christian philosophers not to let others – people with non-Christian world-views – set the agenda, but to pursue their own research programs. What is needed, he says, is 'less accommodation to current fashion and more Christian self-confidence'.[5] Indeed. Why should *Christian* faith be excluded from the search for understanding when other faiths – including modernity's faith in instrumental reason, empiricism and naturalism – are not?

Christian theology takes faith in the revelation of Jesus Christ, attested in the Scriptures, as its ultimate criterion for judging what is true, good and beautiful. While not at all turning our back on the results, assured or not, of modern learning, it is important to acknowledge that all of us, Christians and non-Christians alike, come to the data with interpretive frameworks already in place. The present essay approaches the 'data' concerning language and interpretation with an interpretive framework largely structured by theological concepts. Instead of excluding considerations of Christian doctrine from my inquiry, I intend to make explicit use of them. This is not to turn one's back on philosophy, but to let human reason be guided and corrected by Christian

---

[1] Sperber and Wilson, *Relevance*, 46.

[2] Ibid., 173.

[3] Steiner, *Real Presences*.

[4] Bartholomew, 'Philosophy'.

[5] See his 1983 lecture, 'Advice to Christian Philosophers'.

doctrine, and by the language and literature of Scripture itself. Only by first conducting 'theological investigations' of language and literature *in general* can we then come to discuss, with philosophy, the task of interpreting Scripture.

The most fruitful recent development for the dialogue about language between philosophy and theology is undoubtedly the emphasis on language as a species of human action: speech acts. Examining what people *do* with language represents a fascinating case study for the broader dialogue between philosophy and theology. Of course, the idea that humans do things *in* speaking was well known to the very earliest biblical authors, even without the analytic concepts of speech-act philosophy.

The present essay evaluates the extent to which speech-act philosophy approximates and contributes to what theologians want to say about language. This is not to say that speech-act categories will dominate the discussion. On the contrary, we will see that Christian convictions concerning, say, divine authorship, the canon and the covenant, will lead us to both modify and intensify the typical speech-act analysis. My goal is to let the 'discourse of the covenant' (e.g., Scripture) inform and transform our understanding of the 'covenant of discourse' (e.g., ordinary language and literature).

The first, and longer, part of the chapter explores what I shall call the 'covenant of discourse': a philosophy *and* theology of communication. My hope is to achieve a certain consensus about language and understanding based on a strategic appropriation of certain philosophical concepts that will be amenable to Christian biblical scholars and theologians.

In the second part of the chapter, I turn to the 'discourse of the covenant', that is, to a consideration of the Bible as written communication. Dealing with the canon – a complex, intertextual communicative act – will lead us to modify and develop our understanding of how biblical language works in ways that again go beyond typical speech-act theory. However, the benefit of using speech-act categories to describe the divine discourse in Scripture will also become apparent. Throughout the essay I examine not only what speech acts are, but the implications for looking at language as a form of human action as well, particularly for the sake of interpretation. Here too the leading theme of covenant proves helpful, insofar as interpretation is largely a matter of fulfilling one's covenantal obligation towards the communicative agents, canonical or not, who address us.

The conclusion highlights what follows from our analysis for biblical interpreters. It is not insignificant that the leading categories for describing interpreters – witness, disciple – are drawn from the language of theology. For nothing less will do in describing our properly *theological* responsibility to hear, and to understand, what God and neighbor are saying/doing when they address us. The series of theses running throughout the argument summarize the main claims and seek to provide the contours for the 'mere communicative hermeneutic'. My hope is that they begin to articulate an emerging consensus regarding the theological interpretation of Scripture.

I. The Covenant of Discourse: Speech Acts

'Tis writ, 'In the beginning was the Word.'
I pause, to wonder what is here inferred.
The Word I cannot set supremely high:
A new translation I will try.
I read, if by the spirit I am taught,
This sense: 'In the beginning was the Thought.'
This opening I need to weigh again,
Or sense may suffer from a hasty pen.
Does Thought create, and work, and rule the hour?
'Twere best: 'In the beginning was the Power.'
Yet, while the pen is urged with willing fingers,
A sense of doubt and hesitancy lingers.
The Spirit comes to guide me in my need,
I write, 'In the beginning was the Deed.'
Goethe, *Faust*

Goethe, of course, did not have the advantage of having read Austin or Searle, or for that matter, me! We can therefore forgive him for not having Faust write something like the following:

The mystery of the sign I now have cracked;
'In the beginning was the *communicative act*.'

Much of what I wish to say about the significance of speech acts for contemporary interpretation in general, and for interpreting the Bible in particular, is implicit in these lines from Goethe's *Faust*. They also have the merit of directing our attention to Jesus Christ in such a way that Christ becomes, as Bartholomew puts it in his article, 'the clue to theology and philosophy ... the clue to the whole creation'.[6] Communicative action, as I understand it, indeed takes up and integrates the four possibilities for translating *logos* that Faust considers: word, thought, power, deed. For, as we shall see, word-deeds involve both thought (propositional content) and power (illocutionary force).

To begin with, Goethe roots our thinking about speech acts in theology – Trinitarian theology, to be exact. Faust is, after all, translating a text about the incarnation of the *Logos*. His successive tries at translating *logos*, taken together,

---

[6] Bartholomew, 'Philosophy'.

suggest that the Word is God's-being-in-communicative-action. This approximates Karl Barth's Trinitarian analysis of divine revelation in terms of revealer-revelation-revealedness.[7] God communicates himself – Father, Son, and Spirit – to others. In terms of communication theory: the triune God is communicative agent (Father/author), communicative action (Son/Word), and communicative result (Spirit/power of reception). I shall suggest in due course that the canon too may be considered a species of divine communicative action.

Goethe in this passage also sets us thinking about the relation of God's speech act – the *Logos* – to the words of Scripture. Interestingly, John Macquarrie, in his own free rendering of John 1:1, suggests the following translation: 'Fundamental to everything is meaning'.[8] The question that needs to be asked here is whether the incarnation alone exhausts the divine speech, or whether Scripture itself may be legitimately considered a divine speech act of sorts.

A new interdisciplinary consensus?

For the past fifteen years I have been exploring the potential of viewing language and literature in terms of speech acts.[9] I have been heartened by other wayfarers from other disciplines who have since joined the pilgrimage towards the promised land of a communicative hermeneutic. In May of 1998, participants representing five theological disciplines met in Cheltenham, England, to think together about how speech-act philosophy might afford the conceptual resources with which to meet the contemporary crisis in biblical interpretation.[10] The discussion that follows attempts to set forth these conceptual resources, as well as their philosophical, and theological, basis.[11]

---

[7] Barth, *CD* I, 1.

[8] Macquarrie, 'God?', 400.

[9] The earliest effort was 'The Semantics of Biblical Literature'.

[10] The disciplines, and their representatives, were philosophy of religion (Nicholas Wolterstorff), Old Testament (Craig Bartholomew), New Testament (Anthony Thiselton), biblical theology (Francis Watson), and systematic theology (Kevin Vanhoozer).

[11] Some readers may want to know what, if any, advances the present essay makes on my *Is There a Meaning in This Text?* The new elements include: a 'missional' model of communication; a more consistent use of the concept of covenant, and the concomitant notion of imputation; a reinvigorated, if not entirely new, defense of the priority of illocutions over perlocutions that incorporates William Alston's recent work on illocutionary acts; and a new argument, based on an analysis of biblical covenants, for seeing a greater continuity between oral and written discourse than is often the case in contemporary philosophy and literary theory. Finally, and perhaps most surprisingly, there is an almost complete absence of the term 'meaning'!

Why speech acts? First, because thinking in terms of speech acts approximates the way in which the Bible itself treats human speech. Moreover, as Nicholas Wolterstorff has demonstrated, speech-act categories have the potential to help us appreciate what it means to call the Scriptures God's Word. For me, however, the most important contribution speech-act philosophy makes is to help us to break free of the tendency either to reduce meaning to reference or to attend only to the propositional content of Scripture. Viewing texts as doing things other than representing states of affairs opens up possibilities for transformative reading that the modern obsession with information has eclipsed. Finally, speech-act philosophy commends itself as perhaps the most effective antidote to certain deconstructive toxins that threaten the very project of textual interpretation and hermeneutics.

I am under no illusions about the difficulty of achieving such a consensus. Speech-act theorists themselves are divided over, say, the relative importance of intentions (Grice) over conventions (Searle). The challenge is to specify the most important commonalties – the greatest common denominator, as it were – without diluting the remaining significant differences. So, while we can agree on certain basic presuppositions and principles, some significant differences may persist.

Where do we agree? In my opinion, there is considerable agreement about the following points: 1) We use language to do more than picture states of affairs. None of us believe that the sole point of language is reference or representation. We affirm that language is transformative as well as informative. Hence we are interested in the pragmatics as well as the semantics of language.[12] 2) We reject the idea, rampant among some postmoderns, that meaning and reference are radically indeterminate, as well as the related idea that the author is 'dead' or irrelevant to the process of interpretation. 3) We agree that *action*, rather than representation, should be the operative concept, and that this entails certain *rights* and *responsibilities* on the part of authors and readers. In particular, we see the promise as the paradigm for what is involved

---

[12] In his chapter elsewhere in the present book, however, Thiselton misleadingly associates me with those who see meaning in terms of reference, largely because I used the phrase 'single determinate meaning'. Let me take this opportunity, then, to state that what I think is determinate is the whole communicative act. 'Single' and 'determinate' were intended to shore up the notion that what fixes the meaning of a text is what the author said/did, and that this does not change at the behest of the reader. 'Single determinate meaning' is shorthand for the realist's intuition that the author's intentional action, however complex, is what it is, and cannot be changed by interpreters at a later date. Moreover, determinate communicative acts often have presuppositions, entailments and implications that preclude our viewing interpretation in terms of 'endlessly wooden replication' of a single propositional content.

in speech action (though in the present work I put forward *covenant* as an alternate). 4) We reject the idea, again rampant among some postmoderns, that readers are free to manufacture, or to manipulate, textual meaning in order to serve their own aims and interests.

Where do we differ? Two areas come to mind. 1) Some think that speech-act analysis is most helpful in understanding particular parts of the Bible – for instance, Jesus' parables, or Paul's preaching (Thiselton). Others use speech-act theory in order to recover the notion of authorial discourse and to open up possibilities for reading the whole Bible as divine discourse (Wolterstorff). Still others, while not denying the preceding points, see speech-act philosophy as contributing categories for a full-fledged interpretation theory that resonates well with properly theological themes (Vanhoozer). The continuing discussion thus concerns whether biblical interpreters should be concerned to develop specific strategies for reading Scripture in particular (special hermeneutics) as opposed to applying biblical and theological insights to interpretation theory in general (general hermeneutics). 2) There is also some difference over the role of the interpretive community's response and audience reception of a text. One symptom of this difference may be seen in the various ways we appreciate (or not) the potential contribution of Ricœur's hermeneutic philosophy.[13] Wolterstorff explicitly criticizes Ricœur's theory of 'textual sense' interpretation, whereas Thiselton explores Ricœur's (and Jauss's) suggestion that the meaning of a literary work rests upon the dialogical relation between the work and its audience in each age. The question this raises for biblical interpretation pertains to the mode, and time, of God's speaking: are God's speech acts in Scripture once-for-all, or does God speak anew in each present reading (and, if this is so, does God say the same thing or something different on different occasions?).

My purpose in what follows is to develop some of the leading themes, philosophical and theological, of a hermeneutic of communicative action in order better to display what lies at the core of this emerging interdisciplinary approach. By no means is speech-act philosophy the queen of the hermeneutic sciences, however. How could it be? It was developed in order to deal primarily with oral, not literary, discourse, and quite apart from any concern for a specifically Christian view of persons or language. So, while speech-act philosophy has formulated some key insights and concepts, I shall feel free to make use of other theories (e.g., relevance theory) and concepts (e.g., imputation) as well. The aim is to sketch a model – and it will be no more than a sketch – of what we might call, after C.S. Lewis, 'mere hermeneutics'.

---

[13] I shall later cast this disagreement in terms of the distinction between illocutions and perlocutions and in terms of their relative roles in interpretation and understanding.

Anatomy of communicative action

In order to succeed in some inquiry, says Aristotle, one must ask the right preliminary questions. The overall goal of the Scripture and Hermeneutics Seminar is to address, and resolve, the contemporary crisis in biblical interpretation. Given this goal, I believe the right preliminary questions concern language and communication. What is language? What is communication? These questions are philosophical inasmuch as they pertain to basic concepts – concepts that lie behind, and often govern, the actual practice of interpretation. My strategy in what follows is to explore what I take to be the best answers to such questions, where 'best' is defined in terms of experiential and logical coherence, comprehensiveness, and compellingness on the one hand, and in terms of 'fittingness' with Scripture and Christian tradition on the other.

Language vs. speech

Most theories of linguistic communication have been based on a 'code' model, where language is the code and communication a matter of encoding and decoding messages. On this view, words are signs that represent thoughts: encoded thoughts. The main problem with this model is that it is descriptively inadequate, for several reasons: 1) some of the information conveyed is not actually encoded; 2) understanding involves more than decoding linguistic signals; and 3) words do more than convey information. The code theory leaves unexplained the gap between the code and the meaning that is actually communicated by the language. Mere mastery of a sign system is no guarantee of understanding.

Far more adequate are descriptions of language *use* or 'discourse' (the technical term for language in use). Of course, not just any use is in view. Repeating 'The rain in Spain …' for the sake of improving one's English accent is not yet discursive. (For the same reason, standing on a hermeneutics textbook to reach the top shelf counts as a *use*, but not as an interpretation, of a text.) Let us define 'discourse' as 'what someone sometime says to someone about something'.

Ricœur makes an important distinction between semiotics (the science of the sign) and semantics (the science of sentences). A sentence, or speech act, is not simply a larger sign but an entity of a completely different order.[14] A sentence is the smallest unit of language that can be used on a particular occasion to say something; it is more than the sum of its semiotic parts and requires a level of description all its own.[15] For Ricœur, this distinction between

---

[14] Ricœur, *Interpretation Theory*, 6–7.

[15] We may here note a parallel between the self and the sentence: each is what Peter Strawson calls a 'basic particular', that is, an irreducible concept that cannot be explained by something more basic (see my *Meaning?*, 204).

semiotics and semantics 'is the key to the whole problem of language'.[16] The distinction thus deserves closer inspection.

A simple example shows how the linguistic meaning alone of a sentence-long discourse falls short of encoding what a speaker, *S*, means when she says: 'Coffee would keep me awake.' There is no problem breaking the code of this sentence. The language is clear and stands in good syntactical order. The information conveyed is that coffee, presumably the caffeinated kind, has an accelerating effect on the human nervous system. But what does the discourse – the use of the sentence on a given occasion – mean? Decoding the language is not enough. We need to know something about the circumstances of the discourse. Consider two different scenarios where *S* is asked 'Would you like some coffee?': 1) *S* is studying for an exam late at night and is struggling to stay awake; 2) *S* has finished studying for an exam and would like to retire early in order to be fresh for the exam the following morning. In the first case, the meaning of *S*'s statement 'Coffee would keep me awake' is 'yes'; in the second instance, 'no'. What this example shows is that communication involves more than linguistic encoding; it involves, in ways that we have yet to specify, the broader, unencoded circumstances of someone's use of language.

Communication: The design plan of human language
Words alone have at best only meaning potential. Human languages should not be thought of as free-floating sign systems that enjoy an autonomous existence from their users. Even a dictionary simply reports the common usages associated with a given word. Hence, to study a language apart from studying what language users do with it is a hopeless enterprise.

The philosopher William Alston advocates what he terms the 'Use Principle': 'An expression's having a certain meaning consists in its being usable to play a certain role (to do certain things) in communication'.[17] A language, then, is a vehicle for communication. He claims that 'Interpersonal communication is the primary function of language; its other functions, for example, its use in the articulation of thought, are derivative from that'.[18] By 'speech act' or 'discourse', then, let us refer to language-in-communicative-use.

Using language to communicate is not an arbitrary happening. I have elsewhere argued that the 'design plan' of language is to enable communication and understanding.[19] Here, then, is our first working thesis, a thesis that arises from a theological conviction:

---

[16] Ricœur, *Interpretation Theory*, 8.
[17] Alston, *Illocutionary Acts*, 154.
[18] Ibid., 155.
[19] Cf. my *Meaning?*, 204–7.

1. Language has a 'design plan' that is inherently covenantal.

Language is a divinely given human endowment and serves as a crucial medium for relating with God, oneself, others and the world. For the moment, my focus is on interpersonal communication. My hope is that certain developments in recent philosophy will help us better to understand what we believe about language on the basis of our Christian theological convictions.

A missional model of communication (theology)

The sender-receiver model is well known in communication studies. According to this model, a source (speaker, author) encodes a message into a linguistic signal (speech, text) that serves as the channel which conveys the message (through air, across time) to a destination (listener, reader) who receives the message by decoding the signal.[20] What light, if any, might theology have to shed on debates about the nature of language and communication? While I certainly do not think that everything in our world is a 'vestige of the Trinity', I do think that in this case there is something more than an interesting analogy. The doctrine of the Trinity, I shall argue, stands not as an analogy but as a paradigm to human communication.

The triune God is an eternal communion of divine persons. Presumably, there is some 'communication' between Father, Son, and Spirit – the so-called 'immanent' Trinity. Nevertheless, I propose to develop a theological understanding of communication on the basis of the 'economic', not the immanent, Trinity. The economic Trinity is the technical term for the way in which the triune God progressively reveals himself in history. The economic Trinity is the name for God in communicative (and self-communicative) action. We can thus state our second thesis:

2. The paradigm for a Christian view of communication is the triune God in communicative action.

The so-called 'missions' of the Son and Spirit, authorized by God the Father/ Author, bear a certain resemblance to the 'economy' of the 'sender-receiver' model of communications. They represent God's attempt to reach out to human others in truth and love. The Son is God's 'mission' to the world, as is indicated by the words of Jesus in John 17:18, 'As you have sent me into the world ...'. Jesus' mission, at least in part, was to give to his disciples the words the Father had given him (Jn. 17:8). At the core of Christian theology, then, is the theme of the *word sent*.

---

[20] Cf. Sperber and Wilson, *Relevance*, 4–5.

Irenaeus believed that the Father's work was two-handed: the Word provides form or shape (content); the Spirit provides animation and movement. 'Sending', then, lies at the very heart of Christian thinking about the triune God. And, in a biblical passage that largely accounts for my appreciation of speech-act philosophy, we read God declaring, through the prophet Isaiah, that his word, like rain, is sent to nourish and enliven life on earth: 'so shall my word be that goes forth from my mouth; it shall not return to me empty, but it shall accomplish that which I purpose, and prosper in the thing for which I sent it' (Isa. 55:11). If every piece of human discourse similarly aims at accomplishing *something*, then it follows that every statement is a 'mission statement'.

Does the notion of *missio* entail the code model of communication? That depends on whether the 'Word', to return to Faust, is conceived exclusively as 'thought' (e.g., information) or as 'power' and 'deed' as well. From the perspective of theology, the mission of the Son – God's 'sending' his Word to earth – should be seen in terms of acting, not encoding. For the sending is not simply a conveying of information, but a conveying of God's very person (i.e., a conveying of one's *communicative* as well as *informative* intentions). For what God purposed in sending the Son (and later, the Holy Spirit) involved much more than conveying information. The purpose of the sending of God's Word was as much *transformative* as it was informative. Indeed, the Gnostics (and others since then) erred precisely at this point, in thinking that salvation was indeed only a matter of knowledge. If that were the case, then information alone could indeed save us. But it is not the case. By communicative action, then, I have in mind the *many* kinds of missions on which verbal messages are sent.

Communication as intentional action

The missional model of communication, together with the design plan of language, encourage us to think of discourse in terms of intentional action. Humans typically conceptualize human behavior in intentional terms. Robert Gibbs, a cognitive psychologist, adopts the 'cognitive intentionalist premise': 'people's experiences of meaning are fundamentally structured by their inferences about the intentions of others'.[21] Gibbs believes that there is empirical evidence that demonstrates how human beings are cognitively 'hard-wired' to look for intentions in human linguistic, artistic and cultural products. Just as babies know to focus on their parents' faces and eyes, so listeners and readers attend to embodied intentions. 'People use words to convey to each other first and foremost their communicative intentions, not the semantic meanings of the words or the unconscious causes that might underlie such intentions'.[22]

---

[21] Gibbs, *Intentions*, 326.

[22] Ibid., 42.

Here again we see how one's view of language is mutually conditioned by one's view of what it is to be human. From a Christian vantage point, human beings are neither mechanical automatons nor free spirits, but embodied agents. Christians reject the modern picture of the sovereign subject who enjoys mastery over language and the postmodern picture of the victim of systemic socio-economic or political forces who is more bespoken by than an active speaker of language.[23]

The subject of intentionality is far too complex to discuss thoroughly here. Yet it is far too important a subject to ignore, either. For what an agent does is ontologically and logically tied to the concept of what the agent intended. It follows that understanding is a matter of recognizing the agent's intention, for it is the intention that makes an act one thing rather than another. Whether a slap on the back is a greeting, an attempt to save someone from choking, or a congratulatory rather than an aggressive gesture, all depends on the intent with which the act was performed. On my view, then, authorial intention returns – not as a feature of psychology so much as an irreducible aspect of action. Intentions are embodied in a material medium, enacted via bodily movement or by saying something.

One popular, though misleading, view of intentions is to identify them with an agent's plans or desires ('I intend to be there on time'). What an agent *plans* to do and what an agent actually does are two different things, however. It is perhaps the failure to preserve this distinction, more than anything else, that accounts for the demise in current literary theory of the concept of authorial intention.

Only the concept of intention enables us to view actions as more than mere bodily movements. When we say that someone gives, or attacks, or borrows, or protects, we are not merely describing bodily movements but intentional actions. Similarly, only the concept of intention enables us to view words and texts as more than mere material marks. Only the concept of authorial intention enables us to specify what the author is doing in using (e.g., *tending to*) just these words in just this way.

The so-called death of the author is actually a form of the worst sort of reductionism, where communicative acts and intentions are stripped away from the text, leaving an autonomous linguistic object. This is similar to reducing the wink – a communicative act in its own right – to the blink, that is, to a minor (and meaningless) bodily movement. If we ignore the intention – that factor that accounts for the unity of an action – we lose the act itself: no intention, no wink. Now, each stage of the physiological process of winking – the neural firings, the muscular contraction – could be described

---

[23] For a fuller account of how human beings are communicative agents in covenantal relation, see my 'Human Being', esp. 175–83.

separately, but no one stage is the location of the intention, or the wink. 'We murder to dissect.' Failure to ascribe intentions thus results in 'thin' descriptions. Descriptions are 'thin' when they must rely on lower-level concepts like 'neural firings' rather than higher-level, intentional categories like 'flirting'.

It is important to locate the cause of the text at the right level: neither at the infrastructure (the sign system) nor at the level of the superstructure (the prevailing ideology), but at the level of the completed act, the level to which the author was attending. It is vitally important to resist 'eliminative semiotics': the tendency to reduce meaning to morphemes in motion. Intention cannot be reduced to the non-intentional without losing the phenomenon of action itself.[24] The author's intention is that intrinsic factor that constitutes an act as what it is. A speech act, then, is the result of an enacted communicative intention.

Relevance

A relative newcomer to the scene of communications studies, relevance theory, has made several helpful contributions towards helping us understand communication in terms of intentional action. Dan Sperber and Deirdre Wilson write: 'To communicate is to claim an individual's attention: hence to communicate is to imply that the information communicated is relevant'.[25] According to Sperber and Wilson, communication is less a process of encoding than it is 'a process of inferential recognition of the communicator's intentions'.[26] Communication succeeds when the audience is able to infer the speaker's meaning from her utterance.

Relevance theory builds on insights into the dynamics of conversations associated with the philosopher Paul Grice. Grice's basic idea is that once a piece of behavior is identified as communicative, it then becomes reasonable to assume that the communicator is trying to make herself understood. What a speaker says is evidence of the speaker's communicative intention. Hence the 'cooperative principle': make your conversational contribution such as is required for accomplishing its particular purpose in the particular situation in which it occurs. For instance, 'be as informative as required, but not more so'.

---

[24] Gibbs prefers to think of a continuum rather than a stark contrast between the conscious and the unconscious. What people do, he argues, may be more or less intentional: 'Any individual speech or artistic event actually reflects a hierarchy of intentions, with each level having a different relationship to consciousness' (*Intentions*, 33). I take Gibbs's point as a qualification rather than a contradiction of the position outlined here.

[25] Sperber and Wilson, *Relevance*, vii.

[26] Ibid., 9.

Relevance theory tries to answer three questions: what did *S* intend to say? What did *S* intend to imply? What was *S*'s intended attitude towards what *S* expressed and implied? In many cases, the linguistic meaning of a speech act, by itself, fails to communicate what the speaker means. Grice's cooperative principle, together with its four maxims, help addressees make sense of a communicative act whose linguistic meaning appears irrelevant or ambiguous. The sentence 'Coffee would keep me awake' appears, on the surface – that is, with regard to its linguistic meaning only – to say something about the effect of caffeine on the human organism.[27] A literalist might reply: 'I didn't ask you whether it would keep you awake, I asked if you wanted some.' Such a reply fails to draw what Grice calls an *implicature* from the original speaker's answer. Grice suggests that when hearers are confronted with a discourse that appears to be irrelevant or uninformative, and which therefore violates the cooperative principle, they must derive the intended message ('No thanks, I don't want any coffee') from their understanding of the broader situation in which the conversation takes place. An important question for biblical interpretation is whether there is a counterpart of the 'cooperative principle' for *written* discourse.

According to Sperber and Wilson, communication concerns the conveying of relevant information. On their view, the purpose of communication is to alter the 'cognitive environment' – the set of assumptions a person is capable of representing conceptually and which are accepted as probably true – of the addressee. To communicate successfully, they believe, we need some knowledge of the other's cognitive environment. As Van Leeuwen puts it elsewhere in this volume, 'human communication presupposes existence in a *shared*, meaningful world ... with enculturated contexts of meaning that enable receivers of a language act (including book or text) to infer meaning that is relevant to their existence or situation'.

Every piece of discourse, merely by being expressed, makes a certain claim upon our attention. By addressing us, a speaker manifests her intention to modify our cognitive environment in some way. Simply to say 'Hi!' modifies the addressee's cognitive environment by making her aware of the speaker's presence. We assume that what is said is relevant and that we will benefit from the effort it takes to process the information. The 'presumption of relevance' is that the level of cognitive effects – the communicative pay-off, as it were – is never less than is needed to make the discourse worth processing. In other words, the cognitive *effort* of understanding must never outweigh the

---

[27] For an extended analysis of this example, see Sperber and Wilson, *Relevance*, 11, 16, 34–35, 56.

cognitive *effects* of understanding. We shall return to relevance theory in due course.[28]

Communicative action as locutionary, illocutionary, and perlocutionary

On one level, speech-act philosophy corresponds admirably with the missional model of communication as intentional action. Indeed, the very title of J.L. Austin's seminal lectures, *How to Do Things with Words*, conveys his intention to move us beyond the picture of language as essentially a vehicle for transferring information (the 'FedEx' model of communication). Speech acts, as Austin and others have pointed out, have other agendas than transmitting information.

This is not the place to develop a full-fledged theory of speech acts. There are many such accounts. Suffice it to say, by way of introduction, that most speech-act theories distinguish three distinct aspects or dimensions of what we do with language. Consider the following utterance: 'Jesus is Lord'. The following might all be correct reports of what the speaker did in this utterance: 1) made vocal sounds; 2) spoke with a French accent; 3) said 'Jesus is Lord'; 4) confessed that Jesus is Lord; 5) told his neighbor that Jesus is Lord; 6) explained how her cancer had suddenly gone into remission; 7) made me feel unspiritual by comparison.

To break down this example into speech-act categories: 1–3 are *locutionary* (Austin, Searle) or *sentential* (Alston) acts. Nothing really communicative happens on this locutionary level. Levels 1 and 2, in particular, are wholly indifferent to the *content* of the utterance. Each of the first three fails to describe the communicative intention of the speaker. This latter aspect – the essential aspect of the communicative act – is the *illocutionary* dimension. This was Austin's term for what one *does* in saying something. Levels 4 and 5 report the illocutionary act. Level 6 is somewhat more complicated. It may be a legitimate implicature or entailment of the speech act, though only a consideration of the broader context of the communicative act can make that clear. Something altogether different, however, is happening in 7, which is a report on the *effect*, or by-product, of the illocutionary act. Austin called this the *perlocution*: what effect is produced *by* saying something. As we shall see, the distinction between illocutions and perlocutions is absolutely fundamental to interpreting texts in terms of communicative intentions and communicative acts.

---

[28] Jürgen Habermas makes a similar point about what we might call the 'presumption of *rationality*'. Every competent speech act must meet three validity conditions: it must be true (e.g., it must represent something in the external world); it must be truthful (e.g., it must sincerely express the speaker's intentions or inner world); it must be right (e.g., it must fit appropriately into the context of the social world). These three conditions together make up the presumption of communicative rationality.

If analytic philosophy conducts an anatomy of communicative action, then the notion of illocution must be judged to be its *heart*. Interpretation is essentially a matter of identifying and specifying illocutionary acts: what speakers and authors have *done* in tending to their words as they have. Hence:

3. 'Meaning' is the result of communicative action, of what an author has done in tending to certain words at a particular time in a specific manner.

Philosophy comes into its own as far as biblical interpretation is concerned when it trains its analytic sights on illocutionary acts. Accordingly, I shall have recourse on more than one occasion to William Alston's recent work on illocutionary acts. I shall also try to deepen Alston's account by considering illocutions from the biblical-theological perspective of the covenant. For the moment, suffice it to say that Alston has produced what is probably the single most complete apology for viewing meaning in terms of illocutionary acts. To be precise, he defines sentence meaning in terms of illocutionary act *potential*. A sentence's having a certain meaning consists in its being usable to play a certain role (to do certain things) in communication. The meaning of 'Jesus is Lord' is that one can use it to confess that Jesus is Lord. It has this potential because of its propositional content, with 'Jesus' as subject and 'Lord' as predicate, and because its utterance enables the speaker to assume a certain stance towards that proposition – in this case, an 'assertive' stance.

Searle, Alston and Wolterstorff all take *promising* to be a, if not the, paradigmatic speech act. 'My doing A in the future' is the content of my promise. Yet identifying this concept does not exhaust what is *done* in promising. To promise is to lay an obligation on oneself with regard to some future action. Alston and Wolterstorff in particular emphasize the agent's assuming a normative stance towards the content of that promise. In other words, in uttering a promise the speaker assumes responsibility for the conditions for its satisfaction. Making a promise, then, alters one's normative stance; one is now responsible for doing something for which one was not responsible before making the promise. In Alston's words: 'An utterance is most basically made into an illocutionary act of a certain type by virtue of a normative stance on the part of the speaker'.[29] Assuming a normative stance means that one becomes liable to judgments of appropriateness and rightness. What a speech act *counts as* depends not only on the words used, but also on the intersubjective situation (the circumstances, conventions, rules, etc.) that render language usable.

---

[29] Alston, *Illocutionary Acts*, 71.

Perhaps the purest examples of how people do things with language are what Searle terms 'declaratives' and Alston 'exercitives'. These speech acts are 'verbal exercises of authority, verbal ways of altering the "social status" of something, an act that is made possible by one's social or institutional role or status'.[30] The crucial fact here is that an utterance only brings something about if the utterer has the appropriate authority and makes his utterance in the appropriate circumstances. Examples of such 'exercitive' speech acts would be 'You're fired!' and 'I now pronounce you man and wife'. Another important example, recently examined by Ricœur, is that of the pronouncement of a judicial sentence: 'I *sentence* you to life imprisonment.' 'Sentencing' is, for Ricœur, the place where the universality of law and the particularity of life-situations meet, and hopefully issue in wise, and just, judgment.[31] The point here is that these communicative actions involve much more than a linguistic code or the sheer meaning of words. They involve communicative agents taking responsibility for what they do with their words.

From communicative action to covenantal relation

Communicative action is essentially an interpersonal affair. There is thus a fourth, overarching, dimension to communicative action: the *interlocutionary*. Let us call an interlocutor – either an agent or recipient of communicative action – a *communicant*. Interestingly, even J.L. Austin, a philosopher, had an inkling of the covenantal dimension of illocutions, for he wrote 'Our word is our bond'.[32] Thiselton has helpfully drawn attention to biblical material on the rights and obligations associated with human speech. Of course, in the context of Scripture, as he rightly points out, these 'rights' are not something that attach to autonomous individuals, as in Enlightenment thinking, but appear rather in the context of covenants with others and with the Other: '*covenantal* obligations presuppose a network of *relationality* which has a different basis from that of "rights" for an isolated, orphaned self who is not even "the sojourner-guest within the gates" '.[33]

---

[30] Ibid., 34.

[31] Ricœur insists that the purpose of the judiciary is to ensure that words win out over violence, justice over vengeance (*The Just*, ix). Later, in the same work, he draws attention to a certain parallel between the trial and the process of textual interpretation. The analogy is apt, for as I argue below, interpreting the meaning of a text is essentially a matter of ascribing intentional action to a responsible agent.

[32] Austin, *Words*, 10.

[33] Thiselton, in Lundin, et al., *Promise*, 217. Thiselton also remarks that Cartesian individualism predisposes us to overlook the interlocutionary dimension. For an illocution usually makes a claim not only of relevance, but also of something else, on the listener.

Whereas Thiselton pays special attention to covenantal promising, I tend to see *all* communicative action in covenantal terms. Philosophers are generally more comfortable speaking of cultural and social conventions than covenants. However, only if we allow our theological convictions to deepen philosophy at this point by invoking the design plan of language will a more Christianly adequate description of communication, as a species of covenantal action, be possible. Communicative privileges and responsibilities are best seen in a covenantal framework. Language is a divinely appointed covenantal institution. Hermeneutics, as the discipline that aims to understand the discourse of others, presupposes an interactive, interlocutionary self that exists only in relation to others. What we need to see is that all discourse is a form of interpersonal, communicative – which is to say, covenantal – action. The parties to the covenant of discourse – the communicants – are essentially two: speaker and hearer, or alternately, author and reader.

The 'who': Speaker/author

Deconstruction, it has been said, is the 'death of God' put into writing. The death of God is nothing less than the death of the Author of history. If there is no God, then ultimately history has no meaning, for the course of events would no longer represent God's communicative action but a meaningless, because impersonal, sequence of cause and effect. Similarly, texts, bereft of human authors, would be radically indeterminate for the simple reason that we could not identify what illocutionary act has been performed.[34] Texts without authors would be mere entities, as devoid of meaning as the marks the waves leave upon the sand. Why? Because meaning is the result of intentional (illocutionary) action, not a natural event. There is verbal meaning only where someone means, or has meant, something by using particular words in a specific context in a certain way.[35] The death of the author thus leads to hermeneutic non-realism and to the suspicion that meaning, like God, is merely a projection on the part of the reader/believer. Neither hermeneutics nor theology can afford to follow Feuerbach's suggestion that what we find – God, meaning – is actually only a projection of ourselves.[36]

The theological response to deconstruction is to stress 'the providence of God put into writing'. The missions of the Son and Spirit, not to mention the mission of the Word of God spoken or written (Isa. 55:11), is an outworking of divine providence. Now human authorship is a (pale) reflection of divine authorship. Created in the image of God, humans have been given the 'dignity

---

[34] For the sake of economy, I shall refer to agents of communicative action, be it oral or written discourse, as 'authors'.

[35] See Garcia's excellent article, 'Can There Be Texts Without Historical Authors?'.

[36] For a fuller analysis of this point, see my *Meaning?*, ch. 2.

of communicative agency'. Humans are communicative agents in covenantal relation, creatures able to enter into dialogical relations with others and, to a certain extent, with the world. To be a communicative agent means that one has the ability to set a language system in motion and so bring about an act of discourse.

Think of the author as a historical agent whose action is fixed in the past. What one communicates or does with words depends both on the historical circumstances of the act and on the state of a particular language at a given place and time. In order to make sense of p-a-i-n, for instance, we need to know whether an author was doing something in English or French. Unless we can associate texts with historical authors, they have potential meaning only. The historical aspect does not exhaust the nature of the author's agency, however. The author is also an aesthetic agent who structures his or her text in order to make the communicative act more effective. But we can go even further. The author is a moral agent who interacts with others in what he or she says and does. Authors of narrative, for instance, do not only tell stories, but also instruct people in right living, or give hope to the needy, or warn the unrighteous of the fate that awaits them. Finally, the author is a religious agent who, in relating to his words in a certain way ('Let your yea be yea, and your nay, nay'), either fulfills or fails his God-given responsibilities in the exercise of his tongue. In other words, the way we relate to our everyday discourse, as well as to the discourse of others, will prove us to be either faithful and true, or untrustworthy liars. (The same religious quality pertains, as we shall see, to interpreters too.)

We saw earlier that illocutionary acts involve authors taking normative stances towards the content of their acts. To promise is to undertake to fulfill certain obligations, and hence to make oneself responsible. I now want to generalize this point by suggesting that *the author is the one to whom certain illocutionary acts can be imputed.* Imputation is the operative concept, for it has to do both with the *capacity to act* and with the related notion of *responsibility for action.* It is also a notion that has an interesting pedigree, both in philosophy and in theology. Kant distinguished persons and things precisely in terms of imputation: 'A *person* is the subject whose actions can be *imputed* to him ... A *thing* is that to which nothing can be imputed'.[37] Imputation names, in Ricœur's words, 'the idea that action can be assigned to the account of an agent taken to be its actual author'.[38] The core of the concept of imputation is the attribution or ascription of an action to its author. The Latin *putare* implies calculation (*computare*), a kind of bookkeeping as to who has done what. The metaphor of a balance

---

[37] Kant, *Metaphysics*, 16.
[38] Ricœur, *The Just*, xvi.

book, at the limit the Book of Life (Rev. 20:12), underlies the idea of 'being accountable for'.

Being an author, then, carries certain responsibilities. Yet every person who speaks is an author – that is, a communicative agent. Again we see the confluence of the two themes of language and personhood. It is important to recognize, however, that authors are not only agents, but also *patients*, in the sense of those to whom something is done. For, once the communicative act is complete, its author can do no more. We may here recall relevance theory's insistence that every speech act is a tacit request for someone's attention. Authors must 'suffer' the reception of their works, including the possibilities that no one will pay attention, or that some might pay the wrong kind of attention. What we have said about the author's agency needs to be balanced, then, by an acknowledgment of the author's passivity. The author is both an active agent and a passive 'other' – a significant, signifying, 'other'. The covenant of discourse works in both directions: the author is responsible for her action; the reader is responsible for her response to the other and the other's act.

The 'what': Word, speech or text act

To this point, I have compared language use with action. Speech is both a 'doing' and a 'deed'. 'Communication' can refer both to the process and to the product, both to the action of communication and to the completed act. The attempt to say just what a communicative act is may be helped by reversing the polarities in order to think of action as a form of speech. For actions have speech–act attributes: in the first place, the doing of an action corresponds to the locution. Secondly, actions have propositional content (e.g., '*S* performs act y *on the ball*') and illocutionary force (e.g., kicking).[39] Finally, actions may also have perlocutionary effects ('*S* scores a goal').

Alston helpfully shows how illocutions 'supervene' on locutions. One can only perform an illocutionary act on the basis of locutions – words, sentences – though illocutions cannot be *reduced* to locutions. The same propositional content, say, 'Jesus' walking on water', can be attended to in different ways, and these different ways – asserting, asking, advising – determine the 'direction of fit' between our words and the world.

A text, then, is a communicative act with matter (propositional content) and energy (illocutionary force). Genuine interpretation, to stick with the

---

[39] Alston's analysis is slightly different. For him, the 'content' of an act includes object and performance: 'kicking the ball'. With regard to illocutionary acts, this means that, for Alston, the content of the act includes both its propositional component and its illocutionary force. For Searle (and usually me), 'content' refers primarily to the propositional component of the illocutionary act. In my view, the difference is largely terminological, though it ought to be kept in mind.

analogy, conserves textual matter and energy; deconstruction lets it dissipate. It does not follow from the fact that a text is a determinate communicative action that there is only one correct way to describe it. Opinions as to what an author did may, and should, change as we come to a deeper understanding of the author's language and circumstances, but this is not to say that the author did something that she had not done before. At the same time, it is important to acknowledge that authors may intend to communicate complex, multi-layered intentions. There is an instructive dialogue in the opening pages of *The Hobbit*. The scene is Gandalf's first visit to Bilbo Baggins:

> 'Good Morning!' said Bilbo, and he meant it …
> 'What do you mean?' he [Gandalf] said. 'Do you wish me a good morning, or mean that it is a good morning whether I want it or not; or that you feel good this morning; or that it is a morning to be good on?'
> 'All of them at once,' said Bilbo. 'And a very fine morning for a pipe of tobacco out of doors, into the bargain.'

A bit later Bilbo uses the same locutionary act with a very different illocutionary intent:

> 'Good morning! We don't want any adventures here, thank you!'
> 'What a lot of things you do use *Good morning* for!' said Gandalf. 'Now you mean that you want to get rid of me, and that it won't be good till I move off.'

Bilbo's first 'Good morning' performs more than one illocutionary act. Well and good. I would say that, in this case, his single determinate meaning was, in fact, compound rather than simple. If need be, I would be prepared to abandon the term 'single', though I think it is still implied in the really important qualifying term 'determinate'.

What is at stake in the foregoing is the status of the literal sense. The foregoing analysis suggests the following definition, which is also my fourth thesis:

4. The literal sense of an utterance or text is the sum total of those illocutionary acts performed by the author intentionally and with self-awareness.

There are many ways to study discourse, but not all are germane to the task of describing communicative action. Genuine interpretation is a matter of offering appropriately 'thick descriptions' of communicative acts, to use Gilbert Ryle's fine phrase. A description is sufficiently thick when it allows us to appreciate everything the author is doing in a text – that is, its illocutions.

Typically, historical-critical commentaries describe either the history and process of a text's composition or 'what actually happened'. According to the traditional 'picture theory' of meaning, the literal sense would be what a word or sentence *referred* to. On my view, however, the literal sense refers to the illocutionary act performed by the author. The important point is that the literal sense may require a fairly 'thick' description in order to bring it to light. For Ryle, a thin description of, say, a wink would be one that offers a minimal account only ('rapid contraction of the eyelid'). The description is thin because it omits the intentional context that alone enables us to see what someone is doing. Much modern biblical scholarship, in so doing, yields only 'thin description'. Text criticism gets bogged down on the locutionary level; historical criticism is obsessed with reference. The matter and energy of the Gospels is largely lost by historical-critical commentaries. The most important thing we need to know about a text, I submit, is what kind of communicative act(s) it performs and with what content.

The 'wherefore' and 'whereto': Reader

All speech acts, we declared, are mission statements, words on a mission: to accomplish the purpose for which they have been sent. That purpose, according to relevance theory, is to alter the addressee's cognitive environment in some way. The 'whereto' of communicative action is the reader; the 'wherefore' of communicative action is the reader's transformation (at a minimum, this means the reader will entertain a new thought).

Authors often wish to accomplish something *by* their discourse. The author of the Fourth Gospel, for instance, wants to elicit the reader's belief that Jesus is the Christ by telling Jesus' story. The question is whether this extra effect – eliciting belief – should count as part of the author's communicative action. I think it should not. Alston is right: an illocutionary act may well produce perlocutionary effects, but it does not *consist* in such effects. The only effect that properly belongs to the author's illocutionary act is *understanding* – the recognition of an illocutionary act for what it is. Sperber and Wilson agree: 'For us, the only purpose that a genuine communicator and a willing audience necessarily have in common is to achieve uptake: that is, to have the communicator's informative intention recognized by the audience'.[40] In a neat reversal of Augustine's formula 'Take up and read', we can say that understanding is a matter of reading and *taking up* (the illocution).

R.A. Duff, a philosopher of law, defines intention as 'acting to bring about a result' and distinguishes it from both desire and foresight.[41] A desired consequence is like a perlocution; an unforeseen consequence is more like an accidental effect. G.H. Von Wright similarly uses the term 'result' for results that are conceptually constitutive of an action, and 'consequence' for those further

---

[40] Sperber and Wilson, *Relevance*, 161.
[41] Duff, *Intention*.

entailments that an action produces.[42] The distinction, then, is between what is intrinsic and extrinsic. A result is what occurs in the performance of an illocutionary act ('he *confessed* that Jesus was Lord'). A consequence, on the other hand, is an event that may or may not follow from the performance of an action ('he made me feel unspiritual'). The main point is that consequences are not intrinsic, but *extrinsic*, to actions.

Understanding is a matter of recognizing an author's illocutionary act for what it is. A communicative act succeeds in the illocutionary purpose for which it has been sent simply by virtue of its being recognized. Communication succeeds when the speaker's communicative intention becomes mutually known. The reader need not believe or obey what is said in order to understand it. The reader's role in the covenant of discourse is nothing less than to seek understanding. Our anatomy of communicative action has led us to a fifth thesis, a thesis of decisive importance for the task of biblical interpretation, as we shall see below:

5. Understanding consists in recognizing illocutionary acts and their results.

Communicative action, however, often produces consequences other than understanding. Strictly speaking, these are not part of the illocutionary act that we have argued is the true object of understanding. Of course, there is nothing to stop a reader from inquiring into such unintended consequences. There *is* something that should stop us from calling such inquiries 'interpretations', however, and that is our analysis of what communicative action just *is*.

Communicative action can be 'overstood': readers can respond to texts other than by inferring illocutionary acts. There are often good reasons for overstanding. Gibbs, for example, cites the example of Jules Verne's *The Mysterious Island*, often thought to be a pro-Union and pro-abolitionist novel. Yet many contemporary readers, sensitive to the ways in which ideologies can affect people at a deep level, detect lingering evidence of racism in Verne's work: 'The book appears antiracist when read in terms of Verne's intentional meanings, yet racist when read from a more contemporary viewpoint'.[43] Similar remarks have been, of course, made about the Bible with regard to sexism. While judgments of political correctness may be appropriate, however, it is important not to rush to judgment too quickly. The first step is to identify what has been done; only then is one in a position to evaluate the action. Indeed, *not* to identify what an author has done risks doing the author violence. This underscores the importance of the reader, who is not merely a

---

[42] See Von Wright, *Explanation and Understanding*.
[43] Gibbs, *Intentions*, 267.

passive but an active recipient of an author's communication. To engage in communicative action – to make the communicative-covenantal presumption – is to hope that one will not fall prey to interpretive violence. This is simply the Golden Rule put into hermeneutics. 'To be understood is in itself a source of joy, not to be understood a source of unhappiness.'[44] Readers have an obligation to recognize an author's illocutionary act for what it is.

The citizen of language

Let us briefly gather up the results of our anatomy of communicative action before going on to discuss the implications for interpretation and for our understanding of the communicative action in Scripture.

Throughout this discussion, I have assumed that the most interesting facts about language all pertain to how humans use it to perform certain actions. That our views of what language is are tied up with our views of what it is to be human should by now be taken as a given. It is no accident that Alston's analysis of illocutionary acts led him straight to the notion of speakers' rights and responsibilities. Inherent in the very notion of speech acts is the idea of a speaker to whom acts may be imputed. Examining language in philosophical perspective directs us to the topics of human action and responsibility; theology deepens the analysis by viewing human action and responsibility in covenantal terms. Authors have an obligation to fulfill the responsibilities that they inevitably assume in performing their illocutionary acts. Readers have an obligation to seek understanding: to recognize illocutionary acts for what they are.

A communicant – either author as active agent or reader as active recipient of communication – is necessarily a *participant* in the covenant of discourse. Communicants enjoy what we might call, after Pascal, the dignity – the privilege and the responsibility – of communicative action. Pascal himself marveled at the dignity of causality with which God has endowed the human race. Like God, we are able to bring about new things. Communicative action – the ability to transform the cognitive environment – is no less marvelous. The privilege of communicative action is that we have the capacity to take initiatives in the world with our words and hence have the capacity to make a difference.

The image of the covenant brings to light yet another dimension of the language-humanity relation: the social. Searle defines language as a rule-governed form of human behavior. I have been at pains to show that these rules are moral as well as simply grammatical. But there is a political dimension, too. Speakers are neither sovereign subjects of language as a manipulable instrument (the modern error), nor slaves of language as an ideological system

---

[44] Thomassen, *Ethics*, 79.

(the postmodern error), but rather citizens of language, with all the rights and responsibilities appertaining thereunto.

According to Aristotle, human happiness is achieved not in solitude but in friendship, to which Ricœur adds, 'in the setting of the city'.[45] We wish to live well with others in just institutions. One such institution is the 'city' of language. Citizenship names the way an individual belongs to a *polis*. Citizens of language are communicants in the covenant of discourse. Indeed, what I have called the covenant of discourse spells out *what it is to live justly in the institution of language (discourse)*. We now turn to consider what good citizenship in the city of language means when it comes to interpretation.

Interpretation and communicative action

The model of communication I have been sketching assumes not merely a cooperative principle (so Grice), but also a 'covenantal principle' of discourse. What follows from our anatomy of communicative action for the practice of interpretation? Let the sixth thesis serve to anticipate the ensuing argument:

6. Interpretation is the process of inferring authorial intentions and of ascribing illocutionary acts.

Interpretation and illocutionary ascription

I agree with Alston that to understand a speaker 'is to know what illocutionary act she was performing'.[46] To interpret a text is thus to ascribe a particular illocutionary act, or set of acts, to its author. To interpret a text is to answer the question, 'What is the author doing in her text?'. Interpretation involves coming up with appropriately 'thick' descriptions of what an author is doing that get beyond the locutionary level (e.g., 'he uttered a sentence' or 'he spoke with a French accent') to descriptions of relevant communicative, which is to say illocutionary, action ('he confessed Jesus is Lord').

Guessing what an author *wanted* or *planned* to do in a text is not yet interpretation. Such a guess, in fact, may have little or nothing to do with what an author has actually done. No, what needs to be described is what the author was actually *attending* to – performing intentionally, with the appropriate skill and with self-awareness – in doing things with words.

In the final analysis, interpretation is a matter of justice: of correctly ascribing or imputing to an author what illocutionary acts have actually been performed. Interpretation is a matter of judging what an author has said/done in his or her words. The idea of inferring intentions from completed acts suggests a certain parallel between the process of textual interpretation and the judicial

---

[45] Ricœur, *The Just*, xv.
[46] Alston, *Illocutionary Acts*, 282.

process of a court trial. The basis of the analogy should now be plain: both have to do with *imputing intentions to agents justly*. In the case of textual interpretation, of course, what are imputed are not criminal but communicative, or, to be exact, *illocutionary* intentions.

Interpretation and illocutionary inference

The hard work of interpretation is largely a matter of inferring illocutionary intent from the evidence, which includes both the primary data (the text) and secondary considerations (context). For example, the information transmitted by the locution 'Wet paint' is one thing; the illocution – 'Do not touch' – is quite another. For simpler communicative acts like a 'Wet paint' sign, we infer the illocution almost automatically, based on our appreciation of the situational context.

Relevance theory emphasizes the importance of inferring authorial intentions, too: 'According to the inferential model, communication is achieved by producing and interpreting evidence.'[47] Interpretation is not simply a matter of decoding linguistic signs (e.g., locutions). Nor is it simply a matter of observing the effects of communicative action (e.g., perlocutions). No, interpretation must go on to determine which inferences as to the speaker's communicative intention would confirm the communicator's presumption of relevance. Recall the statement 'Coffee would keep me awake'. What should be inferred about the communicative act that supervenes on this locution depends entirely on the non-linguistic context of the utterance. It is not enough to know the dictionary meanings of the terms used in the sentence; one must know why just these words were used in just this way in just this circumstance. As Sperber and Wilson write: 'The coded signal, even if it is unambiguous, is only a piece of evidence about the communicator's intentions, and has to be used inferentially and in a context.'[48]

Speech-act philosophy and relevance theory coincide at the point where the addressee has to *infer* what illocutionary act has been performed in a particular utterance. To return to the metaphor of the trial: one way to determine an agent's intent is to cross-examine her. Authors are not physically present, of course, to respond to our interrogations, but this need not prevent us from putting our questions to the text. Normally these questions take the form of hypotheses; we ask ourselves whether an author *could have meant* this rather than that. Our hypotheses are put to the test precisely by being brought to the text. Those hypotheses that can account for more aspects or features of the communicative act have more explanatory power. Interpretation thus works through abduction, that is, by inference to the best explanation. An

---

[47] Sperber and Wilson, *Relevance*, 2.

[48] Ibid., 170.

'explanation' is, in fact, a 'thick description' of what an author has done. It 'explains' insofar as it accounts for the relevance and coherence of the text as a completed communicative act.

Overinterpretation is a matter of drawing 'unauthorized' inferences about what a speaker said or did. For example, one might take an insult as a compliment, thus ascribing the wrong illocutionary intent; conversely, one might take a compliment as an insult. The film *Being There* provides particularly striking examples of overinterpretation. Almost every character in the film consistently reads or infers much more into what Chance, a lowly gardener, intended. These mistaken inferences lead in turn to *misinterpretations*, namely, to ascriptions of communicative intentions when others, or perhaps none, are present.[49]

Interpretation and perlocutionary effects

At this point, readers may perhaps be forgiven for thinking that, though the concept of the covenant of discourse has a certain attractiveness, we could perhaps jettison the ungainly analytic philosophical work on illocutions and the unduly weighty baggage of Trinitarian theology to boot. I have anticipated these objections and tried to answer them by demonstrating the usefulness of the concept of illocution and the necessity of a distinctly theological account of the social institution of language. The practical payoff (the relevance!) of our extended discussion of illocutions comes to light in the contrast between interpreting for the sake of an ethical encounter with the other/author and using texts in ways that are less ethical than egocentric or ideological.[50]

Not all action is communicative. Many actions aim to effect a change in the environment merely by manipulating it. Such actions are causal, 'instrumental', or manipulative – what Jürgen Habermas calls 'strategic'. Instead of saying 'Please pass the salt', I can simply reach out and take it. In the same way, one can produce effects on other people through strategic rather than properly communicative action. After all, there are many ways to bring about change in an environment.

The success of *communicative* action wholly depends on bringing about this one effect: understanding. In contrast, the criterion for success in 'strategic' action is simply bringing about an intended result, some change in the world, other than understanding. The intended result may be to produce an effect on a hearer or reader. Perlocutions, like the Holy Spirit with whom I will

---

[49] The standard example of a mistaken inference when no communicative intention is present would be an interpreter reading marks made by waves in the sand as conveying some message or other.

[50] By 'ethical' in this context I have in mind Lévinas's insistence on recognizing the absolute priority of the 'other'. For an introduction to Lévinas's thought, see his *Ethics*.

associate this dimension of communicative action (see below), remain largely on the margins of theories about discourse. Happily, Alston's recent discussion provides help, and not a little light, in the discussion concerning the proper role for the reader's, or for that matter the interpretive community's, response to communicative action.

The real question is whether perlocutionary acts are essentially strategic rather than communicative. Aiming to produce an effect on the reader *other than understanding*, or *other than by means of understanding*, counts as strategic, not communicative, action. An emphasis on perlocutions can become pathological: 1) by aiming to produce effects on the reader independently of illocutions; or 2) by defining illocutions in terms of the effect produced on the reader. Interpreters must bear in mind the following two mandates: 1) do not think of communication in terms of perlocutions only; and 2) do not think of perlocutions as dissociated from illocutions. The danger lies in thinking about communication, and interpretation, in terms of effects produced on communicants. The seventh thesis puts perlocutions in their proper place:

7. Aiming to produce perlocutionary effects on readers other than by means of understanding counts as strategic, not communicative, action.

Austin himself thought that 'it is the distinction between illocutions and perlocutions which seems likeliest to give trouble'.[51] Stated as simply as possible, Austin was not sure whether the (perlocutionary) effect should be deemed an essential part of the (illocutionary) act. Anticipating our discussion of textual interpretation, we can see that Austin's initial confusion has grown exponentially; today, there are many critics and theorists who think of meaning in terms of the effect a text has on a reader (e.g., the reader's response).[52]

For Alston, the distinction is clear-cut. It is the difference between *having performed an action* and *being understood to have performed that action*. What we have here is a variation on Berkeley's idealism: not 'to be is to be perceived', but 'to act is to have been perceived to have acted'. But perhaps the distinction is not so solid. For as communication theorists remind us, communication is not a one-way street. We do not know if we have communicated until we

---

[51] Austin, *Words*, 109.

[52] E.g., Fish, *Text?*, equates textual meaning with the reader's response. A similar confusion may lie behind the 'functional equivalence' model of Bible translation that Van Leeuwen so competently interrogates and critiques elsewhere in this volume. Philosophers who tend to define illocutions in terms of perlocutions include Paul Grice, 'Meaning', and Stephen Schiffer, *Meaning*. For a fuller presentation of Alston's refutation of these views, see his *Illocutionary Acts*, ch. 2.

receive the appropriate feedback. To this, Alston replies yes and no: if you didn't hear or understand my question, then yes, on one level my communicative purpose has been frustrated. But – and this is all-important – *it does not follow that I didn't ask you.*

Alston posits a hierarchy of supervenience in which the 'higher' depends on, but cannot be reduced to, the 'lower', and in which the 'lower' cannot by itself do what is done at the 'higher' level. Such hierarchical ordering is familiar to scientists: cells depend on atoms and electrons, but the properties and behavior of the cell cannot be reduced to, or explained in terms of, atoms and electrons. No, cells supervene on atoms and require their own set of explanatory concepts. Similarly, illocutions supervene on locutions. Requesting someone to pass the salt is something we do *in* doing something else (e.g., saying 'Please pass the salt'). My *asking* depends on, but cannot be reduced to, my *uttering*.

Applying the same reasoning, Alston argues for an asymmetrical dependence of perlocutionary acts on illocutionary acts. To use the concepts just defined, this means that perlocutionary acts *supervene* on illocutionary acts. Acts are illocutionary when they pertain to what we are *doing in* speaking; acts are perlocutionary when they pertain to what we are *doing by* speaking. So perlocutionary acts can be based on illocutionary acts, but not vice versa. Now, communication can take place even where there are no perlocutionary effects; on the other hand, 'if no IA [illocutionary act] is performed, there is no (linguistic) communication, whatever effects one brings about on another person'.[53]

Humans relate to one another in various ways. It is possible to get people to do things other than by communicating with them. I can get a person to leave the room, for instance, by pushing him out the door. This brings about an effect on the 'addressee' of my action, but it is not, strictly speaking, a perlocutionary one, for the simple reason that it does not supervene on an illocutionary act. The same effect would, however, be perlocutionary if the person left as a result of my saying, 'Please leave'. Less straightforward, but still easily handled, is the case of my using a mere locution to get someone to leave. The sheer physical quality of an utterance (e.g., 'Boo!') may produce the desired effect. Clearly, however, this is an instance of strategic rather than communicative action.

Neither Alston nor I are indifferent to the effects produced on communicants. Indeed, most of us communicate with one another not solely for the purpose of having our illocutionary acts recognized, but for purposes that go beyond understanding. We want to modify cognitive environments in order to modify the natural or social environment. We say 'Clean up your room' not

---

[53] Alston, *Illocutionary Acts*, 170.

because we want to be understood, but because we want our addressee's room to be cleaner. Yet their ulterior effects are grounded in the content of our illocutionary acts. And our acts are what they are whether or not they produce perlocutionary effects. Though the distinction may still strike some as technical, the significance of maintaining it will perhaps come to light in our discussion below of the relation of Word and Spirit in interpreting the Christian canon.

Thiselton's work on 1 Corinthians is apt. He draws a contrast between Paul's apostolic ministry, which is largely *illocutionary* (e.g., *testifying* to Jesus Christ) with his Corinthian opponents, who wielded the instrumental (and ultimately manipulative) power of rhetoric:

> I distinguish between *'illocutionary'* speech–acts, which depend for their effectiveness on a combination of situation and recognition, and *'perlocutionary'* speech-acts, which depend for their effectiveness on sheer causal (psychological or rhetorical) persuasive power.[54]

Here we may recall the importance of the author's assuming a normative stance. Many speech acts (e.g., marrying people by saying 'I do') depend upon the identity and status of the speaker. Paul's proclamation of the cross – preaching the gospel – is directly tied to his status as an apostle, as 'one sent' to perform a particular communicative action.

If all truth is only a species of rhetoric, as some postmoderns and apparently some first-century Corinthians believed, then all illocutions become perlocutions. Paul stakes his own apostolic ministry 'on illocutionary promise, not on perlocutionary persuasion'.[55] I take it that Thiselton is arguing that Paul's discourse transforms his readers not by manipulating them, but rather by virtue of his testimony, which is as much to say by his *meaning* (e.g., illocutions), not by sheer manipulation (e.g., perlocutions).

Manipulative uses of language – by authors who employ deceitful rhetoric and by readers who impose their own interpretations alike – constitute a violation of the covenant of discourse.[56] I do not wish to be misunderstood on this point. There is nothing wrong with perlocutions, or with communicative acts having a perlocutionary dimension. What I do resist is the attempt to produce effects on readers via language use that seeks to by-pass the content of illocutionary acts.

---

[54] Thiselton, *Corinthians*, 51.

[55] Thiselton, in Lundin, et al., *Promise*, 226.

[56] Thiselton forcefully argues that self-personhood is obscured, if not lost, by the postmodern assumption that all language use is essentially manipulative. The close correlation once again between one's view of language and one's sense of self should not be overlooked. See his *Interpreting God*, esp. part 1.

II. The Discourse of the Covenant: Canonical Action

I have devoted the bulk of the present essay to thinking philosophically and theologically about language as communicative action, to *general* questions about language rather than to specific questions about biblical interpretation. This is not the place for a full-scale treatment of biblical hermeneutics. However, I do want to suggest a few ways in which my 'mere communicative hermeneutic' may be stretched towards the theological interpretation of Scripture. To what extent does the model of the text as communicative action with communicative intent need to be modified when that text is the Christian canon, the ensemble of texts that comprise the Old and New Testaments?

From 'promise' and 'sentence' to Gospel and Law

The promise is, as we have seen, the paradigmatic speech act for philosophers such as Searle and Alston. Thiselton has rightly called attention to its centrality in Scripture and in Christian theology as well. Fully to appreciate the discourse of the covenant, however, requires us to deal with both *promising* and *sentencing*.

Communicating the covenant

Genesis recounts the beginnings of many human institutions: marriage, the family, work. These are not merely social, but *created*, institutions: God-ordained orders intended to structure human experience every bit as much as those other divine orders, space and time. For our purposes, however, perhaps the most important institution initiated by God is that of the covenant. In speaking, God commits both himself and his addressees to certain obligations. In short: God establishes a personal relationship with men and women by communicating covenants. Subsequent communicative acts of God also take the form of covenants: to Noah (Gen. 9:8); to Abraham (Gen. 15:8); to David (2 Sam. 7). Promising and sentencing are constitutive of the covenant Yahweh instituted with Israel as recounted in the book of Deuteronomy.[57]

The *Shema* of Deuteronomy 6:4 ('Hear, O Israel') is a solemn summons to covenant fidelity.[58] What is called for is not just any readerly response, but the specific response of obedience. The promise that God will bless obedience is accompanied by a divine sentence: 'But if you will not obey the voice of the Lord your God or be careful to do all his commandments and his statutes which I command you this day, then all these curses shall come upon you and

---

[57] See Gordon McConville's essay elsewhere in this volume, especially the section on 'Deuteronomy and Speech-act Theory'.

[58] Cf. Snodgrass, 'Reading', on the importance of a hermeneutics of hearing/doing.

overtake you' (Deut. 28:15). The subsequent 'Deuteronomistic' history of Israel is largely the history of how Israel responds, or fails to respond, to the word of the Lord. The role of the prophets is largely that of 'prosecutors' of the covenant. The prophets are the ones who bring the Lord's case against Israel for having violated the covenant document.

C.H. Dodd spoke of the 'two-beat rhythm' of salvation history, comprised alternately of judgment and grace, law and gospel – in short, the *sentence* and the *promise*. This two-beat rhythm reaches a crescendo, of course, in the cross and resurrection of Jesus Christ. For in Jesus Christ himself – God's Word made flesh – there is a 'Yes' and 'No'. The cross of Christ fulfills the sentence; the resurrection fulfills the promise. In this sense, we could say that Jesus Christ is God's illocutionary act. We may note in passing that only God has the authority to assume the normative status of one who pronounces acquittal on sinners. 'Justification' – the sentence of acquittal – is also a divinely given institution, and is (justifiably!) regarded by Protestants as one of the best divine illocutionary acts.

Oral or written covenant? From speech to Scripture acts

It is now time to consider a potentially fatal objection to the use of speech-act categories in biblical interpretation. It amounts to the claim that, to cite Ricœur, 'With written discourse … the author's intention and the meaning of the text cease to coincide'.[59] More radically, the objection is that the written text enjoys semantic autonomy both from its original author and from its original situation. The text, in other words, is independent – cut off – from the communicative agent who produced it and from the circumstances that provided the setting for the communicative action. Clearly, if this objection can be sustained, we will need to revisit everything we have previously said about the centrality of illocutionary acts for interpretation.

What does philosophy have to say about the oral-written distinction? Interestingly, there is evidence in Ricœur's own work that the distinction is not as hard and fast as the quotation above suggests. Most importantly, Ricœur continues to see writing as a species of discourse: something said by someone to someone about something. To be precise, a text is 'discourse fixed by writing'. I see no reason why writing should lead us to omit the phrase 'by someone'. Ricœur is happy to speak of meaningful human action as a text, so why can we not see texts as meaningful actions?[60] Indeed, upon closer inspection it is clear that Ricœur wishes to avoid both the intentional fallacy and the 'fallacy of the absolute text': 'the fallacy of hypostatizing the text as an authorless entity'.[61] Often overlooked is Ricœur's acknowledgment that discourse fixes

---

[59] Ricœur, *Interpretation Theory*, 29.

[60] See Ricœur, 'Model'.

[61] Ricœur, *Interpretation Theory*, 30.

not only the locutionary but the *illocutionary* act.[62] Ricœur knows that one cannot cancel out this main characteristic of discourse – 'said by someone' – without reducing texts to natural (e.g., non-intentional) objects like pebbles in the sand. It remains a mystery, however, how texts can be considered discourse if they are indeed 'cut off' from their authors. Wolterstorff has amply demonstrated the incoherence of the notion of 'textual sense' interpretation, so I need not pursue the point here.[63] Instead, I wish to pursue a different, more properly theological, argument in favor of conceiving texts as communicative acts.

Let us consider the book of Deuteronomy. All the illocutionary features of the covenant that God instituted orally with Abraham, Isaac and Jacob are *preserved in writing* in the Book of the Covenant delivered by Moses and ratified by the whole nation of Israel. Elsewhere in this volume, Gordon McConville makes the important point that the words that instituted the covenant at Horeb and then Moab are finally deposited in a book, the Book of the Law (Deut. 28:58). Others have argued that the very structure of Deuteronomy is patterned after the ancient Near Eastern vassal treaties.[64] The significance of this parallel is that many Hittite treaties included a provision for the treaty's *inscription*. The fact that the Tables of the Law are written on stone signals their author's insistence on the permanence of the discourse.

According to Deuteronomy, the Book of the Covenant, precisely as written discourse – text – functions as a standing witness against the nation of Israel (Deut. 31:26). The law is sealed in the ark of the covenant, and it was to be written on stone at the threshold of the Promised Land as a permanent reminder of the blessings and curses associated with the covenant (Deut. 27). As such, the text of Deuteronomy calls not for 'wooden repetition', but rather for continual decision, for or against its illocutions. Directives (laws) must be obeyed; commissives (promises) must be trusted.

The covenant, as a written document, continued to have potency, but only when the people attended to it. Time and again, the kings of Israel neglected to read and obey it. The notable exception is King Josiah, during whose reign the Book of the Law was found. Josiah's reader-response was immediate and drastic: he tore his clothes (2 Kgs. 22:11), not because this was the intended perlocutionary effect, but because Josiah realized that the Law was a divine directive that had been disobeyed. A similar response, this time on the part of the whole community, is recorded in Nehemiah 8: mass weeping. These passages attest to the determinate content and the binding force of the written

---

[62] 'To the extent that the illocutionary act can be exteriorized thanks to grammatical paradigms and procedures expressive of its "force", it too can be inscribed' (Ricœur, *Interpretation Theory*, 27).

[63] See Wolterstorff, *Divine Discourse*, ch. 8.

[64] See Kline, *Treaty*.

covenant. We may therefore conclude that *written texts preserve the same illocu-tionary act potential as oral discourse.* If we can take this point as settled, we may now turn to consider whether the biblical canon has features that distinguish it from other types of written discourse.

Anatomy of canonical action

Do the categories of speech–act philosophy apply to the task of biblical inter-pretation? While sentences are the basic tools for performing illocutionary acts, they can become part of something more complex, just as other basic actions (hammering, sawing, drilling) can become ingredients in a more complex act (building a bookcase). Texts are just *communicative acts of a higher order.* The question now becomes: are there specific illocutionary acts that emerge only on the level of the text, and perhaps only on that of the canon? And, if there are, should they be seen as instances of *God's* authorial discourse? Before turning to the level of the canon, however, let us examine first what takes place at the level of the individual books of Scripture, at the level of the literary whole. We can then proceed to examine what might emerge at the higher levels of 'testament' and 'canon'.

Consider how one might describe some of the acts that comprise writing a Gospel: 1) he gripped the pen and moved it in straight and circular motions; 2) he formed Greek characters; 3) he wrote the word '*theos*'; 4) he said 'a virgin shall conceive'; 5) he quoted from Isaiah 7:14; 6) he said Jesus' birth fulfilled Old Testament prophecy; 7) he narrated the events surrounding Jesus' birth; 8) he confessed Jesus as the Christ. Some of these descriptions pertain to illocu-tionary acts; some do not. We need not rehearse those distinctions here. The claim I am now making is that some of Matthew's illocutions can only be inferred from his discourse *taken as a literary whole.*

Ascribing generic illocutions
'Every piece of writing is a kind of something.'[65] Each literary genre does something distinct, and is hence able to affect one's cognitive environment in a different way. Specifically, each major genre enables a distinct way of engaging reality and of interacting with others. The Russian literary theorist Mikhail Bakhtin views genre not merely as a medium of communication, but as a medium of cognition. Different literary genres, he contends, offer distinct ways of thinking about or experiencing the world.[66] In this respect, forms of literature function like metaphors – they are models, indispensable cognitive instruments for saying and seeing things that perhaps could not be seen or said

---

[65] Gabel and Wheeler, *Bible as Literature*, 16.
[66] Bakhtin, *Speech Genres*.

in other ways. The point is that some illocutionary acts may be associated with texts rather than sentences. Accordingly, we need a supplement to Austin: 'how to do things with literature'.

Let us test Bakhtin's hypothesis on narrative. What do narratives do that others kinds of literature do not, and perhaps *cannot*? Mary Louise Pratt argues compellingly that narratives perform the unique act of *displaying a world*.[67] In narrative, the place of propositional content is taken by the plot. Susan Lanser's *The Narrative Act* appeals to speech-act theory as providing a valuable aim in studying point of view, that is, the author's perspective on the world displayed in the text.[68] What Wolterstorff and Alston have shown to be the case with speech acts thus applies to text acts too: authors do not simply display worlds, but in displaying also take up some normative stance towards these worlds (e.g., praising, commending, condemning, etc.). In Lanser's words: 'Much like the biblical parable, the novel's basic illocutionary activity is ideological instruction; its basic plea: hear my word, believe and understand.'[69]

What we may term a generic act – an illocutionary act performed on the level of a literary whole – is the unifying act that orders all the other acts that comprise authoring a piece of written discourse. Take the book of Jonah. It is only when we consider the text as a unified whole that we can discuss what is going on at the literary level. What is the author doing besides 'telling a story'? At the level of the literary whole, it is harder to maintain that the author of Jonah was primarily making truth claims about certain forms of sea-life that swim in the Mediterranean. Interpretations that never rise above the level of reported events are not thick enough. Genuine interpretation involves ascribing illocutionary acts to authors. I believe the author to be *satirizing* religious complacency and criticizing ethnocentrism.[70] The illocutionary act of 'satirizing' emerges only at the literary level, that is, at the level of the text considered as a completed communicative act. Note that *to describe this generic illocution is to describe the communicative act that structures the whole text.*

The example of satire in Jonah illustrates my thesis: some things that authors do only come to light at the level of the text considered as a whole. To identify a text's literary genre is the first step to determining what the author was doing. We simply would not appreciate what Jonah is doing – ridiculing

---

[67] Pratt, *Theory*.

[68] Lanser, *Narrative Act*.

[69] Ibid., 293.

[70] It is striking that, by the end of the book, everyone has repented – the king of Nineveh, the people of Nineveh, even the beasts of Nineveh – save one: Jonah. Jonah stands for those Israelites who had become complacent about their covenant privileges and responsibilities. Indeed, Jonah goes so far as to accuse God of being excessively merciful! As to Jonah himself, he is portrayed as feeling more concern for a plant than for a people (see Jonah 4).

religious ethnocentrism – apart from considering the text as a whole. Note that the literal sense of Jonah is the sense of his literary act: satire. The moral should be clear. Biblical interpreters would do well to ascertain what kind of literature (which literary genre) they happen to be interpreting. Literary genres are relatively stable institutions, and this stability creates the possibility of a shared context between author and reader: a shared *literary* context.

The main point is that some of the author's illocutionary intentions only come to light at the level of the literary whole. Going beyond Alston's analysis, then, I maintain that we should recognize *generic* illocutions: the narrative act, the parabolic act, the apocalyptic act, the historical act, the prophetic act, etc. In other words, the major forms of biblical literature each have their own characteristic illocutionary forces: wisdom ('commending a way'); apocalyptic ('encouraging endurance'); prophecy ('recalling covenant promises and obligations'), and so on. To describe and ascribe generic illocutionary acts, then, is to say what an author is *doing in his text considered as a whole*.[71]

Canonic illocutions?

So much for the diversity of canonical acts. What communicative act, if any, unifies the canon as a whole? Is a 'testament' a genre? Should we think of the canon as a genre unto itself or as a space wherein the diverse literary genres, like elements of a Hittite treaty, interact and affect one another? Or are there new illocutionary acts that emerge only at the canonical level? The question is whether there is perhaps an even higher level of illocutionary action at the canonical level.

I agree with the literary critic Charles Altieri that 'texts are best viewed as actions performed on a variety of levels for our contemplation'.[72] Take, for example, the many things done in making a covenant: the Lord of the covenant identifies himself ('I am Yahweh'); the Lord recounts the history of what he has done for his vassals ('who brought you out of Egypt'); the Lord stipulates what he will do for the people and what they will do for him ('I will be your God, and you will be my people'); the Lord lists blessings and curses for obedience and disobedience ('You will keep possession of the promised land'; 'You will lose possession of the land'); the Lord makes provisions for passing on the covenant to the next generation (e.g., through its *inscription*). Each of these illocutionary acts is performed throughout Scripture; yet all are also ingredients of a larger, testamental, illocutionary act: *covenanting*.[73]

---

[71]   Note that generic illocutions supervene on illocutions at the sentence and paragraph level.

[72]   Altieri, *Act*, 10.

[73]   Interestingly, Austin included 'making a covenant' in his original list of illocutionary acts.

Brevard Childs argues that the canon was intentionally shaped so that it would function authoritatively for future generations in the believing community. The unity of the whole follows, Childs thinks, from its consistent witness to Jesus Christ. I welcome his emphasis on reading each part of Scripture in its larger canonical context, but I doubt that Childs has given a sufficient warrant for the practice. I agree with Paul Noble, who argues that Childs' approach tacitly depends upon and actually requires an explicit affirmation of divine authorship. Indeed, Childs' claim that the meaning of biblical texts can be arrived at only in the context of the canon as a whole 'is formally equivalent to believing that the Bible is so inspired as to be ultimately the work of a single Author'.[74]

This brings us closer to Wolterstorff's proposal about dual-author discourse. I propose to take such a view as a given, and to move on to a consideration of how the divine authorial intent in Scripture may be discerned. The concept of divine authorship is, of course, miles away from the notion of the 'death of the author'. This is as it should be. A Christian view of language and literature will have nothing to do with 'the death of God put into writing' and everything to do with 'the providence of God put into writing'. The main claim to be advanced here is that *God is doing providential things in his Scripture acts*. The divine intention does not contravene, but supervenes, on the intentions of the human authors.

8. To describe a generic (or canonic) illocution is to describe the communicative act that structures the text considered as a unified whole.

There are two complementary senses in which I wish to affirm the canon as God's illocutionary act.[75] First, there is divine appropriation of the illocutions of the human authors, particularly at the generic level but not exclusively there. For example, God still uses the book of Jonah to satirize religious ethnocentrism. (Indeed, the message of Jonah is as relevant today as ever). Yet God may also be doing new things with Jonah and other biblical texts by virtue of their being gathered together in the canon. Could it be that certain illocutions only come to light when we describe what God is doing at the canonical level? More work needs to be done in this area, but for the moment let me offer the following as possible candidates for the divine canonical illocutions: instructing the believing community; testifying to Christ; and perhaps most obviously, *covenanting*.

---

[74] Noble, *Approach*, 340.

[75] I am happy to consider the locutions too as a product of divine discourse, as traditional theories of inspiration maintain, but this is not the focus of the present essay.

Scripture acts: Transforming cognitive (and spiritual) environments

God's word will not fail to accomplish the purpose for which it was sent (Isa. 55:11). Just what kind of purpose did Isaiah have in mind: illocutionary or perlocutionary? Is the Bible really a divine communicative act if readers fail to respond to its illocutions and perlocutions? Is the Bible the Word of God written or does it only *become* the Word of God when God takes up the human words and does something with them? Opinions differ. Everything hinges on whether we wish to include the reader's response (illocutionary uptake, perlocutionary effect) in the definition of communicative action.

Karl Barth appealed to the Holy Spirit as the 'Lord of the hearing', and suggested that it is only when God freely and graciously takes up the human words that the Bible becomes the Word of God for a given hearer. Is the Bible God's Word? Barth and evangelicals have been at loggerheads on this issue for decades: 'is'; 'is not'. Can our anatomy of communicative action move us beyond the impasse? I think so.

On my view, Barth is partly right and partly wrong. He is wrong if he means to deny that God performs illocutionary acts in Scripture. He is right if one incorporates the reader's reception of the message into one's definition of 'communicative act'. Communication, we may recall, can connote both senses: the act of communicating, or the completed communication, including its reception. Human authors, of course, lack the ability to make their readers understand, much less to guarantee the intended perlocutionary effects. There is nothing human authors can do to make sure their recipients 'get it'. God, however, has no such limits: the Spirit is the 'Lord of the hearing'. The Spirit is the energy that enables the Word to complete its mission. My proposal, then, is to say both the Bible *is* the Word of God (in the sense of its illocutionary acts) and to say that the Bible *becomes* the Word of God (in the sense of achieving its perlocutionary effects).

Does not my proposal tie God down to the texts? Does it not compromise God's freedom? No, for God's freedom is the freedom to initiate communicative action and to keep his word. Once God makes a promise, however, he is obliged to keep it, not from some external force, but because God's Word is God's bond.[76] Neither is it any part of my suggestion that, just because God's

---

[76] My colleague Dan Treier has pointed out to me that God's promises are often progressively realized, so that the 'content' of his promising shifts. For instance, God's promise to the Israelites to raise up a king became, at a later time, a promise to set up an eternal messianic throne. Treier therefore wonders whether God might perform different illocutionary acts with the same locution. This is an excellent query to which I cannot do justice in this short space. Given more time, I would want to explore two lines of response. First, I would suggest that God's promises (and other illocutions as well) are 'seminal'; that is, they contain implicitly the grounds for their later

discourse is fixed in writing, we can somehow 'possess' God's Word or master it. On the contrary, one does not 'possess' or 'master' warnings, promises, commands and so forth. We are rather in the situation of Ezra: in reading Scripture we are confronted with a word that seeks to transform, indeed to master, us.

A final objection. Does not this identification of Scripture with God's illocutionary acts demean Christ as God's Word? Again, no, because what Scripture is doing – particularly at the canonical level of communicative action – is *pointing to Christ*, offering appropriately 'thick descriptions' of his meaning and significance for Israel and the church. Is this not what Luke implies: 'And beginning with Moses and all the prophets, he [Jesus] interpreted to them in all the scriptures the things concerning himself' (Lk. 24:27)? It is precisely through responding to the various illocutions of Scripture – belief in its assertions, obedience to its commands, faith in its promises – that we become 'thickly' related to Christ. Indeed, we cannot have the intended effect – union with Christ – apart from the content of Scripture's illocutionary acts (e.g., telling a story; making a promise; pronouncing pardon, etc.).

Sperber and Wilson define relevance as the property that makes information worth processing. On these terms, must we not conclude that, of all words that can be heard, the gospel is the most relevant? Information is relevant, we may recall, when it modifies one's cognitive environment. Well, the gospel does this, and much more. In the first place, instead of making manifest a set of assumptions (so Sperber and Wilson), Scripture manifests *Christ*, the revelation of God and the hope of glory. Just as significant is the fact that the gospel modifies not only cognitive environments, but spiritual environments as well. It is not only that Scripture gives new information, but that it radically transforms the very way we process information. What ultimately gets communicated through the canon is the way, the truth and the life.

---

[76] (*Continued*) development, a development that would be more continuous than discontinuous. Think, for instance, of God's promise to Abraham in Gen. 12:3, 'in you all the families of the earth shall be blessed'. The second, and perhaps more promising, line of response is also more complex. Essentially, it has to do with the *eschatological* nature of God's speech. The first coming of Christ recontextualized the previous divine discourse, just as the Christian canon recontextualized the OT. However, Christian readers of the canon all share the same situation, eschatologically speaking: we live between the first and second comings of Christ. Subsequent to the coming of Christ, then, God's discourse partakes of the same 'already/not yet' eschatological tension as does the Christian life itself. What God is saying to the church in the twenty-first century, then, will largely be in continuity with what he said to the church in the first. I am referring, of course, to the divine illocutions. The perlocutions of the divine discourse will indeed be different, but as I have consistently argued in this essay, perlocutionary effects are not intrinsic to communicative action.

Biblical interpretation and canonical action: Whose action is it?

Perhaps the most important question we can ask of the canon is: *whose* act is it? If interpretation is a matter of ascribing and inferring communicative intentions, *to whom* do we ascribe the illocutions?

Interpretation after Pentecost: Which voice? Whose tongue?

After Pentecost. Just what difference, if any, does Pentecost make for biblical interpretation? What is the Holy Spirit's role in God's triune communicative action? Many Christian traditions affirm the 'inspiration' of the Scriptures. The Westminster Confession of Faith, for instance, accords supreme authority to 'the Holy Spirit speaking in the Scripture'. Much depends on how we parse this phrase: 'the Spirit speaking'. There are, at present, two approaches to interpretation that risk confusing divine communicative action – the Word of God – with the communicative action of the interpretive community: 1) performance interpretation, where the reader assumes the role of the author, and 2) perlocutionary interpretation, where the illocutionary act is by-passed or eclipsed in favor of achieving a predetermined effect other than understanding. Of interest here is how each approach has been brought to bear on biblical interpretation, and how each makes a tacit appeal to the work of the Holy Spirit.

Ricœur, as we have seen, announces the semantic autonomy of the text from its original author. Yet the text remains discourse. So whose discourse is it? Jorge Luis Borges' story 'Pierre Menard' wonderfully illustrates the problem I have in mind. The story is about a twentieth-century French critic, Pierre Menard, who has written, word for word, several chapters of Cervantes' *Don Quixote*. On the locutionary level, Menard has simply replicated Cervantes' act. Yet Menard does not want to merely repeat the seventeenth-century meaning (what Cervantes had in mind), for that is too easy! Instead, he wants to produce the same text *but with an entirely different meaning*. This is an excellent example of what Wolterstorff calls 'performance interpretation'. The basic idea is this: in performance interpretation, we read the text as if *we* had written it. There is no law against doing that, of course, if one fancies conducting that kind of experiment (e.g., 'what would I have meant if I had authored *Ulysses* or *The Lord of the Rings* or 1 Corinthians?').

There is no law against such performance interpretation, but neither is there any understanding. For once the attempt to infer the communicative intentions of the author is abandoned, so is the means for a meaningful encounter with the 'other'. This is deeply to be regretted; it is difficult to learn or grow or be transformed when one is in dialogue only with oneself.

Stanley Grenz works an intriguing variation of the above. He suggests that 'the Spirit speaking in Scripture' refers to the *Spirit's* illocutions, but these are not identical with those of the human authors. The performance interpretation that now counts is that of the Spirit. Grenz views the Bible as the instrumentality or vehicle *through* which the Spirit speaks. He is clear that the authority of Scripture 'does not ultimately rest with any quality that inheres within it as such (for example, its divine authorship or inspired character)'.[77] So the Spirit's speaking is not to be equated with the Spirit's authorship of Scripture. What, then, does it mean to say 'the Spirit speaks'? Grenz answers: 'Obviously, when we acknowledge that the Spirit speaks through the Bible, we are referring to an illocutionary, and not a locutionary, act.'[78] He considers Wolterstorff's account of authorial discourse, only to reject it. The Spirit does not appropriate the authorial discourse, says Grenz, but rather 'the biblical text itself'.[79] What kind of illocution does the Spirit perform? Exegesis alone, while relevant, cannot answer this question. At this point Grenz's analysis shifts somewhat awkwardly, from a grudging concession that the original meaning of the text is not wholly eclipsed, to what he is clearly more interested in: the Spirit's *perlocutionary* act of *creating a world*.

Because Grenz abandons the authorial discourse model and embraces Ricœur's premise that the text takes on a life of its own, he has difficulty specifying just what illocutionary acts the Spirit performs. Indeed, the only *illocutionary* act Grenz actually ascribes to the Spirit is *speaking*: 'The Spirit performs the perlocutionary act of creating a world through the illocutionary act of speaking … by appropriating the biblical text as the instrumentality of the divine speaking'.[80] Speaking, however, is not an illocutionary act! So it is not at all clear how 'speaking' *simpliciter* can produce perlocutionary effects.[81]

The Spirit can, of course, work through many diverse means to accomplish his sanctifying work (e.g., *creating the new world 'in Christ'*). The crucial question, however, is whether the Spirit performs this work independently of Scripture's *illocutionary* acts. Grenz's account fails to explain how we can infer, and to whom we should ascribe, what illocutionary acts have been performed. Consequently, he leaves unanswered the fundamental question of how Scripture's actual *content* is related to the Spirit's accomplishing his further, perlocutionary, effects.

---

[77] Grenz, 'Spirit', 358.

[78] Ibid., 361.

[79] Ibid.

[80] Ibid., 365.

[81] It may be that Grenz does intend to say that the Spirit performs specific illocutionary acts, but if so, it is not clear how these acts are related to the actual propositional content, and illocutionary force, of the appropriated human discourse.

The eclipse of biblical illocutions: Reading for formation

There is much to admire in Grenz's article. I agree with his overall vision that the Spirit leads people to reconceive their identities and world-view by means of the interpretive framework found *in* Scripture that recounts the eschatological event of Jesus Christ. I even agree with his fundamental premise that the Spirit's perlocutionary act is to 'create a world' (though I explain it theologically in terms of the Spirit's ministry of the Word, and philosophically in terms of perlocutions supervening on illocutions). Yet at the same time I am troubled by his analysis, both for philosophical and for theological reasons.

First, the philosophy of speech acts. As we have just seen, Grenz mistakenly identifies the Spirit's illocutionary act as 'speaking through Scripture'. But 'speaking' *per se* is not an illocutionary act. Illocutionary acts have to do with what is done *in* speaking.[82] Moreover, it is the peculiar role of narratives to *display* a world. This is an illocutionary, not a perlocutionary, act. It is, to quote Susan Lanser, the distinctive *narrative* act. Second, as regards theology. The Spirit does indeed perform perlocutionary acts; no disagreement here. Yet the Spirit does so only on the basis of the concrete textual illocutions (the content!) of Scripture. The Spirit's creating a world, then, is not a new illocutionary act, but rather the perlocutionary act of enabling readers to appropriate the illocutionary acts already inscribed in the biblical text, especially the narrative act of 'displaying a world'.

There is a second contemporary approach to biblical interpretation that fails to see the importance of illocutionary acts. It is an approach that focuses on a particular perlocutionary purpose of Scripture – namely, spiritual formation: 'The aim of reading Scripture, to build up Christian faith and practice, should always order decisions about which methods and approaches to adopt'.[83] This is a laudable aim, and essential to the piety of the church. But is it an *interpretive* aim? I do not dispute the aim of spiritual formation. However, I do resist letting this intended perlocutionary effect run roughshod over Scripture's communicative action.[84] Spiritual formation can be the aim, but not the norm, of biblical interpretation. The norm must remain the author's illocutionary intent. Once again, the problem arises from the confusion between illocutionary acts and perlocutionary effects. *To proceed too quickly to perlocutionary effects is to run the risk of making the illocutionary content hermeneutically dispensable.*

It is, of course, important that Christians read the Scriptures for the sake of

---

[82] In Alston's words: 'The issuing of an utterance with a certain content can itself have effects, and so the production of those effects can supervene on that content presentation. But a content cannot attach to the production of an effect by an utterance, so as to make that effect production to be what carries that content' (Alston, *Illocutionary Acts*, 31).

[83] Ayres and Fowl, '(Mis)reading', 528.

[84] See my 'Body Piercing'.

spiritual formation and edification. Yet this aim, while absolutely vital, must not displace the prior aim of coming to understand the text. The thrust of the present argument is that, just as perlocutions can never precede but must always *proceed* from illocutions, so spiritual formation can never precede but must always proceed from the ministry of the Word – that *thought, power, deed* whose mission it is to transform those who receive it.

Ministering the discourse of the covenant: Of pneumatology and perlocutions
'The Spirit speaks.' Yes, but the Spirit 'does not speak on his own authority, but whatever he hears he will speak' (Jn. 16:13). Here is a case where speech-act categories make perfect sense. Insofar as Scripture is inspired, or 'God-breathed', we may say that even the locutions of Scripture are divinely authored. But Jesus' point in John is that the Spirit confines his communicative activity to speaking only what he receives. The Spirit *ministers* Christ, not himself. The Spirit, to use Gordon Fee's fine phrase, is God's – God the Son's – empowering presence.

We are now in a position to understand how God's word accomplishes the purpose for which it has been sent. It accomplishes this purpose because the Spirit accompanies it, speaking not another word but ministering the word that was previously spoken. The Spirit is nothing less than the *efficacy* of the Word. In short, the Spirit renders the word effective by achieving its intended perlocutionary effects. The point that must not be missed, however, is that the Spirit accomplishes these effects not independently of the words and illocutions but precisely *by*, *with* and *through* them. Hence our penultimate thesis, directed primarily, though by no means exclusively, to the task of biblical interpretation:

9. The Spirit speaks in and through Scripture precisely by rendering its illocutions at the sentential, generic and canonic levels perlocutionarily efficacious.

Here, then, where we might least expect it, we see a certain convergence between philosophy and theology with regard to language and the word. The asymmetrical dependence of perlocutionary on illocutionary acts defended by Alston has a theological counterpart in the idea that the Holy Spirit proceeds from the Father *and the Son* – the celebrated *Filioque* ('and from the Son'). Perlocutions 'proceed' from locutions and illocutions, but not vice versa. Uttering a content can have effects, but a content cannot attach itself to the production of effects. Though Alston does not use the term, I think it is fair to say that he believes in the *illocutioque* ('and from the illocution').[85]

---

[85] My argument does not depend on a particular version of the *Filioque*. The analogy with illocutions and perlocutions would work equally well if one adopted alternative suggestions such as 'from the Father *through* the Son'.

This surprising convergence of *illocutioque* and *Filioque* does not prove anything. It is inadvisable to draw general conclusions about the philosophy of language from Trinitarian theology, nor should one formulate one's understanding of the three Persons on the basis of an analysis of speech acts. Such has not been my intent. Instead, I have sought to reinforce insights gained from one discipline with insights gained in another, all the while looking for places where philosophy might approximate our theology, and where theology might adjust our philosophy. Alston's insistence that perlocutions depend on illocutions does support our contention that biblical interpreters should seek to infer illocutionary content before seeking to achieve perlocutionary effects. This is also, I believe, how the Holy Spirit works through biblical interpretation to form the people of God: not by producing effects unrelated to the text's communicative action, but precisely by ministering the divine communicative action, in all its canonical unity and variety.

10. What God does with Scripture is covenant with humanity by testifying to Jesus Christ (illocution) and by bringing about the reader's mutual indwelling with Christ (perlocution) through the Spirit's rendering Scripture efficacious.

Conclusion: The Covenant Community

Theories about language affect human practice, communication and interpretation alike. What we say about language affects what we think about ourselves. Throughout this essay I have assumed that using language is a covenantal affair. I have adopted what we might call the *presumption of covenantal relation*. This goes beyond the presumption of relevance. The latter states that implied in every speech act is the claim that it is relevant. The covenantal presumption states that implied in every speech act is a certain covenantal relation, namely, a tacit plea, or demand, to understand. Language itself cannot make this demand upon us. Language, considered in the abstract, holds no rights. No, the presumption of covenantal relation stems from the fact that we are obliged to do justice to the words of a communicative agent in order to do that *person* justice. Here we may invoke Lévinas's notion that the face 'speaks'. The 'face' says 'Do not kill', and stands for the infinite obligation we have towards our neighbor. Similarly, the 'voice' in the text says 'Hear me', and stands for the obligation we have towards our neighbor, as good citizens of language, to understand what that person is saying and what that person is doing in her saying. Interlocutors therefore 'always share at least one common goal, that of understanding and being understood'.[86]

---

[86] Sperber and Wilson, *Relevance*, 268.

The church is an interpretive community, a people of the book. As such, it is a covenant community in *both* of the senses employed in this essay. The church is first of all a community oriented to the discourse of the covenant, the Christian Scriptures. Yet the church should also be a community that cares about the covenant of discourse *in general*. For, as I argued at the outset, language is a divinely ordained institution with its own divine design plan.

In conclusion, let me highlight three features that I believe should characterize members of the covenant community.

- *Covenant keepers* – we must keep the covenant of discourse, the bonds that language forges between two persons, between person and world, and between human persons and God. We must be promise-keepers and truth-tellers. But we must also be active listeners. For this is the only way to be peace-keepers in the covenant of discourse. There are many forms of violence, but readers must especially be wary of interpretive violence. We must resist imposing our own interpretations on the discourse of others. We must resist ascribing intentions to authors where there is no evidence of that intent, and we must be honest enough to recognize authorial intentions where there is adequate evidence of such. We must cultivate what I call elsewhere the 'interpretive virtues': those dispositions of the heart and mind that arise from the motivation for understanding.
- *Witnesses* – 'Do not bear false witness.' To me, this is the categorical imperative of hermeneutics. To bear false witness – to say that the author is doing something in a text that he or she did not do – is to subject an author to a form of violence. Reductionist approaches – thin descriptions – are similarly distorting because they fail adequately to attend to what the author was in fact doing in a text. Theirs is the sin of omission, of not telling the whole truth. Willful misinterpretation is a violation of the other. Those who participate in the covenant of discourse are thus obliged to bear true witness. Indeed, this is essentially what interpretation is: bearing witness to the meaning of the authorial intentions enacted in the text. This is why it is important to attend to the history of interpretation. God has spoken to previous generations through his Word, and we need to hear what God said to them as well as to the original readers. Indeed, it may be that God speaks to us in Scripture by way of the tradition of its interpretation. This would only be the case, however, if previous generations had rightly discerned God's canonical action in Scripture.
- *Disciples* – Let us not forget Goethe's cautionary tale. Faust's error was to think that interpretation was something confined to one's study, that interpretation was a matter of knowledge only, quite separate from virtue

and spirituality. Yet every text contains not merely information but an implicit call: 'Follow me'. The vocation of the interpreter is to respond to that call and to follow at least until one reaches understanding, and perhaps further. Just as we indicate our understanding by saying 'I follow you', so we indicate our understanding of Scripture when we start to follow in its way. The privilege of biblical interpretation – the Protestant insistence on the priesthood of all believers – finally leads to the responsibility of hermeneutics: to the call to become not masters but 'martyrs' on behalf of meaning, not only hearers but doers, and perhaps sufferers, of the Word.

'In language man dwells.' Well, Heidegger was almost right. The true end of the covenant of discourse and the discourse of the covenant is indeed a kind of dwelling – or better, a mutual *indwelling*. The Bible simply calls it *communion*: we in Christ; Christ in us. I am referring, of course, to the supreme covenant blessing: life with God. Perhaps this blessing will one day be realized without benefit of language. Until then, however, humans are embodied persons who have to walk and talk with one another to have fellowship. It is noteworthy that God is depicted as walking and talking with man in the garden – before Babel, and before Pentecost. For language is not only a medium of communicative action; it is arguably the most elastic, variegated and powerful medium of interpersonal *communion* as well. 'In the beginning was the Word, and the Word … dwelt among us'.

Summary of Theses

1. Language has a 'design plan' that is inherently covenantal.
2. The paradigm for a Christian view of communication is the triune God in communicative action.
3. 'Meaning' is the result of communicative action, of what an author has done in tending to certain words at a particular time in a specific manner.
4. The literal sense of an utterance or text is the sum total of those illocutionary acts performed by the author intentionally and with self-awareness.
5. Understanding consists in recognizing illocutionary acts and their results.
6. Interpretation is the process of inferring authorial intentions and of ascribing illocutionary acts.
7. Aiming to produce perlocutionary effects on readers other than by means of *understanding* counts as strategic, not communicative, action.
8. To describe a generic (or canonic) illocution is to describe the communicative act that structures the text considered as a unified whole.

9. The Spirit speaks in and through Scripture precisely by rendering its illocutions at the sentential, generic and canonic levels perlocutionarily efficacious.

10. What God does with Scripture is *covenant* with humanity by testifying to Jesus Christ (illocution) and by bringing about the reader's mutual indwelling with Christ (perlocution) through the Spirit's rendering Scripture efficacious.

Bibliography

Alston, W.P., *Illocutionary Acts and Sentence Meaning* (Ithaca, NY: Cornell University Press, 2000)

Altieri, C., *Act & Quality: A Theory of Literary Meaning and Humanistic Understanding* (Amherst, MA: University of Massachusetts Press, 1981)

Austin, J.L., *How to Do Things with Words* (Oxford: Clarendon Press, 1962)

Ayres, L., and S.E. Fowl, '(Mis)reading the Face of God: The Interpretation of the Bible in the Church', *TS* 60 (1999), 513–28

Bakhtin, M., *Speech Genres and Other Late Essays* (Austin: University of Texas Press, 1986)

Barth, K., *Church Dogmatics*, I (Edinburgh: T. & T. Clark, 1956)

Bartholomew, C., 'Philosophy, Theology, and the Crisis in Biblical Interpretation', in *Renewing Biblical Interpretation* (ed. C. Bartholomew, C. Greene, K. Möller; SHS, 1; Carlisle: Paternoster; Grand Rapids: Zondervan, 2000), 1–39

Duff, R.A., *Intention, Agency, and Criminal Liability: Philosophy of Action and the Criminal Law* (Oxford: Basil Blackwell, 1990)

Fish, S., *Is There a Text in this Class? The Authority of Interpretive Communities* (Cambridge, MA: Harvard University Press, 1980)

Gabel, J.B., and C.B. Wheeler, *The Bible as Literature: An Introduction* (Oxford: OUP, 1986)

Garcia, J.J.E., 'Can There Be Texts Without Historical Authors?', *American Philosophical Quarterly* 31 (1994), 245–53

Gibbs, R.W., Jr., *Intentions in the Experience of Meaning* (Cambridge: CUP, 1999)

Grenz, S., 'The Spirit and the Word', *ThTo* 57 (2000), 357–74

Grice, P., 'Meaning', *Philosophical Review* 66 (1957), 377–88

Kant, I., *The Metaphysics of Morals* (Cambridge: CUP, 1996)

Kline, M., *Treaty of the Great King: The Covenant Structure of Deuteronomy: Studies and Commentary* (Grand Rapids: Eerdmans, 1963)

Lanser, S.N., *The Narrative Act: Point of View in Prose Fiction* (Princeton: Princeton University Press, 1981)

Lévinas, E., *Ethics and Infinity* (Pittsburgh, PA: Duquesne University Press, 1985)

Lundin, R., C. Walhout and A.C. Thiselton, *The Promise of Hermeneutics* (Grand Rapids: Eerdmans, 1999)

Macquarrie, J., 'God and the World? One Reality or Two?', *Theology* 75 (1972), 394–403

Noble, P.R., *The Canonical Approach: A Critical Reconstruction of the Hermeneutics of Brevard S. Childs* (Leiden: E.J. Brill, 1995)

Plantinga, A., 'Advice to Christian Philosophers' (1983 inaugural lecture to the John O'Brien Chair of Philosophy at Notre Dame)

Pratt, M.L., *Towards a Speech Act Theory of Literary Discourse* (Bloomington: Indiana University Press, 1977)

Ricœur, P., 'The Model of the Text: Meaningful Action Considered as a Text', in *Hermeneutics and the Human Sciences: Essays on Language, Action and Interpretation* (Cambridge: CUP, 1981), 197–221

—, *Interpretation Theory: Discourse and the Surplus of Meaning* (Fort Worth: Texas Christian University Press, 1976)

—, *The Just* (Chicago: University of Chicago, 2000)

Schiffer, S., *Meaning* (Oxford: Clarendon Press, 1972)

Snodgrass, K., 'Reading to Hear: A Hermeneutics of Hearing' (unpublished ms.)

Sperber, D., and D. Wilson, *Relevance: Communication and Cognition* (Oxford: Basil Blackwell, 2nd edn, 1995)

Steiner, G., *Real Presences* (Chicago: University of Chicago Press, 1989)

Thiselton, A.C., *First Epistle to the Corinthians* (NIGTC; Grand Rapids: Eerdmans, 2000)

—, *Interpreting God and the Postmodern Self: On Meaning, Manipulation, and Promise* (Edinburgh: T. & T. Clark, 1995)

Thomassen, N., *Communicative Ethics in Theory and Practice* (trans. John Irons; London: Macmillan, 1992)

Vanhoozer, K., 'Body Piercing, the Natural Sense, and the Task of Theological Interpretation: A Hermeneutical Homily on John 19:34', *ExAud* (forthcoming, 2001)

—, *Is There a Meaning in This Text?: The Bible, the Reader, and the Morality of Literary Knowledge* (Grand Rapids: Zondervan, 1998)

—, 'Human Being, Individual and Social', in *The Cambridge Companion to Christian Doctrine* (ed. Colin Gunton; Cambridge: CUP, 1997), 158–88

—, 'The Semantics of Biblical Literature', in *Hermeneutics, Canon, and Authority* (ed. D.A. Carson and J. Woodbridge; Grand Rapids: Zondervan, 1986), 49–104

Von Wright, G.H., *Explanation and Understanding* (Ithaca, NY: Cornell University Press, 1971)

Wolterstorff, N., *Divine Discourse* (Cambridge: CUP, 1995)

2

Ricœur, Speech–act Theory, and the Gospels as History

Dan R. Stiver

Treatment of the Gospels has been divided between those who emphasize their historical aspect and those who emphasize their literary dimensions. The former tend to focus on the reference or the 'world behind the text', in Paul Ricœur's words – so much so that the narrative world, or the 'world of the text', can be lost. The latter tend to focus so much on the world of the text that the reference can be lost. This tension was earlier expressed in debates concerning the Jesus of history and the Christ of faith, where rarely did the two ever meet. The strict historiographical concerns for the reconstructed historical Jesus could hardly be reconciled with what was seen as the largely fictive picture configured in the imagination of the early church. The dynamics of the debate have shifted due to questioning by critical scholars themselves of the all-embracing hegemony of the historical-critical methods, but the tension between history and fiction remains.[1] Even where literary studies now overshadow old-time historical-critical studies, the pendulum has often simply swung to the other pole where all of the attention is on the textual world, and the question of historical reality is greeted with antipathy.

Part of the problem is that the Gospels do not easily fit into the categories of modern historiography and fiction. What is needed is an approach that allows for the way the Gospels have been artfully configured but also for the way their historicity is crucial. The suggestion by Hans Frei that they are 'history-like', or similar to historical novels, does not do justice to their reference to history; the attempt to treat them neutrally as historical documents, even in the sophisticated

---

[1] E.g., see Peterson, *Literary*, ch. 1; Culpepper, *Anatomy*, ch. 1.

manner of a Wolfhart Pannenberg, often seems to claim too much.[2] Approaches from both sides do not handle well the way that the documents call for faith and may require faith in their understanding. Thus the interplay of faith with the dimensions of history and fiction complicates the picture even further.

What I am proposing in this essay is that two different contemporary philosophies, one Continental and the other Anglo-American, allow for much more nuanced and flexible approaches to the vexed problem of history and fiction in the gospels. Paul Ricœur's hermeneutical philosophy and John Austin's speech-act theory represent significant postmodern philosophies in their own right, but they also have special relevance to this particular issue.[3] Ricœur is one of the foremost theorists of the philosophical significance of narrative, and his work lies behind one of the main approaches in narrative theology, sometimes called the Chicago school of narrative theology.[4] Although Ricœur has explored biblical narratives in the context of other biblical genres, he interestingly has not applied his major work on history and fiction to the Gospels. While Ricœur's three-volume *Time and Narrative* proposes an interweaving of the modern categories of history and fiction that helps us account for the dynamics of temporality, he did not apply the fruits of his reflection to a genre such as the Gospels. Ricœur's treatment of biblical narratives in other contexts, however, gives some guidance as to how *Time and Narrative* could be applied. In Austin's case, several scholars have applied his work to biblical texts – for example, Anthony Thiselton and Nicholas

---

[2] Frei, *Eclipse*, 10; Pannenberg, *Jesus*, 88–106.

[3] For Paul Ricœur, see the volume about him in the Library of Living Philosophers series, Hahn, *Philosophy*; and my forthcoming book, *Theology*. For Austin, see Austin, *Words*; and Murphy, *Postmodernity*. I am using the term 'postmodern' with caution, recognizing that its definition varies widely. I use it on the one hand in a rather negative sense as a philosophy that rejects modernity's assumptions that in order for something truly to count as knowledge, it must be clear and certain. Moreover, it must be based on a strict method, usually in the context of a foundationalist epistemological structure. It assumes what has been called a 'God's eye point-of-view'. Often, it is allied with individualism and dualistic intellectualism that privileges mind over body. Virtually all approaches that are considered postmodern reject all of these assumptions. In terms of a positive affirmation, I see postmodernism as representing, not relativism, but a holistic epistemology. It allows for truth claims, but they are situated and fallible. In this sense, Austin and Ricœur fit. Insofar as prominent approaches like those of Jacques Derrida and Michel Foucault end in relativism, they are not postmodern, but, rather, in David Griffin's words, 'most-modern'. They assume the high standards of modernity and reject the possibility of attaining them, therefore representing the flip side of modernity rather than a genuine paradigm change. See Griffin, 'Introduction', 3. For a fuller account, see Stiver, 'Much Ado'.

[4] See particularly Ricœur's three-volume *Time and Narrative*; and Stiver, *Philosophy*, ch. 7.

Wolterstorff.[5] Michael Goldberg, in particular, has applied it to biblical narratives.[6] So we have some precedents and parameters for drawing on their thought in this way. What I propose in addition is that the approaches of Ricœur and Austin, seen together, mutually support a more integrated approach to the Gospels in terms of history and fiction and allow for the perspective of faith in interpretation without lapsing into fideism.

I will first explore in more detail the gap between historical and fictive approaches to the Gospels. Then we will look at how Ricœur and Austin's thought can be appropriated, giving special attention to the implications of faith in interpretation.

The Gospels between History and Fiction

Hans Frei has argued that, for several centuries, the focus on the world behind the text has eclipsed the world of the narratives themselves.[7] Moreover, Frei said,

> It is no exaggeration to say that all across the theological spectrum the great reversal had taken place; interpretation was a matter of fitting the biblical story into another world with another story rather than incorporating that world into the biblical story.[8]

In attempting to defend the historicity of the Gospels, conservatives often propounded a reconstructed history that attempted to harmonize and homogenize. The resultant narrative, ironically, was not the same as any found in the Gospels – and sometimes it ran far afield from the actual stories. Perhaps the most damaging result was a sincere but misguided focus upon facts rather than theological meaning. Many have noted, consequently, how these self-proclaimed critics of modernity actually fell under the spell of modernity. For example, George Marsden points out how, under the influence of the empiricist philosophy of Scottish Common Sense Realism, conservatives in the nineteenth and twentieth centuries began to see the Bible as an 'encyclopedic puzzle', a 'dictionary of facts'.[9] Nancey Murphy and George Lindbeck also indicate how conservatives labored to lay down an impregnable foundation of historical and propositional verities that could rival the positivistic foundations

---

[5] Thiselton, *New Horizons*; Wolterstorff, *Discourse*.
[6] Goldberg, *Theology*.
[7] Frei, *Eclipse*.
[8] Ibid., 130.
[9] Marsden, *Fundamentalism*, 58.

of the natural sciences, which were growing in prestige.[10] Strange bedfellows these, but before the Scopes Monkey Trial and the evolution controversy that developed in the 1920s, the scientific and evangelical worlds both strove to live up to a notion of science and faith that looked more like Descartes and Locke than the Deuteronomist and Luke. In the meantime, the foundationalist and objectivist assumptions of science, philosophy and theology have become the objects of heavy attack – if not outright demolition. Theologians and biblical scholars still, however, often see the primary significance of the biblical texts as the reliability or unreliability of the atomistic historical facts that the texts connote.

More liberal biblical scholars took up the higher criticism of historical-critical studies and also sought to find the true historical world behind the text. They were much more negative in their assessment, but they were playing in the same ballpark. When they found that the biblical narratives could not live up to the idealized view of modern historiography, according to Frei, they reinterpreted the meaning of the texts in terms of a larger philosophical and theological framework – whether Kantian, Hegelian or Heideggerian.[11] Murphy and Lindbeck point out that in the aftermath of Schleiermacher, more liberal scholars sought, in religious experience, an indubitable Cartesian foundation of their own.[12] In any case, Frei argues that the biblical narratives were eclipsed in favor of some world behind the text or outside the text. Across the board, the biblical world was absorbed by the assumptions of the modern world.

In reaction, literary critics, particularly influenced by New Criticism and structuralist approaches, have tried to recover the literary world of the text. But they have often done so at the expense of reference to the 'world in front of the text', to follow more of Ricœur's terminology.[13] That is, they have reacted so much to the adulation of historical fact that they have quailed before any reference to historical facts at all. Much has been recovered, thereby, of the

---

[10] Murphy, *Liberalism*; Lindbeck, *Nature*, ch. 1.

[11] Charles Wood, *Theory*, engages in a critique of the hermeneutical tradition of the twentieth century similar to Frei's of the eighteenth and nineteenth centuries, specifically addressing the Heideggerian tradition embodied in Hans-Georg Gadamer and others as a key representative of what he criticizes. Wood's dissertation was done under Frei's supervision and was cited as a 'brilliant work' by Frei in *Eclipse*, right after Frei indicates that most commentators have followed the pattern of Schleiermacher and Gadamer, except those influenced by Wittgenstein (342, n. 1).

[12] Ron Thiemann also argues that such an appeal to an original, founding intuition is pervasive in the modern period and cuts across the theological spectrum. Thiemann, *Revelation*, ch. 2.

[13] See Thiselton, *New Horizons*, ch. 13; Culpepper, *Anatomy*, ch. 1.

theological meaning of the text – but it is not at all clear that one can simply ignore the historical dimension of literature like the Gospels. Fiction may be a salutary clue in terms of reading the artfulness of the way the Gospels produce meaning. Nevertheless, the historical relevance of Jesus' life, death and resurrection is not clearly something imposed upon the Gospels from the outside but seems to be an insistent component of their internal message. As a colleague in a conservative seminary with large biblical and theological departments, I can well remember the frustration of older scholars trained on the historical-critical approach who certainly had their criticisms of it. But along with their appreciation for the newer literary methods, they sharply reacted against what they saw as the attempt to sidestep the historical question altogether.

For those desiring to interpret the Gospels in terms of their meaning for faith, little interest remains in returning to the old battles of who best reconstructs the world behind the text. For those, however, with any interest and conviction concerning the basic historicity of the Gospels, a purely literary approach is equally as unsatisfactory. In some ways, it is simply the flip side of the dualism so characteristic of modernity. Richard Bernstein has characterized modernity as oscillating between objectivism and relativism.[14] If one cannot attain pure objectivity, the only alternative is relativism. Likewise, if we cannot attain historical certainty about the biblical texts – defined of course in terms of a modernist conception of historiography – we give it up. The difficulty of avoiding polar opposition is evinced by the fact that both Frei and Lindbeck have been sharply criticized for offering such an inadequate, fideistic response to the historical challenge.[15] Bernstein argues convincingly that a genuinely new paradigm, which most today term 'postmodern', finds a way between the horns of the dilemma. Such a move, however, often involves using old terms in new ways and evokes what he called 'Cartesian anxiety'.[16] Similarly, in biblical studies, the attempt to find an integration between the configuring activity of the imagination and the work of the historian looks impossible and elicits its own kind of religious and scholarly anxiety. Some kind of integration is surely desirable, but so far its attainment has been contested, risky and far short of consensus.

What I am hoping is that the development of various alternatives to modernity in general may offer genuinely new alternatives and frameworks for considering this traditionally troublesome problem. Instead of simply replaying the same ball game, they may offer new moves and perhaps a new game

---

[14] Bernstein, *Objectivism*, 8.
[15] Wallace, *Naïveté*, 87–110; Fodor, *Hermeneutics*, 280–83; Tilley, 'Incommensurability'.
[16] Bernstein, *Objectivism*, 16.

altogether, allowing us to see the issues in a different light and hopefully opening up creative new responses. In this spirit, I am offering the resources of two such alternative postmodern philosophical approaches, namely, the hermeneutical philosophy of Ricœur and the speech-act theory of Austin.

Ricœur's Interweaving of History and Fiction

Ricœur's treatment of history and fiction in *Time and Narrative* must be set within his overall hermeneutical philosophy, but this is easier said than done. Ricœur is notorious for setting off in new directions, writing a major work in an area, and going on without integrating it clearly within the rest of his work. He himself has famously confessed to difficulty in putting all of his work together.[17] Our attention to religious texts is made even more problematic by Ricœur's attempt to keep his philosophical and religious reflections segregated.[18] As a result, Ricœur's work has been largely appropriated piecemeal in theological and biblical studies, yet with provocative effect in many areas such as symbol, metaphor, narrative and ideology critique. His Gifford Lectures *Oneself as Another*, however, have more recently made a comprehensive grasp of his philosophy easier. For here he ties together, for the first time, numerous threads of his work, plus several significant secondary works.[19]

At the heart of Ricœur's hermeneutical philosophy is the paradigm of interpreting a text, a fact that makes his work an intriguing ally for Christian theology, which focuses upon the interpretation of a sacred text.[20] Without delving into the details of the background and scope of his larger philosophical project, it is important here to note the postmodern character of his rejection of foundationalism and objective certainty.[21] Along with his rejection of the idea of a transcendental and transparent self, this points to an entire postmodern epistemology predicated upon the familiar dynamics of interpreting a text.[22]

In the 1970s, he outlined a hermeneutical arc in which the interpreter

---

[17] Ricœur, *Essays*, 41.

[18] Ricœur, *Oneself*, 23–25.

[19] Ibid. Also very helpful are Hahn, *Philosophy*; and Reagan, *Ricœur*.

[20] Ricœur generally thinks in terms of written texts and does not refer to film or recorded speeches, which are consistent with his general approach, as Nicholas Wolterstorff critically points out in Wolterstorff, *Discourse*, 141–43. Ricœur does, however, apply his hermeneutical theory to actions in Ricœur, 'Model,' 131–44. I will follow Ricœur in using the language of texts with the understanding that this broader reference is implied.

[21] See esp. Ricœur, *Freud*.

[22] This is the theme I elaborate throughout *Theology*.

never starts without presuppositions or with absolute objectivity.[23] Rather, one begins with a naïve or first understanding in which one is grasped by a text as much as one grasps a text. In other words, we are not in control of the text. The meaning is at this point a hunch, a guess, a wager. He appeals then to the indispensability of a stage of criticism, but he significantly places criticism and reflection at a second level. Theology and philosophy cannot live by themselves but are given 'food for thought' by primary experiences and the more primary language of symbol, metaphor and narrative.[24] Critical reflection thus always begins too late. Already his approach represents a rejection of the view that primary language and experiences can be replaced and fully translated into second-level theoretical language. As important as critical methodology is, one also cannot linger there, caught 'in the desert of criticism'.[25] Rather, one must move on to one of his more pregnant ideas, namely, to a postcritical naïvety or a postcritical holistic understanding.[26]

It is clear from his later thought in *Oneself as Another* that such a secondary, holistic grasp is the fundamental epistemological stance. Rather than seeing such holistic insight, which he calls in the latter work 'attestation', as secondary and second-rate to science, it is the grounds for the basic convictions undergirding science and any other discipline.[27] In other words, to draw from his important mentor Hans-Georg Gadamer, no method can substitute for such holistic understanding of truth.[28] Where Ricœur goes beyond Gadamer is to allow for critical methodology enveloped, as it were, within hermeneutical understanding.[29] The postmodern nature of such attestation that attempts to transcend the Bernsteinian poles of objectivism and relativism can be seen in his summation:

> To my mind, attestation defines the sort of certainty that hermeneutics may claim, not only with respect to the epistemic exaltation of the cogito in Descartes, but also with respect to its humiliation in Nietzsche and its successors. Attestation may appear to require less than one and more than the other.[30]

He similarly states,

---

[23] Ricœur, 'Model', 197–221; Ricœur, *Interpretation*, 71–88.
[24] See also the conclusion of Ricœur, *Symbolism*, where he elaborates one of his favorite themes, 'the symbol gives rise to thought'.
[25] Ibid., 349.
[26] Ibid., 352.
[27] At times, Ricœur has reflected a 'modern' or pre-Kuhnian view of science, but the tenor of his thought as it has developed lies in a postmodern direction. This is a view I defend in *Theology*.
[28] The reference is to *Truth*, Gadamer's *magnum opus*.
[29] Ricœur, 'Hermeneutics'.
[30] Ricœur, *Oneself*, 21.

As credence without any guarantee, but also as trust greater than any suspicion, the hermeneutics of the self can claim to hold itself at an equal distance from the cogito exalted by Descartes and from the cogito that Nietzsche proclaimed forfeit.[31]

What is especially significant for his emphasis on the self as completely hermeneutical is that such insight irreducible to objective sight or method is also through and through a work of the imagination. Ricœur set out to do a philosophy of the will, but, as one commentator has said, he has actually developed a philosophy of the imagination.[32] In other words, attestation is a creative configuration that cannot be redeemed in wholly objective terms. It cannot meet the high standards of modernity – but then nothing ever has! Rather than succumbing to relativism or despair, Ricœur points to judgment or 'practical wisdom' (a creative appropriation of Aristotle's *phronesis*) that involves critique, reasons and evidence, but which cannot be collapsed into any of them. In other words, they underdetermine the conclusions. He allows for the power of religious convictions because his basic idea was originally rooted in the dynamics of religious testimony. Despite having strong convictions with formidable grounds, people disagree. Again, Ricœur's central metaphor is the common experience of interpreting a text where people have deep convictions about their conclusions. They can offer significant reasons for them but can still differ without being regarded as irrational. One of the most significant postmodern insights is that instead of this dynamic of the conflict of interpretations being a characteristic of disciplines that make a dubious claim to knowledge, this kind of understanding undergirds *all* claims to knowledge, even those of the hardest sciences.[33]

With this general backdrop of Ricœur's approach to humans as thoroughly interpretive or hermeneutical beings, we can see the significance of Ricœur's understanding both history and fiction in *Time and Narrative* as imaginative enterprises, both as acts of creative configuration and 'emplotment'.[34] Rather than facing each other across a continental divide, the one representing positivistic fact and the other the flight of the imagination into the unreal, history and fiction are both fundamentally alike in being 'mimetic' of reality. They are both fundamentally hermeneutical projects. His first move, therefore, was to join together what modernity had cast asunder, which especially involved a transformation of the nature of historiography.[35] It is now much more readily recognized than it was a century ago that historiography is itself a work of the productive imagination, representing a particular cast on a time

---

[31] Ibid., 23.

[32] Evans, *Hermeneutics*.

[33] See Ricœur's collection of essays by that title, *Conflict*.

[34] Ricœur, *Time*, II, 155–56.

[35] Ricœur, *Time*, I, pt. 2.

and place. The surplus of meaning that Ricœur emphasizes with respect to fiction is also at play in historiography, to which any dispute between historians attests. Ricœur's hermeneutical 'principle of plenitude' applies to historiography – namely, a text or an event means all that it can mean![36]

Fiction and historiography both unfold, he believes, in terms of what he calls a threefold mimesis.[37] Mimesis$_1$ represents the prefigured way of being-in-the-world that we bring to any text. Mimesis$_2$ is the creative configuration of a text. Mimesis$_3$ is the appropriative refiguration of a text that involves what Gadamer calls a 'fusion of horizons'.[38] Ricœur's 'narrative arc', like his earlier hermeneutical arc, challenges the traditional hermeneutic conception that application is an optional third step beyond understanding and explanation. Rather, it is an integral aspect of any hermeneutical act. As he says, 'We are not allowed to exclude the final act of personal commitment from the whole of objective and explanatory procedures which mediate it.'[39]

Ricœur earlier distinguished the world of the text as the sense of the text and the application as the reference of the text.[40] Although in *Time and Narrative* he had become uncomfortable with this language borrowed from quite a different domain, he retained the idea that the text has an inherent referential dimension.[41] Regarding his preoccupation with structuralism in the 1970s, which he characteristically both affirmed and rejected, he argued that structural analysis has a place as a critical methodology, but its insistence on remaining within the field of meaning of the text itself means that 'it would be reduced to a sterile game, a divisive algebra'.[42] Ricœur's point may be understood utilizing Gadamer's notion of a fusion of horizons. Gadamer argued that it is not possible to distinguish wholly between our horizon and the horizon of the text. In the parlance of biblical studies, he rejected the sharp distinction between what a text meant and what it means. Rather, any act of understanding involves a creative fusion of horizons, whether we agree with the text or not. 'It is enough,' Gadamer says, 'to say that we understand in a different way, if we understand at all.'[43] Even the understanding necessary to reject vehemently the meaning of a text involves a fusion of horizons. An aspect of bringing our horizon to the text is some nascent sense of what it might mean to appropriate the text in our horizon. We can of course distinguish relatively

---

[36] Ricœur, 'Metaphor', 176.
[37] Ricœur, *Time*, I, 52–87.
[38] Gadamer, *Truth*, 306.
[39] Ricœur, 'Model', 221.
[40] Ibid., 218.
[41] Ricœur, *Time*, III, 157–58.
[42] Ricœur, 'Model', 217.
[43] Gadamer, *Truth,* 297.

between the meaning of a text and our appropriation of it, but some sense of its significance is inherent in our understanding of it in the first place. Ricœur thus posits a dynamic interrelationship between the world of the text and the world in front of the text – that is, the latter as the meaning of the text as I have appropriated it.[44]

All of this is clearest in terms of fiction. The fictional world is obviously an act of imaginative configuration, both by the author and the reader. The fictional worlds of *Tom Sawyer* or *The Brothers Karamazov* are clearly distinguishable from the way they may be appropriated by us as the world in front of the text. Ricœur recognizes that modern fiction sometimes drives to the uttermost extreme the attempt to separate the fictional world from such reference, and he acknowledges that a first and literal reference must be denied.[45] Obviously, the fictional world is not a literal representation of reality. At the same time, what is denied at one level, as in metaphor being based on a first denial of literal meaning, can be affirmed at a second level. The power of the poetic imagination to redescribe reality is ironically inscribed within the first denial of a literal depiction of reality. Following Aristotle, he sees fiction as 'more philosophical' than historiography in that it does not so much illuminate what has happened as it discloses the possibilities of what could happen.[46] It deals more with the universal than with the particular. On the other hand, fiction communicates through its contact with our 'lifeworld'. If it did not touch base with us at some points, we could not understand it.[47]

Ricœur thus uses mimesis in the Aristotelian sense instead of the Platonic. Rather than being a poor imitation of the real, art and literature can reveal or disclose the real. Specifically, they may disclose not actuality but real possibilities, ways in which human beings can be in the world, just as metaphor, in contemporary theory, discloses or even creates new ways of seeing the world.[48] An example for Ricœur would be Jesus in the Gospels, who represents not so much what we *are* but what we *can be*. Ricœur connects such a vision at times with the role of utopia in providing the means of ideology to critique the distortions of the present.[49] He thus conceives of texts as offering to us possible worlds in which we might live.[50]

So while Ricœur first drew fiction and historiography together, his second move was to distinguish them – at least in a relative sense. The narrative arc

---

[44] Ricœur, 'Model', 218.
[45] Ibid., 201.
[46] Ricœur, *Time*, I, 40.
[47] Ricœur, *Time*, III, 191.
[48] Ricœur, 'Metaphor'.
[49] Ricœur, *Lectures*, 180.
[50] Ricœur, 'Model', 218.

applies most clearly to fiction, but it is not irrelevant to historiography. One brings a prefigurational horizon to reading or writing history. History is configured by the imagination, as we have noted. Perhaps more controversially, history can be appropriated or applied. It does not so clearly offer a possible world in which to live, but it offers possibilities in a muted way. It at least offers possibilities for conceiving the past in different ways, in the way, for example, that a revisionist Native American historian writes the history of the European 'discovery' of the Americas.

Historiography is configurational and always represents a perspective. It does not, and cannot, depict what happened as it actually happened, according to the positivist dream, but is irreducibly hermeneutical. It nevertheless attempts to convey a reliable interpretation of what happened and so 'owes a debt to the past' in a way that fiction does not. Ricœur says,

> Unlike novels, historians' constructions do aim at being *re*constructions of the past. Through documents and their critical examination of documents, historians are subject to what once was. They owe a debt to the past, a debt of recognition to the dead, that makes them insolvent debtors.[51]

Historiography rightly draws on 'archives, documents, and traces',[52] but even these are unavoidably matters for interpretation. The historian's depiction of what happened implies in an indirect way possible ways of being in the world. Historians may not intend to convey a 'lesson' any more than a novelist or poet intends a 'lesson'. Nonetheless, they convey ways of understanding and grasping the world that allow for appropriation.

As Ricœur sees it, there is an inherent interweaving between fiction and historiography.[53] Both share elements of one another, but they are not the same. In *Time and Narrative*, he was primarily interested in the way that the narrative or mimetic element contributes to the way human identity is shaped through its passage in time. Narrative allows, he thinks, for a necessary integrating of impersonal chronological time with internal lived time.[54] Human beings are thus essentially storied beings who are continually writing and rewriting their stories out of their experiences and, importantly, out of the historiographical and fictional texts that they encounter.

In *Time and Narrative*, Ricœur focuses on modern fiction and modern historiography and does not deal with the Gospels, which, as we have seen, have been variously interpreted as more akin to fiction or more akin to

---

[51] Ricœur, *Time*, III, 142f.
[52] See the section by that title in ibid., 116–26.
[53] For example, ibid., 181.
[54] Ibid., 22.

historiography. Given that Ricœur has elsewhere paid great attention to various biblical genres, even biblical narratives, it is odd that he has not applied his ideas on the interweaving of fiction and historiography to an issue that cries out for such attention.[55] A former student of mine, Tim Maddox, indicated in his master's thesis some of the implications of *Time and Narrative* for the Gospels. Focusing on the Gospel of Luke, he pointed out that the gospel genre is itself a unique interweaving of fiction and historiography.[56] The Gospels can be seen as inherently configured, sharing important characteristics of both fiction and historiography. The Gospels bear a debt to the past. They are about crucial events in the past and represent creative, mimetic interpretations, to be sure, but nevertheless interpretations of what actually happened. On the other hand, it is evident that the primary focus is not on the debt to the past but on the configuration of a world in which we might live. As John most clearly puts it, 'But these have been written that you may believe that Jesus is the Christ, the Son of God; and that believing, you may have life in his name' (Jn. 20:31, NASB). John van den Hengel points out that Ricœur's own intimations are to see the Gospels as history-like, similar to Frei, but argues like Maddox that his conceptuality offers a fruitful way to understand the historicity of the Gospels in a more integrated way.[57] Such an appropriation of Ricœur better enables us to understand how, in the genre of the first century, many details can be moved around, reshaped and elaborated in order to convey the reality of what Jesus Christ brought to the world. Nevertheless, the writers clearly have a historical interest. The gospel narratives are not only history-like, but they appeal to history itself. For instance, the details of the crucifixion vary, but the testimony to its happening does not. Details of Jesus' life vary, but the general testimony to his miracle working and speaking in parables does not. More specifically, certain events such as the cross and resurrection are implied by the text as non-negotiable referents in a way that others are not. Ricœur himself at one point said that the question about the reference of the resurrection of Christ cannot be avoided.[58] As such, these historical markers are not contrary or imposed from the outside upon the world of the text. They are, rather, required by the world of the text. The debt to the past, as it were, must be 'paid off', but the larger debt is to the configuration of a redemptive world in which we are called to live. The vexing polarities between history and fiction in the Gospels thus can be brought closer together through the matrix of their inherent interweaving as mimetic acts. As van den Hengel concludes on the basis of

---

[55] Ricœur, 'Toward a Hermeneutic'; Ricœur, 'Naming'.

[56] Maddox, 'Paul Ricœur's …'.

[57] Van den Hengel, 'Jesus'. Francis Watson makes a similar point in Watson, *Text*, 56–57.

[58] Ricœur, *Essays*, 44.

Ricœur's thought, 'A literary approach toward the understanding of the Gospel text is, in principle, not opposed to a historical understanding.'[59] Ricœur's framework allows for integration but does not, however, give much guidance about what is historical and what is not. He helps us to see *that* history and fiction can be integrated, but he does not really help us to see *how*. For another way of relating history and fiction in narrative that is clearer on the particulars, we turn to speech-act theory.

Speech-act Theory's Integration of History and Fiction

Speech-act theory derives from the British philosopher John Austin, who understood speech as actions – that is, as things we do with words.[60] One of Austin's primary criticisms is what he called the 'descriptive fallacy', in which we traditionally look at speaking as primarily a descriptive act.[61] In fact, we do very many things with words, and probably most of them are not simple descriptions. He further recognized that even a description is a kind of action that involves the backing of the speaker. The upshot is that speech is much more complex than we ordinarily think; certainly it requires more dimensions of evaluation than simply how accurately it describes or refers. This is significant when it comes to considering the historical issues in relation to the theological meaning of the Gospels.

For our purposes, I will use the categories that James McClendon and James Smith developed on the basis of Austin's work, which Michael Goldberg then utilizes to analyze narratives.[62] They take a simple example of a request to pass bread at the dinner table. 'Primary' conditions involve using grammar and words in a proper way to convey a request, namely, 'Please, pass the bread' rather than, 'I demand that bread pass.' 'Affective' conditions involve possessing requisite psychological and intentional conditions such as sincerity and politeness in the tone of voice and in body language. For example, if someone glares at the person to whom such a request is made, even if the request is made in the proper language, an observer would suspect that something other than a

---

[59] Ibid., 146.
[60] Austin, *Words*. This work is based on the William James Lectures delivered at Harvard University in 1955.
[61] Ibid., 1.
[62] McClendon, *Convictions*; Goldberg, *Theology*. Speech-act theory has been applied to the Gospels by others more in terms of specific actions rather than in terms of the narrative shape of the Gospels. These tend to follow the much more detailed analysis and taxonomy of speech acts by John Searle. See Thiselton, *New Horizons*, 283–312; and Tilley, *Evils*.

simple request is going on. These conditions concern what we are doing in using the language. 'Representative' conditions are the necessary realities that make such a request possible. If people were not at the dinner table but in a football huddle, if there were no bread, if the people were at different tables across a wide room, all of these would undermine such a simple request.[63] In Austin's language, if such conditions are met, then we have a 'happy' or 'felicitous' speech act. The point, though, is that speech acts can be infelicitous or 'misfire' in a variety of ways, not just in terms of the traditional preoccupation with the factual and descriptive aspects of representative conditions.

McClendon and Smith are particularly interested in analyzing 'convictions', which are much more than simple beliefs or declarations of fact. They define them as follows:

> Convictions, then, are persistent beliefs such that, if X (a person or community) has a conviction, it will not easily be relinquished and cannot be relinquished without making X a significantly different person (or community) than before.[64]

They take the example of a conviction that 'God led Israel across the Sea of Reeds.'[65] The primary conditions are straightforward. The affective conditions are significant in terms of convictions because this is much more than a historical observation or opinion. It is stated as a basic religious confession involving such affects as 'awed gratitude'.[66] If such a confession is followed by, 'But I don't really care,' it would misfire because convictions do not allow for relative indifference. The representative conditions come in at this point, but what is significant about speech-act theory is that they are not the only consideration. They arise in the context of the other conditions. Nevertheless, if no dramatic deliverance through the crossing of a body of water occurred, a problem of infelicity arises. More importantly, as McClendon and Smith point out, 'God, the God to whom the context refers, must be God, must exist.'[67]

It is also important to recognize in a postmodern context that the factual conditions do not have to meet the Cartesian conditions of 'clarity and distinctness'. The factual conditions need only be sufficient for the speech act to

---

[63] Austin's terminology was 'locutionary' elements of grammar and syntax; 'illocutionary' elements involve conventions which indicate that the speech act is one of promising, affirming, questioning, requesting, and so on; and 'perlocutionary' elements involve how the speech act is received, that is, the effect intended by the speech act. Austin, *Words*.

[64] McClendon, *Convictions*, 87.

[65] Ibid., 62ff.

[66] Ibid., 72.

[67] Ibid., 66.

succeed. It may not be necessary to know exactly where the Reed Sea was. It
may not even be important that it was the Reed Sea; after all, due to translation, many have long thought that it was the Red Sea that the Israelites crossed.
Moreover, the context of the broader Exodus narrative itself indicates that the
God, Yahweh, who delivered them is a mysterious being who is not all clearly
comprehended, as in Moses' encounter at the burning bush (Ex. 3 – 4). With
the Wittgensteinian parallel to speech-act theory, we can point out
Wittgenstein's radical point that even so-called literal language may have
'blurred edges'.[68] Jerry Gill takes this as the 'principle of sufficient precision',
that is, words have only the clarity necessary to be used adequately, allowing
for a great deal of looseness and ambiguity of meaning.[69] In a religious context,
we could say that it allows for requisite mystery in our religious language.

At this point, we are still thinking of speech acts in a direct sense. Goldberg
is helpful because he applies speech-act theory to written narratives. The shift
from spoken to written language is a significant jump, but the theory has been
widely applied to written language without violating the basic points that
Austin and other speech-act theorists have made. In fact, we just saw that even
a convictional confession like the one we analyzed implies a narrative background. The God who led Israel across the Reed Sea is the God of the
patriarchs–matriarchs and the God of the burning bush, whose identity is
rendered in written narratives. Goldberg also offers the advantage of dealing
with the narratives as narratives rather than transposing them into a
convictional proposition. This does justice to the point that most narrativists
make concerning the irreducibility of narratives, that is, they cannot be fully
translated into propositional language.

Goldberg's approach thus allows us to consider the Gospels in terms of
multiple conditions. Primary conditions refer to issues such as their language,
genre and composition. They are much more complex than a simple speech
act of requesting such as that we earlier analyzed. For example, Alan
Culpepper describes the artful use of irony in the Gospel of John that conveys
something of the nature of the Messiah and his reception by the disciples and
others.[70] William Placher, among many others, has reflected on the literary and
theological significance of the ending of the Gospel of Mark.[71]

The affective conditions in this case are perhaps more relevant to the
readers than to the writers. If the Gospels are understood as expressing narrative convictions that are intended to lead to faith and following Jesus Christ,

---

[68] Wittgenstein, *Investigations*, par. 71.
[69] Gill, *Knowing* , 83–6.
[70] Culpepper, *Anatomy*.
[71] Placher, *Narratives*, ch. 4.

then the text and what we know of the author (which is very little) should support such a purpose. As Goldberg indicates, however, perhaps the greatest test of this condition is the pragmatic one of seeing if the narratives actually do bring about faith and conviction. In other words, do the affective responses fit the intent of the Gospels? Since obviously not all respond, do the Gospels allow for such a variety? Is there thus a consistency between the message and the response, which Austin called 'uptake'? So far we are dealing with what in Ricœur's context we placed under the configuring or 'fictive' dimension. Are the Gospels felicitous in conveying their message and fulfilling their purpose?

The representative conditions, however, relate to the historical dimension. As in the exodus, one can ask what conditions of reality must be true in order for the narrative speech act to succeed. Placing the question in this context allows us to make more nuanced judgments, as we are going beyond the more simplistic issue of whether the story actually happened the way it was described or not. It makes room for differences in historical assessment about the parables, about individual actions of Jesus, and about the general actuality of Jesus. As Frei emphasized, the Gospels render a character.[72] It is not so important that each individual event happened as it is described, but that a coherent character is portrayed. The representative conditions then arise from the story and are not imposed upon the story. One can legitimately conclude that on the grounds of the gospel narratives themselves, Jesus of Nazareth must exist and be roughly like he has been portrayed. In the apt words of Edward Schillebeeckx, he is the 'reflex of the earthly Jesus'.[73] For example, one may conclude that a particular healing need not have occurred in the precise way it is described, but it is crucial that Jesus healed. It may not be so important exactly how long Jesus' ministry was, how many times he visited Jerusalem, or the exact number and nature of the feedings of the multitudes. It *is* important, however, whether Jesus went to Jerusalem, died on a cross, and was raised from the dead. As another prominent narrative theologian George Stroup says, 'The discovery by historians that Jesus did not die on the cross but died fat and happy of old age in Palestine would render the claims of Christian narrative false.'[74] Moreover, as in the case of the Reed Sea, the God depicted in the narratives must also exist. It does not mean that every detail and every event happened as it is described – just that sufficient representative conditions are met for the theological purpose of the Gospels to be felicitous.

As Goldberg also recognizes, such judgments cannot be strictly proven and are probabilistic in nature. 'The judgment of the veracity of historical claims rarely takes the form of a flat yes or no.'[75] It is one thing to determine what

---

[72] Frei, *Identity*.

[73] Schillebeeckx, *Jesus*, 436.

[74] Stroup, *Promise*, 236f.

historical conditions are necessary. It is another to assess their truth. This judgment may or may not be made as a strict historian. We can presuppose here the
significant revisions that Ricœur and others have made to historiographical
method, moving it from a positivistic to a hermeneutical basis. Since such
judgments now are recognized as more than detached historical observations
and presuppose the influence of one's presuppositions, whether they be those
of religious faith or of naturalism, they represent convictions. The historical
judgments are related to everything else that one brings to the table, so to
speak.[76] Despite this 'revisionist' view of historiography, the Gospels are clearly
not the same genre and should not be collapsed into modern historiography,
which does not, explicitly at least, intend to be didactic and evangelistic but
more simply to recount 'what happened'. Thus the assessment of the truth of
the Gospels is a larger issue than what a historiographer might say. In other
words, assessing the historical implications of the Gospels as a historian
involves presuppositions, but this is not the same as a faith response to the
claims of the Gospels as gospel, as good news. The Gospels thus have a historical dimension without being modern historiography. Speech–act theory helps
us 'locate' the significant historical issues in the Gospels in the context of their
wider evangelistic purpose, allowing us to see the Gospels as a distinctive interweaving of historical and mimetic intent.

In the Gospels, the judgments about history thus relate in complex ways to
larger judgments about the validity of the claims that are being made. For
example, a historical judgment about the possibility of Jesus as a miracle
worker relates to an openness to miracles, however they are defined. The
Gospels call for judgments about the nature of the God they are portraying.
For believers, these appraisals relate to whether the God depicted in the narrative fits one's understanding of the rest of Scripture, one's tradition and one's
spiritual experience. As Goldberg is very aware as a Jew, one's tradition can
shape one's judgment about whether the God portrayed in the Gospels is consistent with the God portrayed in the Hebrew Bible.[77] As in many areas,
experts and others will disagree about how to interpret and evaluate literary
and historical issues. Competent readers are required, but competent readers
can conflict. The complexity of such judgments does not necessarily render
them vacuous, however, for in a postmodern context, such conflict of

---

[75] Goldberg, *Theology*, 216.

[76] For a good example of how complex these historical judgments are, even apart from
the context of faith, see the debate between Iain Provan, 'Ideologies', and Philip
Davies, 'Method'. I am focusing not so much on the historians' task *per se* as on
how one estimates what historical issues are at stake in the more holistic response to the
Gospels' appeal for faith.

[77] Goldberg, 'God', 348–65.

interpretations is now seen to be at play in all areas, including the scientific. Again, absolute objectivity and proof has been seen to be a will-o'-the-wisp that is humanly unattainable. As we have seen, Ricœur sees such religious testimonies as of a piece with the dynamics of attestation that attend general philosophical judgments. The difficulty of such epistemological judgments does not, therefore, militate against speech-act theory any more than it does other areas; rather, such difficulty simply places speech-act theory on the leveled playing field of a postmodern era.

What speech-act theory, as applied to narrative, does provide is a way of placing the figurative and historical aspects of the Gospels in a productive relationship to one another. Rather than competing with one another, they support one another in a 'felicitous' way.[78] Historical aspects are not superimposed upon the text from an anachronistic context but stem from the movement of the text itself in what it is 'doing'. Questions of reference and truth arise – but only in their proper place, so to speak. They prevent obsessive preoccupation with the world behind the text but nevertheless call for particular historical, representative conditions. Modern historiographical assumptions, for example, of strict chronology, are not laid upon ancient texts of quite a different genre because they do not fit the 'speech act', or 'gospel act', as it were, that is being made in that historical context. Room is made for the gospel writers and editors to focus upon their distinctive purpose of conveying the character of Jesus and appealing for faith in him, rather than attempting to write a modern historical biography.

An Interweaving of Ricœur and Austin

What conclusions can we draw after having examined the possible contributions of Ricœur and Austin's speech-act theory to the issue of history and fiction in the Gospels? First of all, placing them in juxtaposition underscores minimally that a more nuanced approach is possible. Even if one does not place them in dialogue, they offer two ways of seeing the historical and the mimetic working in concert rather than at cross-purposes.

Secondly, they complement each other in certain ways. In other words, an 'interweaving' of Ricœur and speech-act theory is more helpful than simply

---

[78] Thiselton also indicates the significance of speech-act theory in helping us deal more carefully with the relationship of the biblical texts to history, again tending to treat more specific claims than the narratives as a whole. Thiselton, 'Action and Promise', 144–51. He notes, though, 'The interplay between linguistic action and states of affairs outside language, however, remains exceedingly subtle, complex, and diverse from case to case' (147).

choosing one or the other. Ricœur is crucial in revealing the mimetic imagination at work in any kind of judgment, whether historical or literary. Thus,
even in considering the representative conditions of the Gospels, which deal
with the debt of history to the past, mimesis is involved, presupposing a significant modification to historiographical method. Ricœur provides more detail
in how critical methods of explanation may be utilized but still in the end yield
to integrative understanding. It is also true that Ricœur provides a much more
comprehensive philosophical perspective in general that includes a broad narrative theory as well as extensive treatment of metaphor and symbol set within
a view of the self as a situated, narratively-shaped, embodied being. In terms of
evaluating literary and historical claims, Ricœur's attention to the problems of
power and distortion intensifies the element of critical judgment that is also in
speech-act theory. Murphy elaborated a postmodern 'Anglo-American' philosophy that is based in large part on Austin's thought, but Austin's work, even
as it has been appropriated by many others, pales in comparison to the breadth
and depth of Ricœur's philosophy.[79] In fact, few are more comprehensive than
Ricœur.

Ricœur would be the first, however, to acknowledge that he has not
covered everything adequately and that he could be challenged. For our concerns, speech-act theory helps much more than Ricœur to see how and where
historical issues arise. Ricœur has justly been criticized for being vague on precisely what historical issues are crucial.[80] He helps us understand the dynamics
of evaluating historical matters better than speech-act theory, but speech-act
theory offers a much better framework for adjudging what historical matters to
evaluate and the degree of their importance. Ricœur enables us to see clearly
that history and fiction *can be* interwoven in the Gospels, but speech-act theory
enables us to see much more clearly *how* they are interwoven.

These approaches together, as creatively appropriated in the ways given
above, represent postmodern philosophies that point to a more sophisticated
and flexible treatment of the historical and literary dimensions of the gospel
texts. They do so, moreover, in a way that does justice to their status not just
as literary works but as authoritative sacred texts. They allow for the kind of
conviction and testimony indigenous to religious faith in a supple way that
neither takes the Gospels out of the realm of hermeneutics or literary theory
nor collapses them into simple instances of general theory.

In this way, the role of faith, even the inspiration of the Holy Spirit, can
play its mysterious role without undermining the place for philosophical
theory. Ricœur's approach allows for critical methodology but does not substitute for personal judgment that cannot be reduced to a method. In the end,

---

[79] Murphy, *Postmodernity.*
[80] Vanhoozer, *Narrative,* chs. 6–7; Thiselton, *New Horizons,* ch. 10.

any broad philosophical or religious judgment is *testimony*. Speech-act theory likewise points to the unique dynamic that attends convictional narratives. It helps us understand the rationality of a high level of personal backing that does not presuppose, Enlightenment-style, appeal to an independent or neutral tribunal.

To put it another way, faith and reason do not have to be collapsed into one another, nor do they need to be in sharp contrast to one another. Much as the historical and fictional impulses interweave in the Gospels, reason and faith interweave in a creative and mysterious, yet productive, way.

Bibliography

Austin, J.L., *How to Do Things with Words* (ed. J.O. Urmson and M. Sbisà; Cambridge, MA: Harvard University Press, 2nd edn, 1975)

Bernstein, R.J., *Beyond Objectivism and Relativism: Science, Hermeneutics, and Praxis* (Philadelphia: University of Philadelphia Press, 1985)

Culpepper, R.A., *Anatomy of the Fourth Gospel: A Study in Literary Design* (ed. R. Funk; FF: NT; Philadelphia: Fortress Press, 1983)

Davies, P.R., 'Method and Madness: Some Remarks on Doing History with the Bible', *JBL* 114.4 (1995), 699–705

Evans, J., *Paul Ricœur's Hermeneutics of the Imagination* (American University Studies, 143; New York: P. Lang, 1995)

Fodor, J., *Christian Hermeneutics: Paul Ricœur and the Refiguring of Theology* (Oxford: Clarendon Press, 1995)

Frei, H.W., *The Eclipse of Biblical Narrative: A Study in Eighteenth and Nineteenth Century Hermeneutics* (New Haven: Yale University Press, 1974)

—, *The Identity of Jesus Christ: The Hermeneutical Bases of Dogmatic Theology* (Philadelphia: Fortress Press, 1967)

Gadamer, H.G., *Truth and Method* (trans. J. Weinsheimer and D.G. Marshall; New York: Crossroad, rev. edn, 1991)

Gill, J., *On Knowing God: New Directions for the Future of Theology* (Philadelphia: Westminster Press, 1981)

Goldberg, M., 'God, Action, and Narrative: Which Narrative? Which Action? Which God?', in *Why Narrative? Readings in Narrative Theology* (ed. S. Hauerwas and L.G. Jones; Grand Rapids: Eerdmans, 1989), 348–65

—, *Theology and Narrative: A Critical Introduction* (Nashville: Abingdon, 1982)

Griffin, D., 'Introduction', in *Varieties of Postmodern Theology* (ed. D. Griffin, W.A. Beardslee, and J. Holland; SUNY Series in Constructive Postmodern Thought; New York: State University of New York, 1989), 1–7

Hahn, L.E., *The Philosophy of Paul Ricœur* (The Library of Living Philosophers; Chicago: Open Court, 1995)

Hengel, J. Van den, 'Jesus Between History and Fiction', in *Meanings in Texts and Actions: Questioning Paul Ricœur* (ed. D.E. Klemm and W. Schweiker; Studies in Religion and Culture; Charlottesville: University Press of Virginia, 1993), 133–53

Lindbeck, G., *The Nature of Doctrine: Religion and Theology in a Postliberal Age* (Philadelphia: Westminster Press, 1984)

Maddox, T.D.L., 'Paul Ricœur's *Time and Narrative* as a Model for Historical Reference in Biblical Narrative' (ThM Thesis; Southern Baptist Theological Seminary, 1992)

Marsden, G.M., *Fundamentalism and American Culture: The Shaping of Twentieth-Century Evangelicalism 1870–1925* (Oxford: OUP, 1980)

McClendon, Jr., J.W., and J.M. Smith, *Convictions: Defusing Religious Relativism* (Valley Forge, PA: Trinity Press, rev. edn, 1994)

Murphy, N.C., *Anglo-American Postmodernity: Philosophical Perspectives on Science, Religion, and Ethics* (Boulder, CO: Westview Press, 1997)

—, *Beyond Liberalism and Fundamentalism: How Modern and Postmodern Philosophy Set the Theological Agenda* (Rockwell Lecture Series; Valley Forge, PA: Trinity Press International, 1996)

Pannenberg, W., *Jesus – God and Man* (trans. L.L. Wilkins and D.A. Priebe; Philadelphia: Westminster Press, 2nd edn, 1977)

Peterson, N.R., *Literary Criticism for New Testament Critics* (ed. D.O. Via, Jr.; GBS; Philadelphia: Fortress Press, 1978)

Placher, W.C., *Narratives of a Vulnerable God: Christ, Theology, and Scripture* (Louisville: Westminster/John Knox Press, 1994)

Provan, I.W., 'Ideologies, Literary and Critical: Reflections on Recent Writing on the History of Israel', *JBL* 114.4 (1995), 585–606

Reagan, C.E., *Paul Ricœur: His Life and His Work* (Chicago: University of Chicago Press, 1996)

Ricœur, P., *The Conflict of Interpretations* (ed. D. Ihde; Northwestern University Studies in Phenomenology & Existential Philosophy; Evanston, IL: Northwestern University Press, 1974)

—, *Essays on Biblical Interpretation* (trans. R. Sweeney; ed. L.S. Mudge; Philadelphia: Fortress Press, 1980)

—, *Freud and Philosophy: An Essay on Interpretation* (trans. D. Savage; Terry Lectures; New Haven: Yale University Press, 1970)

—, 'Hermeneutics and the Critique of Ideology', in *Hermeneutics and the Human Sciences: Essays on Language, Action, and Interpretation* (ed. J.B. Thompson; Cambridge: CUP, 1981), 63–100

—, *Interpretation Theory: Discourse and the Surplus of Meaning* (Fort Worth: Texas Christian University Press, 1976)

—, *Lectures on Ideology and Utopia* (ed. G.H. Taylor; New York: Columbia University Press, 1986)

—, 'Metaphor and the Central Problem of Hermeneutics', in *Hermeneutics and the Human Sciences: Essays on Language, Action, and Interpretation* (ed. J.B. Thompson; Cambridge: CUP, 1981), 165–81

—, 'The Model of the Text: Meaningful Action Considered as a Text', in *Hermeneutics and the Human Sciences: Essays on Language, Action, and Interpretation* (ed. J.B. Thompson; Cambridge: CUP, 1981), 197–221

—, 'Naming God', in *Figuring the Sacred: Religion, Narrative, and Imagination* (ed. M.I. Wallace; trans. D. Pellauer; Minneapolis: Fortress Press, 1995), 217–35

—, *Oneself as Another* (trans. K. Blamey; Chicago: University of Chicago Press, 1992)

—, *The Symbolism of Evil* (trans. E. Buchanan; Religious Perspectives, 17; New York: Harper & Row, 1967)

—, *Time and Narrative* (trans. K. McLaughlin and D. Pellauer; 3 vols.; Chicago: University of Chicago Press, 1984–88)

—, 'Toward a Hermeneutic of the Idea of Revelation', in *Essays on Biblical Interpretation* (trans. D. Pellauer; ed. L.S. Mudge; Philadelphia: Fortress Press, 1980), 73–118

Schillebeeckx, E., *Jesus: An Experiment in Christology* (trans. H. Hoskins; New York: Seabury Press, 1979)

Stiver, D.R., 'Much Ado about Athens and Jerusalem: The Implications of Postmodernism for Faith', *RevExp* 91 (Winter 1994), 83–102

—, *The Philosophy of Religious Language: Sign, Symbol, and Story* (Cambridge, MA, Oxford: Basil Blackwell, 1996)

—, *Theology After Ricœur: The Contribution of Hermeneutical Philosophy to Contemporary Theology* (Louisville: Westminster/John Knox Press, forthcoming)

Stroup, G.W., *The Promise of Narrative Theology: Recovering the Gospel in the Church* (Atlanta, GA: John Knox Press, 1981)

Thiemann, R.F., *Revelation and Theology: The Gospel as Narrated Promise* (Notre Dame: University of Notre Dame Press, 1985)

Thiselton, A.C., 'Communicative Action and Promise in Interdisciplinary, Biblical, and Theological Hermeneutics', in *The Promise of Hermeneutics* (ed. R. Lundin, C. Walhout and A.C. Thiselton; Grand Rapids: Eerdmans, 1999), 133–239

—, *New Horizons in Hermeneutics: The Theory and Practice of Transforming Biblical Reading* (Grand Rapids: Zondervan, 1992)

Tilley, T.W., *The Evils of Theodicy* (Washington, DC: Georgetown University Press, 1991)

—, 'Incommensurability, Intratextuality, and Fideism', *Modern Theology* 5.2 (Jan. 1989), 87–111

Vanhoozer, K.J., *Biblical Narrative in the Philosophy of Paul Ricœur: A Study in Hermeneutics and Theology* (Cambridge: CUP, 1990)

Wallace, M.I., *The Second Naiveté: Barth, Ricœur, and the New Yale Theology* (StABH; Macon, GA: Mercer University Press, 1990)

Watson, F., *Text and Truth: Redefining Biblical Theology* (Grand Rapids: Eerdmans, 1997)

Wittgenstein, L., *Philosophical Investigations* (trans. G.E.M. Anscombe; New York: Macmillan, 3rd edn, 1958)

Wolterstorff, N., *Divine Discourse: Philosophical Reflections on the Claim that God Speaks* (Cambridge: CUP, 1995)

Wood, C.M., *Theory and Understanding: A Critique of the Hermeneutics of Joachim Wach* (AARDS, 12; Missoula, MT: Scholars Press, 1975)

3

The Promise of Speech-act Theory for Biblical Interpretation

Nicholas Wolterstorff

Where We Are Now in Theory of Interpretation

Whether one holds that biblical interpretation, when properly conducted, is just a special application of general principles of interpretation, or whether one believes that it requires special principles of its own – either way, reflections on biblical interpretation have always interacted with reflections on the interpretation of other texts. This has particularly been the case in the nineteenth and twentieth centuries. For that reason, I propose introducing what I have to say on the promise of speech-act theory for biblical interpretation with a brief narrative of where we are now in theory of interpretation generally. This will be, need I say, *my* narrative – in other words, others would offer, and in fact *do* offer, different narratives. There's little disagreement on the chronicle; it's mainly on our construals of significance that we differ.

In his magisterial *Truth and Method*, Hans-Georg Gadamer construes Schleiermacher, whom he regards as the founding father of Romantic hermeneutics, as holding that the main goal of text-interpretation is to understand that part of the author's mental life of which the text is an 'expression'. Since any part of an author's mental life can be fully understood only by placing that part in the context of the author's mental life as a whole, the goal expands to understanding the author. In Gadamer's own words, 'what is to be understood is … not only the exact words and their objective meaning, but also the individuality of the speaker or author…'.[1] The text, says Gadamer, is regarded 'as a unique manifestation of the author's life'.[2] Accordingly,

---

[1] Gadamer, *Truth*, 186.
[2] Ibid., 191.

what is to be understood … is not a shared thought about some subject matter, but individual thought that by its very nature is a free construct and the free expression of an individual human being.[3]

Among others, Gadamer draws the following two implications from this view of interpretation that he attributes to Schleiermacher. Firstly, interpretation thus understood can be viewed as reversing the direction of the author's production, the aim being to arrive at a 're-creation of the creative act', a 'reproduction of the original production',[4] a 'reconstruction of a construction'.[5] Secondly, to view interpretation as aimed at recovering 'what the author meant and expressed'[6] is tacitly to treat the text as an aesthetic artifact. Again in Gadamer's own words,

> understanding in this way … means that the structure of thought we are trying to understand as an utterance or as a text is not to be understood in terms of its subject matter, but as an aesthetic construct, as a work of art or 'artistic thought'.[7]

Texts are construed as 'purely expressive phenomena', and 'the discourse of the individual' which generated the text as 'a free creative activity'.[8]

I judge this construal of Schleiermacher to be a substantial distortion of his thought. Near the beginning of his lectures on hermeneutics, now published under the title *Hermeneutics and Criticism*, Schleiermacher remarks that,

> the belonging together of hermeneutics and rhetoric consists in the fact that every act of understanding is the inversion of a speech-act (*Akt des Redens*), during which the thought which was the basis of the speech must become conscious.[9]

This passage, by itself, gives the impression that Schleiermacher distinguishes the speech-act from the thought that is its basis; and so he does – in a way. But almost immediately after making the remark above, Schleiermacher goes on to talk about 'the unity of speech and thought'. He says,

> Language is the manner in which thought is real. For there are no thoughts without speech. The speaking of the words relates solely to the presence of another person, and to this extent is contingent. But no one can think without words. Without

---

[3] Ibid., 188.
[4] Ibid., 187.
[5] Ibid., 189.
[6] Ibid., 192.
[7] Ibid., 187.
[8] Ibid., 196.
[9] Schleiermacher, *Hermeneutics*, 7.

words the thought is not yet completed and clear. Now as hermeneutics is supposed to lead to the understanding of thought-content, but the thought-content is only real via language, hermeneutics depends on grammar as knowledge of the language.[10]

In short, though speech acts for Schleiermacher are expressions or manifestations of acts of thought, those acts of thought are themselves linguistic in character. They are not the *motive* or *intention* behind the speech act, but the *act of thought* corresponding to the speech act, of which the speech act is then the external expression. I think that if Schleiermacher had been offered J.L. Austin's distinction between locutionary and illocutionary acts, he would have seized on it as a way of clarifying his own thoughts, and would have said that the goal of interpretation is to identify and understand the *illocutionary* act, of which the text is then the trace or manifestation. And need I say that identifying and understanding an illocutionary act is not the same as understanding the mental life of the author – let alone understanding *the author*. Schleiermacher does indeed sometimes speak of trying to understand the train of thought that gave rise to the text – and to its counterpart act of thought. But I submit that in speaking thus he always has in mind trying to *account for why* the speech act, and its corresponding act of thought, occurred. That is, he is trying to account for what he sometimes calls 'its necessity'.[11] And surely he's correct in saying that if you want to know not just what a person said, but why he said it, you'll have to uncover at least a little bit of the speaker's train of thought.

Enough of this, however. Though my scholar's conscience would not allow me to let Gadamer's interpretation of Schleiermacher pass by without challenge, for our purposes here it doesn't actually matter who's right. What matters is that a good many theorists of interpretation have held that the goal of interpretation is to discover that component in the author's mental life which motivated the text we have in hand. Typically, this component has been called 'intention'. Prominent in the nineteenth century, but extending on into the present, there's been a long tradition of *authorial-intention* hermeneutics.

This tradition came under heavy attack in the twentieth century with the result that, over the past fifty years or so, few would acknowledge being advocates or practitioners of authorial-intention interpretation. The one significant exception to this is E.D. Hirsch, in his well-known *Validity of Interpretation*. Two objections seem to me to have been particularly influential.

It's been said that authorial intentions are for the most part inaccessible. How do we know, for example, what Rufus of Cornwall's intentions were, or even Aquinas' – to cite another, but far better-known, example of a medieval

---

[10] Ibid., 8.
[11] Ibid., 91.

philosopher? What seems to me a far more weighty objection than this skepti-
cal one is another, second, objection. Suppose we did know what the author
intended (perhaps because he told us). Texts don't always turn out the way
their authors intended them, nor have authors always been correct in understanding their own intentions. Let us suppose, for the sake of the argument,
that a case of the first sort takes the following form: the text doesn't _mean_ what
the author intended it to mean. Such a discrepancy presupposes: 1) that what
the text means is not to be identified with what the author intended it to mean,
and 2) that we the interpreters have an access to the meaning of the text which
is independent of any knowledge we may have of the author's intended
meaning. It follows that the meaning of a text is neither identical with, nor
even determined by, the author's intentions concerning meaning. There's
nothing wrong, of course, with trying to discover authors' intentions. But if
there is such a thing as the meaning of the text, and if it's that we're trying to
discover, that's a different activity from trying to discover the author's _inten-
tions_ concerning meaning.

The reigning hermeneutic orthodoxy in the twentieth century has been
what I call _textual-sense interpretation_. The idea is that, when interpreting texts,
we should aim not at discovering one thing and another in the mental life of
the author, but at discovering the 'sense' of the text. To the best of my knowledge, everybody in the so-called hermeneutic tradition of philosophy is an
advocate of textual-sense interpretation. The honor of initiating this line of
thought, however, belongs to the so-called New Critics of the 1920s and
1930s, prominent among them being I.A. Richards, William Empson,
Cleanth Brooks, René Wellek and William Wimsatt – to name just a few.

At the heart of New Critical thought was the claim that a text, provided it's
genuinely a _work_ rather than a mere assemblage, is a unity; and that that unity is
a key factor in the determination of sense. Words have meanings in a language.
But when they are put together into a text, they regularly acquire new meanings, meanings-in-context. The idea is that the unity of the text as a whole
forces this word here to acquire a metaphorical meaning-in-context, that
word there to acquire a personification meaning-in-context, that paragraph
there to acquire an ironic meaning-in-context, and so on. The totality of the
meanings that the words have in the context of the text is then the _sense_ of the
text. It was an important part of New Critical doctrine to hold that some words
in a text remain ambiguous, and that often this is an important part of the contribution they make to the sense of the text. A famous example of this ambiguity is John Donne's line, in his address to God: 'When Thou hast done, thou
hast not done.' Likewise it was an important part of New Critical doctrine to
hold that metaphorical meanings are open-ended. The sense of a text is thus
not to be understood as fixed and closed, but as incorporating within itself a
certain amount of indeterminacy and openness.

The contribution of the hermeneutic philosophers to the textual-sense tradition of hermeneutics has been to give it a philosophical grounding rather different from anything one finds in the New Critics. Everybody who has any acquaintance at all with the hermeneutic tradition in twentieth-century philosophy is aware of the philosophical anthropology that lies at the heart of this grounding. Let me mention two aspects of that philosophical anthropology.

For one thing, the philosophers of the hermeneutic tradition all follow early Heidegger in giving centrality to the claim that it's in the nature of the human being always to be projecting itself ahead of itself in such modes as expecting, anticipating, planning, and so forth. We not only exist within time in the way that the traditional philosophers, and especially Kant, emphasized. We all live within time in this much more specific way of 'throwing' ourselves ahead of ourselves.

Secondly, all of us are shaped by the traditions in which we find ourselves – so much so that there's no possibility of extricating ourselves even for a time from these traditions so as to employ only our 'homogeneous human nature', as Gadamer calls it,[12] in the performance of some activity. In particular, we in our projectional nature are shaped by tradition; our anticipations and pre-judgments are not generically human anticipations and pre-judgments, but anticipations and pre-judgments shaped by tradition. All of this is as true for interpretation as for any other activity. We approach the task of interpretation with *praejudicia*, which are formed in us by our immersion in tradition rather than being the expression of some homogeneous human nature. The interpreting self is always an anticipating self whose anticipations are formed by tradition.

As I observed earlier, anyone who has read around in hermeneutic philosophy is aware of these philosophico-anthropological themes. What is regularly missed is another theme, which is just as important for my purposes here. The hermeneutic philosophers work with a certain ontology of the sense of the text that they inherited from Frege, by way of Husserl. The sense of the text has the ontological status, so they claim, of being what they call an 'ideal' entity. It's appropriate to hear echoes of Plato in this terminology – even though the sense of a text is a very different sort of entity from those with which Plato populated his realm of forms.

Let me briefly explain their thought. Suppose we assume that the right way to analyze belief and judgment is into a *content*, on the one hand, and the *stance* of belief or the *action* of judgment, on the other hand. The content of the belief that 2+3=5, is *that 2+3=5,* and the content of the judgment that today is warm and sunny, is *that today is warm and sunny.* Let us further suppose that the content of beliefs and judgments are *entities* of some sort, so that believing

---

[12] Gadamer, *Truth*, 232, and *passim*.

something consists of taking up the stance of belief toward that entity which one believes, and judging something consists of performing the action of judging on that entity which one judges to be true. Frege called such entities *Gedanken*, that is, *thoughts*. But as part of his crusade against psychologism in logic and mathematics he insisted, contrary to the connotations of the term, that *Gedanken* are not states of mind. He argued that whereas you and I can believe and assert the same *Gedanke*, we cannot share the same state of mind. Obviously *Gedanken* are also not physical entities. And neither, so Frege argued, are they to be identified with sentences, for the reason that two distinct sentences may express one and the same *Gedanke*. *Gedanken* have to be abstract entities – or as the hermeneutic tradition preferred to call them, *ideal* entities. What distinguishes them from such other abstract entities as properties is that they can be believed and asserted, and that they are all either true or false.

Return now to a passage from Gadamer that I quoted earlier. Gadamer is describing what he takes to be Schleiermacher's view:

> What is to be understood ... is not a shared thought about some subject matter, but individual thought that by its very nature is a free construct and the free expression of an individual being.[13]

In speaking here of a 'shared thought', Gadamer has in mind Frege's doctrine of *Gedanken*. That this is the case is somewhat clearer from the following passage, which occurs a few pages earlier in *Truth and Method*. Here Gadamer is expressing his own view as to the proper goal of interpretation:

> whenever an attempt is made to understand something ... there is reference to the truth that lies hidden in the text and must be brought to light. What is to be understood is, in fact, not a thought considered as part of another's life, but as a truth.[14]

Admittedly the allusion here to Frege's ontology of sense is still sufficiently elusive to allow for doubts on the matter. Later, however, in the section entitled 'Language as the Medium of Hermeneutic Experience', all is revealed. There we find Gadamer saying that 'What is stated in the text must be detached from all contingent factors and grasped in its full ideality, in which alone it has validity.' Speaking more elaborately on the matter, he says this:

> [The] capacity for being written down is based on the fact that speech itself shares in the pure ideality of the meaning that communicates itself in it. In writing, the meaning of what is spoken exists purely for itself, completely detached from all emotional

---

[13] Ibid., 188.
[14] Ibid., 185.

elements of expression and communication. A text is not to be understood as an expression of life but with respect to what it says. Writing is the abstract ideality of language. Hence the meaning of something written is fundamentally identifiable and repeatable. What is identical in the repetition is only what was actually deposited in the written record. This indicates that 'repetition' cannot be meant here in its strict sense. It does not mean referring back to the original source where something is said or written. The understanding of something written is not a repetition of something past but the sharing of a present meaning.[15]

Given these passages, and others to the same effect,[16] I think there can be no doubt whatsoever that in his theory of interpretation Gadamer is embracing Frege's ontology of sense. The same is true of Paul Ricœur. In his *Interpretation Theory*, Ricœur observes that

> for Frege and Husserl a 'meaning' … is not an idea that somebody has in his mind. It is not a psychic content, but an ideal object which can be identified and reidentified by different individuals at different times as being one and the same. By ideality they meant that the meaning of a proposition is neither a physical nor a psychic reality.[17]

Having thus described what he calls this 'anti-historicist' trend, Ricœur then explicitly allies himself with it. 'I must admit,' he says, 'that I take this anti-historicist trend into account in my own efforts and that I agree with its main presupposition concerning the objectivity of meaning in general.'[18]

A good deal of Derrida's writing in the first half of his career was devoted to polemicizing against textual-sense hermeneutics in general, and against this version of it in particular. From among the plethora of objections that he tossed up, let me single out the two that seem to me to be, if they can be made to stick, the most substantial.

Derrida rejects the Fregean-Husserlian ontology of sense that the entire twentieth-century hermeneutic tradition had embraced. This view of interpretation assumes, he says, that

> whether or not it is 'signified' or 'expressed,' whether or not it is 'interwoven' with a process of signification, 'meaning' is an intelligible or spiritual *ideality* which eventually can be united to the sensible aspect of a signifier that in itself it does not need.[19]

---

[15] Ibid., 392.

[16] Ibid., 390–95.

[17] Ricœur, *Interpretation Theory*, 90.

[18] Ibid., 91.

[19] Derrida, *Positions,* 31.

Language on this view is understood as the *expression* of an ideal entity. Likewise it is understood as

> communication, which in effect implies *a transmission charged with making pass, from one subject to another, the identity of a signified* object, of a *meaning* or of a *concept* rightfully separable from the process of passage and from the signifying operation.[20]

Derrida dismisses out of hand this ontology of sense. Meaning for him is purely adjectival. Sentences are meaningful, and that's the end of the matter. There isn't a set of entities existing independently of sentences waiting to become the meanings of sentences; there are no Fregean *Gedanken*.

Secondly, Derrida attacks the assumption of the textual-sense tradition that those texts that we all acknowledge to be genuine works, and not mere assemblages, are unified. When we actually look, we find almost all of them to be in one way or another disunified. This point, innocent though it may seem, strikes at the very heart of standard textual-sense hermeneutics, since, as I noted earlier, it was assumed that the meanings the words have in the text are what is required if, given the meanings they have individually in the language, they are all together to constitute a unity of meaning for the text. If we give up the assumption that texts do have a unified meaning, then obviously we can no longer argue that that unity requires that this word here be regarded as having a metaphorical meaning in the text, that those words there be regarded as having an ironic meaning in the text, and so forth. Give up the assumption of textual unity, and the fundamental strategy of the textual-sense tradition for determining textual sense is undercut.

My own evaluation of Derrida's polemic is that his ontological objection to textual-sense interpretation is both misguided and ungrounded. The Fregean-Husserlian ontology of sense has long seemed to me correct. I agree with Frege and Husserl that the right analysis of judgment is that, in judgment, there is something that one judges to be true that's to be distinguished from both that particular act and the sentence one uses to make the judgment.[21] Never (to the best of my knowledge) does Derrida do anything more than announce that the Fregean-Husserlian ontology is false; nowhere does he mount a substantive argument against it.

By contrast, Derrida's objection to the assumption that texts have unified senses seems to me very much on target. I myself wish to go farther, however: even if we did adopt the assumption of unity, we would still be left with indeterminacy of sense. This is most obvious in the case of irony. Jonathan Swift's *Modest Proposal* can either be read literally, in which case it proposes a

---

[20] Ibid., 23–4.
[21] See ch. 1 of my *On Universals*.

particularly gruesome way of solving the Irish population program (though no more so than some of the population policies actually implemented in the twentieth century), or it can be read ironically. Nothing in the text itself either eliminates or compels either of these two interpretations.[22]

But if one goes along with the traditional twentieth-century rejection of authorial-intention interpretation, and then also rejects textual-sense interpretation, what's left? Derrida's own proposal is what I call 'performance' interpretation, on the ground of its resemblance to the sort of interpretation that takes place in musical performance.[23] Just as a performing musician, given the specifications of a score, imagines and implements one of the many different ways of realizing the score, so the text-interpreter, given the words of the text and their meaning in the language, is to imagine and explore one and another of the many different things that might be said with these words in this order. Words do have meanings in the language, and this limits the possibilities. It is not that anything goes, contrary to what is often charged against the deconstructionists. But the range of possibilities is typically wide indeed.

I do not deny that performance interpretation may now and then be an interesting, and even important, thing to do. As I see it, our English word 'interpretation' covers a rather wide variety of quite distinct activities, with the consequence that the questions 'What is interpretation?' and 'What ought to be the goal of interpretation?' are both misguided. I reject the curious essentialism of the hermeneutic tradition on this point – an essentialism shared, oddly, by its deconstructionist opponents. Performance interpretation does count as a mode of interpretation; and sometimes it's worth doing.

To suggest that it should be the universal mode of interpretation, however, or even the standard mode, seems to me preposterous – or worse, mindless. One notices that Derrida himself, when discussing interpretations of his own texts, bridles at anything in the region of performance interpretation. Though he feels free to engage in a play of interpretation with the great texts of the Western tradition, he does not want the readers of his own texts to engage in a play of interpretation. He wants them to discern what he actually said.[24] And nobody, when reading scientific treatises or legal documents, or the agenda for a faculty meeting, thinks that performance interpretation is appropriate; nobody thinks it's appropriate to engage in a play of interpretation with such texts.

Where does this leave us? It leaves us with that mode of interpretation that, so it seems to me, all of us employ most of the time, and that all of us take for

---

[22] For more extensive and detailed argument of the point, see ch. 11 of my *Divine Discourse*.

[23] See ch. 10 of my *Divine Discourse*.

[24] See, e.g., *Positions*, 50 and 54.

granted to be basic most of the time. This is, namely, what I call *authorial-discourse* interpretation. Authorial-discourse interpretation is interpretation aimed at discerning what the speaker or writer said – that is to say, which illocutionary act he or she performed. Let me say again that our English word 'interpretation' covers a variety of different and legitimate activities; authorial-discourse interpretation is just one of those activities. What I claim for it is not that it is the only *right* mode of interpretation, nor that it and it alone is *truly* interpretation. What I claim is only that it's the mode of interpretation that most of us engage in most of the time, and that we usually assume to be basic to whatever other modes of interpretation we might want to practice.

Let it be noted that to aim at discerning the illocutionary act that someone performed is not to be identified with aiming to discern the illocutionary act that he or she *intended* to perform. Rather, it's to aim at discerning the one that he or she *did* perform, whether or not it was intended. We speak by operating a complex linguistic system. And the system, along with the various ways of operating it, are such that one may say something that one had no intention of saying – inadvertently, absent-mindedly, etc. – and one may fail, for one reason or another, to say something that one did intend to say. Authorial-discourse interpretation, to say it again, aims at discerning what the discourser *did* say. There's nothing wrong with trying to discern what someone intended to say, in contrast to what she did say; editors in publishing houses do that all the time. The two aims are distinct, however; and most of us are concerned most of the time to discern what the discourser did say. What seems to me mistaken in E.D. Hirsch's advocacy of authorial-intention interpretation, in his *Validity of Interpretation*, is not his argument that it's appropriate to aim at discerning authorial intention, but his claims of universality for such interpretation.

I suggest that the way out of our present plight is a hermeneutic of *authorial-discourse* interpretation – not of authorial-*intention* interpretation, to make the point once more, but of authorial-*discourse* interpretation. There's nothing wrong with reflecting on other modes of interpretation, and employing them now and then. But given that all of us most of the time are concerned to discern what our fellow human beings *said* with their words – which illocutionary act they performed – a hermeneutic of authorial-discourse interpretation calls to be placed at the center of our theoretical endeavors.

The Promise of Authorial–Discourse Interpretation for Biblical Interpretation

My objection to textual-sense interpretation is that there just is no such thing as *the* sense of a text; textual-sense interpretation rests on a false assumption.

That's not the situation for authorial-intention and performance interpretation – for these, as I've been saying, are coherent modes of interpretation. And both are sometimes worth practicing. My objection is not to these modes as such, but rather to the universalizing claims made by those who have developed a hermeneutic of these modes. Interpretation aimed at discovering the author's intentions, and interpretation that consists in asking what the words of the text might possibly be used to say, are both relatively minor activities in human affairs. The activity of interpretation aimed at discerning what the author (or editor) did in fact say by inscribing the words of the text is far more prominent.

It might just be, however, that though authorial-discourse interpretation may be the way forward for hermeneutic theory in general – a way of breaking out of the sterile impasse among defenders of authorial-intention interpretation, of textual-sense interpretation, and of performance interpretation – it's not the way forward for biblical interpretation. So let me now move on to indicate why I think it does in fact represent an important way forward for biblical interpretation.

I hold that the full promise for biblical interpretation of authorial-discourse interpretation, and of its corollary, speech-act theory, is opened up for us only if we think in terms of what I call *double-agency discourse* – something never considered, so far as I know, in standard speech-act theoretical discussions. What I have in mind is those cases in which one person performs some illocutionary act by way of another person performing either some locutionary or some illocutionary act. Paradigmatic cases are those in which one person has been deputized to speak on behalf of another, so that the latter performs an illocutionary act by way of the former performing some locutionary act (and perhaps some illocutionary act as well), as well as those cases in which one person appropriates the discourse of another – that is, cases in which one person performs some illocutionary act by way of appropriating the illocutionary act of another.[25] Good examples of this latter sort of double-agency discourse are the seconding of parliamentary motions and the approving quotation of what someone else has said.

Speech-act theory, as applied to the special case of double-agency discourse, enables us to understand Scripture as the manifestation of God speaking by way of human beings speaking, and then of interpreting accordingly. Or to use the jargon: it enables us to understand Scripture as the manifestation of God having performing illocutionary acts by way of human beings having performed locutionary and illocutionary acts, and then of interpreting accordingly by the employment of a double hermeneutic.

---

[25] For elaboration of these two modes of double-agency discourse, see ch. 3 of my *Divine Discourse*.

When I say that speech-act theory as applied to the special case of double-agency discourse enables us to understand how it is that God speaks by way of Scripture, I use the word 'speaks' literally. The theory enables us to understand how it is *literally* the case that God performs illocutionary actions. The biblical claim that God speaks has traditionally been articulated by theologians in terms of a doctrine of divine revelation, of divine inspiration, or, as in Barth's case, in terms of a doctrine of divine efficacy in evoking faith. I submit that none of these activities is to be identified with God speaking; none is to be identified with God doing such things as promising, assuring, commanding and asserting. Revealing something is not the same as saying something, inspiring someone to say something is likewise not the same as saying it, and evoking a response in someone with words is also not the same as saying something. I cannot detail the argumentation to back up these claims here – the argumentation can be found in my *Divine Discourse*. I must content myself with saying that, unlike these three alternatives, speech-act theory as applied to double-agency discourse enables us to understand how it can be that God speaks, or discourses – *literally so!* – by way of Scripture. I know of no other approach that has the same potential.

And that is the fundamental advantage for biblical interpretation of speech-act theory as applied to double-agency discourse. For by enabling us to understand how it can be that God speaks by way of Scripture, it opens up to us the possibility of interpreting Scripture for what God said and says thereby – the possibility of interpreting Scripture for divine discourse.

This advantage also carries with it two additional, and extremely important, advantages. It offers us a way of understanding the unity of Scripture at a deep level, and thereby opens up before us the possibility of interpreting Scripture in the light of that unity. It's my impression, gained by looking at academic biblical interpretation from the outside, that a good deal of its twentieth-century history has consisted of one attempt after another to honor the church's traditional conviction that Scripture is a unity. The program of biblical theology was one such attempt, the program of canon criticism, as exemplified in the work of my colleague Brevard Childs, is another, and so forth. If all of Scripture is God's deputized and/or appropriated discourse, then it's obvious wherein its fundamental unity lies: in its totality Scripture is God's book. It is not God's *collected works*; it is God's *single* work.

Given this conviction, our interpretation is then to be conducted in this light. It may well be, of course, that there are also important unities to be discovered on the human level of Scripture. It may be, for example, that there is a unified biblical theology that comes to expression, or that there are internal indications that these books belong together in a canon; certainly it is the case that there are important intra-textual references and allusions that tie these books together. The presence, and then the discovery, of such modes of unity is not to be sneezed at; nonetheless, the most fundamental thing that unites Scripture will be that, in its totality, it is God's book.

It may be asked how Scripture can possibly be God's single book if it consists, as it does, of some sixty-six or more individual human books. If God speaks by way of the humanly-authored books of Scripture, and if there are sixty-six or so of these in Scripture, doesn't it just follow that there are some sixty-six books of God? Doesn't it just follow that Scripture is not God's (single) work but God's collected works, God's *opera omnia*? My answer is that it does not follow. Consider an analogy: it's entirely possible for me to compose a work of my own by putting together, in a certain order, texts that I have assembled from a number of sources. If so, then these texts, which originally were to be read separately, or as part of some other context, must now be read all together as parts of *my* book, *my* text, *my* single work – for that's what they now are.

A second important advantage of speech-act theory as applied to double-agency discourse for biblical interpretation is that it enables us to move beyond the sterile controversies over infallibilism. It enables us, in our interpretation of Scripture, to acknowledge the infallibility of God's Word without ascribing a similar infallibility to the human words. When I appropriate someone else's discourse for my own, it may well be that I don't accept, and don't wish or expect to be understood as accepting, absolutely everything that the other person says. Similarly, when one person functions as the deputy of another it may well be that the deputizer, if he heard or read what his deputy said, would not accept everything in it. So too then, the fact that the human authors of Scripture express various false beliefs does not prevent God from nonetheless infallibly speaking by way of what they say.

Interpreting Scripture for Divine Discourse is 'Dogmatic' Interpretation

Let me highlight a feature of divine-discourse interpretation of Scripture that will give many, if not most, of the biblical interpreters working within the academy pause in employing this mode of interpretation – whatever its advantages. Interpreting Scripture for divine discourse is an inherently and unabashedly 'dogmatic' mode of interpretation.

In calling this mode of interpretation 'dogmatic' I mean to allude to Gadamer's narrative of the origins of modern hermeneutics. Gadamer follows Dilthey's lead in construing hermeneutic theory from the Reformers up to Schleiermacher as the attempt to free the interpretation of Scripture from dogmatic assumptions so as to allow Scripture to speak for itself. Dogma is to *emerge from* our interpretation of Scripture rather than *governing* our interpretation.

The last dogmatic assumption to be surrendered was that Scripture is a unity. When the eighteenth-century theorists Semler and Ernesti argued that, rather than assuming the unity of Scripture in our interpretation, we should allow such unity as there is to emerge from our interpretation, then finally Scripture and the interpretation thereof came into their own. Then finally, in the words of Dilthey quoted by Gadamer, there is the 'liberation of interpretation from dogma'.[26] Then, 'when it [finally] ceases serving a dogmatic purpose', 'hermeneutics comes into its own'.[27] Rather than interpreting Scripture in the light of dogma, we are to interpret Scripture in the light of itself. What this amounts to, in Schleiermacher's thought, is the hermeneutic circle: we interpret the parts in the light of the whole and the whole in the light of the parts.

Gadamer interprets this campaign against dogmatic interpretation of Scripture by the seventeenth- and eighteenth-century theorists as tacitly assuming that it's possible and desirable to liberate ourselves from tradition and conduct our interpretation of Scripture (and other texts) by employing nothing but the deliverances of our 'homogeneous human nature'. And that assumption is one of the main points of his attack, as indeed it has been in some of my own writings – for example, in *Reason within the Bounds of Religion*. Gadamer argues that interpretation is unavoidably like the dogmatic interpretation against which the seventeenth- and eighteenth-century theorists polemicized in that, when interpreting, we do not simply drink in what's there but employ *praejudicia* that we bring with us to our interpretation, these *praejudicia* having been planted in us by our induction into tradition.

When I said that in calling interpretation for divine discourse 'dogmatic' interpretation I meant to be alluding to Gadamer's discussion, I did not mean to be alluding to Gadamer's claim that our interpreting selves are always tradition-shaped selves – though I vigorously agree with that. I meant to be alluding instead to that long tradition of biblical interpretation in which one employs distinctly theological convictions in one's interpretation. A good many academic biblical interpreters would nowadays accept Gadamer's argument that the interpreting self is always, and even necessarily, a tradition-formed self; what most of them would not be willing to do, however, is employ explicitly theological convictions in their interpretation. It's my impression that even many of those who believe that Scripture is the Word of God would be hesitant to employ, if they would not refuse to employ, that conviction in their interpretation. Given its dogmatic character, divine-discourse interpretation seems to them too parochially Christian a project for good standing in the academy.

---

[26] Gadamer, *Truth*, 176.
[27] Ibid., 177.

I can give such people a modicum of reassurance – though no more than that. Interpreting Scripture for divine discourse requires a double hermeneutic: first one interprets these writings so as to discern the human discourse of which they are the trace; then, and only then, does one move on to interpret for what God said by way of this human discourse. If you make a point by way of approvingly citing what someone else has said, then for me to discern the point you are making I must first discern what the writer you quoted was saying. The guild of academic biblical scholars, insofar as it has engaged in biblical interpretation, has proved skillful at the practice of what I call the 'first' hermeneutic. If there's to be divine-discourse interpretation of Scripture, that practice will have to be employed in pretty much the way it is presently employed by its best practitioners. It's only when we move to the second hermeneutic that explicit use of the theological conviction that Scripture is God's book comes into play. This is not to say that the first hermeneutic can be practiced in neutral fashion – whatever that might be. It's only to say that in the first hermeneutic one does not employ that theological conviction.

Objections and Answers to Objections

Not everyone has immediately warmed to the project of authorial-discourse interpretation, whether it take the specific form of divine-discourse interpretation or not. Objections have been offered. Let me cite three of those and suggest, all too briefly, how I would answer them.

One aspect of authorial-discourse interpretation which I haven't yet mentioned is this: confronted with the words of a text, if we are to determine what an author said by way of inscribing those words we have to ask what it is that he would have wanted to say by way of inscribing these words in the situation in which he did inscribe them. If there were a one-to-one correspondence between locutionary and illocutionary acts, there would be no need to pose such a question – from the locutionary act we could move straight off to the illocutionary act. Obviously there is no such correspondence. The very same sentence that a mad person can use literally to make a mad assertion can be used metaphorically by a sane person to assert a profound truth. So given the sentence, how do I tell which way to go? The answer is that if I know the writer to be a mad person, I go one way; if I know him to be a sane person of insight, I go the other way.

An implication is that interpretation is impossible in the absence of knowledge about the author. If we know nothing about the author – absolutely nothing – then we have no way to determine, for example, which words are being used strictly and literally and which are being used in one and another tropic fashion. Obviously this point is closely similar to Gadamer's point, that the *praejudicia* we bring with us to interpretation not only obstruct correct interpretation but, more importantly, enable it. Where I differ from Gadamer is over what it is that one must bring to interpretation so as to enable it. Gadamer, as an advocate of textual-sense interpretation, holds that we must bring with us pre-judgments concerning meaning. I hold that we must bring with us convictions concerning the author – specifically, convictions as to what he would have wanted to say with these words in the situation in which he inscribed them.

Obviously it's also true that we learn things about authors from texts; we don't just bring things we already know to our interpretation of the text. Things we know about the author enable us to interpret a text. From that interpretation we then typically learn new things about the author and in turn use that new knowledge to interpret the text more closely and also to interpret other texts by the same author. That knowledge we then in turn use – and so it goes, on and on. It's rather like Schleiermacher's circle – except that a spiral is a better metaphor for the process than a circle.

This thesis concerning authorial-discourse interpretation has given rise to two objections. Though both apply to authorial-discourse interpretation generally, let me cite the first in the form it takes for biblical interpretation. It is objected that, for many of the biblical books, we don't know who the author was.

The fact cited is indisputably correct; but it doesn't constitute an objection. One can know a great deal about the author of a text without knowing *who* the author was. Concerning even the most anonymous of texts we know that the author was a human being, acquainted with other human beings, living on the face of the earth, in need of food and water for sustenance, and so forth. In the case of the authors of biblical books we know a great deal more than these generic facts. What we know about them will seldom if ever be enough to enable us to interpret all passages with confidence; it's enough, though, to enable us to interpret many passages with confidence, and it's always enough to rule out certain interpretations as unacceptable.

The application to interpreting for divine discourse of the thesis concerning the role of knowledge of the author is that such interpretation requires knowledge of God – specifically, knowledge which enables us to determine with more or less confidence what God would have wanted to say by appropriating these texts. And this causes some to hesitate over accepting my proposal concerning biblical interpretation. Don't we learn everything we know about God *from* Scripture? I think not. Reliable interpretation for divine discourse can only occur in the context of some knowledge of God. If we knew nothing of God, absolutely nothing, if God were *ganz anders*, more alien to us than the most alien Martian, how could we possibly know when God was speaking literally and when metaphorically, when ironically and when non-ironically? We couldn't even use, in our interpretation, the principle that God does not contradict himself. Here, too, there's the hermeneutic spiral.

Another objection sometimes cited against authorial-discourse interpretation is that, unlike textual-sense interpretation, it cannot take adequate account of the richness and openness of the meaning of texts. Presumably the assumption behind this objection is that when one performs some illocutionary act, one fully understands everything about that act. But surely the assumption is false. Suppose I use the sentence 'the paint is peeling' to make an observation about the present fate of some organization. Then the illocutionary act I have performed is that of asserting, about the organization, that the paint is peeling. No doubt I have *some* sense of what it is I am saying when I perform this act; but why assume that I have a *lucid* grasp of *all* that I am saying? We regularly say more than we know we're saying, and rather often we say things other than what we think we're saying. Illocutionary acts are just as open-ended, and as little determined in their character by what their performers think their character to be, as textual-senses were assumed to be. The linguistic system that we use for discoursing has, as it were, a life of its own.

Should We Practice Divine-Discourse Interpretation?

The fundamental question before us, then, is whether we should practice divine-discourse interpretation in our interpretation of Scripture. The advantages seem to me clear, the objections, insubstantial. But the advantages will seem worth gaining only if one believes that Scripture is in fact a medium of divine discourse. Everything turns on that. If one believes that God spoke by way of these human words, and continues to do so, then one will want to practice divine-discourse interpretation. If one does not believe that, one will reject such interpretation.

The church over the centuries has explored a number of ways of understanding God's relation to these writings; to think of them as the medium of God's very speech is only one of those ways. As with most substantial theological issues, there's no knock-down argument one way or the other; the matter can be decided only by bringing all relevant considerations into the picture and then judging which construal best handles all of those considerations. As for myself, I do believe that Scripture is an instrument of divine discourse. But defending that conviction would require a theological, not a philosophical, essay. And in any case, my project for this present essay was limited to laying out the promise of speech-act theory for biblical interpretation. Whether that promise should be grasped, and in particular, whether it should be grasped in the way I have proposed, is a different – and let me say,

Nicholas Wolterstorff

more important –matter. For that hinges on whether Scripture is in fact, and literally so, the Word of the Lord.

Bibliography

Derrida, J., *Positions* (trans. A. Bass; Chicago: University of Chicago Press, 1981)

Hirsch, E.D., *Validity of Interpretation* (New Haven and London: Yale University Press, 1967)

Gadamer, H-G., *Truth and Method* (trans. and rev. J. Weinsheimer and D.G. Marshall; New York: Continuum, 2nd rev. edn, 1993)

Ricœur, P., *Interpretation Theory* (Forth Worth: Texas Christian University Press, 1976)

Schleiermacher, F., *Hermeneutics and Criticism* (trans. and ed. A. Bowie; Cambridge: CUP, 1998)

Wolterstorff, N., *Divine Discourse* (Cambridge: CUP, 1995)

—, *On Universals* (Chicago: University of Chicago Press, 1970)

—, *Reason within the Bounds of Religion* (Grand Rapids: Eerdmans, 1976)

4

How to Be a Postmodernist and Remain a Christian

A Response to Nicholas Wolterstorff

Mary Hesse

I once wrote a paper entitled 'How to be a postmodernist without being a feminist', and I feel that my problem arising from this Consultation is how to be a postmodernist and remain a Christian. You will detect that I come down somewhat on the postmodernist side of the polarized debate about hermeneutic theory.

Nicholas Wolterstorff has given us a very clear and interesting account of the types of hermeneutic interpretation as he sees them in recent history. First I should like to make a comment on the *textual–sense* interpretation. Wolterstorff ascribes this to the influence of Frege, and it also, of course, lies at the foundation of modern anglophone or analytic philosophy, with its univocal (non-variable) linguistic 'meanings' or 'senses'. As Wolterstorff rightly points out, it implies a *metaphysics* of sense. Meanings are reified, and make up ideal propositions, which have one and only one sense, and are either true or false. There is very little concession to any kind of ambiguity, metaphor, or other trope of language within this account of meaning interpretation.

On the other side of the polarized debate lies a Derrida-like *performance* interpretation where no 'right' understanding of meaning exists. The reader reads as he or she will, and in its most extreme form we find Feyerabend's famous phrase 'anything goes'.

These two positions echo very closely many of the long-running debates within modern philosophy. For example, in philosophy of science they appear in controversies between realism and relativism in theoretical ontology, and between universalizable method and pragmatics in epistemology. In general hermeneutics they are the polarities between standard anglophone logical analysis and Wittgensteinian language-games and forms of life, with their internal and unchallengeable, but relative, truths and values. The polarity is neatly summed up as that between Wittgenstein's early (and later rejected) *Tractatus*, and his *Philosophical Investigations* and subsequent writings.

With regard to Frege's idealism of 'sense', Wolterstorff regards Derrida's polemic against it as 'both mistaken and ungrounded'. I am not sure it is quite fair to say that Derrida has no arguments against Frege, but in any case it seems to me that there certainly are arguments against his metaphysics of textual sense. Frege's theory is itself descended from the metaphysics of the so-called 'Adamic theory' of the seventeenth century. According to this view there is, in principle, an ideal language – the language in which Adam named the animals – and this language would be a perfect mirror of reality. There would be a one-to-one relation between nouns and natural kinds of substances, and between verbs and happenings, and the ideal grammar would accurately reflect the law-like connections between these things. The theory implies a 'fall of language', that is, the collapse of these language-reality correspondences which Adam knew about in the garden, and which were lost in his Fall and in the confusion of languages at Babel. Redemption was to be looked for in science conducted in the spirit of Francis Bacon and the Royal Society of London. The realistic ontology of seventeenth-century natural philosophy was a version of the Adamic theory, and among its mostly Christian practitioners it was therefore believed to be an essentially religious enterprise, with corresponding persuasive power.

Apart from its mythological trimmings, the theory is a very strong ontology of the world, and is still powerful as the widespread belief that science is the only rationally based system of truths to which we can attain. It was accepted by Frege, and is presupposed in modern realist philosophy of science with its belief in the existence of ideal true theories and universalizable causal laws.

I believe, however, that in regard to science it is a theory that has been conclusively refuted in what I will call the Kuhn-Feyerabend revolution of the 1960s. This revolution introduced the concepts of theory-ladenness and the instability and incommensurability of theories, and particularly emphasized the general openness and creativity of scientific language and its metaphorical character – all of which is incompatible with an Adamic or Fregian ontology. The revolution in philosophy of science was in fact the forerunner for a postmodern recognition of creativity, openness and metaphoricality in discourse in general.

Wolterstorff accepts this feature of postmodernism in his paper where he says that a condition for the success of any theory of interpretation must be some recognition of the ambiguity and variability of sense within all natural language texts. In this respect he agrees that even the performance interpretation may be useful in some circumstances. But he considers that none of the earlier theories of meaning are *universalizable* as theories of interpretation. Consequently he proposes an alternative in terms of a theory of *authorial discourse*. I take from his paper the short definition of what an authorial discourse interpretation should be: it should discover 'what authors did in fact say in the text' (not what they *intended* to say, and perhaps failed, but what they actually said). Or, as Wolterstorff also expresses it, 'which illocutionary act they performed'.

Authorial discourse interpretation necessarily introduces the concept of *speech acts* because it recognizes that what speakers in fact say need not be *propositions* ('locutionary acts') which have direct relations of truth or falsity with the world, but may encompass all kinds of speech acts which have no straightforward truth-value: wishes, commands, fictions, performances, value judgements, and many others.

Speech-act theory has indeed provided a much more flexible and realistic analysis of language in general than did the straitjacket of Fregean 'senses'. But there is a problem with it that did not occur to its founders, who simply adopted the Fregean theory of propositions for *locutionary* speech acts. The problem occurs as soon as one asks about the status of the classic *tropes* of language (metaphor, metonymy, irony, etc.). Are these speech acts locutionary or illocutionary? In other words, are they to be accorded propositional truth-values or not? In the strict Fregean interpretation, espoused for example by Searle, these tropes are *i*llocutions with no truth-value. But in all serious natural language texts, and pre-eminently in Scripture, metaphor and the other tropes are pervasive. No theory of interpretation that neglects them can be adequate for biblical hermeneutics.

Can authorial-discourse theory overcome this limitation upon textual-sense theory? The problem arises with speech acts that have the *form* of propositions, in that they must surely be understood to have some relation to *truth*, but which are couched in metaphoric or other tropic language for which criteria of truth are not clear-cut. Take the biblical account of John's baptism of Jesus, when 'A voice came out of heaven'. The writer states that something happened, and a modern interpreter might wish to say that his statement is a metaphorical description of whatever it was that witnesses experienced. And yet it is important to the understanding of the New Testament to consider whether the statement is in some sense *true*.

Wolterstorff rightly objects to the implication of textual-sense interpretation that there is a single correct sense of a text, and he implies that authorial-discourse theory does not have the corresponding implication of a single fact of the matter of what an author actually said. There is room for alternative interpretations. But in addition to trying to determine *what* the writer said, we are also, in the case of metaphoric speech acts, asking whether what he said was *true*. There is no problem here for the textual-sense interpretation, because for a proposition there is a single univocal sense, determined by the ontological fact of the matter, whether or not we can actually determine in reality what this fact is. In the case of my example, textual-sense commentators might conclude that the report 'A voice came from heaven' is literally *false*, and conclude that sense can only be made out of such biblical accounts by interpreting them as fictitious narratives. This matters, because Christian ministers have congregations who want to ask, 'After all this historical criticism and literary interpretation, did God really speak out of heaven? ... did they really cross the Red Sea?', and so on. The greater part of the biblical narrative suggests such questions, except in a minority of cases where we appear to be dealing with verifiable historical facts.

The authorial-discourse account requires some 'ontology' or criteria of truth, other than the Fregean ontology of the textual-sense interpretation. Wolterstorff does something to provide this in the case of Scripture, although the question of 'truth' does not become explicit in his paper. He explains how he finds authorial-discourse theory usefully applicable as a way of understanding how the Bible can be, as a unity, 'God's speech act', even though it is mediated through fallible human writers. He develops a *double hermeneutic*, which depends on the fact that one person can perform a speech act by appropriating in some way the speech acts of others. Thus a Christian may adopt the ontological premise that God speaks (performs illocutionary acts) through the Bible by using 'what the writers say' in the text for his own purposes.

The first stage of interpretation is to interpret what is said by the human writers themselves, given whatever can be found out about their own languages and historical contexts. About this stage Wolterstorff says,

> The guild of academic biblical scholars, insofar as it has engaged in biblical interpretation, has proved skillful at the practice of what I call the 'first' hermeneutic ... that practice will have to be employed in pretty much the way it is presently employed by its best practitioners.

The 'second hermeneutic' is then the theological task of discerning what *God* is saying through the medium of these interpreted human texts. The idea seems to be that the first hermeneutic can be carried out in purely 'humanist' terms of the secular academy, without any theological underpinning, but that the second stage involves some kind of commitment to a Christian ontology, at least in terms of the existence and some of the characteristics of God. Moreover this commitment arises not just from within the biblical text itself (which would involve the hermeneutic circle), but at least partly from other human experience.

A relative distinction between the first and second hermeneutic can certainly be discerned in the practice of biblical scholarship. But I would question whether the distinction is sharp, particularly in the light of postmodern recognition of the 'theory-ladenness' of all theoretical endeavours. An adequate 'first hermeneutic' of, for example, the story of the Red Sea, would surely have to see it as a type and metaphor for what God performs throughout the history of Israel, and indeed throughout all human history. Additionally, the narrative has become the focus for what is believed and re-enacted in the rituals of believing communities. A truth-claim is therefore indirectly being made for beliefs about the character and actions of God even in the attempt to determine what the writer's speech act was. How far the writer himself participated in this whole complex of theological belief is forever impossible to know, and therefore first and second hermeneutics necessarily become intermingled.

This means that any Christian (or Jewish) interpretation of the Bible has to face the objection that the authorial-discourse interpretation is, in Wolterstorff's words, 'inherently and unabashedly dogmatic' and therefore has no place in objective study. In defence against this objection, Wolterstorff refers to Gadamer's claim that all interpretation is informed by pre-judgements arising from our linguistic and cultural traditions, and that in the history of biblical hermeneutics these have necessarily been theological in character.

Gadamer, however, did not only speak about 'dogmatic' pre-judgements, but also about dialogue between interpenetrating horizons of such judgements, where we negotiate meanings between shifting contexts and perhaps shift some of the pre-judgements in the process. Habermas also talks about this kind of 'dialogical discourse' in opposition to the 'monological discourse' of univocal meanings and rigorously deductive argument. If biblical interpretation is to take its place in our postmodernist academies and their surrounding secular societies, is not the model of 'fusion of horizons' a better one than the presupposition that the whole Bible is (Wolterstorff says *literally* is!) God's unitary speech act? This very strong ontology is bound to suggest an internal debate among biblical scholars, theologians and other believers, rather than interpretations that can face and impinge upon secular culture. Perhaps I am asking for apologetics rather than theology here, but perhaps, again, the two cannot be totally separated.

Fergus Kerr, in his paper at the Consultation,[1] quotes Wittgenstein to the effect that he, Wittgenstein, cannot believe that Jesus will come to judge him, and that he could only believe this if he were living quite differently – that is I suppose, in Wittgenstein's terms, if he were living in a different life-form and language-game. Is there not a sense in which this applies to all of us? When we hear a Russian choir singing the Creed, for a moment we believe. If we lived in a monastic community, or in medieval Rome, or in an African charismatic

---

[1] Fergus Kerr gave the following paper at the Consultation – 'Naming Christ: Traditional Theology since Critical Historical Exegesis'.

church, we would perhaps believe most of the time. But, living as most of us do, belief is a continually collapsing act of faith. Such an act of faith is regarded by the secular world as irrational self-indulgence, and yet, as Craig Bartholomew reminds us, even the secular world admits that a Solzhenitsyn, a Havel, a Steiner, or a Luther are constrained to make a believing stand on some non-negotiable truths. Whatever our circumstances or differences, some of us would claim to have similar experiences within the Christian corpus of belief. We are not really in a Wittgensteinian situation of mutually incomprehensible language-games, but rather within Gadamer's horizons, which can be fused at the edges, often with the effect of changing both sides. Perhaps the bottom line of faith for a postmodern Christian should be like Gamaliel's: if it be of God, it will persist, and if not, not.

5

'Behind' and 'In Front Of' the Text

Language, Reference and Indeterminacy

Anthony C. Thiselton

The Metaphorical Force of 'Behind' and 'In Front Of' in Hermeneutics

Most of us are familiar with the metaphor of 'reading between the lines'. It might well be taken as a description for the trained critical faculty of reading texts with a measure of both intuitive insight and political or theological suspicion that looks for a subtext concerning what the text or its author was genuinely 'after'. Such hermeneutical training characterizes most professional or academic courses in biblical studies in universities or seminaries. To take a text at its face value can be misleading, certainly in such genre as mass-advertising or in texts of political rhetoric.

The metaphor of 'what lies behind it' identifies the critical approach which characterizes the suspicious stance of the detective who seeks to 'understand' a situation that involves interpersonal or communicative inter-subjective events where one or more of the participants may have hidden motives or goals. These may be either consciously or unconsciously concealed. R.G. Collingwood, the historian and philosopher of history, identifies the difference between the less productive question: 'Did you murder the victim?' and the more fruitful one: 'What happened to the third button which seems to be torn from your jacket?' Both Gadamer, in his philosophical hermeneutics, and Bultmann, in his theological hermeneutics, write approvingly of Collingwood's attention to a 'logic of question and answer'. Gadamer insists:

Thus a person who wants to understand must question what lies behind what is said. He must understand it as an answer to a question. If we go back *behind* what is said, then we inevitably ask questions *beyond* what it said ... Almost the only person I find a link with here is R.G. Collingwood.[1]

The notion of reaching back 'behind' the text arose, however, in a broader context and in close connection with a specific world-view. It was in the era of the dawn of modern hermeneutical theory in part in the eighteenth century, but more especially in the early nineteenth century, as the era of rationalism gave way to the era of Romanticism. In his search for 'Correct Interpretation' (1742), Johann Martin Chladenius (1710–59) recognized that different people describe or write from different perspectives or viewpoints (*Sehe-Punkt*). A monarchist and a revolutionary may describe the same political event in different terms; even three spectators of a battle may report the event from different angles of view. Hence 'behind' our understanding of the event must lie a recognition of the part played by perspective (*Sehe-Punkt*).[2] Only thus can we reach a 'right' (*richtige*) interpretation.

Chladenius is still writing at that point, however, within a largely rationalist frame. With Friedrich Schleiermacher (1768–1834) and Philip August Boeckh (1785–1867) came an insight associated with the Romanticist movement and with Herder. Not only 'correct' understanding, they said, but also more personal 'divinatory' or intuitive understanding of authors and text, entailed the attempt to recapture the vision that prompted the author to write or to express the vision through some medium. 'Understanding' (*Verstehen*) is not simply scrutinizing a text as an 'object' of enquiry: it is more akin to listening to, and thereby coming to understand, a friend. The interpreter must step out of his or her own frame of reference and try to place himself or herself 'in the position of the author'.[3] I have urged elsewhere that to reduce Schleiermacher's hermeneutics to a system of mere genetic historical reconstruction does violence to the subtlety and complexity of his carefully nuanced and dialectical work.[4] On the other hand, Schleiermacher did define the role of 'New Testament Introduction' as a necessary way of reaching behind the text to 'understand' similarities, differences, genre, motivations and goals that the text presupposed.[5]

---

[1] Gadamer, *Truth*, 370 (emphasis his). Cf. Bultmann, *History*, 130; and Collingwood, *Autobiography* and *Idea*.

[2] Chladenius, *Einleitung*, sect. 308 and 312.

[3] Schleiermacher, *Hermeneutics*, 112–13. See also the new rev. edn, Schleiermacher, *Hermeneutics and Criticism*.

[4] Thiselton, *New Horizons*, 204–55, 474–76 and 558–64.

[5] Schleiermacher, *Hermeneutics*, 38; cf. further, 107 and 113.

Schleiermacher's younger contemporary, Philip August Boeckh, whom Schleiermacher also taught in Berlin, emphasized still more strongly that to reach through 'behind' the text provided clues to arrive at an understanding of the subject matter which might even surpass the conscious awareness and explicit formulations of the author.[6] Both writers had in view not antiquarian research for its own sake, but the deployment of historical research precisely for the sake of reaching the fullest possible understanding on the part of the present generation. Many considered, and some still consider, that Boeckh's *Encyclopedia and Methodology of the Philological Sciences* represents a paradigm of the classical-humanist model of hermeneutics.

Nevertheless, a reaction against this approach took place with the rise of literary and linguistic formalism that captured attention, especially in the United States and Russia, from the 1930s to the 1950s. Some of its origins can be traced to the Russian formalism of the Moscow Linguistic Circle of the 1920s, especially Roman Jakobson's approach to language as a virtually self-contained linguistic system. In turn, the notion of 'meaning' as a product generated by 'differences' within the linguistic or semiotic system, which took the form of semiotic 'forces', drew on the work of Ferdinand de Saussure's *Course in General Linguistics*, published in 1913. Under the pressures of Stalinism Jakobson moved to Prague, where the Prague School approached 'meaning' as the interplay of linguistic forces *within* the text itself. Questions about origins and authors appeared to import intrusive questions about human emotions, agencies and actions that allegedly distorted the pure world of linguistic 'science', even if Schleiermacher had insisted that understanding and hermeneutics was an 'art'.

In the West this formalist, systemic, emphasis set in motion what became known in the early 1940s as 'the New Criticism'. This term appears to have originated in John C. Ransom's work *The New Criticism* (1941). The 'literariness' of linguistic and poetic forces took the centre of the stage. By the end of this decade René Wellek and Austin Warren wrote *Theory of Literature* (1949), which became hugely dominant as a textbook for literary theory in America for the next twenty years. In particular, these authors dismissed the emphasis associated with Boeckh on the author and the author's intention as 'quite mistaken … The total meaning … cannot be defined merely in terms of its meaning for the author and his contemporaries'.[7] In the same vein, William Wimsatt and Monroe Beardsley specifically attacked what they termed 'The Intentional Fallacy' (1954).[8] Two slogans which emerged from such an attack took the form of: 'The Text and Nothing But the Text', and 'The Autonomy

---

[6] Boeckh, *Interpretation*.
[7] Welleck and Warren, *Theory*, 42.
[8] Wimsatt and Beardsley, 'Fallacy'.

of the Text'. The text was seen as an autonomous world of literary, poetic, linguistic, semantic, stylistic and semiotic forces.

The metaphor of reaching '*behind*' the text now seemed to have been over-taken by a preoccupation with the world '*within*' the text. Biblical studies inevi-tably continued for a time with the traditional classical–humanist model, although in due course the dividends of an approach which could prove its worth specifically for some *narrative* and *poetic* texts began to make an impact, especially in Old Testament studies of these genres. The problems which arose from a move away from the more traditional model did not fully emerge until some biblical specialists who had been trained in literary studies adopted the view that formalism, the new criticism and the genetic 'fallacy' began to accord to a phrase or fashion the status of a hermeneutical *dogma*. A number of other-wise respected biblical scholars began to suggest that we now needed a so-called 'paradigm-shift' from history to literature. Little attention was given to the fact that Ransom, Wellek and Warren, and most of the 'new' critics, were concerned with those specific *literary* and *poetic* devices and forces which genu-inely shed light on texts of a particular genre. We may suggest, by way of example, that to view the book of Jonah as a virtually *self-contained satire* on incoherent self-centred theoretical theistic belief is more 'to the point' than speculating about its possible authorship and origins. However, to fail to look 'behind' the text of 1 Corinthians, or 'behind' *as well as* 'within' the world of the Gospels would fatally detach text from the extra-textual world of reality. This would also result in missing nuances about Corinth and Paul, or about Jerusalem and Galilee, which are fundamental for understanding.

In due course, even literary theorists came to recognize that the notion of an 'autonomous' text is an illusion. Its supposed 'scientific objectivity' is deceptive and false. At one level it cannot be detached from the world of human life and reality; at another level, as Chladenius had urged in 1742, the perspective (*Sehe-Punkt*) of readers plays a serious role in determining what counts as significant in viewing a supposedly autonomous text. Hence linguistic and semiotic structuralism collapsed into post-structuralism, and formalism collapsed, in effect, into reader-response theory. Thus Wolfgang Iser drew upon Roman Ingarden (and ultimately Husserl) for the view that readers 'complete' what counts as 'the text' by 'filling in' presuppositions and assumptions that are not explicitly 'given'. Iser regarded the text (in practice more faithfully to Saussure than many who claimed his patronage) as merely potentially meaningful until readers appropriated, completed and 'actualized' it. Iser writes: 'The text represents a potential effect that is realized in the reading process'.[9] 'Actualization' results from 'interaction' between the text and the reader.[10]

---

[9] Iser, *Reading*, ix.

[10] Ibid., 21.

In biblical studies, it was eventually recognized that such an emphasis accorded well with the hermeneutical strategy that Jesus employed in the telling of those parables that projected a narrative-world in which the listener or reader was either gently seduced or abruptly provoked into an active response. Only provocation into a sense of outrage at 'injustice' on the part of a listener to the parable of the labourers in the vineyard (Mt. 20:1–15) could convey the full meaning of the privilege and affront of sheer grace: 'Do you begrudge my generosity?' (v. 15). Indeed it became apparent that the evangelists sometimes arranged their sequence of narrative material to provoke their readers into active response. Only the sense of puzzlement about the disciples' dullness of understanding and expectation in the feeding miracle of Mark 8:1–10, when it *follows* the parallel miracle of Mark 6:30–44, could provoke readers to see (along with the gospel narrator) the limitations of the kind of Christology reached by the disciples.[11]

We need not pursue the subsequent history of reader-response theory. In Umberto Eco it is applied constructively to 'open', 'productive', or 'literary' texts, with a judicious recognition that other texts may be of different kinds, and may perform communicative functions of a more 'closed' or determinate nature.[12] In Stanley Fish this approach is taken to an untenable extreme, which leaves very serious communicative and epistemological difficulties, and has affinities with the neo-pragmatic postmodernist world-view of Richard Rorty.[13]

The positive point that has emerged in broad terms is that the relation between the text *and the present reader(s)* has increasingly become a focus of attention, and rightly so. This has consistently constituted a concern for Paul Ricœur, among others. His early aphorism 'The symbol gives rise to thought' at once focuses upon the issue of *effects*.[14] In his masterly three-volume *Time and Narrative* he retains his life-long concern about 'meaning-effects'.[15] In contrast to the classical-humanist focus (Boeckh, Schleiermacher, Collingwood) of reading *'behind' the text*, and equally in contrast to any formalist world (Ransom, Wellek and Warren) *'within' the text*, writers on hermeneutics have come to describe this concern with what the act of reading sets going or effects (Iser, Eco, Ricœur) as that which is *'in front of'* the text. (In practice

---

[11] Expounded in Fowler, *Loaves and Fishes*, esp. 83–96. (This issue of strategy is not dependent on Fowler's form-critical theories.)

[12] Discussed in Thiselton, *New Horizons*, 524–29.

[13] The anti-theistic implications of this neo-pragmatism are well identified in Vanhoozer, *Meaning?*, 55–62, 168–74; cf. Thiselton, *New Horizons*, 540–50, and also 'Signs'.

[14] Ricœur, *Conflict*, 288.

[15] Ricœur, *Time*, I, ix.

Schleiermacher also showed some concern for this, as we have argued in the study already cited above.)

In a textbook on this subject, W. Randolph Tate explicitly organizes his discussion around these three metaphors. These prepositions, he says, denote respectively the three 'worlds' of textual interpretation. He argues rightly and convincingly that what is needed is an 'integrated' approach which takes all three fully into account, in their distinct but complementary roles. Only this 'integrated' interpretation can be fully adequate, fully responsible, and finally valid.[16] Yet this leads on to further questions about the relation between texts and the extra-linguistic world or extra-textual reality that lies beyond the text and to which the text may point, or which the text may presuppose. This confronts us with a fourth approach to textuality, namely with claims nurtured by a postmodern climate that texts are not 'representational' at all. Indeed 'determinacy' of meaning, it may be claimed, remains tenable only if the classical-humanist model is retained, which would become problematic within many strands of postmodernity.

Why is there Dissatisfaction with Representational or Referential Accounts of Texts and Language?

The present issue is beset with confusions. A first confusion arises because, while it is right to recognize that some poems or complex literary works of art do not primarily draw their meaning from how they refer to persons, events, or objects in the external world, it does not thereby follow that *any* referential account of language has therefore become untenable. Yet many see the latter (except in relatively trivial quasi-mechanical cases) *as a linguistic doctrine* demanded by the former observation. It would be a mistake to invoke the Saussurean notion of 'difference' within a linguistic system as an *alternative* to theories of reference and representation. In general linguistics, the phenomenon of *deixis* reveals that, in certain contexts, ostensive definition cannot be avoided. *Deictic* words include *you, me, here, that one there*, and *next Tuesday*, and the attention given by linguisticians to *deixis* suggests that these mechanisms are by no means trivial.

Ironically, in view of the contrast in Heidegger and Wittgenstein between *saying* (i.e. stating) and *showing*, historically referential *deixis* derives from the Greek *deiknumi*, 'I show', although the cognate noun *deigma* means both a thing shown and a specimen or instantiation.[17] In short, the claim that

---

[16] Tate, *Interpretation*, xv–xxi, 173–212, and throughout.

[17] Heidegger argues that *zeigen*, showing, 'subverts' (*umwerfen*) referential and representational language (*sagen*), *Language*, 47, 107; cf. 'The Nature of Language', in *Language*, 57–108; see also Wittgenstein, *Tractatus*, 5.6, 6.522 and 5.4–7.

referential and representational theories of meaning are flawed does not follow logically from the proposition that such theories of meaning fail to provide a *comprehensive* account of the relation between language and meaning.

The postmodern tendencies to undervalue any referential or representational account of language are often derived from the Kantian principle that all knowledge of all truth-claims is decisively conditional by prior categories of the mind which shape perception and construe cognition. A second stage emerges largely from the legacy of Fichte that ends in social constructionism. A third step arises from Nietzsche's contention that there are no 'givens', but only interpretations.[18] The fourth and final part of the journey comes with Rorty's attempt to give a supposedly positive spin to 'relativism' by substituting the terms 'local' or 'ethnocentric' in order to disguise this fourth step as a modest disengagement from larger truth-claims in favour of allegedly humbler claims about 'my' world, even if this has the effect of following Protagoras in rendering 'my world' as the neo-pragmatic criterion of all other claims to truth. Yet to turn this supposed promotion of the relative or (as Rorty prefers it) 'the local' into a universalizing 'rubbish disposal' exercise (Rorty's language again) constitutes a seduction of promoting a sweeping aside of all referential or representational theory under the pretence of arguing on the basis of local contextual criteria from community to community.[19] In truth, a carefully 'local' understanding would at once accommodate the referential theory, as Wittgenstein did, as applicable to 'the circumscribed region' of Wittgenstein's builders.[20]

Yet the attack on anti-representationalism can reflect an equally misguided mirror image when a proponent of the opposite view seeks to reinstate reference and representation, as well as single determinate meanings, to contexts in language which they simply fail to fit. In spite of my immense admiration for Kevin Vanhoozer's *Is There a Meaning in This Text?*, I find an over-readiness to ask *whether* rather than *when* defences and attacks concerning reference and determinate meaning are theologically constructive or destructive.[21] It tends to demote the importance of non-referential, non-representational, language if we resort to suggesting that the grossly over-simple, over-general, exhausted distinction between meaning and significance could serve as a panacea for all hermeneutical headaches by the revered E.D. Hirsch. Hirsch's attempts to revitalize the humanist model of language contained much of value, but

---

[18] Nietzsche, *Works*, 15, *The Will to Power*, ii, and the aphorism on p. 481, 'All that exists consists of *interpretations*' (emphasis his).

[19] Rorty, *Truth*, 10; cf. 1–10, 19–42 and 153–65.

[20] Wittgenstein, *Investigations*, sect. 1–3 and 27.

[21] Vanhoozer, *Meaning?*, esp. 76–86, 246–65.

unfortunately his conceptual and semiotic tools were too dated and general to address fully the complexities and nuances of the postmodern world.

To begin from elementary common-sense examples drawn from the biblical writings, *Jesus told parables* precisely to draw his audiences into the process of working out meaning, force and application. As Wittgenstein, once again, urged, it is in the *application* of a piece of language in which meaning and understanding, as a communicative act or process, reside; not in some second-level category distanced and demoted into mere connotation or resonance by the term 'significance', in contrast to meaning. The parables of the Old Testament (e.g., Nathan to David, 2 Sam. 12:1–10) and of Jesus himself provide a prototype of what Kierkegaard would call indirect communication addressed to the will for decision, and what Wolfgang Iser would term reader-response in the sense of the reader's filling in what was needed to actualize the potential communicative event. The issue of how precisely the communicative 'sender' encodes the genetic instructions for the transmission of the encoded message was helpfully described by J. Lotman and by Umberto Eco in terms of the degree to which a text was produced as 'open' or 'closed'.[22] Bible translators are utterly familiar with this contrast in dealing with metaphor. 'The moon shall be turned to blood' (Acts 2:20) has all the power, energy and ambivalence of apocalyptic. The insipid 'and the moon blood-red' (*Twentieth-Century NT*) tries to 'close' the meaning on behalf of a puzzled reader and thereby emasculates the apocalyptic.

This brings us to our second category. *Metaphor*, no less than parable, relies on something more than a single determinate meaning and a referential account of language. Paul Ricœur builds upon the interactive model of Max Black, whereby metaphor is more than substitution, more than vivid embellishment, and more than the added sum of two referential propositions. Even if we reduce metaphor to plainer simile, 'my love is like a red, red rose' means more than the mathematical sum of the attributes of love and red roses. Nor is it a rose-like love with enhanced but unstated significance. Multiple meaning and inter-textual allusion conspire to produce a semantic richness to which a hermeneutic of understanding must do justice.[23]

A third category is the variation of hermeneutical agenda that even a historical author may envisage as situated within the boundaries of a spectrum of 'implied' or 'ideal' readers. In spite of the once fashionable but now surely discredited trend of dismissing notions of authorial intention as depending on what some formalists had called 'the intentional fallacy', even the language of literary theorists about 'the implied reader' or 'ideal' reader reintroduced through the back door the notion of an authorial will or decision (rightly

---

[22] Eco, *Theory*, 136–39; also *Semantics*, 68–86; *Reader*, 4–33; and Lotman, *Structure*.
[23] Ricœur, *Rule*, esp. 6–24; *Time*, e.g. vol. 3, 101.

underlined by Kevin Vanhoozer and Nicholas Wolterstorff). This has in view a so-called target readership or target audience whose specific values, needs, assumptions and horizons the author held in view in the production of the text. As my former colleague in the UK Colin Brown (now at Fuller Theological Seminary) used to tell students at the beginning of each year about written assignments, 'If you aim at nothing you are sure to hit it.' The implied reader, Powell and others observe, is 'the reader presupposed by the text'.[24] Malbon speaks of an 'intended readership'.[25] Yet, on the other side, can Scripture address *only* the immediately implied readers? Has 1 Corinthians 2 nothing to communicate to twenty-first-century philosophers seeking to understand the conceptual grammar of revelation, or a university class discussing the personhood and deity of the Holy Spirit?

Here the work of Hans-Robert Jauss, among others, becomes instructive.[26] On one side he accepts the importance of a given tradition of continuity of interpretation which suggests constraints beyond which interpretation becomes idiosyncratic or irresponsible. Meaning is not *grossly* indeterminate and unbounded. Nevertheless, hermeneutical agenda are not simply replicated from era to era. New questions and new thought-forms arise in relation to which new paradigms exhibit both continuity and discontinuity as traditions of interpretation expand. This is far from the 'local' contextual pragmatism of Rorty and Fish. Nevertheless it challenges the notion that biblical interpretation is nothing but the endlessly wooden replication of 'a single determinate meaning'. In my view, the most constructive recent development in biblical studies has been that of scattered attempts to offer a *Wirkungsgeschichte* of exegetical issues – that is, a critical account of how the *reception* of biblical texts has in turn shaped the agenda and pre-understanding of the next generation to be addressed by the text. This is not to be reduced to the mere 'history of interpretation', which is historical and descriptive, rather than hermeneutical and creatively critical. Yet few, to date, have explored this area in more than a very basic way. U. Luz describes the *Wirkungsgeschichte* of the exegesis of Matthew as 'history, reception and actualizing of a text in media other than commentary, e.g. in sermons, canon law, hymns, art and in the actions … of the church'.[27]

---

[24] Powell, *Criticism?*, 20.

[25] Malbon, 'Criticism', 27–8; cf. 23–49.

[26] Jauss, *Literaturgeschichte*; *Aesthetic*; 'Paradigmawechsel'; discussed in my chapters in Lundin, Thiselton, and Walhout, *Promise*, 191–208.

[27] One of the very few examples is Luz, *Evangelium*; see Introduction, sect. 6; Schrage, *Korinther*, is more 'historical'. I have attempted to treat selected passages in my *1 Corinthians*, e.g., esp. 196–204, 276–86, 330–44, 479–82, 531–40, 658–61, 998–1026, 1306–14. Changes of agenda within the Patristic, mediaeval and Reformation eras provide the most telling material.

The significant point for our purposes is that the choice between: 1) a single determinate meaning based on reference and representation; and 2) a radical indeterminacy which sweeps aside reference and representation, provides a contrived, artificial and misleading alternative. In concrete terms, Paul's specific communicative action in 1 Corinthians 2 hinges on redefinition and 'code switching' about what counts as being 'a spiritual person' at Corinth. In my commentary I have argued in detail that whereas many at Corinth applied to themselves the designation 'spiritual people' in a way which appeared to invite 'recognition' and to enhance their status in the eyes of others, Paul himself insists that the nature of authentic 'spirituality' is a Christomorphic experience of the transformative work of the Holy Spirit, as evidenced and tested by conformity with the criterion of the proclamation of the cross. There is nothing 'status-enhancing' about identification with a crucified Christ.[28] However, this is not to exclude the possibility of layered meanings when Basil and Athanasius asked about entailments for the personhood and deity of the Holy Spirit, or when Luther and Calvin enquired about the transformative implications of communicative action initiated by the Holy Spirit. This is more than a matter of 'significance', but does not invite all and sundry to 'complete' whatever meaning arises from any kind of agenda.

This brings us to the title assigned for this paper. What occurs 'in front of' the text, that is, what it sets going, its 'influence, history, reception, actualization …' (Luz) is not a self-generated process, as if the text were reduced to a unit of semiotic or literary production. *Here I not only endorse Vanhoozer's concerns about the theological and anti-theological implications of such views, I go further: such views relate too often to an egalitarian politics that reduces the status of the author to that of another co-reader. Further, it borders upon a mechanistic account of a theory of literary texts which attempts to eradicate such irreducibly personal features as will, purpose, aim, goal, intent and exchange for such mechanistic and market categories as production, effect and criteria of what-is within a prior socially constructed world.* In a world where *everything* has become *socially constructed as media-shaped virtual reality*, it no longer makes sense to return to the language that assumes that *the agency of a personal voice any longer 'makes a difference'. It is precisely at this point that Vanhoozer's 1998 work comes into its own* (if we may hesitate over its neat polarities, over-exclusive alternatives, and uniformly triadic patterns to be correlated with Trinitarian modes of action).

---

[28] 1 Cor. 1:18–25; 2:1–5; 3:1–3; 4:8–13; 12:1–3; 13; and corresponding pages in my commentary, incl. 900–89. 'Code-switching' is discussed in *First Epistle*, 43, 325–26, 396, 587, 996, and elsewhere. See further, below.

Is there Still Value in Drawing Distinctions between Worlds 'Behind' the Text and 'In Front Of' the Text?

Like most creative metaphors, these terms served to open up a new understanding of valid hermeneutical distinctions when they were first employed by Ricœur and others. But, like 'paradigm', 'postmodernity', 'incommensurability' and 'non-foundationalist', these become thinned, flattened, and discoloured by overuse, and we may hope for their replacement by a less sullied currency in due course. The world 'behind' the text does not merely relate to its genetic origin or even to the historical world and value system inhabited by the author. It is a gross oversimplification of F. Schleiermacher's hermeneutics to attribute to him, as is regularly done, the view that interpretation is simply and exclusively the converse of composition, in which the goal is to trace the originating circumstances. I have pointed out elsewhere that Schleiermacher was sufficiently sophisticated to note that an emphasis on cause, effect, genre, vision or goal depends largely on strategic decisions about what specific questions are being addressed *within* hermeneutical agenda. As Vanhoozer implies, the 'world' behind the text has links with whether or how a 'control' or 'directedness' may be said to characterize a text apart from its perception and reception by successive audiences.[29]

As long ago as 1946, Wimsatt and Beardsley speak of a world 'beyond [the author's] power to intend … or control …'; even the 'dramatic speaker' who sets the textual effects in motion at the moment of its recital articulates the text's 'autonomy' with greater privilege than the forgotten author.[30] This reflects not simply a literary overreaction against origination in Romanticism, but also a liberal political overreaction against control on the part of authority figures of status or learning. It is the liberal pseudo-rationalism against which Gadamer protests, in which the individual's 'autonomy' and the doctrine of progressivist social construction lead to the levelling down of all tradition and authority to 'one of us'. Hence Gadamer argues for 'the rehabilitation of authority and tradition' in the light of the fallibility and finitude of individual subjective consciousness.[31]

Undeniably, these overreactions rest on half-truths. The whole communicative act is not completed by the 'sender' alone. Textual actualization entails author or personal sources, code, content, contact, context and reception, appropriation, application or understanding on the part of implied readers, addressees or actual readers. In Christian theology, the definitive givenness of Scripture remains both authoritative and potential in meaning on the ground

---

[29] Vanhoozer, *Meaning?*, 48–90; 229–59.
[30] Wimsatt and Beardsley, 'Fallacy'.
[31] Gadamer, *Truth*, 270–300.

that the same Holy Spirit who inspired the agents who wrote will also inspire the prophets, teachers, congregations and seekers who read. In this sense the creativity of the Holy Spirit, who gives organic birth and life rather than mechanistic replication, confirms Schleiermacher's insistence that hermeneutics and understanding constitutes a creative art, not a science.[32] Like the gift of manna, it is received anew day by day, not stored and siphoned off in mechanistic packages.

Many theorists who have not become obsessed with the 'postmodern turn' now emphasize an 'integrated' hermeneutics. In spite of its 'textbook' level of writing, W. Randolph Tate's *Biblical Interpretation* provides a useful, unintimidating and modest example. His three main parts are headed '*author-centred* (with attention directed to the world behind the text); *text-centred* (with the focus on the world within the text, or the textual world); and *reader-centred* (where the spotlight is trained upon the world in front of the text, or the reader's world)'.[33] 'This model of communication sets the agenda'.[34] Nevertheless, a survey of the contents demonstrates that these three 'worlds' remain inseparable. Are such textual phenomena as the distinction between, for example, narrative, poetry and prophecy simply a textual 'property', or do they not equally reflect an act of decision, direction and purpose on the part of the writer?[35]

In the context of Christian theology, this principle becomes transparent. In the case of catechetical instruction concerning the Two Ways, or doctrinal affirmation concerning the kerygma of the crucifixion of Jesus of Nazareth, such formula as Γνωρίζω δὲ ὑμῖν, ἀδελφοί, τὸ εὐαγγέλιον ὃ εὐηγγελισάμην ὑμῖν, ὃ καὶ παρελάβετε, ἐν ᾧ καὶ ἑστήκατε, δι' οὗ καὶ σῴζεσθε, τίνι λόγῳ εὐηγγελισάμην ὑμῖν εἰ κατέχετε, ἐκτὸς εἰ μὴ εἰκῇ ἐπιστεύσατε (1 Cor 15:1–2) cannot make sense unless they are referential and representational, even if they also generate deeply affective and volitional implications and resonances. This is confirmed by 15:3: παρέδωκα γὰρ ὑμῖν ἐν πρώτοις, ὃ καὶ παρέλαβον, ὅτι Χριστὸς ἀπέθανεν ὑπὲρ τῶν ἁμαρτιῶν ἡμῶν κατὰ τὰς γραφάς.

As Anders Eriksson convincingly and incisively argues, Paul uses shared pre-Pauline traditions as 'rhetorical proofs': 'Traditions constitute agreed upon premises which are the starting-point for argumentation'.[36] Eriksson

---

[32] Schleiermacher, *Hermeneutics*, 100–105; discussed in Thiselton, *New Horizons*, 218–21, 558–62. Gadamer goes further here, although Ricœur emphasizes both creative art and constraining criticism.

[33] Tate, *Interpretation*, xvi (emphasis his).

[34] Ibid., xx; respectively 1–58; 59–142; 143–212.

[35] Ibid., 74–106.

[36] Eriksson, *Traditions*, 3.

acknowledges, with literary theorists and postmodern interpreters, that even argument can have diverse, multiple, rhetorical *effects* upon an audience (i.e. the argument behind and in a text generates a pluralism 'in front' of it). However, this raises the issue of redefinition and code switching.

Most up-to-date interpreters of 1 Corinthians acknowledge that the Corinthians (or many of them) have a different view from that of Paul about what constitutes, or counts as, being 'a "spiritual" person'. Paul does not at this point shrug his shoulders and say, 'Well, "spiritual" for *your* peer-group of addressees is how *you* define it'. He insists on employing allusive or referential criteria that ground the definition (meaning) of 'spiritual persons', 'people led by the Holy Spirit', in terms of the crucified Christ and the cross. *He insists that only a cruciform definition or meaning of 'spiritual' is valid.* A.C. Wire's argument (in her view in criticism of Paul) that Corinth understands with freedom while Paul seeks to speak with authority carries some force.[37] Thus 'redefinition' or 'code switching' applies to the contrast between wisdom and folly in 1:18. Paul transposes the wisdom-folly contrast as it is understood by many at Corinth by 'reversal' and by correlating the former (as they understand it) with self-destruction, and the latter (as they understand it) as effective, operative, saving, power.[38]

The same principle of redefinition and code switching occurs in 1:26, where claims to 'high status' become redefined and reversed in the light of the cross. Honour-shame and grounds for 'glory' are redefined in terms of sharing the status of a humiliated Messiah, not triumphalism of a social or religious nature.[39] Such redefinition is an 'affront' to many. In 2:5–16, Paul borrows the Corinthian sloganizing about *pneuma* and *pneumatikos* to redefine and subvert it in accordance with Christ and the cross as the source of 'spiritual' transformation. 'Spirituality' means more than 'religious experience'.[40] Twenty-seven years ago, I called attention to 'persuasive definition' in the contrasts between the meaning of 'flesh' and 'spiritual' between Paul and his addressees in 3:1–5 and 5:1–5.[41]

How can so much hang upon a rhetoric of redefinition and a strategy of code switching if, in the world behind the text, a single meaning is not at issue, *and also deemed to be communicated as textual effect to the audience?* We cannot impose the 'doctrine' of a literary theory upon the particularities of exegesis as well as logical analysis. Recently Garrett Green distinguished between

---

[37] Wire, *Women Prophets*.

[38] Wilckens, *Weisheit*, 5–41 and 205–24; Schrage, *Korinther*, I, 165–92; Moores, *Rationality*, 5–32, esp. 24–28 (on code-switching) and 132–38.

[39] Pogoloff, *Logos*, 113–27; 153–72; 197–216.

[40] Horsley, 'Pneumatikos'. Pearson, *Terminology*; Lampe, 'Wisdom'.

[41] Thiselton, 'Meaning'.

postmodernity as a cultural *description* of society and '*normative*' or '*doctrinaire*' postmodernity, which is actually 'a philosophical *doctrine*'.[42]

Nevertheless, other biblical texts reflect a 'world behind the text' where double meaning or multiple meaning or even indeterminate meaning plays a role. In Hebrew, the introduction of poetic metre sometimes (not always) gives a cue for such 'play' of language. If God is more than an existent object within the world, such poetic creative hymnic form as 'Holy, holy, holy is the Lord of hosts; the whole earth is full of his glory' (Is. 6:3) transcends representa-tional, referential, 'single' meaning. In Tillich's use of the term, we enter the realm of double-edged symbol, which opens up both reality and our own self-hood. It is not for nothing that Ricœur and Derrida focus largely on Job and on apocalyptic. A referential understanding of the book of Revelation becomes, in George Caird's phrase, an attempt to unweave the glory of the rainbow. As I have argued elsewhere, like Bakhtin and Dostoevsky's *The Brothers Karamazov*, the book of Job offers polyphonic dialogue, which conveys the divine word only through the *plurality* of its voices.[43] In the case of the psalms, when the speaker is *both author and reader* sharing address *to* God, how *could* meaning be single, determinate and 'plain' *for all*? Paul Ricœur is utterly right to complain that too often we give privilege to the *prophetic* model of communication that is, after all, only *one* of five or more which he identifies.[44] This is almost as bad as the misguided attempt of many literary theorists to assimilate *all* modes of biblical discourse into parables, poetry or fictive narrative.

My point is that the will and purpose of the author (to take up terms used by Vanhoozer) utilize code as well as message to indicate the degree of constraint or freedom appropriate to this or that text. Even then, the issue remains one of *degree*. If the degree becomes *boundless*, so that 'anything goes', such a view, as Vanhoozer urges, is anti-theological.[45] 'God' becomes the human projection shaped by human wishes and social construction. Craig Bartholomew identi-fies the point at issue when he links a radically postmodern approach to biblical interpretation with the post-industrial social phenomenon of consumerism. David Clines disarmingly concedes, and indeed claims, that he proposes as 'pluralist' a model of biblical interpretation which constitutes

> an end-user theory of interpretation, a market philosophy of interpretation ... First comes the recognition that texts do not have determinate meanings ... The social axis for my framework is provided by the idea of interpretative communities ... There is no ... standard by which we can know whether one interpretation or other

---

[42] Green, *Theology*, 9.

[43] Thiselton, 'Action and Promise'.

[44] Ricœur, *Essays*, 73–118.

[45] Vanhoozer, *Meaning?*, 49–59, 105–106, 427–29.

is right; we can only tell whether it has been accepted. There are no determinate meanings …[46]

As in Rorty's neopragmatism, the words 'true' and 'right' have been sold out in favour of a pluralism of undecidability elevated to the status of 'ethics' in place of 'God', to be defined by the consumer. Such an approach is often promoted as one based on 'ethics', that is an ethics of pluralism. However, there remains an exclusivist aspect that is disguised as a tolerant pluralism. Few Muslims, for example, could endorse such treatment of Islamic texts as 'ethical'; rather to them it would more probably be judged as simply idolatrous – that is, as equating the sacred with social constructions of 'interest' and instrumental reason on the part of a world-view based on secular liberal political democracy.

The Conflict between Consumerist Hermeneutics and Both Theism and Reasonableness: Two Sides of the Case?

It cannot be accidental that this 'consumerist' hermeneutic is advocated from within what is probably the only department of biblical studies in the UK which does not explore biblical studies within a department of theology (where its entailments for theism are explored) or religious studies (where its entailments for the sacred scriptures of other religions, especially Judaism and Islam are explored) or philosophy of religion (where the philosophical and ethical world-views in which it is grounded are made explicit and assessed). Even dialogue with a robustly 'secular' school of critical theory may more readily demonstrate just how illusory are the pretensions of consumerist approaches to claim to offer a 'descriptive', 'comparative' or value-free approach. For consumerism at the beginning of the twenty-first century relies on a *manipulative* strategy of devising and promoting *virtual reality* generated by the interests of market-forces in which *money*, not even goods nor persons, has become the controlling commodity. For example, the 'desires' of teenagers for designer clothes, or for products connected with films or sports teams, are usually the fruit of careful market manipulation. They have nothing to do with genuine 'democratic choice', as most parents well know. Ironically, the very globalization of market-forces in terms of powerful international conglomerates demonstrates the partial validity of the very concerns of the early Marx in his Paris manuscripts about the dehumanization of persons and agents into

---

[46] Clines, 'Possibilities', 78–80; cf. 67–87; and also cited in Bartholomew, 'Consuming', 83; cf. 81–99.

mere units of production or into 'commodities'. The significance of 'the capitu-
lation of the eastern block to consumer culture', and the manipulative portrayal of such 'innocent' images as children and the family for value-laden
commercial purposes has been noted by Craig Bartholomew.[47] Peter Selby
explores the consequence of regarding money itself as a market commodity.[48]

In his 1998 volume of essays, *Truth and Progress*, Richard Rorty repeats his
endorsement of the pragmatic tradition of James, Dewey and Davidson,
including Donald Davidson's rejection of those aspects of truth-claims which
relate to 'correspondence, coherence [or] warranted assertibility'.[49] Just as A.J.
Ayer, with the brash confidence of a positivist who had disguised himself as a
philosopher of language, swept aside all religious propositions about God as
non-sense, on the ground of unverifiability, so Rorty sees 'the task of getting
reality right' as a task to be consigned to rubbish-disposal because 'there is no
Way the World Is'.[50] Like Clines, Rorty sees the issue of truth as derivative
from prior '*social practices*'; and these are shaped by the responses of those who
judge what is *justified* in relation to these practices.[51] 'Decisions about truth and
falsity are always a matter of rendering practices more coherent or of developing new practices'. Truth, Rorty urges, is *what people accept as a justification,*
usually within the context of a liberal democratic society. Needless to say,
'what people *accept*' as such varies within different local groups. Hence Rorty
prefers the term 'ethnocentric' (in a positive, 'progressive' sense) as against 'relativist' (even if he concedes that the two terms convey virtually the same
content with different associations).[52] Even 'what proves itself to be good' is
deemed to be such in the eyes of consumers. 'Justification is always relative to
an audience'.[53]

In my Presidential Paper to the Society for the Study of Theology (Edinburgh, 1999), I set this consumer-orientated progressivism in contrast to a
grace-orientated eschatology.[54] As Bonhoeffer, Moltmann, Pannenberg and
many others perceive, whereas pragmatism is linked with an illusory confidence in human self-generated progress, eschatology allows for discontinuity,
critique, transcendent reversal, and not least for reversals of the cross which

---

[47] Bartholomew, Introduction to *Christ and Consumerism*, 5 and 7.
[48] Selby, *Grace*. There is no level playing field generated by 'liberal democracy' for
value-laden strings-attached loans to the two-thirds world: it is a time bomb, based on
power.
[49] Rorty, *Truth*, 11.
[50] Rorty, 'Is Truth a Goal of Inquiry?', *Truth*, 25 (cf. also 131).
[51] Rorty, *Truth*, 129.
[52] Ibid., 10; cf. 1–15; 19–42; and 433–62. See also Rorty, *Objectivism*.
[53] Rorty, *Truth*, 4.
[54] Thiselton, 'Signs'.

negate or at least question what is 'conformable' (Bonhoeffer's word) to human consumer-choice. Most especially in first-century Roman Corinth, the major issue for Christians was whether 'the audience' defined truth in terms of the competitive rhetoric which impressed them most and won most applause. Or did the 'affront' of the cross proclaimed by those regarded as dirt to be scraped off the shoes hold a prior claim over those who sought to redefine themselves as 'spiritual people' (1 Cor. 1:18–25; 2:1–5; 4:8–13)?

I have argued this case most recently not only in the paper identified above but also in my detailed commentary on the Greek text of 1 Corinthians.[55] Further, *Paul in no way appeals to an ethnocentric or 'local' perception of truth*, as if 'reasonableness' had nothing to do with issues of epistemological and interpretative judgement. Anders Eriksson and John Moores, among others, have shown that Paul seeks to convey not a rhetoric of mere causal persuasion (bare rhetorical force or perlocution). He conveys, rather, a reasonable chain of inferences from shared promises, that is *shared pre-Pauline traditions which define* Christian identity on the basis of God's grace, the cross and eschatological resurrection.[56] Moores asserts:

> [Paul] does not think (as some modern upholders of the importance of the reception factor do) that the identity of the message in a piece of communication is determined by what it means for those at the receiving end. For him it is rather *their* identity than that of the message which is determined by their response. To subject him to the criteria of present day ... reader-response theory would be to turn *his* ideas on the subject upside down.[57]

Moores is far from being unaware of theories of sign-production – especially in Umberto Eco, Luis Prieto and Pierre Guiraud, and he is familiar with the so-called new rhetoric of C. Perelman. It is precisely his recognition of the importance of semiotic code, however (with its spectrum from closed and tightly matching codes to open codes and code switching), that determines Moores' emphasis not only upon authorial agency, but also upon a 'rationality' that finds expression not merely in deductive and inductive logic but more especially in the 'enthymeme'.[58] This is a shared basis for advocating a reasoned and reasonable case, which in Paul's view embraces 1) appeals to Scripture; and 2) appeals to reason.

Where hearers or addressees already possess precisely the same mindset, belief system and stance as the authorial agent, the code presupposed by each in

---

[55] Thiselton, *1 Corinthians*.

[56] Eriksson, *Traditions*, throughout.

[57] Moores, *Rationality*, 133–34 (emphasis his).

[58] Ibid., 21–32.

the communicative act may be not only matching but identical. But in this case the speech act is not transformative; persuasion need not be involved. Replication, not creative shaping, takes place. This is the perception that lies behind much postmodern dissatisfaction with merely representational or referential accounts of language. Scripture does not merely report or replicate; it also shapes, persuades and transforms. Biblical reading (in the ancient world usually a corporate and oral temporal recital, not a private 'inner' experience) occurs in a context of expectancy of a creative, transformative, impact-making event. Hence, as Moores (taking up and applying Eco) insists, usually 'the superimposition of one code upon another ... is a pervasive feature of sign-production ... To designate such supplementation and superimposition the term "over-coding" is often used'.[59] As Paul Ricœur also emphasizes, the double-meaning-effect of symbol or of metaphor 'gives rise to thought' creatively at a supra-cognitive level as 'surplus of meaning'.[60]

Where a source-signal (e.g., the sound of a musical texture which cannot easily be put into words) cannot readily be interpreted into encoded and decoded texts within the hearer's world, 'under-coding' may have occurred. Interplay in Scripture occurs between:

- *exploratory polyphonic multivalent Wisdom literature* (Job, Ecclesiastes)
- *heart-laments; paeons of hymnic praise or expressions of longing for God beyond words* (Rom. 8:26, 27; 1 Cor. 14:2; Ps. 42:1–3, 5–7, 9)
- *parables, riddles and jokes* (Mt. 5:29; 7:3–5 [the log and speck in the eye]; 13:10–15; Jon. 1:3, 9; 2:2, 4, 10; 4:1–5, 8–11 [satire on a self-centred, self-important, 'godly' prophet!])
- *parallel sequential accounts of events* (Mk. 14:1 – 15:39/Mt. 26:1 – 27:54/Lk 22:1 – 23:48 [the Passion Narrative])
- *shared pre-Pauline creeds and confessions* (both with cognitive declarative content and with commissive self-involvement, 1 Cor. 12:3; Rom. 10:9; 1 Cor. 11:23b–26; 15:3b–5 [6, 7?]; 1 Cor. 8:4b,c [Jesus is Lord; Jesus died for our sins ...; there is One God ...])
- *illlocutionary acts of promise* (e.g., Heb. 6:11b–20; 4:16, based on the stability of covenant security, and Heb. 8:6 – 10:23)
- *multi-functional speech acts* (Heb. 1:1–13: i) a homily; which ii) confesses faith; iii) cites Scripture; iv) provides exegesis; v) recites salvation history; vi) expresses acclamation and praise; vii) teaches; and viii) promotes assurance by stressing the completeness of the finished work of Christ [e.g. 1:3b]).

---

[59] Ibid., 26–7.
[60] Ricœur, *Freud*, 19; cf. 5–33; *Conflict*, 288; cf. 287–334; *Rule*, 6.

Perhaps our traditional emphasis upon 'a single determinate plain meaning' has impoverished the creative potential of our preaching, even violating the biblical example of homily in Hebrews 1.[61]

We cannot conceivably find ways in which a consumer philosophy or consumer hermeneutic of indeterminate meaning open to the shaping of ethnocentric communities may be regarded as compatible with Christian theism, which asserts certain universal truth-claims about 'how things are' (against Rorty). Nevertheless, we must also concede that any approach that limits textual meaning to either a *single* meaning or a *tightly determinate* meaning *in all genres of Scripture in every case* will reduce and emasculate the capacity of Scripture to act *transformatively and creatively*. The proof of this is that even when we accord to authorial agency the indispensable role which Vanhoozer (rightly) gives to it, authors *choose* sometimes to communicate in terms of a goal of *matching* codes through *closed* texts, for example in cases where information or description is more important and more primary than creative shaping or transformation. On the other hand, they sometimes *choose* 'open' texts or a 'switching' of codes, when creative transformation or iconoclasm becomes their aim. *Promise* also presupposes a degree (although not an absolute degree) of specificity concerning conditions, stance and appropriation, or the identity of addressees. Promises to individuals, however, differ from those made to the world. We have noted many communicative modes in which the emphasis lies on projecting a world into which the reader or hearer enters to perform self-involving action for which a rigid protocol has *not* been laid out in advance. Here Gadamer is right: always to insist that some 'method' is laid out in advance is to risk transposing creative understanding into mere response to propaganda. It is to substitute *techne* for *phronesis*.[62]

David Lyon attempts (perhaps too late now) to distinguish between *postmodernism* as a polemic against the 'universal' claims of Enlightenment *rationalism* and epistemology in favour of the local and ethnocentric, and *postmodernity* as a *social* polemic against the solidity of the 'real' in favour of the *virtual reality* of media-construction, sign-construction and local community-construction.[63] *The latter, he urges, replaces means of production by a consumerist culture. Virtual reality* is a construct dependent on the tastes, inclinations and distorted perceptions of consumers. Scripture, we may urge by contrast, proclaims a kerygma that liberates humankind from this illusory 'reality'. Moreover, Scripture is less ready to be associated with the first type of 'postmodernism' in dismissing too readily 'reasonableness' and responsible

---

[61] It is unnecessary to cite the mass of literature on Heb. 1–12 as homily. See, e.g., Lane, *Hebrews*, I, lxx–lxxx; and Übelacker, *Hebräerbrief*. I endorse this in 'Hebrews'.

[62] Gadamer, 'Reflections', esp. 17, 36, 43–6, 53.

[63] Lyon, *Postmodernity*, 6–7.

argument as a God-given weapon against the anxiety of 'anything goes'. That kind of postmodernism is only for 'winners', its 'ethics' remain illusory. In Paul's view it is precisely this that the cross has exposed as 'foolish' and 'weakness', in contrast to the transformative power of the gospel (1 Cor. 1:18–25). It is ironic that Rorty links hermeneutics with 'edification' in contrast to epistemology. As Vielhauer argues, 'to edify (*oikodomō*) oneself' (1 Cor. 14:4) is a self-indulgent, contentless activity.[64] By contrast, Stanley Stowers demonstrates conclusively the importance of reason and reasonableness for Paul, while Alexandra Brown shows the link between transformation, the cross and epistemology.[65]

Concluding Postscript

I have argued that with the proviso that we take full account of textual genre, interpreters need to explore processes behind, within, and in front of the text, more often as complementary than as alternative tasks. Moreover, the interpreter diminishes rather than enhances understanding by setting aside as irrelevant all questions about how the text may relate to the external world in this or that case.

As a speculative but, I hope, suggestive analogy, it may be constructive to compare Aristotle's pre-modern but sophisticated account of causality. When a sculptor creates a marble statue, he suggests, we may distinguish between four kinds of cause, which explain its come into being. The 'efficient' cause lies in the blows of the chisel upon the marble block. This lies 'behind' what comes to constitute the statue. The 'material' and 'formal' causes are the marble and the structure, which we may compare with the actual world of the text itself, as it is structured 'within' this world. Yet crucially, Aristotle observes, there is a 'final' cause at work: the reason why the sculptor makes the statue and what effects upon those who view it are envisaged. In part this retraces what lies 'behind' it; but it also brings into focus the effects which it sets in motion 'in front of' it.

All aspects together combine to make the statue what it is. Yet, as Gadamer and Ricœur insist, hermeneutics moves beyond mere 'explanation' (*Erklärung*) to understanding (*Verstehen*). A higher level and fuller horizon is at issue than knowledge – even if, as Vanhoozer urges against a doctrine of postmodernity, we should not assume that in every case it is less than knowledge. One thinker whom we perhaps too readily ignore here is Bernard Lonergan, who should be

---

[64] Vielhauer, *Oikodomē*.
[65] Stowers, 'Paul'; and Brown, *Cross*.

ranked with those who contribute to this subject. Involved in the processes of experiential understanding, he urges, is 'experiencing, understanding, judging, and deciding' including 'understanding the unity and relations ... and relatedness' of these.[66] Hermeneutics embraces more than this, but it does not embrace less.

Bibliography

Bartholomew, C. and T. Moritz (eds.), *Christ and Consumerism: A Critical Analysis of the Spirit of the Age* (Carlisle: Paternoster, 2000)

—, 'Consuming God's Word: Biblical Interpretation and Consumerism', in *Christ and Consumerism*

Boeckh, P.A., *Encyclopaedie und Methodologie der philologischen Wissenschaften* (Leipzig: Teubner, 2nd edn, 1886)

—, *On Interpretation and Criticism* (Norman: University of Oklahoma Press, 1968)

Brown, A.R., *The Cross and Human Transformation* (Minneapolis: Fortress Press, 1995)

Bultmann, R., *History and Eschatology* (Edinburgh: Edinburgh University Press, 1957)

Chladenius, J.M., *Einleitung zur richtigen Auslegung vernünftiger Reden und Schriften* (Düsseldorf: 1969 repr. of 1742 edn, Stern)

Clines, D.J.A., 'Possibilities and Priorities of Biblical Interpretation in an International Perspective', *BibInt* 1 (1993), 67–87

Collingwood, R.G., *An Autobiography* (Oxford: OUP, 1939)

—, *The Idea of History* (Oxford: Clarendon Press, 2nd edn, 1946)

Eco, U., *A Theory of Semantics* (Bloomington: Indiana University Press, 1976)

—, *Semantics and the Philosophy of Language* (London: Macmillan, 1984)

—, *The Role of the Reader: Explorations in the Semiotics of Texts* (London: Hutchinson, 1981)

Eriksson, A., *Traditions as Rhetorical Proof: Pauline Argumentation in 1 Corinthians* (Stockholm: Almqvist & Wiksell, 1998)

Fowler, R., *Loaves and Fishes: The Function of the Feeding Stories in the Gospel of Mark* (Chicago: Scholars Press, 1981)

Gadamer, H.-G., 'Reflections on my Philosophical Journey', in *The Philosophy of Hans-Georg Gadamer* (ed. L.E. Hahn; Chicago: Open Court, 1997), 3–63

—, *Truth and Method* (London: Sheed & Ward, 2nd edn, 1989)

Green, G., *Theology, Hermeneutics and Imagination* (Cambridge: CUP, 2000)

---

[66] Lonergan, *Method*, 14–15.

Heidegger, M., *On the Way to Language* (New York: Harper & Row, 1971)

Horsley, R.A., 'Pneumatikos vs. Psychikos: Distinctions of Spiritual Status among the Corinthians', *HTR* 69 (1976), 269–88

Iser, W., *The Act of Reading: A Theory of Aesthetic Response* (Baltimore: John Hopkins University Press, 1978)

Jauss, H.-R., 'Paradigmawechsel in der Literaturwissenschaft', *Linguistische Berichte* 3 (1969), 44–56

—, *Literaturgeschichte als Provokation* (Frankfurt: Suhrkamp, 1970)

—, *Toward an Aesthetic of Reception* (Minneapolis: University of Minnesota Press, 1982)

Lampe, P., 'Theological Wisdom and the "Word about the Cross": The Rhetorical Scheme in 1 Cor 1–4', *Int* 44 (1990), 17–31

Lane, W.L., *Hebrews* (Dallas: Word, 1991)

Lonergan, B., *Method in Theology* (London: Darton, Longman & Todd, 1972)

Lotman, J., *The Structure of the Artistic Text* (Ann Arbor: University of Michigan Press, 1997)

Lundin, R., A.C. Thiselton and C. Walhout, *The Promise of Hermeneutics* (Grand Rapids: Eerdmans, 1999)

Luz, U., *Das Evangelium nach Matthäus* (3 of 4 vols.; Evangelisch-Katholischer Kommentar zum NT; Zürich: Benziger, 1989, 1990, 1997)

Lyon, D., *Postmodernity* (Buckingham: Open University, 1994)

Malbon, E.S., 'Narrative Criticism: How Does the Story Mean?', in *Mark and Method: New Approaches in Biblical Studies* (ed. J.E. Anderson and J.D. Moore; Minneapolis: Fortress, 1992)

Moores, J.D., *Wrestling with Rationality in Paul: Romans 1–8 in a New Perspective* (SNTSMS 82; Cambridge: CUP, 1995)

Nietzsche, F., *Complete Works* (18 vols.; London: Allen & Unwin, 1909–13)

Pearson, B.A., *The Pneumatikos-Psychikos Terminology in 1 Corinthians* (Missoula, MT: Scholars Press, 1973)

Pogoloff, S.M., *Logos and Sophia: The Rhetorical Situation of 1 Corinthians* (Atlanta: Scholars Press, 1992)

Powell, M.A., *What is Narrative Criticism?* (London: SPCK, 1993)

Ricœur, P., *Essays on Biblical Interpretation* (London: SPCK, 1981)

—, *Freud and Philosophy: An Essay on Interpretation* (New Haven: Yale, 1970)

—, *The Conflict of Interpretations* (Evanston, IL: Northwestern University Press, 1974)

—, *The Rule of Metaphor* (Toronto: University of Toronto Press, 1977)

—, *Time and Narrative* (trans. K. McLaughlin and D. Pellauer; 3 vols.; Chicago: University of Chicago Press, 1984–88)

Rorty, R., *Objectivism, Relativism and Truth: Philosophical Papers*, I (Cambridge: CUP, 1991)

—, *Truth and Progress: Philosophical Papers*, III (Cambridge: CUP, 1998)

Schleiermacher, F.D.E., *Hermeneutics and Criticism, and Other Writings* (ed. A. Bowie; Cambridge: CUP, 1999)

—, *Hermeneutics: The Handwritten Manuscripts* (ed. H. Kimmerle; Missoula, MT: Scholars Press, 1977)

Schrage, W., *Der erste Brief an die Korinther* (3 vols. of 4; Zürich: Benziger, 1992, 1996, 1999)

Selby, P., *Grace and Mortgage: The Language of Faith and the Debt of the World* (London: Darton, Longman & Todd, 1997)

Stowers, S.K., 'Paul on the Use and Abuse of Reason', in *Greeks, Romans and Christians: Essays in Honor of A.J. Malherbe* (ed. D.L. Balch, et al.; Minneapolis: Fortress Press, 1990), 253–86

Tate, W.R., *Biblical Interpretation: An Integrated Approach* (Peabody, MA: Hendrickson, 1991)

Thiselton, A.C., 'Communicative Action and Promise in Interdisciplinary, Biblical and Theological Hermeneutics', in Lundin, Thiselton and Walhout, *The Promise of Hermeneutics*, 172–83

—, 'Hebrews', in *Eerdman's Bible Commentary* (ed. J.W. Rogerson and J.D.G. Dunn; Grand Rapids: Eerdmans, due 2001)

—, 'Signs of the Times: Toward a Grammar of Grace, Truth and Eschatology in Contexts of So-Called Postmodernity', in *The Future as God's Gift: Explorations in Christian Eschatology* (ed. D. Fergusson and M. Sarot; Edinburgh: T. & T. Clark, 2000), 9–39

—, 'The Meaning of *sarx* in 1 Cor. 5:5: A Fresh Approach in the Light of Logical and Semantic Factors', *SJT* 26 (1973), 204–28

—, *1 Corinthians: A Commentary on the Greek Text* (NIGTC; Carlisle: Paternoster; Grand Rapids: Eerdmans, 2000)

—, *New Horizons in Hermeneutics: The Theory and Practice of Transforming Biblical Reading* (Carlisle: Paternoster; Grand Rapids: Zondervan, 1992)

Übelacker, W.G., *Der Hebräerbrief als Appell* (Stockholm: Almqvist & Wiksell, 1989)

Vanhoozer, K., *Is There a Meaning in This Text?: The Bible, the Reader, and the Morality of Literary Knowledge* (Grand Rapids: Zondervan, 1998)

Vielhauer, P., *Oikodomē: Das Bild vom Bau in der christlichen Literatur vom NT bis Clemens Alexandrinus* (Karlsruhe: Harrassowitz, 1940)

Welleck, R., and A. Warren, *Theory of Literature* (London: Penguin, 1973)

Wilckens, U., *Weisheit und Torheit* (Tübingen: Mohr, 1959)

Wimsatt, W.K., and M.C. Beardsley, 'The Intentional Fallacy', in *The Verbal Icon: Studies in the Meaning of Poetry* (Lexington: University of Kentucky Press, 1954), 4–18

Wire, A.C., *The Corinthian Women Prophets* (Minneapolis: Fortress Press, 1990)

Wittgenstein, L., *Philosphical Investigations* (Oxford: Basil Blackwell, 2nd edn, 1967)

—, *Tractatus Logico-Philosophicus* (London: Routledge, 1961)

6

A 'Polite' Response to Anthony Thiselton

William Olhausen

It is a mark of Professor Thiselton's familiarity with the complexity of language *and* its communicative potential that he has grasped the enormity of the hermeneutic challenge. Taken together with his other extensive publications,[1] Thiselton's chapter represents another forceful plea for the biblical interpreter to wrestle with the diversity of texts. The chapter steers a *via media* between, on the one hand, simplistic and deterministic approaches to meaning and reference for all texts and, on the other, interpretative strategies that prioritize pragmatic or 'local' considerations at the expense of tradition and/or the extra-linguistic world.[2] Quite rightly, in my view, Thiselton resists any positivistic idea that all texts can be analysed purely by a referential or representational understanding of language. Clearly, he wants to defend as meaningful, and potentially 'transformative', diverse texts such as parable, narrative and law, and so on, and make the case for what Taylor terms a 'designative' theory of meaning[3] in certain more 'closed' contexts of discourse.[4]

---

[1] Thiselton's contribution in *The Promise of Hermeneutics* is the most recent.

[2] Elsewhere Thiselton refers to these two extremes as the 'Scylla of mechanical replication' and the 'Charybdis of orphaned indeterminacy'. Thiselton, in Lundin, et al., *Promise*, 137f.

[3] In a very helpful article, Taylor traces the history of the two predominant approaches to meaning in Western thought. He uses the term 'designative' to refer to approaches to meaning most favoured by the Anglo-American (or analytic) philosophical tradition. He uses the term 'expressivist' to denote approaches to language favoured by twentieth-century continental philosophy, which he traces from its development in the Romantic critique of Kant found in the German language philosophy of Hamann, Herder and Humboldt. Taylor, 'Theories', 250.

[4] This commitment is seen most clearly in Thiselton's discussion of Donald Evans' work on the logic of self-involvement. Thiselton, *New Horizons*, 282f.

In this response I make two related suggestions. First I propose supplement-
ing Thiselton's linguistic approach with insights drawn from recent developments in linguistic pragmatics. By way of example, I suggest that Brown and
Levinson's work on 'Politeness'[5] 1) pays careful attention to 'local' or pragmatic considerations that would include the referential dimension of utterances *and* 2) respects the dialogical or conversational emphasis found in
expressivist theories of meaning. In this way, valuable contributions from both
traditions are retained while in its methodology pragmatics avoids the ideological problematic associated with a more deterministic referential theory of
meaning. Secondly, linguistic issues cannot be separated from the question of
theology: our view of one will affect in large part our view of the other.
Despite making the case for a responsible hermeneutics that takes into account
worlds *behind*, *within* and *in front* of the text, the difficult task of developing a
hermeneutic model that integrates an understanding of the role of the Holy
Spirit still remains to be done within Thiselton's programme. While his
chapter continues to affirm the Spirit's significance, it is not immediately clear
why or in what way. In light of this, I conclude the response by drawing attention to the need for an integrated approach to the work of the Spirit.

Language, Meaning and Theology

In this opening section I begin to set out the need for biblical interpretation to
take seriously Bartholomew's belief that 'the ultimate issues in philosophy of
language are theological'.[6] Whatever theory of meaning we select from those
on offer we discover that we get more (sometimes less) than we bargained for,
resulting in theologically skewed readings of Scripture. In saying this I am not
advocating a retreat from the endeavours of philosophy – far from it. Indeed,
following Thiselton's example, I suggest that in the pursuit of biblical hermeneutics we continue to study as many of the insights on offer as possible but
proceed cautiously with a corrective eye always on the biblical text.

It might equally be said that ultimate issues of language are anthropological
because, as Taylor among many others points out, the capacity to use language
defines the uniqueness of being human.[7] Indeed language creates the public
space in which the human and the divine can meet.[8] In this way language
makes sense of a notion like theological anthropology. Not surprisingly,
although it is seldom remarked upon, the Bible as a whole tells us something

---

[5] Brown and Levinson, *Politeness*. Hence, the title for this paper.

[6] Bartholomew, 'Babel and Derrida', 305.

[7] Taylor notes that 'we are constantly forced to the conception of man as a language
animal, one who is constituted by language'. 'Language', 246.

[8] This idea of language creating public space is made well by Taylor in 'Theories', 259.

very important about the way human beings use language. Within the biblical narrative, Babel and Pentecost bracket salvation history, reminding us that the language event as a defining aspect of our humanity is, in a real way, 'fallen',[9] and awaits always the consummation of Pentecost. There is an intimation of this in the hermeneutic tradition of Martin Heidegger, reflected in the recognition of our finitude and historical situatedness.[10] It is understandable, therefore, that theologians have been attracted to the writings of Heidegger, Gadamer and Ricœur, where these central themes of 'being' are discussed. It has been less common for theologians to engage with the designative theories beloved of Anglo-American philosophy. Kevin Vanhoozer[11] and Thiselton are notable exceptions. While both of them have seen merit in Searle's work on speech-act theory, for the present discussion it is Searle's commitment to a version of a referential or designative theory of meaning that is significant. This is because a philosophical commitment to a theory of meaning that connects the propositions of language with extra-linguistic states of affairs represents, in Thiselton's view, an important corrective to the pragmatism[12] of, for instance, Richard Rorty.[13] It has, therefore, been an emphasis in Thiselton's work that certain insights from the analytic tradition can be used to supplement hermeneutic theory.[14] Thus, against much of twentieth-century hermeneutic

---

[9] Vanhoozer maintains that 'fallenness' concerns 'moral and spiritual dispositions' rather than 'social or cultural issues'. Vanhoozer, 'Spirit', 158. While he is right to recover the idea of 'fallenness', I believe he has underestimated the scope of the problem.

[10] Grondin, *Introduction*, 123.

[11] Vanhoozer, *Meaning?*

[12] Pragmatism in this sense is a theory of truth developed by William James and John Dewey. Rorty, *Consequences*, 160.

[13] Recently, as Thiselton is aware, the very idea of 'truth' in any representational sense has come under attack. As Rorty observes: 'If one gives up thinking that there are representations, then one will have little interest in the relation between mind and the world or language and the world. So one will lack interest in either the old disputes between realists and idealists or the contemporary quarrels within analytic philosophy about "realism" and "antirealism". For the latter quarrels presuppose that bits of the world "make sentences true", and that these sentences in turn represent those bits. Without these presuppositions, we would not be interested in trying to distinguish between those true sentences which correspond to "facts of the matter" and those which do not (the distinction around which realist-vs.-antirealist controversies revolve).' Rorty, 'Twenty Five Years', 372.

[14] Cristina Lafont's recent publication is a case in point. In the same way that Lafont has seen in the internal-realist philosophy of Hilary Putnam an important corrective to Habermas's theory of communicative action, Thiselton has found in Austin and Searle a similarly important guarantee in the connection between word and world. Lafont, *Linguistic Turn*; Thiselton, *New Horizons*, 282f.

philosophy, Thiselton defends the referential or representational capacity of language as the basis for the meaningfulness of certain instances of discourse. It is for this reason that Thiselton is suspicious of Rorty. For Thiselton, a designative theory of language offers an objective criterion of meaning, thereby protecting the very possibility of accessing reliably the events of history, especially as these impinge on the gospel kerygma.

This much is clear. But what consequences follow from signing up to a designative theory of truth? The implication is that the meaning of a sentence or, more properly, an utterance, can be pursued apart from a real-life context of use. It is the role of these so-called contextual factors that is the concern of linguistic pragmatics.[15]

Taylor expresses a similar reservation about prioritizing a designative theory of meaning when he says that

> the crucial and highly obtrusive fact about language, and human symbolic communication in general, is that it serves to found public space, that is, to place certain matters before *us*. This blindness to the public is of course (in part anyway) another consequence of the epistemological tradition, which privileges a reconstruction of knowledge as a property of the critical individual. It makes us take the monological observer's standpoint not just as a norm, but somehow as the way things really are with the subject. And this is catastrophically wrong.[16]

Taylor is not arguing for a rejection of the designative aspect of meaning. His concern is to prioritize the intrinsically social aspect of language by adumbrating central notions such as 'dialogue', 'conversation', 'public space' and 'moral agency'. Importantly, to subordinate a designative theory of meaning to an expressivist theory of meaning neither entails the proposition that we cannot talk about historical events nor that historical events cannot be presupposed in our linguistic usage. Instead, we assess the nature of meaning for a given chunk of discourse on a careful case by case basis – very much how the later Wittgenstein and, in turn, Austin, envisaged.

Adherence to the philosophical commitments of a designative theory of meaning becomes problematic when, for example, interpreting Paul's use of the phrase 'spiritual person'. Thiselton observes rightly that Paul '*insists on a cruciform definition or meaning of "spiritual"* '. But it does not follow that because Paul employs referential criteria the cruciform definition of 'spiritual' is somehow guaranteed. No doubt Paul has a specific meaning in mind, and certainly there is a world behind the text. The question is whether that world is accessed by a referential theory of meaning. The validity of Paul's account of

---

[15] Stephen Levinson provides a very helpful introduction to the field of pragmatics in *Pragmatics*, 1–55.

[16] Taylor, 'Theories', 259.

'spiritual' has more to do with his own theological convictions, resting as they do on a revelation concerning the meaning of a crucified messiah. In the same way, the all-important use of 're-definition' or 'code-switching' cannot be more than trivially explained by an appeal to designative factors. Instead we need to study the wider context of this passage both intratextually and intertextually. Paul's is a discourse that flows from belonging in a new relationship with God and made possible by the Spirit of God in light of the life, death and resurrection of Jesus. In his support for a 'grace orientated eschatology', Thiselton also appears to acknowledge that any referential theory of meaning is itself dependent on the context of theology. The tension arises when these roles appear to be reversed. So, while I understand Thiselton's realist concerns, I do not believe they are met by a commitment to a referential theory of meaning. This is the case for at least one of three reasons: firstly, some versions of a designative theory of meaning restrict meaningful language to the correspondence of isolated propositions with observable sense data. Secondly, semantic analysis is often pursued in abstraction from any real-life context. Thirdly, and most importantly, it is a moot point as to whether the philosophical world-view associated with Anglo-American philosophy is an appropriate conceptual tool for the task Thiselton envisages. These approaches tend to deny what is fundamental to language: the hermeneutic imperative to engage, and be engaged by, the 'other' in the dialogue of an on-going conversation.

Politeness

Semiotics within the analytical tradition is treated as three interrelated disciplines: syntax, semantics and pragmatics. While linguists agree that each of these disciplines retains an important role within the communicative act, semantics and, with it, the analysis of formal languages, has been the privileged domain of analytical philosophy since Frege. Increasingly, pragmatics works with actual instances of discourse and provides an account of meaning arising from that empirical data. Politeness theory is an example of this kind of approach. Importantly, pragmatics meets Thiselton's referential concerns without the need to defend *in advance* a referential theory of language. The question, then, is whether there is an approach to meaning that holds off from a dogmatic commitment, either to some form of designative theory of meaning or an existential expressivism. One such area of research that may prove fruitful in developing a more nuanced understanding of language use is politeness theory.[17] As Levinson suggests, 'we can have our cake and eat it'.[18] We can

---

[17] Work in the area of politeness incorporates and builds on the ideas of ordinary language philosopher Paul Grice. Brown and Levinson, *Politeness*, 3–7.
[18] Levinson, *Presumptive Meanings*, 7–8.

proceed with a study of language that is always sensitive to the social context of an utterance *and* is ready to provide an account of indexicals, presuppositions, implicatures and so on. Briefly, Brown and Levinson make the double assumption that all 'competent adult members of a society' possess 'rationality' and 'face'. Rationality is defined as the ability to 'choose means that will satisfy their ends'.[19] 'Face' consists of two related aspects:

- Negative face: the basic claim to territories, personal preserves, rights to non-distraction – that is, to freedom of action and freedom from imposition.
- Positive face: the positive consistent self-image or 'personality' (crucially including the desire that this self-image be appreciated and approved of) claimed by interactants.[20]

Within this schema, certain linguistic acts of communication are intrinsically 'face threatening' – either for the speaker and/or for the hearer. Brown and Levinson have observed that communication is marked by politeness when a speaker attempts to redress the extent of his or her face-threatening act (FTA). The FTA proves to be a useful tool in explicating the strategies that are employed by members of a speech community.

Generally, politeness theory suggests that the goals and purposes of discourse, along with the accompanying strategies, are universals of language usage. Although there is not the space here to develop the significance of this point, it is worth noting that the spectre of relativity might be more apparent than real. And, against any unqualified appeal to reason, notions of 'reasonableness' or 'rationality' are not necessarily morally positive or even neutral notions. Brown and Levinson have produced a model of anthropology that suggests strongly what might be happening, as it were, between the lines of human discourse. Politeness theory may do at least three things for hermeneutics. Firstly, it will show how we belong to, and are shaped by, the speech community in which we reside. Unwittingly, we are obliged to play by some well-defined social conventions just to maintain our sense of status and solidarity. Secondly, by elucidating notions of 'rationality' and 'face', Brown and Levinson's model is able to predict the type of goals and motivations people bring to discourse and, by extension, the interpretation of Scripture. And thirdly, politeness theory may provide some helpful insights and strategies by which to understand specific narratives and discourse chunks found in the biblical texts. For instance, it is clear that in Paul's first letter to the Corinthians the kerygma of the cross stands opposed to the prior demands of 'face'. Thus the anthropology that emerges offers a sociolinguistic account of what Paul

---

[19] Ibid., 59.
[20] Ibid., 61.

calls 'the natural man'.[21] It is in this context that Thiselton captures well Paul's linguistic strategy of 'code-switching' or 're-definition' and its implicit recognition of the need for a complete *reversal* of the Corinthian church's way of understanding the purposes of God in the world. Wisdom, as discerned by the Spirit, is now to be found in the kerygma of the cross. If language is, in some sense, constitutive of our world, then the language of the cross speaks a *new* world; one that is dependent on the Spirit to open our eyes and unstop our ears. It is for this reason that I draw attention to the need for a more developed account of the Spirit in Thiselton's work.

Biblical Interpretation and the Holy Spirit

In a recent paper, Professor Mark Husbands urges us to recognize the presuppositions already present when we call the biblical texts 'Scripture'. The involvement of the Spirit means that the personality of God is a party to the interpretation of the Bible.[22] In principle, this is something with which Thiselton agrees. It is worth repeating some lines from his present paper:

> In Christian theology, the definitive givenness of Scripture remains both authoritative and potential in meaning on the ground that the same Holy Spirit who inspired the agents who wrote will also inspire the prophets, teachers, congregations and seekers who read.

In view of this *theological* commitment, as I have already suggested, more needs to be done to describe what this might mean for our understanding of language and, in particular, biblical interpretation. For instance, what difference has Pentecost made to the ability of human beings to interpret the Bible? Does Pentecost mark the beginning of a new speech community? The New Testament corpus reflects a self-conscious belief that the indwelling of the Spirit in the community of faith does not just confer a change by degree but in kind; that is, the presence of the Spirit has ontological consequences for human agents. After Pentecost the world has changed.

Despite the scope of Thiselton's model of biblical interpretation, one senses that it is at this point that he has not explicated adequately the radical disjunct that Pentecost represents, namely the *new* human capacity for comprehending and appropriating the gospel kerygma.[23] According to Calvin, the role of the

---

[21] 1 Cor. 2:14.

[22] Husbands, 'Spirit'.

[23] For instance, on the last page of *New Horizons* Thiselton writes: 'In a co-operative shared work, the Spirit, the text, and the reader engage in a transforming process, which enlarges horizons and creates new horizons.' However, the preceding pages provide little idea of what such a model might look like.

Spirit in biblical interpretation itself subverts human rational capacities and with them, presumably, the associated demands of 'face'. He writes, '… without the illumination of the Holy Spirit, the Word can do nothing'.[24] Calvin gathers this principle from many texts in both the Old and New Testaments and, clearly, Paul's comments in the second chapter of his first letter to the Corinthians are significant. Commenting on 1 Corinthians 2:14, Calvin writes: 'Whom does he [Paul] call natural? The man who depends upon the light of nature. He, I say, comprehends nothing of God's spiritual mysteries.'[25] There is an important theological principle at stake for Calvin here, which is captured succinctly in the following: 'The Spirit is so contrasted with flesh that no intermediate thing is left.'[26] Calvin appears to be saying that the Spirit affects not just the use of language but also the ability to process or, in Sperber and Wilson's terms, to count particular chunks of discourse as *relevant*.[27] Husbands expresses a similar perspective when he says that 'the eloquence or semantic force of scripture is not a natural or inherent property of the bible, but emerges rather in its *use*'.[28] He continues,

> The uniqueness of this proposal follows from the fact that the understanding of "use" I am working with is not one in which we are to be regarded as the primary agents of meaning. Rather, just as *adam* was brought to life by the constitutive action of *ruach elohim*, the presence and activity of the Spirit is central to God's *use* of scripture.[29]

Taylor's notion of 'public space' is significant in this context. He writes: 'Language creates what one might call a public space, or a common vantage point from which we survey the world together.'[30] What the Spirit speaks through the Word of scripture draws us into a public space with God himself; we can 'survey the world together'. In this way we begin to see how the Spirit draws the reader in to a new way of seeing the world that involves a crucial reorientation, and enabling, to *hear* scripture as God 'uses' it.

---

[24] Calvin, *Institutes*, 580.

[25] Ibid., 279–80.

[26] Ibid., 289.

[27] Sperber and Wilson, *Relevance*.

[28] Husbands, 'Spirit', uses the term 'scripture' to include the inseparable operation and function of Word and Spirit.

[29] Husbands, 'Spirit'.

[30] Taylor, 'Theories', 259.

Conclusion

In this response I have briefly outlined two related concerns. First, I have suggested that biblical hermeneutics will be best served by moving beyond philosophical models of meaning, especially of the referential type. In attending to actual instances of discourse, linguistic pragmatics will explicate ways in which social interaction typically relates (or does not relate) to states of affairs in the world. Thus, while the expressivist dimension of language needs to be given priority, referential considerations are not neglected. Consequently, Thiselton's approach to language may benefit from insights provided by developments in linguistic pragmatics since speech-act theory. Secondly, I have suggested that Thiselton's biblical hermeneutics will profit from a more integrated approach to the work of the Holy Spirit. This theological task arises both from Scripture's own witness and from the anthropology that emerges from empirical linguistic data of the type used by politeness theory. Both these proposals will, I submit, contribute to a clearer theological account of language.

Bibliography

Bartholomew, C., 'Babel and Derrida: Postmodernism, Language and Biblical Interpretation', *TynBul* 49.2 (1998), 305–28

Brown, P., and S. Levinson, *Politeness: Some Universals in Language Usage* (Cambridge: CUP, 1987)

Calvin, J., *Institutes of the Christian Religion*, I (ed. J.T. McNeill; trans. F.L. Battle; Philadelphia: Westminster Press, 1961)

Grondin, J., *Introduction to Philosophical Hermeneutics* (New Haven: Yale University Press, 1994)

Husbands, M., 'Spirit and the "Use": Hermeneutics and Divine Action' (unpublished paper given at Redeemer University College, August 2000)

Lafont, C., *The Linguistic Turn in Hermeneutic Philosophy* (trans. J. Medina; Cambridge, MA: MIT Press, 1999)

Levinson, S., *Presumptive Meanings: The Theory of Generalized Conversational Implicature* (Cambridge, MA: MIT Press, 2000)

—, *Pragmatics* (Cambridge: CUP, 1983)

Lundin, R., C. Walhout and A.C. Thiselton, *The Promise of Hermeneutics* (Grand Rapids: Eerdmans, 1999)

Rorty, R., *Consequences of Pragmatism* (Minneapolis: University of Minnesota Press, 1982)

—, 'Twenty-Five Years After', in *The Linguistic Turn: Essays in Philosophical*

Method with Two Retrospective Essays (Chicago: Chicago University Press, 1992), 371–74

Sperber, D., and D. Wilson, *Relevance: Communication and Cognition* (Oxford: Basil Blackwell, 1986)

Taylor, C., 'Theories of Meaning' and 'Language and Human Nature', in *Human Agency and Language: Philosophical Papers* (Cambridge: CUP, 1985), 248–92 and 215–47

Thiselton, A.C., *New Horizons in Hermeneutics: The Theory and Practice of Transforming Biblical Reading* (Carlisle: Paternoster; Grand Rapids: Zondervan, 1992)

Vanhoozer, K., 'The Spirit of Understanding: Special Revelation and General Hermeneutics', in *Disciplining Hermeneutics: Interpretation in Christian Perspective* (ed. R. Lundin; Grand Rapids: Eerdmans, 1997)

—, *Is There a Meaning in this Text?: The Bible, the Reader, and the Morality of Literary Knowledge* (Grand Rapids: Zondervan, 1998)

7

Before Babel and After Pentecost

Language, Literature and Biblical Interpretation

Craig G. Bartholomew

Protests, then, against the postmodern readings of the Bible are likely to be ineffec-
tual. Unless, that is, those who care about serious reading of the gospels set about exploring ways in which to articulate a better epistemology, leading to a better account
of what happens when a text is being read, a better account of what happens when a
sacred text is being read … *There is a sense … in which this demands a full theory of language. We need to understand, better than we commonly do, how language works.*
Tom Wright[1]

If Derrida can give a gnostic hermeneutic of the human text in the light of the
gnostic logos, then we should have the confidence to give a Christian hermeneutic
in the light of the real one.
John Milbank[2]

Summary of Argument

At our 1998 Scripture and Hermeneutics consultation in Cheltenham, we
identified 'language' as a major issue that would need to be addressed if we
were to help facilitate a renewal of biblical interpretation. In this chapter I
describe how language has come to be central to contemporary philosophy
and hermeneutics. Biblical interpretation always assumes, even if unconsciously, some view/s of language, and I argue that it is vital that interpreters of

---

[1] Wright, *New Testament*, 61–63. Italics mine.
[2] Milbank, *Word*, 79.

the Bible attend to the current debates about language. Using Derrida as a foil, I develop the view that such critical attention to language and interpretation will mean taking theology of language seriously. In particular I suggest that George Steiner's and John Milbank's work in this area holds considerable potential for biblical interpretation.

Introduction

'Language' has been at the heart of the philosophical debates of the twentieth century.[3] This is particularly true of the last few decades of the twentieth century, during which the postmodern debate has come to the fore, and in which issues of language are utterly central. Charles Taylor notes that the pre-occupation with language is a modern phenomenon:

> The whole development, through the seventeenth-century designative theory and the Romantic expressive view, has brought language more and more to centre stage in our understanding of man; first as an instrument of the typically human capacity of thinking, and then as the indispensable medium without which our typically human capacities, emotions, relations would not be. … we have all in fact become followers of the expressive view … we have all been profoundly marked by this way of understanding thought and language … the profound influence of the expressive view in modern culture is what underlies our fascination for language, our making it such a central question of twentieth-century thought and study.[4]

> From where we stand, we are constantly forced to the conception of man as a language animal, one who is constituted by language.[5]

Origins and Development of the Modern and Late Modern Debate about Language

Of course, the debate about language goes back to early Greek philosophy. The Stoics, Aristotle, Plato and Augustine are key foci in any revisiting of the philosophical tradition in terms of language.[6] However, the origins of the debates about language in the twentieth century go back to the linguistic turn

---

[3] Taylor, 'Language', 215, 216.

[4] Ibid., 235.

[5] Ibid., 246.

[6] Eco always stresses the need to revisit the tradition. See, for example, *Semiotics* and *Kant and the Platypus*. Taylor himself, 'Language', 217, points out that the 'slide' into preoccupation with humans as language animals from Aristotle is not that great.

in German philosophy known as the Hamann-Herder-Humboldt tradition.[7] From a Christian perspective it is fascinating that the Christian thinker Hamann developed his view of language in a critical engagement with Kant, that great father of modern thought.[8] The linguistic tradition initiated by Hamann entails two decisive shifts in relation to the philosophy of consciousness embodied in Kant. Firstly, the H-H-H tradition opposes the Kantian view of language as a mere instrument or tool which mediates the subject-object relation. Rather language is thought of as *constitutive* of thought, having a double status as both empirical and transcendental. Secondly, as a result of this, reason is seen to operate in the context of a multitude of natural languages, so that the unity of reason cannot be guaranteed in terms of the 'extraworldly standpoint of a transcendental subject'.[9]

Hamann's critique of Kant had minimal repercussions in Hamann's lifetime. The significance of his critique lies in its anticipation of ideas that took hold two centuries later.[10] Lafont points out that the implications of Hamann's critique came to fruition in both the continental and Anglo-American (A-A) traditions of philosophy of language in the twentieth century.[11] Frege is the Anglo-American equivalent of Humboldt in the continental tradition, and the common ground is that both of these father figures initiated their linguistic turns by distinguishing *meaning and reference*, and arriving at the thesis *meaning determines reference*. Humboldt and the German tradition were more interested in the analysis of natural languages, whereas Frege was more concerned to develop an artificial language. It is only at a later point, in the postanalytic phase

---

[7] Referred to as such by Taylor, 'Theories', 256. Abbreviated hereafter as H-H-H. Taylor refers to this tradition as the 'Romantic' theory or family of theories, and also as the expressive as opposed to designative theory of language. The latter distinction between designative and expressive structures Taylor's whole discussion of language. Taylor refers to Heidegger as the one in particular who has taken up the H-H-H tradition in the twentieth century. Humboldt is hugely influential in the development of this tradition. For a taste of his expressivist view of language see Humboldt, 'Nature'. Humboldt, ibid., 105, says that, 'By the same act through which he [man] spins out the thread of language he weaves himself into its tissues. Each tongue draws a circle about the people to whom it belongs, and it is possible to leave this circle only by simultaneously entering that of another people.'

[8] For an excellent discussion of the relationship between Hamann and Kant see Beiser, *Fate*. It is intriguing to note that John Milbank invokes Hamann in his critique of the autonomy of philosophy in developing a *Radical Orthodoxy*. See Milbank, 'Knowledge'.

[9] Lafont, *Linguistic Turn*, 3. I have found Lafont helpful in outlining these developments.

[10] Lafont, ibid., 5. Beiser, *Fate*, 40, also notes the significance of Hamann.

[11] See Lafont, *Linguistic Turn.*, ix–xviii.

of the Anglo-American tradition in the 1950s and onwards, that the common ground especially as regards linguistic relativism, incommensurability and meaning holism, becomes apparent.

The way in which the H-H-H and the A-A traditions of language come to fruition in the postmodern debate is perhaps epitomized in Habermas's theory of communicative action, in which he utilizes the Humboldt tradition *and* speech-act theory to try and articulate a theory of language and meaning that preserves a universalist or rationalist perspective against relativism.[12]

Relevance of this Debate to Biblical Interpretation

For Christians, as 'People of the Book',[13] the debates about language that continue to be central to philosophy and our (postmodern?) cultures should not be thought to be irrelevant. For, clearly, the Bible as 'the recording witness to God's authority'[14] is a linguistic (written!) artefact and its interpretation will not be unrelated to how we think about language. Linguistics exploded as a discipline in the twentieth century,[15] and the issue of language is at the heart of hermeneutics, as any assessment of the sources of hermeneutics makes clear.[16]

---

[12] Lafont, ibid., xiii, from her more analytical perspective asserts that, 'The pernicious consequences of the thesis that meaning determines reference become especially apparent once this thesis is combined with the fact of the plurality and contingency of natural languages and the worldviews peculiar to them … For this combination necessarily poses serious problems for the possibility of objective knowledge of the world and of intersubjective communication across different languages. If "what there can be" in the world diverges completely for speakers of different languages, if they cannot talk about the same reality, how can they ever communicate? Worse yet, how can these speakers achieve any knowledge about reality?' Lafont argues that Donnellan, Kripke and Putnam's theories of direct reference contain the resources to underpin Habermas's communicative rationality. See chs. 5ff. of Lafont. The struggle between analytic and continental views of language continues!

[13] See Jeffrey, *People*, esp. xi–xx.

[14] Ibid., xv.

[15] Taylor, 'Language', 215, 216.

[16] See Grondin, *Sources*, esp. chs. 1 and 2. Grondin does not mention Hamann, but makes much of Jacobi: 'There is an historic path from Kant to Nietzsche, therefore, the road from Jacobi to Schopenhauer. And it is precisely this road that accounts for the passage from a metaphysical to a hermeneutical universe' (Grondin, ibid., 5). Grondin, ibid., 13, notes that, 'The transition "from metaphysics to hermeneutics" thus alludes to a shift in our relation to language, one that would take adequate distance from the propositional or "presential" conception of our linguistic dwelling in this world.' Of Gadamer, Grondin, ibid., 14, says, 'the transition "from metaphysics to hermeneutics" can be understood as a passage from a restrictive, logical conception of language to a

No one would deny a close relationship between linguistics and biblical interpretation. After all, there are some major examples in the twentieth century of how understandings of language have changed the course of biblical studies. Langdon Gilkey and James Barr are credited with sounding the death knell of the Biblical Theology Movement (BTM) in 1961.[17] Barr's contribution was to critique the understanding of language that underpinned the BTM. Thiselton rightly argues that what Barr did, in effect, was to mediate Saussure's influence into the discipline of biblical interpretation.[18] Word studies have never been the same since! Another more recent example is the influence of tagmemic discourse analysis on the interpretation of narrative Old Testament texts.[19] Longacre utilized this form of discourse analysis to great gain on Genesis,[20] and exegetes like Gordon Wenham have found it very useful indeed.[21]

'Discourse', itself, alerts us to the fact that in the Bible we are dealing with texts and literature – that is, more than words and sentences. In the 1970s, the literary turn occurred in biblical studies when scholars woke up to the fact that the biblical texts are often carefully crafted literature, and that good interpretation must take account of this literary language. The insights such an approach yield are exemplified in the work of Robert Alter, reaching a high point in Meir Sternberg's classic, *The Poetics of Biblical Narrative*.

Consequently, among biblical scholars, there is an awareness of the importance of linguistics and literary studies for biblical interpretation. The same cannot, I suspect, be said about the *philosophies* of language that underlie linguistics and literary studies, and even when it comes to linguistics and literary studies biblical scholars tend to be eclectic and pragmatic. We tend to live in a modern way in this respect, assuming that the science of language and literature is progressing and that we can draw on new and developing trends where necessary. This is not necessarily a bad thing, depending on the context in which the biblical scholar works and what views of language and literature are in the air, as it were. In my opinion, there are in the air at present some toxic views of language that undermine good, healthy biblical interpretation.

---

[16] (*Continued*) more dialogical understanding, one which is attentive to the speculative dimension of linguisticity.' In terms of biblical interpretation Milbank, *Word*, 64, argues that it was Lowth's view of the poeticality of the Hebrews and not philosophy of history that created the space for the development of historical biblical criticism in Germany.

[17] See Hayes and Prussner, *Old Testament Theology*, 239–45. For a useful contemporary critique of Barr and the BTM see Watson, *Text and Truth*, 18–28.

[18] Thiselton, 'Semantics'.

[19] See Dawson, *Text-Linguistics*.

[20] *Joseph*.

[21] See Wenham's two-volume Word commentary on Genesis.

Simultaneously there are views being developed that hold huge potential for biblical interpretation. If a creative course is to be charted for biblical interpretation in our day it is essential that biblical scholars become conscious and informed about language. Even biblical scholars who embrace the postmodern turn wholeheartedly will need to face the fact that 'linguistics is pursued in a number of mutually irreducible ways, according to mutually contradictory approaches, defended by warring schools'.[22] Thus, whatever position one holds on language and interpretation, the pressure is on to account for one's view. This is reinforced by the connection between language and the mystery of being human.[23] How we think about language is a philosophical, and ultimately a religious, question.

Let me elaborate on the logic I am getting at here:

1. Because Scripture is a linguistic artefact, perspectives on language will *always already* be involved in biblical interpretation and exegesis. If one thinks of the history of biblical interpretation one can track the way in which different views of language manifest themselves exegetically. For example, different views of how language functions underlie the early distinction between Antiochene and Alexandrian, i.e. literal and allegorical styles of interpretation.[24] The 'father' of modern biblical criticism, Wilhelm de Wette, was deeply influenced in his aesthetic 'recovery' of the Bible by Herder and Schelling and their poetic views of language.[25] If de Wette opts for more of an expressivist view of language, most historical criticism has been obsessed with a designative approach to the language of the Bible, always in search of the referential behind the text. Segovia rightly says of historical criticism that, 'As an umbrella model or paradigm, historical criticism may be summarized in terms of the medium or text as means with an emphasis on the signified – the text as means to the author who composed it or the world in which it was composed.'[26]

---

[22] Taylor, 'Language', 215.

[23] Ibid., 216.

[24] One has to be careful of generalizations. For a detailed discussion of the roots and varieties of allegorical interpretation see Thiselton, *New Horizons*, 142–78. A good example for our discussion is Thiselton's point about the connection between Philo's allegorical approach and Platonic idealism. Ibid., 162, 163.

[25] De Wette spent his life, as Rogerson, *W.M.L. de Wette*, points out, trying to come to grips with Kant's philosophy. Herder's and Schelling's aesthetics provided a way for de Wette to combine Kant with a poetic recovery of the Bible.

[26] *Decolonizing*, 8.

The influential Biblical Theology Movement was founded on particular understandings of how words worked, as James Barr exposed,[27] even as he mediated Saussure and modern linguistics into biblical studies. The literary turn in the 1970s showed that 'the literary vehicle is so much the necessary medium through which the Hebrew writers realized their meanings that we will grasp the meanings at best imperfectly if we ignore their fine articulations as literature'.[28] Recently Thiselton, Watson, Vanhoozer and Wolterstorff have in different ways used speech-act theory to respond to the challenges of postmodernism and to forge creative ways forward for biblical interpretation.[29] The postmodern turn in biblical studies is at base informed by views of language, deconstruction being one of the most obvious examples. The emerging theological turn in biblical interpretation, anticipated in the twentieth century by Childs, and championing a reading of the Bible as Christian Scripture, cannot of course avoid some view of language. Thus, for example, as we noted, Watson depends on speech-act theory. Language is always, already, involved in biblical interpretation.

2. Often, however this is at an unconscious level, and the result is that biblical scholars sometimes work with naïve, anachronistic and uninformed views of language.[30] Much of the historical critical paradigm, which has dominated biblical interpretation for the last 150 years or so, has often worked with a naïve and wooden view of literary language. An effect of a more informed view of the Pentateuch as literature, for example, led a mainline scholar such as the late Norman Whybray to move from a Wellhausenian view of the Pentateuch to a view of the Pentateuch as probably by one author, albeit written very late.[31]

---

[27] Barr, *Semantics* and *Biblical Words*.

[28] Alter, 'Introduction', 21.

[29] Thiselton, *New Horizons*, 16–19, 364–67, and 'Communicative Action'; Watson, *Text and Truth*, 95ff.; Vanhoozer, *Meaning*, 209–14, 217, 226–7, 326; Wolterstorff, *Divine Discourse*.

[30] As Thiselton similarly says, 'Communicative Action', 137, 'Curiously, the limits of scientific method to explain all of reality seem to be appreciated more readily in the philosophy of religion than in biblical studies. Views and methods that students in philosophy of religion recognize as "positivist", "reductionist", or even "materialist" are often embraced quite uncritically in issues of judgment about, for example, acts of God in biblical narrative. In place of the more rigorous and judicious exploration of these issues in philosophical theology, biblical studies seems too readily to become polarized.'

[31] Whybray, *Making*.

3. As long as the views of language and literature in the air are fairly compatible with a view of the Bible as 'the recording witness to God's authority'[32] there is not of necessity much pressure for believing biblical scholars or theologians to reflect on language and literature from within a Christian framework. So, for example, New Criticism could be seen as compatible with and even helpful for interpretation of the Bible as Scripture. Lyle Jeffrey notes that, 'It is not difficult to see why many modern literary critics who were Christians found even this *regula* of the New Critics epistemologically, ethically, and even theologically a comfortable framework in which to operate, despite its potential impediments to the moral or theological heurism which regularly enough intruded in any case into some Christian critical writing.'[33]

4. With the rise of postmodernism we have witnessed the emergence of views of language, literature and interpretation that are in some cases antithetical to the Bible as 'the recording witness to God's authority'. I will elaborate on and argue for this below, but my point is that it has become important to be conscious about one's view of language and literature in contemporary biblical interpretation. I particularly want to suggest that if Christians want to find a way forward for biblical interpretation out of the current flux and crisis while capitalizing on the best developments, then we will, *inter alia*, have to attend closely to these issues from within a theological perspective, and we simply cannot wait until a new paradigm emerges within which we can then work conservatively or not so conservatively once again.

I do not want to make the late modern mistake of absolutizing language – there is more to biblical interpretation than language. What I do, however, want to suggest in this paper is that the following ingredients will be important in a renewal of biblical interpretation in our day:

- biblical scholars becoming conscious of the role of language in interpretation
- biblical scholars becoming more sophisticated about the views of language that do and can and should shape interpretation
- believing (Christian) biblical scholars becoming discerning about the *theology* of language and how this impacts on language and interpretation

---

[32] See above.

[33] Jeffrey, *People*, 93. See ibid., xviii, 91–6, for a useful discussion of the secularizing tendency of New Criticism.

Derrida, Language and Biblical Interpretation

This may seem very basic but it has, I suspect, radical implications for biblical interpretation as practised in the academy. One of the good things about postmodernism is, in my opinion, the way it confronts us about our understanding of language and how this functions in our interpretation. *An* important reading of postmodernism is, I suggest, to see it as the linguistic turn working out its inner logic.[34] Certainly the issue of language is central to Heidegger, Gadamer, Rorty, Lyotard, Derrida, and others. Deconstruction is a philosophy of language dealing with how words relate to things.[35]

One could use a variety of routes to show how postmodernism confronts us with how we understand language (e.g. the late Heidegger, Gadamer, Rorty, Lyotard, Habermas, Ricœur, etc.). I will use deconstruction, and Derrida in particular, as an example in this paper. It is the postmodernism I know best and is also in many ways the most radical expression of the linguistic turn. An advantage of Derrida for our debate is that he attends to Scripture on many occasions, and in particular to Genesis 22,[36] and to the Tower of Babel narrative.[37]

At the end of *Structure, Sign and Play*, Derrida distinguishes between two interpretations of interpretation.[38] The first, in the tradition of the metaphysics of presence, deciphers the text in search of its true meaning. The second, in good Nietzschean fashion, sets the text in play. Derrida's straightforward reading of Genesis 22 in *The Gift of Death* is a good example of the first interpretation of interpretation. There is nothing unusual about this reading – authorial intention could be said to be firmly in place as a guard rail guiding Derrida's reading of the text.[39] It is Derrida's contemporary application of the reading that is most unusual and disturbing – the extraordinary call of God to

---

[34] See Lafont, above.

[35] I recognize that this is a controversial view. I think Ellis, *Against Deconstruction*, 29, is right in his assessment that 'What his [Derrida's] argument is really concerned with is a much more familiar issue, the relation of words to things, signs to referents, or, in its most traditional formulation, language to reality. Logocentrism, as Derrida calls the error he wishes to diagnose and transcend, is not about the priority of speech over writing but about the relationship of words to their referents.' Keefer, 'Deconstruction,' 75, is, however, probably right in arguing that deconstruction is *more* than a philosophy of language: 'deconstruction in its Derridean form is neither a philosophy nor even, primarily, a set of strategies for dealing with texts: it is a Gnosis.' See our discussion below.

[36] *Gift*, 53–115.

[37] See Bartholomew, 'Babel and Derrida', for references and a detailed discussion.

[38] Derrida, *Structure*, 292, 293.

[39] I allude here to Derrida's statement about authorial intention in *Of Grammatology*, 158.

Abraham: 'Take your son, your only son, Isaac, whom you love ... and offer him' is secularized into a paradigm for the daily call of our neighbours upon ourselves.

Derrida's performative reading of the Tower of Babel narrative is a good example of his second interpretation of interpretation, of setting a text in play. I have discussed this in detail elsewhere.[40] Suffice it here to note that Derrida uses an obscure French translation whereby the text is read as God invoking God's name BABEL over the city. This marginally, marginally possible – but completely unacceptable – reading is telling in terms of Derrida's philosophy of language. Derrida returns repeatedly to the Babel story because, it seems to me, it functions like a metanarrative for him. But, his is a reading of the narrative abstracted from its creation, fall, redemption context in the Hebrew Bible and the Christian canon.[41] Derrida, from a theological perspective, collapses creation and redemption into fall, and language is absolutized and central to the 'fall'.

Derrida's reading of these few Hebrew words may seem a small detail to concentrate on – but is not that to be truly Derridean! The reception of Derrida in Christian academia has been diverse. Mark Taylor and John Caputo have, it seems to me, embraced deconstruction and, in different ways, developed a way of doing theology and interpretation within this framework.[42] Graham Ward argues that Derrida provides us with a postmodern philosophy of language that fits with Barth's theology.[43] Milbank and many others, like Catherine Pickstock and Roger Lundin,[44] see Derrida as nihilistic and profoundly unchristian. The deliberate complexity and instability in Derrida's work makes it hard to evaluate him. As regards interpretation, does Derrida go for deciphering or for setting texts in play? Criticize Derrida for allowing anything to go, and the deciphering pole of his thought gets invoked. Personally, I am of the opinion that Derrida's real sympathies lie with the Nietzschean affirmation of setting texts in play.[45]

---

[40] See Bartholomew, 'Babel and Derrida'.

[41] Ibid.

[42] Milbank, *Theology*, 295, discerns three theological responses to the postmodern critique of metaphysics. The second is exemplified by Taylor and Caputo. They fully embrace the postmodern critique of metaphysics and seek to 'de-Platonize' Christianity. 'Characteristically, the theological content in these endeavours turns out to be small: the transcendental rule of anarchic difference can be renamed God or the death of God. Dionysiac celebration can be declared to include a contemplative mystical moment – and very little has really been added, nothing is essentially altered.'

[43] Ward, *Barth*.

[44] Pickstock, *After Writing*; Lundin, *Culture*.

[45] For a similar view see Ellis, *Against Deconstruction*, 60–66.

If I am right, and if setting a text in play is a 'logical' consequence of deconstructing Saussure,[46] then reading God as pronouncing God's name BABEL over the city is a legitimate example of the hermeneutic implications of deconstruction. Certainly this reading encapsulates Derrida's collapse of creation and redemption into fall. For such a hermeneutic polysemeity and dissemination are truly uncontainable. If this text can be read in this way, then the possibilities for textual interpretation are infinite! But apart from that frightening thought, is not such a perverse reading a clear case of calling good evil and evil good? And, if nothing else does, ought not such a moment cause us to step back from the trendy affirmation and appropriation of deconstruction?

Yes, such a detail ought to be like a red flag, alerting us to the consequences of travelling down this route. Note that I am *not* saying that deconstruction has nothing to teach us, but what I am saying is that there is serious idolatry here and we need to take note of it.[47] It is very hard to see how such a reading of the Babel narrative could be compatible with a view of the Bible as Scripture.[48] This is one of those points at which one realizes how right Thiselton is when he says of Barthes, Foucault and Derrida that, '[t]hese perspectives constitute the most serious and urgent challenge to theology, in comparison with which the old-style attacks from "common-sense positivism" appear relatively naïve'.[49]

The right response to Derrida is to articulate 'better' understandings of language and interpretation, and to consciously inhabit these rather than the labyrinth of deconstruction.[50] 'Better' understandings will, I suggest, involve plumbing the resources of the Christian tradition.

---

[46] See Derrida, *Of Grammatology*, for his deconstruction of Saussure.

[47] Wolters, 'Perplexing History', is helpful at this point in his argument that it is precisely around the points of idolatry in scholarship that the penetrating insights are to be found.

[48] I realize this assumes some view/s of the Bible as Scripture. See below for a brief discussion of the testimony of the Bible and its nature as Scripture.

[49] *Interpreting God*, 16. It is surprising how often this sort of critique of postmodernism is misunderstood. Let me therefore reiterate that I think postmodernism to be also a time of *great opportunity*. However, Hauerwas, *A Better Hope*, 43, is right when he refers to Yoder's view that the crucified Jesus is 'a more adequate key to understanding what God is about in the real world of empires and markets than is the ruler in Rome', and then says that 'Postmodernists cannot help but think such a claim to be the grandest of grand narratives, but I cannot imagine Christians saying anything less. Not only saying it, but also truthfully living and thinking that this is the way things are.'

[50] Note the quote from Tom Wright at the outset of the chapter, and see Scott, 'Steiner', 4, for a helpful articulation of this perspective.

Postmodernism as Confronting Us with Our Ultimate or Religious Orientations Towards the World and Language

To even suggest that academic biblical interpretation should be theologically informed has not always been welcome in the academy. Thus it is intriguing to note how a variety of Christian and non-Christian theorists recognize that postmodern views of language such as deconstruction relate to religious or ultimate perspectives we hold about the world.[51] George Steiner, in his discussion of deconstruction, boldly asserts that deconstruction confronts us with a stark choice:

> It is Derrida's strength to have seen so plainly that the issue is neither linguistic-aesthetic nor philosophical in any traditional, debatable sense – where such tradition and debate incorporate, perpetuate the very ghosts which are to be exorcized. The issue is, quite simply, that of the meaning of meaning as it is re-insured by the postulate of the existence of God. "In the beginning was the Word." There was no such beginning, says deconstruction; only the play of sounds and markers amid the mutations of time.[52]

From Steiner's perspective the wager that real presences underlie language makes a tremendous difference to how we interpret texts, and not least the Bible. In a talk in Birmingham in the UK, for example, Steiner urged British 'Old Testament' – he suggested we change the name of the society – scholars to revisit the issue of the authorship of biblical texts. Steiner explained that on a good day he could imagine Shakespeare going home from work having written one of his profound plays. But never can he do this with God's speeches in Job, and Steiner suggested we revisit the issue of the authoring of these texts.

So much has happened since the fall of the Eastern bloc that it is too easy to forget the importance of the connection between language and truth in that context. For Solzhenitsyn giving his Nobel address in 1966 it was vital to connect language with truth: 'One word of truth outweighs the entire world.' Very much in that tradition is the thinker, playwright and politician Vaclav Havel. For Havel, a correct understanding of the ethics of language flows from our living in the truth. He says,

---

[51] At a popular level Os Guinness similarly refers to John 1: ' "In the beginning was the Word", John's Gospel begins – which means that in the end meaning itself has meaning, guaranteed by God himself and now spoken forth as an effective, liberating Word.' *Time for Truth*, 86. At a theoretical level, Milbank, *Word*, makes a similar case. See discussion below.

[52] *Real Presences*, 120.

Having learned from all this, we should all fight together against arrogant words and keep a weather eye out for any insidious germs of arrogance in words that are seemingly humble.

Obviously this is not just a linguistic task. Responsibility for words and towards words is a task that is intrinsically ethical.

As such, however, it is situated beyond the horizon of the visible world, in that realm wherein dwells the Word that was in the beginning and is not the word of man.[53]

No doubt the link between language and theology could be made in many ways. I will use deconstruction and the doctrine of the two ways to indicate one way in which the religious dimensions of language can be foregrounded. There are a variety of types of deconstruction, helpfully distinguishable as 'soft' and 'boa' deconstructors.[54] Miller and Bloom would be examples of the former and Derrida the embodiment of the latter. Intriguingly all of these deconstructors have in common a doctrine of 'the two ways' when it comes to reading texts.[55]

In *Deconstruction and Criticism* Harold Bloom asserts that the 'praxis of poetry' requires one of two views of language, namely: a magical theory which credits language with plenitude of meaning; or a nihilistic view which discerns a lack of meaning and randomness in language. Bloom associates this theory with Derrida, de Man, Hartman and Hillis Miller. Bloom says that

All I ask is that the theory of language be extreme and uncompromising enough. Theory of poetry, as I pursue it, is reconcilable with either extreme view of poetic language, though not with any views in between. Either the new poet fights to win freedom from death, or from plenitude, but if the antagonist be moderate, then the agon will not take place, and no fresh sublimity will be won. Only the agon is of the essence.[56]

Similarly Hillis Miller describes the two extremes in theory of language as a reciprocal relationship in which nihilism is present always as a latent ghost encrypted in the logocentric system. The two are neither antithetical nor may they be synthesized: 'Each defines and is hospitable to the other, host to it as parasite.'[57]

---

[53] Havel, 'A Word About Words', 389.
[54] I am conflating two typologies here. See Himmelfarb, *On Looking*, 9.
[55] See Jeffrey, *People*, 1ff.
[56] Bloom, 'Breaking', 2.
[57] Miller, 'Critic', 228.

Derrida's view of interpretation is also constructed around two ways, and this manifests itself in a variety of ways. We have already noted the two interpretations of interpretation, deciphering a text and setting it in play. This is paralleled in his discussion of Jabés and the book by his typology of the rabbi and the poet.[58] Derrida's distinction between the rabbi and the poet symbolizes the two types of interpretation.[59] In the third footnote to this essay Derrida says that:

> [t]he 'rabbinical' interpretation of interpretation is the one which seeks a final truth, which sees interpretation as an unfortunately necessary road back to an original truth. The 'poetical' interpretation of interpretation does not seek truth or origin, but affirms the play of interpretation.[60]

Earlier on, Derrida explains:

> [b]etween the fragments of the broken Tables the poem grows and the right to speech takes root. Once more begins the adventure of the text as weed, as outlaw far *from 'the fatherland of the Jews,'* which is a *'sacred text surrounded by commentaries'*... The necessity of commentary, like poetic necessity, is the very form of exiled speech. In the beginning is hermeneutics. But the *shared* necessity of exegesis, the interpretive imperative, is differently interpreted by the rabbi and the poet. The difference between the horizon of the original text and exegetic writing makes the difference between the rabbi and the poet irreducible. Forever unable to reunite with each other, yet so close to each other, how could they ever regain the realm? The original opening of interpretation essentially signifies that there will always be rabbis and poets. And two interpretations of interpretation. ... The book of man is a book of question.[61]

Within this doctrine of the two ways, theology and Christian reflection get damned as irretrievably 'logocentric'. Jeffrey suggests that the roots of this perspective lie in Gnosticism:

> But deconstruction is itself arguably one of the most evidently gnostic varieties of poststructuralist theory. Like its second-century predecessor as much as the antinomian structuralism of Barthes on which it more nearly draws, deconstruction

---

[58] Derrida, *Writing*, 64–78.

[59] Derrida, ibid., 76, makes statements in this essay very similar to his controversial statement that there is nothing outside the text. He writes, 'everything that is exterior in relation to the book, everything that is negative as concerns the book, is produced within the book. ... One emerges from the book only within the book, because for Jabés, the book is not in the world, but the world is in the book.'

[60] Derrida, *Writing*, 311.

[61] Ibid., 67.

ad finem strives to separate its form of knowledge from any reference to external nature, experience, or historical process. The transcendent principle in both ancient gnosticism and modern deconstruction is an absence, not a presence.[62]

Jeffrey is not alone in discerning Gnostic parentage for deconstruction. Milbank,[63] Eco,[64] Watson[65] and Keefer[66] make similar comparisons. Of these, the fullest case is that by Keefer.[67] Keefer argues that deconstruction, like second-century Gnosticism, is antinomian, antihistorical and anti-worldly. Epistemologically, knowledge is cut off from 'positive externality'. The hidden God of Gnosticism is an absence, but this God who is inaccessible is also constitutive of everything. With its concern for salvation, Gnosticism might appear different from Derrida, who manifests no nostalgia for presence. But Keefer argues that any genuine piety is lacking in Gnostic texts. Keefer suggests that the sources for Derrida's Gnosticism might be Nietzsche and Heidegger, Hans Jonas noticed the similarity of Heidegger's thought to Gnosticism. A more specific source may be Lautréamont's *Chants de Maldoror*, which Derrida engages positively in *Dissemination*.[68]

For theological assessment of deconstruction, this comparison of deconstruction with Gnosticism is very important. There may well be much more going on in deconstruction than Gnosticism, but I think this critique is accurate in terms of Derrida's collapse of creation into fall, as epitomized in his reading of the Tower of Babel narrative. Jeffrey rightly asserts that the two ways of deconstruction are an unacceptable framework from a Christian perspective:

Accordingly, for the Christian, theory of poetry cannot responsibly be formulated from either polar view about the nature and properties of language, since such an absolute dichotomization misrepresents reality, either idolizing language (logocentrism) or repudiating it as useful means to understanding (nihilism).

---

[62] Ibid., 356.

[63] Milbank, *Word*, 60–63, 79. Milbank, ibid., 61, notes that Derrida is anti-Platonic in his taking the signifying trace to be an absolutely original moment, but remains Platonic in seeing this imaging as a lapse. 'The further dimension to his scepticism might be described as a kind of Valentinian gnosis, in that it identifies creation with fall and makes both inevitable, though resignation to aesthetic jouissance is the nearest he gets to a motif of redemptive "return." '

[64] Eco, *Interpretation*, 1–43.

[65] Watson, *Text and Truth*, 77, 80, 82.

[66] Keefer, 'Deconstruction'.

[67] Ibid., 83–87.

[68] *Dissemination*, 36ff. Keefer, 'Deconstruction', 86, describes *Chants de Maldoror* as an 'explicitly Gnostic text, in the line … of Carpocrates, the most violently antinomian of the second-century Gnostics.'

Still more disturbing is the way any such misprision as Bloom's masks the nature of the actual *agon* in which men and women struggle to communicate and commune, to know and to be known, to love and seek truth. Neither Dante nor Eliot, for example, could say with Bloom that whichever theory of language one chooses is immaterial for theorizing about poetry so long as it is 'extreme enough and uncompromising'; for the Christian theorist the choice does not lie between sense and nonsense, a surplus of meaning and no certain meaning at all. Rather, it lies more profoundly between life and death (Deut. 30:19), truth and denial of truth (Rom. 1:25). In the imperfect area of human signification, where we see 'as in a mirror enigmatically,' the asymptotic character of fallen language is a source of endless frustration as well as momentary joy.[69]

In a comparable way Brian Ingraffia has argued that biblical theology is eschatological[70] and not guilty of logocentrism in the way Derrida and postmoderns assert. The point is that such a biblical, eschatological framework which refuses to absolutize autonomous reason or language delivers a very different two ways to that of Bloom, Miller and Derrida.

Consider, for example, the doctrine of the two ways in Old Testament wisdom literature. Ray van Leeuwen has done fine work in analysing the diverse ways in which this doctrine manifests itself in Proverbs 1–9 as two ways, two women, two houses, and so on. Van Leeuwen rightly argues that the underlying metaphor is that of a carved world with limits:

> … underlying the bipolar metaphorical system of positive and negative youths, invitations/calls, 'ways', 'women', and 'houses' in Proverbs 1–9, is a yet more fundamental reality which these images together portray. These chapters depict the world as the arena of human existence. This world possesses two fundamental characteristics. First is its structure of boundaries or limits. Second is the bi-polar human *eros* for the beauty of Wisdom, who prescribes life within limits, or for the seeming beauty of Folly, who offers bogus delights in defiance of created limits.[71]

This perspective is disclosed by carefully crafted language, but it is not created by language. At the centre of this vision, and in contrast to the two ways of deconstruction, is Yahweh Elohim, who has created by his wisdom.[72] Language is a creature, and the agon in this view of language is directing it in a way consistent with the fear of the LORD as opposed to the way of folly.

---

[69] Jeffrey, *People*, 8.

[70] *Postmodernism*. See also Andrew Lincoln's important book, *Paradise Now and Not Yet* in this respect.

[71] Van Leeuwen 'Liminality', 116.

[72] See esp. Prov. 8.

Scripture and Language

Do note that I am *not* suggesting that Scripture delivers a full-blown philosophy of language. What I am suggesting is that Scripture *orients us towards* the world and language in a way that is profoundly at odds with Bloom and Derrida. And Steiner, Havel and others are suggesting that we take these clues to language seriously. Indeed there is rather more about language in the Bible than is sometimes recognized. Historically, for better and for worse, the Bible has profoundly influenced the philosophy of language.[73] Indeed, one of the exciting dimensions of postmodernism is the readiness of (non-Christian) theorists to interact with scriptural references to language.[74]

This does *not* mean that the scriptural clues about language are easily discerned or easily fitted into a unified picture, let alone easily related to philosophy and theology of language. Despite, or perhaps because of, its massive influence on the history of the philosophy of language, the theme of language in the Bible has been neglected by most biblical scholars and theologians,[75] and the renewed attention to the theme of language that we seek must do justice to the range and diversity of Scripture.[76] There is the crucial question of *how* we take the biblical clues seriously. Certainly we should be careful of imposing a unity upon the diverse biblical data dealing with language, but my approach anticipates that the different elements of Scripture would interact with each other to open up for us an alternative vision of the world.[77] Analysis of scriptural teaching about language would require a monograph in itself, and it must suffice here to note some of the key places where Scripture deals with language and to indicate the direction such analysis might take.

---

[73] See Eco, *Search*; Steiner, *After Babel*.

[74] See Bartholomew, 'Babel and Derrida', 316, 317.

[75] Although the Tower of Babel narrative obviously has to do with language, a quick survey of commentaries on Genesis indicates that many commentators ignore this dimension. This is also true of biblical/Old Testament theologies and of commentaries on Acts. Among Old Testament theologies, Preuss is exceptional in having a section on 'The Language of Humans'. Unfortunately there is little in this section on theology of language. Among Genesis commentaries, Brueggemann's is a refreshing exception, and it is encouraging to see missiological studies attending to this dimension of Scripture. See Hunsberger, *Bearing the Witness*, 244–55, on 'the Table and the Tower'.

[76] This would need to include data that strikes us nowadays as strange, such as the etymologies of place and name.

[77] Kelsey, *Uses*, remains a useful text for setting out the variety of ways in which Scripture is used in theology. Kelsey recognizes the importance of *how* Scripture is used theologically. The suggestions I am making about pursuing the clues in Scripture could fit with a number of the models he describes, including his own view of the use of Scripture for shaping Christian existence.

In both Genesis 1 and John 1 God is portrayed as *speaking* the creation into existence. These passages, as we have seen, are often referred to for a theological perspective on language. However, one must be cautious here in moving too quickly to a theology of language. God speaking, by fiat, creation into existence, is one *metaphor* among several for creation in Genesis 1. God also makes and brings things into existence through other things, and he names that which he creates.[78] And in John 1 the point of describing Jesus as the Logos is that God has shown himself to us in Christ. If issues of language are present in Genesis 1 and John 1, then they are secondary to these concerns about creation and revelation. As von Rad rightly notes, the idea of creation by word indicates firstly the radical *difference* between creator and creature, and God's naming speaks of his unique sovereignty.[79]

This does not mean that the choice of the speaking metaphor for creation is irrelevant to issues of language.[80] In Genesis 1 the humans made in the image of God are the first to be addressed directly by God, indicating that God creates a creature that can listen to God and answer back.[81] It seems to me, however, that the primary importance of God speaking creation into existence for our understanding of language is that language itself must be understood within that 'orderly cosmic arrangement and wholesome stabilization'[82] that results from God's creative activity. This is what I am getting at in the 'Before Babel' of the title of this paper. A theological account of language must position Babel within the context of creation, fall and redemption. It is the very secondary of human language that is illuminating against the background divinization of language by some postmoderns. Humans too are 'naming persons' (Gen. 2:19, 20), but in a radically secondary way.

The Tower of Babel narrative clearly has to do with language, although commentators generally ignore this. It is not easy to know how to read this narrative, but in its canonical context I suggest that Genesis 11 should be read against, and not in contradiction to, Genesis 10. Thus Babel does *not* present the diversity of languages as judgement, but as God-given.[83] The judgement in

---

[78] Watson, *Text, Church and World*, 137–53, speaks of the speech-act model, the fabrication model and the mediation model of creation.

[79] *Genesis*, 49–51.

[80] See Watson, *Text, Church and World*, 143ff. *Inter alia* Watson notes that the Genesis narrative alerts us unequivocally to the distinction between divine and human speech acts, contra to much postmodernism.

[81] Watson, *Text, Church and World*, 150.

[82] Von Rad, Genesis, 51.

[83] Bartholomew, 'Babel and Derrida', 313. O'Donovan, *Resurrection*, 230, rightly notes that 'The plurality of mankind, like the pluriformity of created order as a whole, is God's first and last word.'

terms of (mis)communication is given expression through language but derives, not from structural problems with language, but from humans seeking idolatrous centres for their lives. Humans, in the totality of their lives, are fallen away from that centre which is God, and it is humans that need redemption, not some structural deficiency in language.[84] Read thus, Genesis 10 and 11 are consistent with the proclamation of the gospel in a variety of languages at Pentecost. Babel and Pentecost are about language and canonically they stand, as it were, like two large inclusios at either end of the canon – although it is surprising how few commentators on Acts recognize Pentecost's backward reference to Babel.

Two of the Ten Commandments are about language use: 'You shall not take the name of the Lord your God in vain', and 'You shall not bear false witness'. The latter commandment is particularly significant for our purposes. Its primary reference is to the fundamental importance of truth telling in a judicial context, but, particularly in Proverbs, this principle of truth telling is extended into other societal contexts.[85] Indeed, Proverbs is a major source for any canonical consideration of language. Already in Proverbs 1–9 the keeping of the heart is closely connected with language (4:23, 24), but from Proverbs 10 onwards the amount of material dealing with 'the mouth', 'lips' and 'words' is astonishing. Language use is one of the fundamental ways the antithetical paths of folly and wisdom manifest themselves.[86] Proverbs, like the ninth commandment, is concerned with language *use*, and as Fretheim perceptively notes, 'What is at stake here is the good order of God's creation.'[87] In Proverbs, as in Genesis, the doctrine of creation is foundational for understanding the human and language, and this must function as an important clue for any Christian understanding of language.

We have already mentioned the relevance of Acts and Pentecost to language. The Gospels and the Epistles also contain much instruction about language use (Matt. 5–7; 1 Cor.; Eph. 4; James, etc.). In all of these contexts,

---

[84] Eco, *Search*, 9, 10, says of Genesis 11 that '[i]t is this story that served as the point of departure for any number of dreams to "restore" the language of Adam. Genesis 10, however, has continued to lurk in the background with all its explosive potential still intact. If languages were already differentiated after Noah, why not before? If languages were differentiated not as a result of a natural process, why must the confusion of tongues constitute a curse at all? Every so often in the course of our story, someone will oppose Genesis 10 to Genesis 11. Depending on the period and the theologico-philosophical context, the results will be more or less devastating.' See Eco, ibid., for the story of the search for the original language.

[85] Childs, *Old Testament Theology*, 83.

[86] About 20% of Prov. 10 – 29 deals with speech (Murphy, *Proverbs*, 258).

[87] *Exodus*, 237.

speech is understood as a way of operating in the world for which the moral subject is responsible. Underlying language use is the direction of 'the heart'.[88] There is a mine of material waiting to be excavated in terms of the Bible and language. Of course, where this theme is being addressed, there is considerable difference of opinion. Kermode,[89] for example, argues that Mark enacts the labyrinth of language. Suffice it, here, to note that Kermode's reading is not uncontested.[90]

To sum up, the biblical texts we have attended to suggest a very different view of language to Bloom and Derrida. The following elements are central to the biblical vision that we have begun to explore:[91]

- Humans and language (and reason) are creaturely, and part of God's ordered creation. Language is something that humans 'do' and is a meaningful activity. The capacity for language is a central element in being a human creature.
- In a fallen world language can be seriously misdirected by humans, as epitomized by Babel.
- Language can be redirected redemptively – Pentecost is the great example of this, where the God-given diversity of languages is used to tell forth the gospel.
- Believers have a responsibility to speak/write the truth in love.[92]

Language is not a simple entity and it is vital that, as we pursue these clues and relate them to theories of language, we recognize the complexity of language.[93] However, a theology of language must, I suggest, do justice to:

- Language as fundamentally good, a gift of God. A Christian perspective must, for example, take account of the capacity for words to be a means

---

[88] See O'Donovan, *Resurrection*, 204–207.

[89] *Genesis of Secrecy*.

[90] Watson, *Text, Church and World*, 78–82.

[91] It is important to reiterate that the unity of Scripture remains a highly contested area and that ideally my argument requires a detour via a careful analysis of 'language' in the different parts of Scripture, so that the diversity and unity are foregrounded.

[92] For a useful discussion of the Christian ethics of truth telling see Bonhoeffer, *Ethics*, 363–72, and Burtness, *Shaping*, 121–66.

[93] The complexities of this process should not be underestimated, and I do not imply here that the direction is simply one way from Scripture to language theory. See Ford, *Theology*, 19–26, for a useful typology of ways of doing theology. The approach I am proposing would fit under Ford's type 4, which gives priority to Christian self-description but still enters into a wide range of dialogues. Ford, ibid., 17, refers to an 'ecology of responsibility' for theology, and this metaphor usefully alerts one to the diverse elements in articulating a biblical theology of language.

whereby humans give themselves to each other at the deepest level, as in Jesus' words in the Eucharist, 'This is my Body.' Augustine rightly speaks of words as 'Those precious cups of meaning.'

- Language as world-disclosing and world-constituting, but not finally world-creating.[94] The following incident that Timothy Radcliffe describes is a fine example of the world disclosive potential of words: 'A Dominican sister from Taiwan told of a girl carrying the burden of a child on her back. Someone said to her: "Little girl, you are carrying a heavy weight." She replied, "I am not carrying a weight, I am carrying my brother." '[95] As Taylor points out, there are some phenomena central to human life, such as feelings, relations and political equality that are partly constituted by language.[96] Such an approach is different from a postmodern tendency to see human life as a linguistic construct. The latter perspective absolutizes language and is in danger of idolatry, and the creative and constitutive power of language needs to be distinguished from language as create-ive in an ultimate sense.

- The capacity of language to disclose, to refer *and* to communicate. We need understandings of language that open up these different and yet not mutually exclusive functions of language. I suspect this also relates to our need for understandings of language that explore language as one mode of being in a world made up of many different dimensions.

- Our everyday use of language – so much postmodernism seems radically out of sync with this, but a Christian view of language must surely do justice to the way in which language functions quite happily much of the time.[97]

- Language as capable of being misdirected, and our responsibility *not* to participate in such misdirection. Ethics must be a priority in our understanding and use of language.

Theology and Language, and Biblical Interpretation

If Steiner and Havel are right in asserting that our religious framework affects our view of language, then it follows that there is a place for Christians pursuing the above clues and consciously thinking through language 'theologically'.

---

[94] I have found Taylor's discussion of language as constitutive most helpful. See, 'Theories of Meaning', 270–73.

[95] Radcliffe, *Sing*, 18, 19.

[96] Ibid.

[97] See Wolterstorff, 'Importance', for a useful discussion of this point.

In this section I will initiate a discussion about theology of language and how it might benefit biblical interpretation.

For a long time now something of a chasm has been in place between biblical studies and theology. Thankfully this is now being subverted by the renewal of theological interpretation of the Bible as Scripture. Brevard Childs, Francis Watson, Stephen Fowl, Richard Hayes, Chris Seitz, Kevin Vanhoozer, Tom Wright, and a growing number of other biblical scholars and theologians are insisting that we need to make *theological* interpretation a priority.

As I have noted elsewhere, there are a variety of views that go under the banner of theological interpretation.[98] A key issue that emerges from the diversity is the relationship between theological interpretation and general hermeneutics. This is a variant of the Yale-Chicago debate.[99] I fully sympathize with the desire to get on with issues like the Old Testament-New Testament relationship and biblical typology, without being delayed endlessly by general hermeneutical discussions. However, I think it is a mistake to think one can avoid the general hermeneutical issues such as philosophy of language. Ontology and epistemology are always already present in theory construction, whether they are acknowledged or not. They function something like scaffolding in building construction, and while we would not want to focus continually on scaffolding it is important to check this out every now and again.

And, naturally, 'Yale-type' proponents of theological interpretation do invoke different philosophies of language. Intriguingly, it is precisely those philosophies of language that biblical scholars mostly appeal to that Derrida finds vulnerable to deconstruction. Derrida subjects Saussure, Searle's speech-act theory and Gadamer to deconstruction, and argues that all three of these theories of language are logocentric and profoundly problematic. Of course, we might rightly differ with Derrida here and therefore dismiss his critique. But, at the very least this begs the question why we, as Christian scholars, are so comfortable with Saussure, Searle and Gadamer.

I am *not* suggesting that we discard Saussure, Searle and Gadamer. But there must surely be room for theological assessment of Saussure, speech-act theory and Gadamerian hermeneutics, and so on. For example, take Searle's understandings of brute facts and institutional facts, and background – do these concepts carry the baggage of Searle's world-view or framework, and if so how? And what does this say about how Christian scholars ought or ought not to make use of them?

---

[98] 'Uncharted Waters', 24–9.
[99] See Stiver, *Philosophy*, 134ff. for a useful summary, and Vanhoozer, 'Spirit'.

A similar situation arises when it comes to reading the Bible as literature. Within literary theory, as Jeffrey makes clear, there is a robust and fertile Christian tradition that remains relevant today. Jeffrey epitomizes the sort of creative development of the Christian tradition we need today, as do Christian thinkers like Roger Lundin, Calvin Seerveld, Michael Edwards and Ruth Etchells. It is this Christian tradition of linguistic and literary analysis that biblical scholars need to tap into, while, of course, remaining in real dialogue with the mainstream, and drawing on the very real insights there.

It seems to me folly to neglect general hermeneutics, for the issues addressed here are unavoidable. At the same time general hermeneutics is never theologically neutral, so that what is required for biblical interpretation is a theologically informed grasp of general hermeneutics. At stake here is our very understanding of (Christian) scholarship and how it develops. I am aware of just how easily the above proposals are misunderstood. With George Marsden, I *am* suggesting that

> mainstream [biblical studies] ... should be more open to explicit discussion of the relationship of religious faith to learning. Scholars who have religious faith should be reflecting on the intellectual implications of that faith and bringing those reflections into the mainstream of intellectual life.[100]

Marsden says of 'the outrageous idea of Christian education' that

> [t]he problem of recognizing the day-to-day significance of this factor is aggravated by the difficulty of talking about something that is missing. Not only is it missing, but its absence is taken for granted. ... How do you portray something that is missing?[101]

The result is that attempts to call attention to this difference get categorized in terms of what is visible – for example, fundamentalism. However, as Milbank rightly asserts, 'if Derrida can give a gnostic hermeneutic of the human text in the light of the gnostic logos, then we should have the confidence to give a Christian hermeneutic in the light of the real one.'[102] Let me therefore give some examples of theologies of language and how they might assist biblical interpretation, lest my proposal be misconstrued. This is a huge area to even

---

[100] Marsden, *Outrageous Idea*, 3, 4. Brackets represent my adaptation of Marsden. Marsden, ibid., 23, suggests that in American education 'in place of a Protestant establishment we now have a virtual establishment of nonbelief'. This reminds me of Walter Brueggemann's comment at a Canadian conference that certain types of biblical scholarship amount to unbelief seeking understanding.

[101] Marsden, *Outrageous Idea*, 77.

[102] Milbank, *Word*, 79.

begin to address, and it is possible here only to describe certain approaches and make some suggestions about future directions that will help biblical interpretation. I will focus on one theistic (Jewish) approach, namely that of Steiner, and one Christian, Trinitarian approach, that of Milbank.

1. Language undergirded by Real Presences: George Steiner's courteous hermeneutic

Language has been the pivot of Steiner's extensive and wide-ranging work,[103] and *inter alia* he has insisted on examining the (transcendent) roots of our understanding of language and the humanities.[104] In *After Babel* and *Real Presences* in particular, Steiner has articulated an expressivist perspective on language that is deeply indebted to Heidegger but moves in a radically different direction to Derrida and some of the other postmoderns who also draw on Heidegger.[105] Steiner's overt use of Eucharistic lexicography (*Real Presences*) to articulate his view of language indicates Catholic influence, which is mediated to an extent by Heidegger, but Steiner's stronger theological commitments also distinguish him from Heidegger.[106]

From the outset of *Real Presences*, Steiner is clear that any coherent account of language and communication needs to be supported by a theology of God's presence. Steiner is acutely aware of the interpretative crisis of our time – secondary critical reflection upon literature and art has become an end in itself, and in this Secondary City we are hindered from encountering art and literature, and thus the Bible, directly. Steiner relates this crisis in artistic encounter and interpretation to a loss of the transcendent. Such a time radically misconceives hermeneutics, which rightly understood is 'the enactment of answerable understanding, of active apprehension'.[107] Steiner discerns theological reasons behind our consumer society's preference for the secondary. We

---

[103] Steiner, 'Responsion', 281. As Krupnick, 'Steiner's Literary Journalism', 46, says, 'His single great theme has been the status of language and the humanities in the wake of the political bestiality of our century.'

[104] Almansi, 'Triumph', 60.

[105] Steiner, 'Responsion', 277, confesses that he is, 'utterly persuaded by Heidegger's finding that we are guests of Being, transient dwellers in a temporality and "thrownness" entirely beyond our grasp, and that this condition makes of us the custodians of language and of certain values and astonishments in the face of life itself'. For Steiner's relationship to Heidegger see Ward, 'Heidegger in Steiner' and Steiner, *Martin Heidegger.*

[106] See Ward, 'Heidegger', 199, 200.

[107] *Real Presences*, 7. See p. 9 for Steiner's emphasis on performance and on ingestion of the text so that it becomes part of the pacemaker of one's consciousness.

prefer not to confront the real presence or the absence of that presence. Amidst all the secondary theory we welcome the one who can secularize the mystery and call of creation.[108]

According to Steiner, humans have great and unbounded freedom when it comes to language. There is no limit to the chain of signs, and it is the way we think about this infinity that shapes our practice of interpretation.

> Inhabiting language ... both the act of interpretation and that of assessment, hermeneutics and criticism, are inextricably enmeshed in the metaphysical and theological or anti-theological question of unbounded saying.[109]

An effect of this, according to Steiner, is that language cannot be verified or falsified.[110] Generally we proceed by appealing to consensus, and tradition (the canonic), but this is never decisive.[111]

The consequent turn to theory to make reading of language scientific is like trying to catch the wind. The principles of indeterminacy and of complementarity, as understood in particle physics, are central to all interpretation. Each text is singular. For Steiner there is a gap, therefore, between all theories and the process of understanding. Theory has value, but only if it is aware of its reductiveness. Theories are best understood as narratives of moments of illumination in dealing with texts.[112] Steiner describes the claim to theory in the humanities as impatience systematized, and he notes that this impatience has assumed nihilistic urgency today.

How have we reached our present state? For Steiner, there has been a monumental break in our understanding of the word–world relationship. Our understanding of language and discourse had been underwritten by trust, by the assumption that being is 'sayable'. According to Steiner this contract was broken in a major way for the first time during the decades from the 1870s to the 1930s. '*It is this break of the covenant between word and world which constitutes one of the very few genuine revolutions in spirit in Western history and which defines modernity itself.*'[113] So decisive is this shift for Steiner that he distinguishes two major phases in our 'inward history', the first being that from the beginnings of recorded history to the later nineteenth century. This is the phase of the 'saying of being'. The second is that which follows this phase, the time of the after-Word, of the epilogue, 'an immanence within the logic of the "afterword" '.[114]

---

108 Ibid., 39.
109 Ibid., 59.
110 Ibid., 61, 68.
111 Ibid., 68.
112 Ibid., 86.
113 Ibid., 93.
114 Ibid., 228.

Steiner discerns this monumental shift in Western consciousness in Mallarmé's understanding of language as embodying 'real absence' and in Rimbaud's deconstruction of the first person singular as encapsulated in his *Je est un autre*. Mallarmé rejects the 'covenant of reference', and argues that non-reference constitutes the true genius of language.[115] 'Where Mallarmé alters the epistemology of "real presence" (theologically grounded) into one of "real absence", Rimbaud posits at the now vacant heart of consciousness the splintered images of other and momentary "selves".'[116]

Steiner identifies four great currents of the 'after-Word' that followed this revolution in consciousness: that of Wittgenstein, post-Saussurean linguistics, psychoanalysis (Freud, Lacan), and the indictment of language in *Sprachkritik* (Fritz Mauthner, Karl Kraus). For Steiner, Nietzsche's 'death of God' and Freud's implicit secularization of the psyche are footnotes to the breach represented by Mallarmé and Rimbaud. In Derrida and deconstruction Steiner discerns the nihilistic consequences of the after-Word: 'In a time of epilogue and after-Word, a critique such as deconstruction *must* be formulated.'[117]

Steiner recognizes the grounds for refuting deconstruction, but the problem is that deconstruction can live quite comfortably with the critique it engenders. In Steiner's opinion, deconstruction is, on its own terms, irrefutable. The real alternative is to ask what would happen if we take theology and metaphysics seriously.[118] Steiner

> chooses not to waste time on polemic: because what Paul Ricœur calls 'the dismantled fortress of consciousness' is not to be 'restored or made foolproof by replacing this or that fallen brick' ... He sees with absolute clarity that the most essential repudiation lying at the heart of the whole deconstructive enterprise is a theological repudiation, and thus, as he feels, the one kind of faith (in unfaith) may only be countered by another kind of faith.[119]

This alternative architecture of language and literature/art is the subject of the third section of *Real Presences*.

In order to articulate a vision of interpretation that does justice to our experience of the other, Steiner invokes the metaphor of *courtesy*. He is worth quoting at length on this point.

> ... the phenomenology of courtesy would organize, that is to say quicken into articulate life, our meetings with each other, with the beloved, with the adversary, with the

---

[115] Ibid., 96.
[116] Ibid., 99.
[117] Ibid., 120.
[118] Ibid., 134.
[119] Scott, 'Steiner', 4.

familiar and the stranger. ... Classically, where branch and leaf are highest, *cortesia* qualifies the last ambush or the final tryst which is the possible venue – the coming, the coming to a place – of God.[120]

We lay a clean cloth on the table when we hear the guest at our threshold. In the paintings of Chardin, in the poems of Trakl, that movement at evening is made both domestic and sacramental.[121]

What we must focus, with uncompromising clarity, on the text, on the work of art, on the music before us, is an ethic of common sense, a courtesy of the most robust and refined sort.[122]

Such courtesy allows the object of interpretation precedence over the reader, thereby reversing the direction of our Secondary City. The movement towards reception and understanding embodies an initial act of trust. The guest may turn antagonistic, but in order to open the door we have to gamble on trust.[123] Steiner discerns three levels of philological reception of a text. Lexical grammatical study is, for Steiner, the opening of the door to a text. The second level is that of sensitivity to syntax. The third level is that of the semantic.[124]

Steiner notes that this passage into meaning always entails interaction with *context*, and the latter is unbounded. However, contra deconstruction,

the fact that there cannot be, in Coleridge's macaronic phrase, any *omnium gatherum* of the context that is the world, does not mean that intelligibility is either wholly arbitrary or self-erasing. Such deduction is nihilistic sophistry.[125]

The dialectic of context alerts us to the impossibility of a systematic theory of meaning in anything but a metaphoric sense. Art and literature are expressions of human freedom and such freedom always has as a corollary the sort of radical doubt of deconstruction. But between the illusion of absolute presence and the play of deconstruction 'lies the rich, legitimate ground of the philological'.[126]

---

[120] Steiner, *Real Presences*, 148.

[121] Ibid., 149.

[122] Ibid., 149.

[123] Ibid., 156.

[124] Cf. here Steiner's fourfold understanding of the hermeneutic motion in *After Babel*, 312ff.: Understanding starts with trust, then comes aggression, then incorporation, and finally the enactment of reciprocity.

[125] Steiner, *Real Presences*, 163.

[126] Ibid., 165.

It is a mistake to ignore the historicity of texts. We welcome them now, but this immediacy is always historically informed.[127] As the metaphor of courtesy implies, a good reading is never complete and final; its falling short guarantees the otherness of the text. But such limitation does not reduce the presence before us to absence or falsehood.

Steiner grounds the experience of otherness in art in the transcendent. There is human creation because there is creation.

> So far as it wagers on meaning, an account of the act of reading, in the fullest sense, of the act of the reception and internalization of significant forms within us, is a meta-physical and, in the last analysis, a theological one. The ascription of beauty to truth and to meaning is either a rhetorical flourish, or it is a piece of theology. ... The meaning of meaning is a transcendent postulate. To read the poem responsibly ('respondingly'), to be answerable to form, is to wager on a reinsurance of sense. It is to wager on a relationship ... between word and world, but on a relationship precisely bounded by that which reinsures it.[128]

Steiner has unfailingly brought an incisive, theological critique to bear on literary and hermeneutical developments. The literary turn in biblical interpretation in the 1970s brought with it many positive developments. Although Steiner has not written extensively on biblical interpretation, in his review of *The Literary Guide to the Bible* he articulated the theological weaknesses of some literary approaches to the Bible with rare precision:

> The question is: Does this 'Literary Guide' help us to come to sensible grips with the singularity and the overwhelming provocations of the Bible – a singularity and a summons altogether independent of the reach of current literary-critical fashions? Does it help us to understand in what ways the Bible and the demands of answerability it puts upon us are like no others? Of this tome ... a terrible blandness is born. ... We hear of 'omelettes,' of 'pressure cookers,' not of the terror, of the *mysterium tremendum*, that inhabits man's endeavours to speak to and speak of God. ... The separation, made in the name of current rationalism and agnosticism, between a theological-religious experiencing of Biblical texts and a literary one is radically factitious. It cannot work.[129]

It is clear to me from the above just what a fertile view of interpretation Steiner's 'courtesy hermeneutic' yields, and just how helpful this is for biblical interpretation. Steiner himself has not published much on biblical

---

[127] See ibid., 168ff., for Steiner's nuanced discussion of biography and intentionality.
[128] Ibid., 216.
[129] Steiner, 'Books', 96, 97.

interpretation, and there has been little exploration of his views by biblical scholars.[130] This is a discussion that needs to be pursued, preferably in dialogue with Steiner himself. Suffice it here to indicate some of the advantages I perceive in Steiner's hermeneutic for biblical interpretation.

Steiner's warm and human hermeneutic[131] is miles away from Derrida's cold hermeneutic which hands us over to the flux.[132] The text is given priority, and there is an ethics of interpretation that acknowledges that one can do all sorts of things with texts, but insists that 'answerable understanding' is the reader's first responsibility. Criticism is allowed a full role in exegesis but it is made subsidiary to the reading of, and encounter with, the text. Texts do have rights,[133] and while right method cannot guarantee the right reading, there is every hope that approached courteously, with all the philological rigour that Steiner insists upon, they will yield their treasures – albeit never completely – to their readers. Steiner resists the polarities of determinacy and indeterminacy of textual interpretation and leaves us with a rigorous and hopeful, but humble, hermeneutic.

Finally, Steiner's approach gives some indication of how interpretation of Scripture may differ from interpretation of other books. There is a tendency for Steiner to treat all 'great works' as canonical in a similar way, but Steiner's comments about revisiting the authoring of Job also indicate an understanding of the peculiar provocations of the Bible. And it is surely right that to read Scripture without making these provocations a focus is woefully inadequate. Here, in my view, considerable progress is made towards the approach recommended by Tom Wright in the quote we began with – a (theological) understanding of how words work, and how we read text and *sacred* texts.

In my opinion, the fact that Steiner's hermeneutic is overtly theological and rooted in the 'grammars of creation'[134] is a strength and not a weakness. It is a moot question whether or not theology is indispensable for this type of hermeneutic, and it may well be that scholars with very different perspectives to Steiner will nevertheless find themselves in agreement with the contours of his hermeneutic. For those of us who cannot accept the rationale behind keeping

---

[130] Carroll, 'Toward a Grammar', is an exception. Vanhoozer, *Meaning?*, makes significant use of Steiner.

[131] Steiner, 'Responsion', 276, defines true criticism and reading as a 'debt of love'. By contrast he notes that he has 'felt our age and climate to be one of *invidia*, of the sneer'.

[132] Caputo, *Hermeneutics*, 186ff., describes Derrida's interpretation of interpretation in this way. Contra my perspective, Wyschogrod, 'Mind', argues that Steiner is closer to Derrida than Steiner's critique suggests.

[133] Contra Morgan, *Interpretation*, 7.

[134] The title of Steiner's 1990 Gifford Lectures, *Grammers of Creation* (London: Faber & Faber, 2001). See Carroll, 'Toward a Grammar', for a summary of the lectures.

theology and biblical studies firmly apart, and who believe that some sort of theology is unavoidable in scholarship, Steiner's integrally theistic hermeneutic is to be welcomed, especially in relation to the unhelpful approaches that abound in our secondary city. There is certainly room for clearer articulation of the theology that underlies Steiner's type of hermeneutic, but, contra Carroll,[135] I think that in general Steiner's grammars of creation is precisely the sort of foundation a biblical hermeneutic requires.

2. Theological, Trinitarian Understandings of Language: John Milbank

The latter half of the twentieth century witnessed a resurgence of Trinitarian theology, and recently this has been brought to bear on theology of language. Marshall[136] regards analytical philosophy as a fruitful dialogue partner for a Trinitarian theology of language and truth, whereas Milbank's approach[137] embraces an expressive view of language.

Both approaches insist on the epistemic priority of Christian doctrine, and Marshall's *Trinity and Truth* is, I think, a good indication of the sort of generic direction our inquiry needs to take. Marshall has drunk deeply at the well of Frei and Lindbeck, and central to Marshall's exploration of epistemology is a commitment to the epistemic priority of the doctrine of the Trinity. He states quite clearly that:

> Believing the gospel (that is, the narratives which identify Jesus and the triune God), therefore, necessarily commits believers to a comprehensive view of the world centered epistemically on the gospel narrative itself. On such a view there will be no regions of belief or practice which can isolate themselves from the epistemic reach of the gospel.[138]

> … the whole ordering of creation will have to fit with – hold together in relation to – what happens in the crib at Bethlehem, on the cross of Golgotha, and with the disciples on the Emmaus road.[139]

Far from Marshall's 'prejudices' taking him away from linguistics and philosophy of language, they lead him into an extended and complex discussion with lingual analytical philosophy and the issues about meaning and truth that

---

[135] Carroll, ibid., 265, finds difficulties theologically with Steiner's grammars of creation. But these are not telling. See O'Donovan, *Resurrection*, for how compelling and creative a view of creation order can be.

[136] Marshall, *Trinity and Truth*.

[137] Milbank, *Word*.

[138] Marshall, *Trinity and Truth*, 118.

[139] Ibid., 123.

originate with Frege and Tarski, Quine, Davidson and Dummett. There is much to learn from Marshall's approach. Christian scholarship is not obscurantist, but rather asserts, as Augustine reminds us, that all truth is God's truth, and we should therefore not fear truth wherever we find it – not even in lingual analytical philosophy. Marshall is particularly instructive in his insistence on the priority and epistemic potential of faith, while never for a moment denying the validity of mainline scholarship. Not all will agree with Marshall's optimism about analytical philosophy, and the benefits of Marshall's approach for biblical interpretation are not immediately apparent. The analytical language tradition that Marshall draws upon remains, I think, within a designative understanding of language, and I suspect that this does not get at the disclosive, constitutive functions of language that the expressivist approach captures.[140] However, it is exciting to see this discussion between Trinitarian theology and lingual–analytical philosophy developing, and it is precisely this sort of dialogue that biblical interpretation urgently needs.[141]

Milbank attends to language in his *The Word Made Strange*. Milbank's work is not easy, but it is important. He is one of few contemporary theologians prepared to challenge the autonomy of philosophy, and in terms of language he is also one of the few to assert the need for a theology of language and then to articulate the parameters of such a theology. Milbank welcomes the linguistic turn with all its radical linguisticality, and argues, similarly to Steiner, that it confronts us with two alternatives: the endless semiosis of postmodernism or a theological account of language.[142] The issue, according to Milbank, is the conception of semiosis itself.[143]

Milbank re-examines the philosophical and theological tradition and finds in the eighteenth century a tradition of language among the Christian thinkers Berkeley, Hamann, Herder and Vico, that he transfuses into the present to provide a theology of language. Milbank reads the linguistic turn ushered in by these eighteenth-century thinkers, not as Enlightenment secularism, but as a delayed coming to fruition of a Christian perspective on language, embodying the move from a metaphysics of substance to a metaphysics/metasemiotics of

---

[140] Naturally, far more needs to be said here. Donald Davidson, with whom Marshall aligns himself, is hugely influential, and has been interpreted in very different ways. See, e.g., Norris, *Deconstruction*, 59–83; Malpas, *Donald Davidson*, Dasenbrock, ed., *Literary Theory*.

[141] See LePore, ed., *Truth and Interpretation*, and Dasenbrock, ed., *Literary Theory*, for articles exploring the relationship between Davidson's philosophy and textual interpretation. Marshall is particularly enamoured of Davidson's work.

[142] Contra Eco, Milbank, *Word*, 112, 113, argues that the choice is between nihilism and theology when it comes to semiosis.

[143] Milbank, ibid., 85, cf. 112, 113.

relation.[144] In his view it is these thinkers who brought to light the view of language implied by Christian doctrine and especially the doctrine of creation. These are clarifications implicit in ancient Stoic doctrine and in aspects of Augustine's thought, but which patristic and mediaeval thinkers were unable to develop while they remained committed to a metaphysics of substance.[145]

Milbank says of these thinkers that

> without succumbing to a hermetic, magical view of language, they nonetheless variously insisted on the indispensability of language for thought, the more than arbitrary relation between signifier and signified, the impossibility of distinguishing 'sign' from 'thing', and an origin of language that is at once both human and divine.[146]

Berkeley questioned the *res/signum* distinction, opening the way for what Milbank calls a realist metaphysic in the deepest sense of knowledge as relational event.[147] Milbank argues for a theological view of language as expressivist, and metaphorical at its source:

> Metaphor is placed by Hamann and Herder at the very genesis of language. But it was only possible for them to combine a very 'bodily' and naturalistic account of linguistic origins with primal metaphoricity because they subscribed to an 'expressivist' ontology. ... The real achievement of a non-instrumental and metaphorical conception of language in Lowth, Vico, Hamann and Herder is part of an untimely theological and antimaterialist strategy. ... If metaphor is fundamental, then religion ceases to be a mystery in addition to the mystery of humanity itself. ... Instead, original metaphor implies either a primal personification of nature ('paganism') or else a primal response to nature as a personal address ('monotheism').[148]

It is not clear in *The Word Made Strange* just how Milbank's theology of language would flesh out in biblical interpretation. Indeed 'Radical Orthodoxy'[149] has not extended its discussion into this area, a gap that one hopes they will fill. However, it is clear from Milbank's references to Scripture

---

[144] Ibid., 97, 112.

[145] See ibid., 88–92, and esp. 90, 91, for the implications of Augustine's philosophy of language for his view of the Bible as almost dispensable for the mature Christian. For elements in Augustine's philosophy that connect with Gadamer see Grondin, *Sources,* 99–110. See Milbank, *Word* 92–7, for his analysis of five elements in the development from patristic and mediaeval times towards a more 'religiously positive' view of language.

[146] Ibid., 85.

[147] Ibid., 101.

[148] Ibid., 106.

[149] I.e. the 'movement'.

in *The Word Made Strange* and in his other books and articles, that his Trinitarian theology of language yields a positive, theological reading of the Bible as Scripture. Two areas are of particular interest for the future of this discussion. Firstly, Milbank alerts us to the importance of the history of philosophy of language. Milbank and Steiner tell the story of language somewhat differently, and if we are to find a positive way forward, it will be necessary to have detailed retellings of the story of language. And for biblical interpretation we will need to discern how the story of language connects with the story of biblical interpretation. Major work remains to be done in this area.

Secondly, Milbank alerts us to the issue of metaphor and language and interpretation. The twentieth century saw a resurgence of interest in metaphor,[150] but to this day metaphorical and analytical approaches to language tend to steer different courses.[151] Milbank's work gives an indication of how a metaphorical view of language might be integrated within an orthodox theology. Here again, major, exciting work remains to be done, with huge implications for biblical interpretation.

Conclusion

I hope it is clear from this chapter just how much language has to do with hermeneutics and biblical interpretation. Both negatively, in terms of resisting unhelpful paths, and positively, in terms of appropriating the promise of hermeneutics in biblical interpretation, biblical interpreters have much to gain from close attention to the philosophy and theology of language, and to linguistics. To its credit, postmodernism has foregrounded the issue of language and has made it virtually unavoidable for those who read texts.

We have suggested that it is the expressive tradition of language that comes to us through Hamann, Herder, Humboldt and Heidegger that holds particular promise for a creative renewal of biblical interpretation. Steiner's *Real Presences* is, in my opinion, a dazzling example of the sort of hermeneutic that a healthy view of language in this tradition can yield. It is this sort of approach to language and the hermeneutic it produces that needs to be understood, appropriated and transfused into contemporary biblical interpretation. *Real Presences* should be compulsory reading for all students of the Bible.

With Steiner we have argued that a theological dimension is a vital ingredient in a contemporary understanding of language and the consequent

---

[150] See, e.g., the recent book by Lakoff and Johnson, *Philosophy in the Flesh*.

[151] Thus, remarkably, an introductory text on philosophy of language like that of Miller, does not even have a reference to metaphor in his index.

development of a hermeneutic. In a day in which Babel has become the much vaunted symbol for wild pluralism, it is important that we recover a theological context of 'Before Babel' and 'After Pentecost' for our understanding of language. We need a grammar of creation. Indeed, one cannot but be aware that the expressive tradition, which Steiner uses to such creative ends, is also the one which, in our late modern context, has been developed in a historicist direction, a logical outcome of which is deconstruction. As with Hamann, I think it is Steiner's commitment to the grammars of creation which enables him to hold the expressive tradition creatively against its historicist deterioration into a cold hermeneutic that hands us over to the flux of history. Stephen Neill perceptively discerned some years ago that New Testament studies is in urgent need of a theology of history.[152] It seems to me that what Steiner has developed is a view of language informed by a theology of creation, and thus of history, which is thereby inoculated against the historicism in Heidegger and the hermeneutic tradition,[153] while developing the latter's creative potential. What Neill said of a theology of history could equally be said of Steiner's *Real Presences*: it will not solve all the problems, but it holds the ring within which solutions may be found.

With a profound sense of the philosophy and history of language, Steiner and Milbank have pointed us in the direction that a theology of language could go, as it pursues the scriptural clues. Exploration and development of this direction will be greatly to the advantage of biblical interpretation. The magnitude of this task confronts us once again with the reality that biblical interpretation takes place at the intersection of the humanities, and that renewal of biblical interpretation will require interdisciplinary endeavour.

Theologically, Steiner relates his hermeneutic, in much quoted and very moving words, to the long day's journey of the Saturday, and suggests that in the utopia of the Sunday the aesthetic will have neither logic nor necessity.[154] A Sunday/Christian perspective more strongly affirms the meaning of meaning, but still, in my opinion, alerts us to the now and not yet, and leaves ample room for the betweenness of suffering and struggle and hope that art and literature and biblical interpretation manifest so powerfully, and with which Steiner is so concerned. As Vanhoozer says:

> We may likewise celebrate the feast of interpretation. The Spirit of Pentecost over-
> comes the cultural and ideological biases that distort communication and so restores
> language as a medium of communion. ... We now enjoy only the first-fruits of

---

[152] Neill and Wright, *Interpretation*, 366.

[153] See O'Donovan, *Resurrection*, 162, for a perceptive note on historicism in Gadamer.

[154] *Real Presences*, 232.

understanding, but we look forward to that day when we will understand as we have been understood. *Veni spiritus interpres!* Come interpreter Spirit![155]

Bibliography

Almansi, G., 'The Triumph of the Hedgehog', in N.A. Scott and R.A. Sharp (eds.), *Reading George Steiner*, 58–73

Alter, R., *The Art of Biblical Poetry* (New York: Basic Books, 1985)

—, *The Art of Biblical Narrative* (New York: Basic Books, 1981)

—, 'Introduction to the Old Testament', in R. Alter and F. Kermode (eds.), *The Literary Guide to the Bible* (London: Fontana, 1987), 11–35

Barr, J., *The Semantics of Biblical Language* (Oxford: OUP, 1961)

—, *Biblical Words for Time* (SBT, First Series, 33; London: SCM Press, 2nd edn, 1969)

Bartholomew, C., 'Babel and Derrida: Postmodernism, Language and Biblical Interpretation,' *TynBul* 49.2 (1998), 305–28

—, 'Uncharted Waters: Philosophy, Theology and the Crisis in Biblical Interpretation', in *Renewing Biblical Interpretation* (ed. C. Bartholomew, C. Greene and K. Möller; SHS, 1; Grand Rapids: Zondervan; Carlisle: Paternoster, 2000), 1–39

Beiser, F.C., *The Fate of Reason: German Philosophy from Kant to Fichte* (Cambridge, MA and London: Harvard University Press, 1987)

Bloom, H. 'The Breaking of Form,' in H. Bloom, et al., *Deconstruction and Criticism* (New York: Seabury, 1979), 1–37

Bonhoeffer, D., *Ethics* (London: Fontana, 1964)

Brueggemann, W., *Genesis* (Atlanta: John Knox Press, 1982)

Burtness, J., *Shaping the Future: The Ethics of Dietrich Bonhoeffer* (Philadelphia: Fortress, 1985)

Caputo, J.D., *Radical Hermeneutics: Repetition, Deconstruction, and the Hermeneutic Project* (Bloomington and Indianapolis: Indiana University Press, 1987)

Carroll, R., 'Toward a Grammar of Creation: On Steiner the Theologian', in N.A. Scott and R.A. Sharp (eds.), *Reading George Steiner*, 262–74

Childs, B.S., *Old Testament Theology in a Canonical Context* (London: SCM Press, 1985)

Dasenbrock, R.W. (ed.), *Literary Theory After Davidson* (University Park: Pennsylvania State University Press, 1993)

Dawson, D.A., *Text-Linguistics and Biblical Hebrew* (JSOTSup, 177; Sheffield: Sheffield Academic Press, 1994)

---

[155] Vanhoozer, 'Spirit', 165.

Derrida, J., *Writing and Difference* (London and Henley: Routledge and Kegan Paul, 1978)

—, 'Structure, Sign, and Play in the Discourse of the Human Sciences', in *Writing and Difference*, 278–93

—, *Dissemination* (Chicago: University of Chicago Press, 1981)

—, *Of Grammatology* (Baltimore and London: John Hopkins University Press, 1976/1997)

—, *The Gift of Death* (Chicago: University of Chicago Press, 1985)

Eco, U., *The Role of the Reader: Explorations in the Semiotics of Texts* (Bloomington: Indiana University Press, 1979)

—, *Semiotics and the Philosophy of Language* (Bloomington: Indiana University Press, 1986)

—, with R. Rorty, J. Culler and C. Brooke-Rose, *Interpretation and Overinterpretation* (ed. S. Collini; Cambridge: CUP, 1992)

—, *The Search for the Perfect Language* (London: Fontana, 1997)

—, *Kant and the Platypus: Essays on Language and Cognition* (London: Vintage, 2000)

Ellis, J.M., *Against Deconstruction* (Princeton: Princeton University Press, 1989)

Ford, D.F., *Theology: A Very Short Introduction* (Oxford: OUP, 1999)

Fretheim, T., *Exodus* (Interpretation; Louisville: John Knox Press, 1991)

Grondin, J., *Sources of Hermeneutics* (Albany: State University of New York Press, 1995)

Guinness, O., *Time for Truth* (Leicester: IVP, 2000)

Hauerwas, S., *A Better Hope: Resources for a Church Confronting Capitalism, Democracy, and Postmodernity* (Grand Rapids: Brazos, 2000)

Havel, V., 'A Word About Words', in *Open Letters: Selected Prose 1965–1990* (London: Faber and Faber, 1991), 377–89

Hayes, J.H. and F.C. Prussner, *Old Testament Theology: Its History and Development* (London: SCM Press, 1985)

Himmelfarb, G., *On Looking Into the Abyss: Untimely Thoughts on Culture and Society* (New York: Vintage, 1994)

Humboldt, W. von, 'The Nature and Confirmation of Language', in K. Mueller-Vollmer (ed.), *The Hermeneutics Reader* (New York: Continuum, 1992), 99–105

Hunsberger, G.R., *Bearing the Witness of the Spirit: Lesslie Newbigin's Theology of Cultural Plurality* (Grand Rapids: Eerdmans, 1998)

Ingraffia, B.D., *Postmodern Theory and Biblical Theology* (Cambridge: CUP, 1995)

Jeffrey, L.D., *People of the Book: Christian Identity and Literary Culture* (Grand Rapids: Eerdmans, 1996)

Keefer, M.H., 'Deconstruction and the Gnostics', *University of Toronto Quarterly* 55/1 (1985), 74–93

Kelsey, D.H., *The Uses of Scripture in Recent Theology* (London: SCM Press, 1975)

Kermode, F., *The Genesis of Secrecy: On the Interpretation of Narrative* (Cambridge, MA: Harvard University Press, 1979)

Krupnick, M., 'Steiner's Literary Journalism: "The Heart of the Maze" ', in N.A. Scott and R.A. Sharp (eds.), *Reading George Steiner*, 43–57

Lafont, C., *The Linguistic Turn in Hermeneutic Philosophy* (trans. J. Medina; Cambridge, MA and London: MIT Press, 1999)

Lakoff, G. and M. Johnson, *Philosophy in the Flesh: The Embodied Mind and Its Challenge to Western Thought* (New York: Basic Books, 1999)

LePore, E. (ed.), *Truth and Interpretation: Perspectives on the Philosophy of Donald Davidson* (Oxford and New York: Basil Blackwell, 1986)

Lincoln, A.T., *Paradise Now and Not Yet: Studies in the Role of the Heavenly Dimension in Paul's Thought with Special Reference to his Eschatology* (Cambridge: CUP, 1981)

Logan, A.H.B., *Gnostic Truth and Christian Heresy: A Study in the History of Gnosticism* (Edinburgh: T. & T. Clark, 1996)

Longacre, R.E., *Joseph: A Story of Divine Providence. A Text Theoretical and Textlinguistic Analysis of Genesis 37 and 39–48* (Winona Lake, IN: Eisenbrauns, 1989)

Lundin, R., *The Culture of Interpretation: Christian Faith and the Postmodern World* (Grand Rapids: Eerdmans, 1993)

Lundin, R., C. Walhout and A.C. Thiselton, *The Responsibility of Hermeneutics* (Grand Rapids: Eerdmans; Exeter: Paternoster, 1985)

—, *The Promise of Hermeneutics* (Grand Rapids: Eerdmans; Carlisle: Paternoster, 1999)

Malpas, J.E., *Donald Davidson and the Mirror of Meaning* (Cambridge: CUP, 1992)

Marsden, G., *The Outrageous Idea of Christian Scholarship* (Oxford: OUP, 1998)

Marshall, B.D., ' "We Shall Bear the Image of the Man of Heaven": Theology and the Concept of Truth', in L.G. Jones and S.E. Fowl (eds.), *Rethinking Metaphysics* (Directions in Modern Theology, Oxford: Basil Blackwell, 1995), 93–117

—, *Trinity and Truth* (Cambridge: CUP, 2000)

Milbank, J., *Theology and Social Theory: Beyond Secular Reason* (Oxford and Cambridge, MA: Basil Blackwell, 1990)

—, *The Word Made Strange: Theology, Language, Culture* (Oxford and Cambridge, MA: Basil Blackwell, 1997)

—, 'Knowledge: The Theological Critique of Philosophy in Hamann and Jacobi', in J. Milbank, et al. (eds.), *Radical Orthodoxy* (London and New York: Routledge, 1999), 21–37

Miller, A., *Philosophy of Language* (London: UCL Press, 1998)

Miller, J.H., 'The Critic as Host', in H. Bloom, et al., *Deconstruction and Criticism* (New York: Seabury, 1979), 217–53

Morgan, R. (with J. Barton), *Biblical Interpretation* (Oxford: OUP, 1988)

Mueller-Vollmer, K. (ed.), *The Hermeneutics Reader* (New York: Continuum, 1992)

Murphy, R.E., *Proverbs* (WBC, Nashville: Thomas Nelson, 1998)

Neill, S. and N.T. Wright, *The Interpretation of the New Testament: 1861–1986* (Oxford: OUP, 1988)

Norris, C., *Deconstruction and the Interests of Theory* (Leicester: Leicester University Press, 1992)

O'Donovan, O., *Resurrection and Moral Order: An Outline for Evangelical Ethics* (Leicester: IVP; Grand Rapids: Eerdmans, 1986)

Phillips, A., *Ancient Israel's Criminal Law: A New Approach to the Decalogue* (Oxford: Basil Blackwell, 1970)

Pickstock, C., *After Writing: On the Liturgical Consummation of Philosophy* (Oxford: Basil Blackwell, 1998)

Preuss, H.D., *Old Testament Theology*, II (Edinburgh: T. & T. Clark, 1996)

Rad, G. von, *Genesis* (London: SCM Press, 1961)

Radcliffe, T., *Sing a New Song: The Christian Vocation* (Dublin: Dominican Publications, 1999)

Robbins, J., *Prodigal Son/Elder Brother: Interpretation and Alterity in Augustine, Petrarch, Kafka, Levinas* (Chicago and London: University of Chicago Press, 1991)

Rogerson, J.W., *W.M.L. de Wette: Founder of Modern Biblical Criticism: An Intellectual Biography* (JSOTSup, 126; Sheffield: Sheffield Academic Press, 1992)

Scott, N.A. 'Steiner on Interpretation', in N.A. Scott and R.A. Sharp (eds.), *Reading George Steiner*, 1–13

Scott, N.A. and R.A. Sharp (eds.), *Reading George Steiner* (Baltimore and London: John Hopkins University Press, 1994)

Segovia, F.F., *Decolonizing Biblical Studies: A View from the Margins* (Maryknoll, NY: Orbis Books, 2000)

Steiner, G., 'Books. The Good Books', *The New Yorker*, 11 January 1988, 94–8

—, *Real Presences* (London and Boston: Faber and Faber, 1989)

—, 'A Responsion', in N.A. Scott and R.A. Sharp (eds.), *Reading George Steiner*, 275–85

—, *After Babel: Aspects of Language and Translation* (Oxford and New York: OUP, 2nd edn, 1998)

—, *Heidegger* (London: Fontana, 1978)

Sternberg, M., *The Poetics of Biblical Narrative: Ideological Literature and the Drama of Reading* (Bloomington: Indiana University Press, 1985)

Stiver, D.R., *The Philosophy of Religious Language: Sign, Symbol and Story* (Oxford: Basil Blackwell, 1996)

Taylor, C., 'Theories of Meaning', in *Human Agency and Language: Philosophical Papers* (Cambridge: CUP, 1985), 248–92

—, 'Language and Human Nature', in Taylor, *Human Agency and Language*, 215–47

Thiselton, A.C., 'Semantics and New Testament Interpretation', in I.H. Marshall (ed.), *New Testament Interpretation* (Carlisle: Paternoster, 1977), 75–104

—, *New Horizons in Hermeneutics* (Grand Rapids: Zondervan, 1992)

—, *Interpreting God and the Postmodern Self: On Meaning, Manipulation and Promise* (Edinburgh: T. & T. Clark, 1995)

—, 'Communicative Action and Promise in Interdisciplinary, Biblical, and Theological Hermeneutics', in R. Lundin, et al., *The Promise of Hermeneutics*, 133–239

Vanhoozer, K., *Biblical Narrative in the Philosophy of Paul Ricœur: A Study in Hermeneutics and Philosophy* (Cambridge: CUP, 1990)

—, 'The Spirit of Understanding: Special Revelation and General Hermeneutics', in R. Lundin (ed.), *Disciplining Hermeneutics: Interpretation in Christian Perspective* (Grand Rapids: Eerdmans; Leicester: IVP, 1997)

—, *Is There a Meaning in This Text?: The Bible, the Reader, and the Morality of Literary Knowledge* (Grand Rapids: Zondervan, 1998)

Van Leeuwen, R., 'Liminality and Worldview in Proverbs 1–9', *Semeia* 50 (1990), 111–44

Ward, G., *Barth, Derrida and the Language of Theology* (Cambridge: CUP, 1995)

—, 'Heidegger in Steiner', in N.A. Scott and R.A. Sharp (eds.), *Reading George Steiner*, 180–204

Watson, F., *Text, Church and World: Biblical Interpretation in Theological Perspective* (Edinburgh: T. & T. Clark, 1994)

—, *Text and Truth* (Edinburgh: T. & T. Clark, 1997)

Wenham, G., *Genesis 1–15* (Waco, TX: Word Books, 1987)

—, *Genesis 16–50* (Texas: Word Books, 1994)

Whybray, R.N., *The Making of the Pentateuch: A Methodological Study* (JSOTSup, 53; Sheffield: Sheffield Academic Press, 1987)

Wolters, A. 'Facing the Perplexing History of Philosophy', *TCW* 17 (1981), 1–17

Wolterstorff, N., *Divine Discourse: Philosophical Reflections on the Claim that God Speaks* (Cambridge: CUP, 1995)

—, 'The Importance of Hermeneutics for a Christian Worldview', in R. Lundin (ed.), *Disciplining Hermeneutics: Interpretation in Christian Perspective* (Grand Rapids: Eerdmans; Leicester: IVP, 1997), 25–47

Wright, C., *Deuteronomy* (NIBCOT, Peabody, MA: Hendrickson; Carlisle: Paternoster, 1996)

Wright, N.T., *The New Testament and the People of God* (Minneapolis: Fortress Press, 1992)

Wyschogrod, E., 'The Mind of a Critical Moralist: Steiner as Jew', in N.A. Scott and R.A. Sharp (eds.), *Reading George Steiner*, 151–79

8

Language at the Frontiers of Language

Gregory J. Laughery

Introduction

Scripture is a literary text made up of a diversity of genres and language uses. As a result biblical interpreters have quite rightly worked with, and been influenced by, various theories of language. However, in view of the scepticism implicit in some of these theories, uncritical acceptance may result in unwarranted suspicion concerning the capacity of Scripture to communicate truths about God, the world and the self. What perspectives on language theory are to be considered useful or dangerous for the faithful art and act of biblical interpretation? How might Christians respond to the driving polemics attached to the current intrigue and infatuation with language? These exceedingly pertinent questions require the careful attention of Christian scholarship should it wish to learn from, but also eschew the perils of, the medley of language theories on offer.

In the contemporary arena of debates about language one is faced with a puzzling question: what is a theory of language? Is it even a possibility, without recourse to a horizon past its own boundary? How is one to talk about language in a post-Pentecost, post-structuralist, postmodern, and now allegedly post-Christian,[1] world?

---

[1] Cupitt, 'post-Christianity', argues that post-Christianity means: there is no longer capital-T truth, existence is in flux, human expression is our redemption, and there is only the stream of language-formed events. It is crucial to understand that Cupitt has not only embraced a theory of language here, but he is advocating a particular worldview in connection with it.

According to one commentator language is a sort of labyrinth playfully deferring meaning,[2] while another argues it is a series of signs that refer only to themselves, eventually leading to an endless erring.[3] 'Meaningless! Meaningless! Everything is Meaningless' reads one translation of the famous words from Ecclesiastes.[4] Perhaps, 'Language! Language! Everything is Meaningless Language' resonates an up-to-date echo of this age-old commentary. All language is suspect and void of meaning. Such a plot may well describe the current state of language theory and what has been referred to as the linguistic turn[5] in philosophy, literature, theology and hermeneutics.[6]

The subject of language has undergone intense investigation and become a central topic of debate within each of the disciplines mentioned above. Language has been variously understood to be ordinary, scientific or religious. It has also been suggested that language is language and is grounded in nothing other than language.[7] There have been the claims, among others, that language is God,[8] a gift of God,[9] and that language is man.[10] Questions of the origin, essence and function of language have come under piercing examination, and a raging discussion has ensued which has led to a variety of perspectives and conclusions that have had an impact on biblical interpretation.[11]

In this chapter I shall not undertake the task of dealing with the breadth and diversity of the language debates and problematics. I should like rather to address two basic, yet complex, questions related to language theory and Scripture. First, I will examine the division between religious language and other language and second, in the light of this, I will ask whether Scripture should be read as any other book or in a special manner.

---

[2] Crossan, 'Metamodel'.

[3] Taylor, *Erring*, 3, marks Nietzsche as being one of the major prophets of post-modernism with his declaration: 'God remains dead. And we have killed him'. See also, 134–35. The death of God, from Taylor's point of view, 'marks the loss of a stable center', which was believed to be the support for individuality and a transcendent selfhood. 'This mortal wounding of the original subject releases the erring of scripture that entwines all things.' In Taylor's perspective, language 'as a ceaseless play of interrelated differences' undermines the possibility of any original subject outside of language.

[4] NIV, Ecc. 1:2. This is not the end of the story in Ecclesiastes, in contrast to what some suppose is the case in the contemporary context.

[5] Stiver, *Philosophy*, 4–7.

[6] Fodor, *Christian Hermeneutics*, 147.

[7] Heidegger, *Poetry*, 190–91. See also his *On the Way to Language*.

[8] Edwards, *Christian Poetics*, 217.

[9] Vanhoozer, *Meaning?*, 205.

[10] Ricœur, 'Language', 230–31, seems to accept this point of view.

[11] See Stiver, *Philosophy*, and Thiselton, *New Horizons*, for erudite discussions of this topic.

Religious Language versus Other Types of Language

Are ordinary language and religious language rivals? Is scientific language a panacea? Is God language a mysticism? Anthony Thiselton points out:

> ... whereas the heart of the problem of religious language has traditionally been perceived to lie in its distinctively 'religious' character, especially since around 1967 the deepest problems of religious language are perceived to lie in the opaqueness and deceptiveness which supposedly characterize all language.[12]

In the context of this discussion, religious language is considered by some to be non-sense.[13] A requisition of special pleading is often thought to be necessary if it is going to have a legitimate place in the world and language.[14] In response to this radical separation and a privileging of ordinary or scientific language, religious language advocates may aim to enlarge the horizons of language (beyond merely the ordinary or scientific) so that religious language might also be considered as cognitive, or at least in some sense meaningful, without, however, dealing with the 'all' language problematic mentioned above by Thiselton. The inordinate disjunction between two types of language seems to have been left intact in this scenario and it is this that I would like to explore further.[15]

Since the time of what has been referred to as positivism, and perhaps even long before,[16] religious language has often been viewed as completely separate from other categories of language. The early work of L. Wittgenstein,[17] followed by A.J. Ayer[18] and others, privileged a verificationist view. Language

---

[12] Thiselton, 'Language – religious'.

[13] Cuppit, 'Post-Christianity'. See Thiselton, *Interpreting God*, 81–118, for an insightful analysis and critique of Cuppit's work.

[14] See Clayton, *Problem*, who argues that some who doubt (following Kant) theistic language, also see difficulties with 'metaphysical explanations' and a 'historicity of knowledge'.

[15] While I agree with Thiselton that the supposed problematic today is with 'all' language (see note 12 above), I would nevertheless argue that an acceptance of an absolute division between religious language and other language will not help in addressing the tyranny of this view.

[16] Braaten, 'Naming the Name', 14, argues that 'the problem of language seems to be as old as creation'.

[17] Wittgenstein, *Tractatus*. The later Wittgenstein, in my opinion, is still empiricist in his orientation to language use or games, however he is not as reductionist as in his early work.

[18] Ayer, *Language*. See O'Connor, 'Ayer', who argues that this is 'one of the most influential philosophical books of the century'. See also Thiselton, 'Language – religious', 316: 'In his *Language, Truth, and Logic* of 1936, A.J. Ayer expounded what amounted to a positivist world view, but clothed in the dress of a theory of language.'

needed to be defined according to strict empirical requirements. As Ayer is a major protagonist of this notion, especially concerning religious language, his position is worth citing at length:

> To test whether a sentence expresses a genuine empirical hypothesis, I adopt what may be called a modified verification principle. For I require of an empirical hypothesis, not indeed that it should be conclusively verifiable, but that some possible sense-experience should be relevant to the determination of its truth or falsehood. If a putative proposition fails to satisfy this principle, and is not a tautology, then I hold that it is metaphysical, it is neither true nor false but literally senseless.

> For since the religious utterances of the theist are not genuine propositions at all, they cannot stand in any logical relation to the propositions of science.

> And if 'god' is a metaphysical term, then it cannot be even probable that a god exists. For to say 'God exists' is to make a metaphysical utterance which cannot be either true or false

> ...to say that something transcends the human understanding is to say that it is unintelligible. And what is unintelligible cannot significantly be described. But if one allows that it is impossible to define God in intelligible terms, then one is allowing that it is impossible for a sentence both to be significant and to be about God.[19]

Ayer's concoction of an effacing of metaphysics and an embrace of scientific-positivistic analysis attempts to render religious language non-sense. This point of view has undoubtedly contributed to the trend of a denial of metaphysics in any form,[20] as well as to a general suspicion towards the referential capacity of all language in the wake of its failure. Yet the contemporary version of this rejection and scepticism is more entangled in theories of language than in scientific-empirical presuppositions *per se*.

It has become indispensable in the light of this emphasis on language theory and its relation to God, Scripture, metaphysics and intelligibility, among other issues, that those who practice biblical hermeneutics be aware of how theories of language are intertwined with and have an influence on the task of biblical interpretation. Language theory is connected to a view of the world and reality that is often the underlying force behind such a theory.[21] As this is the case, it is

---

[19] Ayer, *Language*, 31, 115, 117–18.

[20] Soskice, *Metaphor*, 144.

[21] Devitt and Sterelny, *Language*, 236–37, comment in regard to Ayer and the positivists, 'So, at the same time the positivists are rejecting the metaphysical dispute about the nature of reality, they are making a strong metaphysical assumption about reality: it consists only of the given. Despite their disavowals, they are committed to a

essential that Christian interpreters of Scripture be encouraged to rethink language theories, including their own, in the recognition that each theory has a premise which is connected to a world-view.[22] How does a view of the world 'count' when it comes to a language-view? World-view analysis will not inevitably decide if a language theory affirms or denies God, yet world-view considerations will give some useful indications as to the merit, or lack thereof, of a language theory for the Christian art and action of interpreting God, the world and the self. Responsible Christian scholarship will endeavour to detect which world-views are attached to which theories and whether or not these are hermeneutically in accord with Scripture.

There is no question today of whether Ayer's language theory, or his world-view for that matter, were justifiable. They have been rightly critiqued and, one would suppose, bypassed on the grounds that the verification principle itself is non-empirical.[23] However, what interests me at this stage is not the validity of the critique, but the powerful residue of the theory that seems to remain in spite of it.[24] One still finds, for example, as influential a scholar as Paul Ricœur generally accepting that there is an unmitigated difference between religious language and other language,[25] although he forcefully joins the critique of the positivist position in other respects.[26] In my opinion, Ricœur

---

[21] (*Continued*) powerful and, we claim, thoroughly false metaphysics.' While being in agreement with this evaluation and critique, I would nevertheless disagree with these two scholars on their approach to the problem of language which is entirely 'naturalistic' in both the epistemological and metaphysical sense. See also *Language*, 9–10.

[22] See Wolters, *Creation Regained*, 1–11, on the importance of 'world-view for Christian reflection'. See also Devitt and Sterelny, *Language*, 237, who point out that 'one cannot theorize about anything, least of all language, without implicit commitment to a view of the world'. Also Ricœur, *History and Truth*, 193, states: 'Every philosophical attitude flows from a *Weltanschauung*, from a certain vision of the "world."' (Emphasis his.)

[23] O'Connor, 'Ayer', 230, asserts that Ayer's view has 'been shown to be faulty in admitting as meaningful metaphysical statements of precisely the kind that the principle is designed to outlaw'. Also, Stiver, *Philosophy*, 44–6, points out that one significant factor in the theory's diminishing influence was the internal critique from the positivists themselves.

[24] Gill, *On Knowing God*, 36. See also Thiselton, *New Horizons*, 20, who provocatively suggests an analogy between Ayer and his world-view, 'positivism in linguistic dress' and Barthes and Derrida, among others, who propose 'a post-modernist world-view in semiotic dress'.

[25] Ricœur, 'Language'. Also, *History and Truth*, 165–91.

[26] Ricœur, 'Toward a Hermeneutic', 100–104. See the comments by Fodor, *Christian Hermeneutics*, 147–71, who perceives something of a 'residual positivism' in Ricœur's view of language, while he nevertheless points out some of his differences with a positivistic outlook.

attempts to make religious language credible within what he sees as a 'process of secularization' – a world of technical, factual and scientific language. In some sense I share his evaluation and a concern over the loss of the sacred, though I differ in the way I address the problem. His argument is that religious language has a right or even a priority over other language and therefore has at least a legitimate place alongside it. This view, however, assumes that other language types are unable to speak of God, and this leaves Ricœur reducing God language to the poetic-symbolic.[27] On the issue of religious language, it is argued that Ricœur's orientation is more anthropological (concerned with human possibilities), than theological (about God).[28]

A variety of responses to Ayer and those who adopted similar views of language have developed, but I shall briefly focus on only two of them. In her influential book *Metaphor and Religious Language*,[29] Janet Martin Soskice points out two such ripostes that influenced biblical interpretation: Christian empiricism and idealism.

According to Soskice, Christian empiricism was proposed by Ian T. Ramsey,[30] who attempted to show that religious language was cognitively credible on the basis of empirical arguments, which would in turn, in his opinion, lead to the reanimation of metaphysics. Ramsey recognized that if this was to happen there needed to be an adequate explanation of reference in religious language. One of the ways he formulated this was in terms of 'cosmic disclosure', affirming that this type of confrontation might function in a positive manner for objective reference and claims of transcendence. One of Ramsey's difficulties in this project was being too empirical, or at least being inconsistent with his empirical orientations. Soskice states:

> His difficulty is this – he relies on his empiricism to ground his reference, but he is not justified in terms of the same empiricism in developing the 'disclosure event' with models of God as husband, king, landlord, shepherd, or judge. The disclosure is simply a point of reference with no content and, to be consistent with his empiricism … Ramsey should restrict his claims to what is observable, but this he plainly does not wish to do.[31]

---

[27] Ricœur, 'Toward a Hermeneutic', 100–104, and 'Biblical Hermeneutics'. This does not mean, in Ricœur's orientation, that poetic language is non-cognitive or non-referential.

[28] See Vanhoozer, *Biblical Narrative*, 120–22; 236–38. For another view, see Laughery, *Living Hermeneutics*, 115–20.

[29] Soskice, *Metaphor*, has done much to dispel the illusions that scientific and theological models and metaphors are completely incongruent. Her insights, in this context, make a valuable contribution to a theory of language. I am in her debt for these thoughts on Christian empiricism and the notions of idealism.

[30] Ramsey, *Religious Language*; *Christian Empiricism*.

[31] Soskice, *Metaphor*, 146.

If there is no reason why Christians should eschew empirical reference claims, it is crucial that they recognize, however, that any exclusive focus on them leads to reductionism, which in turn diminishes the broader assertions of Scripture that God communicates in a diversity of ways. An overemphasis on solely empirical concerns results in biblical interpretation being forced into a frame that is unable to contain the picture. Ramsey sought to establish the cognitive character of religious language in the midst of the era of positivism and falsification, rather than questioning the validity of the world-view presuppositions underlying the claims that there was a valid exclusivity between religious language and other types of language in the first place.

Soskice argues that with the failure of empiricist theology, and in the face of scepticism towards cognitive models or claims for religious language, one may find something of an explanation for an idealist thesis.[32] In her opinion, this relates to a broad point of view that can characterize religious language as personal, affective or evocational. Religious language, it is thought, has an impact in an existential sense as it addresses the human situation, but it does not 'depict reality'.[33] Such language has some form of anthropological merit, but it is theologically empty. In this context, the transcendent-immanent God of Scripture disappears behind a cacophony of fictive or human constructs which are continuously recycled as they fail to have any capacity to refer outside themselves. God is so far away that language can never begin to speak God. Biblical interpretation risks becoming a shadow desperately in search of a form that lacks any stability.

The problematic, as I see it, is that both of these developments accept the fundamental division between religious language and other types of language. Christian empiricism seeks to respond to positivistic empiricism with empiricism on its own terms, attempting to observably show that religious language is just as meaningful and cognitive as other language. Idealism argues that there is no need to respond to empirical claims and criteria, as religious language should not have to measure up to such demands. In being freed from these requirements religious language may speak in an entirely different way, hence there is no need to seek to justify it as cognitive or even referentially meaningfull.

In the light of the weaknesses in these two responses to Ayer and his view of language, which in some sense remain relevant in our own context, Soskice appeals to and calls for a theological realism. While I do not agree with all of

---

[32] Ibid., 147. While it is true that Soskice is discussing scientific models, she herself makes an application to the theist and the Christian in this regard.
[33] Ibid., 97–117.

her arguments and conclusions,[34] I appreciate that she has done much to advance the language discussion. I shall sketch out below a somewhat different angle on theological realism and its application to language.

Does embracing an *exclusive* division between different types of language force biblical scholarship into choosing between the false options of religious language versus other categories of language?[35] In my opinion, a theological perspective contributes to a unifying of language that does not discount its diversity. On this account, theology legitimately addresses the issue of the 'all' language problematic.[36] This can be framed in an 'either-or' manner. Scripture makes a powerful and pivotal proposal: God is there as opposed to not being there. If God is there, this then opens the possibility of a 'both-and' paradigm for the world and language that may be described in the following way.

Scripture, for example, affirms that God exists *both* outside the world and language use (transcendent),[37] *and* also that God comes into the world[38] and language use through speaking in creation, to people and through Christ (immanent).[39] There is no warrant to collapse these two truths into one, nor is

---

[34] Ibid., 147–61. I do agree with Soskice that a theological realism should neither be dogmatic nor presumptuous and that a realist perspective accommodates figurative speech, which is reality depicting. I also agree that a realist position holds that the world informs our theory, however I am not convinced that our theories may never adequately describe the world. My view would be that it is possible to sufficiently describe the world and that most of the time that is practically what happens. In those cases, description is adequate.

[35] While no one denies some distinction, as with French and English, is there not also a primordial relationship that has been underplayed with regard to its place in the world and language? Religious language is distinct from other language, yet it is also related to it.

[36] See the quote from Thiselton above (note 12).

[37] Watson, *Text, Church and World*, 144.

[38] Braaten, 'Naming the Name', 29, argues that the problem of contemporary thinking about God is expressed in a 'great divide'. There are those who see anthropomorphic language about God as beyond all concreteness, 'rapt in mystical silence', and those who follow 'the incarnational current deep into history, into the concreteness of human flesh' – God incarnate in Jesus. Braaten rightly affirms the latter, but in my opinion too exclusively, thereby lacking an emphasis on a creational and eschatological perspective.

[39] Jüngel, *God as the Mystery*, 288, remarks with regard to Christ, 'The translation of the model of human speech to God is based on the certainty that God has shown himself to be human in the execution of his divinity. To think of him as one who speaks, to speak of him as one who speaks, is not a "dogmatic anthropomorphism," which comes too close to God, but rather the result of that *event* in which God becomes accessible as God in language, which the Bible calls *revelation*.'

it necessary to wholly distinguish them, as in one fashion or another empiricism and idealist notions tend to do. A definite tension embedded on the level of God and the world, language and human beings, points toward the possibility of a relation-distinction between the identity of God and language. Tension in this scriptural sense is to be embraced, not rejected. To say it another way, God is outside, *beyond*, language, but can be said inside, *within*, language. This is precisely because God in Scripture is revealed in language, although never confused with it. The point here is that God is not reduced to language, but is *both* related to *and* distinct from it as God – hence the relation-distinction tension. Furthermore, I would argue this holds true for the world and for human beings. God is *both* related to the world as creation *and* also distinct from it as God. God is *both* related to human beings *and* also distinct from them as God.[40]

A Scriptured portrayal of this tension relates to daily life, the land, work, justice, economics, social contexts, and so on. The Scripture writes to the whole of life – not just to some sequestered area designated 'religious'.[41] Whether scientific, ordinary or religious, 'all' language has a capacity, in a meaningful, referential, dynamic manner, to point back to the Creator who made the world and who made human beings as images of God. Particles, quarks, atoms, rock, fortress and shelter may all recount something of the complexity and character of God the Creator.[42] Why should any of these, in their specific contexts, be prohibited from referring to God in a general context? What is one to make of the most sophisticated geometrical language formulations? Why should they be forbidden from having the Creator as their referent? Such language types, while often used in specific scientific or mathematical contexts, may also refer to God in a more general creational perspective. As the world is not merely one's own but God's, language boundaries can be refigured. Scientific and religious languages are not so absolutely

---

[40] See Gunton, *The One...*, 167, 207–19, on the relation-distinction between God, world and being.

[41] Wright, *People of God*. See also Wolters, *Creation Regained*, 7, who rightly argues, 'Scripture speaks centrally to everything in our life and world, including technology, and economics and science.'

[42] Ricœur, *History and Truth*, 193, argues, 'in the eyes of the psalmist: it is the trees which "clap their hands" and not the electrons and neutrons'. While this is true, perhaps it is not necessary to paint the picture so reductionistically. If one considers the creational perspective that God made the world and everything in it, as affirmed, for example, in Paul's discussion with the Athenians (recounted in Luke's narrative: Acts 17:22–34), there is no necessity to exclude the language and reality of electrons and neutrons from pointing to the creator God.

divided as Christians may often have been led to suppose.[43] They are *both* related *and* distinct on a creational level. What I want to stress here, from a scriptural perspective, is that language is creational in that it enters the world through the world's createdness. As the world is given by God, so is language. Human language in the world, then, refers back to its Creator and is first of all an attribute of the speaking God who is revealed as the Great Speaker.[44]

On a creational register language is language as, for example, experience is experience. While it is true there are distinct types, this does not signify that one type is utterly disjointed from the other on the level of language or experience. All language has cognitive and non-cognitive, literal, metaphorical, analogical, private and public spheres which are related to and dependent on the contexts in which language is used.

The perspective of the relatedness of all language then, on the level of creation, does not necessitate an obliterating of distinctions. Language games or understanding the world as linguistic may, in some sense, be viewed positively from a Christian standpoint.[45] There is no question that there are different types of language use and that these are relevant in their own specific contexts.[46] Distinctions may be perceived as a good thing and a beautiful dimension of creativity. What often happens, however, is that these contexts are thought to become the totality of language, thereby negating any horizons larger than their own network or language game. If this is the case, language becomes the sole vehicle for understanding, explanation and new understanding – rather than one important, but not comprehensive, reality-world identifier.[47] If there is no referent outside of one's language games, networks and the linguisticality of the world, the hermeneutical circle is indeed vicious and not productive.[48]

---

[43] Stiver, *Philosophy*, 196, states, 'Perhaps the most remarkable implication of recent developments for religious language is the affirmation that despite irreducible imprecision and metaphorical language, religious language is communicable and understandable. Even if religious language possesses more indeterminate and figurative language it is not so unlike other language, even scientific language.'

[44] Vanhoozer, *Meaning?*, 205. See also, Milbank, *Word*, 29, who argues that human language utterance reflects the divine creative act.

[45] Thiselton, 'Language and Meaning'.

[46] Ibid., 1123–46, esp. 1132, where Thiselton argues that religious language 'is not necessarily a special kind of language, but is ordinary language put to a special kind of use'.

[47] Laughery, *Living Hermeneutics*, 55–91.

[48] Ricœur, *Conflict*, 298, argues, 'This circle is not vicious; still less is it deadly.' And on 389, 'The hermeneutic circle can be stated roughly as follows. To understand, it is necessary to believe; to believe, it is necessary to understand. This formulation is still too psychological. For behind believing there is the primacy of faith over faith; and behind

A major difficulty concerning the problematic of 'all' language, in my opinion, resides in this previously described claustrophobia. That is, there is supposedly no way out of distinction. One is caught within a web of distinct language uses that never relate or cohere. Each language game has only its own specific rules, which are not subject to any general ones. In this plot distinction reigns, and relation is underplayed or even thought to be non-existent. Yet for all the supposed flexibility here, the result is disconcertingly one-dimensional.

The problem is not with distinct language categories *per se*, but with not reconnecting the distinctions to relatedness and viewing both as emanating from God the Creator.[49] The fascinating intricacy of *both* relation *and* distinction, in finding its *raison d'être* in the being, character and complexity of God, must be allowed to play itself out in a positive 'both-and' tension, which better explains the world and the phenomena of language than reductionistic polarizations. The creator God, who is capable of creating the universe in all its complexity, explodes such reductionism in having spoken open the world for investigation, creativity, participation and discovery, which in turn produces language use of *both* a related *and* a distinct manner.

This framing of God's transcendence and immanence, in spoken penetration of the created world,[50] opens up possibilities for an 'all' language perspective through a creational context. This is embedded in the Creator-creature relation-distinction (Gen. 1–2). Furthermore, God's transcendence and immanence spoken through the saving Word (Jn. 1) and the event of Pentecost (Acts 2) open 'new' possibilities for language in a salvific context (Eph. 5:1–20). Perhaps the great contemporary language debate centres on the answer to the ancient query, 'Did God really say?' (Gen. 3:1). As suspicion reigns over trust, human beings are devastatingly broken, language misfires,

---

[48] (*Continued*) understanding there is the primacy of exegesis and its method over the naïve reading of the text. This means that the genuine hermeneutical circle is not psychological but methodological. It is the circle constituted by the object that regulates faith and the method that regulates understanding. There is a circle because the exegete is not his own master. What he wants to understand is what the text says; the task of understanding is therefore governed by what is at issue in the text itself. Christian hermeneutics is moved by the announcement which is at issue in the text.' According to Ricœur, 'Toward a Hermeneutic', 103, 'The proposed world that in biblical language is called a new creation, a new Covenant, the Kingdom of God, is the "issue" of the biblical text unfolded in front of this text.'

[49] I would propose that the Babel event in Gen. 11, often understood as the root of language distinction, might be better explained as the root of language confusion. Gen. 10 seems to affirm that distinction was already there, pre-Babel.

[50] See Milbank, *Word*, 74–8, for an illuminating discussion of Hamann's views of language, creation, and God's transcendence. In addition, see Watson, *Text, Church and World*, 137–53, on language, God and creation.

communication and relationship are shrouded in obscurity, leaving humans a mere shadow of what they were.[51] God's goal through Christ in vanquishing suspicion and its insidious corruption is not, however, focused on a redeeming of language, but on the hope of a transformation of the whole world (Rev. 21:1–27), which includes people, and in turn through people, language, communication and relationship.[52] This perspective situates language in a creational, salvific and eschatological context that recognizes its value and importance, without granting it a power or status it does not deserve. Language lacks the capaacity to be its own referent as it can only go so far before reaching its frontier, or boundary.[53] Language is being framed as a traitor when scholars argue that it refers only to itself.[54]

A crucial task for Christian scholarship, as it aims to faithfully interpret the biblical text, is to make effective and rigorous theological contributions to redrawing the boundaries of language theory. I am not intending to say that Scripture presents a detailed philosophy of language, but perhaps biblical scholars have underplayed the possibility that it may provide a paradigmatic world-view perspective that gives an orientation to the world, language and the whole of life. Al Wolters puts it this way:

> [b]iblical faith in fact involves a worldview, at least implicitly and in principle. The central notion of creation (a given order of reality), fall (human mutiny at the root of all perversion of the given order) and redemption (unearned restoration of the order in Christ) are cosmic and transformational in their implications. Together with other basic elements ... these central ideas ... give believers the fundamental outline of a completely anti-pagan Weltanschauung, a worldview which provides the interpretive framework for history, society, culture, politics, and everything else that enters human experience.[55]

---

[51] There is always the possibility that people speaking language misfire. Should this surprise us? Meanings and referents are partially opaque, yet context can help in diminishing this to the sufficient degree that language often functions accurately, but never perfectly. See Carson, *Gagging*, 102–105, on valid communication.

[52] In this case, language has no ontological status of its own. The Word in John's gospel, for example, seeks to redeem people as a person/God, not language. Language, in a scriptural context, is always related to a person/being, never an entity in and of itself or the totality of any person/being.

[53] Ricœur, *Interpretation Theory*, 20, states, 'Language is not a world of its own. It is not even a world.' Ricœur's point here is that language is always dependent on something else. Also see, *Interpretation Theory*, 15–16, where he argues for the miracle of communicative meaning becoming public.

[54] Crossan, *Dark Interval*, 40–41.

[55] Wolters, 'Gustavo Gutiérrez', 237.

It is vitally important to evaluate philosophical, literary, hermeneutical and language world-views in the light of the biblical text, and in so doing to be better able to elucidate their advantages and disadvantages for the faithful art and action of biblical interpretation.[56] While it is true, following Wittgenstein, that 'what we cannot speak about we must pass over in silence',[57] one might complement this with, 'and where we can sufficiently speak we must'.

Should Scripture be Read as any Other Book or in a Special Manner?

There has been a fair amount of lively debate over this question.[58] The recent Scripture and Hermeneutics Seminar: Third International Consultation, was no exception. My aim is to address this controversy, in its contemporary context, through an elucidation of what Ricœur and others have referred to as the question of general and regional hermeneutics, or philosophical and biblical hermeneutics.[59] I shall primarily focus on the work of Ricœur, as in my opinion it can make a useful contribution to this question. The dispute concerning whether one reads Scripture as any other book or in a special way is intricately linked to the hermeneutical orientations just mentioned and to the discussion of language in the first part of this chapter. Language, reading Scripture and philosophical-biblical hermeneutics are not entirely unrelated worlds of investigation. While respecting their differences and in no way attempting to cancel them out, their interrelationship also needs to be recognized. A polarized viewpoint without warrant, or a sophisticated synthesis for its own sake, is in danger of short-circuiting the hermeneutical enterprise. Does a creational perspective play a role in this debate? How might a 'both-and' trajectory work its way out with respect to reading the Bible, and what are the implications for biblical hermeneutics?

---

[56] See Laughery, *Living Hermeneutics*, 105–106. Perhaps, as an unfortunate result of over-specialization, biblical scholars often pay little attention to the ways in which philosophical-general hermeneutics in-forms or de-forms a reading of the biblical text, while philosophers rarely engage themselves with biblical-regional hermeneutics, thereby inadvertently (or perhaps otherwise) risking the loss of a more in-formed or less de-formed reading of that very philosophy.

[57] Wittgenstein, *Tractatus*, 74.

[58] See Laughery, *Living Hermeneutics*, 92–106, for a fuller account than can be undertaken here.

[59] Ricœur, 'Philosophical Hermeneutics', 89–101. See also Frei, 'Literal Reading'; Lindbeck, *Doctrine*, and Kelsey, *Uses*.

Some have argued that of the two hermeneutical orientations, a Christian perspective should privilege a biblical-theological, rather than a philosophical, hermeneutics.[60] Some have even suggested that all texts should be read the way the Bible is read.[61] It is often maintained that Ricœur gives precedence to a philosophical over a biblical hermeneutics.[62] Allegedly, Ricœur supports his biblical hermeneutics with a philosophical point of view that jeopardizes the true referent of the biblical story.[63] That is, Ricœur has attempted to re-frame the ancient text in more contemporary categories in order to make it compatible with current philosophical concerns and queries.

I would suggest the debate over biblical and philosophical hermeneutics might move toward greater clarity if one remembers to differentiate between a reader's imposition of a general-philosophical hermeneutics and having one in the first place (which may or may not then be modified as a result of reading Scripture). Will an interpreter simply impose the general-philosophical hermeneutic and snuff out the flaming arrow of the sense and referent of the biblical text – God, world, Christ, self and other, and so on? Or will this arrow enlighten enough to explain that this is God's Spirit-illuminated word, world and creation, and not one's own, and thereby transfigure a reader's general-philosophical hermeneutics into a biblical hermeneutics, demonstrating that one is obliged to come under an authority greater than oneself ?

There is no doubt a complex interrelationship between philosophical and biblical hermeneutics in the thought of Ricœur.[64] Does this presume, as Frei and others argue, that he gives more weight to the philosophical?[65] Ricœur affirms that the philosophical pole begins the movement to the biblical. In his opinion, the same categories of a 'work, writing, world of text, distanciation and appropriation' apply to both poles.[66] However, Ricœur's position is that in dialogue with the unique character of the biblical text the movement inverses, eventually resulting in the subordination of the philosophical to the biblical. The biblical overpowers the philosophical.[67]

---

[60] Watson, *Text, Church and World*, 1–2.

[61] Vanhoozer, *Meaning?*, 379: 'Christian doctrine, I have claimed, has hermeneutical significance. I prefer to say, not that we should read the Bible like any other book, but that we should read every other book as we have learned to read the Bible, namely, in a spirit of understanding that lets the text be what it is and do what it intends.'

[62] See Frei, 'Literal Reading', esp. 45, 50, 56 for a critique of Ricœur on this. Also Vanhoozer, *Biblical Narrative*, 148–50.

[63] Frei, 'Literal Reading', 50. See also Placher, 'Paul Ricœur', 35–52.

[64] See Wallace, *Second Naiveté*, 27–103; Laughery, *Living Hermeneutics*, 91–121 and 172–95; and Vanhoozer, *Biblical Narrative*, 119–272.

[65] Fodor, *Christian Hermeneutics*, 258–330, has an excellent discussion of Frei and Ricœur.

[66] Ricœur, 'Philosophical Hermeneutics', 89–90.

[67] Ibid., 89–90. See also, Ricœur, 'Toward a Hermeneutic', 104.

In my view, this is because the explanation of God, the world (God's creation), the human condition (a broken God-image), history (God's mighty acts), salvation (Christ), the future (new heavens and earth) are utterly and magnificently unique. The biblical text has the capacity, because of these truths among others, to lead one from understanding, through explanation, to new understanding which culminates in a knowledge of the truth and a saving relationship with God.

On the one hand, Ricœur's view affirms a hermeneutical motion from the philosophical to the biblical, while on the other, philosophical hermeneutics gradually functions within the sphere of a text-related biblical hermeneutics. I shall briefly focus on three points of this gradual movement in Ricœur's hermeneutics: a 'confession of faith', asseverated in the forms of biblical discourse; 'the world of the text'; and the 'naming of God'.[68]

Firstly, Ricœur views the confession of faith, in the biblical text, as interwoven with its forms of discourse.[69] As a result of this vision, it can be said that the biblical text has a structure and genres (such as narrative, parable, gospel, prophecy, etc.), while at the same moment being also a declaration of faith.[70] For Ricœur, it is precisely this declaration that challenges philosophical hermeneutics, resulting in its eventual surpassing, but not effacing, by biblical hermeneutics.

In Ricœur's argumentation the inversing, and eventual subordinating, of philosophical hermeneutics to biblical hermeneutics, comes about through the message or content of the biblical text as expressed in its diversity of forms of discourse. Form and content, in this sense, can be said to synchronize, yet this synchronization does not produce an annihilation of either one or the other. Such is the case because Scripture's content can be identified by the form (narrative, etc.), but the content (God, the great actor of deliverance) is not merely the form.

Secondly, let's consider 'the world of the text' as the world of the biblical text. Ricœur calls this 'thing' of the text[71] the 'object' of hermeneutics.[72]

---

[68] Ricœur, 'Hermeneutique', formulates his views on '*la lecture savante* and *la lecture confessante*' and gives an insightful articulation of biblical genres and the theological import of their confessing characteristics.

[69] See Laughery, 'Reading Jesus' Parables', for how this pertains to the parables.

[70] Ricœur, 'Philosophy', esp. 84–85, where faith is related to a logic of superabundance: '… the thematic of faith escapes from hermeneutics and testifies to the fact that the former is neither the first nor last word'. There is a need for a reliance on a 'constantly renewed interpretation of the sign-events reported by the writings, such as the Exodus in the Old Testament and the Resurrection in the New Testament.'

[71] See Wolterstorff, *Divine Discourse*, 130–52, for a critique of Ricœur's emphasis on the meaning of the text at the expense of the author's intention. Vanhoozer, *Meaning?*, 106–11, addresses this question with much erudition. See also Laughery, *Living Hermeneutics*, 292–321 and 'Reading Ricœur'.

[72] Ricœur, 'Philosophical Hermeneutics', 95.

Hermeneutics, in the first instance, is to be an explaining of the text and the world of the text as a proposed world of possibility and possible habitation. Many texts, it can be said, present a world, but the specificity of biblical discourse, as Ricœur affirms, is to be found in the emblematic characteristic of its referent 'God' and in the presentation of a new world, new birth, new covenant.[73]

Thirdly, there is a biblical text resistance situated in the fact that in the naming of God, the word 'God' cannot be reduced to a philosophical concept of 'being', since it always says more than this. Ricœur appeals to the word as presupposing a total context under which, and towards which, all the diversity of biblical discourses gravitate. To understand this word involves a supervening of the arrow of sense orchestrated by God. For Ricœur, this 'arrow of sense' asseverates a twofold force: firstly, a reassembling of all the signification generated by the biblical discourses, incomplete though they may be, and secondly, the aperture of a vista that eludes the closure of discourse.[74] The naming of God, in Scripture, relates to God's initiative and objectifying of sense.

According to Ricœur, on the grounds of these three points among others, regional-biblical hermeneutics becomes the organon for general-philosophical hermeneutics. It seems however, in my opinion, that this can only be confirmed through the Spirit-illuminated Scripture and its reader in reading the author's literary act inscribed in the biblical text. This scenario works out in the following way. Every interpreter comes to the Bible with a general-philosophical point of view when he or she begins to read it. The reading of the biblical text does not make this the case, as it is already in place on a creational level before one ever reads Scripture.[75] Yet this reading does count for the reader, not in the sense that one makes the biblical text what it is when read, no more than one makes a car what it is when looking both ways before crossing the street. The reader is always *both* related to what is read *and* distinct from it, just as the person crossing the street is related to the car, and distinct from it. The point here is that these relations-distinctions can be said to be true for human beings at the practical level on general hermeneutical grounds. I would argue this is because it is God's world (although it may not always be recognized for what it is), even before one reads the Bible to discover

---

[73] Ibid., 97. In addition, Ricœur, 'Philosophy'.

[74] Ricœur, 'Philosophical Hermeneutics', 97–98.

[75] Interpretation is rooted in the situatedness of the interpreter, however it is not actualized only by this, but also by the created world which precedes it. Interpretation takes place within the borders of creational limits. No interpreter, at least that I know of, begins the hermeneutical journey grounded in the biblical text.

that this is the case. It is, nevertheless, the biblical text that explains how and why the world is the way it is. In moving from general to regional hermeneutical grounds there is, then, an overcoming and re-framing of the general as Scripture explains that this is God's creation. Biblical scholars too often underplay a biblical world-view perspective that frames a place for the scientific, language-orientated and philosophical approaches to the world as it is God's created world. These valid enterprises, the scientific, language-oriented and philosophical, however, need to be put into dialogue with Spirit-illuminated Scripture if they are to have a possibility of both affirming and critiquing their various positions on criteria both related to and distinct from themselves. This is essential if they are to move from understanding, through explanation, to new understanding that it is ultimately God who gives science, philosophy and language their *raison d'être* in the first place. As Acts 17:22–34, in a fascinating *coup de force* affirms, God has created the world and everything in it and it is in God that humans live and move and are.

I would argue that Scripture may *both* be read as any other text, *and* not be read as any other text. Both a one-dimensional forcing, a synthesis that exclusively fuses these two together, and an antithesis that keeps them entirely apart, seem inadequate on the level of the complexity of creation. There is interconnection without effacement. The intriguing value of a 'both-and' approach to this question, as has already been argued with reference to language, is that it respects a creational relation-distinction, which acknowledges a tension, that in this case neither de-prioritizes the biblical, nor dissolves the philosophical.

All texts are texts and their authors may indicate, in one way or another, that this is God's world, but not all authored texts claim to be revelation illuminated by the Spirit.[76] That is, even though it is possible that a variety of texts can affirm in a general way that the world is God's, the Bible remains a special text, not just one of many. Authored Scripture's Spirit-illuminated recounting of events in history, its theological configuration, its referent God, its creation-salvific-eschatological focus, its canonical form, etc., all render it unique. Scripture merits being read as a special book. It is still true, however, that the Bible is a text like other texts: genres, work, written, etc. and therefore that it should be read as any other text might be. On one level the Bible is a special book, on another level it is book like any other. This perspective acknowledges a space for both a biblical-regional and a philosophical-general hermeneutics and a tension between them that is interactive and productive.

My contention is that to force this issue into an 'either-or' where it is not warranted may result in a underplaying of the complexity of Scripture,

---

[76] Gunton, *Theology*, 64–82.

creation and the concurrent relation-distinction that has already been developed with respect to the problematic of language. While it is true that the Bible
presents God as 'either' there 'or' not there, the Bible is not God and therefore
does not 'either-or' frame the question of the Bible being read as a special book
or like any other. Perhaps, as with language, a 'both-and' perspective is in
order, but if this is the case it must be clear where the relations-distinctions
stand.

The relevance of this for biblical hermeneutics moves along the following
lines. A biblical world-view presents the hermeneutical venture as a living one
in motion. Interpreters are situated in the created world, move to the authored
Spirit-illuminated biblical text, and potentially move back to the world with a
biblical view of it. In other words, there is a movement from understanding,
through explanation, to new understanding. However, the trajectory does not
end here in a biblical perspective. A living hermeneutics in motion only comes
to its realized, yet provisionally mediated closure when the biblical text is acted
or lived out into the world. It is only in this sense that a contribution to the
transformation of the world begins and can be brought to finite completion.

Biblical hermeneutics does not culminate with the linking of author and
reader or the connecting of the world of text and the world of reader,[77] but
with the hermeneutical Spirit-illuminated 'what', read and Spirit acted on,
which has *transforming world power* as it continues its motion through the text to
the reader, and through the reader out into the animate world. It is only when
this motion reaches the world, not just the world of the reader, that a living
hermeneutics motion is then reanimated back through the hermeneutical
circle in a broad sense. The animate world, in its relation and distinction to
both biblical text and reader, is a hermeneutical factor that demands consideration. The world of the text and the world of the reader then must finally be in
dialogue with the world God has created. This hermeneutics in motion,
however, is envisaged as stratified – neither static nor iniquitous. In this
context, hermeneutical motion is to be understood as living and having the
capacity to affect the world.

While it is true that the goal of understanding and explanation is what has
been done in the text, which then for a reader has the possibility of becoming
new understanding (Ricœur's passionate claim), this new understanding also
calls for an engagement with God and the world in order to evaluate and cultivate its authenticity. If this is the case, the hermeneutical venture is not entirely
a private matter between text and reader, but in addition to this, it relates to the
world that is distinct from, yet related to both.

---

[77] Ricœur and LaCocque, *Thinking Biblically*, ix–xix, who, I believe, overemphasize
the readerly end. See also, Ricœur, 'Life'.

In this sense the biblical text, through its readers, must be acted out into the animate world (which speaks back), if anything other than self-transformation is to be hoped for that world. Ricœur's use of the biblical realities of new covenant, the kingdom of God and new creation are neither merely poetic possibilities, nor are they solely concerned with self-understanding in the biblical text (they do pertain to and are for both). Such biblical realities, however, also aim at transforming the totality of the world, not merely that of the reader.

Conclusion

The issues of language and reading Scripture addressed in this chapter are indeed something of a minefield. In my opinion, those interested in interpreting Scripture better cannot afford to avoid the arduous questions that language, philosophy, hermeneutics and the world pose for biblical interpretation. It is essential to be keenly aware that each of these will have an effect – sometimes positive, sometimes negative – on how one interprets the biblical text. A variety of language proposals, philosophical overtures or hermeneutical directives are simply anti-God and must be identified and critiqued on their own grounds.

Wolters, Ricœur and Thiselton have all pointed out that world-views are always connected to philosophical perspectives and language theories. Discernment, for a Christian perspective, is indispensable – not only when it comes to the evaluation of language claims and philosophical statements, but also with respect to the underlying world-views that are an integral part of them. The validity of the Christian faith will only suffer should interpreters assume that the minefield is of no concern to them.[78] There remains much work to be done in terms of engaging previous and emergent points of view in all these fields if Christians are going to have a role in developing a theory of language and better ways of reading and living Scripture out into the world.

Language theory, as explained in the 'Introduction' above, is much debated in our contemporary context. In some circles, it seems to be all that matters. Everything is language and language is often considered meaningless. It was only a short step from Ayer's overstated and sweeping rejection of religious language to a suspicion of 'all' language.

I attempted to deal with this problematic in the first part of the chapter. Religious, scientific and ordinary language are related to and distinct from each other in God's created world. They are meaning-full in their specific

---

[78] See Bartholomew, 'Uncharted Waters'.

usage contexts, but this is because they are related to one another and the world in a general usage context that encompasses them all. I have argued that a creational perspective of language, being intimately connected to God, the world and the self, opens up a possibility for a new understanding of 'all' language as both related and distinct on the level of creation. Such an orientation intends to confront any absolute division between language types, without forging a synthesis that dissolves distinction. I would wager, on these grounds, that 'either-ors' do not fit a theory of language, because they do not fit a theory of creation in its high degree of complexity.

This proposal was put forward as a theological realism. As one who embraces such a view, my hope is that this conception creates fecund discussion and moves towards an alternative that goes beyond the powerful residue of positivism, which continues to haunt language theory at the present time. Furthermore, it seems to me that there is an inordinate amount of time spent on language introspection. No doubt investigations of this genre have merit to some degree and they are beneficial, yet if such painstaking elucidation never arrives at working its way out of details and questions of language usage, in order to draw some general conclusions about the whole of life, one is in danger of getting lost in the reticulation of language that is never merely the context or referent for itself.

In addressing the question in the second section on reading Scripture in a special way or as any other text, I aimed to move a polarized discussion forward. There are those who overplay a general-philosophical hermeneutics, while there are others who overplay a regional-biblical hermeneutics. If one makes the biblical text too general, there is a loss of its distinctness from other texts. If one makes it too special, there is a loss of its relatedness to other texts. A general-philosophical hermeneutics that underplays regional-biblical hermeneutics is to be faulted for its comprehensiveness, which has the tendency to envelop Scripture within the context of all other books. While it is true the Bible is a text, it is a text unlike any other. A regional-biblical hermeneutics that underplays general-philosophical hermeneutics is culpable for its narrowness, which has the tendency to focus on the Bible as solely a special book that deals with theology. Granted, Scripture is theological, yet it relates to the interpretation of the world, the self and the whole of life – not just theology. It seems to me there is room for critique and embrace on both sides once one takes into consideration a possible both-and proposal that respects relation-distinction. The problem resides in assuming an either-or approach on the question where it is not warranted by the biblical text.

In addition, this assumption unwittingly (or perhaps otherwise) attempts to resolve too early the tension that exists at a diversity of levels in the hermeneutical process. A diminution of tension on this question, in my opinion, incurs the risk of being reductionistic and therefore entirely excluding one hermeneutical dimension from the other. Scripture, as far as I can tell, itself points beyond itself to resolution, but for the present tension remains. A position of relation-distinction, on such questions, seems to correspond better with Scripture than do polarizations.

It is crucial, in the end, not to leave biblical hermeneutics in the text or with the reader, but to view it in motion and as relevant to the whole of life. As interpreters begin in and with the world, this too is where biblical hermeneutics must provisionally and in a finite manner reach its summation. This orientation does not intend to ignore readerly transformation, but only to situate it in a context that is always larger than itself. When one's understanding is modified by the explanation of the biblical text, one's new understanding is to be passionately lived out in the world.

Bibliography

Ayer, A.J., *Language, Truth, and Logic* (New York: Dover; London: OUP, 1952)

Bartholomew, C. 'Uncharted Waters: Philosophy, Theology and the Crisis in Biblical Interpretation', in *Renewing Biblical Interpretation* (ed. C. Bartholomew, C. Greene and K. Möller; SHS, 1; Carlisle: Paternoster; Grand Rapids: Zondervan, 2000), 1–39

Braaten, C.E., 'Naming the Name', in *Our Naming of God* (ed. C.E. Braaten; Minneapolis, Augsburg–Fortress, 1989)

Carson, D.A., *The Gagging of God* (Leicester: IVP, 1996)

Clayton, P., *The Problem of God in Modern Thought* (Grand Rapids: Eerdmans, 2000)

Crossan, J.D., *The Dark Interval: Towards a Theology of Story* (Niles: Argus, 1975)

—, 'A Metamodel for Polyvalent Narration', *Semeia* 9 (1977), 105–47

Cuppit, D., 'post-Christianity', in *Religion, Modernity and Postmodernity* (ed. P. Heelas; Oxford: Basil Blackwell, 1998), 218–32

Devitt, M. and K. Sterelny, *Language and Reality: An Introduction to the Philosophy of Language* (Oxford: Basil Blackwell, 2nd edn, 1999)

Edwards, M., *Towards a Christian Poetics* (London: Macmillan, 1984)

Fodor, J., *Christian Hermeneutics: Paul Ricœur and the Refiguring of Theology* (Oxford: Clarendon Press, 1995)

Frei, H., 'The "Literal Reading" of Biblical Narrative in the Christian Tradition', in *The Bible and the Narrative Tradition* (ed. F. McConnell; Oxford: OUP, 1986), 36–77

Gill, J.H., *On Knowing God: New Directions for the Future of Theology* (Philadelphia: Westminster Press, 1981)

Gunton, C., *The One, the Three and the Many: God, Creation and the Culture of Modernity* (Cambridge: CUP, 1993)

—, *A Brief Theology of Revelation* (Edinburgh: T. & T. Clark, 1995)

Heidegger, M., *Poetry, Language, Thought* (trans. A. Hofstadter; New York: Harper & Row, 1975)

—, *On the Way to Language* (trans. P. Hertz and J. Stambaugh; New York: Harper & Row, 1971)

Jüngel, E., *God as the Mystery of the World* (trans. D.L. Guder; Edinburgh: T. & T. Clark, 1983)

Kelsey, D.H., *The Uses of Scripture in Recent Theology* (Philadelphia: Fortress Press, 1975)

Laughery, G.J., 'Reading Jesus' Parables According to J.D. Crossan and P. Ricœur', *EuroJT* 8.2 (1999), 145–54

—, *Living Hermeneutics: An Analysis and Evaluation of Paul Ricœur's Contribution to Biblical Hermeneutics* (Doctoral Dissertation, University of Fribourg, 2000)

—, 'Reading Ricœur: Authors, Readers, and Texts', *EuroJT* 9.2 (2000), 159–70

Lindbeck, G., *The Nature of Doctrine: Religion and Theology in a Postliberal Age* (Philadelphia: Westminster Press, 1984)

Milbank, J., *The Word Made Strange: Theology, Language, Culture* (Oxford and Cambridge, MA: Basil Blackwell, 1997).

O'Connor, D.J., 'Alfred Jules Ayer', *The Encyclopedia of Philosophy*, I (New York: Macmillan, 1967), 229–31

Placher, W.C., 'Paul Ricœur and Postliberal Theology: A Conflict of Interpretations', *Modern Theology* 4 (1988), 35–52

Ramsey, I.T., *Religious Language: An Empirical Placing of Theological Phrases* (London: SCM Press, 1957)

—, *Christian Empiricism* (Grand Rapids: Eerdmans, 1974)

Ricœur, P., *History and Truth* (trans. C. Kelbley; Evanston, IL: Northwestern University Press, 1965)

—, *The Conflict of Interpretations: Essays in Hermeneutics*, I (ed. D. Ihde; Evanston, IL: Northwestern University Press, 1969)

—, 'Philosophy and Religious Language', *JR* 54 (1974), 71–85

—, 'Biblical Hermeneutics', *Semeia* 4 (1975), 29–148

—, *Interpretation Theory: Discourse and the Surplus of Meaning* (Fort Worth, TX: Texas Christian University Press, 1976)

—, 'The Language of Faith', in *The Philosophy of Paul Ricœur: An Anthology of his Work* (ed. C.E. Reagan and D. Stewart; Boston: Beacon, 1978), 223–38

—, 'Toward a Hermeneutic of the Idea of Revelation', trans. D. Pellauer, in *Essays on Biblical Interpretation* (ed. L.S. Mudge; Philadelphia: Fortress Press, 1980), 73–118

—, 'Philosophical Hermeneutics and Biblical Hermeneutics', in *From Text to Action: Essays in Hermeneutics*, II (trans. K. Blamey and J.B. Thompson; Evanston, IL: Northwestern University Press, 1991), 89–101

—, 'Life: A Story in Search of a Narrator', in *A Ricœur Reader: Reflection and Imagination* (ed. M.J. Valdés; Toronto: Toronto University Press, 1991), 423–37

—, 'Hermeneutique – Les finalités de l'exégèse biblique', in *La Bible en philosophie* (Paris: Cerf, 1993), 27–51

Ricœur, P. and A. LaCocque, *Thinking Biblically: Exegetical and Hermeneutical Studies* (trans. D. Pellauer; Chicago: University of Chicago Press, 1998)

Soskice, J.M., *Metaphor and Religious Language* (Oxford: OUP, 1995)

Stiver, D., *The Philosophy of Religious Language: Sign, Symbol, and Story* (Oxford: Basil Blackwell, 1996)

Taylor, M.C., *Erring, A Postmodern A/theology*, (Chicago: University of Chicago Press, 1984)

Thiselton, A.C., 'Language and Meaning in Religion', in *NIDNTT*, III (ed. C. Brown; Exeter: Paternoster, 1978 & 1986), 1123–46

—, *New Horizons in Hermeneutics* (Grand Rapids: Zondervan, 1992)

—, 'Language – religious', in *Blackwell Encyclopedia of Modern Christian Thought* (ed. A. McGrath; Oxford: Basil Blackwell, 1993), 315–19

—, *Interpreting God and the Postmodern Self* (Edinburgh: T. & T. Clark, 1995)

Vanhoozer, K.J., *Biblical Narrative in the Philosophy of Paul Ricœur: A Study in Hermeneutics and Theology* (Cambridge: CUP, 1990)

—, *Is There a Meaning in This Text?: The Bible, the Reader, and the Morality of Literary Knowledge* (Grand Rapids: Zondervan, 1998)

Wallace, M.I., *The Second Naiveté: Barth, Ricœur and the New Yale Theology* (Macon, GA: Mercer University Press, 1990)

Watson, F., *Text, Church, and World: Biblical Interpretation in Theological Perspective* (Edinburgh: T. & T. Clark, 1994)

Wittgenstein, L., *Tractatus Logico-Philosophicus* (trans. D.F. Pears and B.F. McGuiness; London: Routledge & Kegan Paul, 1961)

Wolters, A., 'Gustavo Gutiérrez', in *Bringing into Captivity Every Thought* (ed. J. Klapwijk, S. Griffioen and G. Groenewoud; Lanham, MD and London: University Press of America, 1991)

—, *Creation Regained* (Carlisle: Paternoster, 1996)

Wolterstorff, N., *Divine Discourse: Philosophical Reflections on the Claim that God Speaks* (Cambridge: CUP, 1995)

Wright, C., *Living as the People of God* (Leicester: IVP, 1983)

9

'Starting a Rockslide' – Deconstructing History and Language via Christological Detonators[1]

Colin J.D. Greene

Your word, O Lord, is eternal;
It stands firm in the heavens
Psalm 119:89

Introduction

I enter this debate concerning the importance of the philosophy of language to biblical interpretation as a theologian, recognizing that attention to biblical texts raises all kinds of issues about the nature of language. In this chapter I would like to undertake at least a partial deconstruction of positivism and pragmatism, which have dominated the philosophies of history and language, respectively, in modern times. By so doing I hope also to demonstrate the rich potential of a biblically informed, Christological reconstruction of the central issues. In doing so I also acknowledge the inevitability of standing within a particular tradition. In this case, the tradition is a mainstream theological one that

---

[1] Contributing to the Scripture and Hermeneutics Seminar allows me to indulge one of my other favourite pastimes, i.e., love of contemporary music. I should therefore have acknowledged that the title of my chapter for vol. 1 in this series, 'In the Arms of the Angels', was taken from Sara McLachlan's excellent album *Surfacing*. The title of this chapter is taken from one of the tracts from the recently released album *The Hour of the Bewilderbeast* by Badly Drawn Boy.

asserts the cross and resurrection of Jesus as both the central compelling narrative and the essential signifier to the meaning of everything.

Attention to the 'asymmetrical relationship' between the cross and resurrection, I will assert, creates a *via media* between these two extremes of positivism and pragmatism. To make such an assertion is to become immediately embroiled in a debate about the relationship of apocalyptic, a particular genre of language and symbolism, to the historical events it purports to describe. Biblical interpretation inevitably raises questions about the meaning of language because, as Ricœur recognized, there is a double distanciation involved in interpreting biblical texts. The first relates to the distance between the author and the text and the other relates to the temporal, cultural and contextual distance between the horizon of the interpreter and that of the writer.[2] So once we try to provide an adequate account of the meaning of Jesus' teaching about, and relation to, the apocalyptic metaphor, the kingdom of God, we are already immersed in a heated debate about the meaning of language and the ability of such language to adequately reconfigure both the world behind and in front of the text.[3]

Apocalyptic and the Metaphor of the Kingdom of God

This biblical and theological debate, in the course of the last 150 years, has caused much ink (if not blood) to be spilt! Schweitzer first raised the issue of the enigmatic character of biblical apocalyptic in the modern mind[4] and so opened the way to attempts to demythologize and demystify it. Like many others, I remain unconvinced by translation processes that eventuate in a realized or horizontal eschatology (Bultmann) or a moralizing equivalent (Dodd, Harnack and Ritschl). But I do want to embrace, as far as historical reconstruction will permit, the original first-century or Second Temple Jewish meaning of apocalyptic.

Thus I am not prepared, like Robert Funk, Burton Mack, Dominic Crossan and some other representatives of 'the renewed new Quest' for the

---

[2] See the contribution to this volume by Ian Paul.

[3] It should not, therefore, be surprising to readers of *Renewing Biblical Interpretation*, the first volume in this series, that I now return to the issues raised by my chapter in that volume and seek to move the argument forward by offering my own theological account of the relationship of history to language and therefore also suggest a way to avoid the inflation of history as a mediating narrative that enables us to read the world correctly, which, I believe, typifies the foundational ethos of modernity.

[4] Schweitzer, *Quest*.

historical Jesus to translate apocalyptic into an ethical eschatology.[5] They assert that, while Jesus' ministry, sayings and sense of vocation appear to be housed within an apocalyptic world-view, his real intention was to offer a less bombastic, cynically debunking, amusingly fun poking form of radical social critique aimed at generating a new egalitarian reform movement within first-century Judaism. This so obviously, however, does not fit the world-view of early Christianity – riddled as it is with eschatological hopes and horizons.[6]

I want instead, therefore, to begin with a realist eschatology (and by that I do not mean literalist) – that ties eschatology into a basic storyline that lay behind Israel's self-identity as a nation. The more critically realistic the eschatology, the more difficult it will be to extract Jesus from this context and transpose him into an alien world-view – for instance, the modern secular notion of an a-temporal wandering mystic, cynic or teacher of religion.

Accordingly, in my view, there is a lot of sense to N.T. Wright's conviction that the phrase 'kingdom of God' did not refer to some heavenly domain where the dead could rest in peace. Rather, it articulated Israel's basic storyline and hope that YHWH would once again return to Zion and establish himself as King of the nations.

> God's kingdom, to the Jew-in-the-village in the first half of the first century, meant the coming vindication of Israel, victory over the pagans, the eventual gift of peace, justice and prosperity. It is scarcely surprising that, when a prophet appeared announcing that this kingdom was dawning, and that Israel's god was at last becoming king, he found an eager audience.[7]

In Wright's opinion a world-view cannot be understood as a history of ideas project, but refers instead to an overarching metanarrative in which a central defining story, symbols and subversively realized praxis are inextricably linked.[8] In that sense, YHWH and Israel's eventual return to Zion from exile links together Temple, land and Torah (symbols and praxis) and Israel's sense of national identity in one 'reinforcing narrative of hope'.[9]

Wright provides evidence for this interpretation of the eschatology of Second Temple Judaism by noting other substantial retellings of the story with which Jews would have been familiar. So, for example, he refers to Josephus' essentially idolatrous version of the story that ends with the Temple in ruins

---

[5] Funk and Hoover, *Five Gospels*; Mack, *Myth*; Crossan, *Historical Jesus* and *Jesus: A Revolutionary Biography*.
[6] See, e.g., Wright, *Jesus*, 210–14.
[7] Ibid., 204.
[8] See Wright, *New Testament*, 243.
[9] Ibid.

and Vespasian enthroned as the new world ruler. Nearer to home, the author of the Habakkuk commentary sought to reverse the tables with the elect few now representing Israel and executing YHWH's judgement over the nations.[10]

Most important of all, however, was Jesus' subversive retelling of the story with the signs of the kingdom now breaking in through his own symbolic re-enactment of the basic storyline. This was a Jesus who was in some sense unafraid to see his own vocation and calling as deeply messianic, because he believed he personified in himself and his actions the long-awaited return of YHWH and Israel to Zion. This was a Jesus who identified the real enemy not as pagan puppet regimes but the great Satan, who must be defeated before YHWH could once again be King. This was a Jesus who, on this basis, as Marcus Borg suggests, could also have been suffering from elusions of grandeur unless, of course, he was in some mysterious fashion installed as Messiah by YHWH and no one else.[11] When eschatology is inserted into a storied universe, then, it functions as an essential structural element to the whole worldview and is capable of being adapted to different, if at times conflicting, versions of the central metanarrative. Wright outlines the main alternatives concerning how eschatology has been understood within recent biblical scholarship.

The Meaning of Apocalyptic and Eschatology within Recent Biblical Scholarship

1. Eschatology as the end of the world, i.e. the end of the space-time universe (or the transformation of the space-time universe into a new heaven and a new earth where there are both continuities and discontinuities between the former and the latter);
2. Eschatology as the climax of Israel's history, involving the end of the space-time universe;
3. Eschatology as the climax of Israel's history, involving events for which end-of-the-world language is the only set of metaphors adequate to express the significance of what will happen, but resulting in a new and quite different phase *within* space-time history;
4. Eschatology as major events, not specifically climactic within a particular story, for which end-of-the-world language functions as metaphor;
5. Eschatology as 'horizontal language' (i.e., *apparently* denoting movement forwards in time) whose *actual* referent is the possibility of moving 'upwards' spiritually into a new level of existence;

---

[10] Ibid., 199.
[11] See Borg's critique of Wright in this regard in Wright and Borg, *Meaning,* part 2.

6. Eschatology as critique of the present world order, perhaps with proposals for a new order;
7. Eschatology as critique of the present socio-political scene, perhaps with proposals for adjustments.[12]

With respect to all those who have taken different trajectories on the roller coaster of eschatological expectation, I offer another possibility, or (to use Nietzsche's pregnant phrase) an extravagant thesis, which could well be close to that which both Second Temple Judaism and Jesus originally intended.

8. Eschatology does not refer to the literal end of the space-time universe, nor necessarily to the climax of Israel's history, although it most probably does contain elements of this within it. But it uses a set of metaphors that refer to climactic events, most notably the exile and the crucifixion/resurrection, that do, in fact, *tear the fabric of history apart*, consequently offering proposals and possibilities for a new social order.

With this thesis I also offer a particular philosophy of history and language, respectively, that will function as such throughout the rest of this chapter.

The way to test this hypothesis, as Wright indicates, is to ask whether such an eschatological perspective would make sense in the context of Second Temple Judaism. So at this point in the argument we return to the origin of eschatology in cataclysmic socio-political events upon which Israel's whole history was both predicated and decided. We also return to Jewish scholars Gershom Scholem, Walter Benjamin and Martin Buber, whom Jürgen Moltmann has also sought to utilize,[13] who have informed us that 'Jewish messianism is by origin and nature – and this cannot be too much stressed – a theory about a catastrophe. This theory stresses the revolutionary, subversive element in the transition from every historical present to the messianic future.'[14]

The catastrophe was of course the exile, which as Wright recognizes is the hinge on which Israel's covenant hope and election turns. That catastrophe included the defeat, subjugation and enslavement of Israel by the Assyrian Empire. Is it any wonder that Nietzsche postulated that such an event was in fact the end of Israel's dream, the zero point in her history that demanded a complete reassessment of her covenant relationship to YHWH and unfortunately eventuated in a new religion of moral and spiritual servitude born out of

---

[12] Wright, *Jesus*, 208.
[13] See Moltmann, *The Way*, 22–24.
[14] Quoted in Moltmann, *The Way*, 22.

defeat and resentment.[15] In much more restrained fashion, but nonetheless still granting the traumatic theological and political catastrophe of the exile, Gerhard von Rad emphasized that the exile involved the complete breakdown of the traditions and institutions through which Israel's national identity had been sustained.

In terms of the central symbols of the overarching metanarrative, to use Wright's thesis, Temple, monarchy, land and, to a large extent, the practice of the Torah, had all perished. A serious question arose: namely, how was it possible to be Israel in such a situation?[16] Von Rad pointed to the resilience of Israel's prophetic traditions that put this whole catastrophe under the proviso of the former things that had now perished and apparently disappeared (Isa. 43:18), and in compassionate and compelling language pointed to the new thing whereby both covenant and election would be preserved. What was new was the eschatological and, to a certain extent, the messianic.

> The eschatological phenomenon is simplified once more; it is reduced to the extremely revolutionary fact that the prophets saw Jahweh approaching Israel with a new action which made the old saving institutions increasingly invalid since from then on life or death for Israel was determined by this future event.[17]

Of course the prophets could only envision this new event in terms of a re-appropriation of the old saving traditions. So for Hosea it is a new entry into the land, for Isaiah a new Davidic monarchy and a new Zion, for Jeremiah a new covenant, and for Deutero-Isaiah a new exodus. Similarly, this new event revisited Israel's hope concerning the day of YHWH, the return of YHWH in person to Zion, the instigation of a new holy war when all YHWH's enemies would be routed and all nations, indeed creation itself, would pay homage to the King of Kings.[18]

But the nub of the issue is that what is old does indeed die. It tumbles into the abyss caused by the cataclysmic rupture of the fabric of history, and what is new cannot just be predicated on the basis of the old. Israel's future after the exile remained undecided, unfulfilled and essentially an interim experiment. Indeed, as Walter Brueggemann notes, 'Whereas the "storyline" before the exile is clear and singular, the "plot" of Judaism after the exile is much less clear and singular, no doubt reflecting the tentative situation of a community scarred and sobered by displacement.'[19] It was, therefore, not surprising that

---

[15] Nietzsche, 'The Antichrist', 24f.; see also, Genealogy, 34f.

[16] So for instance Ps. 74, 79, and particularly 137.

[17] Von Rad, Old Testament Theology, II, 118.

[18] Ibid., 119–25.

[19] Brueggemann, 'Journey'.

shadowy, ill-defined, eschatologically-orientated, messianic expectations emerged and, more importantly, that another perplexing literary genre we call apocalyptic appeared.

Apocalyptic involved a theological rereading and retelling of Israel's political history – past, present and future – through the lens of highly metaphorical language. But while metaphorical, the language is not gnostic or dualist – unless, like von Rad and Schweitzer and much biblical scholarship since, one reads its language of cosmic meltdown literally. Apocalyptic is a profound speculative hope born out of a powerful combination of mystical experience, socio-political impotence, metaphysical representation, and historical realism and perplexity. It is, therefore, all too aware that history fractures, skews off in different directions, and even at times, due to the pressure of apparently absurd occurrences, appears to turn back on itself. At times of catastrophe, history, 'the all too human' (to refer again to Nietzsche), rips apart, and both the judgement and salvation of YHWH rain down upon Israel and the nations. Many of the former things are washed away, while all Israel waits for the new day of salvation – however and whenever it will come.

Other retellings of the central story similarly combined contemporary political events with theological interpretation, because the future remains the future of the unpredictable kingdom. Apocalyptic could not be expressed in anything other than deeply symbolic and metaphorical language because it refers to decisive, cataclysmic historical events and yet renders them part of a wider cosmic drama – which means, not surprisingly, that meaning is both postponed and deferred.[20]

Jesus, Apocalyptic and the Kingdom of God

The other central question, of course, is whether this thesis can make any sense of Jesus' vocation, ministry and eventual fate. That is an even more difficult question to answer because it depends, at least in part, on two further questions. Do we believe that all we have access to in the New Testament is the early Christian representation or misrepresentation of the Jesus phenomenon?

---

[20] This does not mean, however, that eschatological language or apocalyptic cannot be taken literally. So, for instance, there is a real sense contra Wright that such eschatological hopes went beyond the return of YHWH to Zion and set Israel's history within the context of the history of the cosmos. I have been reminded recently how literally some Jews did take such language particularly through the practice of keeping the bones of the dead in ossuaries to be ready for the final resurrection. Metaphors allow for a fluidity of meaning, but this does not happen by cancelling out the referential and cognitive aspect to such linguistic usage.

And is there in fact some real continuity between Jesus' awareness of his vocation and calling and that which his followers ascribed to him? On the basis that what we find throughout the period from the exile to the sacking of Jerusalem in AD 70, however, is realistic, hard-wired eschatology, we should ask how can both Jesus and the early Christian communities be understood within such a context?

Into just such a context John the Baptist came preaching a baptism of repentance for 'the forgiveness of sins'. Why, because another fiery judgement, maybe even another exile, but certainly another substantial tear in the already over-loaded tissue of history was on the way because the axe was even now laid at the root of the tree.[21] How, then, did Jesus, the one who would baptize with the Holy Spirit and fire (metaphorical language that heralded another apocalyptic event), understand his own role in such a situation, particularly after the arrest of John?

We know that what was distinctive about Jesus' preaching and embodiment of the kingdom was that it was somehow both present and future; that, in fact, *both* dimensions expressed the *imminence* of the kingdom which entailed that the *signs* of the kingdom were already breaking in through his jubilee ministry of good news for the poor, release for the captives and recovery of sight for the blind (Lk. 4:14–30). These were the signs John the Baptist was asked to acknowledge as an indication that his own enigmatic predictions concerning one greater than himself were being fulfilled, and therefore in Jesus, his cousin, the time was ripe.

But what time was that? Wright believes there could be only one answer. So Jesus' announcement of the kingdom, which he recognizes is quite new and distinctive, nevertheless must be understood as a basic variation on the same central storyline.

> We must stress, again, that this message is *part of a story,* and only makes sense as such. And there is only one story that will do. Israel would at last 'return from exile'; evil would be defeated; YHWH would at last return to 'visit' his people. Anyone wishing to evoke and affirm all this at once, in first-century Palestine, could not have chosen a more appropriate and ready-made slogan than 'kingdom of god'.[22]

But based on this thesis Jesus had a very particular idea of messiahship in mind. Similarly, all the essential symbols of the story required radical, subversive

---

[21] The Gospels are not only redolent with the creative use of metaphors and illusion to past events in salvation history, they also provide us with striking instances of rhetoric – particularly in John's Gospel. In what follows I deliberately adopt a more rhetorical style as a way of untapping the reservoir of meaning that metaphors hold.

[22] Wright, *Jesus*, 227.

reinterpretation and the important metaphors could have one and only one set of referents – namely the climax of Israel's history, the return of YHWH to Zion.

We accept that it would be hard for a first-century Jew proclaiming the arrival of the kingdom not to be intimately aware of this basic storyline. But they would also be poignantly aware that in regard to history it had never quite worked out like that, nor was there yet any substantial burden of evidence that it was going to. Similarly, we contend that they could also have been aware that within the variegated and deeply mysterious corpus of writings we call apocalyptic, there appeared to be more than just variations on a single theme. There were whole new overtures and melodies that may, in fact, have been written to find a way of dealing with the torture and fragility of a hope that seemed so often out of sync with real politics and history.

So, what if Jesus *was* or *may have been* operating within some notion of the basic metanarrative of exile and restoration but also had no way of predicting what shape that restoration would take? YHWH's triumphant return to Zion was one, and in some sense the ultimate, possibility, but there could be, if past history was anything to go by, other possible avenues of exploration. There was even possibly a penultimate extension to the storyline about to take place that involved his own unique and distinctive contribution to this chequered history between Israel and her covenant God.

And what was this distinctive calling? To be the conduit, the focus whereby that clearing, that tensile space referred to as the kingdom, would arrive and hold long enough for YHWH to save and comfort his people Israel. And is this not what his baptism on behalf of Israel implied? His vocation, to demonstrate and incarnate that saving reality in the praxis of his preaching, lifestyle, healing and liberating actions and deeds, in turn indicated that even now the febrile fabric of history was being stretched to breaking point by the imminent arrival of the kingdom in his own personage. Indeed, another cataclysmic fissure could appear at any moment when the evil and tyranny that resided in all the dispersed centres of power within a compromised Judaism were flushed out and exposed. Is this not just what the temptations and the infamous Temple incident imply?

That was why the time of both judgement and salvation had arrived – because you could not have one without the other. And the evidence was there, the signs of the new age were already tumbling in, fracturing the space-time continuum that supported the rumble tumble of events we call history, making the miraculous commonplace. That was why the call was out to be the new Israel, to create the clearing of the kingdom, so that YHWH could gather his lost sheep to himself, so that like the waiting Father he could run to embrace all those returning from exile.

Could this not be why Jesus, like the early Christians, appeared to sit so loose on the central defining symbols of Judaism? Because, as we have indicated, Temple, monarchy, land and even to a certain extent Torah (certainly the Pharisaical interpretation of the Law that sought holiness from the outside in), belonged to the old regime. Therefore, such an apparently cavalier attitude to these once central and cherished symbols was *bound* to bring him into conflict with the religious establishment. A conflict that mirrored the apostasy of Israel's former leaders who thought that politics and religion could be expedited separately which, he well knew, had heralded in the catastrophe of the exile.

And this was why it was imperative that he seek out the lost, the marginalized and ostracized members of society, and call them to repentance and faith – because his focus was justifiably sinners, not those whose apparent righteousness blocked their entrance to the kingdom. And this was why it was incumbent upon him, together with the disciples who represented the twelve tribes of Israel, to establish an egalitarian community based on the jubilee principle.

This was also why he, like the prophets, embraced a restoration theology of love, mercy and forgiveness, but would not identify himself with any of the expectations of what was, after all, a fairly confused notion of messiahship.[23] Finally, this is why he took as his way of personifying Israel the suffering servant of Deutero-Isaiah. Because, as he acknowledged to Peter (Mk. 8:27–29; Mt. 16:13–16; Lk.9:18–20), to be this kind of prophet, to become the meeting place between heaven and earth, was to take the reality of sin, suffering and exile upon your own fragile frame. It was to weep over the sins of Jerusalem, to seek the spiritual and therefore also the political and moral regeneration of his nation, and so, when the chasm appeared, to fall into the abyss of godforsakenness in one final act of surrender and atonement.

The nature of metaphor is to marry history with hope and so create the possibility of fluidity of meaning, to defy any one set of referents, to introduce a 'semantic impertinence' (Ricœur) and so set the imagination free to linger long enough in an act of attestation that names the proper object of faith – that is, the love and mercy of the covenant God.

---

[23] In this regard, see the discussion between Wright and Borg in *Meaning*, part 11. For a more substantial investigation of Jewish messianic hopes and expectations see Charlesworth, 'Messianology'.

The Early Christian Communities, Apocalyptic and the Kingdom of God

We must also ask if our rendition of the nature of eschatology coheres with the Christian version of the story. Their story, of course, began with the cataclysmic events of the cross and resurrection, and that is where we should begin also. First I wish to affirm the principle that cross and resurrection must be taken together as complementary, if not symmetrical, aspects of the one saving event. As such they define the true identity of Jesus of Nazareth, and that is both their narrative and metaphorical intent.

Thus, the crucifixion was for the burgeoning Jesus movement as catastrophic as was the exile for Israel. The godforsaken holocaust of the crucifixion precipitated a crisis that left the storyline, symbols and praxis of this fledgling movement in tatters.[24] The confusion, disarray and desertion of the disciples expressed in tangible form the same question that faced the Jews in exile – namely, how was it possible to be this egalitarian reform movement after this tumultuous event? A new exile, a new torture of history seemed imminent.

The apocalyptic signs and language that surround the Synoptic Gospels' account of the crucifixion event require explanation. In contradistinction to Jürgen Moltmann, I am not convinced that these apocalyptic metaphors necessarily refer to the foreshadowing of the universal suffering that will hasten in the end times.[25] Nor do I believe that this is figurative language used to denote the inexplicable. Apocalyptic language describes an apocalyptic event, namely, the sundering of the connection and continuity between the Jesus phenomenon and the messianic future. The crucifixion may have been on the cards as far as Jesus' behaviour in Jerusalem was concerned, but it still represented the *terminus ad quem* of anyone purporting to be a national leader, a prophet, and most certainly a messiah.

If this was the climax this new reform movement was building up to, then it was a maniac leap into the abyss. Unless, of course, that was precisely what it was intended to achieve. So, like the sundered temple veil it severed the jugular of history as the judgement of God upon the nations has a tendency to do and the resulting haemorrhage of meaning rendered history a dead end.

---

[24] I am not suggesting that there is a direct comparison between the central defining elements of Israelite religion and those of the fledgling Jesus movement. Rather I am simply drawing attention through analogical language to the complete disarray that overtook this 'discipleship of equals', to use Fiorenza's phrase, that Jesus appears to have tried to construct as a way of practically representing the new Israel under the aegis of the kingdom.

[25] Moltmann, *The Way*, 151–95.

Another apparently disastrous, but certainly decisive, break in the space-time continuum appeared and the hopes and fears of the generations spilled out into an empty crevasse which no form of historicism could possibly bridge.

The asymmetrical relationship between cross and resurrection is due to the fact that one does not automatically imply the other. Neither the disciples nor scholarship can extrapolate a resurrection event out of the fracture and torture of Good Friday. This is in fact what all the evocative stories and narratives at the end of John's Gospel imply – a complete *novum*, a totally unexpected development of the storyline that no one, least of all the disciples, were pre-dicting. Rowan Williams makes basically the same point when he invokes the category of risk.

> In other words, it is a story of 'risk'; and only at Easter are we able to say, 'he comes *from* God just as he goes *to* God', and to see in the contingent fact of the resurrection – the limited events of the finding of an empty tomb and a scatter of bewildering en-counters – that which is not contingent, the life of God as Father and Son together.[26]

Consequently, in line with all that has been said so far, I would contend, contra Wolfhart Pannenberg, that resurrection is not just a metaphor that refers solely to the prolepsis of the end of the space-time universe.[27] Nor is it shorthand for the disciples' vision of the continued 'aliveness' of Jesus,[28] nor does it merely refer to their corporate experience of faith.[29] Instead, I would affirm that resur-rection refers primarily to the installation, or enthronement, or exaltation of Jesus as the Messiah. He, and no other, has been installed as the Christ by the same God whose kingdom Jesus sought to inaugurate. And only in this way does the exalted Messiah now rule so that what is done in heaven can become reality on earth. All socio-political principalities and powers are now subject to Jesus the Christ who is King of kings (Rev. 17:14). As Peter announced, this crucified Jesus has now been confirmed as both Messiah and Kyrios. Most cer-tainly this would have led eventually, as we see in the Pauline corpus and John's Gospel, to some notion of pre-existence. But what it eventuated in first of all was something quite different.

Throughout the New Testament we encounter passages that inform us that the kingdom is no longer the sole prerogative of YHWH but now also belongs to the Messiah. This is explicit, for instance, in Ephesians 5:5 (the kingdom of the Messiah and of God).[30] The important passage is 1 Corinthians 15:20–28.

---

[26] Williams, *Christian Theology,* 159.

[27] Pannenberg, *Jesus.*

[28] Schillebeeckx, *Jesus.*

[29] Macquarrie, *Christology.*

[30] See also Col. 1:13; 2 Pet. 1:11; Jn. 18:36f.

Here we learn that the Messiah, the first fruits of both the new resurrection life and the new humanity, has been charged with rescuing the whole creation from its bondage to futility, death and decay. The Messiah is still 'on his way' to realizing the kingdom in the affairs of this world and will have only achieved his purpose when the final enemy, death, has also been destroyed.

Again, we encounter the distinctively Christian contribution to the history of eschatological hope. The present and future dimensions of the kingdom interlock. In other words, the *imminence* of the kingdom has not retreated or gone away. It is steadily at hand, ready at any moment to break in again, buckle and splay the fibrous layers of the mean play of history and let the signs of the kingdom break out once again. The exalted Messiah is now the new broker of the kingdom who possesses the power and authority to pour out the eschatological Spirit on all his followers and companions so that they too are kingdom people, visible signs and portents of a new age.[31] Pentecost becomes the new baptism in the Holy Spirit because the installation of Jesus as the Messiah instigates a radically new understanding of the nature of the kingdom and indeed of discipleship.

Precisely at this point, as Wright concedes, we discover the most audacious redefinition of the Jewish hope of the kingdom, the almost total absence of any association with the essential symbols and praxis that defined Second Temple Judaism.

> The story of the new movement is told without reference to the national, racial or geographical liberation of Israel. The praxis of the kingdom (holiness) is defined without reference to Torah. The answers to the worldview questions can be given in terms of a redeemed humanity and cosmos, rather than in terms simply of Israel and her national hope.[32]

Wright offers a useful cameo of the evidence. Thus, John distinguishes the kingdom 'not from this world' from that espoused by the Jewish revolutionaries of the time. Paul disassociates the kingdom of 'righteousness, peace and joy in the holy spirit' from a kingdom tied into dietary restrictions and other such ceremonial rituals. Luke emphasizes that this kingdom is no longer territorially defined but spans the whole world. And the Apocalypse directs our attention to the heavenly Jerusalem where the lamb is on the throne and no Temple is required. What does all this imply?

> Yet, even at a surface reading, this early Christian kingdom-language has little or nothing to do with the vindication of ethnic Israel, the overthrow of Roman rule in

---

[31] Rom. 8:18–27; 2 Cor. 5; Rev. 21.
[32] Wright, *Jesus,* 218.

Palestine, the building of a new Temple on Mount Zion, the establishment of Torah-observance, or the nations flocking to Mount Zion to be judged and/or to be educated in the knowledge of JHWH.[33]

Precisely, so to try and surmount what others would view as a serious if not mortal threat to his whole thesis concerning the central meaning of eschatology, Wright has recourse to the role of metanarratives. In other words, what we locate here is not a new story, but a new moment in the old story, or to use the language of drama, here we are in Act 5, not Act 3, of the one overarching dramatic rendition of the one central story.[34]

At this point I must demur once again and exercise a certain incredulity toward metanarratives, particularly those, as I have indicated elsewhere, that can become (although this is most certainly not Wright's intention) totalizing forms of discourse that imperialistically exclude and deny the validity or viability of other metaphorical referents.[35] This looks, to me at least, impecuniously like a new story and one that recognizes, perhaps reluctantly, an inevitable parting of the ways. Because now the Gentiles, and not solely Israel, are YHWH's target and focus. While this dimension of the story may well have been in place well before AD 70, Judaism was itself redefining its story dramatically after that particular tragedy. In other words, it is at this point that the central story splits into two perplexing and conflicting discourses of controversy and disputation, because both the Jewish and Christian stories are ecclesiologically separated and eschatologically unfulfilled.

No doubt this is, at least in part, something of what Paul is struggling with in Romans 9 to 11. Paul recognized with great personal pain and perplexity that Israel had, at least temporally, refused the invitation to stay within the Christian version of the overarching metanarrative. For to the Jew, the Christian belief in the resurrection of Jesus and the enthronement of him as the Messiah did not create a new act within their story – it founded a new story based on a new movement with a new mission.[36] In other words, a meta-narrative gave way to a continuing history of disputation and religious controversy because the understanding of the kingdom peculiar to both Jesus and the early Christians has to do with the interpenetration of both the present and the future that brings the kingdom within reach of the nations and consequently can no longer be defined solely through Israel's symbols of national identity.

---

[33] Ibid., 219.

[34] The acts being creation, fall, Israel, Jesus and the church (ibid.).

[35] Greene, *Marking*, ch. 14.

[36] The original trace of which was the redefinition of Christians as the followers of a new Way. See also Greene, *Marking*, ch. 6.

While Christians affirmed this interpretation of events post-AD 70, Jews overall did not. To ignore this hiatus and simply conclude that the church is the new Israel is to collude in the kind of religious imperialism that would inevitably produce the baleful legacy of anti-Semitism that emerged once Christianity became the first great world religion.

This is in fact what happens continually within history, because history cannot bear the weight of metanarratives. The vagaries, distortions, silences, misrepresentations, tragedies, downright absurdities and inexplicable farce of history, as Karl Marx (that apparently most historicist of thinkers) realized, elude the meaning imposed upon it by totalizing metanarratives.[37] It is also for this reason that I see no point in trying to apply Troeltsch's criteria of historical verifiability to an event like the resurrection. This is not because this is a unique historical event of which there are no analogues, for all events are in some sense unique and not simply the result of causal interconnections. But cataclysmic events that rupture the tissue of history itself cannot be judged by criteria that presuppose that history is a seamless robe based on the fiction of the homogeneity of all events.[38]

Further Implications for the Philosophy of History

It should by now be clear, and for some alarmingly so, that I am departing from a broad consensus in terms of how history has been understood both by the exponents of modernity and by those who have appropriated their insights in theology. Put starkly, if somewhat simplistically, for most of the modernity project history has remained an over-inflated positivistic myth, at times of gargantuan proportions, extolling the virtues, values and progress of the human spirit while at the same time masquerading under the guise of historical objectivity.[39]

In order to substantiate this thesis, we refer to the latest addition to the modern industry of Jesus research by Dominic Crossan, *The Birth of Christianity:*

---

[37]   Marx, 'Eighteenth Brumaire', 103–50. So, for instance, Marx writes; 'Men make their own history, but they do not make it just as they please; they do not make it under circumstances chosen by themselves, but under circumstances directly encountered, given and transmitted from the past ... And just when they seem engaged in revolutionizing themselves and things, in creating something that has never existed, precisely in such periods of revolutionary crisis they anxiously conjure up the spirits of the past to their service and borrow from their names, battle-cries and costumes in order to present the new scene as world history in this time-honored disguise and this borrowed language' (103–4).

[38]   See Troeltsch, 'Historical and Dogmatic Method', 11–32.

[39]   For a theoretical justification of this position see Greene, 'Angels'.

Discovering what Happened in the Years Immediately after the Execution of Jesus. In entirely commendable fashion, Crossan develops an interdisciplinary approach to critical historical investigation of both the intra- and extracanonical sources that he postulates form the bedrock of early Christianity. This amounts to a three-pronged analysis of the evidence.

First of all, utilizing cross-cultural anthropology he seeks to demonstrate that ancient agrarian societies undergoing a period of extensive commercialization inevitably provoked serious peasant unrest, particularly when encouraged by members of a retainer class. Secondly, historical analysis of Graeco-Roman involvement in first-century Palestine points to a bitter conflict between traditional Jewish values and Roman commercialization. Finally, both of these conclusions are apparently supported by archaeological evidence. Taken together, Crossan asserts that these three historical factors would have inspired a Jesus resistant movement centred on opposition to commercial exploitation aided and abetted by disaffected retainer scribes. This in turn supposedly demonstrates that Jesus advocated an ethical eschatology based on Jewish covenantal traditions of justice and the preferential option for the poor and marginalized.

Not surprisingly, Crossan's thesis soon appears to break down in a number of significant ways. Most notably, as one proceeds the interdisciplinary approach unravels in favour of overtly theological judgements concerning equally problematic historical sources. These include judgements about the significance of a common sayings tradition upon which both Q and the gospel of Thomas are supposedly based; a common meal tradition that apparently links together Jesus' pre-Easter itinerant rural ministry and the early Christian, Jerusalem-based, urban passion and resurrection story; and, even more incredulously, a Cross gospel located within the second-century gospel of Peter.

To be fair, Crossan is no friend of positivistic accounts of history. Rather, he claims that all history is story, that it requires reconstruction of the past through critical interaction with the present, and that this interactivism is the same as what Wright means by critical realism.[40] What remains in dispute, however, is the problematic status of history reconfigured according to an equally tendentious theory of reconstructed sources that automatically privileges the epistemological scope of the historian. It is this error that is always the source of the pernicious fallacy that undergirds all positivism.

History telling is always also history making, and therefore to a certain extent history remaking. In other words, imaginative portrayals and conjectures, which are, to be sure, based on some ascertainable and recoverable historical sources and accounts, nevertheless can only amount to a probable

---

[40] Crossan, *Birth*, ch. 2.

construal of what the available evidence might suggest, or the direction *we* might be orientated towards in our investigations. And it is this dissimilitude that, in fact, makes history interesting.

As Ricœur acknowledges, historical reconstruction most certainly owes a debt to the past we are not at liberty to fictionalize, however that does not and cannot absolve us from the risk of interpretation and the test of appropriation.[41] And neither can it guarantee immunity from the possible contamination of ideological reconstruction of the past in the light of perceived religious or epistemological threats and challenges the historian is facing in the present. Even when a historian allows sufficient credence to the uncertainty, probability and vexing disputability surrounding events, actions, speech acts and interpretations of the past, he or she may not recognize the equally problematic status of the cultural, sociological and historical situated-ness of the interpreter in the present. Nor may a historian necessarily be clear about the philosophical relationship between the 'two horizons', to use Gadamer's suggestive phrase.[42]

So, against the positivism and historicism of modernity, am I in fact opting for the more austere landscape of postmodernity? For we have been confidently informed that we stepped off that particular trajectory of history some time ago, rejecting it as an imperialistic metanarrative of self-delusion and domination. Hence we can no longer believe in history as anything other than an ideological construct rather than the universal carrier of truth and meaning.[43]

A good example of this view in contemporary theology are those who espouse a relativist and consumerist approach to biblical and theological exploration.[44] Interestingly enough, there is a parallel here with Crossan's thesis concerning the socio-political reality of first-century Palestine. For now a new postmodern ethic of commercialization has subverted the old Enlightenment foundational values of truth and meaning, and all we can do is let the market decide which Jesus we should seek to valorize. A Jesus who could not be counter-cultural but, instead, inevitably baptizes the consensus morality of the hapless victims of postmodern kitsch and simulacra.

I wish to repudiate both extremes, while at the same time putting forward the thesis that the reason for their apparent persuasiveness resides in the privatization of religion. Once the ability of religion to provide 'public' meaning, truth and vision had been both seriously truncated and elided, something had to take its place. In my view, the modern impostor has been the philosophies

---

[41] Ricœur, *Time*, III, 142f.

[42] See Greene, 'Angels'.

[43] In this regard see Baudrillard, *Forget Foucault*, 67ff.; 'The Year 2000'; and *Cool Memories*.

[44] See Clines, *Biblical Interpretation*; also *Bible and the Modern World*.

and theologies of universal history. I have argued elsewhere that most, including those espoused by Hegel, Dilthey, Rahner and Pannenberg, with the possible exception of Heidegger, all subsume the meaning of the particular within the metanarrative of the universal.[45] Once this step is taken, the contingency, particularity, and sheer strange otherness of events is forgotten and the fragility of history that cannot bear the imprint of totalizing discourses is ignored.

This does not entail that we should scorn or reject the important discoveries, illuminating hypotheses and occasional refreshing demythologizing of those involved in history telling and writing. But I come back to my conclusion above – history telling is always a case of history remaking, because the space-time continuum that supports the intoxicating dance and revel of past, present and future events knows no inherent supporting logic or immanent entelechy.[46] Or if it does, I submit it is a dangerous move to connect this with a full-blown theology of revelation. So for instance John Goldingay, in commenting on Daniel 11 (a passage where history is reconceived and reconstructed through the medium of apocalyptic), is quite sanguine about the implications of all this for those who want to claim history as the most comprehensive category of revelation.[47]

> The details of Persian and Hellenistic history have no constructive theological meaning. Events unfold as a pointless sequence of invasions, battles, schemes, and frustrations, a tale of selfishness, irrationality, and chance. History is neither the implementation of human purposes, the outworking of a principle of order and justice, the unfolding of a plan formulated in heaven, nor the reflection of the sovereign hand of God at work in the world. Often it seems to be the tale of human beings' unsuccessful attempts to be like God, though for the most part the true God appears to be sitting in the gallery watching history go nowhere.[48]

In reality we are the makers of our own history and the obliterators of that of others. We tell stories that are by no means an idle fiction – rather they are often freighted with ideological constraints and tantalizingly persuasive and potentially destructive world-views.[49] They are powerful articulations of how

---

[45] Greene, *Marking*, ch. 9.

[46] See, for example, the ill-fated attempt by Pannenberg to rewrite human history from the perspective of the doctrine of election in *Human Nature, Election and History* – a project he thankfully abandoned.

[47] See, e.g., Pannenberg, 'Redemptive Event', 15.

[48] Goldingay, *Models*, 305.

[49] A good example of which in recent history has been the nationalistic ideology of Slobodan Milosovich, by which he dragged the Serbian people into three catastrophic ethnically-motivated wars.

we believe things are or should be. In the process, we often deliberately ignore the aporias that should require us to look again at the evidence.

It is indeed ironic, therefore, that for those who have sought to integrate or develop their Christology from the basis of some overarching theory of history, apocalyptic has been a favourite hunting ground.[50] It is my contention that this confidence has been misplaced, because it is apocalyptic that directs us to the fundamental aporia and dispersal of meaning that continually breaks apart the fragile continuities and interconnectivities of history. Apocalyptic remains the torture of history. Under the pressure of cataclysmic events, the earthen vessel of history shatters and the meaning of the past evaporates, spilling out into the sands of time.

How, then, should we articulate a theology of history which in turn would have a radically new bearing on how we understand the nature of language? I suggest a Christological alternative based on the assymetrical relationship between the cross and resurrection of Jesus. To use an analogy developed by Hans Urs Von Balthasar in his atonement theology, history stands under the judgement and mercy of God explicated by the Easter events.[51]

Good Friday, if it was indeed the crucifixion and death of the eternal Wisdom of God, symbolizes the end of history. History as we could possibly know and experience it; history as the forward thrust of a continuous, seemingly random and disjointed, yet also interconnected series of events; history as representatively encompassed in the body of the dying and tortured Jesus, fractures, loses its meaning and momentum and suffers the judgement of God.

Cast into the abyss of Holy Saturday, history, like the Son, dies and descends into the depths. All that remains is a dark and foreboding crevasse, and both the promise and the failure of the past are consigned to its meaningless depths. The mean power play of history, that which is subject to sin, chaos and futility, and so for many, to quote Hobbes, still remains nasty, brutish and short, is dissipated and destroyed. If the Son is dead, his future denied, lost in Hades, then everything mortal and human (including the debris of history) suffers the same fate.

There it would and should remain and we would have no interest in, or contemplate any glory to, the bacchanalian revel we call history if it were not for Easter Sunday. It is here, indeed, precisely because the hollow shell of history has been broken open, that the kingdom praxis of the Messiah is fulfilled, verified and exonerated. The two 'arms of God' outstretched upon the cross in love and forgiveness, his judgement and mercy, grasp again the past and the future folds of the robe of history. The Father, through the ecstasy of the Spirit, raises the Son – and history is reborn. Now and only now can we say

---

[50] So, for instance, both Pannenberg and Moltmann in their respective Christologies.

[51] Von Balthasar, *Mysterium Paschale*.

'comfort, comfort my people', and claim that the warfare of history has ended (Isa. 40:1). The only meaning or purpose to history that could possibly be perceived is through the lens of the resurrection. Without the resurrection, without this particular space and peace in the midst of time, history would remain what to a certain extent it always is. It is at worst a bitter tragedy of failed projects, the destructive menace of ideological conflict, the coercive reality of futile domination systems. Or, at best, it is a positive reminder that the distance from the finite to the infinite is always infinite.

Let me be clear about the theological claims I am making. The asymmetrical relationship between cross and resurrection does not permit a seamless transition from one to the other. Revelation is God's judgement and mercy, both of which are manifest in the fissures, fractures and frustrations of history in every era and we must learn to live with this discordance. Neither do I wish to understand the judgement of God in a purely punitive sense. I do not want to return to the old Reformation juxtapositioning of the wrath and love of God.

Judgement and mercy are twin expressions of the enduring love of God for creation. The judgement of God is manifest in the equivocation, uncertainty and obstinate refusal of the past to be subsumed within some inflexible law of historical determinism. The past is protected in the eternity of God from both our arbitrary interference and our abject fear of reaping its consequences. We most certainly owe a debt to the past, but we are not circumscribed or controlled by it. Nor are we at liberty to ignore the past and become immersed in a debilitating 'presentism' that typifies some aspects of postmodernism.

The judgement of God also relativizes, to a certain extent, the perspective of the interpreter in the present because we must acknowledge the epistemological scope of the future to deconstruct and reinterpret the actions of history makers in the present. Consequently, there can be no overarching, totalizing metanarrative to history understood in the postmodern sense as a grand theory that seeks to legitimize foundational claims for knowledge and truth.

The same is true for the biblical account of God's actions in creation and history. Most certainly there is a compelling story to be told that moves from creation to eschaton. However, none of the crucial episodes in this story are necessarily implied in what preceded them. Creation does not necessarily imply a cataclysmic fall into non-being. The fractured contingencies of a creation now seriously out of sync with its Creator most certainly do not imply election. The total shock, displacement and meaning under erasure of the exile were never intended to be part of the election narrative. And the tentative experiments in restoration could not have anticipated the inevitable renegotiation of the incarnation.

In fact, every episode in the story comes up for constant renegotiation precisely under the shock and pressure of the developments in the storyline that appear to break away from the past with ever greater intensity, eluding the totalizing discourses that would seek to explain this episode as an inevitable part of the whole scheme of things. Only the person who could stand at the end of history would understand the real meaning of its fragile contingencies and scarred and wounded trajectories. Only from this perspective would the enormous resilience of those who in faith, hope and love continually sift through its debris make sense – as they find their eternal rest and peace in the embrace of the kingdom.

Further Implications for the Philosophy of Language

It is surely no coincidence that the positivistic modernity myth of history was accompanied by equally positivistic approaches to the philosophy of language. When philosophies of universal history were in the ascendancy, a unilateral philosophy of language also became fashionable – although the connections were not always recognized.

Logical positivism as represented by such important figures as the early Wittgenstein, Bertrand Russell, G.E. Moore and A.J Ayer, effectively reduced the world and our understanding of it to a series of logical relationships between ascertainable facts.[52] Language, it was claimed, mirrors reality and so the limits of our language constitute the limits of our world. Not surprisingly, metaphysics, religion and indeed ethics were not well suited to such cognitive positivism. The high priests of logical positivism, the Vienna circle, sought to demolish all three.

> It was a revolutionary force in philosophy, for it stigmatized metaphysical, theological, and ethical pronouncements as devoid of cognitive meaning and advocated a radical reconstruction of philosophical thinking which should give pride of place to the methods of physical science and mathematical logic ... Today logical positivism no longer exists as a distinct movement, yet its effects, direct and indirect, recognized and unrecognized, continue to be felt.[53]

The notion of a univocal language based on 'protocol' statements that apparently mirrored demonstrable and measurable facts was a theory of language that understandably worshipped at the high altar of the verification principle.[54]

At heart, logical positivism reflected the Enlightenment bifurcation of the world, undertaken by Hume and Kant, into 'hard facts', where science is the

---

[52] Wittgenstein, *Tractatus*; Ayer, *Language*.

[53] Achinstein and Barker, eds., *Legacy*, quoted in Stiver, *Philosophy*, 42.

[54] See Stiver, *Philosophy*, 42–7.

only credible form of knowledge, and 'soft beliefs', or values, that apply to just about everything else, including art, religion and morality.

Thankfully, the verification principle died the death of its own empirical unverifiablity! However, due to the work of Karl Popper and Anthony Flew, it was mysteriously brought back to life again in the equally positivistic mode of the falsification principle.[55] Due in large part to the influence of the later Wittgenstein, the non-cognitive theory of religious language fell into disrepute. However, if positivism dominated the philosophy of language espoused by the proponents of modernity, then pragmatism is the postmodern equivalent.

In his celebrated book *Philosophy and the Mirror of Nature*, Richard Rorty rejects what he regards as the foundational pretensions of philosophy since Hume, Descartes and Kant that sought to make knowledge the result of a cognitive match between the real world, or states of affairs, and the concepts of pure understanding.[56] The power of Enlightenment epistemology, he claims, resides in its privileged metaphors – particularly the persuasive notion of the mind or rationality, or pure consciousness, as the mirror of reality. The result was a story or a narrative that concentrated on the unearthing of unreal solutions to unreal problems, most noticeably the entire post-Kantian debate about the limits of human knowledge.

Not surprisingly, Rorty claims that Kant's privileging of the a priori categories of the understanding are merely transcribed into the equally privileged equivalents of analytic and linguistic philosophy. So, for instance, most noticeably in the interminable debates about how far language mirrors reality and so can be judged and tested by the equally vacuous criteria of verification or falsification. The exchange of one technical vocabulary for another simply serves to distance philosophy from any semblance of social relevance. The holy grail of post-Enlightenment epistemology, the search for pure concepts of understanding and its linguistic equivalents, should now be abandoned in favour of a wider cultural conversation where we accept that no revered group of metaphors can ever cut the world at its joints. So what is real, true and, for all practical purposes, life-giving, is in the end precisely what Nietzsche recommended – that which can serve the purposes of society's best interest.

Here, of course, the old Enlightenment dichotomy of knowledge versus belief, or fact versus value, has simply been reversed. Now it is knowledge and fact that prove to be the illusory self-serving candidates, while belief, opinion and value strike a more reasonable chord amidst the postmodern cacophony of pragmatic possibilities.

---

[55] Popper, *Logic*; Flew, 'Theology and Falsification'.
[56] Rorty, *Philosophy*.

On the Nietzschean view that Rorty adopts, this process (*i.e. the search for indubitable knowledge*) started out with the victory of Socratic rationalism and achieved its bad apotheosis with Descartes, Kant and their successors. Its last major episode was the rise of Anglo-American analytical philosophy, a movement that has now lost its way among the competing (and wholly undecidable) claims and counter claims. So our best option is to drop the old metaphors – especially those that still trade on ideas of privileged epistemic access, or the mind as a mirror of nature – and try out whatever promising substitutes now come to hand.[57]

Rorty's postmodern pragmatism is echoed in Baudrillard's deconstruction of Marxist theory in favour of a media-induced, consumerist-driven vision of hyper-reality. What Rorty does to epistemology, Baudrillard does to political theory.[58] The Marxist mirror of production is denounced as but another version of the post-Kantian mirror of reality metaphor that is again based on an illusory search for a theory of truth that can separate fact from fiction and knowledge from ideologically-tainted forms of belief.[59] Add to all of this Derrida's post-structuralist exploitation of the lacuna between signifier and the signified in the name of *différance*, his equally punishing deconstruction of the metaphysics of presence, and his preference for 'grammatology' over 'logocentrism', and the possibilities seem endless.

It is, however, worth remembering that the route from positivism to pragmatism was expedited via the later Wittgenstein's ruminations about language games and the general hermeneutical theory of Heidegger, Gadamer and Ricœur. As Jean Grondin recognizes, the latter in particular were part of that transition from a metaphysical to a hermeneutical universe that travelled via Kant, Jacobit and Schopenhauer.[60] In the process, theories that promoted the respective notions of univocal language and universal history that supposedly mirrored reality were superseded by the idea that everything, including, of course, the human subject, is a culturally and historically conditioned 'text', in which meaning is no longer found 'behind', but 'in front' of, our engagement with and interpretation of reality.[61] We have thus moved from an understanding of reality based on the natural sciences to one modelled on the human sciences, to one apparently constructed around the vertiginous pluralism of cultural theory.

In terms of the latter, however, we should take note that not all the representatives of postmodernism espouse the designation relativist, pragmatic or nihilist. Derrida, for instance, categorically rejects such labels.

---

[57] Norris, *What's Wrong*, 168.
[58] Baudrillard, *Mirror; Critique*.
[59] Baudrillard, *Simulacres; Simulations*; 'Ecstasy'.
[60] Grondin, *Sources*, chs. 1 and 2.
[61] Ricœur, *Essays*; 'Model'.

There have been several misinterpretations of what I and other deconstructionists are trying to do. It is totally false to suggest that deconstruction is a suspension of reference. Deconstruction is always deeply concerned with the 'other' of language. I never cease to be surprised by critics who see my work as a declaration that there is nothing beyond language, that we are imprisoned in language; it is, in fact, saying the exact opposite. The critique of logocentrism is above all else the search for the 'other' and the 'other of language'.[62]

The difficulty for the poststructuralists, however, is that they are often hoisted on their own petard – it simply depends on how you read or play with the text. So, for instance, a pertinent critique of the deconstructionalist agenda is to ask how their concern for the 'other' could ever be anything more than an arbitrary assertion or meaningless foil. If meaning is always deferred, then the 'other' is also constantly destabilized, decentred and deconstructed. There simply is no basis in language for establishing the legitimacy of the 'other' over and against the acerbic deconstruction of the interpreter, who, in turn, is vulnerable to the same epistemological destabilizing.[63]

Once again I suggest a Christological equivalent that avoids the postmodern slide toward pragmatism, constructivism and relativism but nevertheless respects the alterity and instability of language and so the inevitable superfluity of meaning that accompanies all forms of discourse.

The verification principle is this; we simply must not balk at the holocaust of the cross. The death of the Logos incarnate means that everything is broken. Primarily, the eternal fellowship of the triune God is broken. Therefore also the space-time continuum that is itself dependent on the Logos marking out the horizons of the creation is broken. Ontology and the possibility of metaphysical representation are broken. History and the ability to link past, present and future as a meaningful episode of human endeavour are broken. Epistemology, the heuristic efficacy of mental constructs, and the desire to know aright are broken. Hermeneutics and the promise of imaginative interpretation are broken. The structure of language and the meaning of meaning are broken. Semiotics and the relationship between signifier and the signified are broken. As the creation story suggests, nothingness hovers at the margins and meaning is constantly deferred.

After the cross and the death of the Logos, nothing remains the same. Here we meet God's judgement in all its finality, the eternal act of deconstruction

---

[62] Derrida, 'Jacques Derrida', 123.

[63] I am grateful to Professor Andrew Lincoln of Cheltenham and Gloucester School of Higher Education, who read the first draft of this chapter, for alerting me to this critique of the deconstructionalist preference for a constant postponement and instability of meaning.

that relativizes and marginalizes all our *epistémes*. It is the ultimate *aporia* that exposes the naked ideology and power play of the human text. Once again the asymmetrical relationship between cross and resurrection means that one does not imply the other and so the whole human project still limps. The complete *novum* of the resurrection, the unpredictable brokerage of the kingdom, God's penultimate 'Yes' to the human situation, is, after all, only partial repair and reconstruction that consequently entails an eschatological elasticity of meaning. We who experience the first-fruits of the Spirit and the privileges of adoption still groan inwardly as we long for our redemption (Rom. 8:23).

But in this epistemological and linguistic gap, this historical lacuna, this textual instability that requires constant imaginative renegotiation, we encounter the hermeneutics of hope. Hope that all our striving after truth, knowledge, beauty and meaning is a reflection of, indeed a referral to, the only transcendental signifier – the cross and resurrection of the incarnate Logos. Because of the cross, and the judgement of God upon the human text, everything is broken and so truth, meaning, wisdom and knowledge constantly elude us. But where hope breaks forth from the power of the resurrection, there the kingdom is still near, the signs of the kingdom still break in, all things are under reconstruction according to the image of the Son, and the liberation of our language to speak the truth in hope, love and fidelity is still possible.

The whole of reality is cast into this dialectical relationship so we should not be surprised that our language alerts us to this heuristic possibility. Where modernity preferred a *theologia gloria* and proclaimed the indubitable reality of foundationalism, postmodernity locates the debris of a false hubris and opts instead for a *theologia crucis*. The former leads to a vacuous triumphalism and the latter to an equally debilitating nihilism. The New Testament holds both in tension and so refuses either option. This entails that the instinctive feel for referral can and does stem from closure and the desire to assuage our ontological anxiety by the construction of some illusory epistemological foundation. However, as Kierkegaard recognized, this merely reflects humanity turned in upon itself. On the other hand, the constant negation of referral and the preference for an epistemological and linguistic vacuum is, after all, simply an exercise in bad faith.

The eschatological horizon of cross and resurrection is the transcendental foundation to which everything is ultimately referred. And only here do we discover the mystery of the other, the meaning of meaning, the fallible yet genuine possibility that we have spoken truthfully and aright, and the necessary erasure of all those mean power plays whereby we seek to exclude, dominate and subjugate our neighbour.

In conclusion, then, it should be quite clear that I have not sought to denounce or repudiate the substantial repositioning in regard to our understanding of history and language, and the integral relationship between the two, undertaken by the exponents of postmodernity. Neither, however, have I sought to cut my theological cloth to fit the fabric of this particular substantial and still ongoing cultural transition. It is my belief that postmodernity hitherto has been almost entirely an exercise in radical deconstruction, decentring and the wholesale dethroning of usurpers and pretenders to the throne of absolute power and truth. The resulting epistemological blitzkrieg has devastated the intellectual landscape of modernity beyond repair, including the ideological internment camp to which religion had been banished.

As the postmodernist Zygmunt Bauman astutely recognizes,

> Religion belongs to a family of curious and often embarrassing concepts which one perfectly understands until one wants to define them. The postmodern mind, for once, agrees to issue that family, maltreated or sentenced to deportation by modern scientific reason, with a permanent residence permit. The postmodern mind, more tolerant (since it is better aware of its own weaknesses) than its modern predecessor and critic, is soberly aware of the tendency of definitions to conceal as much as they reveal and to maim and obfuscate while pretending to clarify and straighten up. It also accepts the fact that, all too often, experience spills out of the verbal cages in which one would wish to hold it, that there are things of which one should keep silent since one cannot speak of them, and that the ineffable is as much an integral part of the human mode of being-in-the-world as is the linguistic net in which one tries (in vain, as it happens, though no less vigorously for that reason) to catch it.[64]

If this analysis of our present situation is correct, as I firmly believe it is, then the invitation is there for biblical interpretation, particularly where it is orientated toward Christological reconstruction, to emerge from its ideological internment camp and start making a substantial contribution to the very necessary debate concerning the 'public' significance and import of religion in the twenty-first century.

Bibliography

Achinstein, P. and S.F. Barker (eds.), *The Legacy of Logical Positivism: Studies in the Philosophy of Science* (Baltimore, MD: John Hopkins Press, 1969)

Ayer, A.J., *Language, Truth and Logic* (New York: Dover Publications, 2nd edn, 1946)

Balthasar, H. Urs von, *Mysterium Paschale* (trans. A. Nichols; Edinburgh: T. & T. Clark, 1990)

Baudrillard, J., *The Mirror of Production* (St Louis: Telos Press, 1975)

—, *For a Critique of the Political Economy of the Sign* (St Louis: Telos Press, 1981)

---

[64] Bauman, *Postmodernity*, 165.

—, *Simulacres et simulation* (Paris: Galilee, 1981)

—, *Simulations* (New York: Semiotext, 1983)

—, 'The Ecstasy of Communication', in M. Poster (ed.), *Jean Baudrillard: Selected Writings* (Cambridge: Polity; Stanford: Stanford University Press, 1988)

—, *Forget Foucault* (New York: Semiotext, 1987)

—, 'The Year 2000 Has Already Happened', in A. Kroker and M. Kroker (eds.), *Body Invaders: Panic Sex in America* (Montreal: The New World Perspectives, 1988), 35–44

—, *Cool Memories* (Paris: Galilee, 1987)

Bauman, Z., *Postmodernity and Its Discontents* (Cambridge: Polity Press, 1997)

Brueggemann, W., 'A Journey: Attending to the Abyss', *The Bible in Transmission* (Bible Society, Spring, 2000), 6–8

Charlesworth, J.H. (ed.), 'From Messianology to Christology: Problems and Prospects', in *The Messiah: Developments in Earliest Judaism and Christianity* (Minneapolis: Fortress Press, 1992), 3–35

Clines, D.J.A., 'Possibilities and Priorities of Biblical Interpretation in an International Perspective', *BibInt* 1.1 (1993), 67–87

—, *The Bible and the Modern World* (Sheffield: Sheffield Academic Press, 1997)

Crossan, J.D., *The Historical Jesus: The Life of a Mediterranean Jewish Peasant* (San Francisco: HarperSan Francisco, 1991)

—, *Jesus: A Revolutionary Biography* (San Francisco: HarperSanFrancisco, 1994)

—, *The Birth of Christianity: Discovering what Happened in the Years Im-mediately after the Execution of Jesus* (Edinburgh: T. & T. Clark, 1999)

Derrida, J., 'Jacques Derrida', in R. Kearney (ed.), *Dialogues with Contemporary Continental Thinkers: The Phenomenological Heritage* (Manchester: Manchester University Press, 1984), 123–4

Flew, A., 'Theology and Falsification', in A. Flew and A. MacIntyre (eds.), *New Essays in Philosophical Theology* (London: SCM Press, 1955), 96–130

Funk, R.W. and R.W. Hoover (eds.), *The Five Gospels: The Search for the Authentic Words of Jesus* (New York: Macmillan, 1993)

Greene, C.J.D., 'In the Arms of the Angels: Biblical Interpretation, Christology and the Philosophy of History', in *Renewing Biblical Interpretation* (ed. C. Bartholomew, C. Greene, K. Möller; SHS, 1; Carlisle: Paternoster; Grand Rapids: Zondervan, 2000), 198–239

—, *Marking Out the Horizons: Christology in Cultural Perspective* (Carlisle: Paternoster, forthcoming)

Goldingay, J., *Models for Scripture* (Carlisle: Paternoster; Grand Rapids: Eerdmans, 1994)

Grondin, J., *Sources of Hermeneutics* (Albany, NY: State University of New York Press, 1995)

—, *Introduction to Philosophical Hermeneutics* (trans. J. Weinsheimer; New Haven: Yale University Press, 1994)

Mack, B.L., *A Myth of Innocence: Mark and Christian Origins* (Philadelphia: Fortress Press, 1988)

Macquarrie, J., *Jesus Christ in Modern Thought* (London: SCM Press; Philadelphia: Trinity Press International, 1990)

—, *Christology Revisited* (London: SCM Press, 1998)

Marx, K., 'The Eighteenth Brumaire of Louis Napoleon', in *Karl Marx and Friedrich Engels: Collected Works*, II (London: Laurence & Wishart, 1979), 103–97

Moltmann, J., *The Way of Jesus Christ: Christology in Messianic Dimensions* (London: SCM Press, 1990)

Nietzsche, F., 'The Antichrist', in *The Portable Nietzsche* (ed. and trans. W. Kaufmann; New York: Penguin Books, 1982), 568–656

—, *On the Genealogy of Morals: A Polemic* (trans. W. Kaufmann and R.J. Hollingdale; New York: Vintage Books, 1989), 13–163

Norris, C., *What's Wrong with Postmodernism: Critical Theory and the Ends of Philosophy* (London: Harverster Wheatsheaf, 1990)

Pannenberg, W., *Jesus – God and Man* (London: SCM Press, 1968)

—, 'Redemptive Event and History', in *Basic Questions in Theology*, I (London: SCM Press, 1970)

—, *Human Nature, Election and History* (Philadelphia: Fortress Press, 1977)

Popper, K., *The Logic of Scientific Discovery* (New York: Basic Books, 1959)

Rad, G. von, *Old Testament Theology*, (2 vols.; trans. D.M.G. Stalker; Edinburgh: Oliver and Boyd, 1962)

Ricœur, P., *Time and Narrative* (3 vols.; trans. K. McLaughlin and D. Pellauer; Chicago: University of Chicago Press, 1984–88)

—, *Essays on Biblical Interpretation* (trans. R. Sweeney; ed. L.S. Mudge; Philadelphia: Fortress Press, 1980)

—, 'The Model of the Text: Meaningful Action Considered as a Text', in J.B. Thompson (ed.), *Hermeneutics and the Human Sciences: Essays on Language, Action and Interpretation* (Cambridge: CUP, 1981), 131–44

Rorty, R., *Philosophy and the Mirror of Nature* (Oxford: Basil Blackwell, 1980)

Schillebeeckx, E., *Jesus: An Experiment in Christology* (trans. H. Hoskins; London: Collins, 1979)

Schweitzer, A., *The Quest for the Historical Jesus: A Critical Study of its Progress from Reimarus to Wrede* (London: A. & C. Black, 1968)

Stiver, D., *The Philosophy of Religious Language* (Oxford: Basil Blackwell, 1996)

Troeltsch, E., 'Historical and Dogmatic Method in Theology', in *Religion and History* (trans. J.L. Adams and W.F. Bense; Fortress Texts in Modern Theology; Minneapolis: Fortress Press, 1991), 11–32

Williams, R., *On Christian Theology* (Oxford: Basil Blackwell, 2000)

Witherington B., III, *The Jesus Quest: The Third Search for the Jew of Nazareth* (Carlisle: Paternoster, 1995)

Wittgenstein, L., *Tractatus Logico-Philosophicus* (trans. D.F. Pears and B.F. McGuiness; London: Routledge & Kegan Paul, 1961)

—, *Philosophical Investigations* (trans. G.E.M. Anscombe; New York: Macmillan, 1958)

Wright, N.T., *The New Testament and the People of God* (London: SPCK, 1992)

—, *Jesus and the Victory of God* (London: SPCK, 1996)

Wright, N.T., and M. Borg, *The Meaning of Jesus: Two Visions* (London: SPCK, 1999).

10

Words of Power

Biblical Language and Literary Criticism with Reference to
Stephen Prickett's Words and the Word *and Mark 1:21–28*

Stephen I. Wright

Stephen Prickett's *Words and the Word* was published in 1986, but his rich and subtle analysis of the relationship between biblical and 'secular' literary criticism over the last three hundred years invites biblical hermeneutics to a programme of literary sensitization that could occupy it for decades yet to come. Not the least of its merits is its profoundly historical tone, telling the story of ideas concerning the poetic and of the mutual influence of biblical and secular criticism with great nuancing. It should encourage biblical scholars to look behind current fashions in the literary-critical world, sometimes over-hastily followed in theological circles, to the mutual interdependence of the disciplines and the tale of where we have been together.[1] This chapter will point to some of the questions raised by Prickett's book for the language of the Gospels, by focusing on just one or two of the literary-critical issues raised in each of his five chapters and relating them to the story of Jesus' exorcism in the Capernaum synagogue (Mk. 1:21–28).

---

[1] Prickett himself has commented more recently that though 'current biblical inter-pretation continues to be heavily influenced by twentieth-century literary and aes-thetic theory and practice, there is still little evidence that the historical centrality of that relationship to biblical studies has been fully recognized, or that its implications for the future have been considered'; 'Bible', 175.

The Transparent Text?

Prickett begins by describing the awed hesitancy with which Coleridge approached Scripture to read it 'as any other work'. Coleridge was aware not just of the cultural distance between his own period and the biblical one, but of the unquantifiable influence which Scripture had exercised on his own culture, and the corresponding difficulty of attaining any kind of objective understanding of it. Prickett contrasts this hesitancy with the confidence of the Good News Bible translators that they could 'understand correctly the meaning of the original' and express it 'in a manner and form easily understood by the readers'. He illustrates this contrast with a discussion of the story of Elijah's encounter with God in the 'still small voice', and of the difficulty which modern translations have with this Hebrew phrase, which might be rendered 'voice of thin silence'. He cites the GNB's 'soft whisper of a voice', the NEB's 'low murmuring sound' and the JB's 'sound of a gentle breeze'. All (unlike the famous AV phrase) fail to capture the mysterious ambiguity of the original, its artless combination of what in more recent times we have separated into 'natural' and 'supernatural'.[2]

The issue opened up here is whether we are ready to stay with the strangeness of a text, aware both of our distance from it and of the impossibility of viewing it from an external standpoint outside of the influence it has itself exercised. Or are we impatient to go through it to some comprehensible, readily uncovered reality beyond? The translators of the GNB aimed for language that was 'natural, clear, simple and unambiguous', but the result in such cases as this was to miss a vital quality of the original. In Prickett's words, 'it is those who would look *through* the text, who, disconcertingly, see least; those who would look at it and discover the detailed patterning of its surface as an artifact, who discover most'.[3]

'Literary criticism' implies above all (one might think) attention to the letters, the *litterae*, but this is precisely what biblical criticism in the wake of the Enlightenment has often not given to its object of study. The desire to *explain* in rational terms, with reference to universals, or to reconstruct a history behind the text, has often taken precedence over frank recognition of the presence of mystery. The relentless pursuit of determinate meaning continues to characterize many biblical commentaries.

There are strange elements in Mark's account of Jesus' first exorcism to which our very familiarity with the story may dull us – and which, indeed,

---

[2] Prickett, *Words*, 4–13. He cites Coleridge's *Confessions of an Inquiring Spirit* (1849; originally entitled 'Letters on the Inspiration of the Scriptures') and the Preface to the Good News Bible (1976).
[3] Prickett, *Words*, 35f.

some popular modern Bible translations keep from us. First we have Mark's famous catchword 'immediately', quite absent from the parallel account in Luke. It comes three times in Mark 1:21–28. No doubt it adds to an impression of breathless urgency in Jesus' mission, as is regularly noted. But this does not mean that it can be smoothly rendered in a translation that is going to sound 'natural' to us – that is, in a sequential narrative based on the conventions of realistic prose, still surviving from their nineteenth-century heyday. The NIV's simple omission of the word speaks volumes. What does 'immediately on the Sabbath'[4] mean (v. 21)? 'On the next Sabbath'? No doubt, but if we render it thus we miss the connection with 'immediately there was in their synagogue' (v. 23) and 'the report of him immediately went out everywhere' (v. 28). There seems to be some (perhaps) theological resonance to the word for Mark which is not captured by our word 'immediately' but is captured still less by omitting to render it at all. This resonance is in tension with the function of the word as a temporal marker. Does verse 21 imply that it was a Friday afternoon when Jesus arrived in Capernaum, and so the Sabbath itself came 'immediately'? This seems too smooth a reading: there was an immediacy about Jesus' entering the synagogue, whether it was a Sunday or a Friday when he arrived in town.[5] Does verse 23 imply that the demoniac entered the synagogue hard on Jesus' heels? Such an interpretation would be in tension with verse 22, which suggests that Jesus has already been teaching there for some time. Again, we sense that there was an 'immediacy' about the appearance of the demoniac, at whatever precise point he entered the synagogue – he may indeed have been inside all along. The occurrence of the adverb in verse 28 is more readily translatable in temporal terms: it can indicate simply that there was no delay in reporting what Jesus had done. But the usage in the earlier verses prepares us to see here, too, something more than the mere wildfire of a rumour.[6] The point

---

[4] Here and unless otherwise stated I am using the RSV translation.

[5] Gundry attempts a fusion of temporal and other connotations which undermines the sense of oddness: ' "Immediately" stresses the quickness with which he didactically takes charge' (*Mark*, 73); 'Mark's "immediately" tells how soon Jesus enters the synagogue on the Sabbath or, more likely since it suits Mark's emphasis on Jesus' teaching, how soon Jesus starts teaching once he enters the synagogue on the Sabbath' (ibid., 80).

[6] A good instance of the kind of 'either/or' exegesis which smooths out the tension in the use of the word 'immediately', here in terms which minimize its meaning, is found in Rawlinson, *Mark*, 17: 'It has been suggested that the call of the disciples took place on a Friday, and that the party entered Capernaum the same day ... It is probable, however, that here, as elsewhere, *straightway* is merely the Marcan particle of transition and need not imply any immediate connection in time.' Rawlinson may be right; but equally, reducing such a word to the status of 'particle of transition' may just be a convenient and over-slick way of gaining 'transparency'.

is that we should neither dismiss the word's temporal function, nor allow it to push aside other connotations.

Another curiosity is the language used to describe the possessed man and his exchange with Jesus. He is (literally) 'a man in an unclean spirit', and though we are told that this is a usage of the preposition *en* in its 'sociative' sense,[7] one cannot help wondering if it would not be better to translate it literally as 'in' rather than as 'with'. This, after all, would convey better what we mean by 'possession': the spirit possesses the man, surrounds and grasps him. If the unclean spirit is imagined as 'inside' him (as is suggested by the translation 'with'), it implies rather that the man possesses and therefore is master of the spirit, which is patently inconsistent with the story.[8] No doubt we have become accustomed to this understanding of *en* as 'with' because in verse 26 the spirit 'came out' of the man. But this accommodation of one verse to another may be another instance of our desire for an easy passage through a narrative. Psychologically, the sense that at one moment a man may be 'in' an unclean spirit and at another the unclean spirit may 'come out of the man' may in fact represent well both the confusion of such a person's state and the struggle of language to express it.

A final point to note under this heading is the summary comment of the onlookers in verse 27: 'What is this? A new teaching! With authority he commands even the unclean spirits, and they obey him.' It has probably struck many readers as odd, and therefore perhaps significant, that according to Mark, the first thing that people comment on after the exorcism is the *teaching* of Jesus. This was apparently even more impressive than the casting-out of the unclean spirit. A 'solution' to this oddity would be to regard the people's words as a summary statement of response to Jesus, fitted into the story without a strict concern for its temporal narrative progression. Put another way, the words stand as a general response to the whole synagogue service: this was the kind of thing people were saying as they eventually went out of the door, not the kind of thing they said at the moment when the man was released.[9] But to see this as a 'solution' may be too simple: it may be an attempt to accommodate the narrative once again to our own canons of realism.

Another possible way of dealing with this surprising return to 'teaching' after the exorcism is that of form-criticism, in which the evangelists are seen as

---

[7] Zerwick and Grosvenor, *Analysis*, I, 102. The usage may be a Semitism (Gundry, *Mark*, 75).

[8] I am grateful to Ray Van Leeuwen for helpfully pointing to the parallel here with the NT usages 'in Christ' and 'in the Spirit'.

[9] Such an approach is represented by Lane, *Mark*, commenting on vv. 27, 28: 'The people were utterly astonished and alarmed at Jesus' word. The same measure of authority with which they had been confronted in his teaching was demonstrated in the word of command to the demon.'

stitching up bits of tradition kept alive in the worshipping activities of the church, but often doing so rather unsuccessfully, so that the breaks between traditional items and the evangelist's editing are often 'obvious'.[10] In such a reading, the evangelists are not credited with an 'authorial' so much as a 'redactional' role, and what appear to us as infelicitous joins or sequences have no greater significance than to point to the rough-and-ready functionalism both of the traditional items and of the Gospels themselves.[11] But this again presupposes a view of what a smooth, 'realistic' narrative sequence would be, and therefore what disjointedness must look like. It does not allow for the possibility of a different way of writing narrative from the familiar conventions we have inherited from more recent times.[12]

Another 'solution' to such a 'problem' would be a theological interpretation, which might ignore the historical issue of how Mark has stitched his sources together, and which would focus on the 'final form' of the text, drawing significance from the priority given by the people – and the evangelist – to the 'new teaching' of Jesus. This, it could be argued, is a remarkable instance of word being privileged over deed;[13] even, of the unchanging calling of the church (the ministry of the word) being seen prototypically in the ministry of Jesus, whose exorcisms and other acts of power were unique attestations of his identity, not to be elevated into a norm for his followers. Other Gospel passages can be adduced in support of this kind of theological reading – notably, the priority given to the declaration of forgiveness for the paralysed man in Mark 2:1–12 (the healing, according to Jesus, functioned subserviently as a demonstration of the forgiveness), and the reluctance of Jesus to offer people 'signs', mighty works which would cause people to marvel but not to look beyond the sign to the reality it indicated. However, this theological approach may again be too easy. It flattens out the peculiar contours of the text. The response of the people does not appear to privilege the teaching above the

---

[10] See the classic works of form-criticism by Dibelius (*Tradition*) and Bultmann (*History*).

[11] So, for instance, Bultmann writes that the words about Jesus' teaching with authority in vv. 22, 27 should be ascribed to Mark, not to earlier tradition, since these are passages 'which conflict with the point' (i.e. the focus on the casting-out of an 'unclean spirit'); *History*, 209.

[12] Though even the realism of modern fiction scarcely exists in any ideal form from which 'symbolic' elements are absent. Important insights here were gained through structuralist analyses. For a clear explication of this see David Lodge's discussion of Ernest Hemingway's short story 'Cat in the Rain', in 'Analysis'.

[13] The comment of Williamson exemplifies this approach: 'It is somewhat awkward to refer to an exorcism as "a new teaching" (v. 27), but this very awkwardness shows the intention to subordinate healing to teaching, linking Jesus' power in both word and deed as evidence of his amazing authority' (*Mark*, 49).

exorcism; it is rather that the teaching and the exorcism are all of a piece. The parallel halves of their comment:

A new teaching!
With authority he commands even the unclean spirits

indicate an equivalence, perhaps almost synonymy between the teaching and the exorcism, that is difficult for us to grasp.[14] There are, then, peculiarities about this passage when we attend to its 'letters', which presumptions of naïve realism, editing of blocks of tradition and theological significance may all fail to address.

If there are blockages in the way of reading the story as straightforwardly realistic narrative, should we then read it as 'poetic'?

Religious and Poetic Language

Prickett draws our attention to an 'extensive' and an 'intensive' tradition of conceiving the 'poetic'.[15] In the former, the 'poetic', as a fundamental mode of human creativity, is held to embrace all language, history and religion. In the twentieth century this tradition is represented prominently by Martin Heidegger and Paul Ricœur. In the latter, the 'poetic' is seen as a separate language-game from other modes of consciousness and discourse, concerned with the non-cognitive aspects of experience. This tradition has found voice theologically in the work of John Macquarrie.

To describe a particular text as 'poetic' may not, therefore, be to say very much that is intelligible or coherent; it is a description that, particularly over the last three hundred years, has meant rather different things to different people. Indeed, the 'extensive' and 'intensive' traditions have a confusing habit of collapsing into each other.[16] Prickett points out, for instance, that to call parts of the Bible 'poetic' has evoked a mode of ancient, primal and thus universal consciousness – but also the primitiveness associated with it. Thus, in different ways, it has seemed necessary to 'demythologize' Scripture in order to distil from it a 'kerygma' that can be expressed in discursive (i.e. non-poetic) terms. The poetic may indeed be an originary and universal mode, but we have often felt the need to leave it behind.

So in a passage like the one we are considering, the ideas of the man being 'in an unclean spirit', and being delivered by Jesus, may be 'demythologized'

---

[14] Gundry is careful to stress that exorcism is not subordinated to teaching here (*Mark*, 74).
[15] Summarized in *Words*, 93f.
[16] Ibid., 72.

so that the passage is seen as being 'really' about the overcoming of 'evil' as modern philosophy understands it. Such a reading effectively allegorizes the story, and evacuates it of its details like so many worthless husks. The primitive mythological or (we might say) 'poetic' character of the tale is seen as an obstacle to its contemporary appropriation. This obstacle is overcome by an appeal to an inner intention or essential message in the text, which renders its outward features secondary and disposable.[17] Concern for the *littera* is once more abandoned.

One may not go so far as a full 'demythologization', yet still fail to do justice to the poetic character of the text. This happens when the man's condition is reinterpreted in terms of mental illness or suffering more generally. Take this statement of William Neil, typical of much of the accommodating liberalism of the nineteenth and early twentieth centuries:

> In the gospels, physical disease and insanity are regarded as the work of demons ...Jesus accepts this view-point as a child of his times ... the basic fact for us in this, as in all the healing stories of the gospel, is that Jesus healed suffering folk.[18]

Prickett discusses Coleridge's concept of 'desynonymy' – the historical process whereby language gradually becomes more differentiated, and (for instance) the Hebrew *ruach* and Greek *pneuma* gradually become separated out into our concepts of 'wind' and 'spirit'.[19] When we 'translate' the description of the demoniac so that he is no longer 'in an unclean spirit' but simply 'insane' or 'suffering', we may be reducing an original, unified terminology which expressed *both* a 'medical' condition *and* a sense of the entrapment of human beings in powers that were greater than themselves, into one half of its original meaning. This manoeuvre can be construed either as failure to grasp the primal, 'extensive' poetic sense of the unity of human experience, or as a recognition of the language as poetic in the limiting 'intensive' sense – as a prelude

---

[17] See Bultmann's 'demythologizing' of the conception of evil spirits: 'This conception rests upon the experience, quite apart from the inexplicable evils arising outside ourselves to which we are exposed, that our own actions are often so puzzling; men are often carried away by their passions and are no longer master of themselves, with the result that inconceivable wickedness breaks forth from them ... Particularly in our day and generation, although we no longer think mythologically, we often speak of demonic powers which rule history, corrupting political and social life. Such language is metaphorical, a figure of speech, but in it is expressed the knowledge, the insight, that the evil for which every man is responsible has nevertheless become a power which mysteriously enslaves every member of the human race' (*Jesus*, 20f.).

[18] Neil, *Commentary*, 358f.

[19] For this example see *Words*, 87.

to rejection of it on grounds of preference for a discourse of whose rationality and cognitive value we can be more confident.

A strong twentieth-century tradition, then, finds contemporary and religious usefulness in such a text only through bypassing whatever 'poetic' character it may possess. An alternative to this bypassing is found in the proposal of Ricœur that we should aim for a kind of recreation of the original primal participation which the 'poetic' language (here, for the sake of argument, that of spirit-possession) expresses.[20] But this proposal is not without its difficulties. Above all, we are still left with the character of the story as, apparently, witness to an event. To construe it as (in some sense) inviting a reader's participation in a similar experience is to look at it obliquely, to say the least. Its language may indeed express a unity of experience that we have lost, but that does not imply that an imaginative re-entering of that experience is an adequate or appropriate way of responding to that language. (One need only think, for instance, of the pastoral disasters that might ensue from inviting people to imagine themselves as having an unclean spirit.) To speak of a story like this as 'poetic', then, may offer insight into an ancient mode of consciousness, uniting what later became separate, but it has not yet constituted any particular solution as to how we should deal with it.

The Prophet and the Poet

Having discussed the 'extensive' and 'intensive' understandings of the 'poetic', Prickett devotes a chapter to the specific understanding of the term developed by the Romantics Wordsworth and Coleridge. For them, the poetic entailed 'a peculiar and indissoluble union of thought and feeling, productive of psychic health and wholeness, which though primal was not pre-rational but *historical* in its mode of consciousness'.[21] Deeply influenced by Robert Lowth's seminal work on Hebrew poetry, his *Lectures on the Sacred Poetry of the Hebrews* (1787), they saw the poet's role as a prophetic one. Conversely, as Lowth had asserted, the prophets were poets, and Jesus was seen (especially in his parables) as continuing this tradition.[22]

In this view, the poet and the prophet are one in their insight into reality, in their awareness of the divine in creation, and in their ability to communicate this vision and sensibility in a fresh language that enables others to share it.

---

[20] On this see *Words*, 84–8. For Ricœur's use of the idea of the poetic cf. Ricœur, *Essays*, 98–104.

[21] *Words*, 94.

[22] Ibid., 108.

Rather than being a condition of language in which all naturally partake (as in the 'extensive' view), the poetic is seen as gift and calling. Rather than having as its domain the purely emotive or aesthetic (as in the 'intensive' view), the poetic is the mode of knowledge in the fullest sense, the means of perceiving and encountering reality. How might this understanding of the poetic take forward our understanding of the language of Mark 1:21–28?

On two levels – like a simple Russian doll – we may discern the poet-as-prophet or prophet-as-poet at work. First, Mark is not only storyteller but also interpreter, shaping the description of the event according to his insight into its meaning. To say that he is creative does not mean that he is making up the event or even freely elaborating upon it. It simply means that he is fashioning order out of an otherwise formless void. As Prickett remarks in a later chapter, it is not the dialectic between fact and fiction that is at stake in reading premodern narrative, but that between form and chaos.[23] How *would* one describe the behaviour and condition of a man 'possessed'? 'Possessed', of course, is our term. For Mark, he is 'in an unclean spirit'. The fact that Luke uses a different phrase, 'having the spirit of an unclean demon' (4:33) – perhaps introducing the word 'demon' by way of explanation for a readership less likely to be familiar with the 'unclean spirit' terminology[24] – shows that the same phenomenon could be described in somewhat different ways. The point is that we should not just assume that, for the eye-witnesses, or for those who handed on the story, or for the evangelists, this was a known and familiar phenomenon for which there was a ready label to hand; that the 'facts' of such an event were easy simply to 'record'. Such assumptions lie behind conceptions of biblical narrative as plainly 'realistic' (whether fictional or historical). Such a view tends to see the evangelists' language as basically conventional, such that we can look the words up in a dictionary and discover their 'meaning' in a particular instance from the 'meaning' they generally possessed at the time.[25] However, it is perfectly conceivable – and it is quite beside my point here to argue that it is any more than this – that Mark (and his sources) were here bringing together *in a new way* a specific case of human misery (sticking, as we must, with our inadequate English terms!) with *both* the Jewish and Hellenistic belief in the existence of powers in the universe that were hostile to God, *and*

---

[23] Ibid., 208.

[24] Cranfield comments that 'unclean spirit' is 'a thoroughly Jewish expression' (*Mark*, 74). Later, Luke is happy to write simply of 'unclean spirits': see 4:36 (at the end of the present passage), 8:29, 9:42, 11:24. Maybe this indicates that having used the fuller expression 'spirit of an unclean demon' in 4:33, he felt that the shorter phrase would be clear enough thereafter.

[25] At work here, of course, is the powerful influence of Saussurian linguistics.

the belief that Jesus was carrying out the punishment of those powers that had been predicted, for example, in 1 Enoch 55:4. In other words, Mark – standing also as surrogate for all those who fed him his stories, since singular authorship is an anachronistic construction when applied to the Bible – can be seen as the poet/prophet in Romantic terms, who has insight into the unseen powers and the meaning of historical events. The historical, rational conditioning of this insight is seen in his use of the familiar *language* of the 'unclean spirit'; its poetic, creative quality is seen in his *application* of the language to what happened in the synagogue.

The poetic creativity of the Markan portrayal of the event might also be discerned in the startling conjunction of singulars and plurals in verses 23–25:

> And immediately there was in their synagogue a man with an unclean spirit; and he cried out, 'What have you to do with us, Jesus of Nazareth? Have you come to destroy us? I know who you are, the Holy One of God.' But Jesus rebuked him [or it], saying 'Be silent, and come out of him!'

Here we see the man's tragic sense of divided identity. Indeed, the 'possession' is just that; he has become the mouthpiece of the spirit, itself glimpsed as just one of many ('us'). As suggested by W. Foerster,[26] we find here a quintessential case of the distortion of God's image in humanity, which Jesus came to reverse. And such a theological reading, though of course consistent with the possibility that the actual words were handed down from those who originally heard them, probably implies the creativity of the tradition and the evangelist: not creation *ex nihilo*, but a Romantic insight into divine meaning, a fusion of the historical event and a dramatic language of personal disorder through which we feel as well as see the true nature and pitifulness of the man's state.[27] The question may be posed whether a theological reading of this kind implies only our own creative insight into the text, and not Mark's. We cannot pursue this central dilemma of Romantic poetics here; we may simply note that whether it is our insight or Mark's, the story is being read as 'poetic' in essentially Romantic terms.

The inner Russian doll is, of course, Jesus the poet-prophet himself. The central figure is not only Mark's main subject; he both reflects the creativity of the tradition and the evangelist, and may be seen as the one who has engendered it. He is the one who teaches with authority: not like the scribes, with their discourse subservient to Scripture and tradition, but with prophetic

---

[26] Kittel, *TDNT*, II, 1ff.

[27] Another possible sign of Markan 'creativity' is the pairing of the questions in v. 24: 'What have you to do with us ... Have you come to destroy us?', which may be modelled on 1 Kgs. 17:18 (LXX) (Gundry, *Mark*, 79).

immediacy. He is the one with direct insight into the man's condition as human space invaded by the enemy. And his word is a word of power, a word which silences the unclean spirit and releases the man it had disfigured. Like a proto-Romantic, his word is no stale convention or repetition of tradition, but a dynamic intrusion into the human condition.

To view the story in Romantic-prophetic terms, then, can take us some way towards appreciating its language. But Prickett invites us further.

'Disconfirmation' and Revelation

The experience of Elijah, for whom God was *not* in the expected media of earthquake, wind and fire, and that of Dante in the *Purgatorio* when Beatrice eventually greets him with astonishing harshness, are taken by Prickett as paradigmatic of the '*disconcertingness* of Revelation'.[28] Literature struggles to express the paradoxes of God's unexpected meetings with men and women, above all the incarnation itself; and Milton's *Paradise Lost*, with its rather tame portrayal of Eden, is seen as a classic case of failure to imagine the truly other.[29] The psychological term 'disconfirmation' is used to describe the feeling of complete disorientation and subversion of expectation that writers do occasionally manage to capture and communicate to their readers.[30]

In other words, there may be a kind of literary or poetic language which goes beyond the Romantic fusions of thought and feeling, historical event and inner purpose; a language that goes even beyond the prophetic in conveying the disturbingly and profoundly new. Efforts to understand and explain the Bible today always court the danger not only of ironing out its ambiguities (as we saw above), but also of missing the presence of such 'disconfirming' language. Already in considering Romantic poetics, we have seen the inadequacy of simple dependence on the conventional language use of the period in our attempt to grasp the meaning of biblical texts. The possibility of 'disconfirmation' invites a bolder suggestion: that we be ready to see in the Bible a language that not only subverts conventional usage, but also aims at replacing it.[31]

So the newness of what went on in the Capernaum synagogue may be missed if we try to understand it as an event which conformed to familiar

---

[28] *Words*, 153.
[29] Ibid., 160f.
[30] Ibid., 161f.
[31] Cf. a seminal work on the linguistic transformations visible in the New Testament, Wilder, *Rhetoric*.

categories; and even if we limit it (in Romantic terms) as reflecting the poetic-prophetic creativity of Jesus and Mark, sensitivity to historical context may end up playing into the hands of theological timidity. Belief in the existence of evil spirits was standard, and exorcisms were commonplace, as the Gospels themselves make clear (Mt. 12:27/Lk. 11:19); but here in Capernaum was this not something dramatically different?

The story can be read as mediating 'disconcerting' revelation – to those in the synagogue, to Mark's readers, to Jesus and to the evil spirits. In the outcry of the unclean spirit, the bystanders hear an uncanny and disturbing declaration of Jesus' identity and mission. In his narrative, Mark has given us no indication that such people would have yet formed any judgement about Jesus and what he was doing; they have simply been astonished at his teaching (v. 22). But now, they see Jesus as exercising a kind of magnetic repulsion in respect of a distraught person who claims strange knowledge about him. It is not only that this, and the subsequent demonstration of Jesus' power, takes speculation about Jesus on to a deeper level. It is also that the condition of the possessed man is revealed in a new way, as somehow the polar opposite of what is being seen in Jesus. The 'unclean' spirit is pitted against 'the Holy One of God'.[32]

For Mark's readers, the revelation appears still stranger. Mark has made no secret of his own view of the identity of Jesus (1:1). But here in the synagogue is the first *public* declaration of something like this view in the narrative of events: and it comes from the mouth of an 'unclean spirit'. Previous and subsequent elements of the narrative make this mystifying: one would expect insight into Jesus from those with prepared and prophetic spirits (John the Baptist; the seed that fell on good soil) – not from those in the grip of evil. There is, however, still more disconfirmation to come. Jesus does not prevaricate with the spirit; there is no nicely-qualified 'Yes, you are right about me, but don't tell anyone just yet'. Instead, there is strong rebuke, a command to silence, and the expulsion of the spirit. To the bystanders, the end of the possessed man's outcry would be (one imagines) a signal for relief. To the readers, it is paradoxical.[33] Mark clearly wants *us* to know of the unique status of Jesus. But here Jesus not only urges, but compels into silence, the first person who seems to have openly declared it.

The narrative permits, and perhaps invites, us also to see this as a revelatory occasion for Jesus: here is his first public encounter with the powers of evil

---

[32] Cf. Gundry, *Mark*, 76.

[33] Jesus' command to silence as a part of the process of exorcism was intended to stop 'the spirit's attempt to reduce him to helplessness through uttering his knowledge of Jesus' name, hometown, intention, and title' (ibid., 77), but this does not remove the strange sense of paradox in the chapter as a whole.

which he had, indeed, come to destroy (for which he had been privately prepared in the wilderness). There is a sense, for him, of 'this is what it will be
like'. And it is revelatory, too, for the evil spirits. The one speaks for the many;
they see that now their time is up.

This is surely an extraordinary encounter and a multi-faceted moment of
vision that is also deeply disconfirming. What the readers have been allowed to
glimpse at the opening of the Gospel is both dramatically enacted and then
mysteriously taken away. Here we have not simply 'exorcism' with a new
authority. The narrative record of this event gives 'exorcism' a new meaning,
revolving around the paradoxes attending the identity of the exorcist. We
should not be lured by the general belief in spirits and the practice of exorcism
in antiquity into understating the originality of such a narrative or the event to
which it points.[34]

The last surprise, perhaps, is that Mark's story still seems to us nevertheless
so 'realistic', even 'matter-of-fact'. This, no doubt, will turn out to be
because our notion of realism has been so deeply formed by the biblical
literature itself. But for a final perspective on this story we turn to Prickett's
final chapter.

Metaphor and Reality

What is the relationship of such apparently 'realistic' language – especially in
the Bible – to reality? Prickett has already shown that the nineteenth-century
literary convention of prose 'realism' does not bring the reader any closer to
'reality' than the so-called 'poetic' outpourings of the same period: both alike
depend on the creative perceptions of the writer. Conversely, for Blake,
Wordsworth and Coleridge, 'the "poetic" was concerned not with a retreat
from reality, but with helping to constitute it'.[35] Prickett points to the fact that
at the heart of even what we call 'literal' language there is a tension that can
appropriately be described as 'metaphorical'. Words never simply mirror
reality; reality is always bigger than the words with which we seek to describe
and constitute it. Against the closed systems of structuralism or the
Wittgensteinian language-game, which in their 'ideal' forms prohibit the
access of new insight or expression, Prickett articulates that metaphorical
quality in language which allows it to speak of a reality outside its own system,

---

[34] Notwithstanding details such as the use by Jesus of the command 'be silent',
'technically used in the language of hellenistic magic to express the *binding* of a
person by means of a powerful spell, so as to render him impotent to do harm'
(Rawlinson, *Mark*, 17).
[35] *Words*, 204.

to give voice to new disclosures, and to transcend historical distance in order to break into the hermeneutical circle of the past. Prickett's final chapter is thus symptomatic of an irreversible twentieth-century trend in which not only philosophy, but also literary criticism, is seen to revolve around the nature of language itself.[36]

We began by noting some elements of strangeness in the narrative which make a simply naturalistic reading problematic, but which – equally – cannot be readily dealt with by drawing attention away from the event to some decodable 'meaning', either historical (the strangeness is a product of poor editing) or theological (Mark is making a 'point'). The metaphorical-tension theory of language which Prickett expounds (drawing on the work of Ricœur and Douglas Berggren, among others) fits the situation precisely.[37] According to this theory, metaphor does not function simply via the direct replacement in a reader's or hearer's mind of the literal 'meaning' by a metaphorical 'meaning'. Rather, the literal meaning lingers, as it were, in *tension* with the metaphorical meaning. It is by this means that language can at least begin to suggest the multifaceted nature of life, though it can never be equal to this task. So in this story – like many, perhaps most, stories – the elements of strangeness invite us to linger with the literal meaning (for instance of the word 'immediately') *at the same time* as looking beyond it.

This tensional character of language itself gives us a better perspective on the subsequent ways of reading the story which we have outlined, following Prickett's chapters. If the story is 'poetic', this need imply neither that the language of 'an unclean spirit' is mere discardable myth, nor that an adequate interpretation depends on a re-entering of the 'primal participation' which gave it birth. Such language is metaphorical not by virtue of the discarding of its character as literal witness, but on account of the inadequacy of all language to express truth. Insofar as the story can be read in Romantic-prophetic terms, the creativity of Mark and of Jesus is seen precisely in the tension engendered between the literal meaning of words and the greater reality to which they are enabled to point. And the 'disconfirming' character of the story may be neither more nor less than the evidence of the peculiar starkness of metaphorical tension in language at that particular historical juncture.

---

[36] Cf. the pregnant statement of Barthes: '[O]nce again [as in mediaeval times] the exploration of language ... corresponds to the exploration of the cosmos. For literature is itself a science, or at least knowledge, no longer of the "human heart" but of human language ... Just as in Western culture grammar was not born until long after rhetoric, so it is only after having made its way through *le beau littéraire* that literature can begin to ponder the fundamental problems of language, without which it would not exist' ('To Write', 51).

[37] *Words*, esp. 221–30; Ricœur, *Rule*; Berggren, 'Use and Abuse'.

To read such a story as 'metaphorical' in this sense is thus to preserve its character as historical witness better than some other interpretative strategies involving metaphorical transfer. Such strategies include seeing the idea of being 'in an evil spirit' as a metaphor for sickness more generally; the deliverance of the man as a metaphor for the power of Jesus compelling people to existential decision; Jesus as prototype – and thus metaphor – for the church in its contemporary ministry.

The notable feature of all such interpretations is that while none of them necessarily or explicitly question that Mark is writing about a 'real' event, the reality of the event tends to be relativized against the reality of what it is held to 'mean', or how it is held to 'apply', today. But the strange contours of the narrative invite us to see reality *both* in 'what happened' *and* in 'what it meant/means'. The available language can capture the event and its startling novelty and significance only obliquely; but this tension between words and reality is a condition of *all* our attempts to describe the real.

The fascinating phenomenon at which Prickett hints is that in modernist biblical criticism, 'miracle' has been turned into 'parable'. Because of discomfort with the idea of irruptions into a 'natural' order of things, language that attempts to express such abnormalities has been either flattened and rationalized, or dismissed, as the child of a more superstitious age. The reality that the writers have been struggling to express has been turned into an edifying parable or metaphor for something that we can cope with more easily. It is intriguing to reflect that during the same period, the power of the *actual* parables of Jesus may also have been allowed to diminish, by treating them (as did Adolf Jülicher[38]) as expressions of general, universal truth rather than invitations to a genuinely new insight. The language of both miracle-stories and parables was implicitly tamed, so that neither was truly allowed to be 'words of power'.

To read a story such as that of the exorcism at Capernaum as 'metaphorical', however, *ought* to mean that we hold in tension the reality of the event which it seeks to describe and the reality of its 'meaning', suggested by the form which the narrator has given it. Neither should be allowed to become the 'real' against which the other is seen as 'mere metaphor'.

The question with which Prickett leaves us is how the *power* of the biblical words may be received and not negated. His closing comments, referring back again to Elijah's encounter with God on Mount Horeb, could equally well apply to the incident from Mark which we have been pondering:

> Our problem is not so much that the original event is inaccessible to us (as it is) but that, in another sense, it is apparently accessible in too many ways. We can seem to

---

38 *Gleichnisreden.*

approach it by a multitude of routes. It is, rather, that at its centre lies an event of such complexity and mystery that it resists translation into any of our preconceived categories or disciplines (as it resisted Elijah's own). As such, it may be taken as emblematic of other events and acted metaphors which occur throughout the Bible and which defy classification. The greatest problem with 'miracles' is, perhaps, that we attempt to classify them as such. What we have seen here (and it is only a fragment of the story) is a conflict between open and closed systems of hermeneutics: those which claim to possess the Word, and those which are capable of being translated by it.[39]

Prickett's elegant discussion – which this chapter, in its brevity, cannot hope to reflect satisfactorily – can be seen as pointing in the direction of an answer: through our grasp of the tensional metaphorical character of language. This can enable us to imagine how writers can successfully communicate truly new reality, 'meaning' that as yet has no words truly 'proper' to it. It can also help us both to understand and to communicate that reality ourselves. The tale of Jesus at Capernaum may be taken as a paradigmatic and vividly symbolic case. The power of the story is felt in the metaphorical tension between the narrative of an earthy event, one Sabbath in a synagogue, and its significance as symbolic of the newest reality of all, the revelation of God in Jesus. That the language of such a story can possess this power is testimony to a source beyond human culture and creativity. The word of power with which Jesus cast out the unclean spirit is the ultimate generator of the words of power with which the story can be told, both then and now.

Bibliography

Barthes, R., 'To Write: An Intransitive Verb?', in *Modern Literary Theory: A Reader* (ed. P. Rice and P. Waugh; London: Edward Arnold, 2nd edn, 1992), 42–51

Berggren, D., 'The Use and Abuse of Metaphor', in *Review of Metaphysics* (Dec. 1962), 237–58; (March 1963), 450–72

Bultmann, R., *History of the Synoptic Tradition* (trans. J. Marsh; New York: Harper & Row, 5th edn, 1963)

—, *Jesus Christ and Mythology* (New York: Charles Scribner's Sons, 1958)

Cranfield, C.E.B., *The Gospel According to St Mark* (Cambridge: CUP, 1959)

Dibelius, M., *From Tradition to Gospel* (trans. B.L. Woolf; London: Ivor Nicholson and Watson, rev. edn, 1934)

Gundry, R.H., *Mark: A Commentary on his Apology for the Cross* (Grand Rapids: Eerdmans, 1993)

---

[39] *Words*, 242.

Jülicher, A., *Die Gleichisreden Jesu* (2 vols.; Tübingen: J.C.B. Mohr [Paul Siebeck], 2nd edn, 1899)

Kittel, G., and G. Friedrich, *Theological Dictionary of the New Testament* (trans. and ed. G.W. Bromiley; Grand Rapids: Eerdmans, 1964)

Lane, W.L., *The Gospel of Mark* (London: Marshall, Morgan & Scott, 1974)

Lodge, D., 'Analysis and Interpretation of the Realist Text', in *Modern Literary Theory: A Reader* (ed. P. Rice and P. Waugh; London: Edward Arnold, 2nd edn, 1992), 24–42

Neil, W., *One-Volume Bible Commentary* (London: Hodder & Stoughton, 1962)

Prickett, S., 'The Bible in Literature and Art', in *The Cambridge Companion to Biblical Interpretation* (ed. J. Barton; Cambridge: CUP, 1998), 160–78

—, *Words and the Word: Language, Poetics and Biblical Interpretation* (Cambridge: CUP, 1986)

Rawlinson, A.E.J., *The Gospel According to St Mark* (London: Methuen, 7th edn, 1949)

Ricœur, P., *Essays on Biblical Interpretation* (trans. D. Pellauer; ed. L.S. Mudge; Philadelphia: Fortress Press, 1980)

—, *The Rule of Metaphor* (trans. R. Czerny, with K. McLaughlin and J. Costello, S.J.; Toronto: University of Toronto Press, 1977)

Wilder, A.N., *Early Christian Rhetoric: The Language of the Gospel* (London: SCM Press, 1964)

Williamson, L., *Mark* (Atlanta: John Knox Press, 1983)

Zerwick, M., and M. Grosvenor, *A Grammatical Analysis of the Greek New Testament* (2 vols.; Rome: Biblical Institute Press, 1974).

11

Reviving the Power of Biblical Language

The Bible, Literature and Literary Language

Brian D. Ingraffia & Todd E. Pickett

... we must convince ourselves that the literary genres of the Bible do not constitute a rhetorical façade which it would be possible to pull down in order to reveal some thought content that is indifferent to its literary vehicle.
Paul Ricœur, 'Toward a Hermeneutic of the Idea of Revelation'

In his essay for this volume, Stephen Wright, following Stephen Prickett's *Words and the Word*, argues for the value of reading the Bible, particularly the Gospels, as literary language. Although postmoderns now readily acknowledge the metaphorical nature of all language, the use of literary language and narrative tends to make us more aware that, in the words of Stephen Wright, 'Words never simply mirror reality; reality is always bigger than the words with which we seek to describe and constitute it.' Wright's main purpose is to avoid the ways in which both historical-critical and theological hermeneutics (that is, liberal and conservative)[1] 'tame' the 'words of power' in the Bible.

Wright concludes that, 'The question of whether any or all of the Bible is "literary language" may not be the right question ... The more important question, perhaps, is how the *power* of the biblical words may be received and not negated.' We, too, hope to revive the power of biblical language to inform and reform a scriptural imagination, and to preserve the power of biblical language to communicate the Word of God, beyond the power of human imagination.

---

[1] Cf. Vanhoozer, *Meaning?*, 307. 'In this respect, empirically minded fundamentalists share something in common with demythologizers such as Origen and Bultmann, namely, an inability to appreciate the *literary* dimension of the text.'

While taking advantage of the 'literary turn' in biblical studies, Wright avoids the reduction of the Gospels to fictional narrative.[2] For Wright, to read the Gospels as 'metaphorical' does not mean that we ignore the purpose of the Gospel writers to serve as historical witnesses. In Wright's own words,

> Discussions of literary form and language cannot in the end provide us with histori-cal conclusions ... To glimpse the metaphorical character of language, as Prickett does, will not in itself tell us the angle of obliqueness with which the language of a *particular* text refers to reality ...[3]

Wright refuses to use a reading of the Bible 'as literature' as a way of denying or ignoring the relationship between meaning and reference, between an event and the representation of an event in language. Ricœur reminds us that the Gospel, as a text, 'expresses a difference and a distance, however minimal, from the event that it proclaims'.[4] Wright does a superb job of carefully reading the language of Mark's gospel as both historical and literary, refusing to reduce the language of the Scriptures to one or the other.

> To read a story such as that of the exorcism at Capernaum as 'metaphorical' will mean to hold in tension the reality of the event which it seeks to describe and the re-ality of its 'meaning', suggested by the form the narrator has given it. Neither should be seen as the 'real' against which the other is seen as 'mere metaphor'.

He concludes, therefore, that, 'The power of the story will only be felt when it is read as striving, tropically, to describe the new revelation of God in Jesus, as something real and historical.'

We would like to continue Stephen Prickett's and Stephen Wright's analy-sis of the relationship between literary language and the language of the Gospels, but our emphasis will be upon the reception of the text through an analysis of the relationship between literary criticism and biblical hermeneu-tics. While our emphasis will be upon the relationship between the literary and the theological, our hope is to follow what Bartholomew describes as the 'more sophisticated and theologically aware models for biblical hermeneutics [which] recognize ... the need to integrate *three key elements or strands* in their approach to the Bible, namely the historical, the literary and the theological'.[5]

---

[2] On this reduction of the biblical narrative to fiction, see Ingraffia, 'Deconstructing', esp. 293 and 299.

[3] Wright's description of the biblical narrative's 'angle of obliqueness' is a wonderfully descriptive phrase which echoes Emily Dickinson's admonition to the poet to 'Tell all the Truth but tell it slant'.

[4] Ricœur, 'Preface', 56.

[5] Bartholomew, 'Introduction', xxvii.

Our contributions to this essay are intended to be both contrasting and complementary. Ingraffia will develop a theological criticism in order to highlight the difference between literary interpretation and biblical hermeneutics. He will reject the modernist call 'to read the Bible like any other text', through an analysis of the relation between general and special hermeneutics, in dialogue with Kevin Vanhoozer and Paul Ricœur.

In contrast but not in contradiction, Pickett will emphasize the close relationship between the interpretation of the Bible and the interpretation of literature, especially the valuable role that literature can play in the interpretation of the Bible. He has chosen to focus, appropriately, upon the relationship between the parable of the great banquet and a poem entitled 'The Guest' by Wendell Berry. Early and often in the history of hermeneutics, the parables have been the site of negotiation between literary and biblical language, since the parables record Jesus' own use of literary language, of story and narrative.

We will conclude with the analysis of the possibility of a more destructive relationship between the Bible and literary rewritings through Robert Alter's description of Franz Kafka's and James Joyce's 'wrenching' of Scripture in their modernist revisions of scriptural narrative.

In dialogue with these prophets and poets, theologians and literary critics, as well as with each other, we will explore some of the multiple implications, both the promises and the dangers, of the literary turn in biblical hermeneutics for Christian literary theorists.

General and Special Hermeneutics in Vanhoozer and Ricœur (Ingraffia)

> Whether one reads Scripture with a general or special hermeneutic will depend on whether one thinks that the Bible should be read as ordinary discourse or as literature.
> Kevin Vanhoozer, *Is There a Meaning in This Text?*

> How does a literary theory formulated to deal with Revelation – sacred Scripture – develop in such a way as to deal with products of the writerly imagination – 'secular criticism'? ... In what way does the perceived authenticity of biblical narrative become a criterion for authenticating secular narrative? Does this transference, among Christians, undermine secular narrative, or, as may seem more likely, does it in the end undermine biblical narrative?
> David Lyle Jeffrey, *People of the Book*

To begin with, I will quickly summarize what Vanhoozer means by 'reading the Bible like any other text'. Vanhoozer makes it clear that he does *not* mean that the Bible shouldn't be read as Scripture. This is the Enlightenment understanding of what it means to read the Bible like any other text. Vanhoozer uses B. Jowett as an example of a biblical scholar working within this paradigm. In this paradigm, we are told that we should read the Bible without any presuppositions, especially the presupposition or 'prejudice' of believers that it contains or communicates divine revelation.[6] The classic, philosophical formulation of this modernist hermeneutic principle is found in Spinoza's 'Tractatus Theologico-Politicus'.[7]

In contrast, Vanhoozer formulates the problem of reading the Bible like any other text from within a specifically theological perspective. Following Ricœur,[8] Vanhoozer reverses the Enlightenment paradigm to argue that we should read every other text like we read the Bible.

> On the one hand … we should read the Bible like any other text, though due consideration must be given to those factors that set it apart (e.g., its divine-human authorship, its canonical shape, its function as Scripture). On the other hand, we should read every other text with the same theological presuppositions that we bring to, and discover through, our study of the Bible.[9]

Vanhoozer begins by highlighting what makes the Bible holy, or set apart from literature, for the believing reader.[10] I will return to these distinctions in order to question the felicity of his expression when he calls believers to 'read every book as we have learned to read the Bible'.[11] In defining what he means by this assertion, Vanhoozer writes that we should read every text 'in a spirit of understanding that lets the text be what it is and do what it intends'.[12]

While I agree that we should do our best to follow the directedness of authorial discourse in reading any text, I disagree that we should let every text 'do what it intends'. In my work as a literary critic, I use a rhetorical criticism in large part because I believe that literature does not simply ask us to imagine a world. I believe authors use works of literature to try to persuade us to follow their vision and understanding of human existence. T.S. Eliot stresses this aspect of literature in his seminal essay on 'Religion and Literature': 'The

---

[6] See Gadamer on the Enlightenment 'prejudice against prejudice' in *Truth*, 239–45.

[7] 'I determined to examine the Bible afresh in a careful, impartial, and unfettered spirit, making no assumptions concerning it …' (8).

[8] See Ricœur, 'Philosophical Hermeneutics', 89ff.

[9] Vanhoozer, *Meaning?*, 455–56.

[10] On 'believing reading', see Thiselton, *New Horizons*, 598. 'It is not that believers understand some new propositional content unknown to unbelievers or to enquirers; it is that they … perceive themselves as *recipients or addressees* of directed acts of commitment, or of promise' (Thiselton's emphasis).

[11] Ibid., 379.

[12] Ibid.

author of a work of imagination is trying to affect us wholly, as human beings
... and we are affected by it, as human beings, whether we intend to be or
not.'[13] As a consequence, Eliot tells us, readers should resist modernist authors
who call us to see the world in purely secular terms. In other words, we should
not allow these modernist texts to do what their authors intended them to do.

Therefore I am troubled by Vanhoozer's assertion that, 'Trust rather than
suspicion is more fruitful when it comes to interpreting testimony.'[14] As a spe-
cialist in postmodernist literature, I find trust to be a very dangerous approach
to take with these texts; in fact, many of these texts are designed in such a way
as to subvert our traditional trust in texts.[15] Vanhoozer is well aware that 'certain texts should neither be admired nor followed, but rather rejected in dis-
gust'.[16] But if we read every text like we read the Bible, doesn't this mean that
we read all texts with the same trust that we as Christians bring to Scripture?
Even with texts written by Christians, although we may want to follow these
texts as 'friends' we accompany and from whom we learn,[17] there is a radical
difference between following a text as a friend and following a text as an
authority.

So while I agree with Vanhoozer's main point, which is that Christians
should develop a hermeneutics which is explicitly theological and specifically
Christian, including a Christian literary criticism, I am troubled by his assertion
that the understanding of any communicative action is possible only with the
aid of the Holy Spirit. Surely non-Christians understand communicative
actions all the time, without the aid of the Holy Spirit?

I would argue that, because of the unique nature of the Bible as divine revelation or divine discourse,[18] we should neither read the Bible like any other
text nor read every other text like we read the Bible.

Tony Thiselton's work can provide a helpful corrective to the diction used
by Vanhoozer concerning the relationship between general and special hermeneutics. Thiselton asserts, correctly I think, that 'Hermeneutics has suffered
grievously from the attempts of theorists to use one particular hermeneutical
paradigm as an explanatory model for a large variety of texts.'[19]

---

[13] Eliot, 'Religion', 348.

[14] Vanhoozer, *Meaning?*, 292.

[15] An excellent example of this strategy is T. Pynchon's *The Crying of Lot 49*. See my
essay 'Is the Postmodern Post-Secular?'.

[16] Vanhoozer, *Meaning?*, 370.

[17] On the development of this metaphor into a sophisticated literary theory, see Booth,
Company.

[18] On the analysis of the Bible as 'divine discourse', see Wolterstorff, *Divine Discourse*.

[19] Thiselton, *New Horizons*, 21.

In answering the question, 'What has biblical hermeneutics to do with literary theory?' Thiselton agrees with Vanhoozer that we should develop a specifically theological hermeneutics. However, I believe that Thiselton is more aware of the dangers of reading the Bible like any other text and of reading every other text like the Bible. Reading the Bible like any other text is based upon an Enlightenment paradigm that refuses to read the Bible as Scripture. Reading every other text like the Bible is based upon a Romantic paradigm that has a tendency to elevate the status of literature to the level of a new scripture and to demote Scripture to the level of myth. Vanhoozer takes this formulation from Ricœur, and I would argue that we see these same Romantic tendencies in Ricœur, especially in his more Heideggerian moments. For all his limitations, as a New Critic, in his theorizing of the relationship between literature and religion, Cleanth Brooks gets it right when he asserts that 'I think we have to distinguish between the functions of literature and religion … be wary of conceptions that would turn literature into an ersatz religion or religion into a kind of fairy tale with ethical implications.'[20]

In 1 Corinthians 2:11, Paul asks, 'who among men knows the thoughts of a man except the spirit of the man, which is in him? Even so the thought of God no one knows except the Spirit of God.' Vanhoozer might take this verse as a confirmation of his belief that the Holy Spirit is needed in order to understand human as well as divine communication, given that he seeks 'to explore the possibility that the Spirit plays a role in general hermeneutics as well' as in biblical hermeneutics.[21] Here Vanhoozer claims to be following Barth.

> Barth asks: 'Is there any way of penetrating the heart of a document – of any document! – except on the assumption that its spirit will speak to our spirit through the actual written words?' … Does it then follow that the Spirit is Lord of the hearing, not only of the Scriptures, but of all texts?[22]

Leaving aside here whether Barth's hermeneutics, in this statement, is too influenced by the Romantics' emphasis upon the role of 'divination' in the interpretation of texts, surely Barth would nevertheless still stress the difference between the spirit of the human author and the Spirit of the Lord. In his development of Barth's statement, Vanhoozer highlights the role of the Holy Spirit in the development of interpretive virtues.

> The Spirit enables us to avoid falling prey to self-deception, not by working a miracle in our rational faculties, but by shedding grace abroad in our hearts. The Spirit's

---

[20] Brooks, 'Religion', 62.
[21] Vanhoozer, *Meaning?*, 407.
[22] Ibid., 414.

work in interpretation does not represent a new faculty or capacity in the reader so much as a reorienting of those faculties that we already have. The Holy Spirit aids understanding in general, not least by cultivating the interpretive virtues in individuals and in the believing community.[23]

This is an admirable emphasis upon the role of the Spirit in the interpretive life of the believer, developing some of the insights of Ricœur.

> Ricœur describes the general process of interpretation in theologically charged terms. A text, he says, both 'reveals' and 'transforms.' That is, it both displays new ways of looking at oneself or the world and thereby transforms the reader's existence. All texts, not only the Bible, have the potential to be both revelatory and transformative. We can learn lessons for hermeneutics in general, Ricœur believes, by attending to how we interpret the Bible in particular.[24]

However, here Vanhoozer reminds his reader of his critique of Ricœur's failure to provide an adequate role for the Holy Spirit in his hermeneutics, aligning Ricœur's hermeneutics more with Bultmann than with Barth. 'Transformative reading is for Ricœur ultimately an innate human capacity that is more related to the power of the imagination than to the Holy Spirit.'[25] While I agree that Ricœur does have a tendency to describe our response to Scripture in Romantic terms which highlight the response of the human understanding, apart from the role of the Holy Spirit, I am also nervous about his tendency, also Romantic, to elevate the status of literature to that of Scripture. In even the best transformative reading of literature, it is 'an innate human capacity that is more related to the power of the imagination than to the Holy Spirit' which is at work.

Consequently, I believe that in 1 Corinthians 2:11 Paul is highlighting the *differences* between divine and human discourse. The spirit of the human author does not indwell us as the Holy Spirit indwells the believing reader of Scripture, for in our interpretation of Scripture, Paul assures Christians that we 'have received … the Spirit who is from God, so that we may know the things freely given to us by God' (1 Cor. 2:12). The same Holy Spirit who inspired the biblical writers is present with us, guiding us in our interpretation of Scripture. This is an astounding claim, whose power should not be diminished by being applied to the reading of literature.

Because of the unique role of the Holy Spirit in the interpretation of Scripture, I believe that we need to consider biblical hermeneutics a special hermeneutics. We should read secular literature differently than the way we

---

[23] Ibid., 415.

[24] Ibid., 414.

[25] Ibid.

read sacred Scripture. While we should first, in something like a 'momentary suspension of disbelief', use all our imaginative and rational powers to open ourselves to the author's way of describing the world, this reading, to experience the author's vision and to learn the author's beliefs, should then be *completed* by a critical response to the author's beliefs based upon our faith. But whereas believing readers should attempt to submit themselves to their best understanding of the divine discourse communicated in the Bible, believing in its promises and obeying its commands, Christian critics should *not* do so with literature.

> Are readers to be admirers and followers but never critics? Should responsible readers turn off all their critical faculties and willingly suspend their disbelief? Or might it not be that responsible reading requires the reader to judge the content of what is read? Is it not the case that certain texts should neither be admired nor followed, but rather rejected in disgust?[26]

In the end, Vanhoozer is aware of this distinction. Because of the unique function of the Bible as a sacred text, because of 'the Bible's character as "Scripture" and "canon" – its nature as a guidebook for the believing community ... the Bible is different, for the kind of response it enjoins is more demanding.'[27]

Informing and Reforming the Scriptural Imagination: The Guest in Parable and Poetry (Pickett)

> The proposed world that in biblical language is called a new creation, a new Covenant, the Kingdom of God, is the 'issue' of the biblical text unfolded in front of this text.
> Paul Ricœur, 'Toward a Hermeneutic of the Idea of Revelation'

In what ways, however, might extrabiblical literature help us interpret the Scriptures? How might other narratives intervene to help us recover and receive the power of biblical language and narratives?[28] A response to these questions requires first that we emphasize the Scriptures as sacred texts whose purpose, in great part, is to nurture in its readers a *scriptural imagination*.[29] Their

---

[26] Ibid., 370.

[27] Ibid., 313, 335.

[28] A question raised by Stephen Wright, 'Words of Power'.

[29] I have settled upon the term 'scriptural imagination' somewhat reluctantly, having considered the alternatives of 'Christian imagination', 'divine imagination', and 'religious imagination' (though this last term I will sometimes use in the essay). As I will make clear, such an imagination is 'scriptural' when it seeks to be shaped by the

effect is to redescribe reality, to present a possible world for the reader to imagine and to act within. It is the metaphorical work that says, 'look at it this way (or like this)'. Emphasizing this imaginative or metaphorical function of the Scriptures, however, does not negate them as historical witness. Rather, this approach implies that much of reality, including history, is and must be 'imagined' or seen within paradigms of one sort or another. In this sense, what Scripture seeks to cultivate in its readers is, in Garrett Green's words, the 'realistic imagination'.

While the 'imagination', historically, has been religiously suspect as the faculty that creates both fantasies and falsehoods, Green in his revision of Kuhn's notions of paradigms reminds us that the imagination inevitably comes into play when we must 'make present ... what is inaccessible to direct experience'.[30] Scientists must imagine both those existing elements of matter that are too small or too large to be seen directly through their instruments. What is not temporally accessible because it is past or future (the beginning of the universe, the impact of global warming) must also be imagined. And what is not *logically* visible, like the soul or the kingdom of God, must similarly be imagined. The function of the imagination, in this large sense of the term, is 'to tell us what the world is like', and we rely frequently upon implicit, imagined models as the conditions for even the most ordinary tasks.[31] For Green, such a 'paradigmatic imagination' is active also in the religious imagination, providing us with the patterns, exemplars, models, myths and metaphors that shape our perceptions and, consequently, influence our actions. The realistic, religious imagination, then, works 'to help us see what is really there and to imagine new possibilities for action'.[32]

Bringing into view the possible world of the 'kingdom of God' is one of the primary ways Scripture seeks to inform the believer's realistic imagination. The kingdom of God is that which, according to the Scriptures, truly exists but needs to be imagined and made manifest. God's interventions in human history – including and especially the incarnation, ministry, death and resurrection of Christ – gave human or earthly shape to the kingdom of God. The genres of the Old Testament, the Gospels, the Epistles, and the Apocalypse of John gave narrative and linguistic shape to the kingdom, providing in turn the (not quite) raw materials for the religious imagination. Consequently, learning to live in the kingdom of God, as George Lindbeck suggests, is like learning a

---

[29] *(Continued)* language and narrative of the Bible. But it also, in a sense, wanders out from Scripture to seek the kingdom of God – the Word that is behind, before and after the scriptural words.

[30] Green, *Imagining God,* 62.

[31] Ibid., 79.

[32] Ibid., 63.

language (a 'linguistic framework') 'that shapes the entirety of life and thought' for believers.[33] Jesus' repeated simile 'the Kingdom of God is like …' is the most obvious example of the effort of Christ and the Gospel writers to shape linguistically and metaphorically the imagination of auditors and readers – an example to which I will return.

In such a scheme, the work of theology is to conceptualize, systematize and generally articulate the rich and often ambiguous images, metaphors, symbols, narratives and other kinds of discourse found in the Scriptures. But, as Stephen Prickett suggests throughout *Words and the Word*, the effort to translate scriptural language and narratives into simplified, less ambiguous language and concepts often hems in the language's rich suggestiveness that, in our terms, is crucial for a religious imagination seeking the fullness and strangeness of the kingdom of God. For, the purpose of reading the Scriptures is not to hold manageable concepts in our hands, but to behold a world full of possibilities for action. To understand is to know how to proceed. In this way, the religious imagination is ultimately an ethical imagination. To put it another way, we can only act within the worlds that we see, and it is through scriptural language chiefly that we come to see the possible world of God's kingdom that we might act in conformity with it.

To speak of scriptural language and the imagination in this way is to suggest that through our reading and meditations on such language we can perfectly receive the paradigms or models of God's kingdom. But, of course, it is not that simple. Language is protean – slipping, sliding and changing shape relative to the cultural conditions of translation and reception, as well as to the contexts brought by the individual reader. Biblical language itself is not immune to such changes as it becomes marked, informed and transformed by its use in cultural and market settings. What can happen to biblical language, Jeffrey reminds us in the words of Walker Percy, is 'a kind of devaluation of language – a cheapening of the very vocabulary of salvation, as a consequence of which the ever fresh, ever joyful meaning of the Gospel can come across as the dreariest TV commercial'.[34] Such a devaluation of the language of Scripture can occur within religious speech communities as well where a familiarity with and zeal for theological concepts causes readers to look *through* scriptural language rather than looking *at* it.[35] The danger here is that the ambiguity and suggestiveness of scriptural language that might provoke a richer and more startling

---

[33] Lindbeck, *Nature of Doctrine*, 32–33. Terrence Tilley has pointed out rightly that Lindbeck's notion of a linguistic framework is rather too sanguine, not taking into account the way in which it is already permeated by surrounding languages (*Five Postmodern Theologies*, 91ff.).

[34] Jeffrey, *People*, 344.

[35] Prickett, *Words*, 35–36.

imagination of the kingdom of God is eclipsed. To revive the power of biblical language in the face of these and other erosions of it is the work, in part, of metaphorical representation, which can upset 'normal' ways of viewing things and startle us into redescribing and reimagining reality.

In this broadly metaphorical way, extrabiblical literature can assist us in reviving and cultivating a scriptural imagination. It does this primarily by carrying biblical language, motifs and ideas (metaphor means 'to carry over') into new or different contexts. Such contexts can both reveal new possibilities for these metaphors and drive us back to Scripture to look at its language with new eyes.

I offer below one example of a text, Wendell Berry's poem 'The Guest', that can be appropriated for the work of informing a scriptural imagination. Of course, examples are never innocent, and we are not claiming that all literary texts can assist us as this one does in reconsidering biblical language. While we think that all narratives – fictional or not – are involved in a 'tournament of narratives',[36] asking their readers to 'look at it this way', some work better than others to allow us to reconsider biblical language and images (whether their authors are sympathetic to such a project or not). It is the ongoing discovery of such texts and the helpful ways of reading them that we want to encourage. While this will seem to some an overly ideological approach to literature, it is our view that readers' intentions can legitimately guide their critical interests in spite of (but not in ignorance of) authors' intentions, however those may be conceived.[37] For while there are many reasons why Christians read, the informing and reforming of the scriptural imagination should certainly be one of them.

Wendell Berry's poem 'The Guest' presents us with the question of how we are to look at the stranger and, as its title suggests, re-presents in a new context the metaphorical and biblical construction of the stranger-as-guest. Although the poem makes several allusions to biblical language and narratives – not the least of which is the parable of the Good Samaritan – it begins and ends with allusions to the parable of the great banquet in Luke 14. In that chapter of the Gospel, Jesus is himself a guest at the home of a 'prominent

---

[36] The phrase is borrowed from Charles Scriven's essay, 'Schooling for the Tournament of Narratives'.

[37] Kevin Vanhoozer, in his book *Is There a Meaning in This Text?*, maintains in the end that reading all other texts as we read the Bible requires that we be primarily interested in the intentions of the author, as Vanhoozer deftly redefines these along the lines of speech-act theory. While Christian readers must respect authors as others by not ignoring their intentions, I differ from Vanhoozer, perhaps, in giving more emphasis to the responsible appropriation of extra-biblical texts for the end of learning to live in the kingdom of God, regardless of their authors' intentions.

Pharisee' on the Sabbath. There, he plays out one scenario and narrates three in an effort to re-form the imaginations of those present concerning hosts, guests and strangers. A brief reading of this chapter will help us see Jesus' own attempt to inform the religious imagination before we look at Berry's own reconsideration of the 'guest' in his poem.

In the one actual situation before Jesus that begins the chapter, there is a man present at the meal who suffers from dropsy. Jesus asks the Pharisees ('experts in the law') whether it is lawful to heal on the Sabbath. The question exemplifies Jesus' strategy of drawing his critics into these dramas, forcing them to play roles and speak commitments so that they might become visible to others and themselves. In this case, the Pharisees' objection would make visible their self-serving legalism against Christ's mercy; to grant approval would be to weaken their power as 'keepers of the law'. In either case, a response would change how those present imagine both them and Christ. Understandably, then, they avoid language altogether – a silence which, of course, still 'says' something.

After healing the man, Jesus goes on to ask in his first fictional scenario, 'If one of you has a son or an ox that falls into a well on the Sabbath day, will you not immediately pull him out' (Lk. 14:5). Again, they have nothing to say, but the question is more rhetorical than the last one and continues to frame the Pharisees' legalism as arbitrary and self-seeking.

The third scenario returns to the setting of the meal and exposes the degree to which the guests are now also implicated in power-seeking actions. The parable Jesus tells is that of guests choosing a seat at the table, a passing moment that is nevertheless fraught with political implications. Jesus' imperative here is simply, 'do not take the place of honor, for a person more distinguished than you may have been invited' (14:8). Here again, Jesus exposes how the self-serving desires of the guests inevitably force them to imagine others as less distinguished. He commands instead that they 'humble themselves' by taking the lowest place, and so see others as possibly more distinguished. This humble description of the self is tentative, one that awaits the judgment of the host, who may reorder the guests as he esteems them. Such a modest imagination of their significance is, in any case, not final: in the kingdom of God, such lowly 'guests' will be exalted. Jesus offers this tentative redescription of the self, however, clearly as a momentary but necessary disorientation of their imaginations. Indeed, all of the scenarios that precede the parable of the great banquet work to destabilize how those present at the meal – both guests and hosts – imagine themselves and others.

The fourth scenario returns to hosts, exhorting them not to invite 'your friends, your brothers or relatives, or your rich neighbors', which will further their desire to be repaid and certainly fix the guest list to only those who can repay in kind (14:12). Instead, says Jesus, 'when you give a banquet, invite the poor, the crippled, the lame, the blind, and you will be blessed' (14:13–14a). The fact that Jesus speaks this at a meal to which, almost certainly, friends, relatives and rich neighbors were invited makes this another awkward, disconfirming moment for those present, to say the least. At this point, Luke writes, 'When one of those at the table with him heard this, he said to Jesus, "Blessed is the man who will eat at the feast in the kingdom of God" ' (14:15). It is hard to tell if this is said with sincerity or in a tone of self-serving piety, but Jesus takes this opening into the possible world of the kingdom of God to inform their spiritual imaginations with a longer parable concerning hosts and guests. Although the common introduction, 'the Kingdom of God is like …', is absent here, the parable's work will clearly be metaphorical in just this way.

In this parable, a man was 'preparing a great banquet', for what occasion we are not told (though a related parable in Mt. 22 has it as a wedding banquet). Jesus' hearers would know that hosts often chose guests as witnesses to an event, and so such guests would need to be credible and esteemed in the eyes of the community. In this case, however, such guests surprisingly find the banquet not worth their time: two of them say they must attend to their recent purchases (land and oxen), and the third claims to have just been married himself. Upon hearing the news, the angry host apparently does not hesitate to invite new guests: 'Go out quickly into the streets and alleys of the town and bring in the poor, the crippled, the blind and the lame.' The servant does so, but finds there is still room. The host commands him to cast the net further, to the 'roads and country lanes', so that his house will be made full and that 'not one of those men who were invited will get a taste of my banquet' (14:21–24).

The parable ends with what sounds like a vindictive tone that we might think unworthy of a parable about the kingdom of God. The host's anger here might either be a bit of realistic detail on Jesus' part or a hint that anger and exclusion are not inappropriate responses to the pride and ingratitude of those who reject God's call. Be that as it may, the part of the parable meant to startle his hearers is certainly the instantaneous willingness of the host to consider as guests those whom no self-respecting host would invite. Such guests are clearly not those who could repay the host with other invitations, and they are not ones worthy of a place of honor – at least not in the actual world of the ancient Near East. But this is the possible world of the kingdom of God, and in such a world, those marginalized by poverty and disease are potential guests worthy of sitting at the banquet. Of course, the word 'banquet' or 'feast' has eschatological connotations, and the parable can be read as Jesus' intimation that someday, such as these (or the Gentile outsiders they are sometimes seen to represent) will be welcomed at God's table, if not man's. (Indeed, the word for 'guest' is simply 'those called' – *tous keklēmenous* – which echoes the language of divine calling.) But the setting of Jesus' telling makes it hard to ignore an ethical force the parable has for those present. Jesus redescribes the

uninvited poor and diseased as guests certainly not merely for allegorical purposes. And here we see that his language straddles a literal/metaphorical line.
Jesus would have been delighted, we imagine, at the admission of the poor literally as guests to the meal. But he also certainly means 'guest' to be a metaphor
for the paradigmatic way in which we are to see the other. In the ancient Near
East, to be invited as a guest promised approval and legitimacy, as well as protection, honor and sustenance. Imagining the other as guest is a paradigm for
treating strangers, especially suffering strangers, as 'guests' in any number of
ways that might offer dignity, protection and care.

Christianity, Julia Kristeva reminds us, figures life as a journey, with all
believers now imagined as strangers and with Jesus as the foreigner of foreign-
ers.[38] Paul's designation of the church as *ekklesia*, 'those called out', echoes the
word for guest in Luke 14, and, as Kristeva notes, substitutes for the more
probable, nationalistic term, 'people' (*laos*).[39] Jesus' earthly association with
marginalized people as well as the metaphorical joining of himself with the
hungry, thirsty, naked, sick and imprisoned in Matthew 25 further served to
transform the status of the struggling underclass. The New Testament concern
for the suffering stranger, of course, extended an ancient Near Eastern tradition of hospitality for the uninvited visitor who might be, in fact, a god or an
angel (as in the case of Abraham and Sarah's visitors). All such recasting of the
other in the Scriptures influenced the creation of shelters or *xenodochia* in early
Christendom where strangers, wanderers and outcasts were welcomed as
guests (though in practice care was often limited to the faithful).[40] In theory at
least, this was the right idea: the scriptural imagination looked at the suffering
stranger and saw an honored guest.

Wendell Berry's poem 'The Guest' brings the language and motifs of this
metaphor into the context of the contemporary urban world, allowing us to
reconsider how imagining the stranger as guest might play out in the possible
worlds of the poem and, ultimately, of the kingdom of God. In this poem, a
speaker narrates and reflects briefly upon his encounter with a suffering
stranger on a city street in Manhattan. We know little about this speaker other
than that he is wealthy enough to own or rent a place in the city, and more
importantly for our purposes, that he has an imagination schooled in the Scriptures. Indeed, it is how he should imagine the even more anonymous stranger
before him that becomes the subject of the poem.

> Washed into the doorway
> by the wake of the traffic,
> he wears humanity

---

[38] Kristeva, *Strangers*, 83.
[39] Ibid., 80.
[40] Ibid., 86.

like a third-hand shirt
blackened with enough
of Manhattan's dirt to sprout
a tree, or poison one.
His empty hand has led him
where he has come to.
Our differences claim us.
He holds out his hand,
in need of all that's mine.

And so we're joined, as deep
as son and father. His life
is offered me to choose.

Shall I begin servitude
to him? Let this cup pass.
Who am I? But charity must
suppose, knowing no better,
that this is a man fallen
among thieves, or come
to this strait by no fault
– that our difference
is not a judgment
though I can afford to eat
and am made his judge.

I am, I nearly believe,
the Samaritan who fell
into the ambush of his heart
on the way to another place.
My stranger waits, his hand
held out like something to read,
as though its emptiness
is an accomplishment.
I give him a smoke and the price
of a meal, no more.

– not sufficient kindness
or believable sham.
I paid him to remain strange
to my threshold and table,
to permit me to forget him
knowing I won't. He's the guest
of my knowing, though not asked.[41]

---

[41] 'The Guest' from Collected Poems: 1957–1982 by Wendell Berry. Copyright 1985 by Wendell Berry. Reprinted by permission of North West Press, a division of Farrar, Straus and Giroux, LLC.

From the beginning, the speaker experiments with various metaphors to imagine the man confronting him. Initially, the stranger appears to him as a kind of debris, washed by the 'wake' of traffic to the thoroughfare's edge. While his position puts him on the margins of human traffic, it also sets him liminally at a 'doorway' – on the verge of someone's hospitality. He wears the dirt of Manhattan, and the speaker with a touch of sarcasm imagines him for a moment able either to poison or fertilize a tree. The ambiguity of the man's squalor is significant, however, for the question is whether death or life – for the man or the speaker – will come out of this encounter between the two. The stranger's silent supplication creates a tableau that not only evokes our own memories of such encounters, but also rhymes with the image of those who called to Jesus from the edges of ancient city streets. That this scene – repeated daily in every city in America and around the world – is set in Manhattan recalls a third context, that of the Native American hosts, who eventually became suffering strangers at the hands of opportunistic European guests.

Whether what stops the speaker here is the memory of Jesus himself as the halted traveler is uncertain. In any case, he does stop for a moment, allowing himself to take in the 'differences' between the two. These differences and the man's tacit request beg the question of how he should imagine himself, the other and the relationship between them. The role of the imagination seems ever more inevitable given the silent and anonymous stranger whose history is unknown and who seems to invite interpretation as he holds his hand out 'like something to read'. The constructions he entertains in the rest of the poem are clearly those of a religious imagination, rummaging for metaphors and stories from the New Testament in an effort to find identities and relations for himself and the stranger.

In the first of these, the speaker imagines a joining as 'deep as son and father', metaphors that invoke the parable of the prodigal son where the son's life is the father's to choose as the stranger's life 'is offered me to choose'. To interpret their encounter through this parable, however, is to imagine certain histories for them that bear with them moral judgments. In such a story, the stranger becomes the prodigal, seeking but not deserving a second chance, while the speaker is allowed to play the forgiving father. But such a construction is moments later resisted by the intrusion of another narrative frame, that of the Good Samaritan, in which 'charity must suppose … / that this is a man fallen / among thieves, or come / to this strait by no fault' of his own. In trying on both of these biblical stories, the speaker realizes that such a situation tempts and maybe requires from him a kind of judgment (or imagination) of the other merely because he can 'afford to eat'.

In between these two biblical allusions comes a third in which the speaker seems to sense that no matter what biblical narrative he may choose, a sacrifice will be required. The request to '*let this cup pass*' and the anticipation of a potential '*servitude*' clearly now type the speaker as Jesus in Gethsemane, facing an inevitable, painful sacrifice. Perhaps confused by the succession of images (father, Samaritan, Christ), or retreating from a too flattering comparison of himself with Christ, the speaker now wonders, '*Who am I?*' The question of how he should respond to the stranger suddenly now also depends upon how he is to imagine himself.

In these final two stanzas, the speaker for a moment 'nearly' believes that he is indeed faithfully re-enacting the parable of the Good Samaritan. But the role is not quite convincing. His abilities as a faithful reader both of the parable and of himself reveal that his offering of 'a smoke and the price of a meal' is 'not sufficient kindness / or believable sham'. Both he and the stranger, he senses, understand that this gift is not an invitation to a previously uninvited guest, but a social contract that insures the man will remain strange both to his table and to his memory. The stranger, then, will not be one who eats at *his* table (*sunanakeimenon* – one who reclines at your table – is the other image for the guest in Luke 14) – even in a metaphorical sense.

The concluding and disconfirming revelation, however, is that the stranger has become a guest after all – 'the guest / of my knowing, though not asked.' The reality and presence of the suffering stranger – in his world, in our world – does not go away. The man has become a guest of the speaker's memory, a ghost-guest, that haunts him in the gap between the possible world he finds in Scripture and the world he authors (or co-authors) in the unfinished, ongoing narrative which is his life.

This story, then, is an example of a speaker whose scriptural imagination in the end fails to inspire him. But in spite of this, both the speaker and the poem itself reveal positively a number of ways in which the religious imagination in contact with life and literature can be driven back to reconsider the narrative and linguistic materials of Scripture. First, the speaker, in spite of his failure, models a consciousness dominated by a scriptural imagination. Scriptural language and narratives intrude upon his twentieth-century life, shaping his perceptions, framing his interpretations and forcing him to interpret his own life within the possible world of the kingdom of God.

Indeed, what the speaker discovers is that his attempt at acting out his scriptural imagination *is* part of the interpretative process. His story teaches that only when we embody the imagined and possible world of the kingdom of God can we finally judge the faithfulness of our interpretations of Scripture. Our resulting actions are necessarily a part of the hermeneutical process, not merely an 'application' of an already interpreted concept. Indeed, it is the speaker's willingness to have his own act interpreted, to allow Scripture to *interpret him*, that makes of his moral failure at least an interpretive victory.[42] Put

---

[42] At the end of *People of the Book,* Jeffrey wonders if understanding comes about, 'not

another way, a hermeneutical integrity has emerged from a moment's failure of moral integrity. He has not imagined this encounter as a seamless extension, integration or application of the biblical narratives, but has recognized the break or gap that his own acts make with that possible world. If, as Jeffrey writes, an effect of sin is the 'evasion of truth about the self',[43] the speaker's honest interpretation of the self is partly redemptive.

Of course, the embodiment of one's scriptural imagination or interpretation is not just an important *part* of the interpretive process, but its end. What Jeffrey notes about representations of reading in medieval religious art might well stand for Christian readers of all generations, that reading should be 'an incarnational process whereby the word becomes ingested ... and gives birth to life, as well as to other words and books'.[44]

While the speaker's scriptural imagination does not, in this case, give birth to life, it does give birth to other interpretations and stories. In particular, the speaker's failed performance has given a new interpretation to the biblical figure of the 'guest'. Certainly, understanding the guest as the ghost of one's memory is not the sense of 'guest' in the parable of the great banquet. And yet, this poem's concluding reversal of 'guest' is not unbiblical. In the speaker's scriptural imagination, the failure to make a guest of the stranger in the way Jesus intended makes 'guest' a word that brings conviction. It is now Janus-faced, with connotations both of mercy and healing, and of regret and failure. As readers and spectators, we are spared his pain, but we ourselves are not left unchanged. Read in the light of a scriptural imagination, this poem changes our future readings of the Luke 14 parable, expanding our interpretation of it in a way unforeseen by the Gospel writer but arguably consonant with his purposes. The parable and its central metaphor of the 'guest' now take on the aspect of prophetic rhetoric, which as Jeffrey observes, takes as its 'culminating point ... an imperative insistence on the reader's option, as well as a reminder of what is at stake in the choosing'.[45] In the metaphorical give and take that has come about through the contact of these biblical and extrabiblical stories, the central metaphor in both stories now reads to our scriptural imaginations as an ethical choice between two experiences of the 'guest'.

Not only has the speaker expanded the connotations of the great banquet's 'guest', but he has to some degree rewritten other parables that ripple through his imagination. If he is not the Good Samaritan, he is also not either of the

---

[42] (*Continued*) because we interpret the text, but because, when read accountably, the text interprets us' (373). See also Thiselton's discussion of how reading interprets the self (*Interpreting God*, 63–5).

[43] Jeffrey, *People*, 359.

[44] Ibid., 230.

[45] Ibid., 37.

other two who passed by without stopping. He has become a fourth traveler, the central, struggling figure of a twentieth-century version of the parable of the Good Samaritan. In the narrative of this incident, he has also given us the story of an urban, rich young ruler, beginning where that biblical story leaves off, with the young man's turning away from Jesus' call. Ethically powerful texts, writes Jeffrey, are 'ones which seem able to generate *new story*, to make old new'.[46] The value of these new stories taking shape in the poem is indeed to draw us back to the ethical power of those old, sacred stories.

Questions remain, however. If the poem's speaker sees with a scriptural imagination, why does he fail to act with 'sufficient kindness'? What, indeed, is sufficient kindness in the parables of the great banquet and the Good Samaritan, and in the translation of the kingdom of God to earth? One might say, for instance, that what the speaker of the poem seems to lack is the attendant feeling of compassion (*splanchnizomai*) that erupts in several places where Jesus encounters needy strangers. How would the action of this poem be different in a version that successfully translated the kingdom of God into modern urban life? Far from leaving us high and dry, such questions raised by the poem work to drive us both back to the language and narrative of the Scriptures and forward to imagine new narratives, fictional and actual, that might be. It is the questions that extrabiblical literature as experiments in life pose, then, that work to open up fresh inquiries into the Scriptures.

Reforming or Deforming the Scriptural Imagination

Of course, the question that looms over our religious readings of both scriptural and extra-scriptural texts is, how do we know when we're imagining scripturally? How do we judge if a literary author is reforming or deforming the scriptural imagination? To take one negative example, the Puritan religious imagination, steeped as it was in the world of the Scriptures, nevertheless erred in imagining the New World as the New Israel, casting the Puritans themselves as its righteous and rightful inhabitants. Much can be and has been said about the hermeneutical wrong turns taken by the Puritans,[47] and it is certainly beyond the scope of this essay to explore these and other misuses of the religious imagination.

However, one guide for regulating the scriptural imagination can surely be taken from Augustine's conviction in *On Christian Doctrine* that useful reading begins with *caritas,* the desire to love God and our neighbors. In our context,

---

[46] Ibid., 373.

[47] See Jeffrey for a recent discussion of the Puritan religious imagination. Ibid., 317–52.

we might turn this around to say that any faithful embodiment of the scriptural imagination should not offend against *caritas*, as the speaker of Berry's poem discovers. Any more precise understandings of what *caritas* looks like will emerge in the stories of our lives and of our fictions that move out from Scripture and back again to it.

Robert Alter, in his recently published study of the response of modern writing to the authority of the scriptural canon, can provide us with a brief example of a fictional response to the biblical text which seeks not to reform the scriptural imagination for a new generation in a new context, but which seeks rather to 'wrench' Scripture apart from its canonical context as a way of undermining, or at least taming, the power and authority of Scripture for the modern imagination. Alter describes how 'Kafka's writing undermines any sense that the Bible is a fixed source of authority or a reliable guidebook', and how in Joyce's writing 'the canonical status of Scripture is subverted, transformed, and reaffirmed in new terms'.[48] In both of these modernist writers, 'the Bible ... is converted into a secular literary text'.[49] While we, as Christian critics, cannot accept this secularization of Scripture, we can nevertheless learn from such secularizations and even parodies of the biblical narrative which, like more faithful rewritings, can drive us back to Scripture to look at its language with new eyes.

Paul Griffiths, following Donald Davidson's theory of metaphor, writes that metaphor 'provokes a shift of the gaze' and 'intimates a train of thought whose ending is unclear'.[50] In other words, it makes us look and move in a certain direction, provoking and unfolding patterns of thought and action not yet determined. With scriptural metaphors and stories in mind, we become, as Thiselton says of the Hebrews, a 'people on the move', watching to see how these will play out in our own lives.[51] And in our movements out among language and stories, we pray to be saved, suspecting that, as Garrett Green writes, 'To save sinners, God seizes them by the imagination.'[52]

Bibliography

Alter, R., *Canon and Creativity: Modern Writing and the Authority of Scripture* (New Haven: Yale University Press, 2000)

---

[48] Alter, *Canon and Creativity*, 95, 181.
[49] Ibid., 182–83.
[50] Griffiths, 'Egyptian Gold', 7.
[51] Thiselton, *Interpreting God*, 153.
[52] Green, *Imagining God*, 149.

Bartholomew, C., 'Introduction', in *Renewing Biblical Interpretation* (ed. C. Bartholomew, C. Greene and K. Möller; SHS, 1; Grand Rapids: Zondervan; Carlisle: Paternoster, 2000), xxiii–xxxi

Berry, W., 'The Guest', in *Upholding Mystery: An Anthology of Contemporary Christian Poetry* (ed. D. Imapastato; Oxford: OUP, 1997), 202–3

Booth, W.C., *The Company We Keep: An Ethics of Fiction* (Berkeley: University of California Press, 1988)

Brooks, C., 'Religion and Literature', in *Community, Religion, and Literature* (Columbia: University of Missouri Press, 1995), 50–62

Eliot, T.S., 'Religion and Literature', in *Selected Essays* (San Diego: Harcourt Brace Jovanovich, 1960), 343–54

Gadamer, H.-G., *Truth and Method* (New York: Crossroad, 1985)

Green, G., *Imagining God: Theology and the Religious Imagination* (Grand Rapids: Eerdmans, 1989)

Griffiths, P.J., 'Seeking Egyptian Gold', *The Cresset* 63.7 (2000), 6–17

Ingraffia, B.D., 'Is the Postmodern Post-Secular?: The Parody of Religious Quests in Thomas Pynchon's *The Crying of Lot 49* and Don DeLillo's *White Noise*', in *Postmodern Philosophy and Christian Thought* (ed. M. Westphal; Bloomington: Indiana University Press, 1999), 44–68

—, 'Deconstructing the Tower of Babel: Ontotheology and the Postmodern Bible', in *Renewing Biblical Interpretation* (ed. C. Bartholomew, C. Greene and K. Möller; SHS, 1; Grand Rapids: Zondervan; Carlisle: Paternoster, 2000), 284–306

Jeffrey, D.L., *The People of the Book* (Grand Rapids: Eerdmans, 1996)

Kristeva, J., *Strangers to Ourselves* (New York: Columbia University Press, 1991)

Lindbeck, G., *The Nature of Doctrine: Religion and Theology in a Postliberal Age* (Philadelphia: Westminster Press, 1984)

Prickett, S., *Words and the Word: Language, Poetics and Biblical Interpretation* (Cambridge: CUP, 1986)

Ricœur, P., 'Philosophical Hermeneutics and Biblical Hermeneutics', in *From Text to Action* (trans. K. Blamey and J.B. Thompson; Evanston: Northwestern University Press, 1991), 89–101

—, 'Preface to Bultmann', in *Essays on Biblical Interpretation* (ed. L.S. Mudge; Philadelphia: Fortress Press, 1985), 49–72

—, 'Toward a Hermeneutic of the Idea of Revelation', in *Essays in Biblical Interpretation*, 73–118

Scriven, C., 'Schooling for the Tournament of Narratives: Postmodernism and the Idea of the Christian College', in *Theology Without Foundations: Religious Practice and the Future of Theological Truth* (ed. S. Hauerwas, N. Murphy, and M. Nation; Nashville: Abingdon Press, 1994)

Spinoza, B., 'Tractatus Theologico-Politicus', in *The Chief Works of Benedict de Spinoza*, I (trans. R.H.M. Elwes; New York: Dover, 1951), 1–278

Thiselton, A.C., *Interpreting God and the Postmodern Self: On Meaning, Manipulation and Promise* (Grand Rapids: Eerdmans, 1995)

—, *New Horizons in Hermeneutics: The Theory and Practice of Transforming Biblical Reading* (Grand Rapids: Zondervan, 1992)

Tilley, T., *Five Postmodern Theologies* (New York: Orbis Books, 1995)

Vanhoozer, K.J., *Is There a Meaning in This Text? The Bible, the Reader, and the Morality of Literary Knowledge* (Grand Rapids: Zondervan, 1998)

Wolterstorff, N., *Divine Discourse* (Cambridge: CUP, 1995)

12

Naming the Father

The Teaching Authority of Jesus and Contemporary Debate

David L. Jeffrey

> For this reason I bow my knees to the Father of our Lord Jesus Christ, from whom
> the whole family in heaven and earth is named ... (Eph. 3:14–15)

In the novel *Midnight's Children* (1981) by Salman Rushdie, a young Catholic
priest advises one of his flock, during her time in the confessional, concerning
'the colour of God':

> 'Blue,' the young priest said earnestly. 'All available evidence, my daughter, suggests
> that Our Lord Jesus Christ was the most beauteous, crystal shade of pale sky blue.'

When the penitent expresses some dubiety over this point, her somewhat distraught confessor reflects inwardly that what he has spoken was prompted,
after all, by high theological authority, that of his Bishop:

> 'Remember,' thus spake the Bishop, 'God is love; and the Hindu love-god, Krishna, is
> always depicted with blue skin. Tell them blue, it will be a sort of bridge between the
> faiths ...'[1]

But in the ensuing debate with his Portuguese-Indian parishioner the priest's
new palette transfers its pigment poorly; in the end he has to give it up.

One is reminded, in reading Rushdie (as surely he intends) that other such
attempts at 'bridging' – even those with a much more wide-ranging and
enduring effect – have also come at last to be rejected. The Aryan insistence

---

[1] Rushdie, *Midnight's Children*, 118.

that Jesus had blond hair and blue eyes, or that, on account of his insuperable antiquity, God the Father ought to be depicted as having a long and flowing white beard – these too, in the end, have had to be abandoned.

Selectively – that is, as fashion permits – ecclesiastical culture eventually tends to let go of most such awkward projections of social consciousness, even with a kind of relief. Yet while they remain comfortable illusions and so institutionalized they can involve a serious problematization of the sources of religious authority – or at least confusion about that authority. The Aryan-Christ example makes this clear, and almost everyone is now willing to be warned by it. Yet this sort of problematization is likely to recur in other guises, especially when it is the very notion of an authoritative source beyond social consciousness which is being questioned. When this more radical questioning becomes highly visible, as now again it is, the fact if not the form of the questioning makes clear that it is not merely a matter of style or cultural translation which is at issue. More deeply, the issue is a quest for hermeneutic constraint of the textual sources.

And so it is with current 'imaging' controversies in the nominally Christian West. As with either the Aryan or the blue Jesus, or with Blake's 'Ancient of Days', the new feminist imagings of God are more popularizable than some other theological inventions, and perhaps quite precisely because of the shift in religious authority they are seen to represent, even at the vernacular level. Stories normalizing 'goddess religion' appear almost daily. Venues may vary, but not the theme. A Catholic cathedral in Sacramento celebrates a Mass with diaphanously veiled dancers and a version of Psalm 23 in which the feminine pronoun is used exclusively: 'she restores my soul'. In the new service book of the United Church of Canada (by far Canada's largest Protestant denomination), baptism is no longer required to be in the name of the Father, Son and Holy Spirit. One declares now in the name of the 'Crea-tor, Liberator and Healer' or, alternatively, in the name of 'God, Source of Love; in the name of Jesus Christ, Love incarnate; and in the name of the Holy Spirit, Love's power'. In the first one hundred pages of the Canadian text there is only one reference to God the Father. One prays instead to 'Mother and Father God', or more simply 'Mother God'. Like the *Inclusive Language Lectionary*, on which it is modelled, this new type of liturgy has prompted both celebration and condemnation. Among the latter reactions, one critic has representatively described such institutional gestures as a 'systematic attempt to remove sexuality from males and to impose it on God'.[2] Elizabeth Achtemeier's point retains an instructive pertinence, I believe, for both sides in the contemporary debate.

---

[2] Anyone reflecting on *An Inclusive Language Lectionary*, and service books developed from it, should still consult Achtemeier's review. Arguments attacking Achtemeier typically have not dealt with the substantive hermeneutic and theological issues. Recent examples include Dell'Olio, 'Why Not?', a largely sophistical attempt to argue that 'even if Jesus's explicit use of a term may serve as justification for its use by

In a culture in which no subject so predominates as sex, it should not be surprising that gender and sexuality are more frontally present, so to speak, in our syncretisms than the colours blond or blue, or the white-beards of antiquity either.[3] Nor are we to imagine, presumably, given the tumult of our cultural identity wars, that there can now be an identity more firm and long-standing than one based upon our own consensual habits, or more persuasive than those arising from our personal, polymorphous 'bridging' efforts. A recent article by Margaret Merrill Toscano succinctly makes a general hermeneutic point of departure: its title is 'If I Hate My Mother, Can I Love the Heavenly Mother? Personal Identity, Personal Relationships, and Perceptions of God'. In it, Toscano shares her assumption concerning how both theology and 'reading' are to be done:

> In this essay I mix personal narrative with theological analysis not only because I see this as effective methodology but also because my thesis assumes that all of our theological constructs are based on personal and cultural preference.[4]

Toscano's assumption is, of course, often expressed with greater sophistication. Elisabeth Schüssler Fiorenza, for example, has it that

> The insistence that feminist christological discourses must be rooted in Christian Scriptures is encumbered by the same theoretical problems and methodological difficulties that have impeded the attempts of dominant biblical scholarship to reconstruct 'New Testament' christology.[5]

But in either formulation, the point is the same.

Christology is explicit in the preoccupations of more scholarly feminist theological writing to the degree to which there is candour about what is most directly at issue in the deeper theological debate. What Schüssler Fiorenza and others wish to subvert, even dismiss altogether from our language about God,

---

[2] (*Continued*) Christians, it does not follow that the absence of the explicit use of a term renders the use of that term by Christians illicit' (198). Cf. Vigano, *God*. Most feminists put it, nonetheless, in ways that underscore their largely sociological justification. See, e.g., Schneiders' representative preface: 'As women have become aware of their inferior status and actual oppression in family, society, and Church, they have also become aware that the gender of God, God's presumed masculinity, has functioned as the ultimate religious legitimization of the unjust structures which victimize women', in Schneiders *Women*.

[3] Schneiders, earlier in her text, insists that 'it is important to be aware that the question of the gender of God is a thoroughly modern issue' (2).

[4] This article is published in *Dialogue*, a Mormon journal.

[5] *JESUS*, 76.

is not merely the Hebrew Scriptures but the teaching authority of Jesus in the Gospels specifically. Textually, on the face of it, this has proven very hard to accomplish without engaging in nearly intolerable levels of sophistry. To their credit, Schüssler Fiorenza and her colleagues have been candid about that.[6] Sandra M. Schneiders' contention, finally, that Christianity is ultimately inhospitable to women – however debatable in itself, and indeed disputed by many female biblical scholars – is another such evidence of sober reflection on the central problem:

> The established fact that Jesus' preferred address for God was 'Abba,' the caritative form of 'Father,' raises two questions. Did Jesus experience God and therefore present God as exclusively masculine? Did Jesus intend to present God in patriarchal terms? If the answer to either question is affirmative, the New Testament has little to offer to women.[7]

Academically, the usual *bête noir* theologian for Schneiders and others is Joachim Jeremias.[8] The hermeneutic implications of their opposition to Jeremias and his ilk, perhaps needless to say, cut a much wider swath. Scholarship in hermeneutics in the last two or three decades has done much to help us recognize that the sort of exegesis which attempts to get at the meaning a text had for its author is not determinative for the sort of interpretation which the 'horizon' of a contemporary reader may unavoidably colour. It is clear that none of us are innocent of local colour in our imaginations concerning anything – even texts in which, to the exegete, there is an astonishing degree of perspicuity.[9] Nor is all of this coloration without redeeming virtue. And most Christians would want to insist that the Holy Spirit still speaks to the church, that there is thus a correlative authority to the authority of Scripture in the magisterial teaching of the historic church. But what about situations in which, all hermeneutic operations of credible reason having been vested, there still appears such contradiction to source texts as cannot, without the most radical sort of sophistry or denial, be rationalized to the text? Such, I think, is the actual situation of moment that confronts creedal orthodoxy, evangelical and Catholic, concerning the Fatherhood of God.

---

[6] Schneiders, *Women*, 7.

[7] Ibid., 37.

[8] Jeremias, *Abba*.

[9] Charting this territory two decades ago was Thiselton, *Two Horizons* – still a useful book.

Hermeneutic and Translation

In an earlier article on inclusive language I tried to show how the biblical doc-trine of the Fatherhood of God is even more central to Christian identity than it was to faithful Jewish identity.[10] It had seemed to me then that attacks upon the naming of God as Father – including those which attempt to reduce this central plank of biblical theology to a prejudiced cultural metaphor which sup-posedly 'excludes' women – were, in principle at least, attacks on two indis-pensable foundations of Christian identity: Scripture and the traditional teaching of the universal church. I want to develop this commonsensical point further, and along a line of hermeneutic reflection to which I had not then given sufficient scope.

Let me begin by drawing attention to the obvious. The assignation of 'Mother God' or goddess vocabulary to previously Trinitarian liturgies helps to make it apparent to all concerned that what is at stake is not, as is often argued, a matter of translation. Something much deeper – and possibly more violent – is involved. In biblical scholarship there is a historical analogue for this propaedeutic violence, however, and it also manifested itself initially as merely disagreement about translation.

During the tense but outwardly civil years of the Weimar Republic in Germany (1918–33), two distinguished scholars were working on a new German translation of the Bible. They were Martin Buber (1878–1965) and Franz Rosenzweig (1886–1929). Among the most respected members of the European Jewish intellectual community, Buber and Rosenzweig were none-theless acutely aware of their vulnerability to a growing hostility to Jews and their religion. It was becoming harder and harder, for religious Jews especially, even to get their work published by mainstream publishers and journals.[11] In a scattering of articles announcing their new translation, they made many favourable comparisons and complimentary references to the German stan-dard version of Martin Luther, at least partly in a sincere effort to be diplomati-cally positive toward their Christian fellow-Germans.

In the most remarkable of these essays (1926), Franz Rosenzweig, in an evident tip of the hat to Jesus, wrote this provocative first sentence: 'Trans-lating means serving two masters. It follows that it cannot be done.'[12] He then promptly admitted the obvious dilemma: translation nevertheless *must* be done if Scripture is to be served. But (as he went on to suggest) it ought not to be done in such a way as to transfer authority from the text to the reader, to

---

[10] 'Inclusive Language'. For the full article from which this version was adapted, see Packer, ed., *Best Essays*, 135–52.

[11] Boas, 'Shrinking World'.

[12] 'Scripture and Luther'. See also the subsequent essay by Buber, 'On Word Choice'.

reduce the text merely to a mirror for the reader's own subjective or ego-determined prejudices. For then what we would have would not be, in any responsible sense of the word, a 'translation'. It would be instead a new and different book.

Rosenzweig's point applies to contemporary attempts to present biblical and liturgical revision as 'new translations'. In many cases such revision is rather a matter of creating new textual authority, rewriting Scripture and the creeds so as to give some of those uncomfortable with these texts new means to assert and establish institutional control or, to put it in the more familiar way, to 'develop doctrine'. The actual question at issue here, as Humpty-Dumpty famously said to Alice, is about 'which is to be master – that's all'.

As Buber and Rosenzweig were working on their translation, German Lutherans were likewise occupied. In this instance the most visible bugaboo was not gender but race. A notable reluctance to use the words 'Jew' and 'Israel' had begun to be evident in the German church in the early years of the Nazi era. It expressed itself in the de-Judaizing of biblical language in the liturgy and hymns, in changing worship references from 'Jews' to 'people of God', and in eschewing readings which made the Jewish identity of the 'chosen' people too transparent to disguise by 're-translation' alone. This felonious and often fraudulent strategy had, predictably enough, voluminous academic defence. The ploy, as Wolfhart Pannenberg has observed, was already an old one – insistence that religious language was in any case simply a projection of prevalent social experience onto images of divinity. On this view, whether or not anything accountable to the plausible meaning in the original text was left, change in social conditions would require a change in religious language. (Feuerbach, Nietzsche and Heidegger were often cited as philosophical authorities who justified such a move).[13]

What we are now experiencing is essentially the same phenomenon. In Pannenberg's terse summary, 'As the Nazi Germans were bothered by Jesus' Jewishness, so are our contemporary feminists bothered by the contingency of language about God as father.'[14] In both cases, and for similar reasons, response to the irritation which takes the form of erasure of the offensive 'name' is an act of propaedeutic linguistic violence. It portends further degradation of status, legalized or institutionalized opprobrium, and the potential for other kinds of attack.

Of course I do not mean to say that every German professor or pastor saw it that way from the beginning. It is entirely probable that many among those who wished the words 'Jew' and 'Israel' to disappear from worship and the biblical record would have insisted, in 1933, that nothing in what they were

---

[13] See Keller, *Religion*, 103ff. Also the comments by Pannenberg, 'Feminine Language?'.
[14] Pannenberg, 'Feminine Language?', 29.

doing was preparing the public for acquiescence in the annihilation of Jews. Their claim, after all, was that the changes simply made the text 'more inclusive'.

Consciousness and Conscience

We need not press this analogy to the limit. Rather, I would simply ask a brief series of plausibly connected – albeit contentious – questions, the answers to which, I think, are by now both evident and constructively provocative. Why, in our own tremulous time, does the idea of fatherhood – especially of a goodly, godly, and finally a divinely modelled exemplar of fatherhood – excite such hostility among would-be revisers of Christianity? Why is it that those made angry, sometimes angry enough to wish annihilation of any vestige of worthy images of fatherhood, imagine that what we need as a replacement exemplar of positive authority is a 'mother goddess' – a figure whose religious tradition in every non-biblical culture is that of 'fertility worship'? And which has, as its typical concomitant, fertility sacrifice – the sacrifice of children?

These are, of course, elaborations of one question. The answers most often given, and credibly so, point to the poor record of human fatherhood in our recent past, even among Christians. Few will deny that the flight from responsibility and the incidence of even predatory cruelty on the part of many fathers has been a direct cause of a more general rejection of the institution of fatherhood. Indeed, one may wonder if such 'bad' fathers have not presaged our present crisis by rejecting the biblical relationship of sexuality to parenthood long before they became fathers.[15] If so, that this too is a pre-textual condition with hermeneutic implications should be apparent.

Let us then approach the stumbling block in a somewhat more tentative way. Might it be that responsible fatherhood constitutes a framework of circumspection, perhaps particularly sexual circumspection? Is it possible that part of the reason that fatherhood is under attack is not just the actual plague of irresponsible fathers, but that fatherhood *per se* is seen as a species of authority that, in its highest exemplar, the Fatherhood of God, implies a limit, even a tacit limit contrary to our culture's most cherished credo – that sexual autonomy is the highest human good? Is it not the case that what rampant sexual appetite wants, and what *un*circumscribed sexuality, in attempting to legitimate itself, tries to achieve, is what Freud reasonably characterized as 'the death of the Father'? Death of the Father (Freud), death of the Author

---

[15] See here Miller, *Calling God 'Father'*, esp. chs. 5 and 10, with which I am substantially in agreement.

(Barthes), death of God (Nietzsche and a great chorus of seminarians) – are they not, in spiritual terms, diverse manifestations of a common impulse?[16]

But this is not a Christian impulse. In none of its manifestations, whatever flimsy garb of institutional propinquity it wears, is it capable of bowing the knee to God the Father or to Jesus Christ his only-begotten Son. If it appears to do so, it will be in pretence – at its most unwitting a self-deception, at its most informed and articulate a cynical deception of others. And nowhere, in the church or out of it, will we be immune to confusion about what is really being worshipped – or, to put it more clearly, what is being obeyed. For the issue here, both ecclesial and hermeneutic, is quite precisely the issue of authority and as such it is, strictly speaking, a matter neither of sex nor of gender, but rather of role.

On what authority may we dare to reflect upon the deeper motives of revisers and, as it may seem on occasion, disguisers, of biblical language? After all, many of the most flagrant of such revisers have already dismissed from their counsel the teaching authority of the historic church, and that on principles they declare to be non-negotiable. In a remarkably large number of cases, they substantially control the present institutional church, especially in Protestant-ism. Perhaps, some say, anti-authoritarians though they may be, these folk represent the authority 'set over us' in our time, and we must accept that.

Yet one authority remains by which we are obliged to ask questions about evident revision of biblical language. In the canonical or global sense, this is, of course, Scripture itself – especially when we ask out of a competence in and respect for the languages and the textual tradition of Scripture. This perspective has been the basis of a great deal of rational and, for those who have ears to hear, credible constraint upon hermeneutic and linguistic anti-authoritarianism. With varying degrees of scholarly precision, this is particularly apparent in respect of 'naming the Father'. Yet rarely in biblical textual scholarship has textual evidence proved more contentious.

It has already been shown that God is called Father more than 250 times in Scripture. We have been reminded that in Scripture God is most jealous of his

---

[16] The notion of ex-Catholic theologian and feminist Mary Daly that the emancipation of women requires the emasculation of God ('Since God is male the male is God') certainly misconstrues the Scriptures ('Qualitative', 21). But St Thomas Aquinas, commenting on the verses in Ephesians (3:14–15) which afford the epigraph for my remarks here, reminds us that the analogy or derivation in Paul is central to our sense of the meaning of *human* fatherhood. Aquinas writes: '*Fatherhood* and *generation* are superlative in God, comparative in creatures' (*Summa Theologica*, 1a.xxxiii.2). He continues, 'Now fatherhood and sonship at full strength are the Father's and the Son's who are one in nature and glory' (*ST*, 1a.xxxiii.3). It is not difficult to see that hatred for the one notion of fatherhood may entail hatred for the other.

name, and names himself, forbidding this prerogative to any other.[17] It has
been shown that in Scripture God is rarely given plausibly feminine characteristics, and that he is never called 'Mother'.[18] Masculine metaphors for God are
persistent and characteristic,[19] though not in such a manner as would give them
sexual content.[20] In fact, Yahweh proves to be unique among the deities of the
universally patriarchal cultures of the ancient Near East (even those which
practised goddess worship were culturally patriarchal) in that he is not *sexually*
male.[21] His fatherhood over us is, notably, by adoption – a point definitive for
Paul's understanding of Christ, as well as for Jesus' self-understanding as the
Christ.[22] We have seen that feminist metaphors for God, by contrast, especially
when used in the context of 'goddess' language, can ironically replace non-
sexist metaphors with overtly sexual, and thus sexist, ones.[23] It has also been
pointed out, and frequently, that for some the real agenda in much of this conflict over interpretation, translation and the language of worship is a repudia-
tion of the Bible as the authority above all authorities of Christian life as well as
for patterns of worship.[24] The critical strength of these arguments by biblical
scholars and theologians is not wanting. Yet their lack of influence upon all but
the 'converted' so to speak – even within the church – has been a source of
frustration and discouragement to them and, one gathers, to others.

---

[17] See Bloesch, *Battle*, who anchors his entire argument on this point. A fine supplement to Bloesch, from a linguistic point of view, is Mankowski, 'Necessary Failure'.
For another Catholic analysis, relating the Exodus 20 passage to the first article of the
historic creeds, see Pastor, 'Credo'.

[18] Bloesch, *Battle*; Pannenberg, 'Feminine Language?'; Achtemeier, 'Review'; also
Hook and Kimel, 'Pronouns'; and Podles, *Church Impotent*.

[19] Bloesch, *Battle*; Achtemeier, 'Review'.

[20] See '1992 Synod Summary: Language, Gender, and God'; see also Frye, 'Language'.
From a Catholic perspective, Reardon, 'Father', shows how Aquinas among others
utterly rejects the idea that 'Father' is metaphor: '... classifying the Father's proper name
as only metaphorical is not in practice at least to explain it; it is rather to explain it away.
It makes God's revelation nothing more than a restatement of our ignorance of him, so
that we are back where we started, as though there never had been a divine revelation
in Jesus Christ' (146). This seems to me to be the decisive point.

[21] Bloesch, *Battle*, *passim*; Frye, 'Language', 8.

[22] Rom. 8 – 9:8; Gal. 4:4–7; Eph. 1:5. See here the fine article by Thompson, 'Mercy';
as well as her *Promise of the Father*; also Kereszty, 'God the Father'; and Widdicombe,
Fatherhood of God, who shows in ch. 11 how adoption is *the* issue among the early
Church Fathers.

[23] Frye, 'Language', 8.

[24] For Paul Ricœur, the terms 'Father' and 'Son' are part of the fundamental symbolism of Christianity. They are performative terms which make possible (cf. Rom. 8 – 9)
our being Christian. See his *Conflict in Interpretation*, 487–91; cf. Bloesch, *Battle*; Frye,
'Language'; Jeffrey, 'Inclusive Language'.

Why has this scholarship been so ineffective? In my own view, part of the frustration for many involved in the ecclesial aspect of this debate has occurred because of a tacit concession that the dispute can be engaged as a matter internal to the church. That is, we have not been as clear-minded about this as many of our feminist interlocutors. We have tended to regard the prolonged debate, often out of politeness as well as a commitment to practical charity, as yet another example of conflict in interpretation among faithful believers. But neither hermeneutically speaking nor theologically speaking is this issue now accurately so represented. It is not finally comparable to disagreements over ecclesial practice for ordering the understanding of sacraments, for example, or to differences concerning our sense of the role of human freedom in responding to God's offer of grace in Christ. For if the teaching of Jesus is to have any authority, acceptance of the Fatherhood of God becomes a matter of definitive discrimination between those who may in any meaningful sense be called Christian and those who, however religious in their reasoning and practice, are not in the most crucial of matters following Christ. Unambiguous acceptance of the Fatherhood of God, I want to say here (to this extent in agreement with Schneiders and others), is not open to revision by those who would be Christian because it is, unambiguously, the central and persistent teaching of Jesus *about* God, and the transparent mode of his own relationship *to* God.

Textual Consistency

Narrative analysis of the Gospel of Matthew alone makes it impossible that we should construe resistance to biblical characterization of God as Father to be motivated by a Christian impulse. From the account of Jesus' own baptism, where the words of institution are pronounced by the Father from heaven in such a way as to confirm that Jesus is the Son in whom he is well pleased (Mt. 3:17), to the Great Commission in which Jesus commands his followers to go into the world and to teach all nations, baptizing them in the name of the Father, Son and Holy Spirit (Mt. 28:19), there is evident consistency on this matter in the life and teaching of the Lord.

His teaching actually begins with Jesus identifying his faithful ones as children of the Father – those who will take up his cross so as to love their enemies and do good to those who hate them (5:44) will by this obedience be filiated to God as Father. Obedience is required so 'that you may be sons of your Father in Heaven' (5:43), and radical obedience is not less high in its imitative aims than filial resemblance: 'Therefore you shall be perfect, even as your Father in heaven is perfect' (5:48). Our heavenly Father is, Jesus assures us on the basis of his own matchless intimacy with him, so deeply caring that he is aware of the needs of his children before they ask (6:18). If he provides for the creatures of his world (6:26), how much more his own children (6:32)? What the children of the heavenly Father are to seek most from him is not these natural gifts of his providence, however, but 'first the kingdom of God and his righteousness'. This too is a condition of accountable hermeneutic and reading practice where Scripture is concerned. After all, Jesus says, 'not every one who says to me "Lord, Lord" shall enter the kingdom of heaven, but he who does the will of my Father in heaven' (7:21).

Much is said in the preambles of the inclusive lectionaries and new worship books about 'the movement of the Spirit'. What Jesus tells his disciples about the Holy Spirit is that, at moments when their own words cannot persuade those who would mislead or condemn them, then it will be the 'Spirit of your Father who speaks in you' (10:20). This speaking will clearly be to point to the authority of Jesus as true Son of the Father. Accordingly, 'whoever confesses me before men, him will I also confess before my Father who is in heaven' (10:32). However scandalous it appears to our judgement, whoever denies Jesus in so many words, that person Jesus will deny (disclaim) before his 'Father which is in heaven' (10:33). When we are told that the 'Spirit speaking in our times' requires evident contradiction to the Spirit of the Father who Jesus assured us would speak to his faithful always, we are at a point where application of the apostolic injunction is urgently necessary: 'Beloved, do not believe every spirit, but test the spirits [to see] whether they are of God' (1 Jn. 4:1).

It can be an irritation, understandably, to those who present themselves as more intelligent or, because of certain learning, more wise than others, that recognition of the truth of Scripture and authority of Jesus is not theirs alone to control. Jesus prayed, 'I thank You, Father, Lord of heaven and earth, that You have hidden these things from the wise and prudent, and revealed them unto babes' (11:25). It is not only within Free Church traditions that this passage has been taken as a caution against contradicting theological *droit de seigneur*. No Christian who is thinking straight ought to be bent away from the teaching authority of Jesus or the witness of Scripture at any point merely by the educational credentials, cleverness or institutional prominence of an evidently contradicting authority. (Nor by an autobiographical assertion of 'bad associations' or personal woundedness, however these may most legitimately prompt our compassion.) Moreover, we ought to be zealous to protect children in particular from the religious abuse, however 'well intended', of those who would usurp Jesus' guidance concerning the trustworthiness of their heavenly Father. Children may grasp the value of God's Fatherhood more truly than anyone. 'Take heed,' he says to us, 'that you do not despise one of these little ones, for I say to you that in heaven their angels always see the face of my Father who is in heaven' (18:10).

If it is true that in this world no one truly knows the Father but the Son, nor truly knows the Son but the Father (11:27), it is nevertheless also the reward of those who are faithful that their righteousness will one day 'shine forth as the sun in the kingdom of their Father' (13:43). In the meantime, all in the church are bound in a reciprocal covenant with the Father through Jesus. This covenant entitles us to his care in the world, but it is also a covenant by which we will be judged in the next (18:19, 35). It is in the Father's disposition alone to reward the faithful (20:23). When we pray, as Jesus taught us, 'Our Father which art in heaven', we pray to be conformed to the will of the Father – so perfectly accommodated to that will that we accept that our own forgiveness is conditional upon our reflecting his forgiveness in our dealings with others (6:9–15; cf. 18:21–35). Jesus is serious about our loving our enemies. Recrimination against our ecclesiastical opponents is thus also a clear violation of his principle.

Textual Cues

Let's return then to my main point, which I have posed as a question. Do we have any hermeneutic basis, any authority, for resisting resisters of Jesus?

> Now when He came into the temple, the chief priests and the elders of the people confronted Him as He was teaching, and said, 'By what authority are You doing these things? And who gave You this authority?' But Jesus answered and said to them, 'I also will ask you one thing, which if you tell Me, I likewise will tell you by what authority I do these things: "The baptism of John – where was it from? From heaven or from men?" ' And they reasoned among themselves, saying, 'If we say, "From heaven" He will say to us, "Why then did you not believe him?" But if we say, "From men," we fear the multitude, for all count John as a prophet.'
>
> So they answered Jesus and said, 'We do not know.' And He said to them, 'Neither will I tell you by what authority I do these things.'
> (Mt. 21:23–27)

We ought most diligently to study what Jesus was doing here. There is always going to be debate (human wilfulness being what it is) between those who see religious belief and practice in terms of revelation and those who want to see it in terms of the projection of evolving social consciousness, particularly their own consciousness. There is nothing novel, historically speaking, in the predicament of this moment in the western Christian church. Ours is a recurrent symptom of a systemic spiritual decadence or deviance, and it affects us in many more ways than in the issue here under discussion.

The decisive point is engaged in the parable that Jesus tells immediately following this challenge to his authority. Here is a story of two sons, one of whom is quick (and perhaps glib) to proclaim his allegiance to do the will of his father. The other son is resistant to the point of initial denial of his father's will.

Nevertheless, in the end, the one who readily proclaims his vocation fails to work in the vineyard of his father (we are not told what he was doing instead). The resistant son surprises us by repenting and fulfilling the call of his father. When Jesus asks 'which of the two did the will of the Father' (21:31), he is asking about actual obedience, not about the verbalization of piety. This word is a sword that cuts two ways.

Either way, the issue of obedience remains. Jesus is not ambiguous in his claim that his own authority derives from his Father, rather than from his creative imagination or from a projection of some social or political pragmatism.[25] That he is the Son of God, not just a man among men, is the essence of his rebuke to the Pharisees (22:45). We are to call no one but the Father 'father' in this religious sense, 'for One is your Father, who is in Heaven' (23:9). And in these matters there is a judgement coming that is not a matter of either social consciousness or human politics. On that day (which moment only the Father knows [24:26]), those who have accepted the revealed authority of Jesus concerning the Father's gift of reconciliation through him – and who persevere in obedience to the will of God – will hear the words, 'Come ye blessed of my Father' (25:24).[26] Others, presumably, will not on that day have such a Father.

At the Last Supper (26:20–29), in Gethsemane (26:39–42), as in the great prayer of Jesus recorded in John 17, it is his own obedience to the Father which characterizes everything that his atoning sacrifice means. He prays specifically that, on the witness given by the Father, we shall be united to him and the Father in love and faithfulness. This same Jesus whose prerogative it was to summon from his Father legions of angels to smite his oppressors, chose in obedience rather to be faithful to the Father's will in sacrificing his life. Nowhere do we see that he made that issue, or any language concerning it, a matter for 'comfort zone' compromise.

---

[25] Some have wanted the text to be much more ambiguous than it is on any rational construal. An example is Wainwright's *Toward a Feminist Critical Reading of the Gospel*. Wainwright's strategy is largely to eschew commentary on most of the Matthew texts I have cited (e.g., 336). When she does comment upon one, e.g., Mt. 12:50, she simply begs the question (98–99) and defies the integrity of the text attributed to Jesus by reducing it to a mere affirmation of inclusivity. What Jesus is recorded as saying, most evidently, is a description of the adoptive filiation by which obedience to the will of the Father makes those who obey 'kin' to Jesus himself.

[26] In the powerfully suggestive 'theodramaturgy' of Balthasar, *Glory of the Lord*, VII, the Father's omnipotence is revealed dramatically but ironically in his making the expression of his paternal love dependent upon the Son's obedience. In adoption, this Fatherhood 'by assent', through a willed acceptance of the Father's authority, is held out to us. See also the good discussion of Balthasar in Turek, 'As the Father'.

I do not wish to suggest that there is not a great deal more that might be said on this subject. Clearly there is, and I myself would be grateful for it, especially for that which in the spirit of fraternal correction would point my own heart and mind to a more accurate obedience. What I do mean to say is that, so far as I can tell, for a Christian – one who would follow Christ in his teaching and in his example (cf. Lk. 9:23) – the authority of Jesus concerning the Fatherhood of God is irrefragable authority. Opposition to it is not therefore an intramural debate, and we must learn, as graciously and yet as clear-mindedly as possible, to acknowledge that.

The perennial problem of translation – which is to say, interpretation – is inextricable from the question of authority. Franz Rosenzweig's dictum about tension in translation is helpful in that it declares not against the possibility of translation, but against any imagination that we can avoid in such work the choice of 'which is to be master'. Or, rather, Master.

Conclusion

Let me conclude with a brief observation and summary. Striking a note of dissonance, even in the social consciousness of our time, two most improbable recordings appeared at the top of the pop music charts in Europe and Britain in 1999 – the CD 'Abba Pater' (with Pope John Paul II chanting prayers) and Cliff Richard's phenomenally successful 'Millennium Prayer' (a version of 'Our Father Who Art in Heaven' sung to the tune 'Auld Lang Syne'). At the turn of the millennium, from out of the vast unchurched proletarian ranks (especially the ranks of the young) there seems to have come, as it were unbidden, some sort of deep yearning for ultimate Fatherhood. Have the makers of the new lectionaries noticed this cultural phenomenon?

Even if they have, one may reasonably doubt that it will much alter their particular altar. There is now a substantial, if ageing, vested interest in feminized prayers, deities and priestly vestments. Institutionally, there has come about a *de facto* 'development of doctrine' (*pace* Newman) for which a tradition of sorts has been established, and with it the anxious jealousies of institutional prerogative. In most North American churches committed to the inclusive lectionary, the feminizing of God and erasure of the actual language of Jesus has after all been consistently and persistently part of a larger disenfranchisement of what has come to be regarded as an inflexibility in biblical teaching. Historically, the desire for a 'softening' of biblical language appeared first in the seminaries and only then in the pulpits. Avoidance of language which invokes the presence or idea of authority – whether textual, theological or ethical – has been a principal preoccupation in biblical and theological studies, just as it has in education, politics and ethics in the secular sphere. Discomfort with Father language in particular closely mirrors gender warfare and generational conflict in the secular culture, notably and at least initially, as voiced among intellectual elites in the West. (It is certainly not a universal phenomenon.) Yet response to 'comfort zones' in the culture concerning these issues is so strongly at odds with both the language and the self-characterization of Jesus as Son of God the Father that the theological dissonance is no longer able to be harmonized either by rhetoric or by diplomacy. Visible discrepancy between the two nomenclatures confounds, creating an intellectual barrier to coherent thought about Scripture that, in my opinion, must be overcome if the project of a rich and accountable biblical hermeneutic is not itself to become incoherent.

That which rejects the overwhelming teaching of Jesus, I think we must be prepared to concede, is anti-Christ, not Christian. It may hurt us to admit it, but not to admit it would be to deceive ourselves and others. Goddess religion, for example, is certainly religion. But it is not Christian religion, nor can it be made to cohabit with it without spiritual adultery. The incorporation of mother-god language and the corresponding deletion of the Fatherhood of God from the prayer life and hymnody of any church will make of those who use that language refusers of the teaching authority of Jesus. On *his* authority, such refusal is a matter of the gravest consequences for those who so choose.

How can academic theologians and biblical scholars best help those who seem prone to be led in this path to consider the consequences? By faithfully pointing them again and again to the words of Jesus. It is his authority which is decisively the basis for our adoption by the Father, and it is on his authority that we have the means to recognize those who would (and those who would not) seek membership in his family in such terms as he has offered. 'Whosoever shall do the will of my Father which is in heaven,' said Jesus, 'the same is my brother and sister and mother' (Mt. 12:50). That makes the conditions of our inclusion, academic theologian and layperson alike, clear enough.

Bibliography

'1992 Synod Summary: Language, Gender, and God', *Year Book of the Diocese of Sydney* (Sydney, Australia, 1993), 446–63

Achtemeier, E., 'Review of *An Inclusive Language Lectionary*', *Interpretation* 38 (1984), 64–66

Balthasar, H. Urs von, *The Glory of the Lord*, VII (San Francisco: Ignatius Press, 1989)

Bloesch, D.G., *The Battle for the Trinity: The Debate over Inclusive God-Language* (Ann Arbor: Servant Publications, 1985)

Boas, J., 'The Shrinking World of German Jewry, 1933–1938,' in *Leo Baeck Institute Yearbook* 31 (1986), 241–44

Buber, M., 'On Word Choice in Translating the Bible: In Memoriam Franz Rosenzweig', in *Scripture and Translation* (trans. L. Rosenwald, with E. Fox; Bloomington, IN: Indiana University Press, 1994), 73–89

Daly, M., 'The Qualitative Leap Beyond Patriarchal Religion', *Quest* 1 (Spring 1975), 20–40

Dell'Olio, A.J., 'Why Not God the Mother?', *Faith and Philosophy* 15.2 (1998), 193–209

Frye, R.M., 'Language of God and Feminist Language', *Reports from the Center of Theological Inquiry*, no. 3 (Princeton: Princeton Seminary Publications, 1988), 1–25.

Hook, D.D. and A.A. Kimel, Jr., 'The Pronouns of Deity: A Theological Critique of Feminist Proposals', *SJT* 46 (1993), 297–323

Jeffrey, D.L., 'Inclusive Language and Worship', *JBMW* 4.2–3 (2000), 10–16

Jeremias, J., *Abba: Studien zur neutestamentlichen Theologie und Zeitgeschicte* (Göttingen: Vandenhoeck & Ruprecht, 1966)

Keller, A., *Religion and the European Mind* (London: SPCK, 1934)

Kereszty, R., 'God the Father', *Communio* 26 (1999), 258–77

Mankowski, P., SJ, 'The Necessary Failure of Inclusive Language Translations: A Linguistic Elucidation', *The Thomist* 62 (1998), 445–68

Miller, J.W., *Calling God 'Father': Essays on the Bible, Fatherhood, and Culture* (New York: Paulist Press, 1999)

Packer, J.I. (ed.), *Best Essays in Theology: 1988* (Chicago: CT Publications, 1989)

Pannenberg, W., 'Feminine Language About God?', *The Ashbury Theological Journal* 48.2 (1993), 27–29

Pastor, F.-A., SJ, ' "Credo in Deum Patrum": sul primo articolo della fede', *Gregorianum* 80.3 (1999), 469–88

Podles, L.J., *The Church Impotent: The Feminization of Christianity* (Dallas: Spence, 1999)

Reardon, P.H., 'Father, Glorify Thy Name', *Pro Ecclesia* 7 (1998), 138–51

Ricœur, P., *Conflict in Interpretation* (trans. D. Ihde; Evanston, IL: Northwestern University Press, 1974)

Rosenzweig, F., 'Scripture and Luther', in M. Buber and F. Rosenzweig, *Scripture and Translation* (trans. L. Rosenwald, with E. Fox; Bloomington, IN: Indiana University Press, 1994), 47–72

Rushdie, S., *Midnight's Children* (London: Jonathan Cape, 1981)

Schneiders, S.M., *Women and the Word: The Gender of God in the New Testament and the Spirituality of Women* (New York: Paulist Press, 1986)

Schüssler Fiorenza, E., *JESUS: Miriam's Child, Sophia's Prophet: Critical Issues in Feminist Theology* (New York: Continuum, 1994)

Thiselton, A.C., *The Two Horizons: New Testament Hermeneutics and Philosophical Description with Special Reference to Heidegger, Bultmann, Gadamer, and Wittgenstein* (Exeter: Paternoster; Grand Rapids: Eerdmans, 1980)

Thompson, M.M., ' "Mercy upon All": God as Father in the Epistle to the Romans', in *Romans and the People of God: A Festschrift for Gordon Fee in Honor of his 65th Birthday* (ed. S.K. Soderlund; Grand Rapids: Eerdmans, 1999), 203–16

—, *The Promise of the Father: Jesus and God in the New Testament* (Louisville: Westminster John Knox Press, 2000)

Toscano, M.M., 'If I Hate My Mother, Can I Love the Heavenly Mother? Personal Identity, Personal Relationships, and Perceptions of God', *Dialogue* 31.4 (1998), 31–51

Turek, M.M., ' "As the Father has Loved Me" (Jn. 15:9): Balthasar's Theodramatic Approach to a Theology of God the Father', *Communio* 26 (1999), 295–318

Vigano, A., *God our Father/Mother* (London: St Paul's, 1999)

Wainwright, E.M., *Towards a Feminist Critical Reading of the Gospel According to Matthew* (Berlin, New York: de Gruyter, 1991)

Widdicombe, P., *The Fatherhood of God from Origen to Athanasius* (Oxford: Clarendon Press, 1994)

13

Back to Babel – That Confounded Language Again

A Response to David L. Jeffrey

Kathryn Greene-McCreight

To God be the glory, great things He hath done,
So loved He the world that He gave us His Son,
Who yielded His life an atonement for sin,
And opened the Lifegate that all may go in.
Praise the Lord, Praise the Lord!
Let the earth hear His voice!
Praise the Lord, Praise the Lord!
Let the people rejoice!
O come to the Father through Jesus the Son,
And give Him the glory, great things He hath done.

This is the hymn that closed our worship on Sunday at St John's, New Haven.
An old chestnut. Certainly one that could not be used in a politically correct
congregation, for all of its masculine language. And what a pity, for this hymn is
grand: 'Great things He hath taught us, great things He hath done, and great our
rejoicing thro' Jesus the Son; but purer and higher and greater will be Our
wonder, our transport, when Jesus we see ...' A quintessentially revivalist hymn.

In his article on 'Naming the Father,' David Lyle Jeffrey makes reference to
another 'hymn', this one more contemporary, a nouveau-revivalist one might
say.[1] Bobby McFerrin's hauntingly beautiful rendition of the Twenty-Third

---

[1] It is hard to imagine the other songs which Jeffrey mentioned hitting the top of the pop
music charts in the USA. The coasts which control the music industry, indeed the cities
which largely control the music and television industries in the US, Los Angeles

Psalm has become popular among feminist Christians and neo-pagans who want to reach out for the feminine Divine. The psalm opens traditionally, moving on to using female pronouns in reference to the Lord: 'The Lord is my Shepherd, I shall not want, She makes me to lie down in green pastures, She leads me besides still waters, She restores my soul ...' and closes with a feminine Trinitarian doxology. This setting of the psalm was used several years ago at Yale Divinity School when Henri Nouwen preached his last sermon there. After the service, the women who had organized the music were in the hallway outside of the chapel gleefully proclaiming how 'controversial' the psalm had been. This is instructive. Whereas the first hymn is meant for praise, the second in this instance was meant to make a point, to teach that women have power to name God the way they want regardless of whom they will offend or whom they will please.

It appears that Jeffrey does not approve of such tampering with pronouns, and yet he is not immediately explicit as to the whys and wherefores of his dis-approval. He does say that the 'biblical doctrine of the Fatherhood of God is ... central to Christian identity' and that to negotiate around (he uses the more aggressive word 'attack') the fatherhood of God is to weaken the foundational status of Scripture and tradition for Christian theology. While not immediately apparent as an issue in the McFerrin psalm, this is a serious charge, and one worth listening to. To those who would prefer to erase Father language for God, or who would substitute ways of naming God other than Father, Jeffrey would say that specifically naming God as Father is biblical, and as such it is foundational to Christian identity in a way that no other name can fill in for or substitute. And where Jeffrey would say that erasing Father language is an attack on Scripture and tradition one can imagine one group of his interlocu-tors, at least some of his truly honest ones, saying a hearty 'Amen'.

But now, let us play the devil's advocate. Let us for a moment say that attacks on the naming of God as Father are in fact biblical. Let us argue that such attacks allow us to see God as truly God is, freed from the shackles of patriarchy. Instead of God the Father, we might say God the Parent, or better still, God the Mother. What can be so wrong with this? What is wrong, after all, with expanding the metaphors for God, with widening our expressions for God's wondrous working in our midst?

I can imagine that Dr Jeffrey might say that the problem lies not necessarily in the expansion but more in the constriction and, more importantly, the substitution of the modes, which themselves are divinely taught. That the

---

[1] (*Continued*) and New York, are overwhelmingly secular and it is almost unthinkable that 'Abba Pater' with Pope John Paul II chanting prayers or 'Millennium Prayer' would ever make it out of a studio in the United States. Maybe Britain is more religious than we thought. Bobby McFerrin's appeal is reggae, not Christian per se.

Fatherhood of God is, after all, instructed by our Lord rather than simply a social construct is crucial to Jeffrey's argument. This is the key to Jesus' response to the chief priests and elders who are questioning him about his authority – whether it is from God or from humans. In Matthew 21, Jesus is asked by whose authority he teaches, and he returns the question in good rabbinic style with a question. He tells the chief priests and rabbis that if they answer his question he will answer theirs. By whose authority, heaven's or earth's, was the baptism of John? This, of course, sets the chief priests and elders into a tizzy, because they know the people believe that John was a prophet, but if they say that he was from God, Jesus will ask them why they didn't follow him, but if they say his authority was just earthly, the people will be upset. So they answered shrewdly that they did not know, and Jesus returned the same answer.

Here Jeffrey says,

> There is always going to be debate (human wilfulness being what it is) between those who see religious belief and practice in terms of revelation and those who want to see it in terms of the projection of evolving social consciousness, particularly their own consciousness. There is nothing novel, historically speaking, in the predicament of this moment in the western Christian church. Ours is a recurrent symptom of a systemic spiritual decadence ...

But is this so? Are we really in the same position as the chief priests and elders who question Jesus' authority? On the one hand, yes. We always have those who doubt Jesus' divine authority with us. We always have those with us who see it, as Jeffrey says, 'in terms of the projection of evolving social consciousness'. Yet even here this is different from Matthew's apparent situation. The chief priests and elders were the outsiders to Matthew's community of believers. They were precisely the unbelievers. But now we find the unbelievers within our community, indeed at times even the leaders of our ecclesial bodies, the ones telling us what to say and when to say it and what we must mean by it.

Back to the question of naming the Father, because it does follow immediately from this problem of where we assign authority, to the human or to the divine. I would like to submit a small thesis with regard to God-language. And here I do mean specifically God-language, not language regarding people, for these are, theologically speaking, two entirely different problems. In language regarding people the matter of sexism is indeed a burning issue. But my small thesis does not include language regarding people. My thesis is that at stake in our attempts to inclusivize God-language is rarely if ever a simple matter of sexism. Rather, they are more often driven by the sinking assumption, whether consciously or subliminally grasped, that Feuerbach was right: God is indeed the projection of ourselves onto a cosmic screen. If Feuerbach was right, and patriarchy rules, then by all means, inclusivizing a patriarchal god may help to tumble the wall of patriarchal structures here on earth. Many good souls are convinced that sexism is indeed at the core of the attempts at and debates over inclusive language and feminist theologies. Men have had the power to project themselves onto that cosmic screen, and now women should have a turn. Many good souls, with noble intentions, passionately set out to change liturgies, Scripture and hymns – all so they are not masculine poison to God's holy name. If God really is 'man writ large', as Feuerbach believed, then women indeed should worry about their well-being. If God really is patriarchy inscribed on the celestial screen, then women had better use all the power in their hands to re-inscribe the goddess.

But if Feuerbach was not correct, the possibility exists that there could conceivably be no need to inclusivize God-language at all – just human language which does bear marks of sexism. 'Father' language for God may actually say something about God that 'Mother' language cannot say, or simply does not say. God as Father may actually say something on its own, apart from patriarchy, apart from sexism, insofar as it would not be a projection of the human male self onto the divine screen, to be 'healed' by the projection of the human female self onto the divine screen. The possibility exists that our language could really be healed of its divisions, a true Pentecost, rather than scattered into so many Babel divisions, my offences and yours.

What then would come of our attempts to perfect our devotion in inclusivizing? To purify our liturgies? To cleanse our language? What would be the theological status of these ceaseless rounds of trying on our own to approach God with clean tongues and a pure heart, as if we could somehow get ourselves there by tweaking the pronouns and gutting the genders? The ghost of Pelagius, who had such overwhelming confidence in the human capacity to reach out in love to the divine, is always with us. But it does seem that the ghost of Pelagius is especially present in our day – at least in this one instance where we assume that Feuerbach was right. And thus the question from the chief priests and rabbis from Matthew 21 resurfaces: by whose authority Jesus? Ironically, if we say 'humans', we have cut ourselves off from any power to redeem us from patriarchy. On the other hand, if we say 'From the Father', we know we have a mediator powerful to save.

O come to the Father through Jesus the Son
And give Him the glory, great things He hath done!

14

On Bible Translation and Hermeneutics

Raymond C. Van Leeuwen

Christians read the Bible as God's Word. But few of them, including ministers of that Word, read it in Hebrew, Aramaic and Greek – its original languages. Muslims, on the other hand, universally study Arabic to read the Koran. And Jews learn Hebrew, at least for *bar mitzvah*, and have revived spoken Hebrew as the *Umgangssprache* of an entire nation. But we Christians read translations, a myriad of translations – all of them called Holy Bible, though the holy words do not all agree. In consequence, the very words of Scripture seem to matter less and less.

This paper is in part a meditation on the untranslatable proverb, *Traduttore, Traditore – Translator, Traitor,*[1] in part a reflection on the type of book we translate as Bible, in part an appeal to reform our notions of the Bible translator's task. Throughout, it is an urgent call to return to the linguistic sources of Christian faith and to a perpetual renewal of Christian preaching and commentary – because translation is necessary, but never enough.

My thesis is that the dominance of 'functional equivalence' in Bible translation urgently needs supplementation by translations that are more direct and transparent to the original languages. It should be said at the outset that translations serve a variety of purposes and audiences. Thus there should be a variety of types of translations.[2] My concern is that *one* type of translation has come to

---

[1] Ironically, *Webster's Third New International Dictionary* defines the obsolete English 'traditor' as 'traitor' and secondly as 'one of the Christians giving up to the officers of the law the Scriptures, the sacred vessels, or the names of their brethren during the Roman persecutions'. The English cognate of *Traduttore*, 'traducer', draws out some of the pejorative connotations of translation.

[2] For example, it makes sense to 'distinguish between translations where the translator is free to elaborate or summarize and those where he has to somehow stick to the explicit contents of the original' (Gutt, *Translation*, 122).

dominate, and that dominant type of translation is less apt for Scripture in literate societies than is commonly supposed, particularly with respect to study by educated persons. Moreover, with few exceptions, the tendency to replace biblical metaphors with abstractions ill serves readers of all stripes.

The translator's task is to negotiate the difficult tension between faithfulness to the original text and the requirement to 'make sense' in the target language. In approaching this problem, I take some cues from the 'relevance theory' of Dan Sperber and Deirdre Wilson (*Relevance*), which brings together a variety of developments in linguistics from Grice's 'implicatures' to speech-act theory and pragmatics. Central to this theory is the idea that optimal relevance or 'meaning' is produced when an utterance or text provides 'maximal contextual effects' at a 'minimal processing cost'. For example:

1) If it's raining, I won't go to the lecture this morning ...
2) It's raining ...
3) I won't go to the lecture this morning.

Sentence 2, as observation or communication, is relevant as you wake up, because it has a contextual implication for your behavior, 3.[3] The basic, mutually interactive principles may be summarized as follows:

1) Other things being equal, the greater the contextual effects, the greater the relevance.
2) Other things being equal, the smaller the processing effort, the greater the relevance.[4]

The interpretive notion of 'contextual effects' requires that the receiver or interpreter of an utterance or text possess adequate tacit or implicit, contextual and cultural assumptions. (For the example above, a culture in which lectures are given would be assumed, as well as perhaps that the student has a cold and no umbrella.) Goatly[5] sums up the required knowledge as follows:

> Information is relevant to you if it interacts with your existing beliefs/thoughts (which Sperber and Wilson call *assumptions*). [These are:]

---

[3] The example is from Goatly, *Language*, 138.

[4] Goatly, *Language*, 138 (punctuation and numbers adjusted). Compare Gutt, *Translation*, 30: 'The central claim of relevance theory is that human communication crucially creates an expectation of *optimal relevance*, that is, an expectation on the part of the hearer that his attempt at interpretation will yield *adequate contextual effects* at *minimal processing cost.*'

[5] Goatly, *Language*, 137–38.

1. Knowledge of the language system
2. Knowledge of the context: situation and co-text
3. Background schematic knowledge: factual and socio-cultural.

Put another way, the contextual effects of an utterance or text require prior knowledge on the part of the receiver or interpreter. That is, human communication presupposes existence in a *shared*, meaningful world, created and ordered by God, with enculturated contexts of meaning that enable receivers of a language act (including book or text) to infer meaning that is relevant to their existence or situation. (I use the terms 'existence' and 'situation' because I take the latter to be a subset of the former. Existence is life in the created and enculturated world and all that makes it possible, including universal and individual features.[6] Situation is a narrower concept characterized by *immediacy* of place, time and 'relevance'.) In general, the Bible is relevant to 'existence' because it describes and prescribes the 'world' ('is' and 'ought') and depicts life in a multitude of secondary genres and narratives about characters who are other than us. Moreover, the Bible (and its translations) constitute a macro-genre which is more than the sum of its parts. Only in a mediated way – hermeneutics, if you will – does it speak to our 'situations' and secondary genres (which may correspond to biblical situations and genres).

The task of translation arises because the receivers of a communication actually lack '1. Knowledge of the language system'. A translation tries to make up this lack, but it cannot, except indirectly, make up for lack of knowledge of types 2 and 3: 'Knowledge of context' and 'Background schematic knowledge'. However, if a translated text is long and rich enough, the *carefully* translated text may itself be a relatively adequate source of knowledge of types 2 and 3 above, *given the assumption of a spiral of reading and rereading* – which is how we learn the paradigmatic and syntagmatic senses of words and their referents in reading our own native languages. One learns the 'meaning' of things and words from 'living' with(in) the extended literary context. We learn that certain authors use words 'a certain way'.

In a sense, rendering a foreign text into another language is an attempt to reduce the processing cost for the reader, who does not have to take the trouble to learn a foreign language. And yet, the serious reader of a translation cannot forego the obligation of learning the text's 'world' of natural and cultural realities, its characters and world-view. In this connection, in dealing with a sacred text like the Bible, the question as to the *nature* and *mode* of the communication's relevance becomes especially acute. Is the Bible's relevance

---

[6] See O'Donovan, *Resurrection*, chs. 2 and 3, on the divinely ordered world of universal 'kinds' and 'ends' in relation to the particular or historical 'ends' of individual social entities and persons.

primarily 'existential' or 'situational' in nature?[7] That is, are the 'contextual effects' of a book like the Bible to be sought primarily in the reader's immediate situation (including his expectations concerning 'ease of processing')? Or are they to be found *indirectly* and *mediately* through long-term engagement with that other 'world' which the Bible generates over hundreds of pages? We must not only ask, 'How does the Bible generate relevance or meaning for readers?' but also, 'How can people foreign to the language and cultural world of the Bible enter into and appropriately infer meaning from it?' What factors make understanding possible? And what must the translator do and not do to make understanding possible?

Before such questions can be discussed, some caveats are in order. Translation is a very difficult task, and thanks are due to those who have mightily labored in this field, such as Eugene Nida, whom I discuss below. Most translations mingle features that range from 'functional equivalent' or 'free' to 'literal' or 'direct'. The differences among translations are generally a matter of degree, of what goals the translator strives for, and of whether the normative emphasis is on the source or the target language. There is *no* translation that is sufficient (including 'woodenly' literalistic ones, whose problems are not the focus of this paper). The church has always understood this and has supplied believers with biblical preaching and commentary by Spirit-gifted teachers and preachers (Eph. 4:11–16) who have learning in the original languages, cultures and thought modes of Scripture. Where this has not been the case, the understanding of Scripture among the people of God has suffered.

I am arguing for a type of translation that is more consistently *transparent* (a term I prefer to 'literal'), so that the original shines through it, to the extent permitted by the target language. A translator must, in a learned and aesthetically appropriate way, *use* the resources of the target language so as to maximally capture the details of the original, even if there is some increase in processing effort required on the part of readers with regard to the Bible's 'foreign' expressions and images. It is common for written works to create a context of meaning through cross-references and allusions, sometimes over very long stretches of text containing a variety of sub-genres. Here the epic, novel or Bible functions as a macro-genre. For this type of non-immediate 'contextual effect' to work in translation, translators of the Bible must be constantly aware of parallel passages, expressions and images. Where this does not happen, existential, non-immediate 'contextual effects' are obscured with damage to the text's actual message: the reader will miss what the text actually says. Awareness of secondary genres is not enough in translating Scripture.[8]

---

[7] For this distinction, see the extended parenthesis and note 6 above.

[8] Cf. de Vries, 'Bible Translation'.

Where possible, for example, metaphors and similes should be preserved in the target language and not turned into abstractions. Such metaphors and meanings can disclose themselves to all who are 'afar off' for three reasons. First, the Bible is adequate in size and repetition of crucial meaning complexes and contexts to elucidate what its key terms and metaphors mean. Second, the world which the Bible represents in its own culturally specific way is yet *one* world, created by *one* Lord, inhabited through time by *one* humanity, whose history and meaning from beginning to end are disclosed by the history of Israel in Christ.[9] Within this shared, comprehensive context, we can learn to understand the other's otherness. Third, the Scriptures themselves demand, and the Lord supplies, teachers to help the church to understand God's Word. This does not negate the individual reading of Scripture (say, by the Ethiopian eunuch), but means that members of the body need one another in their diversity of gifts, just as the Ethiopian needed Philip. Individual*istic* reading of the Bible is unbiblical.

There exists a history of Bible translation going back to the Greek LXX, the Old Latin and Vulgate, and the Syriac Peshitta and Aramaic Targums. In English, the most distinguished line of translation goes back through the RSV to the KJV and William Tyndale, who laid much of the KJV's foundation.[10] This English tradition has leaned toward what has somewhat inexactly been called 'literal translation' – that is, translating foreign words into English words and syntax in such a way as to preserve as much of the sense, style and tone of the original *as comports with the requirements of good English*. However, in the last fifty years, under the aegis of groups like the American Bible Society and the missionary Wycliffe Bible Translators, a contrary type of theory and practice has come to dominate Bible translation.[11] This theory of 'dynamic equivalence' or,

---

[9] On this second hermeneutical point, see O'Donovan, *Resurrection*, 160–62.

[10] No good translation can be 'word for word.' This is not in dispute. The dispute concerns, I think, the degree of 'directness' with which the original is translated (understanding 'directness' in Gutt's sense of rendering contextual effects with appropriate means in the target language), and in the degree to which translation interposes implicit interpretation of non-linguistic matters between the reader and the Scriptures. When this is done, Scripture no longer speaks for itself, and the reader's right to inference is curtailed. In my judgment the Tyndale/KJV tradition does this a good deal less than do virtually all recent translations in English. For instance, note the care taken by the KJV to indicate added words with italics. Ironically, close reading of the NASB, which claims to be 'literal', shows that it is often less literal than commonly supposed.

[11] I use the term 'theory' with respect to ideas or notions of translation in a non-technical sense, because there is no coherent 'theory' of translation that is generally accepted. (See Gutt, *Translation*, 1–2, who attempts to provide one.) Certain widespread principles and practices of translation may, however, be labeled with the rubric 'dynamic equivalence' or 'functional equivalence'.

more recently, 'functional equivalence' arose from missionary work involving the translation of the Bible into hundreds of languages, many of them without previous literacy.[12] This theory has also come to dominate (*de facto* if not always *de jure*) recent translations of the Bible for (mostly Western) cultures whose history of literacy spans centuries. The almost universal hegemony of this type of translation is the concern of this paper.

Consider an example of the contrast between this older tradition of translation (RSV) and the newer 'functional equivalent' type (NRSV). It illustrates the point made above about preserving metaphors and images – and also exposes a problem typical of 'literal' translations (see note 13). Here is Psalm 1:1.

> Blessed is the man
> who walks not in the counsel of the wicked,
> nor stands in the way of sinners,[13]
> nor sits in the seat of scoffers. (RSV)

A look at the Hebrew shows that this translation is not truly 'literal' (e.g., word order is not imitated, though it could have been). But it does preserve the images, so that the verbs (walk, stand, sit) instantiate a gradual move towards the immovable stasis of sin. Among other features preserved, 'the way' is a

---

[12] My focus in this paper is on the problem of translating the Bible into the languages of societies with traditions of literacy and reading. The task of creating an original translation of the Bible for a newly literate society raises issues that partly overlap and partly diverge from our present focus. But it should be noted that the theory and practice of dynamic equivalence translation grew out of the work of translating the Bible into 'aboriginal' languages, with their oral cultural context. See Nida, *Bible*.

[13] Today, when taken by itself, the expression 'to stand in the way of ...' usually suggests the idea of presenting an obstacle to someone or something. One might avoid this confusion by rendering line 3, 'nor stands *within* the way of sinners'. Solving such translational problems is a matter of linguistic sensitivity and creative artistry and cannot be taught or prescribed by rule. And yet, the problem here may be somewhat imaginary. Given the powerful parallelism of Ps. 1:1, the alert reader is able to infer that RSV 'stand in the way of ' does *not* here have its idiomatic meaning of 'present an obstacle to'. The *context* enables the reader to resolve the apparent ambiguity of the phrase. On this crucial point, see C.S. Lewis, *Studies*, 11–12. Lewis refers to 'the insulating power of the context' which enables readers to select the appropriate meaning for a word or phrase, while eliminating the word's other legitimate meanings as irrelevant. 'When we see the notice "Wines and Spirits"', says Lewis, 'we do not think about angels, devils, ghosts and fairies ...' Part of the insulating power of context in Ps. 1:1 is created by the 'formal' device of parallelism, which the translator can easily reproduce. Indeed parallelism (the paradigmatic axis of meaning according to Jakobson, 'Statements') is a universal means of generating and clarifying meaning. Note, e.g., the opening lines of T.S. Eliot's 'The Wasteland'.

biblical image (either positive or negative) that has a significant redolence all through Scripture, and profoundly portrays the journey aspect of life (cf. Jn. 14:6; or Acts 9:2; 19:9, 23, etc., where 'the way' has become a name for the Christian life). This powerful and richly suggestive imagery, however, is thwarted in the NRSV translation which here comprises a 'functional equiva-lent' translation – in spite of the translators' avowed intent of continuing the Tyndale/KJV tradition and of working under the maxim, 'as literal as possible, as free as necessary'.[14] Here words, meanings and images are unnecessarily abandoned:

> Happy are those
> who do not follow the advice of the wicked,
> or take the path that sinners tread,
> or sit in the seat of scoffers.

Here, not only is the movement in the parallel verbs lost, but in attempting 'gender inclusivity' (plural 'those' for singular 'the man'), the Psalm's overall movement from the individual to the group is lost.[15] The reader is robbed of the suggestive power of parallel phrases (e.g., 'in the x/y/z of 1/2/3 ...') and images which make it possible to read more deeply and infer meaning more richly.

The abandonment of biblical metaphors in many translations follows natu-rally from functional equivalent theory, because the target languages often do not use such expressions. But it is the *foreignness* of metaphors that is their virtue. Metaphors make us stop and think, 'Now what does *that* mean?' It may be tempting to reduce processing cost by rendering 'God is my rock' as 'God is my firm support', but the cost of such short cuts is inordinately high. Meta-phors are multifaceted and function to produce active thought on the part of the receiver. One must think through a metaphor, and it is this very process that gives the metaphor its power to take hold of the receiver as the receiver takes hold of it.

Many translators rightly assume that the biblical metaphor of God as shep-herd will be difficult to process for people from a society without sheep. But to

---

[14] Cited from Lewis, *English Bible*, 379. The NRSV translators claim to continue the KJV tradition except for three items: '(1) removing archaisms like "thee" and "thou," (2) making the text more "gender inclusive," and (3) including scholarly advances in understanding the lexical meaning of biblical Hebrew and Greek.' I owe this summary of Metzger et al., *Making*, 8 and *passim*, to Al Wolters. My sense of the NRSV is that in spite of these goals, it is essentially a functional equivalent translation, partly because of the requirements of 'gender inclusive' language.

[15] A point made by James Barr in a Midwest Society of Biblical Literature meeting at Calvin Seminary, Grand Rapids, Michigan in the early 1990s.

render Psalm 23 as 'The Lord is my pig herd ...' is problematic. There have been rumors of a translator in a tribal context who actually rendered John the Baptist's utterance on first seeing Jesus something like, 'Behold the little pig of God!' As Nida acknowledges, such translations are inappropriate even within societies that keep pigs and not sheep. For one thing, throughout the Old and New Testaments, pigs are considered unclean, the polar opposite of holiness and a holy God. Sheep are acceptable sacrifices to Yahweh, but pigs are ritually and symbolically abhorrent. One cannot simply translate words into 'functional equivalents' in the target language: the normative context for biblical meaning is the whole Scripture and *its* world. Bible readers need to learn what sheep (and much else besides) are and were in ancient Israel.

There is another reason why rendering metaphors with abstractions or paraphrases is problematic in Bible translation. Metaphors in ordinary language, as Lakoff and Johnson have demonstrated, display a coherence among themselves; they possess a mutual coherence which ultimately embodies frameworks of meaning on the level of basic world-view. Within such frameworks, some fundamental metaphors function as 'root metaphors' that determine the roles of subsidiary metaphors in the system of meaning.[16] If this is true of ordinary language in a culture, it is all the more true of carefully crafted literary works such as the Bible and its parts.[17] Metaphors are the warp of the fabric by which the Bible weaves its tapestry depicting the world and Christ.

An example of distortion in meaning and loss of biblical coherence occurs when the Greek metaphorical phrases 'the old man' and 'the new man' are translated as 'your old self' (cf. Rom. 6:6) and 'the new self' (Col. 3:9–10, NIV).[18] Paul here is referring to putting on *Christ*, 'the new man', the second *Adam* – which is of course Hebrew for 'man' (cf. Rom. 13:14; Gal. 3:27; Rom. 5:12–21; 1 Cor 15:44–49; Eph. 4:22–24). The NIV has here obscured Paul's presentation of *Christ* (not the ancient or modern reader's 'self') as the last Adam who establishes a new humanity in himself, so that our 'life is hidden with Christ in God' (Col. 3:3). It is better that Christian readers realize that they do *not* understand what the text is saying when they encounter a phrase like 'the new man', than that they assume they know when they do not. Teachers, preachers and commentators exist to help readers over their initial cultural and metaphoric difficulties, even as Philip did for the Ethiopian eunuch. This is not 'elitism' but the recognition that the church is a body of

---

[16] Lakoff and Johnson, *Metaphors, passim*; Goatly, *Language*, 41–81. This point by Lakoff and Johnson remains valid, even though one may reject their ontological and epistemological framework.

[17] See Van Leeuwen, 'Liminality'.

[18] It is crucial to note that metaphors are referential and communicate truth about actually existing things, and persons, including God. See Soskice, *Metaphor*.

many members with multiple tasks. The alternative is to turn the translator into commentator as well, with readers unable to know what is commentary and what is Scripture.

In what follows, my general concern about the problematic dominance of 'functional equivalence' Bible translations is focused with regard to three particulars. First, they conflate the problem of the Bible's peculiar mode of relevance with the reader's desire or 'need' for 'ease of processing' meaning. Such translations focus on the reader's subjectivity *as it exists before it encounters the biblical text*. They seem to assume that the text itself has little role in 'creating' its reader, or that readers have little need to *become* competent and 'worthy' of the texts they read.[19] Second, they underestimate the manner in which large, comprehensive *literary* works and their contexts generate interpretive 'clues' for meaning (that is, this theory has an oral or *situational* focus inappropriate to the Bible's literary, 'existential' character and 'macro-genre').[20] Third, since functional equivalent translations are mainly based on a 'code' theory of linguistics, they tend to underestimate the inferential task of the reader, and inhibit this task by prior interpretative decisions on the meaning of words when they provide a presumed 'functional equivalent'.

Relevance and Processing Cost

Most current translations seek to foster immediate ease of processing by reducing linguistic difficulties – which is good. But sometimes cultural and interpretative difficulties are also reduced, even to the extent that meaning suffers. Indeed, some translations add matter to the original to explain cultural and factual matters.[21] Alternately, the 'translation' itself constitutes explanation. Such explanations in the form of purported translation are often more problematic than a 'transparent' rendering of the original. For instance, Jeremiah 4:4a takes a basic Israelite ritual act and uses it as a metaphor for a chastened and sacrificial heart: 'Circumcise yourselves to the Lord, and remove the foreskin of your heart [singular] ...' (RSV, modified). Somewhat remarkably, considering the importance of circumcision for the Jewish faith, the *Tanakh* translation of the Jewish Publication Society renders this verse as follows, 'Open your hearts to the Lord, Remove the thickening about your hearts ...'[22]

---

[19] De Vries ('Bible Translation') describes the fascinating process by which native co-translators in Papua New Guinea edited the biblical translation *away from* their native oral genres to better accommodate the new, written macro-genre of Scripture.

[20] See the parentheses above on these terms.

[21] Gutt, *Translation*, provides some dramatic examples.

[22] The *Tanakh* does provide a footnote referring to the literal 'Circumcise' at the word 'Open'. But at the parallel in Deut. 10:16 it does not.

The metaphorical 'foreskin' has apparently become an obscure medical condition ('thickening about the heart') requiring open-heart surgery.

In functional equivalent translations, the ideal is that the Bible not read like a *foreign* book – which is odd, for foreign is what the Bible inescapably is. In short, the focus of 'functional equivalence' is on the subjective expectations of the target audience and its ease of 'understanding'. In contrast, the (not perfectly realized) focus of older translators, such as William Tyndale and his heirs, was on the biblical text as normative object. In doing so, they preserved many oddities and ambiguities, images and metaphors of the sort that give rise to thought and change people. Their tendency to translate similar words and phrases in similar ways (not, however, in a 'concordance' fashion),[23] helped generations of readers to discover the intense intertextuality of the biblical books. They also produced an *English* language classic that had a profound cultural (and thus 'spiritual') effect on the English-speaking peoples until recently – in spite of not following functional equivalent principles.

In contrast, most recent Bible translations for industrialized, Western peoples, seek to achieve an immediate relevance by accommodating to the linguistic and conceptual expectations of potential readers.[24] Such translations provide a more easily 'readable' Bible. But they sometimes domesticate and flatten the Bible for an audience of people whose expectations are shaped by TV, pulp fiction, the blandishments of consumerism, remnants of pagan Greek thought in theology, American individualism and the post-Kantian dichotomy of 'facts and values'. Such approaches – sometimes abetted by marketing that creates 'niche' Bibles – may silence the foreignness of Scripture and erase crucial otherness in God's book. For instance, Paul's term *sarx* is oddly foreign to us ('flesh'), so translations relegate it to a footnote (a reasonable solution) or, less acceptably, eliminate it altogether (GNB translates *sarx* as 'our human

---

[23] An example is the variety of ways in which words like Hebrew *nephesh*, 'soul, life, self, throat, appetite ...' and *leb* 'heart, mind' are rendered in the KJV tradition. Here especially translation is prone to traduce, for 'soul, life, and heart' are fundamental world-view concepts. Such concepts are especially liable to being (mis)understood in terms of the translator's world-view. Thus Hebrew *nephesh* and NT Greek *psyche* have historically been understood in terms of the 'immortal soul' tradition of Greek thought. Such world-view confusion has done immeasurable damage to the Christian church over the centuries. Jesus does not 'save souls' but human persons or 'lives'. See Cullmann, *Resurrection*.

[24] Rare exceptions are the Jewish translations that seek to embody principles of stylistic imitation that were established by Martin Buber and Franz Rosenzweig in their famous German translation of the Hebrew Bible. Nida (*Toward*, 23) considers such translations for 'scholars' and not for 'common people'. In English, see now Everett Fox's (less successful) Pentateuch translation and Buber and Rosenzweig's *Scripture*.

nature' at Rom. 7:5 – which is certainly as open to misunderstanding as 'flesh'). Such an approach can distract from the uncomfortable (and salvific) questions of existence that the Bible raises. It is susceptible to the readers' assumption that biblical meanings are really the same as our (cultural) meanings, and that the essential questions of existence are in fact those raised by the terms of our own culture, our immediate situation, or inner subjectivity.[25] It is true historically that Paul's term 'flesh' has often been misunderstood in terms of Greek or Gnostic world-views foreign to Paul's meaning. But the solution to such misunderstanding of Paul is by informed Christian *teaching* and commentary.

In short, the dominant notion and practice of Bible translation seems to me often to violate the basic hermeneutical principle of respect for the other. In the words of A. Thiselton,

> ... hermeneutics nourishes respect as *respect for the otherness of the Other* ... [Citing Gadamer:] 'It is the Other who breaks into my ego-centredness and gives me something to understand.' ... interpreters conditioned by their own embeddedness in specific times, cultures, and theological or secular traditions need to *listen*, rather than seeking to 'master' the Other by netting it within their own prior system of concepts and categories. This premature assimilation of the Other into one's own prior grooves of habituated thought constitutes the 'control' and advance commandeering that Gadamer calls 'Method'.[26]

We may contrast contemporary discomfort with a genuine 'Other' (a deep irony in our time of superficial 'multicultural' celebration of 'difference') with the eager desire to be challenged, corrected and 'reformed' by the Bible as Other which characterized the Reformers.[27]

How does functional equivalence theory compromise the voice of the other in translation? To a certain extent, it does this by confusing the task of

---

[25] See the acute and poignant discussion of the missionary problem of translation by the great anthropologist, Evans-Pritchard (*Theories*, 12–14). In spite of sincere labors, he concludes that much of what missionaries 'teach natives is quite unintelligible to those among whom they labour ... The solution often adopted is to transform the minds of native children into European minds, but then this is only in appearance a solution' (14).

[26] In Lundin, et al., *Promise* , 133–34; cf. 221–22.

[27] See Thiselton, *New Horizons*, 186–90, and the quotation from T.F. Torrance (193, original not available to me): ' "Where we feel ourselves under attack from the Scripture, where our natural reason is offended by it, and where we are flung into tumults, is *the very point where genuine interpretation can take place and profound understanding be reached.* It is then ... that we can let ourselves be told something which we cannot tell ourselves, and really learn something new which we cannot think up for ourselves." '

translation with that of interpretation (in practice the confusion is sometimes unavoidable, but one should not make a virtue out of a necessity). Even more problematic is that functional equivalence theory believes that a translation should produce in the average reader an effect *equivalent* to the effect produced in the ancient readers of the original biblical texts. This requires that the translator understand not only the source and target languages, but the *minds* of both ancient and modern readers! The theory is perhaps best summed up in the words of Eugene Nida, its single most influential advocate.[28] Nida, with his co-author Taber, caricatures older translations as follows:

> The older focus in translating was the form of the message, and translators took particular delight in being able to reproduce stylistic specialities, e.g. rhythms, rhymes, plays on words, chiasmus, parallelism, and unusual grammatical structures. The new focus, however, has shifted from the form of the message to the response of the receptor ...

> Correctness [of translation] must be determined by the extent to which the average reader for which a translation is intended will be likely to understand it correctly.

> ... a translation of the Bible must not only provide information which people can understand but must present the message in such a way that people can feel its relevance (the expressive element in communication) and can then respond to it in action (the imperative function).[29]

Nida defines the 'message' which is translated as ...

> the total meaning or content of a discourse; the concepts and feelings which the author intends the reader to understand and receive.[30]

At first glance this seems a compelling account of the translator's task. Unfortunately, it can lead to shortcomings when applied to Bible translation. The shift to the 'response of the reader' may foster the shift to the subject and her

---

[28] Already, in 1947, Nida published *Bible*. With many others, I am grateful for Nida's considerable contributions. My concern here is that he has been too successful! Consequently, the limitations of functional equivalence, especially in practice, have been overlooked, and the church's need for a more 'transparent' form of translation has gone unmet. See most recently, Porter and Hess, *Translating*, for critical responses to Nida and his influence on translation theory and practice.

[29] Nida and Taber, *Theory*, 1, 24.

[30] Ibid., 205. For further discussion of these quotations, see Gutt, *Translation*, 66–9.

situation, which increasingly characterizes modern and postmodern cultures (including at least the American church). Increasingly the reading subject is seen as the norm in establishing meaning.[31] Nida's perspective here, at least as worked out by current translations, seems to assume that readers from one culture and historical situation can simply stand in the place of those who lived thousands of years ago and be affected in the same way as those others – and that we can somehow know what those readers felt, thought and did – not by creating a corresponding system of (target language) words, but by searching for equivalent concepts or functional effects.

This seems to me an implicitly a-historical theory of understanding. We and the other are essentially the same, so much so that we accommodate the other to our pre-understandings and situation. But modern Americans or British people are not ancient Israelites living under the heel of Persia or Rome. We stand in a different place – historically, culturally and linguistically – and we must *infer*, somehow, what these ancient documents given by God intend to say to us. In seeking to ease the cost of processing the communication, we risk denying its otherness, while misunderstanding what enables us, nonetheless, to understand.

Moreover, with Gutt, it must be asked, what constitutes 'equivalence' in translation or in response? A rich, happy American *cannot*, and should not, hear God say the same thing through Psalm 137 ('By the waters of Babylon there we sat down and wept ...'), as an ancient Israelite in or shortly after the exile. The inscripturated speech acts of God are often indirect and require Holy Spirit-filled inference on the part of readers.[32] For readers to do their interpretative, inferential job, the translated words and images must be as faithful as possible. To translate a 'meaning' or 'effect' rather than *words* is often to interpose the translator's cultural subjectivity between a complex structure of meaning-effects and the reader. Even an Inuit who has never seen one can infer approximately what a sheep is, given enough (con)text or teaching. In cultures where there are no sheep, perhaps some sort of loan word needs to be created, with appropriate explanatory footnotes. It does not suit to substitute an Inuit word for 'seal' in the place of some word for 'sheep'.

Nida suggests that the duty of the translator is to eliminate what is foreign in the text:

> Translating consists in producing in the receptor language the closest natural equivalent to the message of the source language, first in meaning and secondly in style ... By 'natural' we mean that the equivalent forms should not be 'foreign' either in form

---

[31] Whang, 'To Whom', offers a sharp critique of the reliability and validity of 'reader-response' criteria in translation.

[32] Cf. Wolterstorff, *Divine Discourse*.

... or meaning. That is to say, a good translation should not reveal its non-native source.[33]

Nida is entirely correct with respect to the linguistic meaning of forms in the target language. However, as the sheep/seal, lamb/pig examples suggest, it is often not possible to avoid 'foreignness', even on a linguistic level, without distortion of the original meaning.[34] The Bible is not and cannot be a modern English or French or Kingandou (Central African Republic) document. Bible readers and Nida himself know this well – as his often penetrating analyses show. Granted that irrelevant linguistic foreignness should be eliminated, the foreignness of Scripture (in some cases even linguistic foreignness) remains crucial to its message and to our task as readers to understand the *other* as other.

The most important, most characteristic concepts of a culture are often those most resistant to translation. When asked about the meaning of Akkadian *paṛsu* (a term central to the ancient Mesopotamian world-view), Erica Reiner, editor of the *Chicago Assyrian Dictionary*, cited her predecessor, the great Benno Landsberger. 'Someday,' he declared, 'we will translate *parsu* as *parṣu*!'[35] Central terms in Scripture, like *ḥesed* (KJV, 'steadfast love') and *ṣedaqah*

---

[33] Nida, 'Principles', 19. See also Nida's 1947 work, *Bible*, 5, 'If possible, he [the translator] does not want this book to bear the marks of a foreign language ... His goal is to translate in the same form in which the people speak, in a style which seems so natural to them that it speaks intimately and personally to their own hearts' (5). Though Nida's statement speaks of 'form' and 'style', it is questionable whether meaning and form can be neatly separated. Consequently, Nida's view unwittingly fosters the frequent attempt by translators to remove the hermeneutical gap by linguistic means. The alien Bible must become something that is naturally at home in every human heart.

[34] De Waard and Nida (*Language*, 38) acknowledge this when they reject 'little pig of God' for 'Lamb of God' in a Melanesian context. But they do this only because 'there are certain important religious symbols which, though often obscure in their meaning, are necessarily important for the preservation of the integrity and unity of the biblical message'. Among such symbols are '[e]xpressions such as "Lamb of God," "cross," and "sacrifice." ' I would suggest that such 'important religious symbols' are far more pervasive in Scripture than the small list of atonement-related items they mention. Indeed, they object to 'circumcision of the heart' (Rom. 2:29) as something 'rarely understood' by readers. But this locution is also essential 'for the preservation of the integrity and unity of the biblical message'. Can one understand the Scriptures (e.g., the controversy with Judaizers) *without* knowing what circumcision is?

[35] Personal conversation at a Midwest American Oriental Society meeting, Garrett-Evangelical Seminary, Evanston, Illinois, late 1980s. As of this writing, the relevant *CAD* volume has not yet appeared. W. von Soden, glosses *parṣu* as '*Amt; (Kult)ordnung, Ordnungen, Ordnungsfunktionen, göttliche Kräfte*' (*Akkadisches Handwörterbuch*, 835). *Parṣu* is so difficult because it covers ideas we moderns do not put together: office, ritual order, cosmic order and functions, and divine powers.

(KJV, 'righteousness') have a range of meaning that is foreign to English. They are doors to a new world. That is why entire books are written about them. They need to be explained, their meanings lived into. Ordinary churchgoers have an intuitive sense of this when they talk of 'shalom' or of 'agape-love' – the latter somewhat mistakenly, following their pastors. Of course the danger of pious, 'meaningless vocabulary' is real.[36] But that is a moral-intellectual failing, not a failing of language itself. My evangelical students often use 'salvation' and 'saved' in a non-biblical, Gnostic sense, having learned the same in church. They need to learn the biblical meanings.

Nida's legitimate desire to eliminate *linguistic* foreignness arises from an intention to facilitate 'ease of processing' on the reader's part, to create translations that speak directly to the 'heart' of readers, as he explicitly says elsewhere.[37] But in practice, it can lead to the elimination of important cultural and theological foreignness. Moreover, to speak to the heart of readers is a goal that is appropriate only to some parts of Scripture – not to most of Leviticus, for example. No amount of linguistic accommodation can override the fact that some parts of the Bible require a great deal of work *before* their content can be comprehended.[38] Indeed, many, if not most, biblical passages cannot be made lucid or 'clear' for a reader who does not have the cultural or geographical or other knowledge which provides the requisite context for meaning. Indeed, even on the 'heart' level, without the Holy Spirit, Scripture is *de facto* foreign to a humanity in rebellion.

Relevance and the Nature of the Literary Text

It is a fundamental feature of large texts, including the Bible, that they generate their own, largely indirect, 'relevance' by creating a literary world anchored in the divinely created world,[39] and that the translator of such texts must trust them (especially the Bible!) to reward the hard work of entering into that world.[40] The Bible is not just a book to read, but rather a book to read, study, and, as it were, *to live in*.

This biblical manner of generating meaning through extended interrelated text (which incidentally tells the story of reality from creation to as-yet-to-be-realized re-creation) renders problematic another aspect of functional

---

[36] As Nida argues, *Toward*, 29.

[37] See note 33 above.

[38] Cf. Gutt, *Translation*, 165ff.

[39] Among many, see C. Walhout (in Lundin, et al., *Promise*, 71–84) who importantly distinguishes the referential and mimetic aspects of literary narratives.

[40] Cf. Thiselton, *New Horizons*, 35–46, 63–75.

equivalence theory. Modern linguistics, stemming from Saussure, developed first of all as a theory of oral language, rather than of second-order written language. Oral communication depends on face-to-face situations that provide a non-linguistic manifold of 'contextual effects'. Such shared situations, with their 'textual effects', facilitate immediate understanding based on the relevance of the communication to participants.

But an obvious feature of texts is that immediacy of shared meaning no longer exists to connect authors with the readers of texts. For textual hermeneutics, a fundamental question is thus, 'What "contextual effects" (both extra- and intra-linguistic) enable a reader to understand or make valid inferences from her reading of a culturally and linguistically distant text?' Functional equivalence thinking seems to seek to create a sense of oral-like or situational immediacy, which *begins* with the reader's pre-understandings and situation or perceived need.[41]

This attempt at situational immediacy appears in a crucial metaphor which suggests that Nida understands Scripture in an almost instrumental, technical way. He uses the example of an aircraft maintenance manual, whose correct translation is a matter of life and death:

> One specialist in translating and interpreting for the aviation industry commented that in his work he did not dare to employ the principles often followed by translators [i.e., pre-functional equivalence] of the Bible: 'With us,' he said, 'complete intelligibility is a matter of life and death.' Unfortunately, translators of religious materials have sometimes not been prompted by the same feeling of urgency to make sense.[42]

In dynamic equivalent *practice*, whether Nida intends this or not, the inference seems to be that there should be no ambiguity, no lack of clarity. The foreign language reader of a manual must be able to understand and act on its instructions while maintaining an aircraft. The translator may need to add explanatory phrases and clauses, and perhaps even diagrams, to make the manual lucid to the foreign mechanic – even if those clauses, phrases and pictures are not in the original.[43] In this type of translation it is necessary to merge commentary and illustration into the translation. Not surprisingly, in translators' prefaces to

---

[41] Learning new words and foreign concepts is actually an interactive process of 'assimilation' of the other to what is already 'known' and of 'accommodation' of the already 'known' to the new and foreign. Sometimes the 'accommodation' is so radical that one must speak of a 'paradigm shift' or 'conversion'. See Goatly, *Language*, 28–9.

[42] Nida and Taber, *Theory*, 1. See Gutt on this passage (*Translation*, 62–3). For Thiselton's critique of a 'handbook' or 'closed' understanding of the biblical text, see *Promise*, 152–82, esp. 153 and 171.

[43] Gutt, *Translation*, provides some extreme examples.

newer Bible translations from the TEV to the NIV, one encounters an emphasis on 'clarity' that has a Cartesian ring.[44] The theory drives translators to supply clarity where it is not appropriate.

Nida's image evokes Scripture as a 'handbook', or technical manual – presumably one that contains life or death instructions on how to obtain eternal salvation. Unfortunately, this image reinforces the evangelical tendency to neglect the variety of genres and functions in Scripture and to read the Bible as a quasi-scientific book of useful, factual information (though Nida himself is well aware of genre).[45] Literature in general reveals a spectrum of 'open' and 'closed' functions.[46] An instruction manual is 'closed' in that it wishes to preclude 'interpretation' and ambiguity of meaning. Stephen Prickett comments, 'The modern English translations ... seem to be quite unanimous in *rejecting* any ambiguity or oddity perceived in the original.'[47] But the Bible is in most of its parts and as a whole an 'open' book collection: the task of interpretation is demanded, the whole is 'dialogic' (as in Job) and the truth arises and is to be found in the interaction of the complex whole and its parts. Can the gospel be stated simply? Yes, and some parts of the Scriptures do that. But even the 'simple' parts of the Bible have depths, nuances and wisdom that readers are meant to 'grow' into. We grow in our knowledge of Scripture just as we grow in the knowledge of a friend, a musical composition, or of God and the creation itself.

For dynamic equivalence practice, then, as it follows a handbook or a quasi-oral, situational model of the text, words are not as important as the 'meaning' or 'message' of the original texts and their larger meaning units. This meaning is determined by 'experts', the translators and the exegetes they consult. Moreover, the criteria for meaning is not 'what the text says' but *the type of response it is hypothesized to have produced in the original readers and which must now be equivalently produced in the readers of a translation.* The readers' response is so urgent, that unclarity is not tolerated. How something is *said* for Nida is not so important as what is *meant*, and that meaning must be readily transparent to the reader.

Thus, Nida cites the passage in Romans 1:17, which, he says, in the traditional translation was commonly misunderstood by 'a high percentage of people':

---

[44] See Lundin in *Promise*, on the Cartesian tradition that has dominated biblical hermeneutics up to the present, also in evangelical circles. The Reformation concept of *claritas* (noted below) has room for ambiguity and difficulty, but the functional equivalent concept of 'clarity' seems not to, as Prickett argues in *Words*.

[45] On these characteristics of evangelicalism, see Marsden, *Fundamentalism*.

[46] For these concepts, see Thiselton in Lundin, et al., *Promise*, 152–54.

[47] Prickett, *Words*, 7, cf. 6–9. He illustrates his point with the 'still small voice' passage in 1 Kgs. 19:8–12.

most traditional translations have 'the righteousness of God is revealed from faith to faith,' and most readers naturally assume that this is a reference to God's own personal righteousness. Most scholars are agreed, however, that this is not God's own righteousness, but the process by which God puts men right with himself.[48]

However, the interpretation of 'most scholars' is actually Nida's representation of one version of the powerful tradition stemming from Luther's Reformation. Of late, the Reformation understanding of 'the righteousness of God'[49] has been increasingly disputed. While this interpretation does not deny the importance of human justification by grace, it asserts that 'the righteousness of God' in Romans 1:16 and elsewhere probably *does* refer to God's character displayed in action.[50] At stake is the significant question whether the primary focus of Romans as a whole is on God (theology and theodicy) or on human salvation (anthropology). However, my point here is not so much which interpretation of Romans 1:17 is right or wrong, but that functional equivalent translations like the NIV and TEV have made an interpretative choice which prevents readers from seeing that Paul may be saying something other than their translation says he says.

In Romans 6:2, Christians are to be 'dead to sin'. According to de Waard and Nida,

Dead can only be understood in the sense of 'not responding to,' and *sin* must be related to 'the impulse to sin.' Literal translations of 'dead to sin' are usually quite meaningless. Accordingly, in most languages it is necessary to employ an expanded phrase such as 'unresponsive to the temptations to sin' or even 'to be just as though dead as far as being tempted to sin is concerned'.[51]

---

[48] Nida and Taber, *Theory*, 2.

[49] Luther translated, 'die Gerechtigkeit, die vor Gott gilt ...' On the linguistic level, unlike the KJV, Luther leaves the reader without the means to determine whether the genitive is objective or subjective. Such translational choices either *permit* understanding and foster the necessary task of interpretation, or they preclude them. Similarly, the NIV's rendering, 'a righteousness from God is revealed ...' forecloses on interpretation. Curiously, it renders the parallel construction in 1:18 as 'The wrath of God is being revealed ...' The two changes ('from' to 'of' and the addition of 'being') erode the signifying parallelism. Similar is the NIV's rendering of *pistis (Iesou) christou* as 'faith in (Jesus) Christ' (Rom. 3:22, etc.) The strong possibility that it refers to 'Jesus Christ's faithfulness' (subjective genitive) is excluded, without a note to this valid translational option. Again, translation without commentary, even in the form of notes, is not really possible, as de Waard and Nida often admit (e.g., *Language*, 34, 108, 155).

[50] See N.T. Wright's lucid, chapter-long treatment in *Paul*, 95–111.

[51] De Waard and Nida, *Language*, 157.

But this assumes that readers cannot explore a new metaphor within an extended context. The suggested translations obscure the central reality of the Christian life described in Romans 6, that Christians have died and risen 'in Christ' (an unchangeable historical reality) and that they die and rise with him in their daily existence, by presently putting to death the 'old man' (see above) and putting on the 'new'. Examples of functional equivalent translations precluding or hindering interpretation, often on fundamental matters such as Paul's use of 'the righteousness of God', are easy for readers of the original languages to come by.[52] Thus, in Ecclesiastes (and only in Ecclesiastes), the NIV has translated *hebel* as 'meaningless'. *Hebel* is the most important keyword in Ecclesiastes, appearing some 37/38 times (one case is uncertain), and its translation dramatically affects how one reads the entire book. *Hebel* means something like 'breath, mist, fog' (cf. Jas. 4:14, 'What is your life? A mist ...'). Ecclesiastes uses the word metaphorically to characterize existence in general (Ecc. 1:2; 12:8) and many things in particular as a 'breath, mist, fog'. The metaphor does not fit well in English usage and it has been traditionally rendered as 'vanity' (KJV, RSV, after Vulgate *vanitas*). While we must admit the great difficulty of translating *hebel* in Ecclesiastes, its translation by the NIV as 'meaningless' precludes all but one interpretation – loosely, that life without God is 'meaningless' – not only of this word, but of the entire book.[53] Once again, my point is not primarily whether the NIV's interpretation is right or wrong, but that functional equivalent 'translation' has dictated one meaning when another, quite contrary, meaning may be correct. Indeed, the translators here may have replaced God's word with their own. Surely at least a note on *hebel* was called for.

There are a myriad ways in which the attempt to 'clarify' the translation may destroy the purposeful difficulty of the text – a difficulty, complexity or ambiguity that is designed to stimulate initial puzzlement, then thought and reflection on the part of the reader. Sometimes the linguistic difficulty of the Hebrew text is part of the message, as when Job uses language that is often obscure or ambiguous because of rare words, or often because simple lines are capable of multiple readings: this difficulty is part of Job's 'message' or 'meaning'. This wisdom book is meant to be an unending puzzle that forces humans to realize their cognitive and moral finiteness, and to trust in God when they cannot understand.[54]

More often, however, the problem engendered by the text is not at all a matter of linguistic difficulty. It seems to me a mistake for translators to try to

---

[52] On this matter, see Prickett, *Words*, 4–36; and Barr, 'Modern'.

[53] See Longman, *Ecclesiastes*. For a contrary and, in my judgment, correct, view see Provan, *Ecclesiastes*.

[54] On this, see O'Donovan, *Resurrection*, 84–5, cf. 136.

'solve' these 'non-linguistic' difficulties for the reader. Consider the pivotal story of Amnon's rape of Absalom's sister, Tamar, which sets the stage for Absalom's revolt (2 Sam. 13). One of the characters, Jonadab, is described as very 'wise' (*hakam*). However, Jonadab counsels Amnon in a way that makes the latter's rape of his half-sister possible. This seems to counter the idea that Jonadab is 'wise' in the biblical sense of god-fearing and morally upright (e.g., Prov. 9:10; Job 1:1; 28:28). Hence, recent translations reject the normal translation of *hakam*, 'wise' (KJV; cf. LXX *sophos*; Vulgate *prudens*), instead telling us that Jonadab was very 'shrewd', 'clever', or the like (2 Sam. 13:3; cf. NIV, NRSV, REB, NJB, *Tanakh*). However, as Bar-Efrat has shown in a masterful close reading of this story, the text means what it says here: Jonadab was indeed 'a very wise man' in the biblical sense, contrary to many readings. The tragedy – one of many in this story – is that his wisdom fails him, and that he does not anticipate the outcome of his specific counsel.[55] Much in the larger narrative in 2 Samuel (beginning with David's adultery and murder of Uriah) has to do with the failures and limitations of even the best human wisdom (cf. Prov. 16:9; 20:24; 21:30–31). Jonadab's failure illustrates this: 'Do not boast about tomorrow, for you do not know what tomorrow will give birth to' (my 'literal' translation of Prov. 27:1; conversely, see Mt. 6:34). In their desire to make things 'clear' for the reader, the translators have in fact robbed the biblical story of that complexity that pushes the reader to insight and wisdom about the limits of the human condition. In short, the difficulty of Jonadab's wisdom is a productive difficulty, part of what enables the Bible to make readers 'wise unto salvation' (*sophisai eis soterian*, 2 Tim. 2:15).

Code and Inference

A third shortcoming of functional equivalent theory is that it seems too narrowly based on the code aspect of communication.[56] Code theory has achieved a virtually canonical status among students of linguistics. According to code theories, a speaker and her hearer share a common linguistic code; the speaker encodes her thought in sounds and the hearer decodes the sounds in his mind to replicate the speaker's intended meaning.[57] In the case of written language and its translation, this theory is applied to the written signs of the text. For Nida, the criterion for translational correctness is that the average reader 'will be able to understand it [i.e., the encoded 'message' or meaning] correctly', and that the translation 'must present the message in such a way that people can

---

[55] Bar-Efrat, *Narrative*, 245–55.
[56] See de Waard and Nida, *Language*, 11–19.
[57] Sperber and Wilson, *Relevance*, 3–7.

feel its relevance ... and can then respond to it in action ...'(Nida as quoted above).

Yet, things are not quite so simple. Sperber and Wilson do agree that 'language is a code' in which sounds are paired with 'semantic representations'.[58] In a limited sense, language is a mutually shared system of sounds or signs encoded and decoded. But Sperber and Wilson emphatically disagree that meaning is something transferred from one mind to another. Code theory is only a partial account of what goes on in communication, and in some regards it is simply wrong, in spite of its near canonical status. Sperber and Wilson argue that,

> there is a gap between the semantic representations of sentences and the thoughts actually communicated by utterances. This gap is filled not by more coding, but by *inference.*[59]

This passage is crucial because it enables us to account for essential features of communication that code theories miss. It forces us to analyze the crucial role of non-linguistic factors in communication. It also enables us to more clearly understand the respective responsibilities of those who make utterances and those who receive them. Sperber and Wilson insist that a sentence is not an actual communication or utterance. Rather, a sentence is a linguistic abstraction of an utterance. An utterance can be spoken in a panic, in a rainstorm, with a heavy cold, to a friend or an enemy. A sentence, as written, removes from the utterance all but the semantic representations of meaning. *Thus it cannot in itself communicate meaning that is relevant to the hearer or reader.* This idea also implies that meaning is not something poured into a bucket of signs at one end of the brain chain and poured out into another brain at the other end. While it is true that thoughts are encoded in sounds or letters, the meaning at the other end is something *inferred*, based on a complex of contextual factors.

Let me give an example or two. Suppose an insomniac were asked, 'Would you like some coffee?' just before bed time, and she responded simply,

  1) Coffee would keep me awake.[60]

The hearer would correctly infer a meaning something like the following, *even though this is not 'what is said'*:

  2) No thank you, I do not want coffee now.

But suppose the same offer of coffee were made to Homer Simpson struggling to stay awake at his job in the nuclear power plant. When Homer replies,

  1) Coffee would keep me awake,

---

[58] Ibid., 9.
[59] Ibid. (emphasis mine).
[60] Ibid., 11.

we know he means 'yes yes, bring me coffee' and probably, 'don't forget the donuts' as well. Note that in each case, there is a gap between what is said as sentence and what the utterance in a face-to-face context means. And in each case this meaning needs to be inferred from a host of extra-linguistic factors. In the present example, one cannot expect to create an 'equivalent response' in a reader not in the situation of Homer Simpson, or in a reader who does not drink coffee. What *might* be possible is that readers gain wisdom, inferentially, about coffee and other things.

One more example illustrates the gap between sentence and actual utterance in context, and shows that this gap is even phonetic and morphological. I have in mind a relatively common American English utterance, which I gratefully borrow from Moisés Silva.[61] The utterance is '*Djeet?*' By itself this seems meaningless, not even English. But a bit of context makes it immediately understandable: A college student spots his girlfriend talking to friends outside the cafeteria. He walks up and says, '*Djeet?*' She responds, 'Not yet,' and they go off to lunch together. As sentence we think and teach, 'Did you eat?' But what the student utters is '*Djeet?*' These examples illustrate both the gap between utterance and sentence, and the indispensable role played by context and inference in communication.

It is clear, then, that meanings inferred by hearers and readers are heavily context-dependent. Meanings are *deductions* of relevance or significance based on what is said, even when they do not correspond to what is said. They are inferences based on the assumed *relevance* of an utterance when 'contextual effects' are coupled with an appropriate level of processing difficulty. Communication presupposes a shared commitment to relevance for specific purposes. Successful communication requires a shared set of *expectations* between speaker and hearer, writer and reader (see above). Without these expectations, encoding and decoding proceed at cross-purposes, and misunderstanding results.

Conclusions

How do these basic aspects of communication affect our understanding of Bible translation? An obvious feature of the Bible is that, in the Protestant canon, it comprises sixty-six small, ancient books, themselves containing a myriad of smaller linguistic units. It belongs to no one's current 'situation' or immediate world. Its message is indirect; God speaks in Scripture to be sure, but through a considerable hermeneutical gap. It seems to me that Scripture, in its great diversity and comprehensive cosmic narrative, speaks more to the general 'existential' human condition than it does to readers' specific

---

[61] Silva, *Biblical Words*, 144.

situations. (The word of God concerning Jerusalem in Isaiah's day is, after all quite contrary to God's word concerning Jerusalem in Jeremiah's day.) In contrast, oral or situational communication requires and provides an immediate context that renders utterances relevant and meaningful, as we saw above.

Written communication, then, quickly loses its original context. This is true even of letters which are written to address specific people and issues. The Corinthians to whom Paul wrote are now all dead and gone. Yet for nearly two thousand years, people have read these letters and found them 'relevant' and meaningful. Writings exist long after their first contexts are gone. Yet they continue to be meaningful and relevant. It is worth pondering why this is so, and how it is possible.

My short, simple answer is that unlike ephemeral oral utterances, written works are able to combine sufficient linguistic material so as to create a literary world that implies in significant ways the world and the mental worlds which we humans inhabit. Literary works give sufficient data for readers to infer meaning, even though the practical immediacies of our oral, lived world are not those of the texts' original writers and readers. We latter-day readers of the Corinthian correspondence still struggle with the weather, enmity, money, the nature of true spirituality, life in the body, greed, sex in high and low places, and the difficulty of passing on life and faith to the next generation. We believe in and seek to serve the same God in the same creation. We hope for the same resurrection from the dead.

The Bible is complex. And yet, for all its diversity, the Old Testament – to speak only of it for a moment – possesses a coherence of 'world-view' and language.[62] One of the indices of this fact is that the language, imagery, narratives and poetry of Scripture are pervasively cross-referential.[63] Much of the New Testament material consists of quotations, paraphrases, or allusions to Old Testament texts. The Old Testament itself uses a language rich in stock phrases and themes that get endlessly varied and enriched in new contexts. This book does not suffer from the modern 'anxiety of influence'. Rather, it uses the language and realities of the past in constantly new and rich ways. Paul says in Galatians that Christians are 'sons of Abraham' through faith in Jesus the Christ, or Anointed One. This makes no sense unless you know who Abraham was, what the conventions and symbolism of sonship are (they include women), and what it means to be anointed in ancient Israel.

My argument is thus that the massive text we call the Bible is itself the primary context of meaning within which we must find the meaning of each

---

[62] I am aware that many will not agree with this assertion. I will not argue it here.

[63] I avoid the term 'intertextual' here, because it has become laden with a variety of strong ideological meanings. Among many works, one may consider Fishbane, *Biblical*; Hays, *Echoes*; and Goppelt, *Typos*.

smaller unit of text. This is nothing new: the Reformers insisted that the Bible was 'its own interpreter'. And though this proverb, like all proverbs, highlights only an aspect of a more complex reality, it speaks its truth profoundly. The Bible creates a world of meaning, and we need to enter it and make ourselves at home in its strangeness, all the better to understand our world, which is insufficiently strange to us. In this indirect way, the Bible, and our Lord who speaks in and through it, still speak to us today.

If this is so, then attempts to translate each passage of Scripture to be immediately meaningful to modern or traditional peoples with a minimum of processing effort are of limited value, particularly for the *leadership* of God's people. Such translations may succeed in transmitting the basic Bible stories and other genres, and I admit there is great virtue in this. Yet growth in biblical understanding ultimately requires 'transparent' translation. It is true that *no* translation suffices to 'explain' such basic contrastive concepts as holiness, cleanness, and uncleanness in Leviticus.[64] Yet these concepts are essential to understanding many biblical stories – from Samson's encounter with the dead lion to Jesus' encounters with lepers, 'unclean spirits', and the woman with a flow of blood. Leviticus requires commentary in light of the entire biblical story, and vice versa. Such commentary requires translations that are carefully accurate and transparent. Thus, for the NIV to speak of 'evil spirits' in place of 'unclean spirits' is to miss the point that the 'Holy One' has come to make the world (especially people) a holy place in which God's glory can dwell (Mk. 1:23–27; Isa. 6:3). Again, the extended genealogies in Matthew and Luke require commentary based on the entire story of Scripture. There is no way to gain the relevant context for understanding these extended utterances, except by reading the Bible whole, in terms of its culture and world, and as much as possible in its (carefully) translated words.

To my mind these facts imply a fundamental point regarding our relation to Bible reading and translation. *Bible reading and translation without (written and spoken) commentary based on thorough study of Hebrew and Greek is inadequate.* Translation is no substitute for commentary. The church and synagogue have recognized this from their beginnings. Both have continuous traditions of commentary and preaching based on the biblical text, even when Targums and translations of various sorts have been used. These functions are not accidental but essential. They may be performed poorly, but performed they must be, for the sacred word of God is always more than our renderings of it. Understanding and interpretation require a community gathered by the Word and Spirit to work in the Word and Spirit.

In my judgment, functional equivalent translations are liable to confuse the complementary tasks of translation and commentary – to the detriment of

---

[64] See Wenham, *Leviticus.*

both. The motivation of the translators is good: to maximize ease of processing in the target language, so that readers will not be scared off by the difficulty of the translated text. There is an important place for such translations, and I myself have contributed to the most recent of them, the *New Living Translation*. And yet I consider them most successful as an aid to evangelism and for unsophisticated readers. Such translations have played a role in the conversion and even Christian growth of many. But when it comes to in-depth study of the Bible and to deeper insight for theology, world-view and life, such translations may become a hindrance. They accommodate the Bible to contemporary tastes, while the Bible insists that we increasingly grow in our accommodation to it. The Bible, I believe, is worth our best efforts at becoming better 'processors' of its meaning – though the word 'processors' smacks too much of a technical procedure such as in 'decoding'. Understanding is something more.

The Bible is a massive book that is adequate and contextually relevant for its most important purposes. I affirm the perspicuity and *claritas* of Scripture in the subtle and careful ways the Reformers developed these ideas.[65] Yet it is a book that requires not just reading, but rereading and explication and comment and interpretive appropriation over time. Moreover, the Bible is a book that communicates on multiple levels, to readers of varying levels of sophistication and competence. Relevant here are the distinctions developed by R.T. France between *surface meaning* and *bonus meaning* and between *naive* and *sophisticated, experienced readers*.[66] He writes:

> I am sure that a distinction between surface meaning and a bonus meaning for the initiated or alert is realistic; any adult reader of children's classics ... will be well aware that the surface meaning may be communicated to the great delight of the more naïve audience, while at the same time a whole world of more esoteric pleasure is in store for those who share the author's private adult viewpoint and erudition. It is a poor author who aims to communicate only with the lowest common denominator of his potential readership.[67]

Professor France illustrates his point extensively using Matthew 2. He concludes:

---

[65] See Thiselton's account in *New Horizons*, 179–85.

[66] France's term 'surface meaning' is somewhat problematic, for it may suggest 'superficial', and that would be a mistake. I prefer to speak of immediate or direct meaning, that which the text obviously and straightforwardly says. Such direct meaning is by no means superficial, but of first importance. Preachers and biblical scholars too often ignore it, while the 'naïve' believer often 'gets' its profound significance.

[67] France, 'Formula-quotations', 241, discussed in Gutt, *Translation*, 70–72.

... what any given reader will find in a chapter like Matthew 2 will vary with his exegetical background. What I want to suggest is that Matthew would not necessarily have found this regrettable, that he was deliberately composing a chapter rich in potential exegetical bonuses, so that the more fully a reader shared the religious traditions and scriptural erudition of the author, the more he was likely to derive from his reading, while at the same time there was a surface meaning sufficiently uncomplicated for even the most naïve reader to follow it.[68]

One can enjoy the stories of Homer as a child, and such readers are served by abridged, simplified versions of the classic. In the same way, my wife and I once read a classic story Bible to our boys after dinner. But we soon graduated to a full-blown Bible translation, and we delighted in the back and forth questioning and comments that arose from encounter with a richer and more accurate text.

Translations which focus on immediate ease of processing for unsophisticated readers function like a story version of Homer. The story is there (though some stories are censored as being too scandalous for kids), but the complexity, ambiguity and richness of meaning and thought that enable adults to *grow* is too often lost. We also lose the particular cultural and literary details which enable readers to enter more fully and precisely into the beauty, thought and world-view of the Bible, and which make *misreading* more difficult. We lose those angular and strange features of the text that force us out of our cultural complacency, out of that little bubble of time and place we call home. We lose the Bible as the book and word of Him who is Other than we are, who nevertheless became an ancient Jewish *man* in all his particularity and otherness.

Bibliography

Bar-Efrat, S., *Narrative Art in the Bible* (Sheffield: Almond Press, 1989), 239–82

Barr, J., 'Modern English Bible Versions as a Problem for the Church', *QR* 14 (1994), 263–78

Cullmann, O., *Immortality of the Soul or Resurrection of the Body?* (London: Epworth Press, 1958)

de Vries, L., 'Bible Translation and Primary Orality', *BT* 51 (2000), 101–14

de Waard, Jan, and E.A. Nida, *From One Language to Another: Functional Equivalence in Bible Translating* (Nashville: Thomas Nelson, 1986).

Evans-Pritchard, E.E., *Theories of Primitive Religion* (Oxford: OUP, 1965)

---

[68] France, 'Formula-quotations', 241

Fishbane, M., *Biblical Interpretation in Ancient Israel* (Oxford: Clarendon Press, 1985)

France, R.T., 'The Formula-quotations of Matthew 2 and the Problem of Communication', *NTS* 27 (1981) 233–51

Goatly, A., *The Language of Metaphors* (London and New York: Routledge, 1997)

Goppelt, L., *Typos: The Typological Interpretation of the Old Testament in the New* (Grand Rapids: Eerdmans, 1982)

Gutt, E.-A., *Translation and Relevance: Cognition and Context* (Oxford: Basil Blackwell, 1991)

Hays, R.B., *Echoes of Scripture in the Letters of Paul* (New Haven: Yale University Press, 1989)

Jakobson, R., 'Closing Statements: Linguistics and Poetics', in T.A. Sebeok, *Style in Language* (Cambridge, MA: MIT Press, 1960)

Lakoff, G., and M. Johnson, *Metaphors We Live By* (Chicago: University of Chicago Press, 1980)

Lewis, C.S., *Studies in Words* (Cambridge: CUP, 2nd edn, 1967)

Lewis, J.P., *The English Bible from KJV to NIV* (Grand Rapids: Baker, 2nd edn, 1991)

Longman T., III, *The Book of Ecclesiastes* (NICOT; Grand Rapids: Eerdmans, 1998)

Lundin, R., C. Walhout and A.C. Thiselton, *The Promise of Hermeneutics* (Grand Rapids: Eerdmans; Carlisle: Paternoster, 1999)

Marsden, G., *Fundamentalism in American Culture* (Oxford & New York: OUP, 1980)

Metzger, B.M., R.C. Dentan and W. Harrelson, *The Making of the New Revised Standard Version of the Bible* (Grand Rapids: Eerdmans, 1991)

Nida, E.A., *Bible Translating: An Analysis of Principles and Procedures with Special Reference to Aboriginal Languages* (New York: American Bible Society, 1947)

—, 'Principles of Translation as Exemplified by Bible Translating', in *On Translation* (ed. R.A. Brower; Harvard Studies in Comparative Literature 23; Cambridge, MA: Harvard University Press, 1959)

—, *Toward a Science of Translating: With Special Reference to Principles and Procedures Involved in Bible Translating* (Leiden: E.J. Brill, 1964)

Nida, E.A., and C. Taber, *The Theory and Practice of Translation* (Leiden: E.J. Brill, 1969)

O'Donovan, O., *Resurrection and Moral Order: An Outline for Evangelical Ethics* (Grand Rapids: Eerdmans, 2nd edn, 1994)

Porter, S.E., 'The Contemporary English Version and the Ideology of Translation', in Porter and Hess (eds.), *Translating*, 18–45

Porter, S.E., and R.S. Hess (eds.), *Translating the Bible: Problems and Prospects* (JSNTSup 173; Sheffield: Sheffield Academic Press, 1999)

Prickett, S., *Words and the Word: Language, Poetics and Biblical Interpretation* (Cambridge: CUP, 1986)

Provan, I., *Ecclesiastes and Song of Songs* (NIV Application Commentary; Grand Rapids: Zondervan, 2001)

Silva, M., *Biblical Words and Their Meaning: An Introduction to Lexical Semantics* (Grand Rapids: Zondervan, rev. and exp. edn, 1994)

Soskice, J.M., *Metaphor and Religious Language* (Oxford: Clarendon Press, 1985)

Sperber, D., and D. Wilson, *Relevance: Communication and Cognition* (Oxford: Basil Blackwell, 2nd edn, 1995)

Thiselton, A.C., *New Horizons in Hermeneutics: The Theory and Practice of Transforming Biblical Reading* (Grand Rapids: Zondervan, 1992)

Van Leeuwen, R.C., 'Liminality and Worldview in Proverbs 1–9', *Semeia* 50 (1990), 111–44

Wenham, G., *The Book of Leviticus* (Grand Rapids: Eerdmans, 1979)

Whang, Y.C., 'To Whom is a Translator Responsible – Reader or Author?', in Porter and Hess (eds.), *Translating*, 46–62

Wolterstorff, N., *Divine Discourse: Philosophical Reflections on the Claim that God Speaks* (Cambridge: CUP, 1995)

Wright, N.T., *What Saint Paul Really Said* (Grand Rapids: Eerdmans, 1997)

15

Illocutionary Stance in Hans Frei's
The Eclipse of Biblical Narrative

An Exercise in Conceptual Redescription and Normative Analysis

Neil B. MacDonald

Introduction

Hans Frei's *The Eclipse of Biblical Narrative* has received much critical acclaim
since its publication in 1974. Alasdair McIntyre wrote that it was 'a brilliant and
disquieting book which raises dangerously powerful questions for every
teacher of the humanities'.[1] In particular, Frei's account of the history of the
transition from pre-critical to critical biblical hermeneutics in the eighteenth
century has been a seminal influence on how theologians think about biblical
hermeneutics, and about biblical narrative in particular. Nevertheless, as one
would expect of a work that has been the subject of extensive discussion, some
of the discussion has been critical of certain aspects of the work. It is one such
criticism that I take as the point of departure of this paper. First, I examine a criticism that Kevin Vanhoozer makes of Frei's *Eclipse* and conclude that it is
unfounded though implicitly understandable. Second, drawing on the work of
Meir Sternberg and Nicholas Wolterstorff, I argue that there remains a conceptual weakness in Frei's framework for describing the transition from pre-critical
to critical hermeneutics. Third, I attempt to resolve this conceptual difficulty by
augmenting Frei's framework with the historical and conceptual framework
Wolterstorff provides in his seminal essay 'The Migration of the Theistic Arguments: From Natural Theology to Evidentialist Apologetics'.[2] In particular, I

---

[1] McIntyre, 'Interpretation', 51.
[2] Wolterstorff, 'Migration'.

will seek to draw on the Reformed-epistemological concept of basic versus non-basic belief implicitly employed by Wolterstorff's history of theological ideas. In essence, I argue that Frei's framework has to be augmented with the illocutionary stance of historical truth-claiming, specifically the concept of belief understood in terms of epistemic stance. This renders his framework capable of explaining the history of the shift from pre-critical to critical hermeneutics. The ultimate rationale behind the essay is as an exercise in conceptual and historical methodology. This means that one criterion by which the proposal should be judged is whether the framework contains sufficient conceptual parameters capable of explaining the historical shift in hermeneutics that Frei describes. I will end the essay with some brief remarks on this matter.

A Discrepancy in Frei?

In Chapter 1 of *The Eclipse of Biblical Narrative* Hans Frei drew a contrast between pre-critical and critical hermeneutics, famously, in the following way:

> ... if it seemed clear that a biblical story was to be read literally, it followed automatically that it referred to and described actual historical occurrences. The true historical reference of a story was a direct and natural concomitant of its making literal sense. This is a far cry from taking the fact that a story makes best sense at literal level as *evidence* that it is a reliable historical report.[3]

It is clear from *The Eclipse of Biblical Narrative* that these sentences are central to Frei's understanding of the course of the history of biblical interpretation before and after what he takes to be the watershed of the eighteenth century. The pre-critical stance assumed that if 'a biblical story was to be read literally then it followed automatically that it referred to and described actual historical occurrences'.[4] The critical stance assumed that if the story made 'best sense at literal level' then this was '*evidence* that it is a reliable historical report'.[5] Some commentators have detected discrepancy in Frei's comparison between pre-critical historical reference and critical historical reference. Vanhoozer writes:

> Frei reads the Gospels as history-like narratives. He insists that the literal sense of such texts is not to be equated with historical reference. But it is just here that we detect a certain tension in Frei, for the *literal* reading of these texts has traditionally affirmed a *historical* reference. Indeed, Frei admits as much. For pre-critical readers of

---

[3] Frei, *Eclipse*, 2.
[4] Ibid.
[5] Ibid.

Scripture, 'the true historical reference of a story was the direct and natural concomitant of its making literal sense.' For post-Enlightenment readers, however, the fact
that a biblical story made sense at a literal level was seen as evidence for its historical
factuality. Biblical critics saw this as an opportunity to examine the biblical referent
and question its truth. Biblical critics and exegetes began to fit the Bible into their
categories of reality rather than vice-versa.[6]

Vanhoozer's statement on Frei's position on pre-critical and critical historical
reference is as precise and as comprehensive a statement as one will find in the
theological literature. The question is: is it correct to say, as Vanhoozer does
say, that 'in defending the literal sense, [Frei] seems to have cut ties with the
question of historical reference, even though the latter was originally an ingredient in pre-critical literal reading'?[7] If the answer is yes, therein lies the source
of the tension that Vanhoozer detects in Frei. For, as Vanhoozer correctly
notes, Frei certainly 'admits' that 'the literal *reading* of these texts has traditionally affirmed a *historical* reference'.[8] And, indeed, there is a history of ideas in the
Eclipse that seems to bear witness to Frei's acknowledgement.

The Transition from Pre-critical to Critical Biblical Hermeneutics

According to Frei, one fundamental element in the pre-critical interpretation
of the Bible was the basic presumption of the *identity* of the world rendered by
the biblical narratives with the world of extrabiblical thought, experience and
reality. For a pre-critical exegete the two designated worlds were one and the
same, such that the latter world was to be interpreted in terms of the 'one real
world detailed and made accessible in the biblical story – not the reverse'.[9]

To anticipate: an exegete such as Calvin did not doubt for a moment that
the world in which he breathed, ate and slept was the very same world which
God had created; the very same world in which Jesus Christ had been crucified, dead and buried and had risen again on the third day; the very same world
in which Jesus Christ would come again in glory to judge the living and the
dead. Not for a second did Calvin doubt any of these articles of faith. Since the
biblical world was the source of Calvin's understanding of the world in which
he lived – it was after all the world he experienced in every waking second as
God's world – it followed that the world on which Calvin stood with his two

---

[6] Vanhoozer, *Biblical Narrative*, 175.
[7] Ibid.
[8] Ibid.
[9] Frei, *Eclipse*, 3.

feet was to be interpreted in terms of the 'one real world detailed and made accessible in the biblical story – not the reverse'.[10]

What happened to destroy the cohesiveness, indeed unity and comprehensiveness, of the pre-critical perspective? Frei locates the 'seeds of disintegration' as planted in the seventeenth century by radical thinkers like Spinoza; but he also traces the source of the breakdown of the original unity back to conservatives who, as he comments ironically, were biblicists to their boots: Johannes Cocceius (who like Spinoza was of the seventeenth century) and Johann Albrecht Bengel of the eighteenth century.[11] Both Cocceius and Bengel 'tried to locate the events of their day vis-à-vis the narrative framework of the biblical story and history, and to locate by means of biblical sayings the present stage of the actual events they experienced and predict future stages as well as the end of the actual history'.[12] An analogy might be that of the astrologer who uses his or her astrological manual as a means of understanding the present and predicting important events in the course of a person's life. There was a certain sense in which it could be said that, when Cocceius and Bengel used the Bible in this way, they were using the Bible as an astrological manual, though in Christian good faith. For, as Frei puts it, this kind of prophecy was a new cultural development: its emphasis was on the events, 'on their likely course and on the hidden signs and references to this "real" world of past and future history, spread through the Bible'.[11] There came into existence

> a kind of detachment of the 'real' historical world from its biblical temporal framework. The real events of history constitute an autonomous temporal framework of their own under God's providential design. Instead of rendering them accessible, the narratives, heretofore indispensable as a means of access to the events, now simply verify them, thus affirming their autonomy, and the fact that they are in principle accessible through any kind of description that can manage to be accurate either predictively or after the event. It simply happens that, again under God's providence, it is the Bible that contains the accurate descriptions.[14]

But the damage is done. The Bible may be confirmed as possessing the most impressive record of accurate prediction concerning events in the real world, that, of the available descriptive 'predictors' (astrology included), it has the most impressive record of accurate prediction both 'before and after the event'. But in being thus confirmed, it is implied that the events in the real world constituted the measure against which the Bible could be tested and

---

[10] Ibid., 3.
[11] Ibid., 4.
[12] Ibid.
[13] Ibid.
[14] Ibid., 4–5.

vindicated. Or, putting it in a more biblical vein: the world of the events one experienced independently of the Bible could in principle come to sit in judgement of its very veracity. Frei described the effect in the following words:

> There is now a logical distinction and reflective distance between the stories and the reality they depict. The depicted biblical world and the real historical world began to be separated at once in thought and sensibility, no matter whether the depiction was thought to agree with reality (Cocceius and Bengel) or disagree with it (Spinoza).[15]

In the pre-critical perspective, the biblical world and the real historical world are one and the same, the same world in which Calvin breathed, ate and slept; all three, as he experienced it, under the providential eye of his Maker. Accordingly, there is no conceivable 'epistemic space' in this world, no 'geographical point' as it were, that does not take place within the realm of the biblical world. It is as if, logically, there is no outside this world, and this precisely because 'every where' and 'every thing' cannot but be inside God's world. Consequently, to the pre-critical mind, it is as if there is no conceivable vantage point from which one can criticize the biblical world: one would have to get outside it, but that, so it appears (and may indeed be the case) is impossible. As Frei puts it:

> For Calvin, we have reality only under a description or, since reality is identical with the sequential dealing of God with men, under the narrative depiction which renders it, and not directly or without temporal narrative sequence. The reason for this is obvious. We are, as interpreters as well as religious and moral persons, part of the same sequence. We are not independent observers of it from outside the temporal framework in which we have been cast. We have no more external vantage point for thought than for action.[16]

---

[15] Ibid., 5. Though, as Frei points out, using the Bible like an astrological manual during this period was 'hardly an unprecedented preoccupation'. He argues that – in the fuller context of the cultural and intellectual developments of the era (presumably meaning, among other things, the rise of science) – it was a 'sign' (as it had not been in the pre-critical period) of the separation, at least in principle, of narrative and reality. Ibid., 4. To recapitulate: it was not necessary for the separation to take place that one's use of the Bible in this way resulted in failure; all that was necessary was the very engagement in the practice (i.e., it did not matter whether one's predictions were fulfilled or not). In the proto-Enlightenment context of the seventeenth century, the very engagement in biblical prediction gave rise to what it had not in the pre-critical period: the concept of measuring the Bible from the vantage point of the world. Frei, of course, argues that the pre-critical position was one of measuring the world from the vantage point of the Bible.

[16] Ibid., 36.

In the seventeenth and eighteenth centuries, with the advent of the critical perspective, this original unity – a once seamless garment – begins to come apart: there is now a 'logical distinction', and in consequence, a 'reflective distance between the stories and the reality they depict'.[17] Previously, an identity between the two worlds akin to a logical identity had been ingrained in pre-critical biblical thought and sensibility almost as a regulative principle of thought. Now, increasingly from the seventeenth century onwards, what had hitherto simply not been reflected upon – the possibility that this world might *not* be the same world which God had created, might *not* be the very same world in which Jesus Christ had been crucified, dead and buried and had risen again on the third day, might *not* be the very same world in which Jesus Christ would come again in glory to judge the living and the dead – that some or all of these things might *not* be true – becomes a matter for urgent reflection. What was inconceivable to the pre-critical mind becomes the conceivable. What was once thought to be an unsplittable identity becomes, in the thought and sensibility of the early Enlightenment mindset, separable in principle into two. What was once thought to be an original unity of one becomes a disjunction of two. One could go so far as to say that one no longer *experienced* the world of one's immediate experience as the world rendered by the biblical narrative. The world that a thinker such as the early Enlightenment philosopher John Locke experienced in the second half of the seventeenth century was quite simply a *different* world from the one Calvin had experienced in the sixteenth.[18]

To reiterate: in the wake of the logical disjunction there appears a 'reflective distance between the stories and the reality they depict'. That is, the identity of the two designated worlds could no longer be presumed true without

---

[17] Ibid., 5.

[18] As Frei puts it: 'the transition from Luther and Calvin' to Anthony Collins – a friend and disciple of Locke – 'is a voyage from one world to another'. Ibid., 90. Clearly the reasons Locke posited and experienced a disjunction between biblical narrative and reality are complex. For about a thousand years, western intellectuals had consulted a unified textual tradition when faced with the question of what to believe on matters of morality and religion. In the wake of the Reformation, personified among other things in Luther's challenge to the church, the European cultural and intellectual tradition split into warring fragments. Amid the proliferation of confessional documents in the sixteenth and seventeenth centuries, religious knowledge and belief had to be re-united around another standard. Locke sought to resolve the moral and religious crisis faced by European intellectuals after the Reformation by making an appeal to reason: Let reason be your guide! In the specific case of affirming the historicity of biblical narrative, appeal to the central miracles of the Christian faith was crucial for Locke. This is essentially the account that Wolterstorff gives in *John Locke*, 2–3. See also Popkin, *History*, ch. 1, for background to the epistemological crisis faced by the churches of the Reformation with the fragmentation of tradition.

justification, without *evidence*. There is now an obligation to prove that the events in question really happened such that the two designated worlds are in fact – turn out to be – the same world, this world. To be sure, the reflective distance between story and reality did not *exclude* the possibility that one could – with good reason – come to believe that story agreed with reality: though one did not *presume* the original identity, one could deploy *argument* and *evidence* as a means to affirming it; conversely, one could deploy argument and evidence in the opposite direction: to show that the two designated worlds were not identical, and could not be identical, because the central biblical narratives did not in fact concur with reality as it had been or was. Frei describes this 'logical distinction and reflective distance' between narrative and reality as 'increasing steadily' (throughout the eighteenth century), 'provoking a host of endeavours to bridge the gap'.[19] One of these endeavours was, naturally enough, an 'enormous amount of inquiry into the factual truth (or falsity) of the biblical stories'.[20] Frei cites John Locke as someone who had no doubt of the historicity of the narrated events precisely because he believed he had 'bridged the gap' between narrative and reality; which is to say, he believed himself to have provided good reason for believing in biblical historicity.[21]

To summarize: there is a history of biblical hermeneutics in *The Eclipse of Biblical Narrative* which clearly presumes that true historical reference was a 'natural concomitant' of a pre-critical reading of the Bible. There is a history of ideas in the *Eclipse* which more than bears witness to Vanhoozer's claim noted at the beginning of this section: Frei acknowledges that the literal reading of these texts traditionally affirmed a historical reference.

The Relation between Literal Reading and Historical Reference in the Pre-critical Period

Yet, as Vanhoozer notes, Frei also claims in the *Eclipse* that the literal sense of the narrative is not to be equated with historical reference. This, as was seen earlier, is the rationale behind Vanhoozer's assertion that 'in defending the literal sense, [Frei] seems to have cut ties with the question of historical reference, even though the latter was originally an ingredient in pre-critical literal reading'.[22] The question is whether the former does, in fact, imply the latter. I submit it does not. To say that the sense of the narrative is not to be equated with historical reference does not commit Frei to the position that historical reference was lacking in the pre-critical period. Frei does not deny the

---

[19] Frei, *Eclipse*, 5.

[20] Ibid.

[21] Ibid., 6.

[22] Vanhoozer, *Biblical Narrative*, 175.

presence of historical reference during this period; *he simply denies that the meaning of the story was identified with it.* Frei is absolutely comfortable with presence of historical reference during the pre-critical period, in Calvin and Luther, for example.

When Frei attributes to Calvin the belief that we could have reality 'only under a narrative' – the biblical narrative – he takes Calvin to mean precisely that the earth on which he stood – this world – was continuous with, identical with, the world narrated in the Bible. As Frei puts it: biblical narrative 're-mained the adequate depiction of the common and inclusive world'.[23] Hence, in accordance with the history of ideas in the section above, the 'common and inclusive' world was precisely the world in which these narrated events *had happened.* This is what Frei means by saying that biblical narrative was taken in the pre-critical period to be '*automatically* identical with reference to historical truth',[24] that the 'true historical reference of a story was *a direct and natural concomitant* of its making literal sense'.[25]

History-likeness, Historicity and History-telling

It has thus been established that Frei's account is not susceptible to the criticism Vanhoozer makes. This is not to say that it is not susceptible to other criticism. Frei is absolutely right in his claim that literal sense is not to be equated with historical reference. He gets entirely right his characterization of the pre-critical period. *Where Frei goes wrong is in his account of the transition from pre-critical to critical biblical hermeneutics.* He gets it right on the pre-critical period; he gets it wrong on the critical period.

When Frei describes the *effect* of the steadily increasing logical distinction and reflective distance between narrative and reality, he argues that, in the wake of this steadily increasing distinction and distance, the locus of the meaning of the narratives shifted from the stories themselves to the external historical referent.[26] Locke's 'new philosophy' is affirmed as the fundamental rationale behind an ostensive-referential analysis which subordinates 'explicative interpretation' – interpreting the meaning in the text itself – to 'critical-

---

[23] Ibid., 3.

[24] Ibid., 11 (emphasis mine).

[25] Ibid. (emphasis mine).

[26] Frei, *Eclipse*, 51. In ch. 5, entitled 'Hermeneutics and Meaning-as-Reference', Frei also makes the case that the meaning of the text itself shifted to an external referent that he identifies as 'ideal'. But since the paradigm-case of this referent – under the influence of the philosophy of Christian Wolff – was instructional (moral) teaching in the

historical explanation' – making history 'the *test* of the meaning of the stories':[27]

> ... Locke's theories, refracted through such deist controversies as that on prophecy and through later supernaturalist and historical-critical exegesis, exemplified a massive scholarly movement for which there was a direct convergence of the meaning of the biblical narratives with the shape of the events to which they refer.[28]

In other words, Frei appears to identify the watershed in biblical hermeneutics in the eighteenth century as one in which the meaning of the biblical narratives shifted from the stories themselves to their ostensive referent in the realm of actual historical event.

I said that Frei did not get it wrong in his characterization of the pre-critical period, but that he got it wrong in his characterization of the critical period. *He did this on two counts*: 1) meaning did not cease being the stories themselves in the critical period; 2) it did not become identical with the historical referent itself in the critical period. The reason for 1) is that meaning *could not* cease to be the stories themselves. The reason for 2) is that it is a logical corollary of 1): if the meaning of the narratives could not be other than the narrative itself, then it could not become identical with something else, be it a historical or an ideal referent. The shift that Frei attributes to the period of transition between pre-Enlightenment and Enlightenment hermeneutics represents a *philosophically* or *conceptually* indefensible position. It is not merely that it is historically false – it represents a philosophically or conceptually impossible historical explanation.

---

[26] (*Continued*) Bible, 'which could in turn be either dogma or general religious ideas (meaning as ideal reference)' (ibid., 101), the predominant presumption of the second half of the eighteenth century was that the 'primary reference' of biblical (historical) narrative was 'historical rather than ideal' (ibid.). Since I am concerned only with Frei's account of the history of the hermeneutics of biblical narrative in the eighteenth century, I will confine myself to meaning as historical referent. Nevertheless, what I have to say about his account would, according to the logic of my case, apply no less to ideal reference.

[27] Ibid., 93.

[28] Ibid., 95. Other examples of Frei's thesis that meaning converged on historical reference are the following. He writes of 'the confusion of history-likeness (literal sense) and history (ostensive reference)'. Ibid., 12. Again: '... their meaning is determined by their reference or failure to refer beyond themselves to certain events'. Ibid., 41. Speaking of biblical narrative, he writes that 'the historical subject-matter was now taken to be its true meaning'. Ibid., 51. He speaks of 'meaning as historical or ostensive reference'. Ibid., 86. Finally: 'Everything conspired to confine explicative hermeneutics to meaning as reference – to equate meaning with knowledge of potential or actual reality'. Ibid., 102.

Whatever happened in the transition, it could not have been this particular shift. (Therein lies the rationale behind engaging in *conceptual redescription* in the section below – hence also the rationale behind my subtitle.)

One cannot speak highly enough of the broad sweep of Frei's history, or of the brilliance of his historical observations on this or that thinker as regards their place and influence within this history: John Locke, Anthony Collins, J.S. Baumgarten, to name but three. The difficulty, as I have intimated, emerges when one attempts to place the more detailed history of ideas in the context of his general conceptual framework for understanding the history of biblical hermeneutics. The point has been well made by Meir Sternberg. Sternberg argues that Frei's conceptual framework is fundamentally flawed as a means of understanding the historical transition from pre-critical to critical biblical hermeneutics. This is because it attempts to understand the transition in terms of two conceptual categories – history-likeness (meaning) and historicity (truth-value) – when a third – history-telling – is necessary.[29] The fundamental rationale behind Sternberg's criticism is that, without the category of history-telling 'which relates to the truth-claim of the discourse',[30] one has insufficient conceptual resources for distinguishing between fiction-telling and historical truth-telling. The two concepts of history-likeness and historicity cannot do this by themselves. History-likeness, as Sternberg implies, is logically neutral as regards fiction and history, but goes 'as a rule' with the former.[31] Either way, it is not a condition of history-telling. Historicity, which relates to truth-value, has 'least to do with meaning and interpretation'[32] and, like history-likeness, cannot of itself render a character in a text a real character – no matter that the description happens to be true. Nicholas Wolterstorff has made a similar point in *Divine Discourse: Philosophical Reflections on the Claim that God Speaks*:

> Whether some discourse, or the text produced thereby, counts as fiction is not determined by the truth or falsehood of the designative content of that discourse.

---

[29] Sternberg, *Poetics*, 81. There is no doubt but that Frei was alive to the distinction between fictional and historical narrative, and contrary to such critics as Gary Comstock, pursued the truth question. See Comstock, 'Truth', 118. William C. Placher declares himself puzzled by the criticism since 'Frei so often acknowledged the appropriateness of the truth question'. See Frei, *Theology*, 23. But it remains the case that he did not have the conceptual resources in *Eclipse* to make the distinction.

[30] Sternberg, *Poetics*, 81.

[31] Ibid.

[32] Ibid.

The designative content of a specimen of history or biography may be massively false while yet being history or biography; conversely, the designative content of a specimen of fiction may be massively true while yet being fiction. Truman Capote's 'realistic fiction' *In Cold Blood*, is an example of this latter point.[33]

In other words: 1) what makes a genre historical cannot have anything to do with whether or not it is true; 2) historicity does not of itself determine genre: a non-fictional novel is still a *novel!* The point is: whether a book is massively true or massively false has little or nothing to do with whether it is a work of fiction or a work of history. The conclusion implicit in Wolterstorff is identical to that of Sternberg. When Sternberg criticizes Frei in terms of what is necessary for the interpretation of texts in general, he is making essentially the same point as Wolterstorff: history-likeness and historicity are not sufficient in order to determine whether a text is history-telling or fiction-telling.

Therein lies the significance of Sternberg and Wolterstorff's respective observations in the present context. It is a *normative* one: the three *distinct* categories of history-likeness, historicity (truth-value) and history-telling (or truth-claiming) apply to *all texts in all cases at all times.* One could just as little distinguish history-telling from fiction-telling *without the illocutionary stance of history-telling before* the Enlightenment as one could *after* the Enlightenment. This means, *inter alia*, that the three categories *applied just as much to the history of pre-critical exegesis of the Bible as to the history of critical exegesis of the Bible.* Hence, whatever shift took place in biblical hermeneutics in the eighteenth century, it cannot be explained in terms of a shift from meaning (history-likeness) to referent (truth-value*). Both concepts operated in some sense or another on both sides of the watershed.* Hence, somewhat ironically, Frei's decision to separate the meaning of biblical narrative from historical reference when describing the pre-critical period is endorsed: according to the analysis offered by Sternberg and Wolterstorff, the categories are logically and conceptually independent; hence they cannot be equated. What the analysis does not endorse is his characterization of the critical period. If both concepts *necessarily* operated in a logically independent manner on both sides of the watershed, then it cannot be right to say that the critical exegete *collapsed* meaning into the historical referent. This was to attribute to him or her an action that he or she, quite simply, *could not conceptually be described as doing.*

It is not, therefore, that Frei has identified a watershed in biblical hermeneutics in the eighteenth century when there was in fact none. That fact is not in question. What has been criticized is Frei's conceptual apparatus for

---

[33] Wolterstorff, *Divine Discourse*, 81.

describing it: his conceptual framework is inadequate as a means of describing the transition from pre-critical to critical hermeneutics.[34]

The Distinction between Basic and Non-basic Belief

Is there a way of preserving Frei's momentous historical insights in the *Eclipse* while at the same time integrating them into a more adequate theoretical description? I think there is. In a seminal essay on the history of ideas of the rationality of religious belief entitled 'The Migration of the Theistic Arguments: From Natural Theology to Evidentialist Apologetics',[35] Wolterstorff has examined the historical context of the emergence of the 'conviction that *unless one has good reasons for one's theistic beliefs, one ought to give them up*'.[36] He contends that

> after the demise of antiquity, the evidentialist challenge to religious belief first became part of the mind-set of Western intellectuals at the time of the Enlightenment. It belongs to the mentality of the *Aufklärung*. Specifically, I suggest that the proto-Enlightenment figure John Locke first articulately issued the evidentialist challenge to the religious believer, doing so as himself a Christian who thought he could meet the challenge.[37]

---

[34] The significance of Sternberg's and Wolterstorff's respective insights for biblical hermeneutics and theology in general should not be underestimated: what is implied is that the concept of historical truth-claiming is absolutely necessary for the hermeneutics of biblical narrative. Historical truth-claiming cannot be avoided; otherwise, we do away with the very identity of biblical narrative, failing to distinguish it from fiction. This realization on my part was a motive-force for writing this paper. A fascinating question remains: why did Frei not, as Sternberg points out, have the conceptual resources to distinguish between historical and fictional narrative? Why, in effect, does he appear to have resisted the necessity of the concept of historical truth-claiming? One can only guess, but one reason might have been that he could not see how to affirm historical truth-claiming without affirming what might be called historical evidentialism – some kind of historical apologetic. This seems to me to be a common fear. It has been my experience that one only has to speak positively of the concept of historical truth-claiming (never mind arguing for its necessity!) to find oneself accused by some theologians of compromising Christian orthodoxy. The accusation is, of course, completely without foundation – as any Reformed epistemologist will know. The rationality of affirming the historical truth-claims of the Gospel narratives, for example, does not depend on historical apologetic. Therefore it is perfectly rational to affirm the former and not the latter. I myself have presented a case for viewing the great Karl Barth as essentially a historical truth-claiming theologian without in any sense turning him into a liberal in the traditional sense. See MacDonald, *Karl Barth*.

[35] Wolterstorff, 'Migration'.

[36] Ibid., 38.

[37] Ibid., 38–9.

One of Wolterstorff's objectives is to show that the evidential apologetics of the Enlightenment was 'fundamentally different' from the mediaeval and, indeed, early modern project of natural theology. In this respect the emergence of evidential apologetics during the seventeenth and eighteenth centuries testified to a fundamental shift in epistemic stance from a 'faith seeking understanding' paradigm to what may be termed a 'faith requiring justification' one. The 'faith seeking understanding' paradigm constituted the fundamental rationale behind the respective theological epistemologies of Augustine, Anselm and Aquinas. But it was no less central to Calvin's basic epistemic stance. As Wolterstorff puts it, on the matter of epistemic stance, Calvin is closer to Aquinas than to Locke. Pre-Enlightenment theologians such as Aquinas and Calvin did not attach foundationalist conditions to theistic beliefs. To be sure, both Aquinas and Calvin are 'deeply convinced of the success of natural theology as polemic (and apologetic)'.[38] However, 'even if the polemic of belief with unbelief should fail because the arguments all prove to lack the force of demonstration, the failure would imply nothing whatsoever as to the acceptability of the believer's faith.'[39] Wolterstorff contrasts this epistemic stance with that of an Enlightenment thinker such as Locke: for Locke, 'the failure of evidentialist apologetics implies that the believer must surrender his faith'.[40] Though Wolterstorff does not explicitly use the terms, the fundamental difference that he discerns between natural theology and evidentialist apologetics can be explained in terms of the Reformed epistemological concept of basic versus non-basic belief.[41] Natural theology occurs in the context where theistic belief is construed as a basic belief, a basic belief being one that is believed not on the basis of any other belief, that is, as a foundational belief itself. Therefore there is no need to justify the belief in terms of some further belief(s). In contrast, evidentialist apologetics occurs in a context where theistic belief is construed as a non-basic belief, a non-basic belief being a belief that *is* based on some further belief(s).[42] Such a belief or

---

[38] Ibid., 80.

[39] Ibid.

[40] Ibid.

[41] It is to be acknowledged that Wolterstorff seems to prefer the conceptual apparatus of immediate/mediate belief to that of basic/non-basic belief. See Wolterstorff, 'Belief?', 149–50. My judgement is that the latter distinction fits more naturally with Frei's account of biblical hermeneutics and, in particular, Frei's account of Calvin's belief that this world is the world which God had created, etc. It seems to me to be more natural to call Calvin's belief here a basic one rather than an immediate one. The basic rationale behind Wolterstorff's conceptual apparatus in his essay remains unaffected.

[42] Alvin Plantinga provides an introduction to the concept of basic belief in his 'Belief?', 41–2. The concept of basic belief is to be distinguished from the concept of a

beliefs are taken to be more basic and taken to be *evidence* for the non-basic belief (hence the rationale behind the terms 'evidentialist' and 'evidentialism' in Wolterstorff's essay). I submit, then, that implicitly the distinction between basic and non-basic belief is crucial to Wolterstorff's account of the history of the rationality of theistic belief.

In what way might such an account augment Frei's framework? The shift that Wolterstorff discerns in theistic belief occurred in close historical proximity to the one Frei detected in biblical hermeneutics. It would therefore not be surprising if they were in some way historically or even conceptually connected. Both Sternberg and Wolterstorff have pointed to the fact that Frei's hermeneutical framework needs to be augmented with the concept of historical truth-claiming. Clearly, simply to add this concept to the framework leaves us with the same problem that beset Frei's account. Historical truth-telling was true on both sides of the history. Therefore, it cannot, *per se*, explain the transition. However, historical truth-claiming, it seems to me, *presupposes that one believes what it is one is claiming about history*. It is conceptually connected with the concept of belief. What I want to propose is that the shift took place in the domain of belief and, in particular, one's epistemic stance toward belief.[43]

---

[42] (*Continued*) properly basic belief. A properly basic belief is a basic belief which it is rational to hold other than on the basis of any further belief. In the present context the latter does not apply. The question whether it remained rational in the face of the evidentialist challenge to affirm belief in the historical truth-claims of biblical narrative as a basic belief is beyond the scope of this essay. The focus of this essay is confined to the historical facts as they occurred, not whether it would have been rational had they been otherwise.

[43] This does not mean that the pre-critical position on the epistemic stance of belief was one of mere personal conviction or existential commitment rather than one of rationality. There is no doubt but that the Enlightenment, in the context of the rise of modern science, viewed knowledge as superior to mere belief. But we find the same distinction present in the pre-critical period. Aquinas, for example, acknowledged a similar distinction between belief and knowledge or *scientia*: for Aquinas, belief or faith in some sense fell short when measured by the standards of knowledge. Hence, to convert one's belief in God into knowledge was to replace an incomplete epistemic position to a more complete one. For Calvin too, belief was not to be cut asunder from rationality or argument. The difference between the two periods is that for the former, *scientia* is a necessary condition of the rationality of belief; for the latter, *scientia* at best is a sufficient condition (demonstrability of the truth of one's belief may be sufficient for rationality but it is not necessary). What therefore would be at issue as regards the rationality of epistemic stance (were we asking the question) is the rationality of believing and affirming the historical truth-claims of biblical narrative without having taken recourse to historical apologetic. (It should be added that such a position does not exclude argument: one only has to look at Calvin's attempt to harmonize the synoptic Gospels to see this.)

As we have seen, in Frei's account the shift is construed as one in which the meaning of the stories shifted from the stories themselves to their historical referents: the meaning – or point – of the stories *changed*. The crucial factor in the account I am offering is that the meaning of the stories *remained basically the same*. Rather, what changed in the wake of the 'steady increase' in the 'logical distinction and reflective distance' between narrative and reality was this: the *belief* that the biblical stories referred to and described actual historical occurrences changed from being a *basic* belief to being a *non-basic* belief. A belief that did not, indeed could not, be justified, became one that obliged evidence of one kind or another. If one were to phrase this in the language of historical truth-telling or historical truth-claiming, one could say that the historical truth-claiming of a pre-critical interpreter such as Calvin was done from the epistemic stance of *basic belief*. In contrast, what we find in a thinker such as Locke is historical truth-claiming done from the epistemic stance of non-basic belief. The change or shift occurred at the level of *epistemic stance* as regards historical truth-telling, not at the level of the meaning of the text itself.

This theoretical adjustment to Frei's explanation of the shift dovetails more or less exactly with the account he gave in the introduction to the *Eclipse* and which constitutes, I believe, the essence of his case. As I said, Calvin did not doubt for a moment that the world of his experience – the world in which he ate, walked and slept – was the world which God had created, the world in which Jesus Christ had been crucified, dead and buried and rose again on the third day. For Calvin, as for others of his time, 'if a biblical story was to be read literally, it followed automatically that it referred to and described actual historical occurrences'.[44] *It could not be otherwise*. It was not a question of justification. They believed in the biblical narrative as a matter of basic belief. They told it as a matter of basic belief. In contrast, if one takes, as Frei does, John Locke as a representative of the historical Enlightenment, it is implicit in Frei's account that the world which he experienced – the extrabiblical world – was separable in principle from the world rendered by the biblical stories. As Frei explains, the former world came to possess – vis-à-vis the world rendered by the biblical stories – an autonomy all of its own against which the latter world could be measured. This created the possibility of an external independent epistemic vantage point from which the reliability of the story as historical report could be doubted. To be sure, Locke ultimately affirmed the proposition that the world of his experience was the world in which God had created the heavens and the earth, and so on. Like Calvin before him, he affirmed the truth-claims of biblical narrative. As Frei says: 'Locke had no doubt of the historicity of the narrated events.'[45] The crucial difference is that, unlike

[44] Frei, *Eclipse*, 2.
[45] Ibid., 6.

Calvin, he attempted to provide reasonable grounds for his belief. He did not believe in the biblical narrative as a matter of basic belief. Belief in it was rather a matter of justification. I conclude that epistemic stance construed in terms of the distinction between basic and non-basic belief is able to explain the shift in biblical hermeneutics that Frei describes: therein lies the fundamental difference between pre-critical and critical hermeneutics.

Conclusion

My objective in this essay has been the modest one of showing how Frei's problematic account in *The Eclipse of Biblical Narrative* can be integrated into a more coherent, because more comprehensive, conceptual framework – one incorporating the distinction between basic and non-basic belief. The more ambitious task still before us is to show that the distinction between basic and non-basic belief is borne out in those whose work is pivotal to the thesis – including, of course, Calvin. Though Paul Helm has warned against employing conceptual frameworks which may bear at best only a distant resemblance to what Calvin actually said,[46] in the case of Calvin's doctrine of Scripture there does appear to be warrant for attributing to Calvin some such understanding of the Bible in terms of basic belief. Calvin speaks of the authority of Scripture as residing 'in a higher place than human reasons, judgements or conjectures, that is, in the secret testimony of the Holy Spirit'.[47] Whether one can extrapolate in this respect from Calvin to pre-critical interpreters in general is a matter for future research, but I am confident that it can be done. Beyond this, the lesson seems to be that Frei's original framework was comprised of insufficient conceptual parameters as regards a theoretically satisfactory historical framework capable of explaining the transition between pre-critical and critical hermeneutics. Whether the parameters I have provided are sufficient in this respect is, as the question of extrapolation, a matter for further examination. It may be that some additional parameters are necessary. Brevard Childs has characterized the shift between pre-critical and critical hermeneutics as one in which the final form of the biblical text was supplanted by a highly edited and reduced form of the text.[48] Whether this is a phenomenon independent of the shift in the epistemic stance of belief, or at the very least a highly correlated factor accompanying the shift from basic to non-basic belief, might be a suitable point of departure for testing whether one has an adequate model or not.

---

[46] Helm, *Faith*, 197–201.
[47] Calvin, *Institutes*, 78.
[48] Childs, *New Testament Canon*, 154–56.

Bibliography

Calvin, J., *Institutes of the Christian Religion*, I (ed. J.T. McNeill; trans. F.L. Battle; Philadelphia: Westminster Press, 1961)

Childs, B., *New Testament Canon: An Introduction* (London: SCM Press, 1985)

Comstock, G., 'Truth or Meaning: Ricœur versus Frei on Biblical Narrative', *JR* 66 (1986), 109–25

Frei, H.W., *The Eclipse of Biblical Narrative: A Study in Eighteenth and Nineteenth Century Hermeneutics* (New Haven, London: Yale University Press, 1974)

—, *Theology and Narrative* (ed. G. Hunsinger and W.C. Placher; New York: OUP, 1993)

Helm, P., *Faith and Understanding* (Edinburgh: Edinburgh University Press, 1997)

MacDonald, N.B., *Karl Barth and the Strange New World within the Bible: Barth, Wittgenstein, and the Metadilemmas of the Enlightenment* (Carlisle: Paternoster, 2000)

McIntyre, A., 'Interpretation of the Bible', *Yale Review* 65 (1975–76), 251–55

Plantinga, A., 'Is Belief in God Properly Basic?', *Nous* 15 (1981), 41–51

Popkin, R., *The History of Scepticism from Erasmus to Spinoza* (Berkeley, London: University of California Press, 1979)

Vanhoozer, K., *Biblical Narrative in the Philosophy of Paul Ricœur: A Study in Hermeneutics and Theology* (Cambridge: CUP, 1990)

Wolterstorff, N., 'Can Belief in God be Rational if it has No Foundations?', in *Faith and Rationality: Reason and Belief in God* (ed. A. Plantinga and N. Wolterstorff; Notre Dame: University of Notre Dame Press, 1983), 135–86

—, *Divine Discourse: Philosophical Reflections on the Claim that God Speaks* (Cambridge: CUP, 1996)

—, *John Locke and the Ethics of Belief* (Cambridge: CUP, 1996)

—, 'The Migration of the Theistic Arguments: From Natural Theology to Evidentialist Apologetics', in *Rationality, Religious Belief, and Moral Commitment* (ed. R. Audi and W.J. Wainwright; Ithaca, NY: Cornell University Press, 1986), 38–81

16

Metaphor, Symbol and the Interpretation of Deuteronomy

J. Gordon McConville

Introduction: Language in Deuteronomy Studies

Whereas evaluations of Deuteronomy's language have in the past focused on its characteristic vocabulary and phraseology, I want to consider instead how its linguistic features, especially its metaphors and symbols, are assimilated into the book at the highest level of discourse, namely the book as a finished entity, and even beyond that, in terms of its setting in the Old Testament canon. The justification for doing this is that Deuteronomy has not only a definable self-contained structure, but also a sharp hermeneutical self-awareness, and even provides for its own re-reading.

The critical study of Deuteronomy has always been closely bound up with its language. That is, its characteristic literary style, phraseology and use of vocabulary, classically described by S.R. Driver,[1] has been a factor in its identification as a distinct literary and theological entity within the Old Testament. Driver's analysis appears to have presupposed that there was a special Deuteronomic linguistic reservoir. The use of language in describing Deuteronomic theology followed from this premise. Because of its linguistic peculiarities, it could be shown not only that Deuteronomy itself was a separate theological entity, but also that wherever else the same type of vocabulary and style occurred, there 'Deuteronomic' influence was also present. And since the vocabulary of law ('the statutes, ordinances and commandments', and, embracing all of these, 'torah') is prominent in the book, the result has been a tendency to interpret Deuteronomy as a book of

---

[1] Driver, *Deuteronomy*, lxvii–xcv.

law, often with a further implication of legalism. These features of the book have
then been used to distinguish it from other books of the Old Testament.[2]

Examples of the effect of this method abound. It has affected the study of
Deuteronomy itself. M. Noth established a distinction between theological
categories of history and law that corresponded to the formal distinctions
between narrative and *paranesis* (exhortation).[3] The differentiation between
'Deuteronomic' and 'Deuteronomistic' followed from this. After Noth, G.
Minette de Tillesse traced redactional layers through Deuteronomy in which
the respective use of singular and plural address served to identify subtly different theological perspectives, though still related to law.[4] In still other studies,
specific vocabulary is regarded as a key to theological points of view (for
example, Lohfink's discovery of a layer based on the term *yarash*, 'inherit').[5]

In the Historical Books, now known as the Deuteronomistic History
(DtrH), the position is similar. R. Smend established one of the prevailing
models of interpretation of these books – postulating several redactional layers,
again subtly distinguished from each other, by means which include the recognition of redactions by their distinctive vocabulary.[6] T. Veijola's studies of the
narratives of the kings also exemplify the point.[7]

In Jeremiah studies, the prose sections of that book have long been known
to have similarities of vocabulary and style with Deuteronomy, such that the
dominant critical view is that Jeremiah is a Deuteronomistic product.[8] In this
context, to give a specific example, the New Covenant passage (Jer. 31:31–
34) is sometimes seen as a desperate rehash of the Deuteronomistic attempt to
regulate Israelite society by adherence to torah.[9] The role played by language
in the criticism of Jeremiah is clearest, oddly enough, where the
Deuteronomistic origin of the book is contested. John Bright's well-known
defence of its Jeremianic origin proceeded by demonstrating differences
between the vocabulary of the prose and that of Deuteronomy.[10] In this
concern to preserve the unique contribution of the prophet, Bright adopted

---

[2] Thus where the Priestly literature (P) has been seen as essentially a theology of divine
presence, Deuteronomy (D) was above all a theology of law; so still Blum, *Komposition*.
[3] Noth, *Deuteronomistic History*.
[4] Minette de Tillesse, 'Sections'. Cf. W. Mittmann's treatment of Deut. 1:1 – 6:3;
Deuteronomium 1:1 – 6:3.
[5] Lohfink, 'Kerygmata'.
[6] Smend, 'Das Gesetz'.
[7] Veijola, *Dynastie*; *Königtum*.
[8] Hyatt, 'Deuteronomic Edition'; Carroll, *Jeremiah*; Thiel, *Jeremia 1–25*; idem, *Jeremia
26–45*.
[9] Carroll, *Jeremiah*, 611–12.
[10] Bright, 'Prose Sermons'.

the same view of language exhibited in Driver's first analysis of Deuteronomic style. The linguistic deficiency of the attempt was felt by H. Weippert, who attempted to put Bright's thesis on a firmer footing by demonstrating distinctive usages across larger stretches of text.[11] She too, however, may not have entirely escaped the same pitfall.

The way in which literary and theological entities are identified by means of language varies and undergoes development. Wordstock and style can be a way into an enquiry, which then proceeds by the assumption that the 'Deuteronomist' has incorporated other material into his work. W. Thiel's work on Jeremiah is a case in point, leading to the complaint of W. McKane that it was a case of 'heads I win, tails you lose'.[12] That is, if a phrase in Jeremiah had affinities with Deuteronomic vocabulary, it was Deuteronomic. But if it didn't it was still Deuteronomic, because the Deuteronomist had taken it over. Veijola also appears to want to have it both ways. In one place he declares that style is the only criterion for determining the history of redaction, while in another he says: 'one cannot expect the [presence of peculiar characteristics of DtrN, i.e., the nomistic Deuteronomist] in every text, as the Deuteronomists, of course, did not only speak with their own phraseology'.[13] Noth may be the progenitor of this way of thinking, because of his idea of the Deuteronomist as a historian who re-used existing materials. In his thesis, the books of Samuel had little Deuteronomistic vocabulary, but they were still subordinated to the Deuteronomistic author's overall purpose.

These developments show, however, that the use of wordstock in itself as the basis for theological interpretation comes under strain in the application. Somehow, context has to be considered as well. In some cases, the criterion of vocabulary and style ends up in uneasy tension with the context set up by the hypothesis. T. Mettinger's belief that the phrase '*lipne Yahweh*' ('before the LORD'), which recurs in Deuteronomy 12 – 18, 'may be a sort of linguistic fossil, bearing no semantic cargo of importance' is a case in point (since his argument depends in part on the Deuteronomic style).[14] And W. Dietrich's study of DtrH, which comes close to a 'final form' treatment, remains constrained by a preceding redaction-critical analysis that owes much to vocabulary as a guide to theology.[15]

---

[11] Weippert, *Prosareden*.

[12] McKane, 'Poetry and Prose', 224.

[13] Veijola, *Königtum*, 13, cf. 110–11 (the translations are mine).

[14] Mettinger, *Dethronement*, 53.

[15] Dietrich, 'Niedergang'. Cf. Crüsemann, *Torah*, 274, and n. 339, who opposes the use of Deuteronomic language alone as a key to the setting and function of Deut. 26:17–19.

Language in context

In contrast to these common features of critical thinking about the Deuteronomic literature, modern trends in the realms of language and litera- ture promote the importance of discourse contexts in determining meaning. To say this does not afford simple answers to the kinds of critical questions raised in the foregoing, however. Those works that we have mentioned have some notion of context. The question is how context is constructed. I have suggested already that contexts are sometimes established in the train of obser- vations based on language and style. (I will notice an example of this below, in the Deuteronomic theology of the divine name, in which the context for the interpretation of individual texts is not a book, or even a set of books, but a religious-political movement constructed hypothetically on the basis of the interpretation of key texts.)

In this paper I want to think about context in ways that do not depend at the outset on vocabulary and phraseology as keys to meaning-units. In doing so I am supposing that interpretations based on these criteria may impose quite artificial boundaries between types of usage. Indeed, texts that share similar vocabulary and style might actually say quite different things, or even be opposed to each other in certain respects. I take this premise to be a gain of speech-act theory, with its recognition that similar 'locutions' might mean dif- ferent things depending on the communicative intention of the author or speaker. Recognition of Deuteronomy's characteristic style may point us to matters of occasion and effect, but it cannot substitute for an enquiry into these as essential elements in the book's interpretation.

We now turn to the interpretation of Deuteronomy, with an eye on the role that an understanding of language might play in it. An underlying issue is the definition of limits. I take it that Deuteronomy may be read in the first instance as a discrete entity, and therefore as a valid context within which to read the discourse in it. The definition of it depends on a number of factors: it has a clear beginning and ending; it has a structure that is intelligible in the light of formal parallels in the ancient world; it has characteristic themes; and, as we have seen, it has a characteristic style.

Deuteronomy and Metaphor/Symbol

We begin with a consideration of metaphor and symbol.[16] Deuteronomy uses a number of important metaphors and symbols in individual ways when

---

[16] Stiver, *Philosophy*, gave me an important stimulus in thinking about this topic.

compared with their use in other parts of the Old Testament. In my view, this feature of the book is of the greatest importance for its interpretation. The problem confronting the interpreter, however, is how to know what the force of any metaphorical usage is. I mean by this that metaphors may have a strong element of what is called 'semantic shock' or 'semantic impertinence'. That is, when they are fresh they have a capacity to surprise the hearer or reader in such a way as to suggest new horizons of meaning. On the other hand, when metaphors become worn they no longer pack that first punch; as 'stock' metaphors they can simply enter the familiar linguistic pool. Anthony Thiselton, in the present volume, shows how Paul's argument concerning a 'spiritual person' in 1 Corinthians involves 'code-switching', that is, using terms in a way that challenges the audience's pre-understanding of what those terms might mean. In that case, knowledge of the specific setting of the writing has helped determine the force of the terms in question. Ian Paul, furthermore, in his consideration of Ricœur's treatment of metaphor, proposes that Ricœur has paid insufficient attention to the 'moment of semantic impertinence' in the world of the writer and first audience. Ian Paul shares with Ricœur the concept of metaphor as a process. The life cycle of a metaphor, from coinage to assimilation into the common speech, can expand 'the world which language can describe'.

Determining the setting of Deuteronomy with any degree of certainty is highly problematical, as it is for many writings of the Old Testament. This means that the questions just aired have to be pursued with some openness of mind concerning the extent to which author and audience shared a particular pre-understanding of concepts addressed in the book. It follows that a theoretical issue is raised to which we must return. First, however, we will consider some of the important metaphors and symbols in the book, to see whether a discernible pattern emerges. The following topics in Deuteronomic theology (among others) might be considered in relation to this issue: kingship, treaty, land, the divine name, the brotherhood of Israelites, circumcision. In each case, I think, something distinctive and interesting is being said by the way in which language is used.

Kingship and Zion

I suggest that Deuteronomy offers a sustained view of what is involved in an appropriate polity for Israel. It does so by addressing the issue of kingship, which in Israel is bound up with other metaphors and symbols, notably that of Zion, the holy mountain on which, in the familiar vision of many Psalms and the book of Isaiah, Yahweh has installed his chosen king, and dwells himself in his temple (cf. Ps. 2). Kingship is a widespread concept in the ancient Near East, and the typical pattern among Israel's nations is for the king to have a powerful role in all aspects of the national life.[17] The language of kingship is also extended into the sphere of the gods, so that gods can be thought of as kings (e.g. Baal, in the *Palace of Baal* and the *Baal-Yam* and *Baal-Mot* epics). Indeed, the metaphors of court, battlefield, jurisprudence and bureaucracy – all involving kingship – are fully exploited in ancient Near Eastern religious language.[18] The Old Testament participates in these ancient Near Eastern habits of language, in the sense that Yahweh too is 'king' in Israel (1 Sam. 8:5), and David is his 'son' (Ps. 2:7). The Davidic kings at their most powerful are not far from the ancient Near Eastern pattern.

However, human kingship is played down in Deuteronomy (Deut. 17:14–20). The king is a student of torah, and deprived of the usual trappings of absolute power. This is at least a challenge to the kind of kingship represented by Solomon (1 Kgs. 10). The challenge to the style of kingship that we know from the story of the Davidic dynasty goes deep: Israelites as such are 'sons of Yahweh' in Deuteronomy, and Yahweh is the 'father' of Israel (14:1, cf. 1:31; also Exod. 4:22).[19] The *qahal* (the assembly of Israel gathered at religious festivals) appoints officials (16:18) and is ultimately responsible for administering torah. The prophet stands over all this, with a 'Mosaic' responsibility for interpretation of torah (18:15–18). Implicitly (and explicitly in Deut. 33:5), it is Yahweh who is king in Deuteronomy. It is he who delivers from slavery and is responsible for the royal duties of righteousness and justice.

To view the intervention (in Deut. 17:14–20, with its ramifications) from a linguistic point of view, it looks like an attempt to redefine what 'king' might mean. This impression is reinforced by a reading of Deuteronomy in its wider context (with DtrH), and also by its cumulative attitude to the theology of Zion.

Along with the diminution of kingship, the theology of Zion is expressly avoided in Deuteronomy. Instead of Zion we have 'the place that the LORD your God will choose to put his name and make his habitation there' (Deut. 12:5). What is the significance of this cumbersome and oft-repeated periphrasis? Is it merely a transparent fiction, necessitated by the artificial setting of Deuteronomy in the Mosaic era?[20] I suggest that it goes deeper, and

---

[17] Ahlström, *Administration*.

[18] Handy, *Host*.

[19] The shift in Deuteronomy compared with 'Zion' texts implies that what is involved in the divine fatherhood here is a democratization of God's special relationship with and care for people. A similar point may underlie Exod. 4:22, where Israel as Yahweh's first-born son makes a contrast in the wider narrative with Pharaoh's first-born son, who will be at the centre of the Passover drama. It is Deuteronomy that develops the implications of the concept, however.

[20] So, e.g., Clements, *Deuteronomy*, 28.

is part of a theology of place and 'journey' that refuses to see any one place as having a final or supreme function in Israel's life.[21] It therefore corresponds to the severely circumscribed role permitted the king, as part of a quite distinct understanding of the religious and political life of the people.

The treatment of Horeb in Deuteronomy is also part of this theology of place. Is Horeb just an alternative name for the place at which the law was given? Or is there a special reason why 'Sinai' is almost entirely avoided in Deuteronomy (except in 33:2, the blessing of Moses)? Is it to avoid certain connotations of Sinai in some context, perhaps the Sinai-Zion parallel set up in texts like Psalm 68:18 (17)? Alternatively, a connection with the god *sin* has been suggested.[22] While such suggestions are somewhat speculative, the significance of the choice of the term 'Horeb', along with the avoidance of Sinai, seem to fit with the tendency in Deuteronomy to deny supremacy to particular places of religious significance. Sinai, like Zion, retreats here. 'Horeb' sounds like a nondescript place, a 'dry place', desert as opposed to land, not even conspicuously a mountain (though Perlitt takes this point too far). The place is diminished, even though the events that occurred there remain crucial.

In this theology of place the journey from Sinai to Zion (Ps. 69) has been reconceived as a journey from Horeb (the dry place) to an unnamed place. Indeed, this is only a section of the journey, which reaches in fact from a hoarier antiquity (Abraham) into an open future. The whole journey has thus placed the key event, the giving of torah to Israel, in a new framework, with distinctive ideological features. I am suggesting that a deliberate, distinctive use of language and symbols has played a major part in this.

Finally, in connection with the relation between symbolism and the ideology of kingship, we may consider the formal similarities of the book to both treaty and law code. The connection with the kingship theme lies in the fact that law- and treaty-making in the ancient Near East are in the province of the king, and treaty-making is part of the means by which the king sustains his power. The issue that concerns us here is how the treaty metaphor has been assimilated to a theological or ideological purpose.

Deuteronomy 13 is a key text in this regard, because it depicts apostasy from Yahweh in terms strikingly similar to those in which Assyrian treaties, especially the vassal treaties of Esarhaddon, portray the disloyalty of vassals to Esarhaddon's successors on the throne.[23] What does this echo mean? According to one highly influential view, the imitation of Assyrian habits

---

[21] McConville and Millar, *Time and Place*, 89–139.

[22] See Perlitt, 'Sinai'.

[23] See Dion, 'Suppression'.

implies an echo of the whole royal-scribal milieu in which the Assyrian documents were produced. The significance of the symbolism, consequently, is to affirm the authority of Yahweh and his king (Hezekiah and/or Josiah), in opposition to the hegemonic claims of Assyria in Judah in the seventh century BC.[24]

However, this aspect of our exploration of the kingship metaphor illustrates the difficulty involved in attempting to understand the book's metaphors by reference to a specific historical (or rhetorical) situation. The date and setting of Deuteronomy used to be regarded as one of the assured results of criticism, but there is much less confidence on the matter today. In modern criticism, Deuteronomy has been dated to various times in the history of Israel and Judah.[25] The nodal points are the late Judean monarchy and the exilic period, with a current predilection for the latter (an option canvassed by F. Hölscher in the 1920s). However, even where the connection between Deuteronomy and late Judah is maintained, there are disparate opinions about its purpose. Specifically, is it in favour of Josiah's reform or actually in contention with it? Deuteronomy can be construed as an affirmation of the kingship of Yahweh alone, rejecting not merely the power of Assyria, but the whole Assyrian conceptualization of politics and religion, including the idea of the king as chief executive in all the affairs of the nation. As such it would hardly be the chosen instrument of a Josiah, who although promoting a Yahwistic reform, was committed to a centralized administration with himself at the apex of the pyramid. The analysis of Weinfeld has not reckoned sufficiently with this discrepancy between the nature of Josiah's reform and the programme of Deuteronomy.

It is not necessary in this context to argue for a date or setting of Deuteronomy. The point is rather to say that investigations of historical settings for Old Testament writings typically produce limited results. This is simply a fact of life in Old Testament studies. I do not mean to be pessimistic about historical study as such. On the contrary, the historical milieu is bound to enter into interpretation to the extent that it can be understood. In this case it furnishes basic concepts in the intellectual and religious environment. It also provides a backdrop against which to evaluate possible communicative intentions of the text. The limitations of our historical knowledge, however, have implications for the concept of 'semantic shock', which on some estimates requires an understanding of the situation of first use. However, in the interpretation offered here, the characteristics of Deuteronomy's polity for Israel have been identified mainly by comparison with other Old Testament texts. The meaning of the metaphor, therefore, has been pursued by a primarily 'canonical' method.[26]

---

[24] Weinfeld, *Deuteronomy*, 99–100.

[25] For a recent survey, see Tigay, *Deuteronomy*, xix–xxiv.

With this in mind, we turn now to the other metaphors and symbols mentioned above.

Land/inheritance

Land is one of the great themes of Deuteronomy. Its usage here is distinctive compared with other parts of the Pentateuch by reason of the idea of land as an 'inheritance' of Israel (Deut. 4:21; cf. Lev. 25:23, in which the land remains Yahweh's, and the Israelites are strangers and tenants). It may be called a 'symbol' in the sense that it includes actual specified land, yet land and its possession also stand for the covenant relationship between Yahweh and Israel in all its dimensions. It includes visions of plenty that recall the blessings of creation (8:7–10), and it stands in parallel with the broader ideas of 'good' and 'life' (6:23–24). As 'place', it conveys belonging, and also comes into close connection with place as place of worship (see 26:9, where 'place' has a certain pregnant ambivalence; cf. 1:31). 'Land' thus becomes inseparable from the Deuteronomic vision of a people keeping covenant, worshipping and enjoying blessing in the context of community, justice, peace and joy (16:13–15).

Brotherhood

Deuteronomy's view of the people of Israel is nowhere more clearly expressed than in its notion of it as a brotherhood. It also has a direct bearing on the idea of inheritance. Brotherhood in Deuteronomy is a striking extension of the more common usage of the idea, which may be exemplified in Psalm 133 ('How very good and pleasant it is when brothers dwell together in unity'; see also Ps. 133:1, a probable reference to a practice by which brothers who have inherited shares of the family property agree to operate it as if it were a unit). The Deuteronomic idea has in common with the Psalm the notion of shared

---

[26] James Barr reflects interestingly on the way in which the study of individual texts, in its various dimensions, relates to 'canonical' study. The traditional critical methodologies had theological significance implicit in them. Critical commentators 'interpreted the text within the context of the other relevant texts'; *Biblical Theology*, 143. In doing so they looked for a 'deeper' or 'higher' level of meaning, which 'would come when one asked about the ultimate axioms and assumptions that were implicit in the text and that were, potentially, significant for regulative statements within theology' (ibid.). He then brings a canonical dimension to the issue, when he writes of the felt inadequacy of a 'theology' of an individual book of the Bible: 'One may perhaps argue thus: since no one book can be authoritative on its own, therefore the theology of any one book can never probe the more profound questions. This is perhaps one way of expressing the effect of the canon', ibid., 144.

inheritance, but it extends this boldly to the sharing of the whole land by the whole people. The idea then affects the orientation of its laws – for example, its law of slave-release (15:12–18), which is undergirded by the brotherly status of all Israelites, in contrast to other release laws (Exod. 21:2–6; Lev. 25:39–46).

In a remarkable case of Old Testament 'inclusive language', 'brother' in this law includes 'sister'! This appears at the opening of the law: 'If a brother – a Hebrew man or a Hebrew woman'. There is a considerable surprise element in this phrase. In the Book of the Covenant (or BC, that is, Exod. 20:22 – 23:19, generally regarded as an earlier code, on which Deuteronomy draws), the status of women in the context of slavery is clearly different from that of men. Deuteronomy's 'feminist' programme is broader than just this instance. (It appears in the recurring command to provide for the widow, orphan and stranger; in the telling expansion of the Sabbath command in Deut. 5:14d – 'so that your male and female slave may rest as well as you', cf. Exod. 20:10; and in the laws concerning sex and marriage in Deut. 22:13–30; 24:1–4, which I believe demonstrate a concern to protect the woman [*pace* Carolyn Pressler[27]]). The opening line of the slave-release law, therefore, is not accidental or out of place, but in keeping with a direction in the book that is observable elsewhere. And this suggests that it has an intended element of 'semantic shock', designed to press a case for a higher view of women in Israel. (Curiously, some modern inclusive devices, such as NRSV's 'If a member of your community, a Hebrew man or a Hebrew woman', miss the force of this.)

'Circumcision of the heart' (Deut. 10:16; 30:6)

This appears to be a bold neologism. It gives rise to the familiar question in Old Testament study whether Deuteronomy, along with the prophets and certain Psalms, aims to abolish the physical and material rituals in favour of 'spiritual-ized' forms (cf. Ps. 40; 50; Amos 5:21–24; Mic. 6:6–8). (H. Hermisson used the term '*Entdinglichung*' for this spiritualizing process.[28]) Here, too, there is a danger of superimposing assumptions from theories of religious development on linguistic criteria.

By way of drawing some conclusions from our study so far, we have seen that Deuteronomy illustrated how metaphors and symbols could be used so as to suggest new ideas to reader or audience in rather forceful ways. It must be said, however, that the business of sensing the connotations of language and terminology in an ancient text is slippery. Our texts come to us from worlds of meaning that we only partially understand. However, as I have already

---

[27] Pressler, 'Violence'; *View*.

[28] Hermisson, *Sprache*.

suggested, both historical and canonical lines of enquiry have a place in the attempt to recover the meaning of biblical language.

Further on Meaning in Context

We have explored issues in establishing contexts within which to interpret biblical language. However, the establishment of contexts for texts, both in life and in literature, is complex and contested. The recognition of the possibility of historical and canonical dimensions of context does not in itself guarantee that texts will be understood in the best way. In what follows we will take an example of the danger of assigning a false context to an important linguistic usage in the interpretation of Deuteronomy.

The name of God

Deuteronomy's laws of worship have a distinctive formula involving the 'name' of Yahweh (e.g. 12:5). This formula has been taken as evidence of a Deuteronomic 'name-theology', a phenomenon associated with the reform of religion in the reign of King Josiah, according to which Yahweh does not himself dwell at the sanctuary. He has, instead, merely put his name there as a kind of representative, or hypostasis.[29] The name-theology is therefore the pre-eminent feature of a Deuteronomic theology of the divine presence. The interpretation has been supported by a reading of Deuteronomy—Kings in which the dominant theology is spiritualizing and the view of God is transcendent, as opposed especially to the 'immanent' God of P. The portrayal of the ark of the covenant in Deuteronomy as a (mere) container for the two stone tablets of the law (10:5), in contrast to the Priestly picture in which it is part of the furniture of the 'holy of holies' in a configuration suggesting the enthronement of the deity (Exod. 25:22), plays an important role in the reconstruction. So too does Solomon's prayer in 1 Kings 8:27–30, which invokes the Deuteronomic concept of the name dwelling at the chosen place in respect of the temple (v. 29), while at the same time acknowledging that the temple cannot contain the divine presence (v. 27).[30]

In the present context, we cannot offer a full response to the issues of interpretation raised here. (I have pursued them more fully elsewhere.[31]) However, the analysis serves to illustrate the question of how to establish the right context

---

[29] See von Rad, *Studies*, 38–39, for a classical statement of the point.
[30] So Weinfeld, *Deuteronomy*, 195.
[31] In McConville and Millar, *Time and Place*, 111–16.

(literary, theological, historical) within which to understand particular expressions, since it has attempted to do precisely this. However, it seems to me to suffer from handicaps that fall in the realm of the topic under consideration.

First, while the narrative in Kings continues from the narrative in Deuteronomy (via Joshua, Judges and Samuel), it does not follow that the connotations of the 'name' language in 1 Kings 8:27–30 should be carried over to Deuteronomy 12:5 (even granting DtrH as the correct literary context for the interpretation of Deuteronomy, and assuming the Kings text is being correctly understood). There is a hint of an illegitimate transfer of meaning here. In the immediate context of the expression 'place the name' in Deuteronomy 12:5, the contrast between the name of Yahweh and the 'names' of other gods (12:3) is a key element. This suggests that the issue is who rules here, rather than the mode of the divine presence. The use in the context of the expression 'before Yahweh' implies on a plain reading a real presence of the deity, or at least that this is not a tract opposing the same (*pace* Mettinger's 'linguistic fossil', noted above).[32] The assumption of literary and conceptual unity in the block Deuteronomy—Kings has therefore led (I believe) to the individual text being misread. (I return to this point in the next section, on narrative.)

The supposition that large blocks of literature use linguistic expressions in entirely consistent ways has an obverse, namely a tendency to think of linguistic contexts in sharply polarized terms, where the use of a term or phrase becomes a signal for the presence of a whole system of ideas, in contrast to some other system of ideas. In this connection, Deuteronomy is contrasted with the Priestly literature, for example on the meaning of the ark of the covenant (the other example cited above). The issue here, as in the first example, concerns the consequences of a failure to read the individual texts in their own right. The result in this case is that a polarization of meaning may be falsely set up. (The portrayal of the ark in Exodus is part of that book's strong focus on the topic of divine presence in worship, whereas in Deuteronomy it is an incidental part of an argument that has more to do with Israel's fitness, or not, to be the covenant people.) The identification of Deuteronomy with Kings, and its disjunction from Exodus, have in common not only the belief that the books of the canon can be confidently divided up into homogeneous blocks, but also the fallacy of assuming that every reference to a phenomenon conveys the writer's whole concept of it.

The example I have pursued prompts a further reflection on the idea of canonical interpretation, namely that the internal relations of the canonical parts are in principle multiplex. Far from literary blocks existing in watertight compartments, a number of possible literary and theological contexts for a

---

[32]   See Wilson, *Midst*, 131–97, for a treatment of 'before the LORD', in response to the position represented by Mettinger and others.

book exist and should be taken into account. For example, is the Exodus narrative, with its important treatments of the meaning of the divine name (Exod. 3:13–15; 6:1–9), as pertinent a literary and theological context for Deuteronomy (and its handling of the 'name') as the Historical Books that follow it? In that case, the meaning in Deuteronomy may have more to do with the affirmation of Yahweh's supremacy in the life of Israel in contrast to other gods, and his demonstration of his character by means of his deliverance of Israel from slavery in Egypt (all of which are important Deuteronomic themes).[33] This question could arise as a strictly 'canonical' one. That is, it need not in principle call into question the concept of a Deuteronomistic History as a thesis in historical criticism. Such a thesis, however, does not avoid the canonical mandate to interpret Deuteronomy within the larger nexus consisting of the primary Old Testament narrative, Genesis—Kings, with all the resonances for interpretation that this brings with it.

Narrative

The question of the narrative setting of Deuteronomy has been raised sharply in the preceding section. Furthermore, the topic of narrative is closely related to that of metaphor and symbol with which I began, since it is often in narrative contexts that metaphors and symbols take on their particular force.[34] In one sense the narrative of Deuteronomy might be understood straightforwardly as the surface narrative, in which Moses: utters speeches to the Israelites assembled on the plains of Moab, on the way from Egypt and Horeb to the promised land, presides over a covenant renewal there, and dies on Mt Nebo.[35] This is a fruitful topic in itself, since the 'journey' metaphor has important implications for the religion and ethics advocated by the book. However, as we have seen, Deuteronomy sits within a narrative context larger than its own immediate one, and that recognition poses dangers to interpretation as well as offering some opportunities.

It may be helpful, therefore, to explore the narrative idea differently, in a way that looks beneath the surface of the text. This approach looks for what G. Lindbeck calls 'narrationally structured symbolic worlds', or '[the Bible's] projected world or worlds'.[36] Lindbeck is referring here to a way of approaching biblical interpretation that has representatives in R.B. Hays and now

---

[33] See Seitz, 'Call of Moses'.
[34] Stiver, *Philosophy*, 136–39.
[35] The significance of the journey for ethics is explored helpfully by J.G. Millar in *Now Choose Life*. Also relevant is Lohfink, 'Zur Fabel'.
[36] Lindbeck, 'Interpretation', 33, 35.

Stephen Fowl.[37] The projected worlds of the Bible have a connection with the surface narratives of texts, but are not dependent on strictly narrative types of discourse, because they have to do with the symbol-systems within which events, discourses and persons are found to make sense.

It will be clear from the foregoing that such an approach to Deuteronomy is promising. Indeed, in our remarks on its view of moral and political order we have begun to sketch what the book's symbolic world looks like, and we have seen that it can be compared and contrasted in turn with alternative symbolic worlds.

The narrative framework of the symbols poses a new set of questions, however. The setting of Deuteronomy within a (surface) narrative that leads to a centralized political-religious synthesis in Jerusalem raises the problem of the diversity of the symbolic worlds of the Old Testament. This is because, in the surface narrative, the Davidic achievement in establishing Jerusalem as the religious and administrative centre of all Israel follows from expectations and prescriptions in Deuteronomy (Deut. 12:8-9; cf. 2 Sam. 7:1). At a deeper level, however, as I have argued, the symbol-system of Deuteronomy contrasts with that of the 'Zion-theology' associated with David and his capital. The surface narrative, therefore, stages the tension between the two somewhat different symbolic worlds.

This account of things stands in contrast to the common view, which I have attributed above to von Rad and Weinfeld, that the Historical Books (Joshua—Kings, or DtrH) continue or explicate the theology of Deuteronomy in a rather straightforward way. That is, in terms of our example of kingship (as of name-theology), the two blocks share a common view. However, it seems to me that the narrative plays off Deuteronomy's refusal to countenance absolutes in time and space against the Historical Books' postulates of king and Zion. The 'clash of symbols' (not my pun[38]) refuses to sanctify a status quo, but holds unlimited possibilities open. It follows, then, that to identify the setting of metaphors and symbols in narratives may not lead in a simple way to greater clarification of the meaning of the text. Rather, it may pose deeper questions about how interpretation might deal with such contrasting symbol systems within the biblical canon.

Deuteronomy and Speech-act Theory

In the previous section we found that an examination of the symbolic worlds of the Old Testament raised the problem for interpretation caused by its

---

[37]   Hays, *Vision*; Fowl, 'Learning'.

[38]   The term comes from Akers, 'Clash'.

diversity of texts and ideas. Diversity within Old Testament theology has been one of the foremost concerns of twentieth-century writing on the subject and has fundamentally influenced the way in which it has been approached.[39] Canonical criticism did not of itself resolve problems posed by diversity, but only set up the textual relationships within which interpretation might be pursued. Those relationships were complex, however, and we saw that the narrative frameworks could expose deep disparities of symbolic content. Is it possible that diversity in the Old Testament texts poses a greater threat than canonical criticism recognizes?

The issue is the more complicated because, in recent writing, what have been perceived as the many voices of the Old Testament have found an echo in explicitly pluralistic readings.[40] The difficulty of the problem posed to interpretation by the claims of diverse readings is addressed by Lindbeck, who thinks that diverse interpretations of Scripture yield a picture of 'apparently self-enclosed universes isolated not only from each other but from extratextual reality'.[41] This is a problem especially for the Protestant belief that Scripture is self-interpreting.[42] One possible answer, he thinks, is that proposed by Wolterstorff in his application of speech-act theory to the idea of divine speech, on the grounds that it may afford a means of 'exiting' the text in order to obtain an external control on its meaning.[43] This, in my view, offers a very promising avenue into the interpretation of individual books and blocks of text within their larger contexts, and perhaps in dialogue with them.

The application of speech-act theory to Deuteronomy is evocative because it resonates with themes and features of the book itself. It is, more than any other Old Testament work, a theology of word. The central theologumenon is the words of the covenant made at Horeb, and the central concern is how to make those words continue to be effective in succeeding generations of Israel.

The words spoken at Horeb conform to the conditions of a speech-act: they are delivered in a certain context of authority and relationships by an authorized speaker and aim to produce a stated effect, namely the formal acquiescence of the people of Israel in the terms of the covenant. The covenantal context is demonstrated not only by its use of the word covenant, but by features of the book that go beyond the level of vocabulary. N. Lohfink, in an important article, argues that Deuteronomy 'shows' covenant by means of its speeches. He calls this type of portrayal '*szenische Darstellung*', as distinct

---

[39] The classic encounter between G. von Rad and W. Eichrodt can be described as a methodological debate in which this issue is paramount. See also Goldingay, *Diversity*.

[40] Brueggemann, *Theology*, is the best example of this.

[41] Lindbeck, 'Interpretation', 43.

[42] Ibid., 44.

[43] In Wolterstorff, *Discourse*; Lindbeck, 'Interpretation', 40–51.

from an explicit explanatory type of portrayal. That is, Deuteronomy does not have to spell out that the language it uses in particular contexts is covenantal language. Rather, he says of speech-acts (*Sprechakte*) that they '... *erst durch Konventionen und Kontext eindeutig werden*' ('that they become unequivocal through conventions and context').[44]

Evidence for the covenantal context of the book is also found in the structure of its main part (Deut. 1 – 28), which resembles an ancient Near Eastern vassal-treaty, and in its use of certain linguistic formulae. The parties to the covenant are Yahweh and Israel, and the issue faced by Deuteronomy is the need for Israel to respond 'today' to the call to obedience and blessing that is constituted by the words that are being spoken. The covenant is mediated by Moses, who is in some respects like the 'king' of the ancient Near Eastern treaties (and whom some scholars see in precisely such a role). The vital difference is that he is not himself the source either of covenant or law, or the giver of the land that is elsewhere the corollary of such a role.

The realization of the covenant requires specified appropriate situations. The classical situation is Horeb itself (Deut. 4:9–14), but this is echoed in the book by further situations of covenant making, namely: at Moab, where the action of the book takes place (note 28:69 [29:1]; 26:17–19, the 'performative' words of this covenant); a unique event at Shechem (Deut. 27); and then at covenant renewal ceremonies to be repeated in perpetuity in the land at the place of worship chosen by Yahweh (Deut. 31:9–13). Authorized personnel in the latter two cases are the Levites/levitical priests and elders (27:14; 31:9–13).

The theory in its application to Deuteronomy may be developed in two further ways. First, far from simply recording a single past event, the book is carefully structured so as to ensure that the speech-acts, by which Israel was created to be the people of God, continue to be effective. The succession of covenant situations is of the essence of the Deuteronomic concept. Indeed, the progression from Horeb to Moab is the hermeneutical key to understanding the book. The relationship between these two covenants is subtle. At the beginning of Moses' second major speech, he addresses the people (at Moab) as if it was they, and not the previous generation, who were actually standing at Horeb (5:2–3). The contrast 'not your fathers' (v. 3), at odds with the chronology in Deuteronomy 1–3, is a rhetorical effect reinforcing the command to re-enter the covenant 'today'.

This, then, is one of the key trajectories in the book – one that binds the new generation afresh to the covenant established once in the past. And it is not limited to the single progression from Horeb to Moab. Rather, that progression becomes paradigmatic for all re-enactments of the covenant. This is clear because of the second stage of progression, namely to the seven-yearly

---

[44] Lohfink, 'Bund', 220–21.

renewal at the Feast of Tabernacles (Deut. 31), and also because of the theme of passing on the covenantal narrative and commands to 'your children' – that is, all subsequent generations. Furthermore, the teaching role of Moses himself becomes paradigmatic. It is often observed that Deuteronomy differs from BC in its concept of the relationship between the Decalogue and the other laws in the respective law codes. While BC does not appear to make a distinction in principle between these, Deuteronomy ascribes the former to the direct words of God while the laws that follow are cast as teachings expressly attributed to Moses (Deut. 4:13–14). The purpose of this device is to sanction an ongoing teaching function in the community, conceived as forging a link with the initial covenant event. (This can be variously understood as the role of the prophet, the successor of Moses [Deut. 18:15–18], or as the Levites who have responsibility for the Book of the Covenant, or even as the heads of families who are to teach their children.)

Second, to the spatial and temporal trajectory just described must be added another – namely the progression from the spoken to the written word. The words spoken at Horeb and Moab are deposited in a book, the Book of the Law (28:58, 61; 31:9). The speech-act, therefore, becomes written, in a book that has an institutional matrix. Assessments of Deuteronomy must in the end reckon with its writtenness. Its form as authoritative 'book' has widely been seen as standing at the fountainhead of the 'canonical' tendency in the Old Testament (understood in the sense of the historical origin of the concept).[45] Such accounts think of it (as also in the case of Perlitt, above) as an intellectual-ized and systematizing kind of theology. This common misconception arises from a failure to understand the force of the covenantal setting. On the basis of this Lohfink rightly argued, against L. Perlitt, that the term *bᵉrit* (covenant) could not be equated with the term *torah* (resulting in an understanding of cov-enant *as* law) simply on the grounds of their occurrence in parallelism.[46] Lohfink, therefore, has used speech-act theory to re-establish a context for Deuteronomy in the thought-world of covenant, as a corrective to the pre-vailing idea that the book is the product of essentially literary and scholarly processes.[47] The covenantal setting in Deuteronomy is part of its attempt to forge a link with the decisive events of the past, enshrined in new decisive moments. The writtenness of the speech-acts is not a function of legalism, but forges a link between such moments in the present and the great decisions of the past.

---

[45] Wellhausen, *Prolegomena*, 402; Blum, *Komposition*, 200–1, 288; Crüsemann, *Torah*, 282.

[46] Lohfink, 'Bund', 238.

[47] Lohfink, 'Bund'; he is in dialogue especially with Perlitt, *Bundestheologie*. See also Poulter, *Rhetoric*.

We may conclude the following from this application of speech-act theory to Deuteronomy. First, as Lohfink indicates, the covenantal setting of the speeches affords a means of controlling the interpretation of the text (he uses the term '*eindeutig*', or 'unequivocal'). In fact, our approach to the text by way of speech-act theory resonates with our discussion of metaphor and symbol above, for it has independently highlighted aspects of meaning that were uncovered there. This is especially notable in relation to Moses (in that Moses takes a role associated with kings, yet is not a king; and in that his teaching function is 'democratized' in its transmission, which becomes the responsibility ultimately of heads of families [Deut. 6:6–9]).

Second, in its rehearsal of the twin progression from Horeb to Moab and from speech to writing, it facilitates its repeated use as language of faith and instruction in ongoing and new situations. The speeches of Moses become the language that helps create the world of faith, and sustain faith. In this respect, too, speech-act theory offers support to the view outlined above, insofar as it disclaimed a concept of Deuteronomy as institutionalizing a centralized administration by means of law. Writing is rather a means of sustaining a vision, not a systematizing as such, of a sort that can readily be negatively contrasted with the 'Spirit'.

Deuteronomy as Hermeneutic

One might derive a further consequence from the transition from speech to writing and say that Deuteronomy is essentially hermeneutical. It builds into its vision the fusion of many horizons by means of the trajectories just described. This in turn affords another reflection on Deuteronomy within the canon. One way of thinking about the tension between Deuteronomy and the Zion theology of the Historical Books is to see the former as a way of evaluating the events reported in the latter. Moses and David, Moab and land, ideal and real, stand in creative tension. A fusion of horizons is involved when the record of the kingdoms is measured by the vision of possible land-histories in the speeches and events set outside the land and prior to occupation. The gaze into further possible futures, at the end of both Deuteronomy and Kings, invites further fusions.

Deuteronomy's hermeneutical significance also reaches back to the books that precede it canonically, and with which it is bound into a (surface) narrative whose closure is coterminous with that of Deuteronomy. The hermeneutical point concerns Deuteronomy's relation, as covenant and law, to other law codes. The striking differences of detailed application between the codes can be put to the account of Deuteronomy's self-understanding. This is preferable to the view of Levinson that the book sweeps away all that went before it, which entails the difficulty that the other codes remain unswept away, and that Deuteronomy belongs with them in a single collection.[48] Rather, the progression from the Book of the Covenant (Exod. 21–23) to Deuteronomy not only involves an act of reinterpretation in itself, but it canonizes the activity of reinterpreting the tradition.

These two points might be thought to be somewhat in tension with each other. On one hand, Deuteronomy provides for itself to be propagated – a tendency that stands under the rubric of Deuteronomy 4:2 ('You shall not add to the word which I command, nor take from it'). On the other hand, it offers itself as an example precisely of reinterpretation, its own example (namely its variation from BC) implicitly permitting a wide degree of freedom. There is no text for this tendency, which is taught instead by the structure of the book (the two covenants) and by its canonical relationship with Exodus. The tension, however, is more apparent than real, since all fresh hearing of Deuteronomy is bound to entail translations into new situations. The safeguard around the canonical literature in Deuteronomy 4:2 is thus balanced by permission, indeed a mandate, to bring it in appropriate ways into the lives of diverse believing communities. (Lindbeck's understanding of 'analogy' is helpful in this connection.[49])

Conclusion

Our study has ranged over a number of topics that arise when theories about language and meaning are applied to Deuteronomy. It has identified a number of avenues that might be explored separately. However, some conclusions may be drawn that bring a degree of unity into the investigation.

In our examination of metaphor in the book, I argued that, while historical investigation was important for identifying broad settings, canonical considerations were essential in sharpening our understanding of their force. However, canonical readings were complex, and had to understand the levels at which symbol and narrative work. Surface narrative (being one kind of 'canonical' nexus) often merely poses, or exposes, theological questions and tensions for exploration. Deuteronomy, as a discrete element within a surface narrative (or narratives), and within a canon (or canons), has still a right to be heard in its particularity. In fact, some of Deuteronomy's leading metaphors apparently belonged to a somewhat different projected world from that of the Historical Books, with which it was joined in a larger surface narrative.

---

[48] Levinson, *Deuteronomy*. See my response, 'Unification'; and his in return, 'Hermeneutics'.

[49] Lindbeck, 'Interpretation', 37.

A further mechanism for understanding Deuteronomy in its individuality is speech-act theory, because it draws attention to specific illocutionary possibilities. An application of it to the book also confirmed lines of interpretation found in the analysis of Deuteronomy's metaphors. Finally, it discloses an important factor in the book, namely its character as a paradigm of interpretation – not only with regard to itself, but also to canonical readings of the Old Testament (Bible).

Bibliography

Ahlström, G., *Royal Administration and National Religion in Ancient Palestine* (SHANE, 1; Leiden: Brill, 1982)

Akers, B., 'A Clash of Symbols: Both Jew and Greek in Origen's *Synthesis*', *Diakonia* 24 (1991), 157–69

Barr, J., *The Concept of Biblical Theology: An Old Testament Perspective* (London: SCM Press, 1999)

Blum, E., *Studien zur Komposition des Pentateuch* (BZAW, 189; Berlin: de Gruyter, 1990)

Bright, J., 'The Date of the Prose Sermons of Jeremiah', *JBL* 70 (1951), 15–35

Brueggemann, W., *Theology of the Old Testament* (Minneapolis: Augsburg-Fortress, 1997)

Carroll, R.P., *Jeremiah* (London: SCM Press, 1986)

Clements, R.E., *Deuteronomy* (Sheffield: JSOT Press, 1989)

Crüsemann, F., *The Torah: Theology and Social History of Old Testament Law* (Minneapolis: Fortress Press, 1996)

Dietrich, W., 'Niedergang und Neuanfang: die Haltung der Schlussredaktion des deuteronomistischen Geschichtswerkes zu den wichtigsten Fragen ihrer Zeit', in *The Crisis of Israelite Religion: Transformation of Religious Tradition in Exilic and Post-Exilic Times* (ed. B. Becking and M.C.A. Korpel; OTS, 42; Leiden: Brill, 1999), 45–70

Dion, P., 'The Suppression of Alien Religious Propaganda in Israel during the Late Monarchical Era', in *Law and Ideology in Monarchic Israel* (ed. B. Halpern and D. Hobson; JSOTSup, 124; Sheffield: Sheffield Academic Press, 1991), 147–216

Driver, S.R., *Deuteronomy* (ICC; Edinburgh: T. & T. Clark, 1895)

Fowl, S., 'Learning to Narrate our Lives in Christ', in Seitz and Greene-McCreight (eds.), *Theological Exegesis*, 339–54

Goldingay, J., *Theological Diversity and the Authority of the Old Testament* (Grand Rapids: Eerdmans, 1987; Carlisle: Paternoster, 1995)

Handy, L.K., *Among the Host of Heaven: The Syro-Palestinian Pantheon as Bureaucracy* (Winona Lake, IN: Eisenbrauns, 1994)

Hays, R.B., *The Moral Vision of the New Testament* (New York: HarperCollins, 1996; Edinburgh: T. & T. Clark, 1997)

Hermisson, H., *Sprache und Ritus im altisraelitischen Kult: zur 'Spiritualisierung' der Kultbegriffe im Alten Testament* (Neukirchen: Neukirchener Verlag, 1965)

Hyatt, J.P., 'The Deuteronomic Edition of Jeremiah', *VSH* 1 (1951), 71–95

Knoppers, G.N. and J.G. McConville (eds.), *Reconsidering Israel and Judah: Recent Studies on the Deuteronomistic History* (Winona Lake, IN: Eisenbrauns, 2000)

Levinson, B.M., *Deuteronomy and the Hermeneutics of Legal Innovation* (New York, Oxford: OUP, 1997)

—, 'The Hermeneutics of Tradition in Deuteronomy', *JBL* 119 (2000), 269–86

Lindbeck, G.A., 'Postcritical Canonical Interpretation: Three Modes of Retrieval', in Seitz and Greene-McCreight (eds.), *Theological Exegesis*, 26–51

Lohfink, N., 'Bund als Vertrag im Deuteronomium', *ZAW* 107 (1995), 215–39

—, 'Kerygmata des Deuteronomistischen Geschichtswerks', in *Die Botschaft und die Boten* (ed. J. Jeremias and L. Perlitt; Neukirchen: Neukirchener Verlag, 1981), 87–100

—, 'Zur Fabel des Deuteronomiums', in *Bundesdokument und Gesetz: Studien zum Deuteronomium* (ed. G. Braulik; Herder Biblische Studien, 4; Freiburg: Herder, 1995), 65–78

McConville, J.G., *Deuteronomy* (Leicester and Downers Grove: IVP, forthcoming)

—, 'Deuteronomy's Unification of Passover and Massôt: A Response to Bernard M. Levinson', *JBL* 119 (2000), 47–58

—, and J.G. Millar, *Time and Place in Deuteronomy* (Sheffield: Sheffield Academic Press, 1994)

McKane, W., 'Relations between Poetry and Prose in the Book of Jeremiah with Special Reference to Jeremiah III 6–11 and XII 14–17', *VTSup* 32 (1980), 220–37

Mettinger, T., *The Dethronement of Sabaoth: Studies in the Shem and Kabod Theologies* (ConBOT, 18; Lund: Gleerup, 1982)

Millar, J.G., *Now Choose Life: Theology and Ethics in Deuteronomy* (Leicester: IVP, 1998)

Minette de Tillesse, G., 'Sections "Tu" et Sections "Vous" dans le Deutéronome', *VT* 12 (1962), 29–87

Mittmann, W., *Deuteronomium 1:1 – 6:3 literarkritisch und traditions-geschichtlich untersucht* (BZAW, 39; Berlin: A. Töpelman, 1975)

Noth, M., *The Deuteronomistic History* (JSOTSup, 15; Sheffield: JSOT Press, 1981)

Perlitt, L., *Bundestheologie im Alten Testament* (WMANT, 36; Neukirchen: Neukirchener Verlag, 1969)

—, 'Sinai und Horeb', in *Beiträge zur alttestamentlichen Theologie* (ed. H. Donner, R. Hanhart and R. Smend; Göttingen: Vandenhoeck & Ruprecht, 1977), 302–22

Poulter, A.J., *Rhetoric and Redaction in Deuteronomy 8: Linguistic Criticism of a Biblical Text* (Dissertation; Cambridge University, 1989)

Pressler, C., 'Sexual Violence and Deuteronomic Law', in *A Feminist Companion to Exodus to Deuteronomy* (ed. A. Brenner; Sheffield: Sheffield Academic Press, 1994), 102–12

—, *The View of Women Found in Deuteronomic Family Law* (BZAW, 216; Berlin: de Gruyter, 1993)

Rad, G. von, *Studies in Deuteronomy* (London: SCM Press, 1953)

Seitz, C., 'The Call of Moses and the "Revelation" of the Divine Name: Source-Critical Logic and its Legacy', in Seitz and Greene-McCreight (eds.), *Theological Exegesis*, 145–61

—, and K. Greene-McCreight, *Theological Exegesis: Essays in Honor of Brevard S. Childs* (Grand Rapids: Eerdmans, 1999)

Smend, R., 'Das Gesetz und die Völker': ein Beitrag zur deuteronomistischen Redaktionsgeschichte', in *Probleme biblischer Theologie: FS Gerhard von Rad* (ed. H.W. Wolff; Munich: Kaiser, 1971), 494–509; ET: 'The Law and the Nations: A Contribution to Deuteronomistic Tradition History', in Knoppers and McConville (eds.), *Reconsidering Israel and Judah*, 95–110

Stiver, D., *The Philosophy of Religious Language: Sign, Symbol and Story* (Oxford: Basil Blackwell, 1996)

Thiel, W., *Die deuteronomistische Redaktion von Jeremia 1–25* (WMANT, 41; Neukirchen: Neukirchener Verlag, 1973)

—, *Die deuteronomistische Redaktion von Jeremia 26–45* (WMANT, 52; Neukirchen: Neukirchener Verlag, 1981)

Tigay, J.H., *Deuteronomy* (Philadelphia, Jerusalem: Jewish Publication Society, 1996)

Veijola, T., *Das Königtum in der Beurteilung der deuteronomistischen Historiographie* (Helsinki: Suomalainen Tiedeakatemia, 1977)

—, *Die Ewige Dynastie* (Helsinki: Suomalainen Tiedeakatemia, 1975)

Weinfeld, M., *Deuteronomy and the Deuteronomic School* (Oxford: Clarendon Press, 1972)

Weippert, H., *Die Prosareden des Jeremiabuches* (BZAW, 132; Berlin: de Gruyter, 1973)

Wellhausen, J., *Prolegomena to the History of Ancient Israel* (Edinburgh, 1885 [German edn 1878])

Wilson, I., *Out of the Midst of the Fire* (SBLDS, 151; Atlanta: Scholars Press, 1995)

Wolterstorff, N., *Divine Discourse* (Cambridge: CUP, 1995)

17

Words of (In-)evitable Certitude?[1]

Reflections on the Interpretation of Prophetic Oracles of Judgement

Karl Möller

How are we supposed to read prophetic oracles of judgement? And what did the prophets think they were doing in conveying their message of divine punishment?[2] Usually, these questions are answered in one of the following ways. The prophets – and I am thinking here of the often so called 'classical prophets' of the eighth century BCE – are conceived either as harbingers of doom, whose task consisted simply, and solely, in announcing the inevitable punishment of God. Or their words are understood in a subjunctive sense as opening up for their audiences the possibility of 'becoming something other', as Jeffrey has put it. In this latter view, in which the interpretative focus has moved away 'from the determinism of the surface text to the open world of the text within',[3] oracles of judgement are understood as warnings.

In the present essay, I intend to explore and illustrate how insights gained from the study of the philosophy of language might be brought to bear on this controversy over the interpretation of prophetic judgement oracles.[4] In

---

[1] Steiner once coined the phrase ' "evitable" certitude' in order to describe the relation of the genuine prophet – as opposed to that of the diviner – to the future. He notes that to the prophet 'the future is entirely present ... in the literal presentness of his speech-act. But at the same moment ... his enunciation of the future makes that future alterable' (Steiner, *After Babel*, 153).

[2] Houston posed this question a few years ago (cf. Houston, 'Prophets').

[3] Jeffrey, *People*, 40.

[4] Of course, it will also become apparent that the conflicting views are themselves already, and inevitably, based on particular philosophies of language.

particular, I will focus on the contributions made by rhetorical criticism understood in an Aristotelian sense as the 'art of persuasion', speech-act theory as developed by Austin and Searle, and theories that stress the metaphorical nature of all language as well as the role of the creative imagination for the process of interpretation.

It should be noted, however, that this delineation actually implies a rather narrow definition of rhetorical criticism. The tendency to define the approach in too restrictive terms has recently been criticized by Amador, who has complained that biblical critics have not even come close to unleashing the potential of Wuellner's 'awesome array of theoretical and methodological insights' put forward in his seminal article 'Where Is Rhetorical Criticism Taking Us?'.[5] Drawing our attention to a variety of routes a rhetorical-critical approach might take, Amador lists both speech-act theory (under the rubric of sociolinguistic approaches) and the 'metaphor approach' as possible options. In response to this, I would point out, first, that I agree that a wider definition of rhetorical criticism is called for. However, as one of the aims of the present article is to indicate how the approach, even in its narrow and precision-lacking form, can contribute to the study of prophetic judgement oracles, I shall stick to the definition that is most commonly used in the field of Old Testament studies. Secondly, it will become clear later on that one of my contentions is precisely that the above mentioned approaches need to be combined if we are to avoid reductionist readings of the texts under consideration.

It should also be noted that this is not to be seen as yet another quest for *the* 'correct' method.[6] Nor do I expect that closer attention to issues brought to the fore by the philosophy of language will settle the question of the interpretation of prophetic judgement oracles once and for all. Indeed, both rhetorical criticism and speech-act theory have been applied to our textual corpus to different effects. What the present study is attempting to demonstrate is how the approaches mentioned above can provide us with more sophisticated conceptual tools for our task. Unfortunately, the use of less suitable, or deficient, tools can lead to undesirable consequences, and we need to ask ourselves whether, and to what extent, that may have been the case in the interpretation of the prophetic literature.

---

[5] Amador, 'Rhetorical Criticism', 195.
[6] See Barton, *Reading*, 5–6, for a criticism of the never-ending quest for a method that will unlock all the mysteries of the biblical texts.

Prophetic Judgement Oracles – Words of 'Evitable' or Inevitable Certitude?

In his exploration of *The Rhetoric of Revelation in the Hebrew Bible*, Patrick recently claimed that 'conventional interpretation' has taken prophetic judgement oracles to be calls for repentance in disguise, as it were.[7] Indeed, this is one of the views that Westermann challenged in his magisterial *Basic Forms of Prophetic Speech*. Taking issue, for instance, with Steuernagel's understanding of the prophetic message, Westermann complained that 'Steuernagel succumb[ed] to a *traditional view* that has not been overcome down to this day, i.e., [that] the prophets are preachers of repentance.'[8] However, the original German edition of Westermann's work was published in 1960, and the situation has since changed considerably, not least as a direct result of his influential effort. Thus, while forty years on it is still true to say that the repentance theory has not been overcome, there is now a very strong tradition that understands prophetic judgement oracles as unambiguous announcements of an irreversible and inevitable divine judgement.[9]

This is exemplified, for instance, by much of twentieth-century interpretation of the book of Amos. Following in the wake of Wellhausen, exegetes such as Weiser, Wolff, Smend and Schmidt have affirmed the negative thrust of the prophet's message. Often Amos 8:2, 'The end has come upon my people Israel; I will never again pass them by' (NRSV), has served as the hermeneutical key for the interpretation of the book, leading to the claim that this is what Amos' prophetic ministry was all about: Yahweh, the God of Israel, would put an end to his people, and this, the dire message that his spokesman had no choice but to proclaim, needs to be understood as one of inevitable certitude indeed.[10]

It is important to note that this understanding has had far-reaching consequences not only for the interpretation of the book but also for investigations into the text's genesis.[11] That is to say, scholars who understand Amos

---

[7] Patrick, *Rhetoric*, 122.

[8] Westermann, *Basic Forms*, 19 (emphasis mine).

[9] For detailed discussion and research review see Fleischer, *Von Menschenverkäufern*, ch. 6; cf. also Hasel, *Remnant*, 173–76; Hunter, *Seek the Lord*, 7–38; Martin-Achard, *Amos*, 143–59; and Markert and Wanke, 'Propheteninterpretation'.

[10] See especially Weiser, *Profetie*, 310f.; Wolff, *Joel and Amos*, 103; Smend, 'Nein', 415; and Schmidt, 'Grundgewißheit', 540, for this line of interpretation.

[11] Crüsemann once complained about the radicalization of Amos' message, achieved by means of literary-critical and theological operations, which turned the prophet into the messenger of a God who murders entire nations, and who therefore may safely be seen as theologically outdated (Crüsemann, 'Vorwort', 10).

as proclaiming the end of Israel have usually found it impossible to attribute passages that sound a different note (especially, but not only, the salvation oracle in 9:11–15) to the same prophet. Cripps, for instance, decreed that 'a promise of restoration such as is outlined in [9:]11–15 is quite incongruous after the threat of absolute destruction which is characteristic of the main body of the prophecy of Amos'.[12]

I do not wish to paint simply in black and white, being of course aware that literary-critical and historical considerations have also played their part in denying this and other passages to the prophet Amos. Yet it needs to be stressed that, for instance, Wellhausen's influential and oft-quoted verdict,[13] that in Amos 9:11–15 we are dealing, in stark contrast to the rest of the book, with 'roses and lavender instead of blood and iron',[14] is not a literary-critical judgement. Indeed, his statement illustrates that whether this salvation oracle could have originated with the same prophet depends to no small degree on how one understands the nature and purpose of Amos' message in general and that of the manifold judgement oracles in particular. As Nägele says, an important – perhaps even the decisive – question is whether it is at all conceivable that Amos would or could have uttered words of salvation such as these.[15]

Some scholars, such as Buber and Fohrer, to name but two representatives, have challenged the view that judgement oracles are to be understood as mere announcements of an inevitable judgement, arguing instead for the repentance theory rejected by Westermann. Buber thought that the prophets, even when uttering an unconditional announcement of judgement, aimed or may have aimed at repentance. He contended that 'behind every prediction of disaster there stands a concealed alternative'.[16] However, Buber's view that, for instance, Amos sought to move his audience to repent, was rejected by Smend on the grounds that it cannot be demonstrated from Amos' words.[17] What Smend meant was that Amos does not (or at least hardly ever, depending on what one makes of Amos 5:4–5, 14–15) explicitly urge his audience to repent. In this understanding, it is the surface text that determines what the discourse

---

[12] Cripps, *Book of Amos*, 67.

[13] Nägele, in an investigation of that passage's history of interpretation (*Auslegungsgeschichte*), comes to the conclusion that Wellhausen's reading has influenced subsequent exegesis enormously (Nägele, *Laubhütte*, 172).

[14] Wellhausen, *Propheten*, 96.

[15] Nägele, *Laubhütte*, 172. See Patrick, *Rhetoric*, 158, who claims that 'they are not imaginable in the mouth of Amos'.

[16] Buber, *Prophetic Faith*, 134; see also Fohrer, 'Bemerkungen', 480–81.

[17] Smend, 'Nein', 416. Patrick, *Rhetoric*, 144, also emphasized that 'the actual words of Amos thwart the effort to classify him as a "prophet of repentance" '.

means. That is to say, the discourse most certainly cannot mean what is not explicitly encoded on the level of the surface text.

As I have indicated elsewhere, I believe this understanding to be badly flawed.[18] It is marked, and marred, by a literalism that looks no deeper than the text's surface grammar as well as by what has been called a 'verbal atomism' that neglects the wider context and the actual use of language.[19] What is needed is a more nuanced and multifaceted interpretation that takes into account recent insights into how language functions in an interpersonal encounter between prophet and audience or text and reader. The philosophy of language has provided many such insights in a century that has been dubbed the century of the linguistic turn,[20] and it is to these that we now turn, focusing on rhetorical criticism, speech-act theory and metaphorical theories of language.

The Prophets as Masters of Persuasion: The Contribution of Rhetorical Criticism[21]

Recent years have seen a growing interest among Old Testament scholars in rhetorical-critical approaches. While these can take many different forms, it has become customary to differentiate between two major orientations, which have been labelled, respectively, the 'art of composition' and the 'art of persuasion'.[22] The former approach is associated with Muilenburg and those following in his wake. It is largely an attempt to overcome the shortcomings of form

---

[18] Cf. Möller, 'Rehabilitation', 45–7.

[19] Stiver, *Philosophy*, 11.

[20] Cf. Rorty (ed.), *Linguistic Turn*.

[21] For more extensive treatment of the issues discussed in this section see the introduction to my forthcoming *A Prophet in Debate*.

[22] Trible, *Rhetorical Criticism*, 32, 41. Again, this is not to imply that these are the only options available to rhetorical critics but that these are the only ones that have gained currency in Old Testament studies. Amador, 'Rhetorical Criticism', has rightly suggested that more work by biblical rhetorical critics is needed on genre, social movements, symbolic convergence, sociolinguistics, metaphor, narrative, argumentation theory, feminist critical rhetorics, critical rhetoric and the rhetoric of inquiry, all of which are being pursued in rhetoric and communication departments. Amador complains that 'antiquarian in aspect (only the rhetorical handbooks and textbooks of authors from the second century BCE to second century CE are consulted), synthetic in approach (no distinction between the wide varieties of ancient rhetorical theories is made, but all are meshed together and drawn from randomly), tropological in focus (concentration is made overwhelmingly upon identifying argumentative structures and compositional styles), the new rhetorical criticism has become a method limited in scope and purpose' (ibid., 195).

criticism[23] by paying increased attention to the unique stylistic or aesthetic qualities of a text in contrast to the concentration on typical and conventional features that characterizes form-critical studies.[24]

The label 'art of persuasion', on the other hand, has been applied to works in the tradition of the 'new rhetoric'.[25] Instead of focusing on stylistics, as the Muilenburg school does, the main interest in this case is in rhetoric as argumentation. Thus, this is a communication-theoretical approach that understands 'all literature ... as *social* discourse'.[26] Recapturing the classical Aristotelian definition of rhetoric, it regards:

> speaking and writing [indeed, language in general] not merely as textual objects, to be aesthetically contemplated or endlessly deconstructed, but as forms of *activity* inseparable from the wider social relations between writers and readers, orators and audiences, and as largely unintelligible outside the social purposes and conditions in which they were embedded.[27]

As Bitzer has pointed out, rhetorical discourse is designed to address a specific 'exigency which amount[s] to an imperative stimulus'[28] and which the rhetorical discourse aims to modify. Rhetoric thus defined 'is a mode of altering reality ... by the creation of discourse which changes reality through the

---

[23] See especially Muilenburg's programmatic essay 'Form Criticism and Beyond'.

[24] In Schleiermacher's terms, hermeneutics must combine a 'grammatical' with a 'technical' approach. Whereas the 'grammatical' dimension refers to the linguistic system at large, the 'technical' approach seeks to ascertain how language is modified by a particular utterance or a particular speaker (Schleiermacher, *Hermeneutics and Criticism*).

[25] In this case, the programmatic works are Perelman and Olbrechts-Tyteca's *The New Rhetoric* as well as, in the area of biblical studies, Wuellner's 'Where Is Rhetorical Criticism Taking Us?'. As the term 'new rhetoric' indicates, Perelman and Olbrechts-Tyteca's work is part of what might be described as a revival movement. This had become necessary because the discipline's fortunes throughout history, which I do not have the space to outline, have been mixed. Useful accounts can be found in Kennedy's works (see the bibliography) as well as in Corbett's *Classical Rhetoric*.

An important medieval work that has been described as 'an *ars rhetorica* and a rhetorical interpretation of the "plain meaning" ... of the Hebrew Scriptures' (Rabinowitz, 'Introduction', lx) is Judah ben Jehiel's *Book of the Honeycomb's Flow*, published in 1475/76. According to Rabinowitz 'no such systematically rhetorical a treatment of the Hebrew Scriptures by a qualified Hebraist is attested until late in the nineteenth century' (ibid.).

[26] Wuellner, 'Rhetorical Criticism', 462f.

[27] Eagleton, *Literary Theory*, 179 (emphasis his).

[28] Bitzer, 'Rhetorical Situation', 251.

mediation of thought and action.'[29] This focus on functional and social aspects not only moves the discussion beyond the pre-occupation with the typical (which is what Muilenburg's project was all about); it also transcends any literalistic fixation on the surface text.

In developing a rhetorical-critical approach, many have followed Kennedy's model, which proceeds in five steps.[30] These involve identifying 1) the rhetorical unit(s) in the text; 2) the rhetorical situation and the specific exigency which called the discourse into existence,[31] and which determines the rhetorical choices made by the author (rhetorician),[32] 3) the rhetorical genre(s) employed by the author,[33] 4) the rhetorical strategy[34] and the style chosen to address the rhetorical problem; as well as 5) the rhetorical effectiveness of the utterance in question.[35] These steps need to be applied in circular fashion so that insights gained by the application of the latter ones can lead to a better understanding of the issues dealt with in the initial ones.

It will not be possible, within the confines of the present study, to present a full-fledged rhetorical-critical analysis of Amos' words of judgement. Some

---

[29] Ibid., 250.

[30] See Kennedy, *New Testament Interpretation*, 33–8; Wuellner, 'Rhetorical Criticism', 455–60; and Bible and Culture Collective, *Postmodern Bible*, 150–56. I have offered a full account of these steps in the introduction to *A Prophet in Debate*.

[31] Cf. Bitzer's comment that 'any *exigency* is an imperfection marked by urgency; it is a defect, an obstacle, something waiting to be done, a thing which is other than it should be' ('Rhetorical Situation', 252).

[32] Lausberg, *Elemente*, 21.

[33] Biblical rhetorical critics, following Aristotle, usually distinguish between 1) *judicial* rhetoric, which asks hearers/readers to judge past events, 2) *deliberative* rhetoric, where the audience is invited to make 'a *deliberative* assessment of actions that would be expedient or beneficial for future performance' (Black, 'Rhetorical Criticism', 254) and 3) *epideictic* rhetoric, which treats the audience as spectators pursuing the aim of reinforcing certain beliefs and values. However, there are two dangers here. First, it is sometimes overlooked that rhetoricians might also use generic hybrids, and secondly, Black has suggested as early as 1965 that Aristotle's conception is inadequate, arguing for a much wider variety of argumentative genres (Black, *Rhetorical Criticism*).

[34] Integral to Aristotle's system of rhetoric are the 'proofs', among which he lists *ethos*, *pathos* and *logos*. These correspond respectively to the moral character of the rhetorician, her ability of 'putting the hearer into a certain frame of mind' and the speech itself (see *Rhet.* 1.2.4). Commenting on these concepts, Wuellner aptly notes that 'rhetorical criticism makes us more fully aware of the *whole* range of appeals embraced and provoked by rhetoric: not only the rational and cognitive dimensions, but also the emotive and imaginative ones' (Wuellner, 'Rhetorical Criticism', 461).

[35] At this point, the leading question is whether, or to what degree, the utterance is a fitting response to the exigency that occasioned it.

general comments, therefore, will have to suffice. First, it needs to be stressed that the approach can take different routes in respect to its point of departure. Thus, while many rhetorical critics prefer to work with the text as it now stands, it would also be possible, in the manner of the traditional form-critical approach, to attempt to go back to Amos' original utterances. But whichever option one chooses, one needs to be aware that the choice affects the identification of the rhetorical units to be analysed (step 1). Form critics have usually assumed original prophetic utterances to be short, self-contained sayings, whereas most rhetorical critics tend to detect longer and more fully developed 'speeches'.[36] Yet again, any decision made at this point impacts upon one's judgements about the text's rhetorical genre (step 3) and strategy (step 4). It stands to reason that interpreters who treat a passage, such as Amos 3, as a series of five individual oracles will come to different conclusions about their rhetoric than those who are interested in elucidating the rhetoric of the 'speech' as a whole.

Secondly, and even more importantly for our purposes, we should not lose sight of the fact that identification of a text's rhetorical genre is not always straightforward. Matters become even more difficult when we seek to determine the purpose behind the use of a certain genre. Kennedy has argued, and this is often taken for granted, that the predominant rhetorical genre 'reflects the author's major purpose'.[37] But is this necessarily the case? For example, does the fact that most of Amos' oracles are accusations or announcements of judgement, thus apparently exemplifying the judicial genre, indicate that Amos' 'rhetorical task was to bring ... his audience under judgement', as has been suggested by Patrick?[38]

I do not think that this necessarily follows and believe, *pace* Kennedy, that the predominant rhetorical genre reflects not so much the author's purpose as his or her strategy for communicating the message that the audience needs to hear. In our particular case, if Amos' aim in majoring on the nation's wrongdoings and painting a picture of unfolding death and calamity was to

---

[36] There is no agreement as to whether the prophetic books contain the actual speeches delivered by the prophets (as has been argued, for instance, by Shaw, *Speeches*, for the book of Micah and Gitay, 'Study', for Amos 3) or whether the 'speeches' found in the prophetic literature are of a secondary nature, having been put together by the prophetic editors and redactors. The latter position is the more common one, and it is the one I have advocated in *A Prophet in Debate* (see also Patrick, *Rhetoric*, 125).

However, texts such as Amos 1:3 – 2:16 (which is treated as a single utterance by most modern commentators) do call into question the older dictum that the prophets only ever uttered short, pithy oracles.

[37] Kennedy, *New Testament Interpretation*, 19.

[38] Patrick, *Rhetoric*, 145.

warn the people of the impending divine judgement, thus attempting to cause
them to repent and thereby avert Yahweh's punitive intervention, we would
be dealing with deliberative rather than judicial rhetoric. If this were the case,
we would have to conclude that the surface text with its predominant focus on
the divine judgement would not, in itself, be decisive in determining the
author's purpose or intention.

Thus, in order to understand how the text worked, or may have worked, it
is necessary also to take into account factors such as the social conventions in
place at the time of making the utterance. This is essential because they would
have influenced not only the audience's perception of and response to that
utterance, but also the choices the rhetorician had to make – that is, which rhetorical genre(s) to employ, which strategy and rhetorical style to choose, and so
on. However, as these issues will be addressed in the subsequent discussion of
speech-act theory, I want to move on and offer some brief comments on
Patrick's reading of the book of Amos. In particular, I intend to highlight how
his understanding of the history of the text, the nature of Amos' ministry and
the generic value of the judgement oracles, to name but a few factors, all to
some extent influence each other in what is a hermeneutical circle *par excel-
lence*. In stressing this, I am not suggesting that Patrick ought to have broken
out of that circle, which, as Schleiermacher and others have taught us, is not
possible,[39] but simply that it *is* a circle and that, if any of its constituents are re-
envisaged, this has implications for the understanding of the other parts as well
as for one's appreciation of the whole.

One of the key reasons why Patrick and I differ in our understanding of
Amos' oracles of judgement is that we take different routes right from the
beginning – that is, from step one of the rhetorical-critical enquiry. Patrick is
interested in 'approximating the original oral prophecies' and claims that, if
that is our aim, 'we must "deconstruct" the extant text, removing all
nongenuine material'.[40] Accepting what he considers to be 'a reasonable and
rather common judgment as to what can be ascribed to Amos',[41] Patrick goes
on to deny the authenticity of the heading (Amos 1:1), the doxologies
(1:2; 4:13; 5:8–9; 9:5–6), the Judah oracle (2:4–5) and the salvation oracle in
Amos 9:11–15.

---

[39] Schleiermacher once put it in these terms: 'Complete knowledge *always*
involves an apparent circle, that each part can be understood only out of the whole
to which it belongs, and vice-versa' (Schleiermacher, *Hermeneutics*, 113; emphasis
mine). On the hermeneutical circle see also Thiselton, *New Horizons*, *passim*.
[40] Patrick, *Rhetoric*, 131.
[41] Ibid., 132.

While I agree that the book consists of collections of speeches that have been arranged by what he calls 'traditionists',[42] I nevertheless would like to point out that to accept the so-called 'common consensus' concerning what does and does not originate with Amos is problematic. Patrick fails to see that, in accepting this 'consensus', he is endorsing judgements made, at least in some cases, on the basis of a reductionist understanding of language that does not go well with the functional perspective characteristic for rhetorical criticism. As we have seen above, it is precisely because Amos' words of judgement cannot mean what cannot be deduced from their surface grammar that, it is often argued, the prophet could not have made statements such as those found in Amos 9:11–15.

Rather than taking these judgements for granted, I intend to re-enter, and hence reshape, the hermeneutical circle by raising a few 'what ifs'. For instance, *what if* we approached a text, such as the book of Amos, with a philosophy of language in which the literalism characteristic for many historical-critical readings has been replaced by a functional, sociolinguistic view of language? *What if* we resisted the tendency to look for a 'single-minded' surface text or, more to the point, a 'single-minded' prophet, bent solely on 'bringing his audience under judgement', and whose words have to be retrieved from amidst the textual data as we now have it? *What if* we allowed for more complex intentions on the part of the rhetorician or author? Would we then still come to the same diachronic conclusions concerning the history of the text? Indeed, *what if* earlier historical-critical scholarship had taken a less literalistic route rather than seeing the existence of so-called 'observable discrepancies'[43] as a prompt to deal with these by means of numerous diachronic hypotheses? Finally, *what if* we momentarily set aside conclusions about the text's genesis, reached partly on the basis of question-able premises, and re-entered the hermeneutical circle by re-evaluating the textual data as it has come down to us?

All this is not to suggest that we ought to abandon historical criticism or concentrate purely on synchronic issues, setting aside the diachronic quest altogether. Far from it. The point of listing these 'what ifs' is simply to under-line my contention that any modification made to any of the constituents of the hermeneutical circle will, or must, lead to a reconsideration, and possibly a re-conceptualization, of the other components.[44] Indeed, a reconsideration of

---

[42] Ibid., 131.

[43] See my critique of Barton's claim that biblical literary critics did not begin by decid-ing that texts must be a conglomerate of various sources but came to such conclusions on the basis of 'observable discrepancies' in Möller, 'Renewing', 154f.

[44] Wolters has made a similar point talking about nine levels of biblical interpretation (i.e. textual criticism, lexicography, syntax, diachronic literary analysis, synchronic lit-erary analysis, historical analysis, ideological criticism, redemptive-historical analysis

the 'common judgement' about the text of Amos, its history and the question of what is or is not 'Amosian', is all the more important if, as has been argued, the traditional historical-critical approaches are flawed. Given these recent criticisms, what is now needed is 'a critical assessment of the aims, presuppositions and methodological procedures of historical criticism',[45] as well as a new look at the texts.

Elsewhere I have recently made a case for re-entering the hermeneutical circle from a synchronic point of view, momentarily setting aside all judgements about the history of the text. Employing a rhetorical-critical approach and working with the book of Amos in its present form, I have argued that it captures or presents the debate between the prophet Amos and his original eighth-century Israelite audience. Although we cannot go into the details of that argument here, I have concluded that Amos is not portrayed as the preacher of indiscriminate judgement that he is often thought to have been.

Taking into account, for instance, the prophet's radical re-interpretations of Israel's theological traditions (see the new twist given to the election theme in 3:2; the 'worship theology' in 4:4–5; 5:4–6, 21–24; the creation theme in 4:13; 5:8; 9:5–6; the concept of the day of the LORD in 5:18–20; and the exodus tradition in 9:7), I have argued that Amos is portrayed as struggling – and, it seems, failing – to make his contemporaries think the unthinkable: that Yahweh, their God, might *do* the unthinkable, and turn against them.[46] This is neither a judge nor the messenger of a judge speaking. If the prophet's task had been, simply and solely, to bring the Israelites under the divine judgement, then much of Amos' rhetoric would have been unnecessary. For instance, there would have been no need for him to appeal to his audience's emotions, warning them that the punishment would lead to a time of lamentation and wailing (5:1–3, 16–17; 8:10). Once again, it is hard to imagine a judge, or indeed a plaintiff, taking this line of approach. Where it does fit, however, is a deliberative context. That is to say, it befits anyone who desires to shock the audience and propel them into taking appropriate measures to prevent the threatened outcome.

---

[44] (*Continued*) and confessional discernment) and arguing that, on the one hand, each level 'rests upon' the others, with textual criticism being at the bottom and confessional discernment at the top, but also that 'interpretative judgments on one level often … "hang on" decisions made on a higher level', thus suggesting two reverse directions of influence (see Wolters, 'Confessional Criticism'; the quote is from p. 108).

[45] Möller 'Renewing', 149. For a summary of some philosophical, literary-critical, theological and socio-religious criticisms that have been levelled against the historical-critical approach see pp. 150–59 of the same article.

[46] See Möller, *Prophet*; and *idem*, 'Word', for further details.

Yet, defending his judicial interpretation of Amos' judgement oracles, Patrick has sought to explain the need for rhetorical invention by suggesting that 'the extension of the prophecy of judgement to the people [as a whole] entailed an analogical leap'. This, he argues, made it necessary for Amos to convince the people of the necessity of corporate punishment.[47] And this the prophet attempted to do by drawing his audience's attention to the seriousness of the problem, that is to the fact that their society was characterized by systemic injustice, which violated the very order the people lived by.[48]

To be sure, there are passages that lend themselves well to such an interpretation – but there is also much material that would seem irrelevant and out of place if the prophet's objective was purely a judicial one. Indeed, Patrick himself occasionally feels compelled to concede that what we are dealing with in the book of Amos 'is not so much a *pronouncement* of judgment as it is an *argument for the possibility* of judgment'.[49] He even notes that 'the prophecy of judgment is at once an effort of getting the people to see themselves as YHWH sees them, and a kind of test to see whether they can be reformed rather than destroyed'.[50] This is much more akin to what I have been arguing for in that it comes fairly close to allowing for a deliberative objective on Amos' part.

However, rather than moving into a detailed discussion at this point, let me summarize why I believe Patrick has not applied the rhetorical-critical approach to its full potential. First, by adopting the traditional form-critical understanding promoted by Westermann and others, Patrick too quickly went down the judicial path. Rhetorical criticism, especially when applied in combination with speech-act theory (as in Patrick's study), would have allowed him to explore alternative interpretative options[51] had he been less unswerving in following Westermann. Secondly, Patrick also too quickly assumed that the predominant rhetorical genre (i.e. the fact that there are quite a few judgement oracles in the book of Amos) is indicative of the prophet's major purpose. As I have maintained above, the predominant genre might also reflect the rhetorician's rhetorical strategy, and given that the book of Amos contains quite a lot of material that would appear to be out of place in a judicial context, it seems more likely that the overall purpose was not a judicial one.

Thirdly, I believe Patrick was ill-advised to accept, right from the outset, what he calls the 'common judgement' as to what can be ascribed to the prophet Amos. To be sure, there is a world of difference between Patrick's 'deconstruction' of the text and the views of those who can find little more than

---

[47] Patrick, *Rhetoric*, 138f.

[48] Ibid., 135, 146f.

[49] Ibid., 138 (emphasis mine); see also p. 146.

[50] Ibid., 147.

[51] We shall come back to this in the subsequent discussion of speech-act theory.

sporadic traces of Amos' authentic words in the book that bears his name.[52] In fact, Patrick does not even go along with Wolff's influential analysis, according to which the book consists, in addition to the prophet's own words, of a variety of material connected with the old school of Amos, the Bethel-exposition of the Josianic age, a deuteronomistic redaction and a postexilic addendum featuring a word of salvation.[53] Nor does Patrick show any interest in the ongoing speculation about the number of textual layers in the book.[54] Thus, his 'deconstruction' of the text turns out to be rather a moderate exercise. Yet, this notwithstanding, I still believe that it is problematic to advocate a new approach and at the same time accept the results yielded by earlier approaches that worked with different presuppositions or, more specifically, different philosophies of language.

However, let me now end this section by highlighting some of the benefits of a rhetorical-critical approach. By applying a communication-theoretical perspective and, more specifically, by paying attention to issues such as the exigency that occasioned the utterance, the rhetorical genre and the rhetorical strategy adopted by the rhetorician, the approach transcends any literalistic fixation on the surface text that characterizes some traditional historical-critical readings. For instance, rhetorical criticism can help us see more clearly that the form-critical identification of the texts in question as 'judgement oracles' does not, in itself, 'solve' the question of their purpose and use. This, however, is precisely what form critics have been aiming for. Westermann's *Basic Forms of Prophetic Speech* is a good example of this. Finding the roots of the prophetic judgement speech in Israelite legal practice, he argued that judgement oracles are best understood not as reproaches or warnings but as what we might call a judge's final verdict.

However, neither this genealogy of the prophetic judgement speech nor the conclusions drawn from it have remained uncontested. As Tucker has pointed out in his foreword to the reprinted English edition of Westermann's work, Koch has denied 'both a judicial background and a legal pattern in the

---

[52] For instance, Fritz, 'Amosbuch', 41, regards almost the entire book as a '*vaticinium ex eventu*', and Ringgren, 'Israelite Prophecy', 204, claims to 'know at least one scholar who is prepared to write off the entire book, with the exception of two or three verses, as a Deuteronomistic composition'.

[53] Wolff, *Joel and Amos*, 106–13.

[54] Wolff (ibid.) distinguished six layers, Coote, *Amos*, three, and Jozaki, 'Secondary Passages', eight. He was outdone recently by Rottzoll, *Studien*, 285–90, who even discovered twelve strata, thus providing a striking example of what Sternberg has called an 'incredible abuse … of frenzied digging into the Bible's genesis, so senseless as to elicit either laughter or tears' (Sternberg, *Poetics*, 13).

speeches'.[55] It has also been stressed that even if we could be sure about the origin of the speech form, there is no reason to assume that the prophets' use of it corresponds closely to its original use. Form critics themselves have therefore come to the conclusion that we need to distinguish between the original meaning, or significance, of a speech form and its use or function in the prophetic literature.[56]

By focusing on pragmatics rather than typicality and convention, on language-in-use rather than origins and *Sitz im Leben*, rhetorical criticism takes us a few steps further than that. It enables us to see not only *that* form and function need to be held apart, but also *how* rhetoricians use language in general – and speech forms in particular – as an instrument with which to persuade or convince[57] their audiences of their course. However, speech-act theory, especially when combined with rhetorical-critical analysis, in my opinion has the potential to take us further still, and it is to a discussion of its capacities and application that we now turn.

Coming to Terms with Prophetic Speech Acts

Speech-act theory, as conceived by Austin, Grice, Searle and others,[58] 'was developed to supersede the old logical-positivist view of language which assumed that the only meaningful statements are those which describe a state of affairs in the world'.[59] Attempting to correct what he thought of as the 'descriptive fallacy', Austin distinguished between 'constatives' (descriptive statements) and 'performatives' (statements that 'get something done').[60] Focusing on the latter, Austin differentiated between three kinds of performative statements, i.e. 'locutionary', 'illocutionary' and 'perlocutionary' acts.[61] The first is

---

[55] Tucker, 'Foreword', xiii. For Koch's own understanding of the prophetic judgement speech see Koch, *Formgeschichte*, 251–54.

[56] Fohrer, 'Bemerkungen', 480; see also *idem*, 'Form'.

[57] For a distinction between the two, cf. Perelman and Olbrechts-Tyteca, *New Rhetoric*, 26–31.

[58] Cf. Austin, *Things*; Searle, *Speech Acts*; *idem*, *Expression*; Grice, 'Logic'; and *idem*, 'Utterance-Meaning'.

[59] Thus Selden and Widdowson, *Reader's Guide*, 148.

[60] The general distinction is made in the first lecture (Austin, *Things*, 1–11). Lectures 2–4 deal with what Austin called 'infelicities', reflecting his basic distinction between constatives, which can be true or false, and performatives, which are either 'happy' or 'unhappy' (cf. pp. 12–52). In lectures 5–7, Austin then discusses criteria for distinguishing performatives from constatives (pp. 53–93).

[61] For the basic distinction cf. lecture 8 (pp. 94–107). The subsequent lectures (9–10, pp. 108–31) follow this up by providing criteria for distinguishing 'illocutions' from 'perlocutions'.

defined as 'the performance of an act *of* saying something', an illocution is 'the performance of an act *in* saying something' and a perlocution is 'the performance of an act *by* saying something'. Thus we can, for instance, 'distinguish the locutionary act "he *said* that ..." from the illocutionary act "he *argued* that ..." and the perlocutionary act "he *convinced* me that ..."'[62]

This distinction is a useful conception in that it helps us differentiate between what a prophet *said* – for instance, 'the end has come upon my people Israel; I will never again pass them by' (Amos 8:2; NRSV); what he was *doing* in making that statement (i.e. issuing a threat or declaring a verdict, depending on how one understands statements like this one); and what the *effects* of that speech act were (or might have been).

Patrick has applied these concepts to the study of prophetic judgement oracles, arguing that they are judicial acts that fall into Austin's category of 'verdictives'.[63] He explains that 'when a duly authorized court finds a person guilty of a crime, the accused *becomes* guilty before the law and within the society under that law. The linguistic act changes the person's status. ... the judicial act changes the relationship of the convicted to her community and to the authority governing that community.'[64]

According to Patrick, who, as we have already seen, follows Westermann's genealogy of the prophetic judgement speech, Amos took the prophecy of judgement of individuals and applied it collectively, to the people of Israel as a whole.[65] This, in Patrick's view, 'was a daring analogical extension of verdictive utterance, and required imaginative, constant rhetorical invention to succeed'.[66] An example of this rhetorical invention are the ubiquitous accusations, which were designed to convince the accused of their guilt, to make them 'face the darkness, accept its inevitability and rightness'.[67] However, the accusations only starred in a supportive role, as Amos' real 'task was to bring ... his audience under judgement',[68] to quote once again the words that sum up Patrick's understanding of the prophet's ministry.

---

[62] Austin, *Things*, 102 (emphasis mine).

[63] Patrick, *Rhetoric*, 121–22, 130. Verdictives, statements that give a verdict, are one of the five classes of performatives that Austin proposed. The others are 'exercitives' (statements that exercise powers, rights, or influence), 'commissives' (statements that commit one to doing something), 'behabitives' (statements that have to do with attitudes and social behaviour), and 'expositives' (statements that are expository) (Austin, *Things*, 147–63).

[64] Patrick, *Rhetoric*, 130.

[65] Ibid., 131, 133; see also Westermann, *Basic Forms*, 169–81.

[66] Patrick, *Rhetoric*, 133.

[67] Ibid., 145.

[68] Ibid.

Patrick thus essentially restates the well-known view that Amos was a preacher of judgement. This he does by taking recourse to speech-act theory without, however, using it to its full potential or indeed taking into account those facets that would have challenged his own interpretation. Being apparently unaware of the instructive work by Eagleton and Houston on prophetic judgement oracles,[69] Patrick simply classifies them as verdictives without exploring other possibilities. This is disappointing because, applying the same insights generated by Austin's speech–act theory, Eagleton and Houston have come to completely different conclusions.

As Lohfink has noted, a crucial aspect of speech-act theory is its insistence that a speech act is determined not only by words and syntax but also by social, situational and textual conditions.[70] To use one of Austin's many instructive examples, the words 'I do' take on special significance, or *count as* something quite specific, only under certain circumstances – that is, when spoken in a wedding ceremony.[71] Thus, in order to understand a speech act, we need to be familiar with the social conditions that determine what it counts as. While many scholars claim that prophetic judgement oracles ought to be understood as unalterable verdicts, Houston and Eagleton have shown that in Old Testament times they were not always thus understood but could in fact be taken as warnings.

An interesting example is found in Jonah 3:4–9. The story is familiar: Jonah has by now arrived in Nineveh, and if ever there was a prophet who was keen to see his audience punished in accordance with the divine 'verdict', it surely was him. 'On the first day, Jonah started into the city. He proclaimed: "Forty more days and Nineveh will be overturned" ' (Jon. 3:4). This is as unconditional as it gets. Jonah doesn't even bother to spell out the reasons for the punishment, let alone attempt to convince his audience of their guilt. But to his great dismay, the message did not count with his audience as an unalterable divine verdict. 'The Ninevites believed God. They declared a fast, and all of them, from the greatest to the least put on sackcloth' (v. 5). Indeed, their king decreed: 'Let everyone call urgently on God. Let them give up their evil ways and their violence. Who knows? God may yet relent and with compassion turn from his fierce anger so that we will not perish' (vv. 8–9). Eagleton comments that,

---

[69] Eagleton, 'Austin'; and Houston, 'Prophets'.

[70] Lohfink, 'Bund', 221.

[71] See also, in this context, Wittgenstein's insistence that words have meaning only in what he called 'forms of life', i.e. when used in particular contexts (Wittgenstein, *Philosophical Investigations*).

in the terms of J.L. Austin's *How to Do Things with Words*, prophetic utterances of Jonah's sort are 'constative' (descriptive of some real or possible state of affairs) only in what one might call their surface grammar; as far as their 'deep structure' goes they actually belong to Austin's class of 'performatives', linguistic acts which get something done.[72]

Thus far, Eagleton is in complete agreement with Patrick in that both regard prophetic oracles of judgement as performative speech acts. However, they part company when it comes to classifying them according to Austin's five classes of performatives. Whereas Patrick, influenced by Westermann's form-critical conceptions, is adamant that they are to be seen as verdictives, Eagleton effectively refuses to be drawn, treating these oracles as hybrids that fit into two of Austin's classes in that they could be both verdictives and exercitives. The latter have been defined by Austin as statements that exercise powers or rights or that influence, and the examples he mentions include 'appointing, voting, ordering, urging, advising, warning', and so on.[73]

Eagleton, who, as we have already seen, defines performatives as 'linguistic acts which get something done', points out that

> what [prophetic judgement oracles] get done is to produce a state of affairs in which the state of affairs they describe won't be the case. Effective declarations of imminent catastrophe cancel themselves out, containing as they do a contradiction between what they say and what they do.[74]

Thus, in the illocutionary act of talking about an unconditional judgement (whether this is construed as warning or as declaring a verdict does not really matter in this case), these oracles perform, or may perform, the perlocutionary act of leading the addressees to repentance (note that it is the addressees who 'decide' what the speech act counts as), thereby paradoxically cancelling out what was said in the first place. However, this is only one possible scenario, as the following example will illustrate.

Even a judgement oracle directed against an individual, which according to Westermann is very closely related to 'regular judicial procedure',[75] could trigger a reaction similar to the one of the Ninevites. This is illustrated, for instance, by David's reaction to Nathan's unconditional oracle of judgement delivered in the aftermath of the Bathsheba episode. Nathan simply informs

---

[72] Eagleton, 'Austin', 233.

[73] Austin, *Things*, 150.

[74] Eagleton, 'Austin', 233.

[75] Westermann, *Basic Forms*, 130–36 (the quote is from p. 135); see also Patrick, *Rhetoric*, 128–30.

David, it seems, that 'the sword will never depart from your house, because you despised me [i.e. Yahweh] and took the wife of Uriah the Hittite to be your own' (2 Sam. 12:10). The prophet could hardly have been less ambiguous, and yet what follows sheds new light on what one would have thought his intention was in proclaiming his message. 'Then David said to Nathan, "I have sinned against the LORD." Nathan replied, "The LORD has taken away your sin. You are not going to die" ' (v. 13). Thus, to recapitulate, the prophet announces an unconditional oracle of judgement, the recipient does not take this to be unconditional at all but repents and thereby apparently averts the judgement, which confirms that the message was indeed not unconditional after all.

However, this is of course not the full story in that Nathan goes on to say that 'because by doing this you have made the enemies of the LORD show utter contempt, the son born to you will die' (v. 14). In this case the judgement is not averted, for the message is confirmed to have been unconditional and one may assume that Nathan's intention was no more than to announce what will happen. It should be noted, though, that this again did not prevent David from seeking to forestall the judgement by fasting and weeping – thus once more not taking Nathan's word as the final one until he was left with no other option (v. 22).

These examples show that, in proclaiming unconditional oracles of judgement, a prophet may, or may not, have had the intention of announcing a final verdict. Or he may, or may not, have intended to warn his audience of an impending judgement thus attempting to lead them to repentance. Yet again, whatever the prophet's intention, the audience's reactions in the examples cited above indicate that it was possible, if not indeed natural, to take judgement oracles as warnings. Indeed, from Jonah's point of view, his brief communication with the Ninevites may well have been an example of a speech act 'going wrong' because, as Wolterstorff notes, only

> if all goes well on both sides, the interpreter, in discerning what counts as what, will perforce discern the content of [the] implemented action plan [...] But everything may not go well, even on the discourser's side. What he casually brings about may not count as what he thought it would count as – not count as the speech action that he intended to perform. Or it may count as quite a bit more than he had in mind; and with that more, he may be less than happy.[76]

But as Houston notes, 'if a type of response is indicated in the literature which was certainly familiar with prophecy, that is because it is *appropriate* to the type

---

[76] Wolterstorff, *Divine Discourse*, 183, 184.

of utterance as such'.[77] To put this in Wittgensteinian terms, one might say that this kind of response is appropriate to the particular language game exemplified by prophetic oracles of judgement because, as Wittgenstein has pointed out, language tends to follow public rules, which are a requirement for meaningful communication.[78] However, as far as the prophet's intention is concerned, Houston has argued that 'the question whether the intention of judgement prophecy is to condemn absolutely or to awaken repentance is transcended'.[79] This is because 'the possibilities of inexorable doom and of mercy evoked by repentance were always implicit in the use of the genre of the oracle of doom'.[80] Steiner, too, emphasizes that the prophet's

> enunciation of the future makes that future alterable. If man repents and changes his conduct, God can bend the arc of time out of foreseen shape. ... The force, the axiomatic certainty of the prophet's prediction lies precisely in the possibility that the prediction will go unfulfilled. From Amos to Isaiah, the true prophet 'does not announce an immutable decree. He speaks into the power of decision lying in the moment ...'[81]

Thus, speech–act theory, with its distinction between locution, illocution and perlocution, overcomes any literalistic fixation on the surface text. It thereby demonstrates the inadequacy of an approach towards language such as Smend's, who effectively took the surface text to determine what the discourse means, and does.

The above examples also illustrate that, as Hart has pointed out, a positivistic approach 'misses all that is most truly human, reducing the other to a categorial abstraction whose particular qualities, concerns, hopes, fears and pains ... are deliberately overlooked'.[82] Hart underlines that emotional, volitional, psychological and spiritual elements all need to be taken into account in our bid for understanding. Speech–act theory – *if* it is bent

---

[77] Houston, 'Prophets', 185 (emphasis mine). It is interesting to note in this context that Zech. 1:4 quite generally understands the former prophets as preachers of repentance: 'Do not be like your forefathers, to whom the earlier prophets proclaimed: This is what the LORD Almighty says: "Turn from your evil ways and your evil practices." ' Petersen, *Haggai and Zechariah 1–8*, 132f., comments that 'one may infer that the author of Zech. 1:4 has viewed such texts as Jer. 11:18; 25:5; 35:15; Ezek. 33:11 as typical of pre–586 prophetic language'.

[78] Wittgenstein, *Philosophical Investigations*.

[79] Houston, 'Prophets', 187.

[80] Ibid., 186.

[81] Steiner, *After Babel*, 154, the latter part being a quote from Buber, *Prophetic Faith*, 103.

[82] Hart, 'Imagination', 321.

on classifying a particular speech act according to Austin's categories of performatives, thereby reducing it to a rather narrowly defined type of action – may therefore well be in danger of underestimating the complexity of the communication event. Yet it should be noted that Austin stressed the preliminary character of his classification, which he hoped would lead him to a better understanding of the nature and function of performatives, and that, according to his own admission, he was 'far from equally happy' about them.[83]

Finally, I would like to point out that speech-act theory clearly challenges Kennedy's view that a text's dominant rhetorical genre necessarily reflects the author's major purpose. As the above discussion has shown, what looks like, and maybe was meant to be, judicial rhetoric, may yet be understood by the audience as deliberative rhetoric – as an attempt to make them rethink their position and take appropriate action. More to the point, however, Nathan's example indicates that, regardless of the initial impression given by unconditional oracles of judgement, this may have been the intention of the rhetorician all along. However, if, or better when, this is so – as we have seen, this can be difficult to determine – one would have to conclude that the main genre, or the way in which the surface text is cast, is indicative not of the author's purpose or intention but of his or her rhetorical strategy.

The Prophets and the Creative Imagination: Observations on the Metaphorical Nature of Language

It has been noted that 'every act of communication involves *both parties* in some responsible activity',[84] and in the above discussion I have already drawn attention to the audience's contribution, pointing out that it may well be the addressees who, in the end, 'decide' what a speech act counts as. Looking at interpretation from a discourse-analytical angle, Green has similarly argued that 'every engaged reading is … participation in a communicative event whereby we join in the generation of meaning and are shaped in the give and take of active discourse'.[85] Discourse analysis, according to this conception, 'is interested in *how* language-in-use invites such participation and formation'.[86]

In a century that has witnessed what has been described as 'metaphormania',[87] it is hardly surprising that one of the key factors that has been

---

[83] Austin, *Things*, 149f.

[84] Hart, 'Imagination', 309 (emphasis mine).

[85] Green, 'Discourse Analysis', 177.

[86] Ibid.

[87] Johnson (ed.), *Philosophical Perspectives*, ix.

identified as inviting the participation of the interpreter is the metaphorical nature of language. This is because, as Stiver has emphasized, both creating and *understanding* metaphor are inventive, and thus supremely active, acts.[88] Philosophers of language have therefore drawn attention to the role of the imagination, which, as Hart notes, 'is bound up with the extension of language through metaphor',[89] and which plays a key role in our bid to understand the other's discourse. As again Hart observes, 'the imagination functions analogically, tracing meaningful connections, identifying the presence of the like in the very core of the unlike, offering metaphorical construals of the unfamiliar in terms of the familiar'.[90]

Before we discuss how this impacts on the interpretation of prophetic judgement oracles, it should be noted that the current interest in metaphor and the analogical way of knowing is the result of a radical turn, initiated by Richards and Black, whose insights have since been appropriated and developed by many others.[91] Prior to this turn, it was Aristotle's reductionist understanding that profoundly influenced the assessment of metaphor.[92] Degrading metaphor (understood as a deviation from 'normal' speech) to a mere ornament to language, a figure of speech, Aristotle affirmed 'the superiority of univocal or literal language over the symbolic'.[93] Following in the wake of Aristotle, the history of the philosophy of language has witnessed many disapproving assessments of the nature and function of metaphor. To mention just one example, Hobbes thought of it at best in terms of an aberration, at worst as pathological. According to his view, metaphor is deceptive because it is a word used in a sense other than the one normally intended.[94]

In marked contrast to this understanding, some philosophers of science now stress the pervasiveness of metaphor even in scientific discourse[95] (the conception of light as a wave would be an obvious example). Metaphor, in Stiver's words, is thus 'not an optional addition to univocal language'[96] but is of vital importance for scientific conceptualization and understanding. Soskice has furthermore suggested that in the background of much of our language

---

[88] Stiver, *Philosophy*, 117 (emphasis mine).

[89] Hart, 'Imagination', 329.

[90] Ibid., 320.

[91] See Stiver, *Philosophy*, 114ff.; and Avis, *God*, 74–76, for further details.

[92] Avis, *God*, 98.

[93] Stiver, *Philosophy*, 10.

[94] Hobbes, *Leviathan*, 13. For a historical account of how metaphor has been understood see Ricœur, *Rule*, 8–64.

[95] See, for instance, Hesse, *Revolutions*.

[96] Stiver, *Philosophy*, 119.

there are metaphors that provide a framework even for our literal language,[97] which suggests that without metaphor there would be no language at all. Hesse has even argued that all language is metaphorical,[98] and Avis has pointed out that

> metaphor is the '*instinctive and necessary*' way in which the mind explores reality and orders experience, using intuitive comparisons whereby the less familiar is assimilated to the more familiar and the unknown to the known.[99]

But how then does all this affect our reading of prophetic oracles of judgement? To start with, attention should be drawn to Wolterstorff's illuminating contention that it was imagination that enabled, for instance, the recipients of Jonah's oracle to respond to the prophet's words in the way they did. Wolterstorff points out that,

> if between locutionary and illocutionary acts there were a one to one relationship, such that for each locutionary act there was just one illocutionary act that the locutionary act could count as, and vice versa, then no imagination would be required on the part of listeners or readers in determining which illocutionary act the locutionary act they're confronted with counts as, nor would any imagination be required on the part of speakers or writers in determining which locutionary act to perform so as to perform the desired illocutionary act.[100]

However, as such a one-to-one correspondence between locutionary and illocutionary acts does not exist, we do require the constructive contribution of imagination, which, as Hart has noted, presents to the interpreter

> 'meaningful' or 'imaginable' states of affairs or worlds for our indwelling and consideration ... by showing us 'how things would be if' certain things were true, imagination breathes life into concepts in a way which not only makes them easier to grasp ... but actually has a degree of persuasive force which disarms our scepticism and makes 'belief in' possible.[101]

This, I believe, is an excellent description of what prophets such as Amos were trying to do.[102] Creatively employing and transforming received forms of

---

[97] Soskice, *Metaphor*, 63.

[98] Hesse, 'Cognitive Claims', esp. 1–3.

[99] Avis, *God*, 97 (emphasis mine).

[100] Wolterstorff, 'Response', 335f.

[101] Hart, 'Imagination', 319.

[102] See Carroll R., *Contexts*, 176, who suggests that 'the biblical text through its language and style offers its readers a world, a world which can often be an alternative and powerful picture of reality that can challenge the present'.

speech as well as established theological traditions and popular beliefs,[103] Amos, in the manner of a true poet (indeed, this is where the label is most appropriately applied to the prophets), attempted to make his audience 'see reality with new eyes', to put it in Eco's words.[104] Shelley once said that 'poetry lifts the veil from the hidden beauty of the world',[105] but it may also, as the prophecies of judgement indicate, uncover its hidden horrors. Yet regardless of whether the poetic vision is a positive or an abhorrent one, it certainly, to quote once more from Hart's illuminating article,

> enlarges our vision, tracing patterns, threads and connexions which stretch out be-
> yond the horizons of our known world, and leading us out … into the complex
> structure of things until, at last, we find ourselves in quite unfamiliar territory, our
> imagination stretched, sometimes to breaking point.[106]

These words again masterfully describe what we find in texts such as the book of Amos. A few examples should suffice to illustrate this. Given that the prophet confronts his audience with a God portrayed as a roaring lion (Amos 1:2; 3:8); who turns the day of the LORD, the great and much anticipated day of the salvific intervention of Israel's God, into a day of darkness and horror (5:18–20); who despises the religious festivals and cannot stand the people's offerings and the sound of their songs (5:21–23) and is going to turn the festivals into mourning and the singing into weeping (8:10); who gets involved in the destruction of the temple (9:1; also 3:14); who hunts his people down without mercy (9:2–4) and even denies them their privileged status associated with the exodus (9:7), I believe we can safely assume that Amos' hearers did find themselves in what would be fittingly described as unfamiliar theological territory. Nor do I think would it be an overstatement to say that their imagination must indeed have been stretched to breaking point. This, I submit, was one of the effects of the world projected by the prophet's message. It turned the audience's world upside down, and I wholeheartedly agree with Lindbeck, who urged that, 'to neglect these tacitly present projected worlds and focus only on *what texts explicitly say* [note again that this is what Smend and others have been arguing for] … is to ignore a *major* dimension of their meaning.'[107]

However, this brings us back to the question of Amos' intention in confronting his hearers with the dire message that he felt compelled to announce. What, then, did he think he was doing in majoring on the divine judgement?

---

[103] See Dell, 'Misuse'; and Smith, 'Continuity'.
[104] Eco, 'Political Language', 107.
[105] Shelley, 'Defence', 33.
[106] Hart, 'Imagination', 316.
[107] Lindbeck, 'Postcritical Canonical Interpretation', 36 (emphasis mine).

And how can we find out what his intentions were? Some brief comments on these issues are necessary. But, before we consider them, it should be noted that Wolterstorff, favouring what he calls 'authorial discourse interpretation', has underlined that most of the time our goal of interpretation is, and ought to be, discerning what the discourser is saying, not what she *intended* to say. Yet he admits that 'considerations of intention will have to go into the discerning of that intentional action which is an act of discourse'.[108] Thus, Wolterstorff makes the 'bid for understanding *what the other said*' the primary focus of interpretation but agrees with Schleiermacher that we also need to 'understand something of the discourser's motivations and purposes'.[109]

In discussing the metaphorical nature of language and the corresponding role of the imagination for interpreting or understanding somebody else's discourse, I have thus far put some emphasis on the audience's contribution. For instance, we have noted that, in addition to certain social conventions, it may have been the audience's imagination that enabled them to react to Jonah's words in the way they did. Yet I have also suggested that Amos, in reinterpreting the people's cherished theological traditions, attempted to make them see reality with new eyes. In making that suggestion, I have therefore made an attempt to understand something of Amos' motivations and purposes. To be more specific, what I am proposing here is that the use of prophetic oracles of judgement may have been part of Amos' appeal to the audience's imagination. As I see it, Amos is presented by the text as being confronted with the problem that his hearers simply do not see the magnitude of their guilt. Nor can they imagine that their God would ever turn against them. Carroll R. captures the problem well in noting that

> false readings of history and national realities (4:6–11; 6:13), hollow hopes (5:18–20), self-deluding confidence (6:1–3; 9:10), and politico-religious ambitions and jealousies (7:10–17) as well as abuses at the cult and in society, all blind the mind and make it impossible to comprehend what God is like and to discern where he is in history and where history itself is going.[110]

These were the problems Amos faced. And one important way of tackling them was his attempt to shatter the people's world-view by painting a picture of an alternative world, the contours of which I have already alluded to above.[111]

---

[108] Wolterstorff, 'Response', 339f. (the quote is from p. 340).

[109] Ibid., 340f. Lindbeck therefore goes too far, in my view, in considering the appeal to authorial intention illicit (Lindbeck, 'Postcritical Canonical Interpretation', 49).

[110] Carroll R., 'God', 67–8.

[111] See Möller, *Prophet*, for further discussion.

Based on these considerations I would conclude that there is sufficient evidence to suggest that the prophet's message is not one of inevitable certitude. That is to say, taking into account the non-judicial material of the book, such as Amos' appeals to the people's emotions; the fact that in the Old Testament traditions there is evidence to suggest that prophetic oracles of judgement were not necessarily taken to be irreversible announcements of an unalterable fate; and that Amos' aim may have been to challenge his audience's perception of reality by painting a picture of a radically different world, I believe we would be mistaken to delimit the function of prophetic judgement oracles to giving a judicial verdict.

Yet in talking about purposes and intentions, I should also stress at this point that my own intention in this essay was not to offer a full-blown interpretation of Amos' message, which would not have been possible within the confines of the present study. What I did intend to show, though, is that the question of how to interpret prophetic oracles of judgement is a complex issue that requires a multifaceted approach if we are to avoid monolithic readings.[112] Perhaps even more to the point, however, such interpretation requires both imagination and *phronesis* (that is, good judgement), to put it in Wolterstorff's terms.[113]

Imagistic Thinking and the Rewriting of the Encyclopaedia

The aim of the present article was twofold. In the first instance, I sought to illustrate how different perspectives on language, as exemplified by rhetorical criticism, speech-act theory and metaphorical theories of language, can enrich biblical interpretation or, as in our case, more specifically the interpretation of prophetic judgement oracles. Of course, none of these theories will have the last word in the debate; nor indeed should they. Yet I believe the above discussion has shown that Stiver is justified in claiming that 'an understanding of the philosophy of language … can sharpen the debate … The philosophy of language … can rarely settle truth claims. [But] it can enhance discussion and lead to greater sensitivity to the role of language'.[114] And this, I should like to add,

---

[112] Compare Stiver's more general comment that, for instance, speech-act theory 're-veals how complex apparently simple language can be … It also shows how simplistic was the traditional concentration on the descriptive type of language at the locutionary level alone' (Stiver, *Philosophy*, 83).

[113] Wolterstorff, 'Response', 336.

[114] Stiver, *Philosophy*, 204.

can lead to more nuanced readings that are more likely to do justice to the multiple dimensions of the texts in question.

In our specific case, rhetorical criticism with its functional or pragmatic focus, among other things, helps us distinguish between purpose and strategy and also enables us to see that a text's predominant genre does not necessarily reflect the author's purpose. Speech-act theory contributes to the discussion by drawing our attention to the sociolinguistic dimension of language. That is to say, it makes us aware of how social conventions contribute not only to the audience's perception of somebody's discourse but also to the rhetorical choices made by the discourser in an attempt to generate the desired reaction. Metaphorical theories of language and the emphasis they put on the imagination in turn remind us that there is more to language than the communication of facts or the description of reality (past, present or, as in the case of prophetic judgement oracles, future). Language may also be used 'poetically', with a view to generating alternative perceptions of reality (again this applies to the perception of a possible past, present or future reality), and we would be the poorer for missing this dimension in a quest for *the* univocal meaning of the texts under consideration.[115]

---

[115] I therefore find myself in agreement with Eco, who underlines that the number of possible interpretations is unlimited. However, he is quick to add that not all of them are equally successful (Eco, *Grenzen*, ch. 1.7). See also Miller, *Thomas Hardy*, ix, who similarly rejects the idea that 'all readings are equally valid or of equal value. Some readings are certainly wrong. Of the valid interpretations all have limitations. ... Some approaches reach more deeply into the structure of the text than others.'

However, to return to the suggestion that there is an unlimited number of possible interpretations, Smith has recently argued for a creational hermeneutic that traces the need for interpretation back to creation rather than the fall, as is commonly done. He notes that 'interpretation has long been a sin. Understood as a postlapsarian phenomenon from which humanity must be redeemed, hermeneutics has traditionally been linked with the curse and banishment from the Garden. Interpretation, in short ... is itself a fall ... from immediacy to mediation, from reading to hermeneutics. [...] Hermeneutics [therefore] is something to be overcome by redemption, whereby the curse of interpretation will be removed in a hermeneutical paradise where interpretation is absent' (Smith, *Fall*, 17).

Smith goes on to show how this understanding shapes: a) the evangelical theology of Koivisto and Lints, who have argued for a 'present immediacy model', in which 'the curse of interpretation is lifted here and now'; b) the hermeneutic of Pannenberg, who advocates an 'eschatological immediacy model', according to which 'interpretation is a state of affairs from which humanity must be redeemed'; and c) the 'violent mediation model' of Heidegger and Derrida (ibid., 20–2). Smith notes that for Heidegger 'human being-in-the-world is "essentially" fallen' while according to Derrida 'misunderstanding and misinterpretation are built into the structure of the sign and system of signifiers.

Secondly, I have also drawn attention to some of the consequences that a 'surface text-centred' literalism has had for some traditional historical–critical readings of the prophetic books. It appears that the adoption of what has been dubbed the 'old logical-positivist view of language'[116] has contributed to the tendency to seek diachronic answers for questions that may never have arisen in the first place had exegetes operated with a functional or, more generally, a more flexible and dynamical view of language. As noted above, diachronic answers have often been seen as the only way to account for what Barton has described as 'observable discrepancies' in the text. Yet one wonders just how many of these 'observable discrepancies' were in fact engendered by what Gunn and Fewell have called an 'aesthetic preference for rationalistic, literal reading of [the biblical] literature'.[117]

Shelley once perceptively observed that 'reason respects the differences, and imagination the similitudes of things',[118] and it appears that the dominance of reason at the expense of imagination has led to what often amounted to almost an obsession with differences and discrepancies, tensions and

---

[115] (*Continued*) Every interpretation is a decision; every decision is "structurally finite" and, as such, "structurally violent." Hermeneutics, which is constitutive of human being, is always already violent and a violation; thus to be human is to do violence' (ibid., 21, 22).

Rejecting a postlapsarian interpretation of interpretation, Smith advocates what he calls a 'non-Platonic' and 'demythologized' Augustinian hermeneutic, which 'understands interpretation and hermeneutical mediation as constitutive aspects of human being-in-the world' made necessary by 'aspects such as the finitude and locality of human existence.' However, Smith adds that this 'creational-pneumatic hermeneutic does not understand [the] necessity and inescapability of interpretation as a violent state of affairs but rather as an aspect of a good, peaceful creation' (ibid., 22). He also points out that 'such an "interpretation of interpretation" *re*-values embodiment and ultimately ends in an ethical respect for difference as the gift of a creating God who loves difference and who loves differently' (ibid., 23).

As far as the fall is concerned, Smith maintains that it did not effect 'the appearance of interpretation but rather the distortion or corruption of interpretation' (ibid., 27). All this raises a number of important questions, which, however, cannot be pursued in the present context. Instead I would like to refer, finally, to Smith's reading of the tower of Babel episode, which is equally interesting. He notes that 'the hermeneutical structure of creation is good; it produces goods: a plurality of interpretations and a diversity of readings. The sin of Babel was its quest for unity – one interpretation, one reading, one people – which was an abandonment of creational diversity and plurality in favor of exclusion and violence' (ibid., 33).

[116] Selden and Widdowson, *Reader's Guide*, 148, as quoted above.

[117] Gunn and Fewell, *Narrative*, 8.

[118] Shelley, 'Defence', 23.

contradictions. Stressing that 'the modernity that stems from the Enlightenment assumes a dichotomy between rational discourse ... and imagistic thinking', Avis has pointed out that this has resulted in a privileging of '*logos* over against *eidos*' by those who stand in the tradition of the Enlightenment.[119] And this in turn has contributed to no small degree to the literalistic fallacy critiqued in the present essay.

In order to counterbalance the traditional historical-critical preference for analytical and vivisective thinking, we need to promote an imagistic approach that goes beyond the text's surface grammar in an attempt to make sense of the textual data as it has come down to us before reverting to diachronic solutions. Of course, we need to be aware of the danger of 'evading ... the challenges of historical criticism', as Barton once put it, complaining that rhetorical criticism 'can nearly always "demonstrate" a rhetorical structure in any given text and so invalidate historical-critical arguments based on its apparent (or evident) formlessness'.[120]

What is needed therefore is 'an integrated model in which reason and imagination could be seen as two interrelated aspects of the mind working as a whole, analytically and synthetically', to put it in Avis's words.[121] That is to say, we need to combine historical and literary methods and perspectives so that the two can complement and challenge each other. Barton is right, on the one hand, to stress that the newer literary approaches ought not to be used with the intention of avoiding the challenges of historical criticism. But it also needs to be underlined that historical critics, too, need to face up to the challenges presented, for instance, by approaches that work with other philosophies of language.

This, I believe, is now more important than ever, and that is despite the fact that we have witnessed the break-up of the dominant historical-critical paradigm. While this has opened up unforeseen opportunities for alternative readings, it has not resulted in a critical assessment of the results historical-critical study has yielded. All too often, these are either ignored or simply taken for granted. Thus, we now find ourselves in a situation where some advocate reader-centred approaches that couldn't care less about the historical location of the texts, while others build their rhetorical, theological or sociological readings upon the foundations laid by those whose presuppositions, aims and methods are clearly at odds with the new interpretative strategies.

However, if there is a need for new approaches, and if these can be justified by appealing to the inadequacies of the traditional methodologies, then it

---

[119] Avis, *God*, 22.
[120] Barton, *Reading*, 201.
[121] See Avis, *God*, 20.

just will not do simply to accept the results yielded by the approaches that are deemed to be in need of supplementation or revision. On the contrary, we need to reckon with the possibility that not a few of our 'assured results' might be flawed,[122] and we would do well, I believe, in heeding Eco's advice that 'the cultivated person's first duty is to be always prepared to rewrite the encyclo-pedia'.[123] This, after all, is what the hermeneutical circle is all about in that any new reading – any reading that proceeds from a different angle or approaches the text with additional knowledge or information at its disposal – will, or ought to, lead to a reappraisal of the other constituents that make up that circle.

Bibliography

Amador, J.D.H., 'Where Could Rhetorical Criticism (Still) Take Us?', *CRBS* 7 (1999), 195–222

Aristotle, *The Art of Rhetoric* (trans. J.H. Freese; LCL, 193; Cambridge, MA: Harvard University Press, 1926)

Austin, J.L., *How to Do Things with Words* (Oxford: Clarendon Press, 2nd edn, 1975)

Avis, P., *God and the Creative Imagination: Metaphor, Symbol and Myth in Religion and Theology* (London: Routledge, 1999)

Barton, J., *Reading the Old Testament: Method in Biblical Study* (London: Darton, Longman & Todd, 2nd edn, 1996)

Bible and Culture Collective, The (G. Aichele, F.W. Burnett, et al.), *The Postmodern Bible* (New Haven: Yale University Press, 1995)

Bitzer, L.F., 'The Rhetorical Situation', in *Rhetoric: A Tradition in Transition in Honor of Donald C. Bryant* (ed. W.R. Fisher; Michigan State University Press, 1974), 247–60

Black, C.C., 'Rhetorical Criticism and Biblical Interpretation', *ExpTim* 100 (1988–89), 252–58

Black, E., *Rhetorical Criticism: A Study in Method* (New York: Macmillan, 1965)

Buber, M., *The Prophetic Faith* (trans. C. Witton-Davies; New York: Macmillan, 1949)

---

[122] See Möller, 'Renewing', 162.
[123] Eco, 'Force', 21.

Carroll R., M.D., *Contexts for Amos: Prophetic Poetics in Latin American Perspective* (JSOTSup, 132; Sheffield: JSOT Press, 1992)

—, 'God and His People in the Nations' History', *TynBul* 47 (1996), 39–70

Coote, R.B., *Amos among the Prophets: Composition and Theology* (Philadelphia: Fortress Press, 1981)

Corbett, E.P.J., *Classical Rhetoric for the Modern Student* (New York: OUP, 3rd edn, 1990)

Cripps, R.S., *A Critical and Exegetical Commentary on the Book of Amos* (London: SPCK, 1929)

Crüsemann, F., 'Vorwort', in M. Schwantes, *Das Land kann seine Worte nicht ertragen: Meditationen zu Amos* (München: Chr. Kaiser, 1991), 8–11

Dell, K.J., 'The Misuse of Forms in Amos', *VT* 45 (1995), 45–61

Eagleton, T., 'J.L. Austin and the Book of Jonah', in *The Book and the Text: The Bible and Literary Theory* (ed. R.M. Schwartz; Oxford: Basil Blackwell, 1990), 231–36

—, *Literary Theory: An Introduction* (Oxford: Basil Blackwell, 2nd edn, 1996)

Eco, U., *Die Grenzen der Interpretation* (München: Deutscher Taschenbuch Verlag, 1995)

—, 'Political Language: The Use and Abuse of Rhetoric', in U. Eco, *Apocalypse Postponed* (ed. R. Lumley; London: Flamingo, 1995), 103–18

—, 'The Force of Falsity', in U. Eco, *Serendipities: Language and Lunacy* (trans. W. Weaver; Italian Academy Lectures; New York: Columbia University Press, 1998), 1–21

Fleischer, G., *Von Menschenverkäufern, Baschankühen und Rechtsverkehrern: Die Sozialkritik des Amosbuches in historisch-kritischer, sozialgeschichtlicher und archäologischer Perspektive* (BBB, 74; Frankfurt: Athenäum, 1989)

Fohrer, G., 'Form und Funktion in der Hiobdichtung', *ZDMG* 109 (1959), 31–49

—, 'Bemerkungen zum neueren Verständnis der Propheten', in *Das Prophetenverständnis in der deutschsprachigen Forschung seit Heinrich Ewald* (ed. P.H.A. Neumann; WdF, 307; Darmstadt: Wissenschaftliche Buchgesellschaft, 1979), 475–92

Fritz, V., 'Amosbuch, Amos-Schule und historischer Amos', in *Prophet und Prophetenbuch. Festschrift für Otto Kaiser zum 65. Geburtstag* (ed. V. Fritz, K.-F. Pohlmann, et al.; BZAW, 185; Berlin: de Gruyter, 1989), 29–43

Gitay, Y., 'A Study of Amos's Art of Speech: A Rhetorical Analysis of Amos 3:1–15', *CBQ* 42 (1980), 293–309

Green, J.B., 'Discourse Analysis and New Testament Interpretation', in *Hearing the New Testament: Strategies for Interpretation* (ed. J.B. Green; Grand Rapids: Eerdmans, 1995), 175–96

Grice, H.P., 'Utterance-Meaning, Sentence-Meaning, and Word-Meaning', in *The Philosophy of Language* (ed. J.R. Searle; London: OUP, 1971), 54–70

—, 'Logic and Conversation', in *Syntax and Semantics*, III, *Speech-Acts* (ed. P. Cole and J.L. Morgan; New York: Academic Press, 1975), 41–58

Gunn, D.M. and D.N. Fewell, *Narrative in the Hebrew Bible* (OBS; Oxford: OUP, 1993)

Hart, T., 'Imagination and Responsible Reading', in *Renewing Biblical Interpretation* (ed. C. Bartholomew, C. Greene and K. Möller; SHS, 1; Carlisle: Paternoster; Grand Rapids: Zondervan, 2000), 307–34

Hasel, G.F., *The Remnant: The History and Theology of the Remnant Idea from Genesis to Isaiah* (AUMSR, 5; Berrien Springs, MI: Andrews University Press, 3rd edn, 1980)

Hesse, M.B., *Revolutions and Reconstructions in the Philosophy of Science* (Brighton: Harvester Press, 1980)

—, 'The Cognitive Claims of Metaphor', *The Journal of Speculative Philosophy* 2.1 (1988), 1–16

Hobbes, T., *Leviathan* (London: Dent, 1914)

Houston, W., 'What Did the Prophets Think They Were Doing? Speech Acts and Prophetic Discourse in the Old Testament', in *'The Place Is Too Small for Us': The Israelite Prophets in Recent Scholarship* (ed. R.P. Gordon; SBTS, 5; Winona Lake, IN: Eisenbrauns, 1995), 133–53

Hunter, A.V., *Seek the Lord! A Study of the Meaning and Function of the Exhortations in Amos, Hosea, Isaiah, Micah, and Zephaniah* (Baltimore: St Mary's Seminary & University, 1982)

Jeffrey, D.L., *People of the Book: Christian Identity and Literary Culture* (Grand Rapids: Eerdmans, 1996)

Jehiel, J. ben, of Mantua (Judah Messer Leon), *The Book of the Honeycomb's Flow (Sēpher Nōpheth Ṣūphīm)* [1475/76] (ed. and trans. I. Rabinowitz; Ithaca, NY: Cornell University Press, 1983)

Johnson, M. (ed.), *Philosophical Perspectives on Metaphor* (Minneapolis: University of Minnesota Press, 1981)

Jozaki, S., 'The Secondary Passages of the Book of Amos', *Kwansei Gakuin University Annual Studies* 4 (1956), 25–100

Kennedy, G.A., *The Art of Persuasion in Greece* (Princeton: PUP, 1963)

—, *The Art of Rhetoric in the Roman World 300 B.C.–A.D. 300* (Princeton: PUP, 1972)

—, *Classical Rhetoric and Its Christian and Secular Tradition from Ancient to Modern Times* (Chapel Hill: University of North Carolina Press, 1980)

—, *Greek Rhetoric under Christian Emperors* (Princeton: PUP, 1983)

—, *New Testament Interpretation through Rhetorical Criticism* (Chapel Hill: University of North Carolina Press, 1984)

—, *A New History of Classical Rhetoric: An Extensive Revision and Abridgment of The Art of Persuasion in Greece, The Art of Rhetoric in the Roman World and Greek Rhetoric under Christian Emperors with Additional Discussion of Late Latin Rhetoric* (Princeton: PUP, 1994)

Koch, K., *Was ist Formgeschichte? Methoden der Bibelexegese* (Neukirchen-Vluyn: Neukirchener Verlag, 3rd edn, 1974)

Lausberg, H., *Elemente der literarischen Rhetorik* (München: Hueber, 8th edn, 1984)

Lindbeck, G.A., 'Postcritical Canonical Interpretation: Three Modes of Retrieval', in *Theological Exegesis: Essays in Honor of Brevard S. Childs* (ed. C. Seitz and K. Greene-McCreight; Grand Rapids: Eerdmans, 1999) 26–51

Lohfink, N., 'Bund als Vertrag im Deuteronomium', *ZAW* 107 (1995), 215–39

Markert, L., and G. Wanke, 'Die Propheteninterpretation: Anfragen und Überlegungen', *KD* 22 (1976), 191–220

Martin-Achard, R., *Amos: L'homme, le message, l'influence* (Publications de la Faculté de Théologie de l'Université de Genève, 7; Genève: Labor et Fides, 1984)

Miller, J.H., *Thomas Hardy: Distance and Desire* (Cambridge, MA: Belknap/ Harvard University, 1970)

Möller, K., 'Rehabilitation eines Propheten: Die Botschaft des Amos aus rhetorischer Perspektive unter besonderer Berücksichtigung von Am. 9,7–15', *EuroJT* 6 (1997), 41–55

—, ' "Hear this Word against You": A Fresh Look at the Arrangement and the Rhetorical Strategy of the Book of Amos', *VT* 50 (2000), 499–518

—, 'Renewing Historical Criticism', in *Renewing Biblical Interpretation* (ed. C.G. Bartholomew, C. Greene and K. Möller; SHS, 1; Carlisle: Paternoster; Grand Rapids: Zondervan, 2000), 145–71

—, *A Prophet in Debate: The Rhetoric of Persuasion in the Book of Amos* (JSOTSup; Sheffield: Sheffield Academic Press, forthcoming)

Muilenburg, J., 'Form Criticism and Beyond', *JBL* 88 (1969), 1–18

Nägele, S., *Laubhütte Davids und Wolkensohn: Eine auslegungsgeschichtliche Studie zu Amos 9,11 in der jüdischen und christlichen Exegese* (AGJU, 24; Leiden: E.J. Brill, 1995)

Patrick, D., *The Rhetoric of Revelation in the Hebrew Bible* (OBT; Minneapolis: Fortress Press, 1999)

Perelman, C., and L. Olbrechts-Tyteca, *The New Rhetoric: A Treatise on Argumentation* (trans. J. Wilkinson and P. Weaver; Notre Dame: University of Notre Dame Press, 1969)

Petersen, D.L., *Haggai and Zechariah 1–8: A Commentary* (OTL; London: SCM Press, 1985)

Rabinowitz, I., 'Introduction', in J. ben Jehiel of Mantua (Judah Messer Leon), *The Book of the Honeycomb's Flow (Sēpher Nōpheth Ṣūphîm)* [1475/76] (ed. and trans. I. Rabinowitz; Ithaca, NY: Cornell University Press, 1983), xv–lxx

Ricœur, P., *The Rule of Metaphor: Multi-disciplinary Studies of the Creation of Meaning in Language* (trans. R. Czerny, et al.; London: Routledge and Kegan Paul, 1978)

Ringgren, H., 'Israelite Prophecy: Fact or Fiction?', in *Congress Volume, Jerusalem 1986* (ed. J.A. Emerton; VTSup, 40; Leiden: E.J. Brill, 1988), 204–10

Rorty, R.M. (ed.), *The Linguistic Turn: Essays in Philosophical Method* (Chicago: University of Chicago Press, 1992)

Rottzoll, D.U., *Studien zur Redaktion und Komposition des Amosbuchs* (BZAW, 243; Berlin: de Gruyter, 1996)

Schleiermacher, F., *Hermeneutics: The Handwritten Manuscripts* (ed. H. Kimmerle; trans. J. Duke and J. Forstman; AAR Text and Translation Series, 1; Missoula: Scholars Press, 1977)

—, *Hermeneutics and Criticism and Other Writings* (trans. and ed. A. Bowie; Cambridge Texts in the History of Philosophy; Cambridge: CUP, 1998)

Schmidt, W.H., 'Die prophetische "Grundgewißheit": Erwägungen zur Einheit prophetischer Verkündigung', in *Das Prophetenverständnis in der deutschsprachigen Forschung seit Heinrich Ewald* (ed. P.H.A. Neumann; WdF, 307; Darmstadt: Wissenschaftliche Buchgesellschaft, 1979), 537–64

Searle, J.R., *Speech Acts: An Essay in the Philosophy of Language* (Cambridge: CUP, 1969)

—, *Expression and Meaning: Studies in the Theory of Speech Acts* (Cambridge: CUP, 1979)

Selden, R., and P. Widdowson, *A Reader's Guide to Contemporary Literary Theory* (New York: Harvester Wheatsheaf, 3rd edn, 1993)

Shaw, C.S., *The Speeches of Micah: A Rhetorical-Historical Analysis* (JSOTSup, 145; Sheffield: JSOT Press, 1993)

Shelley, P.B., 'A Defence of Poetry', in *Peacock's Four Ages of Poetry, Shelley's*

Defence of Poetry, Browning's Essay on Shelley (ed. H.F.B. Brett-Smith; Oxford: Basil Blackwell, 2nd edn, 1923), 21–59

Smend, R., 'Das Nein des Amos', *EvT* 23 (1963), 404–23

Smith, G.V., 'Continuity and Discontinuity in Amos' Use of Tradition', *JETS* 34 (1991), 33–42

Smith, K.A., *The Fall of Interpretation: Philosophical Foundations for a Creational Hermeneutic* (Downers Grove, IL: IVP, 2000)

Soskice, J.M., *Metaphor and Religious Language* (Oxford: Clarendon Press, 1985)

Steiner, G., *After Babel: Aspects of Language and Translation* (Oxford: OUP, 3rd edn, 1998)

Sternberg, M., *The Poetics of Biblical Narrative: Ideological Literature and the Drama of Reading* (Bloomington: Indiana University Press, 1987)

Stiver, D.R., *The Philosophy of Religious Language: Sign, Symbol, and Story* (Oxford: Basil Blackwell, 1996)

Thiselton, A.C., *New Horizons in Hermeneutics: The Theory and Practice of Transforming Biblical Reading* (Grand Rapids: Zondervan, 1992)

Trible, P., *Rhetorical Criticism: Context, Method, and the Book of Jonah* (GBS; Minneapolis: Fortress Press, 1994)

Tucker, G.M., 'Foreword', in C. Westermann, *Basic Forms of Prophetic Speech* (trans. H.C. White; Cambridge: Lutterworth Press; Louisville: Westminster/John Knox Press, repr. 1991), ix–xvi

Weiser, A., *Die Profetie des Amos* (BZAW, 53; Gießen: Töpelmann, 1929)

Wellhausen, J., *Die kleinen Propheten übersetzt und erklärt* (Berlin: de Gruyter, 4th edn, 1963)

Westermann, C., *Basic Forms of Prophetic Speech* (trans. H.C. White; Cambridge: Lutterworth Press; Louisville: Westminster/John Knox Press, repr. 1991)

Wittgenstein, L., *Philosophical Investigations* (trans. G.E.M. Anscombe; Oxford: Basil Blackwell, 2nd edn, 1958)

Wolff, H.W., *Joel and Amos: A Commentary on the Books of the Prophets Joel and Amos* (trans. W. Janzen, et al.; ed. S.D. McBride, Jr.; Hermeneia; Philadelphia: Fortress Press, 1977)

Wolters, A., 'Confessional Criticism and the Night Visions of Zechariah', in *Renewing Biblical Interpretation* (ed. C.G. Bartholomew, C. Greene and K. Möller; SHS, 1; Carlisle: Paternoster; Grand Rapids: Zondervan, 2000), 90–117

Wolterstorff, N., *Divine Discourse: Philosophical Reflections on the Claim that God Speaks* (Cambridge: CUP, 1995)

—, 'A Response to Trevor Hart', in *Renewing Biblical Interpretation* (ed. C.G.

Bartholomew, C. Greene and K. Möller; SHS, 1; Carlisle: Paternoster; Grand Rapids: Zondervan, 2000), 335–41

Wuellner, W., 'Where Is Rhetorical Criticism Taking Us?', *CBQ* 49 (1987), 448–63

18

Metaphor and Exegesis

Ian Paul

Introduction

I remember, as an undergraduate in a college Christian Union in the early 1980s, singing what I thought at the time was a rather odd worship song, *Pierce my ear, O Lord my God*.[1] The strangeness of the lyric was perhaps heightened by the fact that the group's leader, sitting on the other side of the room, did indeed have a pierced ear and earring, and I wondered what his (mildly defiant) statement of 'street credibility' had to do with the worship of God. Even when I understood the significance of Deuteronomy 15:17 and the piercing of the slave's ear in its social context, the words left me feeling uncertain.

My experience highlights some of the difficulties of handling metaphor in the context of biblical exegesis.

In the first place, biblical metaphors are widely used in hymns and songs, and the language of metaphor is prominent within devotional discourse, especially within traditions which perceive Scripture as addressing modern readers very directly or as being a key means by which God addresses the modern reader.[2] The temporality of hymnody has a kind of 'today and every-day' quality about it, as the great events of biblical history are re-actualized in the singing of the hymn, and this resonates with the open temporality of metaphorical imagery.[3] This explains the prominence of archetypal and metaphorically suggestive ideas of harvesting, gathering, looking, standing,

---

[1] 'Pierce my ear' by Steven Croft, copyright © 1980 Dayspring Music. No. 433 in *Songs and Hymns of Fellowship*.
[2] On the immediacy of Scripture as a feature of Pentecostal/charismatic hermeneutics, see Stibbe, 'This is That'.
[3] See Lacocque 'Apocalyptic Symbolism', 8.

opening, walking, and so on, within hymnody. And the verses which seem to 'speak' to people most clearly are the ones dominated by metaphorical images: Isaiah 43:2 ('When you pass through the waters…'); Jeremiah 29:11 ('For surely I know the plans I have for you…'); Revelation 3:8 ('I have set before you an open door'); and so on.[4]

But, in the second place, it is clear that such metaphors are not always handled well. For example, in Mark 4 Jesus tells a parable about the kingdom, beginning 'A farmer went out to sow…'[5] This has popularly been known as 'The Parable of the Sower', as reflected in the heading it is given in the NIV translation. But in Jesus' explanation of the parable, in Mark 4:14, the farmer is passed over entirely, and the focus is almost exclusively on the growth of the seed in the different soils as metaphorically depicting the different responses that people will give to his message.[6] In Jeremiah 18, the relationship between God and his people is described metaphorically as that between a potter and the clay. Popular appropriation of this, as exemplified in the chorus 'Change my heart, O God', suggests that this image is one which implies total passivity on the part of God's people: 'You are the potter, I am the clay/mould me and make me, this is what I pray.'[7] But a reading of Jeremiah 18 that makes passivity the exclusive point of the metaphor is not faithful to the ambiguities of the passage, and sits uneasily with the wider biblical picture of God's relation with his people.

As a preliminary to the discussion of the exegesis of metaphor, it is important to note that any critical engagement should remain secondary to and supportive of the primary aim of enabling proper engagement with metaphor itself. If metaphorical discourse does have the power to engage and transform, analysis of how and why it does this must not be allowed to rob it of the very power that makes it so important.

---

[4] Within my own tradition (charismatic evangelical), it is common practice to cite a verse of Scripture as being the particular thing God is wanting to say in a situation. I find it interesting to note how often God wants to speak through a small number of verses that share a certain metaphorical openness …

[5] Parables have sometimes been described as extended metaphors, or narrative metaphors, and involve a (usually implicit) metaphorical predication, in this case the identification of people who make different responses to the message of the gospel with the different kinds of soils.

[6] I am here classing sayings of the form 'You are the salt of the earth' (a metaphor with explicit predication), 'An Iron Curtain has fallen across Europe' (a metaphor where the predication is implicit in the reference of the phrase) and 'He eats like a horse' (often formally called a simile), all as metaphors. Their common features will be seen more clearly in what follows.

[7] Eddie Espinosa, copyright © 1982 Mercy Publishing. No. 53 in *Songs and Hymns of Fellowship*.

The Problem of Metaphor

If practitioners have had problems handling metaphor, then this is more than matched by the problematic nature of metaphor for philosophers of language in the western tradition. Metaphor has long been the Cinderella of language.

Aristotle held metaphor in the highest regard; to master speech, one must be the master of metaphor.[8] In fact, classical discussion of metaphor formed part of the first systematic reflections on language. Plato made an influential attack on the whole discipline of rhetoric, but he seems to have been more concerned about those who use verbal trickery, rather than the legitimate use of rhetoric within philosophy.[9] Rhetoric in the Roman period was more interested in considerations of style than philosophy, and these two aspects continued to be separated throughout the Middle Ages.[10] The rise of scientific method and the ascendancy of empiricist thinking in the seventeenth and eighteenth centuries completed this separation and thus definitively undermined the status of metaphor.[11] Metaphor was denigrated as, on the one hand, denying a 'proper' description of the world, and so confusing people, and, on the other, as being a tool of deception. Here we see the association of metaphor with 'deceptive' rhetoric. Perhaps the most eloquent and influential attack came from John Locke, in his *Essay Concerning Human Understanding*:

> [I]f we would speak of things as they are, we must allow all the art of rhetoric, besides order and clearness, all the artificial and figurative application of words eloquence hath invented, are for nothing else but to insinuate wrong ideas, move the passions, and thereby mislead the judgment, and so indeed are perfect cheats, and therefore ... are wholly to be avoided.[12]

Ironically, the detractors of metaphor could not deny its appeal. Hume, while arguing that the beauties of poetry 'are founded on falsehood and fiction, on hyperboles, metaphors and an abuse or perversion of terms from their natural meaning', admits that to remove these features entirely would produce a work 'which, by universal experience, has been found the most uninspired and disagreeable'.[13] One advocate of the abolition of metaphorical language in favour of a more 'scientific' diction decried the 'mists and uncertainties of our knowledge' created by metaphor, and called for writers to use a 'close, natural, naked way of speaking'.[14]

---

[8] Aristotle, *Poetics*, 1459a.
[9] Plato, *Gorgias*, 454e.8.
[10] See Soskice, *Metaphor*, 12.
[11] See Lundin, 'Metaphor', 20.
[12] Locke, *Essay*, 147.
[13] Cited by Lundin, 'Metaphor', 21.
[14] Thomas Sprat, cited by Lundin, 'Metaphor', 20, and notes.

The argument against metaphor became further fixed and systematized as a result of Kant's separation of knowledge into the 'useful' and the 'aesthetic'. Kant 'jealously reserved the title of "knowledge" for "pure natural science" alone, and denied to art any significance as knowledge'.[15] Metaphor's flimsy epistemological claims (as they were perceived at the time) put it firmly in the area of the aesthetic, and the subsequent dominance of positivist epistemology confirmed metaphor as having no epistemic claims. Romanticism, while apparently asserting the importance of the aesthetic, and so possibly providing a place for metaphor along with other elements of the 'poetic', actually accepted the 'profound, unresolved dualism' of Kantian thought.[16] The epistemological subordination of literature to science finds its clearest expression in the comment of Frye:

> In literature, questions of fact or truth are subordinated to the primary literary aim of producing a structure of words for their own sake … In literature, what entertains us is prior to what instructs, or, as we may say, the reality-principle is subordinate to the pleasure principle.[17]

It is difficult to overestimate the impact of this legacy as we approach the exegesis of metaphor. The whole discipline of hermeneutics continues to labour under this Kantian bifurcation. On the positivist side, metaphorical texts are all too easily sidelined by the preference for more rational and propositional texts, while on the romanticist side, the evocative power of metaphorical imagery is in danger of becoming detached from the epistemic claims of the metaphors themselves.

Ricœur's Hermeneutic of Metaphor

To find a rehabilitation of metaphor that engages with the whole range of historical criticisms, we can do no better than look to Paul Ricœur. He has done more than anyone to bring together recent developments in the understanding of metaphor within a comprehensive hermeneutical framework, and he does so in a characteristic 'mediating' style that engages with the widest possible range of thinkers.

He was influenced in his early years by existentialists such as Sartre and Marcel, and then by the phenomenology of Husserl. His abiding concern has been to explore the fullness of human being: how can we understand the self

---

[15] Lundin, 'Metaphor', 21. See also Lundin, et al., *Responsibility,* 8f.
[16] Gadamer, *Truth and Method,* 74 (cited by Lundin, 'Metaphor', 21).
[17] Frye, *Anatomy,* 74–5.

without reducing the self to an object within our system of understanding? This concern has taken him on a journey through psychological and literary structuralism (in his works *Freud and Philosophy* and *Interpretation Theory*); the study of myths and symbols expressing guilt and evil in indirect ways (*Symbolism of Evil* and *Fallible Man*); then on to questions of interpretation, especially of the linguistic correlates of symbol and myth, metaphor and narrative (*Conflict of Interpretations, The Rule of Metaphor, Time and Narrative*); and finally he returns to the question of selfhood once more (*Oneself as Another*).

Ricœur's theory of metaphor therefore stands at a crucial point in his own thinking. On the one hand, metaphor is that irreducible feature of language that corresponds to and gives access to the meaning of symbolism, which in turn is essential to understanding the fullness of human existence. On the other hand, the identity of the self in history is given through the imaginative construction of narrative, and this creative leap is, in fact, a metaphorical process. The creation of metaphor in language thus stands at the furthest point of the 'long path' or 'detour' through hermeneutics by which the self gains self-understanding by understanding the world around.[18]

Ricœur's concern with the fullness of human existence leads to a persistent ambiguity towards critical methodology. We cannot appropriate the symbols and myths, the metaphors and narratives, that explain human existence *directly*, since we are then vulnerable to a naïve, overly-subjective understanding of them. Criticism is vital here in approaching these with 'suspicion'. The metaphor that Ricœur employs is that of destroying the idols of human imagination. But we then have to go on to enable the symbols – rightly understood – to live, and this requires what Ricœur calls 'a hermeneutic of retrieval'.[19] This involves going beyond the aridity – the 'desert' – of criticism, to make a commitment to a particular understanding of the text, a hermeneutical wager of faith.[20] This is a sharp warning that theorizing *about* metaphorical imagery must be secondary to a (post-critical) appropriation *of* that imagery.

The anatomy of metaphor

The crucial element of Ricœur's thinking about metaphor is the introduction of diachronic analysis – analysis of changes in language over time and with use – in considering the process of the creation of a metaphor. At once, this puts

---

[18] Mudge, 'Ricœur', 38–69.

[19] This is sufficiently central to Ricœur's thought for commentators to have suggested that it is this that characterizes Ricœur's thought. See, e.g., Thiselton, *New Horizons*, 344–78.

[20] This concept is most fully expressed in the early parts of Ricœur's *Freud and Philosophy*.

the discussion about 'proper' meaning of words into perspective; words mean different things not only in different literary and social contexts, but also at different times. This means that there can be no rigid assertion of *the* proper meaning. This is not to say that meanings in language are completely fluid, but simply to say that they are not completely static. The meaning of a word may well evolve over time, and associations that are at one time metaphorical and novel, even appearing to be 'deviant', with time become an accepted part of 'normal' speech. In the nineteenth century, the idea of the 'inflation' of the economy was a metaphor coined to describe the (thought to be unjustified) increase in prices of goods and commodities within that economy. Nowadays, it is commonplace to talk simply of 'inflation', and it has little if any metaphorical connotation.[21]

Ricœur takes Max Black's interaction theory of metaphor and Monroe Beardsley's theory of verbal opposition and moves them one stage further.[22] If a metaphor provides a new insight, then where does this insight come from? It comes from an imaginative, creative association of the different elements, which is predicative in nature, if metaphor is, as Black says, providing us with a cognitive element that is not reducible to equivalent literal statements. In formulating a metaphor linking 'man' and 'wolf', I am making an assertion about the nature of the two of them. Ricœur also adds to Black's theory in noting that the effect of metaphor is two-way; in saying that 'man is a wolf', we not only see 'man' through the screen or filter of 'wolf', but our view of 'wolf' is also altered. Man is seen to share some characteristics of the wolf, and the wolf becomes an embodiment of certain characteristics of man.

In reply to the comment that there is something deviant about metaphor, Ricœur agrees, but he argues that it is precisely through this deviance, this 'semantic impertinence', that predication takes place.[23] Indeed, it is only through recognizing that there is a semantic impertinence that we even notice that what we are reading is metaphorical, not literal. There is, in fact, a logical inconsistency at the heart of metaphor, since we are asserting both 'it is not' and 'it is like' in the 'it is' of the metaphorical statement.

It is perhaps Black's formulation of 'focus' and 'frame' that makes it congenial for Ricœur to draw on Jakobson to develop his notion of 'split

---

[21] It may be noted that, in the twentieth century, two areas of language growth have been in the developing disciplines of economics and sociology, largely by metaphoric extension, in order to provide a whole new vocabulary of reality.

[22] See Black, *Models* and Beardsley, *Aesthetics*.

[23] This is a term that Ricœur uses self-consciously, as a gentler term to replace Beardsley's phrase 'logical absurdity', in *Interpretation Theory*, 50. His theory of metaphor is further expounded in *Rule*.

reference'.[24] It is this that reinforces the essentially referential and cognitive aspect of metaphor, beyond being a semantic innovation. Jakobson had noted, in the context of studying speech disabilities, two dimensions to speech. He called these the 'similarity' and the 'contiguity' dimensions. The similarity dimension has to do with the relation that a word in a sentence has with other possible alternatives that could have been selected from the 'code' of the language; it is a relation between words that is essentially internal to the linguistic code. The contiguity dimension has to do with the relation of a word to other words in the sentence, and the way these words are combined will be shaped by the context, by the sentence's relation to the world external to language. Thus, says Jakobson, every word has two references: to the code (internally) and to the context (externally).[25] Within Ricœur's explication of metaphor, it is the semantic impertinence that splits open these two dimensions of reference. The contiguity dimension is unchanged, in that the terms involved in the metaphor continue to have the same (literal) relation to the world beyond language. But the similarity dimension is changed, in that the relation between the terms has switched from being one of disconnectedness (at some level) to kinship under the force of the 'is' of the metaphoric predication. The reference within the code is then the reference to a world, to a set of relations that have been refigured by the semantic impertinence of the metaphor. This refigured understanding of reality is what Ricœur calls 'the world in front of the text'. Metaphorical language contains a 'surplus of meaning',[26] and this provides new cognitive space for the reader to inhabit.

Ricœur's theory is not without its critics. But he makes some important observations about the wider enterprise of hermeneutics, as well as offering insights that have a direct bearing on the subject of exegesis.[27] Ricœur's hermeneutic of metaphor begins to offer some answers to the questions about why it is that the metaphorical texts of Scripture are so potent. And his anatomy of metaphor opens the possibility of a method of exegesis, and so an arena for debate between conflicting interpretations. In his later work, Ricœur is not always faithful in allowing space for questions of validation, but his emphasis on method sets him apart from the thinking of Gadamer, and it in turn holds out the possibility of arbitration between conflicting views.[28]

---

[24] The door has been opened to this idea through Ricœur's reading of Monroe Beardsley's concept of secondary signification.

[25] Jakobson, 'Two Aspects', 244.

[26] This is the subtitle of *Interpretation Theory*.

[27] For a more detailed analysis of Ricœur's work, its implications for hermeneutics and its application to the book of Revelation, see Paul, *Value*.

[28] See Gadamer, *Truth and Method* and Thiselton, *New Horizons*, 348.

The Exegesis of Metaphor

I will focus here on the implications of the two central features of Ricœur's theory – the need for diachronic analysis and the role of semantic impertinence.

Diachronic analysis

Ricœur's insistence on retaining an element of diachronic analysis in interpretation comes in the context of his criticisms of a purely structuralist approach to language.[29] Ricœur is, in fact, a convinced user of structuralist methods, but his protest is against the exclusive use of a method that is based on a fiction – the 'code' of language with which structuralism concerns itself does not in fact exist except as an abstraction. What we have in reality are actual utterances, and (unlike the code) these have a temporal dimension to them. So we must take that temporality seriously. Moreover, study of these utterances shows that the code evolves over time, changing and reshaping and enlarging its boundaries. And one of the main ways in which its boundaries are extended is in the coining of metaphor to describe the familiar in new ways or to describe for the first time the unfamiliar in terms of the familiar. As metaphors successively extend the boundaries of language, individual metaphors may then become an accepted part of the lexicon and so lose their metaphorical nature.[30]

In relation to the study of Deuteronomy, Gordon McConville asks:

> Is Deuteronomy innovating by its use of language, or already perpetuating stock metaphors? By the same token, do the major symbols of Israelite religion function here as in other places, or are they being understood in quite new ways? The answer to this question affects the study of the book deeply …[31]

This is a question precisely about the diachronic (rather than synchronic) aspect of language. As McConville suggests, it is a question both about language itself ('Is Deuteronomy innovating …?') and about the relation of that language to the state of the world at the time of inscription ('do the symbols function here as in other places …?'). Ricœur's anatomy of metaphor depicts it as bringing together a particular *subject* (such as 'man') together with the *vehicle* (such as 'wolf'), which results in a certain *tenor* (man seen as a wolf in the metaphorical juxtaposition). The diachronic question about language has to do

---

[29] This is set out most clearly in *Interpretation Theory.*
[30] Contra Davidson, *Inquiries.*
[31] Quotation from the paper upon which McConville's contribution to this volume, 'Metaphor, Symbol and the Interpretation of Deuteronomy', is based.

with the relation of vehicle and tenor (what was the prior linguistic relation between the terms 'man' and 'wolf'?) and the question about its world has to do with the relation of both vehicle and tenor to the subject (how was 'man' perceived at the time? how does this new characterization transform that perception?).

The significance of these two kinds of questions will vary from one text to another. Questions about Israelite pottery may shed some light on Jeremiah 18. The context of exile and return sharpens the significance of the metaphors of water and fire in Isaiah 43, but they are such archetypal images that their precise historical significance is neither here nor there – it feels much the same to drown then as now! The question of whether first-century Palestinian farmers sowed first and then ploughed, or ploughed first and then sowed is of dubious value in the exposition of Mark 4. But the situation of Laodicea and its hot spring water supply is of enormous significance in the exegesis of Revelation 3:16.[32]

In relation to the development of language, diachronic analysis will be of especial importance where metaphors appropriate ideas and vocabulary from other sources, whether they are earlier in Scripture or are extrabiblical. So the narrative symbolization of Revelation 12 is decisively affected by an understanding of the Apollo mythology that underlies the structure of the story.[33] And examples of 'inner-biblical exegesis' or 'inner-biblical allusion',[34] where one biblical text appropriates another explicitly or implicitly, will need to take account not only of the appropriated text in its original context, but also its *Wirkungsgeschichte* ('history of effects') in order to see the effect of the appropriation at the time the appropriation took place.

For any metaphor, the possibility must remain open that these diachronic considerations may be of vital importance, and so they must be included in any exegetical methodology.

Semantic impertinence

Ricœur links his understanding of semantic impertinence with the notion of what he calls 'split reference': language is opened up by metaphor, and the phrase or sentence now has two meanings, the literal and the metaphorical, and these each have a corresponding reference, the literal and the metaphorical reference.[35] He has been criticized for this; J.M. Soskice accuses him of having a 'dual notion' of truth, whereas she argues that there is only one kind of truth,

---

[32] See Rudwick and Green, 'Lukewarmness'.

[33] van Henten, 'Dragon Myth'.

[34] For these terms see Eslinger, 'Inner-Biblical Exegesis'.

[35] See *Rule*, ch. 7.

not a separate category called 'metaphorical truth' which is some sort of poor
relation to truth as normally conceived. But Ricœur's approach is helpfully
elucidated by Nicholas Wolterstorff when he distinguishes between the
noematic content (from the Greek *noema*, meaning mind or thought); and its
designative content.[36] When people at different times and in different countries
assert that 'The queen is dead,' their statements (if taken literally) share the
same noematic content, but they may be speaking about quite different people
– the designative content differs. In metaphor, the noematic content is what
Ricœur is calling the literal sense; the designative content is what he refers to as
the metaphorical sense.

   This distinction has important implications for the exegesis of metaphor.
When a statement is taken literally, the predication involved is total. If
someone were to say to me, 'Here is that old boot you were looking for,' and is
referring to a football boot that I had lost, then there is a total ontological identification between 'that old boot' and the object in question. But if the statement is metaphorical rather than literal – the person is in fact referring to an
elderly relative – then there is only a partial identification between the vehicle
of the metaphor ('old boot') and the subject in question (my elderly relative).
My elderly relative is like an old boot only in some respects and not in others.
Similarly, when Churchill declared that 'an iron curtain has descended across
the Continent [of Europe]'[37] he surely intended to characterize the division of
Europe on the formation of the Eastern Bloc by certain aspects of a curtain
(division, closing off, perhaps even finality) but not by others (warmth, deco-
rative effect). When Jeremiah portrays God as a potter and his people as clay,
only some of the characteristics of the potter/clay relationship carry over.
God's sovereignty and power, his initiative and purpose are there, but what of
the passivity of the clay? The idea of submission is clearly present (mention of
'the stubbornness of [their] evil heart', v. 12), but the point of the illustration is
in fact to challenge Judah to participate in God's plans, to sense the working of
his hands and work with him. (Even God's sovereignty is qualified. When a
pot fails, then the potter is to blame, as he is in complete control of what he is
working with. Not so with God.) It might then be legitimate to preach on this
passage by offering the two halves of the metaphorical prediction, the 'is like'
and the 'is not'. In what ways is God calling his people to be like clay (passive,
submissive and mouldable)? And in what ways is God calling his people not to
be like clay (lacking understanding, unresponsive, perhaps even unprotesting)?
Similarly, those who hear the message of the good news are challenged in

---

[36] Wolterstorff, *Divine Discourse*, 152.
[37] From an address at Westminster College, Fulton, MO, USA, 5 March 1946. *The
Oxford Dictionary of Quotations* (1985), 150, notes that Churchill was not, in fact, the
first to use this phrase – but he was, undoubtedly, the one who popularized it.

Mark 4 to choose to be like the good soil – though the one thing soil cannot do is choose what it is like.

To recognize the limits of metaphorical predication in this way provides an important control on the exegesis of metaphor. The more metaphorical the text, the more important is this limit-defining exercise. This is in no way a negative exercise. Metaphors do not exercise their power because of an ambiguity arising from the lack of semantic limits, but rather because of their transferability (especially as the vehicle is archetypal) and because the metaphorical predication refigures the world and so offers new possibilities for living. Thus a text like Revelation, the most extensively metaphorical text in the New Testament, has long been a 'happy hunting-ground for bizarre and dangerous interpretations'[38] precisely because of a lack of such limits. Revelation does, in fact, offer a powerful and compelling reading when such limits are respected. The key question is how to discern the contours of the metaphorical predication – how can we know which aspects of the vehicle fall into the 'is like' and which fall into the 'is not' of the semantic impertinence? There is not a short answer; consideration of this must include the study of literary context and forms, questions of structure and rhetorical context, as well as those aspects of historical context mentioned above.

Ricœur's theory does not, then, offer a blueprint or a formula for the exegesis of metaphor – but he does offer a framework. It is a framework that both explains the paradoxes of metaphor and suggests a systematic approach to exegesis. And it is a framework that has its place within a wider hermeneutical theory, one which some commentators regard as among the most significant of the twentieth century.

Metaphor, Exegesis and the Hermeneutical Task

To look at the implications of this approach to exegesis, let us look at one of these highly metaphorical passages – Revelation 12. It is an interesting chapter to consider, not only because it is generally recognized as being of pivotal importance within the book itself (Rev. 12:1 is universally cited as a significant structural pivot within the book as a whole), but also because it begins the section in Revelation with the most sustained narrative coherence.

As we have seen, the exegesis of any metaphor must explore the nature of the semantic impertinence, that is, the shape of the metaphorical predication, with reference to both diachronic and synchronic aspects of language. This will involve analysis of historical and literary contexts of the images themselves (the vehicle of the metaphor), the subject of the metaphor (the referent), and

---

[38] Boring, *Revelation*, 4.

the subject as depicted by the metaphor (the tenor), which is the result of the process of metaphorization.[39]

Vehicle

The primary symbolization occurs within three sections of the text of chapter 12: verses 1 to 6; verses 7 to 9; and in the continuation of the original narrative in verses 13 to 17. The most obvious source of imagery is the Old Testament: the woman in labour in Isaiah 26 and 66 and Micah 4 and 5; the heads and horns of the beasts of Daniel 7 and 8; the coming king of Psalm 2; Michael's role as champion in Daniel 10; God's judgement of the evil one in Psalm 37; the fusion of serpent, devil and Satan from Genesis 3, Job 1 and Zechariah 3; the eagles' wings of Exodus 19; and the eschatological time periods of Daniel 7 and 12.[40] The diachronic aspect of analysis demands that these images be considered within the interpretative context of the first-century Christian community in Asia Minor. So the messianic significance of Psalm 2 must be considered alongside its Old Testament context. The distinctive phrase 'there was no longer any place' of Psalm 37:36 is also found in Daniel 2:35, where it receives a particular eschatological significance, and in the Qumran commentary on the psalm in 4Q 171 where the antitype of the evil man becomes particularized as the Wicked Priest destined for eschatological judgement. The verbal parallel of Revelation 12:8 seems, then, to be continuing an already-defined interpretative tradition.

Outside the Old Testament, a major influence on the shape of the narrative of 12:1–6, 13–18 is the Python/Apollo myth, as A.Y. Collins has persuasively argued.[41] Again, exegesis of the narrative symbolization must take into account the interpretative significance of this myth as imperial propaganda.[42]

Subject

The two main subjects to consider are the Christian community, including its relations with Judaism, and Roman Imperial power – in particular the significance of the imperial cult within first-century Asia Minor. Here, historical critical study plays an important role – but it is not always controlling in the exegesis of the metaphors. In the process of metaphorization, aspects of historical detail are lost and may not affect the rhetorical power of the text – that is, the

---

[39] I have explored this in greater detail in *Value*.
[40] For a full study of these texts and the related questions of methodology in detecting allusions to the OT in Revelation, see my 'Use'.
[41] See Collins, *Combat Myth*.
[42] See van Henten, 'Dragon Myth'.

contours of the world opened up by the text. For example, the precise significance of the date of final composition of the text is frequently overstated, and a carefully argued position may have little actual effect on exegesis.[43]

Tenor

The portrayal of the expectant (Jewish) messianic community as the woman of 12:1, and Gentile believers as 'the rest of her seed' (12:17) creates a world in which God's historic people have a privileged status, and so offsets to some extent the harsher language of the 'synagogue of Satan' (2:9).

The polemical inversion of the Apollo myth displaces the emperor as the bringer of peace and order and instead identifies him with the chaos monster, opposed to God's true agent of peace. Entering the world opened up by the text would have involved an explicit departure from the accepted majority view, and those entering would thus constitute a 'cognitive minority'. The majority's perception of the power of Rome as bringer of order and stability is overturned by the minority view of Rome as the agent of violence and chaos.

Revelation characterizes the empire as being fundamentally opposed to God's people where this opposition has cosmic, and not just local, significance, and will be decisively broken in eschatological judgement. It also characterizes the empire as a power that bullies and seduces, with whom it is possible to collude. Both these characterizations would have been relevant to Revelation's first readers in different ways, depending on whether they needed comfort in the face of persecution or challenge in the light of their own complacency. But both are a feature of the world opened up by the text, so the question of whether there was 'persecution' of Christians at the time of the writing of Revelation does not have as decisive a significance for the rhetorical effect of the text as is sometimes supposed.

There is a subtle but important difference in the temporality associated with the figure of the male child (12:5) and the cosmic activity of the dragon manifested in the particular actions of the beasts from the sea and land (13:1, 11). The snatching of the child, explained as the victory over the dragon in heaven, has pivotal and cosmic significance ('Now have come …' 12:10), whereas the beasts appear to be simply particular manifestations of the dragon's cosmic power. This suggests the unrepeatability of the former event and the repeatability of the latter. Imperial power is here characterized by violence ('make war', 13:7), obsession with image (13:14–15) and economic control (13:16–17).

---

[43] Garrow, *Revelation*, 76–9, argues for a date in Titus's reign. But the historical features of this time that he claims are of significance could for the most part be true of the empire at other times, and in any case hardly appear to affect his exegesis.

World

What space does this reading of Revelation give to readers then and now? What sort of world is opened up by this exegesis of the text?

Firstly, it is a world in continuity with biblical tradition. The first readers, as followers of the lamb, constitute 'the rest of [the woman's] seed' (12:17). They share with her the vulnerability (12:2) and struggle (12:4; 13:7) and protection (12:6, 14) of the faithful messianic people of God. Whatever the ethnic disruptions in identity, there is a clear continuity of theological identity. This paradox of continuity and discontinuity is expressed elsewhere in the New Testament in the metaphors of adoption (Rom. 8) and grafting (Rom. 11).

Secondly, it is a world of counter ideology to the prevailing ideology of the surrounding society (12:1–6). Within the narrative of chapters 12 and 13, the inversion of the secular myth to form the narrative of the community is prior to the challenge to remain faithful and receive the seal of the God in preference to the mark of the beast (13:18). The community is equipped with its story and identity before it faces the crisis of decision.

Thirdly, it is a world set in the fold of time that is created by the proleptic enactment of the eschatological victory of God's Messiah over his primeval adversary (12:9, 10).

Fourthly, this period of proleptic victory is the space that is created in fulfilment of specifically Jewish messianic hopes (12:7–8), before it becomes a place of light for the whole world.

Fifthly, it is a world that is made real existentially by participation through praise (12:10–12), as praise is the community's declaration of God as king and his Messiah as victorious – truths that will only be fully expressed at the end.

Sixthly, it is a world that embraces the ambiguity of patient endurance and confidence of victory (13:10).

Finally, it is a world that demands allegiance in the social, political and economic spheres as well as the personal (13:16, 17), and the mythology created by the metaphorization of the world is irrevocably sectarian in its call to decide – follow the lamb or follow the beast.[44]

---

[44] Highwater, *Mythology*, explores the 'mythology' of morality, taking homosexuality as (an example of) the metaphor of 'transgression' for the crossing of socially acceptable moral boundaries. He focuses on the resultant sectarian classification of society into 'insiders' and 'outsiders'. In deconstructing the myth and its associated sectarianism, it is an open question as to whether Highwater is effectively returning to the view that 'mere' metaphor can be dispensed with, and replaced by an analytical/propositional alternative.

Conclusion

An exegesis of the metaphors of Revelation following some of the contours of Ricœur's hermeneutic may not solve all the problems associated with Revelation's imagery, but it does begin to make some headway. Such an interpretative strategy does not bypass hard exegetical labour – indeed, it highlights the need for detailed work which is too often neglected. But a methodologically robust understanding of the world opened up by the text for its first readers is essential for constructive engagement with the world opened up by subsequent readings in new contexts.

Bibliography

Beardsley, M., *Aesthetics* (New York: Harcourt, Brace and World, 1958)

Black, M., *Models and Metaphors: Studies in Language and Philosophy* (Ithaca, NY: Cornell University Press, 1962)

Boring, E., *Revelation* (Interpretation; Louisville: John Knox Press, 1989)

Collins, A.Y., *The Combat Myth in the Book of Revelation* (Missoula, MT: Scholars Press, 1976)

Davidson, D., *Inquiries into Truth and Interpretation* (Oxford: Clarendon Press, 1984)

Eslinger, L., 'Inner-Biblical Exegesis and Inner-Biblical Allusion: The Question of Category', *VT* 42 (1992), 47–58

Frye, N., *The Anatomy of Criticism* (Princeton: PUP, 1957)

Gadamer, H.-G., *Truth and Method* (London: Sheed and Ward, 1975)

Garrow, A.J., *Revelation* (London: Routledge, 1997)

Highwater, J., *The Mythology of Transgression: Homosexuality as Metaphor* (Oxford: OUP, 1997)

Jakobson, R., 'Two Aspects of Language and Two Types of Aphasic Speech Disorder', in *Selected Writings II: Word and Language* (The Hague: Mouton, 1971)

Lacocque, A., 'Apocalyptic Symbolism: A Ricoeurian Hermeneutical Approach', *Biblical Review* 26 (1981), 6–15

Locke, J., *Essay Concerning Human Understanding*, II (Oxford: OUP, 1894)

Lundin, R., 'Metaphor in the Modern Critical Arena', *ChrLit* 33.1 (1983), 19–35

Lundin, R., et al., *The Responsibility of Hermeneutics* (Exeter: Paternoster, 1985)

Mudge, L., 'Paul Ricœur on Biblical Interpretation', *Biblical Review* 24/25 (1980), 38–69

Paul, I.B., *The Value of Paul Ricœur's Hermeneutic of Metaphor in the Interpretation of the Symbolism of Revelation 12 and 13* (PhD thesis, Nottingham Trent

University/St John's College, Nottingham, 1998, to be published in revised form as *Power to See the World Anew: Paul Ricœur, Metaphor and Revelation 12–13* [Carlisle: Paternoster, forthcoming])

—, 'Image, Symbol, Metaphor', in *Studies in the Book of Revelation* (Edinburgh, T. & T. Clark, forthcoming)

—, 'The Use of the Old Testament in Rev 12', in *The Old Testament in the New* (ed. Steve Moyise; Sheffield: Sheffield Academic Press, 2000)

Ricœur, P., *Freud and Philosophy* (New Haven: Yale University Press, 1970)

—, *Interpretation Theory* (Fort Worth: Texas Christian University Press, 1976)

—, *The Rule of Metaphor* (London: Routledge, 1978)

Rudwick, M.J.S. and E.M.B. Green, 'The Laodicean Lukewarmness', *ExpTim* (1957), 176–78

Songs and Hymns of Fellowship (Eastbourne: Kingsway Music, 1987)

Soskice, J.M., *Metaphor and Religious Language* (Oxford: Clarendon Press, 1985)

Stibbe, M., 'This is That: Some Thoughts Concerning Charismatic Hermeneutics', *Anvil* 15.3 (1998), 181–93

Thiselton, A., *New Horizons in Hermeneutics* (London: HarperCollins, 1992)

van Henten, J.W., 'Dragon Myth and Imperial Ideology in Revelation 12–13', *SBL Seminar Papers* 33 (1994), 496–515

Wolterstorff, N., *Divine Discourse* (Cambridge: CUP, 1995)

Cheltenham and Gloucester College of Higher Education

School of Theology and Religious Studies

The College is pleased that the partnership with the Bible Society in the Scripture and Hermeneutics Seminar is continuing and delighted that the second volume is now published. We are grateful to the contributors and editors for their work on this volume and trust that readers will find it stimulating. Christians are 'word' people in many ways, and I am certain that the church must continue to consider how it understands and uses language.

The year since the first volume in this series was published has been an extremely active one for the School of Theology and Religious Studies. In January 2001 the School moved to refurbished accommodation at Francis Close Hall, giving the staff high-quality office accommodation. This campus is where St Paul's College, Cheltenham was established in 1847.

This new base facilitates strengthening of the School's range of undergraduate and postgraduate programmes. Masters programmes now include the MA in Old Testament, MA in New Testament, and MA in Theology and Society.

To enhance research activity in the School, an International Centre for Biblical Interpretation has been established. The official launch was held in June 2001. The Revd Dr Tom Wright, who is Canon Theologian at Westminster Abbey, spoke on the topic of 'Paul's Critique of the Caesar-Cult'.

Also in June 2001 the Scripture and Hermeneutics seminar held a fourth consultation in Cheltenham. The theme was 'The Use of the Bible Ethically and Politically' and papers from that consultation are being prepared for volume 3, to be published in November 2002.

Dr Fred Hughes
Head, School of Theology and Religious Studies
Cheltenham & Gloucester College of Higher Education
Francis Close Hall,
Swindon Road, Cheltenham, Gloucestershire GL50 4AZ, UK
www.chelt.ac.uk/ah/sotrs

The British and Foreign Bible Society

In 2004, the British and Foreign Bible Society (BFBS) will celebrate its bicentenary. The Society originated in the early years of the nineteenth century in a context of evangelical revival and social reform associated with people such as John and Charles Wesley, George Whitefield, Samuel Wilberforce and the Clapham Sect. Wilberforce organized a number of campaigns, ostensibly aimed at the 'reform of manners'. The use of the phrase was itself a piece of opportunism, seizing on a passage in a speech by King George III to Parliament. The formation of the BFBS was one of the elements in Wilberforce's broad-ranging campaign to put the biblical narrative back in the centre of British public life. The purpose of this was to create a new imagination opposed to the cynicism and callousness that allowed social evils such as the slave trade to flourish. Wilberforce was not a biblical scholar. He recognized, however, that genuine social and political reform did not take place in a vacuum but must be earthed in a moral and religious vision of what constitutes a just and humane society.

Over the last 200 years the BFBS, as the founding member of the now worldwide United Bible Societies fellowship, has been deeply concerned with Bible distribution, making the Scriptures available to increasing numbers of people in a language they can understand and at a price they can afford. If and when the Society intersected with the world of biblical scholarship, it was over issues of translation and cultural relevance. It is a source of some considerable irony that, during the period when the distribution and translation work of the Bible Societies was flourishing, particularly overseas, historical-critical biblical scholarship was contributing to the increasing marginalization of the Bible and the churches in the public sphere in the West. That, of course, was not intentional, and it is as well to remember the sanguine comment of Paul Tillich, who said that it is to the credit of the Christian churches that Christianity was the first worldwide religion to allow its primary text to go through the fires of historical-critical research. We are not yet at the end of that process. In our postmodern context, the traditional boundaries between what were previously discrete disciplines (such as philosophy, theology, cultural and literary theory, and socio-political analysis) are being obscured and sur-mounted all the time. Thus it is even more crucial to address questions to do with the credibility, authority and relevance of the Bible in the context of contemporary society.

It is for this reason that we at the BFBS are delighted to be partners in a new and exciting interdisciplinary project we are calling 'The Scripture and Hermeneutics Seminar'.

The hermeneutical recovery of the diverse and variegated traditions of the biblical story in the context of an equally diverse, pluralist and multi-cultural society remains high on our agenda. Consequently, we want to work in and with the world of critical scholarship to allow debate and reflection to flourish for the mutual benefit of all, so that the Book is once again open and able to address the complex realities of living in the third millennium.

The publication of the first volume, *Renewing Biblical Interpretation*, was understandably a significant milestone in the work of the Seminar. We are, similarly, delighted to commend the second volume, *After Pentecost – Language and Biblical Interpretation*, as further testimony to the wide-ranging and intellectually challenging nature of our shared endeavour.

Revd Dr Colin J.D. Greene
Head of Theology and Public Policy (BFBS)

Name Index

Subject Index

Renewing Biblical Interpretation

Craig Bartholomew, Colin Greene, Karl Möller, Editors

Renewing Biblical Interpretation is the first of eight volumes from the Scripture and Hermeneutics Seminar. This annual gathering of Christian scholars from various disciplines was established in 1998 and aims to re-assess the discipline of biblical studies from the foundation up and forge creative new ways for re-opening the Bible in our cultures.

Including a retrospective on the consultation by Walter Brueggemann, the contributors to *Renewing Biblical Interpretation* consider three elements in approaching the Bible—the historical, the literary and the theological—and the underlying philosophical issues that shape the way we think about literature and history.

Hardcover
ISBN 0-310-23411-5

ZONDERVAN™

GRAND RAPIDS, MICHIGAN 49530
www.zondervan.com

paternoster
press

CHELTENHAM
&
GLOUCESTER
College of Higher Education

bible society

We want to hear from you. Please send your comments about this book to us in care of the address below. Thank you.

GRAND RAPIDS, MICHIGAN 49530

w w w . z o n d e r v a n . c o m